Approaches to Auschwitz

APPROACHES TO AUSCHWITZ

THE HOLOCAUST
AND ITS LEGACY

RICHARD L.
RUBENSTEIN

•

JOHN K.
ROTH

John Knox Press
ATLANTA

Library of Congress Cataloging-in-Publication Data

Rubenstein, Richard L.
   Approaches to Auschwitz.

   Bibliography: p.
   Includes indexes.
   1. Holocaust, Jewish (1939–1945)—Causes. 2. Anti-
semitism—History. 3. Christianity and antisemitism.
4. Holocaust (Christian theology) 5. Holocaust (Jewish
theology) 6. Auschwitz (Poland : Concentration camp)
I. Roth, John K. II. Title.
D810.J4R778   1987   940.53'15'0392404386   86-27749
ISBN 0-8042-0778-X
ISBN 0-8042-0777-1 (pbk.)

© copyright John Knox Press 1987
10 9 8 7 6 5 4 3 2
Printed in the United States of America
John Knox Press
Atlanta, Georgia

Acknowledgments

Acknowledgment is made for permission to quote from the following sources:

To A D Peters & Co Ltd for Gitta Sereny, *Into That Darkness*, published by Andre Deutsch Ltd. Reprinted by permission of A D Peters & Co Ltd.

To the American Academy of Political and Social Science for John K. Roth, "Holocaust Business: Some Reflections on *Arbeit Macht Frei*," Vol. 450, July 1980.

To Atheneum Publishers, Inc. for André Schwarz-Bart, excerpted from *The Last of the Just*. Copyright © 1960 Atheneum House, Inc. Reprinted with permission Atheneum Publishers, Inc.

To Basic Books, Inc., Publishers, for excerpts from THE NAZI PERSECUTION OF THE CHURCHES, 1933–1945 by John Conway. © 1968 by George Weidenfeld and Nicolson Ltd. Reprinted by permission of Basic Books, Inc., Publishers.

To Beacon Press for excerpts from Charlotte Delbo, *None of Us Will Return*, copyright 1968; Emil Fackenheim, "Transcendence in Contemporary Culture," in Herbert W. Richardson and Donald R. Cutler, eds., *Transcendence*, copyright 1969; Lawrence L. Langer, *The Age of Atrocity*, copyright 1978; Richard L. Rubenstein, *The Age of Triage*, copyright 1983.

To Beit Lohamei Haghetaot, for excerpts from Yitzak Katzenelson, "The Song of the Murdered Jewish People," Hakibbutz Hemeuchad Publishing House, 1980.

To Bloch Publishing Company, for Joseph H. Hertz, ed., *The Authorized Daily Prayer Book*, copyright 1948.

To Cambridge University Press for G. W. F. Hegel, *Lectures on the Philosophy of World History: Introduction, Reason in History*, translated by H. B. Nisbet, W. E. George, and Duncan Forbes, copyright 1975.

To Columbia University Press for Arthur Hertzberg, *The French Enlightenment and the Jews*, copyright 1968.

To The Crossroad Publishing Company for excerpts from THE TREMENDUM: A Theological Interpretation of the Holocaust by Arthur A. Cohen. Copyright © 1981 by the author. Reprinted by permission of The Crossroad Publishing Company.

To *Dissent* for "Socialism and the Jews," by George Lichtheim, Vol. 15, July–August 1968.

To Éditions de Minuit for Charlotte Delbo, *Une connaissance inutile* (pp. 48–49, 60, 145 and 185–191) and *Mesure de nos jours* (pp. 17, 57–66, 83, 184, 187, 199–200 and 212).

To *Encounter* for "Philosophy, the Holocaust, and the Advance of Civilization," by John K. Roth, *Encounter*, Vol. 46, Spring 1985.

To FAITH AND PHILOSOPHY for John K. Roth, "The Silence of God," Volume I, Number 4 (October 1984), pages 407–420. Used by permission of FAITH AND PHILOSOPHY.

To Farrar, Straus & Giroux, Inc., for Elie Wiesel, NIGHT, translated by Stella Rodway (New York: Bantam Books, 1982); English translation © Mac Gibbon & Kee, 1960. Reprinted by permission of Farrar, Straus & Giroux, Inc.

To Fortress Press for Eberhard Busch, *Karl Barth: His Life from Letters and Autobiographical Texts*, translated by John Bowden, copyright 1976. For Franklin Sherman and Helmut T. Lehmann, eds, *Luther's Works*, vol. 47, copyright © 1971 by Fortress Press. Used by permission.

To The Free Press for excerpts from THE CRIME AND PUNISHMENT OF I. G. FARBEN by Joseph Borkin. New York: The Free Press, a Division of Macmillan, Inc., 1978.

To Harcourt Brace Jovanovich, Inc., for an excerpt from THE ORIGINS OF TOTALITARIAN-ISM, copyright 1951 by Hannah Arendt; renewed 1978 by Mary McCarthy West. Reprinted by permission of Harcourt Brace Jovanovich, Inc., publisher; for an excerpt from THE NEW TESTAMENT: AN INTRODUCTION by Norman Perrin, U.S.A. edition published 1974 by Harcourt Brace Jovanovich.

To Harper & Row, Publishers, Inc., for Philip P. Hallie, *Lest Innocent Blood Be Shed*, Harper & Row, Publishers, Inc., 1979; Richard L. Rubenstein, *The Cunning of History*, Harper & Row Publishers, Inc., 1975.

To Harvard University Press for Benjamin Ferencz, *Less than Slaves: Jewish Forced Labor and the Quest for Compensation*, copyright 1979.

To Holocaust Library for Léon Poliakov, *Harvest of Hate*, copyright 1979.

To Holt, Rinehart & Winston for Elie Wiesel, *Legends of Our Time*, copyright 1970.

To Indiana University Press for Emil Fackenheim, *Quest for Past and Future: Essays in Jewish Theology*, copyright 1968; for Elie Wiesel, "Why I Write," pp. 201–2, in *Confronting the Holocaust*, ed. Alvin H. Rosenfeld and Irving Greenberg, copyright 1978.

To *Journal of Social Philosophy* for John K. Roth, "That Time in Poland," September 1982.

To Kraus International Publications for excerpts from *The Holocaust: Ideology, Bureaucracy, and Genocide: The San Jose Papers*. Edited by Henry Friedlander and Sybil Milton. Millwood, New York: Kraus International Publications, 1980. Reprinted by permission. Permission also granted by the National Conference of Christians and Jews.

To KTAV Publishing House, Inc., for *Auschwitz: Beginning of a New Era?* by Eva Fleischner, ed., copyright 1977; for "The Fall of Jerusalem and the Birth of Holocaust Theology," by Richard L. Rubenstein in *Go and Study: Essays in Honor of Alfred Jospe*, ed. Samuel Z. Fishman and Raphael Jospe, copyright 1980; for *Vatican Diplomacy and the Jews during the Holocaust 1939–1943* by John F. Morley, copyright 1980.

To Franklin H. Littell for excerpts from *The Crucifixion of Jesus*, published by Harper & Row, 1975, rights owned by Franklin H. Littell and used by permission.

To Little, Brown and Company Publishers for excerpts from *The Terrible Secret: Suppression of the Truth about Hitler's "Final Solution,"* by Walter Laqueur, 1980.

To the Los Angeles Times for excerpt from "Reagan Appointee J. Peter Grace Is Under Fire," by Lee May. Copyright 1982, Los Angeles Times. Reprinted by permission.

To Macmillan Publishing Company for *Judenrat: The Jewish Councils in Eastern Europe Under Nazi Occupation* by Isaiah Trunk, copyright © 1972 by Isaiah Trunk, used by permission. Reprinted with permission of The Free Press, a Division of Macmillan, Inc. from ACCOUNTING FOR GENOCIDE by Helen Fein. Copyright © 1979 by Helen Fein. Reprinted with permission of The Free Press, a Division of Macmillan, Inc. from THE FAITH AND DOUBT OF HOLOCAUST SURVIVORS by Reeve Robert Brenner. Copyright 1980 by Reeve Robert Brenner.

To McGraw-Hill Book Company for *Morality and Eros* by Richard L. Rubenstein, copyright 1970 by Richard L. Rubenstein.

To Oxford University Press for Paul Mendes-Flohr and Jehuda Reinharz, THE JEW IN THE MODERN WORLD, copyright 1980.

To The Pickwick Press for Arthur C. Cochrane, *The Church's Confession under Hitler*, 2d ed., copyright, 1976.

To Polak & Van Gennep, Publishers, for Ignaz Maybaum, *The Face of God after Auschwitz*, copyright 1965.

To Prentice-Hall, Inc., for THE NAZI YEARS: A DOCUMENTARY HISTORY by Joachim Remak, © 1969 Prentice Hall, Inc., Englewood Cliffs, NJ 07632. Reprinted by permission of the publisher.

To Princeton University Press for Sarah Gordon, *Hitler, Germans, and the "Jewish Question."* Copyright © 1984 by Princeton University Press.

For
Betty and Lyn

Preface

Auschwitz—how and why has it scarred the earth? This book does not answer that question completely. None can. Its pages, however, are offered to help comprehend the meaning of that place and its continuing significance. These approaches are by no means our creation alone. Literally hundreds of scholars have informed our interpretations. We have sifted and synthesized the best Holocaust scholarship so that sheer volume will not render it inaccessible. In addition, that process gave us a distinctive outlook on Auschwitz. Some background will explain that claim.

From 15 to 19 November 1979 the American Academy of Religion held its annual meeting in New York City. One session focused on "Academic Teaching and Study of the Holocaust." Its organizer was Richard L. Rubenstein. During the afternoon's discussion, he observed that it would be useful to have a book that did not then exist: an interdisciplinary volume which could be a unifying text for the numerous college and university courses that concentrate on the Nazi attempt to exterminate the Jews.

As the panel ended, one of its members approached Rubenstein with a question. "Are you writing the book you described?" he asked. "No," Rubenstein replied. "Would you consider trying to write it with me?" the questioner continued. As John K. Roth heard the answer—"Yes, I might"—his eyes caught those of another person nearby. R. Donald Hardy, Jr., then an editor at John Knox Press, had heard the symposium. Intrigued by Rubenstein's comments about a book on the Holocaust, he soon got together with us. With the subsequent backing of John Knox's editorial director, Richard A. Ray, plans to coauthor *Approaches to Auschwitz* were underway.

Books are conceived more easily than they are written. This one took seven years, primarily owing to the vast historical material we had to master. Don Hardy and Dick Ray are no longer at John Knox Press, but the latter's successor, Walter C. Sutton, picked up their enthusiasm for the project and urged us along to its completion. We are indebted to each of them, but particularly to Walt Sutton for his patience and encouragement. What energized us all was the conviction that this book would be significantly different from any other that has been published about the Holocaust thus far. Pivotal in that appraisal is the fact that one of us is Jewish, the other Christian. While we have relied on original historical scholarship done by others, it is also important to note that we bring to this work decades of training and research in social theory, religious studies, and philosophy. Neither of us witnessed the Holocaust firsthand. Our study of that event, however, totals nearly forty years.

Rubenstein's *After Auschwitz* (1966) sparked an outpouring of American interest in the Holocaust. Certainly that book decisively influenced John Roth, who was a graduate student when it first appeared. Ten years later, we found ourselves together as Fellows at the National Humanities Institute, Yale University. Mutual interests grew into friendship and then into the intuitive understanding and trust that sound literary collaboration requires. Convinced that each had something important to say about the Holocaust and persuaded that no single voice, discipline, or tradition can offer all that is needed on this subject, we were ready to become a team when the opportunity arose.

Both of us have long experience in teaching college and university students about the Holocaust. We think that *Approaches to Auschwitz* can be especially effective in that setting. We hope it will reach a wider audience as well. The book does not pretend to cover every topic that should be addressed where the Holocaust is concerned. Having gone some distance in that direction, we judge that no single volume could ever do so. But these pages do contain a considerable historical sweep. If they sometimes survey the horizon, on other occasions they focus on particular times and places in detail. They move beyond the historical, too, exploring how religious, moral, and literary expressions have been affected by Auschwitz. The arguments we present on all fronts are likely to be controversial, but we value serious debate more than convenient agreement.

We share a pragmatic orientation, which means that our book should have no further justification here. Either it will strike a responsive and productive note in its readers, corroborating the merit of our distinctive interpretation, or it fails the test. To the extent that our efforts do succeed, they are indebted not only to the individuals named and alluded to above but also to other persons who deserve special credit. In 1982, for example, John Roth served as visiting professor of Holocaust studies at the University of Haifa, Israel. Substantial portions of the book were written there. Thanks are due to Elie Wiesel, who arranged the appointment; to Sigmund Strochlitz, who financed it; and to Bela and Lidia Vago, Asher Cohen, and Nehama Friedman, who made the University a wonderful place to work. With tireless good humor, Carol Bovett, Pat Padilla, and Lillie Walls typed and retyped our many drafts. Michael Berenbaum and Lonnie D. Kliever carefully read our work. Their valued advice improved the book immensely. Under the able supervision of Joan Crawford, the editorial staff at John Knox Press—including Barbara M. Blatt and especially our helpful copyeditor, Nancy A. Hardesty—provided the assistance we needed. John G. Gibbs, Acquisitions Editor, encouraged some meaningful revisions. We are grateful to all of them, too.

Survivors of the Holocaust cannot escape it. In their own ways, neither can scholars who write about Auschwitz. Such enormous destruction can drive to despair those who try to comprehend why darkness possesses such power. The human record we display has discouraged and saddened us. Yet a hopeful equilibrium remains. It does so largely because we are each sustained by a loving wife. They are also friends. Our book, then, is dedicated to them as a post-Holocaust sign that Christians and Jews can be brothers and sisters who care very much for one another.

Richard L. Rubenstein   John K. Roth
Tallahassee, Florida   Claremont, California

OTHER BOOKS BY RICHARD L. RUBENSTEIN

After Auschwitz
The Religious Imagination
Morality and Eros
My Brother Paul
Power Struggle
The Cunning of History
The Age of Triage

OTHER BOOKS BY JOHN K. ROTH

Freedom and the Moral Life
Problems of the Philosophy of Religion
The American Religious Experience (with Frederick Sontag)
American Dreams
God and America's Future (with Frederick Sontag)
A Consuming Fire
The Questions of Philosophy (with Frederick Sontag)

Contents

PART FOUR: THE AFTERMATH AND THE FUTURE

Comprehension does not mean denying the outrageous, deducing the unprecedented from precedents, or explaining phenomena by such analogies and generalities that the impact of reality and the shock of experience are no longer felt. It means, rather, examining and bearing consciously the burden which our century has placed on us—neither denying its existence nor submitting meekly to its weight. Comprehension, in short, means the unpremeditated, attentive facing up to, and resisting of, reality—whatever it may be.

Hannah Arendt
Preface to the First Edition
The Origins of Totalitarianism (1950)

APPROACHES TO AUSCHWITZ

Prologue

What Is the Holocaust?

On 23 February 1930 a twenty-one-year-old law student died in Berlin. Like many other young men in the Germany of his day, Horst Wessel, a Lutheran preacher's son, had rebelled against his bourgeois upbringing and joined the "Brownshirts" (*Sturmabteilung*, Storm Detachment) of the *Nationalsozialistische Deutsche Arbeiterpartei*, the National Socialist German Workers' Party, better known as the Nazi party. Wessel's political activities included participation in bloody street battles with Communists. Of greater significance, Wessel was in love with a former prostitute and had moved in with her. Abhorring notoriety, their landlady sought to evict them by enlisting help from a Communist gang. One winter night the gang broke into the couple's room. Much to the landlady's dismay, a former intimate of Wessel's girlfriend gunned him down.

History frequently pivots around small events. Horst Wessel's demise is a case in point. His death would have been inconsequential had he not written a poem sometime before. Entitled "Raise High the Flag," it had been set in march-time to a Viennese cabaret song from the turn of the century. As Wessel was dying, Joseph Goebbels, the mastermind behind Nazi propaganda, saw an opportunity to turn a lovers' triangle into political power. Wessel's lyric immortalized those who had given their lives for the Nazi cause. Arranging to have the "Horst Wessel Song" sung at the conclusion of a Nazi meeting, Goebbels envisioned that it would become "the hymn of the German revolution." He was correct

That same February a Jewish doctor, Sigmund Freud, went about his work in Vienna. Only a few weeks earlier he had finished a small book that would be among his most famous. In English it is called *Civilization and Its Discontents*. Among its final words are these: "Men have gained control over the forces of nature to such an extent that with their help they would have no difficulty in exterminating one another to the last man."[1] Freud was also correct. Horst Wessel's song would help to prove the point.

As the Nazis sang in the Berlin *Sportpalast* that February night in 1930, an infant destined to be at least as well known as Freud was fast asleep. The revolution glimpsed by Freud's premonition and rallied by Wessel's song would profoundly mark this Jewish girl, Anne Frank. Years later she lived for months in her Amsterdam hiding place writing the diary that is still read by millions. One of its last entries, dated 15 July 1944, testifies: "I see the world gradually being turned into a wilderness, I hear the ever approaching thunder, which will destroy us too." Anne Frank also affirmed "that people are really good at heart," and she went on to say that her gloomy forecast would not be the last word. "If I look up into the heavens," she wrote, "I think that it will all come right, that this cruelty too will end, and that peace and tranquillity will return again."[2] Anne Frank was correct, too, but how far is not clear. She was right about the gloomy part. As for the rest, perhaps the best one can say is that the jury is still out.

Horst Wessel, Sigmund Freud, and Anne Frank—these people never met. Yet they are linked together in ways that must be grasped if we are to comprehend what it means to live in the late twentieth century. What links them is an event now called the Holocaust.

What Is Meant by the Holocaust?

The Third Reich's system of concentration camps, murder squadrons, and killing centers took more than twelve million defenseless human lives. All of these deaths were tragic and should be mourned. Between five and six million of them were Jewish, and it will bear remembering that the Jews were the only group that Hitler targeted for extinction. Not every Nazi victim was Jewish, but the Nazi intent was to rid Europe, if not the world, of Jews. Hitler went far in fulfilling that goal. Two-thirds of Europe's Jews were dead by the end of World War II. Thus, the Holocaust refers—not exclusively, but primarily—to the Nazi destruction of the European Jews. It also refers to more than that sentence can suggest. Some further references to Freud, Wessel, and Anne Frank will clarify that fact and illustrate the scope of meaning reflected by the word "Holocaust" in the following chapters.

The event designated as the Holocaust is named by more than one term. Many of Horst Wessel's peers, for example, took part in what the Nazis called the Final Solution (*Die Endlösung*). Wessel's friends had lived through a period when hopes for imperial expansion were shattered by Germany's humiliating defeat in World War I. The aftermath was one of political and economic instability coupled with yearnings for a renewed sense of German identity. Nazi political instincts capitalized on these conditions. Their tactics included an ideological campaign that implicated the Jews in all of Germany's problems. Jews, the Nazis proclaimed, were unnecessary, unwanted, undesirable. In short, they were superfluous. Nazi propaganda accorded Jews this status not because they were impoverished. Nor were Germany's Jews uneducated, unskilled, or unproductive. People can be considered redundant for those reasons, of course, and some of the Nazis' Jewish victims fitted into such categories. Most, especially in Germany, did not. On the contrary, they were able men and women. Thus, the Holocaust reveals that it is as easy for talented people to lose their places in the world as it is for those who cannot cope with the complexities of technological civilization. Even those who facilitate and adapt to the modern world may be spewed out by it. A surplus or redundant population, therefore, is not simply a matter of numbers. It can be any population that for any reason can find no viable role in the society where it lives. The Nazis were determined to put Jews into that category. They succeeded.[3]

Surplus people, including the sort that the Jews became, appear to be a product intrinsic to the process of economic modernization that has governed the world for the past four centuries. Their presence, to be more specific, is one of the most important social consequences of the triumph of an attitude of value-neutral, calculating rationality as the predominant mode of problem solving in practical affairs generally and in economic enterprises, capitalist or socialist, in particular. This practical rationality seeks to solve the problem of surplus people by governmental intervention. As governments implement solutions aimed at population elimination, the measures can range from segregation and incarceration, to eviction and expulsion, and ultimately to outright extermination. The Nazis planned brutal treatment for groups they labeled "subhuman," such as Slavs and Gypsies, but to advance their aims they degraded Jews to "nonhuman" status. After experimenting with various techniques that failed to achieve the desired results, the National Socialists unblinkingly embraced the most radical alternative: systematic, state-sponsored total annihilation.

The line that moved from Horst Wessel's song to a clear definition of "the Jewish problem" in Germany, then to gas chambers in death camps, was neither simple nor direct. As one perceptive historian describes it, the road to Auschwitz was twisted.[4] But a road there was, and interpreting the signs that map it out shows why and how an entire people came to be so unwanted, so superfluous, that no effort was spared to destroy them. Such investigations pertain not only to the 1930s and 1940s. They take us back into the European and American past and then forward to our own day and beyond as we seek to identify peoples and forces struggling through scenarios that have striking similarities. The Holocaust points to a reality larger than itself. By referring to the Nazis' particular attempt to exterminate the Jews, the term also puts us on the trail of tracking down the global forces that bring to power those who find state-sponsored population elimination—more or less radical as circumstances require—to be the most expedient means in achieving a Final Solution for their problems.

Two Hebrew words, *Churban* and *Shoah*, also name the Holocaust. Both signify catastrophic destruction. According to Uriel Tal, the term *Shoah* was used by Polish Jews as early as 1940 to designate their plight under Hitler. The roots of this word, however, go back much further. Indeed, they are biblical. The term is found in the Psalms, in Isaiah's prophecies, and in Job's lamentations. Its meanings are multiple. Sometimes it refers to dangers that threaten Israel from surrounding nations; at other times it refers to individual distress and desolation. If catastrophic destruction is signified in each case, Tal argues, "all Biblical meanings of the term *Shoah* clearly imply Divine judgment and retribution."[5] Those ancient meanings, however, are called into question by the Final Solution. In contemporary usage, *Shoah* conveys the old sense of destruction but adds a profound element of doubt and even despair where religious tradition is concerned.

Freud's best-known book about religion is entitled *The Future of an Illusion.* "In the long run," he wrote, "nothing can withstand reason and experience, and the contradiction religion offers to both is only too palpable." If Freud believed it would be "an indubitable advantage to leave God out of the question altogether, and to admit honestly the purely human origin of all cultural laws and institutions," he also knew that religion had ruled human society for centuries. In particular, it had "contributed much toward restraining the asocial instincts."[6] But not enough, Freud believed, for even the best intentions toward mastery of aggression and self-destruction created hostility as well.

It is a moot issue whether one can leave God out of the question altogether where *Shoah* is concerned, but it is certain that religion must occupy a central place in any sound approach to Auschwitz. It must do so from a perspective that incorporates history, politics, economics, and sociology. Such a perspective can be developed only by taking very seriously what men and women have in fact believed about themselves, their people, and their destinies. At least in that sense, God also is present in the *Shoah.* Here again the particularity of an event, the loss of six million Jewish lives under Hitler, as well as the loss of nine million other innocent lives, sends out waves that move back and forth in time. The *Shoah* prods us to understand Jewish uniqueness, a history of volatile anti-Jewish sentiment in Christianity, and the impact of Auschwitz not only on Jewish and Christian religious consciousness that follows after but also on human self-understanding generally.

The Nazis named the Holocaust before the worst took place. While their Final Solution was under way, the Jewish victims sensed catastrophe, usually too late, and they were correct: *Shoah* happened. Both the Final Solution and *Shoah* are better known as the Holocaust, but like the others, that name did not appear out of thin air either. A contemporary dictionary will define "holocaust" as a great or total destruction by fire, and the entry may indicate the word's derivation from the Greek *holokaustos,* meaning "burnt whole." Once more, biblical roots are important. In the Septuagint, a Greek translation of Jewish Scripture dating from the third century B.C.E. (before the common era), *holokauston* is used for the Hebrew *olah*, which literally means "what is brought up." In context the term refers to a sacrifice, often specifically to "an offering made by fire unto the Lord." Not everyone invests the destruction of the European Jews with special religious significance, however. Some people protest that the Final Solution should not be called the Holocaust precisely because the latter term conveys religious connotations that are repulsive. Walter Laqueur for example is not alone when he finds the term "singularly inappropriate," arguing tersely that "it was not the intention of the Nazis to make a sacrifice of this kind, and the position of the Jews was not that of a ritual victim."[7] Yet the term will not go away, for millions of defenseless human beings were sacrificed and burned.

Horst Wessel and Sigmund Freud testify that history involves powerful social forces that dwarf individuals. Those powers of domination must be studied on a macrocosmic level if they are to be grasped adequately at all. At the same time, the perspective of an Anne Frank must not be overlooked either. It shows that history's drama is also enacted by individual persons. What those individuals choose and fail to choose, how they act and fail to act, make a great deal of difference. Individuals have an identity because of the social reality into which they were born, but how they shape their identities in response can vastly alter those circumstances. The stories of people who survived and who died—victims, killers, and those who stood by—are essential, too, for trying to comprehend the Holocaust. Only by keeping individuals in focus can one avoid the oversimplifications of sweeping generalizations or identify the exceptions that prove a rule.

The Holocaust, then, means Final Solution and "catastrophe." Strictly speaking, it neither begins nor ends with Jews. The history of human instinct is longer than that of Jewish history; the implications of both reach well beyond Jewish destiny, too. And yet Jewish particularity remains at the center of this story. Their sacrifices, as a people and as individuals, show what the scope of human conduct can be, even as they also prod us to ask: what is worth living and dying for?

How Has the Holocaust Been Interpreted?

Names for an event have different meanings. Likewise, the Holocaust itself calls forth varied interpretations. Even to mention all of them here is impossible, but consider some of the more important ones to delineate further the perspective found in this book. The burgeoning scholarship and reflection on the Holocaust appear in many languages. In English works, at least three main trends deserve notice. They correspond to our themes of Final Solution, catastrophe, and sacrifice.

Two dominant approaches to the Holocaust-as-Final-Solution are Raul Hilberg's *The Destruction of the European Jews* (1961, revised 1985), on the one hand, and Lucy Dawidowicz's *The War Against the Jews, 1933–1945* (1975) plus Yehuda Bauer's *A History of the Holocaust* (1982), and Martin Gilbert's *The Holocaust: A History of the Jews of Europe during the Second World War* (1985) on the other. These works all trace a program of destruction from a historical point of view. Hilberg concentrates on the Nazi side. His analysis implicates virtually every segment of German society in a process that moved from definition of its Jewish targets, to concentration and seizure of them, and then to their ultimate destruction. Dawidowicz, Bauer, and Gilbert differ from Hilberg in placing much more emphasis on Jewish experience. If Hilberg drives home the National Socialists' ability to overcome nearly every obstacle that stood between them and annihilation of the Jews, Dawidowicz, Bauer, and Gilbert show how the Jews, against all odds, tried to continue their Jewish lives. Still other historical works concentrate on how diverse nations or institutions, neither Jewish nor German, reacted to the threats of Nazism and of the Holocaust in particular. Collectively, these studies rightly maintain that a firm grounding in history—broadly conceived to include politics, economics, and social change—is fundamental in any sound approach to the Holocaust.

When first confronted with the horror of Auschwitz, one may ask: how could it happen? Historical research reveals how and, to a large extent, why the Final Solution *did* happen. The story is millennia long. In special ways, religion marks it indelibly, bringing the makings of catastrophe. Those ingredients lodge in tensions between two groups, one spawned from the other, who have seen themselves as God's chosen people. A second major strand of Holocaust scholarship focuses specifically on these Jewish-Christian relationships. It tends to see Auschwitz as the culminating offspring of religiously inspired antisemitism, of "faith and fratricide," to cite the title of Rosemary Radford Ruether's influential book in this field.[8] The past casts shadows on the future of religion, too. Franklin H. Littell, for example, writes about "the crucifixion of the Jews," and he finds the Christian tradition so drenched in guilt as to face an unprecedented credibility crisis.[9] Meanwhile Jewish religious leadership shares Emil Fackenheim's perplexity concerning "God's presence in history."[10] What is at stake, however, is not restricted to religion alone. To play a variation on Freud's theme, human consciousness may encounter multiple illusions via the Holocaust, religious factors counting as only one of their dimensions, and the future may not be very bright as a result. Science, technology, education, professional skills of all kinds—these were also instrumental in unleashing catastrophe during the Third Reich. Religious influences figured into those relationships, just as today uncertainty about where human power may lead is attended by clashing gods who vie for loyalty.

Competition for loyalty led to sacrifice and thus to the acts of individuals. So a third major body of reflection on the Holocaust deals with the men and women who enacted and went through the process of destruction. Biographies of Hitler, for example, continue to multiply, some of them—Robert G. L. Waite's *The*

Psychopathic God: Adolf Hitler (1977) comes to mind—drawing upon Freud's psychology to illuminate Hitler's character. Autobiographical statements by Jewish survivors such as Elie Wiesel's *Night* (1958) and Primo Levi's *Survival in Auschwitz* (1958) portray life in the Nazi camps. The Nazi perspective is also represented, not only by the volumes of testimony preserved from the postwar trials at Nuremberg but also in memoirs such as Rudolph Höss's *Commandant of Auschwitz* (1947). Fact is illuminated by fiction too. Novels such as André Schwarz-Bart's *The Last of the Just* (1959) and Jean-François Steiner's *Treblinka* (1966) evoke the moods and feelings of Jews struggling to survive, while Tadeusz Borowski's *This Way for the Gas, Ladies and Gentlemen* (1959) and William Styron's *Sophie's Choice* (1979) affirm that men and women of diverse nationality, Polish and even American, are touched profoundly by the Holocaust.

The Holocaust is defined largely by the stories that are told about it. Whether factual or fictional, historically documented or symbolically expressed, these tales remain to check and to be balanced by the insights provided by scholarly treatments that take a broader view. With their emphasis on sacrifice, such narratives are a necessary ingredient to explorations of the Holocaust as Final Solution and as catastrophe.

How Shall We Interpret the Holocaust?

The Third Reich lasted from 1933 to 1945. Auschwitz, which epitomizes the Holocaust, functioned as a labor and death camp from 1940 through 1944. But these momentous years were centuries in the making. It is crucial to keep this question in mind: why did the Holocaust fail to occur before the 1940s? For most of their history, Jews have been viewed as an alien presence by those around them. Hence, the first major part of this book, which tracks the historical roots of the Holocaust, begins in the Greco-Roman and early Christian worlds, specifically with the Jewish experience of being "outsiders" in those circumstances. While emphasizing the objective innocence of the victims, plus the hideous disparity between the merit of Jewish life and its treatment by non-Jews (Gentiles) in the West, we find—contrary to conventional interpretations—that it is less helpful to regard Jews as passive objects on whom Gentiles have visited antisemitism irrationally than to see the historical situation as a seething conflict involving active parties on all sides. In a word, Jews and Christians could not help but disconfirm each other's religious traditions. The unhappy effects of that tragic fact escalated until the world reached Auschwitz.

Since the triumph of Christianity in the fourth century, Raul Hilberg emphasizes, there have been three fundamental anti-Jewish policies: conversion, expulsion, and annihilation. "The second," says Hilberg, "appeared as an alternative to the first, and the third emerged as an alternative to the second. . . . The missionaries of Christianity had said in effect: You have no right to live among us as Jews. The secular rulers who followed had proclaimed: You have no right to live among us. The German Nazis at last decreed: You have no right to live."[11] This dynamic will become evident as we move through the Middle Ages to the eve of the French Revolution.

After this beginning, we shall outline the Jewish situation in Europe from the triumph of Christianity, through the Middle Ages, to the eve of the French Revolution. Although constantly on precarious ground religiously and culturally, owing to their refusal to embrace the dominant majority's Christian ways, Jews had some security because those same ways mitigated against systematic mass murder. Perhaps even more importantly, we shall suggest, at this time the Jews of Europe could find a place where they were an economically complementary population. They were not, however, destined indefinitely to be an elite minority that filled needed commercial and professional roles left vacant by the dominant population.

Modernization of Europe's economy was, as some have called it, the great transformation.[12] Displacing the social structures and mores of subsistence agriculture, a revolutionary form of human consciousness evolved toward preeminence from the sixteenth century onward. Bent on liberation from the dead hand of the past, its yearnings for progress emphasized organization, industrialization, and specialization—all driven by the Enlightenment's rational methods, which stressed efficiency and cost-effectiveness. Modernization brought forth mass production, but that activity not only resulted in more manufactured goods and wider trade than ever before, it also enhanced the food supply. Populations grew, though not necessarily because they were needed. In fact, the great transformation made overpopulation a persistent threat to the system, especially in a changing value environment that increasingly calculated the worth of everything by the price it could fetch in the marketplace, an outcome that tended to make money more important than persons. Carried to extremes in the Holocaust, such attitudes deny in practice, if not in theory, that there is anything sacred about human life. Rather it is simply another component to be calculated in cost-benefit analysis. Such thinking, unfortunately, contains no credible restraint to its own excesses. Vast dislocations attended the modernizing process. In addition to mass production, it led to mass migration, mass politics, and in due course to mass murder. Steps on the way were found in political upheavals such as the French Revolution. In some regions, these Enlightenment efforts emancipated the Jews, but the irony of the long run was that no group would pay more dearly for the modernization of Europe's economy and society than the Jews.

Having traced some of the early historical roots of the Holocaust in Part I, we focus more explicitly on Nazi-Jewish relations in Part II. Largely helpless to prevent their fate, Jews became increasingly superfluous during the nineteenth century, their competition in the marketplace unwanted because, official decrees to the contrary notwithstanding, Jews were still an alien minority. By the end of the nineteenth century, those attitudes were reflected in biological, racial, and nationalistic theories that transmuted older anti-Jewish sentiments into new forms of political antisemitism. They were also manifest in a series of devastating Russian pogroms carried out in the 1880s with the blessing of a state that wanted to rid itself of Jews. The political leaders of Czarist Russia in the late nineteenth century pursued a goal not so different from that of the Nazis. Only the means employed were less radical and less systematic. The social, economic, and political forces unleashed by accelerating modernization in Europe had already moved far along to seal the fate of European Jewry several decades in advance of Hitler's rise to power. Population pressures made the last quarter of the nineteenth century a period of mass emigration from Europe generally. Open frontiers around the world, many pioneered by imperialistic interests, provided essential safety valves. But as these openings disappeared in the twentieth century, European space for Jews, emancipated or not, would become even more disastrously hard to find.

The unification of Germany under Bismarck in 1870, coupled with the Russian pogroms of 1881, formed one fateful watershed for Europe's Jews. World War I created another. More than inaugurating the twentieth century as one of mass death, it also proved mass extermination to be a politically acceptable method for modern states to use in restructuring society. In addition, when the Germans interpreted their own defeat as a "stab in the back" fomented by a Jewish world-conspiracy, the stage was set for the beginnings of the Nazi party and the emergence of its political messiah, Adolf Hitler. As the Great Depression struck, European nationalism never waned. Fascism was on the rise, and Jewish circumstances became increasingly problematic. Particularly in Poland, which had by far the largest Jewish population of any European nation between the two World Wars, the situation for Jews worsened every year. Gradually caught in the closing vise between a Poland that wanted its Jews to leave and a Germany that would eventually murder them, millions of eastern European Jews learned to their sorrow what the Jewish political scientist, Hannah Arendt, would mean when, following Max Weber, she referred to Jews as a pariah people.[13] That category consists of persons with no country of their own; it refers to people who may be granted privileges but who lack the fundamental rights guaranteed to a society's full members. Hitler's regime removed every privilege from the Jews' pariah status. Without political citizenship, stripped of their membership in a community ready and able to defend their rights, the Jews had no rights whatsoever, a fact that bears a sober warning: no consideration of abstract "human rights" impeded the National Socialists' state-sponsored program of systematic population elimination. The Jews became an utterly surplus population to be diminished by expulsion if not by death. Before Hitler finished, approximately six million of the nine million Jews in Europe in 1939 were dead, and more than 90% of Poland's 3.3 million Jews perished. Our study of the Holocaust therefore convinces us that it is imperative to explore how and why a people can become so helplessly redundant. Failure to do so obscures both the uniqueness of Auschwitz and how that uniqueness is also part of a much larger and continuous social pattern.

When the Nazis came to power in 1933, their commitment to antisemitism was clear, but their practical policies toward Jews were not. It is one thing to have antisemitic feelings and quite another to make those feelings effective in a political regime. Hence it took time for the Nazis to work out a coherent anti-Jewish program. From 1933 to 1938 hoodlum violence mixed with "paper violence," but increasingly the latter proved decisive in ways that the former could not. With the help of an expanding bureaucracy to expedite such matters, German Jews were dismissed from government positions, eliminated from professions and from commerce, and stripped of basic legal protection. The objective behind this paper violence was not harassment and degradation for their own sake but rather to drive Jews out of Germany, albeit with as little as possible in their possession. With the help of the emerging power of the SS (*Schutzstaffel* or protection unit), Hitler created refugees.

The outbreak of World War II in September 1939 required new strategies because it foreclosed opportunities for expulsion of Jews and eventually brought millions of Jews under German authority in eastern Europe and the Soviet Union. From the Nazi viewpoint, this war was a "holy" struggle aimed at giving the Germanic peoples their rightful dominion over the European continent. Populations that did not belong were either to serve Germans as slaves, or to be eliminated, or both. As mobile death squadrons (*Einsatzgruppen*) fanned out with advancing Nazi troops all along the eastern front, attention behind the lines was given to a strategy of ghettoization, which would ultimately feed the death and slave labor camps of the Reich. The Nazis sacrificed countless victims—for example, Slavs, Poles, Gypsies, Russian prisoners of war, homosexuals, the handicapped, and the mentally ill—but the Jews, ranking lowest in Hitler's racial hierarchy, were especially targeted. The Nazi policy toward these people, aimed at total domination, was symbolized by orders "to dig mass graves, strip, climb into the graves, lie down over the layer of corpses already murdered and await the final *coup de grâce*."[14]

Under Nazi domination, the ghettoized Jewish communities had to organize themselves. The dilemma that faced the leadership was how to survive when one could do so neither by total compliance with Nazi commands nor by military resistance against them. The vast majority of Europe's Jews perished in the process, though not without resistance. Some did survive the ghettos and the camps. The story of their struggle has magnificence. Unfortunately, that distinction was achieved against overwhelming odds, in part because the Nazi state revealed a potential for bureaucratically organized, systematic domination that exceeded moral comprehension. The Jews had developed survival strategies of compliance and endurance that had worked against less radical threats in the past. These techniques, sadly, were no match for the state power of the Nazis. The unimaginable happened—without the help of computers and other technological advances that are ours now.

Although the Nazis did not parade their death camps openly, the extermination of the Jews was no secret either. It bears remembering, however, that awareness of the Final Solution involved numerous stages and decisions. On all sides, they were momentous. Dissemination of news about the Holocaust, for example, was complicated not only because the Nazi regime suppressed the truth but also because such reports as did exist could not readily be repeated with impunity or seemed so horrible as to be beyond belief. In short, one could learn the truth and yet disguise, doubt, dismiss, or deny it; and even when one surmised or knew that a report was authentic, questions remained about what, if anything, should be done. Thus, the third major portion of our study concentrates on responses to the Holocaust, then and now. That story begins with an examination of the ways in which Christian churches reacted to Hitler's policies. Although exceptions exist, a majority of Christian institutions and individuals either stood by as the Holocaust unfolded or actively contributed to the Jews' demise. But if Christian complicity is part of the catastrophe represented by Auschwitz, religious institutions were not alone in failing to do all that they could to alleviate the plight of persecuted minorities. Western governments knew about "the Jewish problem," even talked about it during the thirties, but generally did little to relax restrictive immigration policies in favor of Jewish refugees. Intent though they were on refusing Hitler victory during the war, serious questions remain as to whether they did everything possible to minimize the Nazi toll on the Jews. Nor were business communities and the professions left with clean hands. Granted new freedom to experiment by the Nazis, German science made unprecedented use of human subjects, destroying most of them in the process. Under Hitler, Germany industry capitalized on the fact that profit can be made from human misery. It modernized slavery, finding ways to get the most for the least by working people to death. Moreover, the Nazi experiment proved that a highly advanced society, steeped in music, art, philosophy, and literature, is not immune to propaganda that teaches people to kill.

A common reaction greets such revelations with shock and surprise: such realities should not be, but if they did occur they must surely be an aberration, a deviation from the norm. We advance a very different thesis. Without question the Holocaust is shocking, and it is so because it did not have to be. But it is equally important to understand how irresistible the Holocaust was, how rational were the responses of standing-by that characterized so many of the institutions and individuals of the Western world. Here we must make a special effort not to be misunderstood. In arguing for the irresistibility of the Holocaust and for the rationality of responses of the sort that have been mentioned, our intention is not to condone or to legitimize mass death. Quite the contrary, our points instead are, first, that any tendency to see the Holocaust and the responses concurrent to it as purely contingent or irrational ignores the fact that there was a certain logic at once forceful and compelling at work within them. Second, it is crucial to see how the content of that logic developed and unfolded, because only by doing so can one become clear about the modern powers of destruction that threaten human life and about what is necessary to check them.

Defenseless life was sacrificed by the Nazis—that much is clear. What is more problematic is whether the Holocaust was a crime and, if so, in what senses? Postwar trials held by the victorious Allies and by the Israelis, too, provide verdicts in the affirmative, but the fact remains that had the Nazis triumphed instead the world might have concluded otherwise. One issue, then, is whether the reality of law and morality that transcends the boundaries established by political power has itself been victimized at Auschwitz. Practically speaking, answers to that question depend on what individuals believe. True, those beliefs do not determine reality completely, for the existence of God or of normative principles may not depend on us at all. Nonetheless, it does appear that the efficacy of God's reality or of moral principles that govern human conduct may indeed depend on human convictions that God is real and that norms exist which cannot be violated with impunity. In spite of the ultimate defeat of the Nazis, what they did to the Jews at Auschwitz is sufficient to drive home a telling point, namely, that the rights of the defeated dead are of precious little consequence. Functionally, normative status belongs much more to decisions governed by power politics and cost-effective economics, which tend to hold nothing sacred unless it is expedient to do so.

Literature and art during and after Auschwitz have much to teach us about such dilemmas and about the struggle that continues to determine what values shall have priority. The Holocaust cannot be encountered without despair over the power of many traditional views about the good, the true, and the beautiful to sustain themselves against the might of human destructiveness. And yet that is not the only story. The Holocaust once more reveals some of the grandeur of humanity, including the perserverance to suffer and die for matters of faith and to survive to fight for the insistence that no human being ought to be considered surplus. The range of possibility is wide in such matters. The literature and art of the Holocaust help us to explore it and to see something worthwhile about ourselves along the way.

Nearly all of this literature raises questions about the silence of God, which reveals once again the centrality of religious factors in understanding the Holocaust. The question is whether God, particularly through nonintervention, may have sacrificed Divinity in the Holocaust, at least in terms of the ways that Jews and Christians have tended to think about Divinity. Put otherwise, the Holocaust is a season of the "death of God," which is simply a verbal instrument, utilizing the vocabulary of religion, to point to the functionally radical secularity of our times. No sensitive religious thinker can approach Auschwitz without sharing in that experience. How Christians and Jews respond to it, and how their responses affect what they say to one another in a post-Holocaust setting, constitutes an important chapter in the quest for identity undertaken by individuals and groups in the late twentieth century. Our secular world is, to use Max Weber's term, largely "disenchanted." That is, our lives are not those of children of God, and the powers that actually govern our world are not divine. Rationalization and intellectualization reduce creation to naturalistic categories, moral absolutes to relativistic conventions, and inalienable human rights to boundaries established by those who have the power to define social reality. Although religious conviction lives on after the Holocaust, more intense and authentic in some circles than it was before, there can be little doubt that the Holocaust has left the world more profane and less sacred than before. That fact is not cause for celebration, for it may mean that human life is worth less than it used to be.

Finally, the legacy of the Holocaust is a staggering human agenda for the future. Today's world is one in which the credibility of traditional moral and religious norms has been threatened perhaps beyond repair. And yet this world contains a population that continues to grow enormous. As it does so, the specter of scarcity grows larger, too. If the twentieth century has been one of progress, as we are so often told, a more realistic appraisal finds that many of its advances cheapen life and enhance capabilities and even reasons for destroying it. Do we have the resources, individually and collectively, to check such forces, if not to turn them around? Our book ends by reflecting on that question.

What Can Be Done?

At least three governing theses emerge from the preceding outline of the way in which this book interprets the Holocaust. First, to grasp both the Holocaust's uniqueness and its place in a larger and continuing social evolution, attention must focus on the fact that some populations have come to be judged surplus, redundant, unwanted. Any people may fall into this category. They actually do so when, for any reason, they cannot find a viable role in the society they inhabit. The forces that conspired to render Jews superfluous in the Third Reich were religious, racial, cultural, and not least of all economic. When people become surplus, one solution to that problem is expulsion. The Final Solution is to kill them. Second, the Holocaust-as-catastrophe is best characterized by the fact that the Nazi state revealed a potential for bureaucratically organized, systematic domination that exceeded the comprehension of the liberal, enlightened imagination of the day. That power resulted in a radical state-sponsored program of population elimination, a fact that helps to define the Holocaust's continuities and discontinuities with events before and after. Third, it is crucial to understand that the ensuing sacrifice of defenseless lives—both by the overt killers and by those who stood by—was rational, not in terms of some absolute standard of value but in the sense that it had a compelling logic of its own.

To the extent that these propositions are valid, humankind faces a profoundly problematic future. It includes fundamental uncertainties about morality and law, about state power and "progress," about wealth and well-being, about God and religion, and about too many people and not enough resources. A fourth thesis waits to be found in this labyrinth, and it may be located by reflection on what can be done. One thing that can be done is *genocide*, which was an all-but-inevitable consequence of the National Socialist emphases on antisemitism, German nationalism, and conquest of new territory for the German people. Often used in conjunction with the Holocaust, genocide is a recent term, coined by Raphael Lemkin in 1944. Significantly, as Lemkin defined it to mean "the destruction of a nation or of an ethnic group," he observed that genocide denoted "an old practice in its modern development."[15] Lemkin saw that the plight of the Jews under Hitler was not a simple repetition of past historical patterns. Yet precisely what was new and unprecedented in these circumstances? Far from resolving that issue to everyone's satisfaction, Lemkin's discussion initiated a continuing debate about whether the Holocaust is better understood as an instance of genocide or whether it is a singular event that belongs in a category all its own.

The problem is that genocide covers a multitude of sins. The destruction of a nation or of an ethnic group can happen, for example, through deprivation of the means to live and procreate or through killing them outright. In short, the methods of genocide can be diverse. Even killing can be slow and indirect—starvation, for instance—as well as quick and immediate. The destruction process, moreover, can be as subtle as it is prolonged. Procedures to curtail birth rates and to increase mortality can have a genocidal effect over time. Eventually a people can also disappear if their culture is decimated by eliminating intellectual leadership, dismantling institutions, and suppressing literacy.[16]

Variations on the theme of genocide also include another basic distinction. There is a difference between genocide understood as the annihilation of a national, religious, or ethnic identity, and a more radical form that makes no exceptions for the giving up of such identity through assimilation or conversion. The difference is that between seeing the potential victim of genocide as having a fixed and immutable nature versus one that could be altered by choice or acculturation. Furthermore, it needs to be noted that genocide is a term that covers more or less extreme cases of depopulation. There is no precise measurement of when a people has been functionally destroyed, nor is it always crystal clear when an attempt in that direction is underway.

The Jews were permanent Nazi targets. They lacked any options for changing their identities to guarantee their safety within the Third Reich. Nazi propaganda portrayed the Jews as less than subhuman, in fact as not human at all. They

were considered disgusting parasitic vermin and at the same time the embodi-
ment of absolute evil that must be eliminated to complete the Nazi drama of salvation. Hence they were the only group Hitler destined for *total* destruction by
unrelenting, mass murder. Hitler and his cohorts, of course, were not the first
people who wanted thoroughly to eliminate the Jews from their midst. The Nazis, however, were quite ready to resort to measures to ensure this end absolutely, whereas their predecessors lacked the wherewithal and/or the resolution
to do so. Thus they launched a program of population riddance whose systematic character was distinctive. The end the Nazis had in view was less purely
novel than it was an outlook that evolved naturally from the past. To some extent, even the means necessary to achieve the Nazis' goal had ample precedents.
The *implementation* of these means to achieve the Final Solution, however, was
National Socialism's unprecedented contribution. These considerations make
clear that events much milder than the Holocaust can be cases of genocide. At
the very least, then, it is appropriate to see Hitler's destruction of the Jews as an
extreme case of genocide, as "the farthest point of the continuum." As such,
Yehuda Bauer suggests, a special designation is appropriate. "Holocaust" can
designate the murder of the Jews carried out by Hitler. It can also be "a generic
name for an ideologically motivated planned total murder of a whole people,"
which, thanks to Hitler, can never again be the unthinkable possibility that it
once was.[17]

Only in the twentieth century under Hitler and the Nazis did the direct and
total killing of a people biologically identified as Jewish become an implemented human intention. Closely related but not identical practices have been
pursued before and since, but the Holocaust remains what Fackenheim has
called it, namely, an "epoch-making event."[18] Consider two modern attempts
at population elimination to clarify further some similarities and differences.
First, as Americans sought their own *Lebensraum* by expanding westward in the
nineteenth century, millions of Native Americans were destroyed—more than
40% of the population died. Nevertheless, this genocide was not on a par with
the fate of the European Jews under Hitler. Missionizing efforts toward the Indians and the establishment of reservations show that American intentions stopped
short of a truly Final Solution. Such points are made not to minimize the destruction of Native American life in the United States, but rather to clarify how
civilization has "advanced" to new levels of destructive consciousness in our
own day.

A second important benchmark is found in the early twentieth-century case of
the Armenians. In 1853 Czar Nicholas I of Russia labeled the Ottoman Empire
the "sick man" of Europe. This crumbling Turkish regime, which once
stretched from Persia to Hungary, was a congeries of nationalities without an
adequate base of unity that could enable it to compete with the nationalistic con-
sciousnesses that were rising in other European states at the time. The Armeni-

ans, a Christian minority in this predominantly Muslim culture, had long been present in the empire, but in the late nineteenth century, as they began to assert themselves collectively, they became increasingly the targets of pogroms and massacres.

The empire's decline greatly concerned an enlightened group of Turkish officers whose party achieved a 1908 victory—welcomed by Muslims, Christians, and Jews alike—under the promise of "Freedom, Justice, Equality, Fraternity." Political instability was unrelieved, however, and by 1911 a dominant faction emerged with the conviction that a strong and unified Turkey was incompatible with a continuing acceptance of minority demands, including those of the Armenians. Finding cultural pluralism contrary to their aims of political rationalization, which, like all rationalization, is governed by the principle of "least effort," this group moved for "Turkification." There was liberal opposition to this program, but it fell to a coup in January 1913 leaving Turkey under military dictatorship.

Uneasy about losing power to Russian influence, Turkey went to war as Germany's ally. By the winter of 1915, the Turks were in combat against Russian units, many of which were Armenian, along a front that included Turkish provinces with a substantial Armenian population. The stage was set to take a decisive step in the Turkification process. Thus, under the pretext of Armenian disloyalty, the government informed the governors of certain border provinces that a decision had been taken to exterminate all Armenians living in Turkey. There could be no exceptions, for those Armenians innocent today might well be guilty tomorrow. Thus an estimated two-thirds of the 1.8 million Armenians living in Turkey in 1914 were either annihilated outright or marched off to die in the desert.

The scale of Turkish ambitions was more modest than those of the Nazis later, and the Turks lacked some of the detailed biological and demonizing ideology that informed Hitler's policies toward the Jews. But present in the Turkish-Armenian encounter was a calculation of means and ends in which premeditated genocide of a radical kind emerged as the remedy of choice. The point to underscore, which will be apparent in the Holocaust as well, is that genocide—including the development of efficient, cost-effective methods for executing it—is as much an expression of the rationalization of the economy and society as any other bureaucratically managed assembly-line operation. Genocide does not happen without governmental sponsorship. Yet governments seldom elect genocide as an end in itself. Instead it is a means of eliminating a target population that challenges an economic, political, cultural, religious, or ideological value of the politically dominant group. To speak of the rationality of genocide is *not* to condone it. On the contrary, to recognize that genocide can be "rational" in the sense of being the most efficient, economical way to solve a "problem" is to raise urgent questions about the "progress" and political power that human energy has achieved. For genocide represents the ultimate expression of the revolution of rationality with which the problem of population redundancy began in the first place.

In the cases of both the Armenians and the Jews, a basic condition for genocide had been in place for centuries. As Helen Fein puts it, both of these minorities "had been decreed by the dominant group that was to perpetrate the crime to be outside the sanctified universe of obligation—that circle of people with reciprocal obligations to protect each other whose bonds arose from their relation to a deity or sacred source of authority."[19] At least in the case of the Jews, of course, this being outside had for centuries certain components that left them inside as well. Christian consciousness could find a place for Jews as potential converts. Pariah status, therefore, could still leave one a place of sorts; it did not necessarily entail mass death. Yet before National Socialism was through, that was precisely what did happen.

The Armenian genocide and the Jewish Holocaust are distinctively twentieth-century phenomena rooted in ancient traditions that yield pariah status but also require factors that came to fruition only in recent decades. The Armenian disaster happened because the calculating rationality of the "Young Turks" in power determined that the most cost-effective way to modernize the Turkish state entailed extermination of a minority group. The Nazis made similar calculations to facilitate their aims for the Third Reich. The difference was that their efforts reached far beyond established German frontiers and sought a Europe—ultimately a world—that would be *Judenrein*, free of Jews altogether. That goal was practically conceivable only through a sophisticated, bureaucratic orchestration of modern technology and transportation. The Nazis were ready when the twentieth century brought the required elements together in an environment of economic upheaval and mass warfare in which everything was permitted.

Knowing what has been done takes us back to the question: what can be done? In particular is there anything that study about the Holocaust can accomplish to make human life less under threat, to keep genocidal tendencies at bay? Many advocates of study about the Holocaust assume that there is. Frequently appealing to George Santayana's pronouncement that "those who do not remember the past are condemned to repeat it," they suppose that study of what has happened can safeguard against such massive wasting of life in the future. Evidence in favor of such a view is not overwhelming, however, because population elimination continues at the very time when the Holocaust is studied by more people than ever before.

Study about the Holocaust can provide some understanding of what happened in a particular time and place, why it happened, and how that happening fits into a broader historical pattern. Such understanding, unfortunately, does not constitute a map for the present and the future, at least not one to guarantee that people will stem the tides that kill. It does show something about the strength of those tides. One of the things that stands out is the fact that those who control the use of violence in any political regime can go far in acting with impunity against others within their jurisdiction. Only when power from the outside was brought to bear, either directly or in support of insurgents from within, could the plight of Armenians, Jews, and more recently the Cambodians be stopped. Study of the Holocaust, then, should be undertaken without sanguine illusions. It reveals a world more complex, more obsessed with power, more difficult to humanize than one might have guessed before.

The result is that the Holocaust leaves us with tortuous questions. What priorities shall we establish? What ends shall we seek? Which ones are realistic and which ones are naive? What shall count as good? Where can courage be found? Can the individual do anything that matters? Are communities of moral concern significant any more? What will become of the twentieth century?

What is the Holocaust? We started with that question, and it will rise up again at the end, for responses to it hang in suspense. The Holocaust was Final Solution, catastrophe, and sacrifice. All the forces that made it so are still at large in the world, some of them with greater power than ever. The issue is whether there are other powers, too, and whether they can muster enough authority to keep the Holocaust from being a prelude to something worse, which ultimately might include omnicide, the death of all life on earth, via nuclear war.

Horst Wessel's song honored the dead, but it moved men and women to kill. That song is silent now, but there are others to take its place. They form the counterpoint to Anne Frank's diary, which still moves others to bring out the good that she saw within the human heart. *Civilization and Its Discontents*, the struggle between Eros and death, was Sigmund Freud's concern. His study works in between, trying to discern what makes people love and hate.

No one can be sure that attempts to understand the Holocaust will change anything very much, just as Freud could not be sure that his research would have a happy outcome. Indeed the study of final solutions, catastrophes, and sacrifices may produce despair or even help to show the way for turning potential victims into corpses. But without seeing what Horst Wessel's song can do, it is also unlikely that Anne Frank's diary can be read without a sentimentality that obscures its power to yield a more realistic and intense yearning that might conserve life, that might save men and women from the threat of economic redundancy and help to foster the right of all persons to a place of dignity and social utility within their communities. A fourth thesis that lurks in the Holocaust and its aftermath is this: in spite of all the risks involved in seeking to understand approaches to Auschwitz, we can ill afford not to make the effort.

PART ONE

EARLY HISTORICAL ROOTS

Chapter 1

The Jew as Outsider: The Greco-Roman and Early Christian Worlds

Holocaust history begins in a world that had no Jews at all. This fact suggests that the Holocaust leaves some questions beyond answering, for the path that must be followed to explore how Auschwitz came to be will not finally lay to rest issues about why existence is structured so that Auschwitz was possible. Granted, philosophical, scientific, and theological theories are not lacking to respond to that ultimate "Why?" and some of them make more sense than others. But it is also true that the more one learns about the Holocaust, the more understandable it becomes, the more one may be left to wonder.

"Man," said the French philosopher Albert Camus, "is not entirely to blame; it was not he who started history; nor is he entirely innocent, since he continues it."[1] Jewish history, which has so distinctively marked the world, is a case in point.[2] The biblical accounts of creation in Genesis, for example, do not identify Adam and Eve as Jews. Whether one takes them to be actual persons or mythic figures, they are man and woman in a pre-Jewish world. And yet that appraisal is not all that must be said, for the story of Adam and Eve is also a Jewish story, one that begins an ancient account that ponders why there are Jews as well as why the world and human life in general exist.

Genesis, the first of five biblical books forming the Pentateuch or the Torah, is a blending of oral and written instruction much older than the final written codification that scholars place around 550 B.C.E. Insofar as Jewish identity hinges on that written testament, it is a human creation forged as tribes of diverse origin blended their shared experiences and memories into a unifying, articulated self-consciousness. But these experiences and memories, and even their articulation in a final written form, are not solely the results of conscious choices. Events and experiences happen to people; the forces of life are not completely under human control but instead move in and through us partly at their own bidding. Jews do not account for themselves any more than Adam (man) and Eve (woman) can do so.

Religiously speaking, Jews have affirmed that God accounts for their existence. We shall see some of the awesome effects that have followed from that conviction, but first let us probe a gray zone where the world vacillated between having and not having "the Jewish question." Even the best recent scholarship cannot fix the dates precisely, but biblical history appears to begin between the year 2000 B.C.E. and 1900 B.C.E. when tribes of people, reputedly led by a patriarchal figure eventually named Abraham, migrated southwestward from Haran in Mesopotamia into the land of Canaan. No one is sure why these journeys occurred, but the biblical tradition asserts it was because Abraham felt that his God had so directed. Lured by a divine promise that he would become the father of a great people, Abraham and his seminomadic followers stopped at the site of Shechem. There, the Bible tells us, God promised to give the surrounding land to Abraham's offspring. Periodic famines kept these people on the move. Under Abraham's successors, Isaac and then Jacob (the latter eventually identified as Israel), they moved about the hill country of Canaan until hard times once more drove them southwest, this time into Egypt.

A majority of modern biblical scholars regard these accounts not as literal historical records but as a reconstruction brought about as a congeries of strangers formed a community by adopting a common faith at Sinai. As the well-known story of the Exodus and the theophany at Sinai is recounted in Scripture, the "Hebrews" who were enslaved in Egypt appear to share common tribal and religious roots. In reality, the Bible offers ample hints that the group who escaped from Egypt with Moses did not possess a common inheritance. For example, referring to Moses' band in the wilderness, Scripture speaks of "the rabble that was among them" (Num. 11:4).

For several centuries before the Exodus, people from Canaan and Syria had entered Egypt, some as hostages and prisoners of war, some as merchants, and some who had been forced to take up residence in Egypt after engaging in activities hostile to their Egyptian overlords. The name "Hebrews," then, probably designated a number of alien peoples who shared a common condition and social location in Egypt but were from varied backgrounds. Each group of resident aliens retained something of its own identity, especially insofar as their indigenous religious traditions involved elements of ancestor worship. Not all were slaves, but their situation tended to deteriorate over time. In some respects, the situation of the Hebrews was similar to that of members of a modern multiethnic metropolis, in which diverse groups share common problems in the present but remain distinct because of differences in origin, religion, and culture. Once unified, they explained their experience by the cycle of stories involving Abraham, Isaac, Jacob, and even Moses himself. When Moses arrived on the scene, however, the Hebrews were less than Jewish.

Biographical data about Moses is restricted to biblical sources, but it seems clear that he was a charismatic leader born during the reign of Seti I, Pharaoh of

Egypt (1308–1290 B.C.E.). Tradition has it that Seti I, fearing that the Hebrew slave population was becoming too large, decided for reasons of security to limit its growth by eliminating all newborn Hebrew males. Moses survived. Put into the Nile in a reed basket fashioned by his mother, according to Scripture he was discovered and adopted by an Egyptian princess. Although nurtured in the Pharaoh's court, Moses also identified with those who were oppressed. Thus, when he took revenge on an Egyptian soldier who killed one of them, he had to seek refuge in the desert.

Again, no one knows with certainty what happened to Moses as he lived there with a tribe called the Midianites. The Bible, however, speaks of Moses' encountering a strangely burning bush. The bush was not consumed. Instead, as Moses approached to discern it better, he was left with the conviction that the God called Yahweh ("The One who causes to be") was directing him to return to Egypt and to liberate the captives. Conviction was mixed with reluctance and skepticism about this mission, but Moses went, and under his leadership the Hebrew clans fled.

Until this time, the Hebrews probably shared a common yearning for liberation and a common hatred of their overlords but little else. This was enough to unify them for the escape. As soon as they were beyond the reach of the Egyptians, however, a compelling basis for unity beyond shared antipathy and a desire to flee had to be found if the band of fugitives and outcasts was to survive the natural and human hazards of the wilderness. Fortunately, the escape provided a further shared experience, the Exodus itself.

In the ancient Near East, where the distinction between group membership and religious identity was unknown, there could be only one basis for communal unity. The diverse peoples could only become a single people if they were united by a common God who was the author of their shared experience. This new basis for unifying the ethnically diverse band was proclaimed in the prologue to the Ten Commandments: " 'I am the LORD your God, who brought you out of the land of Egypt, out of the house of bondage' " (Exod. 20:2).

The God of the new religion, moreover, had to be one whose power exceeded that of Pharaoh, the Egyptian god-king. Nor could any of the diverse peoples among the escapees claim that its particular ancestral god (or gods) was the true God of the entire band without arousing the mistrust and hostility of the others. Ancestral gods were an impediment to unity. The Hebrews shared a common historical experience more than kinship. Only a God who was regarded as the author of their shared experience could unify them. The Bible reflects this emphasis: " 'You shall have no other gods before me. . . . for I the LORD your God am a jealous God' " (Exod. 20:3–5).

Yahweh's insistence on exclusive worship had both political and religious implications. It united those who accepted worship of Yahweh into a community and barred them from returning to the disuniting worship of their ancestral gods.

After they had been unified under the new God, it was natural for the assorted peoples to claim that they had been kin all along and to read back elements of continuity between their common God and their ancestral gods. Hence, Yahweh, the God of Moses, was identified as the God of Abraham, Isaac, and Jacob, too.

Thus, in the desert at Mount Sinai, probably about 1300 B.C.E., the Hebrews, though still far from being a people united under an earthly king, took formative steps toward a distinctive identity. Their unifying pact with Yahweh, it is crucial to underscore, was a *covenant*. This agreement proffered through Moses to the people by Yahweh, set forth the terms of an agreement that bound God and the Hebrews together, albeit on an asymmetrical footing. God's deliverance of the people from Egyptian bondage, Moses told them, had not been an end in itself. God expected something more: " 'Now therefore, if you will obey my voice and keep my covenant, you shall be my own possession among all peoples; for all the earth is mine, and you shall be to me a kingdom of priests and a holy nation' " (Exod. 19:5–6). The people accepted this status of being God's chosen people. It was the proper response to their liberation.

We can better understand this crucial action of covenant and election by noting that the structure of the biblical covenant between God and the followers of Moses resembles that between a suzerain and his vassals in Hittite treaties of the fourteenth and thirteenth centuries B.C.E.. In these treaties, the ruler grants his vassal protection but stipulates what is expected of the vassal in return. In both the Hittite and the biblical versions, blessings and curses, the former as reward for compliance and the latter as dire consequences of disobedience and rebellion, are emphasized.

In the Hittite world the solemnity of these pacts was often dramatized in elaborate ceremonies. Biblical scholars note that the account in Deuteronomy reflects the procedure of such a treaty ceremony. A recital of the historical events that moved the vassal to enter into the covenant is followed by proclamation of the law to be obeyed, then by a statement of mutual obligations between God and Israel, and finally by the crucial blessings and curses. Although the Hebrews were not yet politically united, they had become one people in agreeing to obey the commandments of their God. Having entered this covenant, the people were warned that disobedience could not take place with impunity, for Yahweh is a jealous God who tolerates no rivals.

Did God or only Moses speak at Sinai? Did divine revelation bring Jewish identity to the fore, or was that consciousness forged more by forces of human politics that used religious ingredients to secure a base of power? The historical record can be read in more than one way, but of this much we can be sure: the existence of a Jewish people who fell under Hitler's threat three thousand years later does depend on the tradition that God acted in history in the Exodus and at Sinai. That action, moreover, singled out a people whose destiny would not only be linked with the land of Israel but also would set them apart from every other human group that has walked the face of the earth. With Moses, if not with God, the world received "the Jewish question." Nothing was ever the same again.

Anti-Jewish Policies in the Greco-Roman World

Space permits no detailed account of the next millennium of Jewish history. Suffice it to say that Moses did not live to enter the "promised land" of Canaan, the land of Israel, which came to be construed as part of the pact between Yahweh and the Hebrew tribes. Joshua succeeded in dominating that territory, but pressure from hostile elements remained intense. In waging wars of defense, however, the Hebrew confederation was ultimately solidified under its first king, Saul, and later under the more expansive rule of David and Solomon (1000–922 B.C.E.). For a time an Israelite empire prospered, but Solomon's death brought political division, and two states emerged: Israel in the north and Judah in the south. Existing in a buffer zone between Egypt and Mesopotamia, these small powers were constantly threatened by political struggle in the Middle East. In 722 the Northern Kingdom fell to the Assyrians. When the Babylonians seized hegemony from the Assyrians, Jerusalem and the Southern Kingdom fell to them in 586, and the Jews were dispersed and exiled. A century later, under Persian rule, they were permitted to return to their homeland. Jerusalem and the Temple were restored. Politically, Jewish life remained under Persian authority until the conquests of Alexander the Great (356–323 B.C.E.) brought Jews under Greek control.

Jewish life has enriched human experience in countless ways and out of all proportion to its numbers. Yet viewed in one way, these ancient Jews seem singularly unimportant in the world's history. Admittedly their ways of life differed from other groups around them, but their political power was less than overwhelming. Most people knew little about them. It would even be hard to document that Jews were consistently singled out for special discrimination and persecution in the world of pre-Christian antiquity. This is not to say that they were specially favored or even that there was nothing to approximate either the anti-Judaism that emerged from the triumph of Christianity or the racially-oriented antisemitism that would follow in nineteenth- and twentieth-century Europe. Some of the seeds of that hostility were planted in the Greco-Roman era prior to the birth of Christianity. It will be well to note them.

As we do so, let us take a moment to clarify some concepts. Uses of the term "antisemitism" are now so frequent that one might suppose them to be of long standing. In fact, the term was first popularized in the late 1870s by a German racist ideologue named Wilhelm Marr. He employed it in speaking about the largely secular anti-Jewish political campaigns that were widespread in Europe at the time. The word derives from an eighteenth-century etymological analysis that differentiated between languages with "Aryan" roots and those with "Semitic" ones. This distinction, in turn, led to the assumption—a false one—that there are corresponding racial groups. Under this rubric, Jews became Semites, thus paving the way for Marr's usage. He might have used the conventional German *Judenhass*, but that way of referring to Jew-hatred carried religious connotations that Marr wanted to deemphasize in favor of racial ones. Apparently more "scientific," the term *Antisemitismus* caught on and eventually became a way of speaking about all the forms of hostility experienced by the Jews throughout history.[3] Antisemitism, then, is both one thing and many. Hatred of Jews is at its heart, but the driving motives behind that hatred can be diverse: economic, racial, religious, social, and mixtures in between. To reckon with antisemitism, then, is to do much more than to deal with "prejudice," for its causes reach deep down into fundamental social, economic, and religious structures.

Religious, and therefore social, factors became the ancient seedbed for modern antisemitism, as Alexander the Great sought to bring his empire under the domination of Greek culture. As far as the Jews were concerned, that policy had impact not only in the Jews' ancient homeland but also upon the now widely scattered Jewish enclaves that could be found throughout the Mediterranean world. Jewish immigration—much of it forced by exile, but some of it voluntary—had for centuries dispersed this people, and even when there was opportunity to return to the homeland, significant numbers decided that their interests were best served by remaining in the Diaspora. Some of these Jews assimilated completely. In most cases, however, a Jewish identity that differentiated Jew from non-Jew (Gentile) was sustained. The decision to remain different, needless to say, could lead to friction between a Jewish minority and any dominant power whose aspirations for empire were predicated on cultural homogeneity. It should be noted, however, that Jews who had migrated to the East did not generally experience such tension. In both China and India, for example, Jews led essentially peaceful lives as a group. In particular, they experienced none of the violence that would be the fate of the Jews later on in Christian and, to a lesser degree, in Muslim lands.

Where Greek power dominated, the typical view held that anything non-Greek was barbarian. Thus, a people who worshiped but one God exclusively— and that one intolerant of any rivals and therefore very different from those of the Greeks—might not do so with impunity. Religious belief, moreover, never stops with theological affirmation. It penetrates into cultural practices, and thus the Jews were different once again in their observance of a special Sabbath, in their rites of circumcision, in their restrictions on diet and marriage, and in their conviction that Jerusalem was the Holy City.

Cultural collision could hardly be avoided, and one of its early scenes was in the Egyptian city of Alexandria, which was becoming a commercial and intellectual center. Alexander himself invited Jews to settle there. Thousands accepted, and many of them prospered while occupying a specially designated area where they could live by their own religious law. Resentment, however, was not far behind. Fueled by Egyptian dislike of tolerance shown to the Jews and by Jewish refusal to accommodate to Greek religious and social standards, an early form of antisemitism found a home in Alexandria. The basic charge was that Jews were misanthropic, distrustful, and hateful toward other peoples, a libel whose virulence would spread and intensify with time.

Tension between Greek and Jewish ways was not restricted to the Diaspora. Greek culture had made substantial inroads in the Jews' Holy Land. Matters came to a head in 167 B.C.E. when a Syrian ruler, Antiochus IV Epiphanes, dedicated the Temple in Jerusalem to Zeus. Numerous Jews had been sympathetic to assimilating Jewish life into Greek ways, but this step went too far. Led by Judas Maccabaeus, a successful revolt ensued. Rededication of the Temple, now commemorated by the Jewish holiday of Hanukkah, occurred in 164 B.C.E. and a century of national independence followed. Both within the Jewish homeland and in the Diaspora the hellenizing trends were reversed. A Jewish revival ensued, replete with an expansionist war led by the Judean John Hyrcanus, who forcibly converted some of the vanquished. During his rule (134–104), the Pharisees, a party both religious and political, achieved prominence.

Jewish successes, however, did not mean that all was well. If the ethical demands of Jewish monotheism attracted voluntary converts in the now declining and even decadent Greek world, these gains were hardly welcomed by everyone. Gentile intellectuals especially launched anti-Jewish attacks alleging that Jews hated strangers, and they were absurdly superstitious; they practiced ritual murder, but they were also atheists. Tension mounted, although its seeds would not produce their most devastating harvest until much later.

The influence of Greek culture outlasted the political might of Alexander the Great. After his death in 323, the Mediterranean political situation was destabilized, even though the powers vying for authority were united by strands of Greek culture. By the beginning of the second century B.C.E., however, Rome had gradually moved in to fill the power vacuum. Soon Roman authority dominated the Mediterranean world. How did this development affect Jewish life?

What occurred was basically a continuation of relationships as they had been under Greek dominance. Certainly in the pre-Christian era there was no official state antisemitism on the part of the Romans. Although Jewish religious practice was at variance with theirs, Jews were if anything granted special legal and religious privileges in a regime that was quite tolerant of religious diversity. Thus, a large Jewish community in Rome, second in size in the Diaspora only to that of Alexandria during the first century B.C.E., could enter the city's business life, win converts, and participate in political life. So long as they posed no serious threat to the government's stability, their lives were reasonably secure. A continuing vilification of Jews by intellectuals remained a concern, but those views, fraught with political dangers though they were, did not come to dominate official government policy at that time.

Nonetheless, Jewish life under Roman authority could hardly be described as tranquil. The first Jewish pogrom may have occurred, for example, in Alexandria during Caligula's reign in 38 C.E. Somewhat later, in Antioch, Ephesus, and numerous cities bordering on Palestine, as the Romans now called the region that contained the former Jewish homeland, the Jews experienced outbreaks of violence, often provoked because of Jewish refusal to join mainstream religious practices. Inside Palestine itself the situation was not more comfortable. By midcentury many Jews found the burden of Roman rule intolerable, and none more so than the nationalists known as Zealots. Open rebellion broke out, and at first the Jews were successful. By August 70, however, Roman power, which abhorred political insurrection and was efficient at crushing it, had prevailed, and the Temple in Jerusalem was in ruins. The last Jewish stronghold, Masada, fell three years later. The Jews who died there—nearly a thousand men, women, and children—did so by their own hand rather than permitting the Romans to enslave or kill them. There will be more to say about the fall of Jerusalem shortly, but for now suffice it to note that a less militant Jewish population survived, and under the leadership of Rabbi Yochanan ben Zakkai, the Jewish religion was transmuted. It centered no longer on sacrifices at the Temple presided over by hereditary priests. Instead local synagogues, which would produce a rabbinic civilization stressing study, the sanctity of life, and obedience to God's will as it came to be interpreted by scribes and sages throughout the centuries, rose to the fore. Still, Jewish visions of independence were not dead altogether. Under the emperor Trajan and again under Hadrian there were Jewish rebellions —the Kitos War (115–117) and the Bar Kochba War (132–135), respectively— against Roman power. With the crushing of these revolts, Israel's life as an effective political force in antiquity came to an end.

To summarize the major points that should be drawn from the historical sketch set forth above, it is clear, first, that a two-way street existed where relationships between Jews and Gentiles were concerned in the pre-Christian world. While Jews were complementary from an economic point of view, their ways of life were still alien, not in superficial ways but in terms of the most fundamental social, political, and religious matters. Second, although the balance of power was always heavily weighted in favor of non-Jews, the Jews remained a minority people primarily because they chose to be, and they did so not least because of a religious persuasion that they were chosen by God for a special purpose and destiny. Their covenant with God could not be violated with impunity, or so many of them believed. One result of sustaining this covenant was that Jewish life could understandably be perceived as foreign to the dominant political and cultural forces of the day. That status could not be held with impunity either. It was a step toward making the Jews tragically superfluous.

It should come as no surprise that tensions might build to the point of hatred and violence, unless one holds a view of human society more protean or of human nature more sanguine than history makes credible. At the same time, however, it is important to note what did not transpire in these ancient civilizations. Plenty of vilification and brutality could be found—more than a million Jews lost their lives in the Judeo-Roman War of 66–70 alone—but the antisemitism that existed then was not mainly engendered by racism, nor by economic prejudice, nor did it involve unrelenting elimination of political rights, let alone a systematic plan for total Jewish annihilation. It can even be argued that this early antisemitism was not even primarily theological, at least not in the sense that would emerge once Christian power was on the scene, although it did have much to do with a Jewish separatism and yearning for independence that was rooted in religious practice.

If there was no enduring state antisemitism in antiquity, despite the extreme violence of the Jewish rebellions against Roman rule, nonetheless it must be underscored that a potent antisemitic mood was in the air from the third century B.C.E. onward. Primarily cultural and literary though it was, its attitudes exacerbated the pariah status of Jews, leaving them vulnerable in a struggle for survival against the Romans. Those struggles left the Jews largely landless and powerless. Their fate would become still more precarious as Jewish history came to be read through Christian eyes. To that account we turn next.

The Birth of Christianity and the Beginning of the Jewish-Christian Schism

The birth of Jesus and the birth of Christianity are not identical, although the narratives about the former in the Gospels of Matthew and Luke do bring the two close together. According to the New Testament book of Acts, it was at Antioch, and some time after the death of Jesus, that Jesus' disciples for the first time were called Christians. The span between events and written records of them may not have been stretched out so far as in the cases of Moses and the Pentateuch, but there is a gap between the historical Jesus and the Christian New Testament. The earliest of those canonical writings are some of the letters by Paul, and they precede by only a few years the first of the Synoptic Gospels, Mark, which is dated approximately 70 C.E. Along with the accounts by Matthew and Luke, Mark appears to draw on an earlier source, often named Q, which may have been in existence by midcentury. The birth narratives, then, are far from being eyewitness accounts of historical events, but clearly they are the accounts of witnesses who heard and saw something special in Jesus of Nazareth and testified about it. The fact that they did so changed the world no less than the liberation of Hebrew slaves from their Egyptian bondage.

Jesus, whose name is the hellenized version of the Hebrew *Joshua* or *Y'ho'shua* (meaning "the Lord saves"), preached a message proclaiming the imminent coming of the kingdom of God and the conditions for inclusion in it. Neither Jesus nor his early followers intended to establish a new religion, although their intentions did entail purification and reform of the Jewish faith. As his public ministry continued, however, some of Jesus' disciples began to view him as the Messiah traditionally promised to the Jews by God. The coming of the Messiah, foreshadowed centuries before in the prophetic writings of Isaiah and Jeremiah and fervently longed for throughout Jewish domination by the Romans, would redeem Israel and bring in the kingdom of God. How and when this divinely appointed king would carry out his work was a matter of diverse conjecture, and Jesus was not alone in having messianic expectations placed upon him.

To be regarded in this way was a mixed blessing, for Jewish and Roman leaders alike knew that subversive agitation might breed in such thinking. Thus, when Jesus eventually made his way from Galilee to Jerusalem, danger was real. How much danger no human mind could have known in advance; what ensued left the world shaken. What really happened to Jesus during those seven days is no easy matter to discern, for the claims are so varied, the testimonies so conflicting, and the resulting controversies so acrimonious throughout history that the interpretations about the facts, let alone the facts themselves, are among the elements that decisively changed the human condition. Stating the matter as simply and as neutrally as possible, the following outline can highlight some of the points that are the most crucial for linking Jesus' demise with Auschwitz.

Following the Gospel narratives, which means that one must be alert to the interpretive points that the writers wish to make at least as much as one must be concerned to piece together a chronology of factual occurrence, Jesus entered Jerusalem amid a popular demonstration by his followers near the time of Passover, the Jewish holiday that celebrates the Exodus. At such a time, both nationalistic and eschatological hopes ran high, and there can be little doubt that some of Jesus' followers—and assuredly the later interpreters—regarded Jesus' entry into the city as a sign that the kingdom of God might indeed be at hand and that Jesus himself would be instrumental in its arrival.

Such feelings were intensified by the next recorded episode, which finds Jesus driving the money-changers and sellers of sacrificial animals from the Temple. Such commercial practices, carefully restricted to the outer court of the Temple, were quite acceptable to most Jews, but Jesus cleansed it nonetheless. Not surprisingly, such actions raised questions about Jesus' authority. Thus, whether the ensuing events happened as written, the Synoptic Gospel narratives follow the cleansing of the Temple with a series of parables, discussions, and speeches that pushed the conflict between Jesus and his opponents to new heights when he predicted the destruction of Jerusalem and the Temple.

The official religious leadership of the Jews, the New Testament reports, now felt compelled to intervene, and such steps were taken on the night after Jesus shared a last meal with his followers. The precise date of this supper—prior to, after, or precisely on the first night of the Passover celebration—is disputed. A pre-Passover dating seems safest, even though it is clear that the later interpreters wanted to identify Jesus as closely as possible with the lambs that were slaughtered for the festival. In any case, Jesus was arrested and brought before the Jewish High Court (Sanhedrin).

At this point the historical facts blur even more. The Gospels offer a picture of a nighttime trial replete with false witnesses, Jesus' confession that he is the Messiah, and a death sentence for him on the charge of blasphemy. The literary effect is to contrast the messianic Jesus with the rage, cruelty, and falsehood of his opponents. These stories, however, cannot be taken simply at face value. Jewish procedure was certainly at variance with the New Testament's version of Jesus' case. Nowhere is there an instance of anyone else ever having been accused of blasphemy and sentenced to death by the Jewish authorities because of messianic claims, a fact that is noteworthy in a situation where such claims were not uncommon. Add to this the fact that if Jesus had committed blasphemy, the Jews had the right to execute him but would have done so by stoning. Instead, Jesus was turned over to Pontius Pilate, the Roman procurator, and ultimately crucified, a form of punishment that was exclusively the prerogative of Roman courts of law and reserved for political criminals.

Roman, not Jewish, power put Jesus to death. An uneasy governor, Pontius Pilate, saw Jesus' execution as the most expedient way to deal with a Jewish messianic pretender who might have a further destabilizing effect in a city that was already chaotic enough during the Passover season. If Pilate's decision to eliminate Jesus as a political suspect was encouraged and welcomed by some of the Jewish leadership for similar reasons, their numbers were small, and by no means did they represent the feelings of the entire Jewish populace, many of whom shared Jesus' antipathy toward the pro-Roman Temple leadership. According to the New Testament, however, Pilate did not accede completely to the wishes of those Jewish leaders. Overriding their protests, he insisted that the identifying inscription on Jesus' cross should read: Jesus of Nazareth, the King of the Jews (John 19:19). Whether historical fact or literary device, the point would not be missed by Christian readers: Pilate's irony conveyed the truth, but Jewish blindness was so extreme that it killed the redemption of Israel.

Jesus was a thoroughly observant Jew.[4] He opposed neither the written nor the oral law, although his interpretations differed from those of some Jewish leaders. His emphasis was on love of one's neighbor, on the need for repentance, on liberation for the oppressed. He eschewed violence and was repaid with a violent death that left his followers dismayed and scattered. Indeed his demise would probably have given him no more than a footnote in history had it not been for the fact that his disciples came to believe—and were able to convince others—that Jesus was resurrected from death.

For a time the followers of Jesus also continued to be practicing Jews but with the difference that they believed the Messiah, expected by all observant Jews, had actually come in Jesus of Nazareth. Moreover, their experience at the Jewish feast of Shavuot (Pentecost), which commemorated the giving of the Law at Mount Sinai, left them convinced that Jesus remained spiritually present among them and that his return to rule over God's kingdom on earth would not be long in coming. These beliefs were expressed and celebrated in worship that closely resembled existing Jewish rituals even while they were supplemented by scriptural interpretations that pointed to Jesus as the Messiah (the Christ in Greek) and by a commemoration of Jesus' last supper with his disciples prior to the crucifixion, which focused attention on Jesus' continuing presence and expected return.

It is crucial to note that from the outset an ardent missionary zeal characterized these early Jewish Christians. Their efforts to win converts aimed first at their fellow Jews. Jewish authorities wavered between toleration of the new sect and repression of it, but competing religious beliefs bred animosity within the ranks of the Jews themselves. One dimension of struggle revolved around the issue of whether being a follower of Jesus necessitated one's first being a Jew. The view that came to dominate—represented initially by Peter and then even more powerfully by Paul, a former Jewish persecutor of Christians who converted—was negative. Gentiles, without becoming observant Jews, could be Christians. The result was that Christianity spread, establishing communities in Rome itself by the time of Paul's execution there in 64.

Under Paul's influence, the Christian message offered to the Gentiles exerted considerable attraction. Especially among the poor and enslaved, an emphasis on equality before God, on love and charity, coupled with an exclusive sense of chosenness or election that embraced the believer who confessed Jesus as Lord, provided a hope for eternal life and therefore a status on earth that was welcome. But these benefits were not without cost, for in their early years communities of Christians were targets of Roman persecution, accused, as Jews have been, of threatening social order and political stability.

In spite of persecution, Christianity grew. One cause and effect of that growth was the emergence of written narratives about Jesus. These writings had both instructive and evangelistic purposes. They also had to deal with some ticklish problems. None was more crucial than the issue of who bore responsibility for the crucifixion of Jesus. That issue was critical because it was precisely at this juncture that the relationships between Christians, their elder Jewish siblings, and the prevailing Roman authorities stood out in boldest relief. To emphasize Rome's responsibility in Jesus' death could have unfortunate results by intensifying suspicion that the followers of Jesus were indeed undesirable anti-Roman elements. It is not accidental, therefore, that the Gospels united in playing down Pilate's role in favor of a much stronger portrayal of nearly fanatical Jewish thirst for Jesus' blood.

Other reasons for such an interpretation are not far to find, nor should they be particularly shocking when one remembers that Christianity was carved out of Jewish religious experience in such a way that each posed a threat to the other, a threat made more intense, not less, by their extremely close relationships. Already we have noted that the Jewish establishment did not always welcome Christians with open arms. By the year 90 C.E. most Jews had made a definitive religious break with Christians, who were now considered to be the greatest apostates from Judaism. Christians would more than return the favor. One crucial way of doing so involved the destruction of Jerusalem and the Temple at the end of the Judeo-Roman War in 70. We return now to that event.

The Fall of Jerusalem and the Roots of the Holocaust

The Judeo-Roman War of 66–70 C.E. and its aftermath can be seen as the Holocaust of ancient times. Rebellion against Rome broke out in Palestine in the year 66. Under normal circumstances, Rome would have been able to subdue the revolt in a few weeks. In war, however, events seldom unfold as expected. The Jewish revolt became a bloody conflict that dragged on for four long years. As the Romans overcame the Jews, slaughter, rapine, famine, and desolation were the order of the day. Of overwhelming importance for Jewish destiny was the destruction of Jerusalem's Holy Temple. The Talmud records that for seven years after the fall of Jerusalem "the nations of the world cultivated their vineyards with no other manure than the blood of Israel."

The Jewish historian Josephus records that 1,197,000 Jews were killed or taken captive by the Romans.[5] Nevertheless, Rome had no interest in exterminating the Jews as did the German government under Hitler. The victor's interest was so to reconstitute the Jewish community that it would henceforth submit peacefully to Roman rule. This could only be accomplished by a radical transformation of the Jewish community's religious and political leadership. Those who had led the Jewish people before the war were no longer acceptable to the Romans. The old aristocracy and the hereditary priesthood were excluded from any leadership role in the reconstituted community. So too were the Zealots who were chiefly responsible for starting and sustaining the war. Only one group was acceptable to Rome, the pacifist wing of the Pharisees under Rabbi Yochanan ben Zakkai, who was known to have opposed the war and to have counseled a policy of submission to Caesar.[6]

Yochanan's counsel was bitterly opposed by the Zealots, who were initially convinced that God would enable them to overcome their world-conquering foe. Yochanan and his disciples were more realistic. They understood that it was impossible for the Jews to defeat Rome. Moreover, they saw no pressing reason why they should, believing that the ultimate fate of the Jewish people was not dependent upon military strength but on reverent obedience to God's law. As long as Rome permitted the Jews religious autonomy, Yochanan was willing to accept Caesar's rule.[7]

The legend of how leadership of the Jewish community passed to the Pharisees is recorded in an ancient tradition that has been engrained in the consciousness of every rabbi, whether Orthodox or liberal, to this day. The tradition has undoubtedly been embellished. Nevertheless, it reveals a great deal about the psychology and character of Judaism. According to the legend, during the siege of Jerusalem, Yochanan determined to escape and save what he could.[8] Because Jewish law forbade keeping the dead in Jerusalem for even a single night, Yochanan's followers were able to carry their master out of the city in a coffin, pretending that he was dead. Once outside the city Yochanan was brought to the Roman commander and soon-to-be emperor, Vespasian. When the future emperor asked Yochanan in effect what were his terms, Yochanan is said to have replied, "I ask nothing of you save [the rabbinical academy at] Yavneh, where I might go and teach my disciples and there establish a house of prayer and perform all the commandments."[9] In the face of the catastrophic defeat of his own community and the victor's overwhelming power, Yochanan wanted only a center of religious learning and prayer.

There was wisdom in Yochanan's choice of surrender and petition for a center of learning and prayer. Prolonged resistance could have meant group suicide and the end of Judaism. Having fought a long and bloody war, the Romans had no intention of permitting the reconstitution of a Jewish power base capable of challenging them in a future crisis. The Romans wanted a submissive community that would be incapable of again becoming a military threat. Because they were scholars rather than soldiers, Yochanan and his rabbinic colleagues were eminently suited to lead a conquered Jewish community. It must, however, be stressed that Yochanan was neither a turncoat nor a crass collaborationist. In the midst of utter defeat, he was determined to save what he regarded as essential for the preservation of Judaism.

An agreement was struck between the Romans and the Pharisees. The Pharisees foreswore all resort to the use of power in their dealings with their Roman overlords. The Romans permitted the defeated community religious autonomy. Within a relatively short period, a majority of the Jews would cease to live in the homeland of their ancestors, but, wherever they dwelt, they were to be led by the disciples and heirs of religious leaders originally placed in power by their conquerors. This does not mean that the rabbis came to lead the Jews against the people's will. On the contrary, no other group within Judaism had a viable program for coping with the conditions in which the Jews found themselves after 70. Still, those conditions would not have existed had it not been for a catastrophic military defeat.

After becoming the leaders of the Jewish community, the rabbis claimed that they were the heirs of biblical Judaism, a claim that most Jews accept to this day. Nevertheless, as a result of the fall of Jerusalem, the Jewish people experienced a religious revolution that was to affect Jewish life for the next two thousand years. Instead of an altar of stone upon which bloody offerings were slain, Jewish religious life emphasized the bloodless study of a Book. The Jews were taught by their rabbis to turn inward and, through a life of study and prayer, to become reconciled to their God. And so it came to pass that a brave and warlike people who had dared to enter into combat with the world's greatest empire forsook the sword for the Book. Every aspect of Jewish life for the next two thousand years was decisively shaped by that political arrangement between Rome and the rabbis.

By surrendering to the Romans, Yochanan took a calculated risk that Caesar could be trusted. The Zealots were unwilling to trust Caesar. When it became apparent that Jerusalem's fall was inevitable, led by Eleazar ben Yair, the Zealots withdrew to the mountain stronghold of Masada where they held out until May 73. Finally, Eleazar exhorted his followers to kill themselves rather than surrender. For Eleazar, a life of utter powerlessness was not worth living. The historian Josephus records that Eleazar, anticipating the degradations a powerless people would have to endure, told his followers: "Wretched will be the young, whose strong bodies can sustain many tortures; wretched, too, the old, whose age cannot endure afflictions! One man will see his wife dragged away by violence, another hear the voice of his child crying to a father whose hands are bound."[10]

According to Josephus, all 960 defenders of Masada, with the exception of a few women and children, died by their own hands or those of kin. At Masada the Zealots preferred death to life in a world where their lives would be entirely dependent upon the whim of hostile strangers. By contrast, the rabbis were prepared not only to accept the risks of powerlessness but to create a religious culture predicated upon the disciplined renunciation of the use of force. Such a policy entailed the necessity of submitting at regular intervals to acts of murderous aggression. Yochanan and his spiritual heirs trained the Jews so to live that their defenselessness became their only defense. Periodically, they were abused and slaughtered, but somehow a remnant managed to survive until the twentieth century when a new kind of Caesar arose, a Caesar who was determined to exterminate every single Jew within his grasp. Unlike the Caesars of old, the new Caesar respected no limits. The Jews were absolutely without defense against the assembly-line methods he used to annihilate them. In his worst nightmares, Yochanan could not have imagined what was to be the fate of his people nineteen centuries after he helped to set them on the path of powerlessness.

Other long-range consequences of the fall of Jerusalem are important to our story as well. Before 70 many Jews had settled outside of Palestine. After 70 the process of out-migration became irreversible. Within a relatively short period, the majority of the Jews came to live in other people's lands. As a minority, the

Jews were compelled to maintain themselves by doing work which complemented that of the indigenous majority. Although generalizing for all Jewish communities over a period of almost two millennia is difficult, in general the Jews served as a "middle-man minority," that is as merchants, traders, artisans, physicians, and moneylenders. The religion of the Book gave the Jews the skills of literacy and calculation required to survive as an economically complementary population in a world where commerce was poorly developed. This was especially true after the breakdown of the Roman Empire and the beginnings of the feudal Middle Ages. As a rule, Jews were permitted to settle wherever the need for their skills outweighed the natural hostility felt by an indigenous population toward a community of strangers.

The fact that the Jews were strangers facilitated the development of their role in commerce. Success in commerce requires impersonal calculation. A merchant must be able to calculate accurately the profit required to remain in business. He cannot put emotional considerations of kinship solidarity ahead of financial calculation. Simply put, a merchant must to a certain extent treat every person impersonally, that is, as a stranger. It is, however, difficult to treat one's own kin or fellow villagers impersonally. Claims of kinship and mutual support are too insistent to be ignored. That is why in many precapitalist cultures, commerce and the professions have often been carried on by ethnic minorities, such as the Chinese in Southeast Asia, the Indians and Pakistanis in Kenya, Uganda, and other parts of Africa, the Armenians in the urban areas of Turkey, and the ethnic Germans in eastern Europe. Sometimes religious differentiation can have comparable results as was the case in France after the Reformation. For centuries France's small Protestant community has been disproportionately represented in banking and finance. Only with the arrival of an economic system such as capitalism in which *all persons* are treated more or less impersonally, at least in business and finance, have members of the indigenous majority begun to take over the commercial, professional, and financial roles formerly played by the ethnic minorities. Whenever this kind of transformation has taken place in relatively homogeneous societies, whether in Africa, Asia, or Europe, a movement has arisen among the majority calling for the elimination of the "middle-man" minority.

Moreover, success in commerce seldom enhances an ethnic minority's popularity, especially among those majority populations in which business and finance are poorly understood. There is almost always the suspicion that the minority is somehow engaged in sharp or dishonest business practices, a not uncommon reaction of consumers to business persons in any society. This was especially true in the case of medieval Jews in Christian countries where usury was regarded as a greater sin than adultery. Jews were identified both with Judas, the disciple who for money betrayed his Master with a token of love, and with the devil, the very opposite of all that Christ stands for. It is hardly accidental that in precapitalist societies one usually finds a strong distaste for commerce and a preference on the part of elite members of the majority for what are considered more "honorable" careers. Had it not been for the defeat of 70, the Jews would undoubtedly have shared the same distaste for commerce and moneylending and a preference on the part of elite members of the majority for more "honorable" careers. As it was, they had no choice but to do whatever work was available to them.

Rabbinic Judaism was not the only new religious tradition to emerge as a consequence of the fall of Jerusalem. Gentile Christianity as we know it also came into being as a direct consequence of that event. The importance of the fall of Jerusalem for both Judaism and Christianity has been stated succinctly by the late Norman Perrin, one of America's most distinguished New Testament scholars:

> The destruction of Jerusalem and the Temple by the Gentiles sent a shock wave through the Jewish-Christian world whose importance it is impossible to exaggerate. Indeed, much of the subsequent literature both of Judaism and Christianity took the form it did precisely in an attempt to come to terms with the catastrophe of A.D. 70.[11]

Before the fall of Jerusalem the Christian church was essentially Jewish in leadership with Jerusalem as its headquarters. After 70 Rome became the church's spiritual center as the church divested itself of its Jewish leadership and became the essentially Gentile church it remains until this day. The fall of Jerusalem marks the final parting of the ways for the two religious communities.

Many scholars share our opinion that the Gospels contain extensive evidence of the Christian response to the fall of Jerusalem.[12] At least three and possibly all of the Gospels are thought to have been written after the fall of Jerusalem. Some scholars assign a date before 70 for the writing of Mark, generally agreed to be the oldest Gospel, but even these scholars seldom date it before 66, the year the Judeo-Roman War began. In any event, early Christians came to agree that the fall of Jerusalem was a terrible punishment visited by God upon the Jewish people for having rejected Jesus and for having been responsible for his crucifixion.

The classical response of the post-70 church to the fall of Jerusalem is anticipated in the parable of the Wicked Tenants, the tale of the householder who planted a vineyard, "let it out to tenants, and went into another country" (Matt. 21:33). When the land rents fell due, he sent three servants, one after another, to collect from the tenants. The wicked tenants assaulted the first and murdered the second and third servants. Finally, the landlord sent his own son to collect the rents. He, too, was killed. As Matthew tells the story, Jesus asks his listeners, " 'When therefore the owner of the vineyard comes, what will he do to those tenants?' " Significantly, Jesus' listeners themselves reply: " 'He will put those wretches to a miserable death, and let out the vineyard to other tenants who will give him the fruits in their seasons' " (Matt. 21:40–41).

The parable of the Wicked Tenants is immediately followed in Matthew by the parable of the Marriage Feast. In this parable Jesus is depicted as likening the kingdom of heaven to a marriage feast given by a king for his son. Twice the king sent forth his servants to invite the guests. On both occasions those invited refused to come. Some even dared to abuse and kill the messengers. Jesus is then reported as saying: " 'The king was angry, and he sent his troops and destroyed those murderers and burned their city' " (Matt. 22:7). According to most scholars, both of these passages contain clear references to the fall of Jerusalem and were composed as a response to that event.[13]

Perhaps the most intense expression in the Gospels of the view that Jewish misfortune is a manifestation of God's punitive wrath is to be found in the terrible scene found only in Matthew in which Pontius Pilate, finding no fault in Jesus, nevertheless condemns him to death in order to appease the Jewish mob, washes his hands before the crowd, and proclaims, " 'I am innocent of this man's blood . . .' " (Matt. 27:24). Matthew describes the response as follows: "And *all* the people answered, 'His blood be on us and on our children' " (Matt. 27:25, italics added).

A political motive seems evident for the Gospels' insistence that the Jews rather than the Romans were wholly responsible for the crucifixion. The church had every reason to dissociate itself from the defeated rebels against the victorious empire. It became necessary to tell the story of the trial and execution of Jesus in such a way that Jesus was not portrayed as yet another Jewish insurrectionist. Hence, in the Gospels the Jews are clearly depicted as the real villains at Jesus' trial. By contrast, the Romans are exculpated.[14]

The moral is clear. It is constantly reiterated. No difference of opinion separates the Jewish Christianity of Matthew from the Gentile Christianity of Mark and Luke. *All four Gospels agree that the Temple was destroyed, Jerusalem ruined, and the Jewish nation slaughtered, not by the profane strength of the Roman empire, but by a just, righteous, all-powerful, avenging God, who was determined to teach the Jews the true cost of rejecting God's Son.*

Nor was the young church alone in interpreting the Jewish catastrophe as God's punishment. Another tradition tells of Yochanan's seeing a desperately hungry Jewish girl on the road to Emmaus. Out of desperation for something to eat, she was extracting undigested barleycorn from the excrement dropped by an Arab's horse. Some time later, alluding to Deuteronomy 28:47–48, he commented on what he had seen to his disciples: "Because you did not serve the Lord your God when you had plenty, therefore you shall serve your enemy in hunger and thirst. Because you did not serve the Lord . . . by reason of the abundance of all things, therefore you shall serve your enemy in want of all things."[15] Yochanan had a clear theology of history. In many respects it was very much like that of his Christian contemporaries. That is hardly surprising. Both the Jews and the Christians were nurtured spiritually by Scripture to believe that God is the sovereign Lord of history who controls the destiny of all nations. Both believed that God had entered into a covenant with the chosen people and that Israel's ruin was explained by both as due to her failure to keep the covenant and God's inevitable response. Where they differed was in the view each held of the sin for which Israel had been chastised. As noted, the Christians believed that Jerusalem fell because the Jews had rejected Jesus Christ. For the rabbis Jerusalem fell because the nation failed to obey God's commandments as they were interpreted by the Pharisees.

After the twentieth-century Holocaust, theologians began to seek for the religious meaning, if any, in that event. That effort became known as Holocaust theology. Nevertheless, essential elements of Holocaust theology are at least as old as the fall of Jerusalem. Moreover, insofar as the Gospels are concerned with the religious interpretation of the fall of Jerusalem, they can be seen as the oldest classical expression of Christian Holocaust theology, just as Rabbi Yochanan's interpretation of the same event constitutes the oldest rabbinic expression of Jewish Holocaust theology. There are, of course, even older attempts to offer a religious interpretation for catastrophic Jewish misfortune, namely, the interpretation by the prophets of the capture of Jerusalem by the Babylonians in 586 B.C.E.. These interpretations form the scriptural basis for both Jewish and Christian Holocaust theology.

Let us look for a moment more closely at the Holocaust theology of the Gospels. In the aftermath of the Judeo-Roman War, Christians had no doubt that Jesus himself had pronounced the dire judgment against Jerusalem ascribed to him in the Gospels. In this, Jesus was only following a tradition of Moses and the prophets. Consider, for example, the words of Moses to the children of Israel in which he gives expression to the idea that Israel is a nation chosen by God:

> "It was not because you were more in number than any other people that the LORD set his love upon you and chose you, for you were the fewest of all peoples; but it is because the LORD loves you, and is keeping the oath which he swore to your fathers, that the LORD has brought you out with a mighty hand, and redeemed you from the house of bondage, from the hand of Pharaoh king of Egypt. Know therefore that the LORD your God is God, the faithful God who keeps covenant and steadfast love with those who love him and keep his commandments, to a thousand generations, *and requites to their face those who hate him, by destroying them; he will not be slack with him who hates him, he will requite him to his face.*" (Deut. 7:7–10, italics added)

Consider also the words of the prophet Amos:

> Hear this word that the LORD has spoken against you, O people of Israel, against the whole family which I brought up out of the land of Egypt:

> "You only have I known
>   of all the families of the earth:
>   *therefore I will punish you*
>   *for all your iniquities.*" (Amos 3:1–2, italics added)

Finally, note the words of Micah as he declares to the rulers of Israel what are to be the consequences of their infidelity to the covenant:

> Hear this, you heads of the house of Jacob
>   and rulers of the house of Israel,
> who abhor justice
>   and pervert all equity,
> who build Zion with blood
>   and Jerusalem with wrong. . . .
> *Therefore because of you*
>   *Zion shall be plowed as a field;*
> *Jerusalem shall become a heap of ruins,*
> *and the mountain of the house a wooded height.*
>   (Mic. 3:9–10, 12, italics added)

The "house" to which Micah refers is, of course, the Holy Temple.

Thus, a firm scriptural basis was already available for the view that the destruction of Jerusalem was God's punishment. All that was sacred to the young church moved Christians to interpret the Jewish catastrophe as incontrovertible evidence of God's rejection of the Jews and their religious institutions. The unparalleled misery of the defeated Jews seemed to confirm Christians in their belief that the church rather than the synagogue was the true successor of the fallen Temple.

Consider, for example, the situation of thoughtful Gentile Christians in Rome about the year 75. Even those who did not have direct contact with the Jews knew that the Jewish mainstream had actively rejected such distinctively Christian beliefs as Jesus' messianic status, atoning death, resurrection, and heavenly lordship. Christians regarded these beliefs as decisive for their eternal salvation. Moreover, Jewish unbelief was no small matter because it came from people who were kin to Jesus and shared with Christians a common faith in the authority of Scripture.

Because of their superior numbers at first, Jews could and often did express their rejection of Christian belief with harsh and undiplomatic arguments, as well as with outright persecution of those Christians who had not broken completely with the Jewish community. Such conduct was bound to be a source of anger to Christians. Today, as a result of the findings of social psychologists in the field of cognitive dissonance, we are able to understand how a group is likely to respond to those who present disconfirming information or who seek to discredit beliefs in which the group has a very strong emotional investment.[16] The social-psychological theory of cognitive dissonance holds that if a person or a group has an important stake in an item of information that does not fit together psychologically with a second item of information, an attempt will be made to make the dissonant items consistent with each other. This process is known as dissonance reduction. An obvious method of dissonance reduction is to discredit the source of the dissonant item of information. An even more radical method would be to eliminate the source entirely. Both methods have been employed in the history of religion. Nevertheless, one must remember that the fundamental motive for even the most abusive attempts at dissonance reduction is the defense of the integrity of values or beliefs that are perceived as indispensable to the survival of one's community. We see this process of dissonance reduction at work in the Fourth Gospel, where Jesus is depicted as condemning the Jews who do not believe in his mission. This Gospel is believed to have been written between 80 and 100 by a tightly knit group whom scholars designate as "the Johannine School." The account which follows reflects the way that school dealt with the vexing problem of Jewish unbelief a few years after the fall of Jerusalem. Jesus is depicted as saying to Jews who challenge his authority:

> "If God were your Father, you would love me, for I proceeded and came forth from God; I came not of my own accord, but he sent me. Why do you not understand what I say? It is because you cannot bear to hear my word. *You are of your father the devil, and your will is to do your father's desires.* . . . He who is of God hears the words of God; the reason why you do not hear them is that you are not of God." (John 8:42–44, 47, italics added)

From the perspective of social psychology, the author(s) of the Fourth Gospel are attempting to discredit the disconfirming other in this highly important passage. Apart from all consideration of class, ethnic, and economic conflict between believing Jews and Christians, there has always been an enormous potential for mutual hostility in the profound challenge each faith poses for some of the most deeply held beliefs of the other.

The passage we have cited from the Fourth Gospel attributes a satanic character to those Jews who reject Jesus. The motives for such an attribution are understandable in the light of the theory of cognitive dissonance. The issue dividing mainstream Judaism and Christianity was not negotiable. Either Jesus was or was not the Messiah. In the apocalyptic atmosphere of the Judeo-Roman War and its aftermath, Christians did not hesitate to defame those who rejected Jesus. After all, they were convinced that the salvation of humanity was at stake. Still, the defamation was destined to have tragic consequences for the next two thousand years. There is no defamation of comparable severity of one religion by another. The ascription of a satanic nature to Jews had the effect of legitimating even the most obscene violence against them. If every single man, woman, and child of the Jewish community is of the devil, and this is the meaning of the defamation, then no one need have any qualms about how they are treated. Whatever violence is perpetrated against them can be defended as God's work. Nor, as we shall see, were the National Socialists reticent about using this legitimation of their antisemitism.

Given the fateful conflict between Christianity and mainstream Judaism, Christians living in the last decades of the first Christian century had every motive to regard the fall of Jerusalem as an expression of divine judgment against the Jews. If the events demonstrated that the unbelieving Jews had been rejected by God, Christians had no reason to be concerned with Jewish arguments against faith in Jesus as the Messiah. Thus, *the supreme Jewish disaster of ancient times was quite plausibly seen by Christians as empirical confirmation of the faith which the Jews had rejected.*

Moreover, if one applies the categories of the Christian thought-world to the Nazi Holocaust, that event can be interpreted as further punishment of the Jews for having rejected Jesus. As a matter of fact, no other interpretation of the Holocaust is strictly consistent with the classical Christian theology of history.[17] This fact will be of especial importance when we consider the role of the Christian church in the rise of modern antisemitism and the vexing question of the response of the Christian churches to the Holocaust. We will be unable to avoid the question of the extent to which belief in the divine origin and justice of catastrophic Jewish misfortune influenced the behavior of Christian leaders in the period culminating in the Holocaust. The question is important because, as we have seen, the view that Jewish disaster confirmed Christian truth was not peripheral to Christianity but was an overwhelmingly important component in the birth of the Gentile church. Nevertheless, at no time in the two-thousand-year history of the encounter between the church and the synagogue did the church ever have extermination of the Jews as its objective.

The fall of Jerusalem affected the Holocaust of modern times in yet another way. The fundamental assumption motivating Yochanan's decision to submit to Rome was his belief that Caesar and his heirs could be trusted not to use their power to destroy the Jews and Judaism as long as the Jews honored their part of the agreement. For two thousand years, Yochanan's calculated risk was justified. Even the Catholic monarchs of Spain, Ferdinand and Isabella, permitted the Jews to leave when they decided to eliminate Spain's Jewish population in 1492. The arrangement between the Jews and Caesar finally broke down in the twentieth century. As the legally constituted leader of the German Reich, Adolf Hitler was an heir to the power and authority of Caesar. It was he who finally used the power renounced by the Pharisees to bring about the degradation and annihilation of every single Jew within his grasp. Under National Socialism the government of Germany no longer had any interest in Jewish submission as did Vespasian and his successors. The Germans had become far too skilled in doing the kinds of things the Jews had been doing for centuries to have any further need for them. With more logic than humanity, the wartime National Socialist elite understood that they had the power to bring about a Final Solution to the

Jewish question, that the problem of an unwanted population could be "solved" by extermination. *The extermination of the Jews during World War II must thus be seen as part of the price, albeit long delayed, that the Jewish community paid for having lost the war against Rome in 70. What the Zealots feared, and much worse, came to full fruition in the Europe of World War II.*

Chapter 2

The Triumph of Christianity and the "Teaching of Contempt"

A century after the death of Jesus, the schism between Christians and Jews was well defined. Each group struggled for life and influence as a minority in an empire that had reason to look askance at both. Neither group was above trying to curry Roman favor at the expense of the other, and competition between them for converts was persistent. Christians claimed to be the true heirs of the promises God first made to Israel. To Jews such claims were anathema. Taking Jesus to be the Messiah and gradually even to be a divine being, the very incarnation of God, Christians could regard Jews as blind and even perverse, fully deserving of every misfortune that befell them and not least because that misfortune might manifest God's judgment. By and large, Jews were neither impressed nor persuaded by such indictments, but they were definitely opposed to them, and the conviction that their own way was the true one was driven deeper. Perhaps involuntarily but nonetheless unavoidably pitted together as rivals who disconfirmed each other, neither side had the upper hand but both held uncertain status under Roman authority. That latter situation, however, would soon change dramatically. As a result, Christians and Jews would continue as rivals, but henceforth the power between them would become radically asymmetrical. Even less than before would Jews be able to choose to be different with impunity.

From the Church Fathers to the Reformation

Certainly both the Jewish and the Christian religions have a better face than the one we have been tracing, but the Holocaust is the night side of history's cunning, and thus we must continue to see how the rivalry of Christians and Jews helped take both groups into the gas chambers of the Nazi death camps. Christian power increased during the second century after the death of Jesus, but that of the Roman Empire rapidly declined. Civil war was almost continuous by the middle half of the third century. Several strong emperors halted the decline. One of them was Constantine (280–337), who converted to Christianity early in the fourth century. Whatever Constantine's motives, political considerations were not missing from them. Although Christians constituted only about 10% of the empire's population at the time, they had put together a vital and dynamic organization, the Christian church. For some time, it had functioned almost as a state within a state. The church handled disputes, provided for the poor, maintained lines of communication from place to place, in addition to canonizing its own sacred writings into a New Testament and making headway toward rationalizing its fundamental doctrines. All of this had taken time, and the effect was less than tidy and systematic, but by 200 nearly every city in the empire had its bishop and body of priests, and one of them, the bishop of Rome, had asserted his authority to be the spiritual leader of the entire church. By wedding himself to the Christian faith and its institutions, Constantine strengthened his political grip. From its origins as a Jewish sect and an underground target of Roman persecution, suffering its worst devastations only a century earlier, Christianity had triumphed as the state religion.

These developments did not bode well for Jews, and one of the reasons was that, as Christians worked to ground their faith firmly in Roman soil, considerable attention continued to be paid to the relationships between Christianity and the Jewish tradition. What emerged was a more structured, more official position toward Jews, one that scholars now call a "teaching of contempt."[1] Built upon foundations that extend back into pre-Christian antiquity, and advanced by the first-century competition between the two rival faiths, this teaching achieved ever greater dominance as Christian authority and Roman power joined hands. Its vestiges still exist today.

We have noted how Jews and Christians created dissonance for each other. Each tradition claimed to possess accurate and exclusive knowledge of God's will. That will, moreover, they took to be decisively revealed in particular events and through particular persons. They agreed on some of these matters but just enough to make their disagreements enormous, for each tradition looked forward to a time when all persons would acknowledge and serve its truth, something that could only be done if people abandoned one tradition for the other. Existing in such close proximity, mutual disconfirmation sowed seeds of doubt and threatened each other's established beliefs, values, and sanctioned modes of behavior. One function of religious leaders and teachers is precisely to reduce such dissonance for their people. Both camps worked hard to achieve that end. Jews, for example, could and did argue convincingly that Jesus simply did not qualify as the Messiah, let alone as God incarnate, an analysis reinforced by the fact that Jesus was, after all, one of their own. To Christian ears, that strategy defamed Jesus intolerably. So, a favorite dissonance-reducing strategy employed by Christians was to elaborate the defamation of Jewish character.

For instance, through the teachings of Church Fathers such as Justin, Tertullian, Origen, Gregory of Nyssa, and John Chrysostom, a theology of supersession or displacement insisted on pariah status for Jews.

At least two claims were central to this perspective: first, God was essentially finished with the Jews; second, the Christian church had replaced the Jewish people as a new Israel with a special historic destiny. To make the case, a variety of arguments and charges were made. One approach was not to look at Jewish rejection of Jesus as an isolated instance but rather as the gravest and ultimate example of age-old Jewish perversity. Jewish history, it was claimed, had been a repetition of apostasy, which resulted even in the shunning and killing of prophets sent by God to correct Jewish evildoing. Indeed the Torah was given to Jews not as a blessing but as a check on their viciousness. Of course, there were exceptions. Not all Jews fitted this description, but the ones who did not were the forerunners of the Christian church, not the patriarchs of Jewish failure.

The decisive Jewish sin, the indictment continued, was the willful murder of the Messiah. For this deicide no retribution could be too great, and thus all Jewish favor with God was lost. No more were the Jews a chosen people except in the sense that they had been cast permanently into exile. Their Holy City ravaged, their Temple ruined, neither would be rebuilt. Jewish misery would continue to the end of time. One hope remained. When Jesus returned in glory, Jews would have a final chance to repent, a teaching that also gave impetus to conversion attempts whose success could count as evidence that the kingdom was not far off.

The language in which such views were expressed was often impassioned, especially in the eastern regions of the Roman world where Christians encountered Jews in the greatest number and were at times persuaded to give up their Christianity in favor of Judaism. Gregory of Nyssa (331–396), for instance, spoke of Jews as "murderers of the Lord, assassins of the prophets, rebels and detesters of God, they outrage the Law, resist grace, repudiate the faith of their fathers. Companions of the devil, race of vipers, informers, calumniators, darkeners of the mind, pharisaic leaven, Sanhedrin of demons, accursed, detested, lapidators, enemies of all that is beautiful." Somewhat later, in Antioch where Christians were probably tempted to associate with the numerous and influential Jews of that city, John Chrysostom (344–407) sermonized as follows: "Brothel and theater, the synagogue is also a cave of pirates and the lair of wild beasts. . . . Living for their belly, mouth forever gaping, the Jews behave no better than hogs and goats in their lewd grossness and the excesses of their gluttony. They can do one thing only: gorge themselves with food and drink."[2]

Anti-Jewish polemics were not an end in themselves. They also served to undergird Christian triumphalism, the sense that Christians were favored partners in a new covenant that would vindicate Christian faith and God's sovereignty.

By putting Jews down, Christians thought they exalted themselves. But in spite of rhetoric that often knew no bounds, Christian restraint toward Jews remained important, too. Under pagan Roman law, Jews had been both Roman citizens and a protected national group with a right to their own forms of worship. The policies of Christian Rome minimized Jewish freedom—for example, severe laws were passed against Jewish attempts to convert Christians and against interference with Christian attempts to convert Jews—but within prescribed boundaries Jewish existence and religious practices were permitted.

In sum, ancient Christian logic entailed a volatile ambivalence about Jews. If the Jews were a dissonance-producing threat and as such hated and attacked, they could also be useful. Their existence as outsiders made plain that the church was victorious. Their conversion to Christianity provided a potential for further corroboration of Christianity's triumph. For those who failed to see the light, God's punishing justice would suffice. Implicitly if not explicitly, then, the aim—never unrelated to an awareness that Jews were a disconfirming threat—was essentially to rid Christendom of Jews. If the church's methods could never have been those of National Socialism, nonetheless implications of its theology about the Jews were not lost on those who made way for Auschwitz.

Christian hostility toward Jews was not simply the result of gratuitous malice vented by an immoral rabble. Nor is the facile explanation that the church was intrinsically evil or psychologically demented an adequate account. Rabble, corruption, and psychological pathology there were. The more telling fact to reckon with, however, is that the most thoroughly anti-Jewish positions were advanced by the church's greatest saints and most rational thinkers. Some of them have been mentioned before, but Jewish-Christian circumstances from the beginning of the medieval period until the eve of the French Revolution can be illuminated in outline by observing attitudes toward Jews held by Augustine (354–430) and by the Protestant reformer, Martin Luther (1483–1546). Among other things, these examples suggest that every tendency to interpret antisemitism merely as an expression of a psychological disorder on the part of its advocates is a misleading simplification. Such interpretations overlook the fact that, insofar as Jews persisted as disconfirming "others," Christians had substantive reasons, as logical as they were unfortunate, for anti-Jewish hostility. Christians also had the power to dictate what status that hostility would entail for the Jewish minority. Let there be no misunderstanding: that hostility was deplorable. Yet even the extremity of Christian vilification of Jews suggests how deep-seated the reasons for it were and how seriously they were taken.

Jewish and Christian traditions confronted each other with disconfirming evidence of the truth of their claims, which in both cases were rooted in historical reality. The spread of Christianity certainly could put the credibility of Judaism into question, but no less so the unyielding persistence of Jews in their faith left

Christianity's triumph incomplete. The anti-Jewish stance of leading Christian thinkers, therefore, can best be explained by the desire to defend what they regarded as supremely important, the authority and integrity of their religious tradition. The point is not to claim that these tactics were morally justifiable or that they were consistent with all Christian teachings. It is to claim that a logic governed Christian anti-Judaism just as later on a developed rationale would govern Nazi efforts to exterminate Europe's Jews.

Augustine of Hippo remains an intellectual giant in Western civilization. His formative influence on Christian theology was profound, and no Christian thinker between Paul and Thomas Aquinas has exerted greater influence. *The City of God* is Augustine's magisterial theology of history, and in it the Jews play a fundamental role. Augustine could not withhold all affection for the Jewish people because God's work of redemption had been carried on through their history, culminating in the Passion and resurrection of Jesus. At the same time, Augustine identified Jews as enemies of the church. Their dispersion and misery were the results of blind refusal to acknowledge Christian truth. By permitting their continued existence, however, God's grace to Christians was all the more evident, for the Jews dispersed remained as a witness-people. Their ongoing history and fate testified to the necessity and significance of Christ's coming; the misery of their experience also underwrote the conviction that God's power cannot be mocked. Augustine still enjoined Christians to love Jews and thus to lead them to Christ, but Christian ambivalence toward Jews persisted. Since Jews were potential converts, the official view was usually that their lives should be spared. Debasing Jewish life, however, was much less discouraged, for Jewish suffering appeared to vindicate the church's authority. Jewish resistance to Christian pressures for conversion, then, was not permitted with impunity. The church, for example, asserted itself in the legal domain to ensure that Christian-Jewish contacts would be carefully regulated. Intermarriage was prohibited. Jews were excluded from the army, from most administrative posts, and from the legal profession. Commerce remained open to them, however, and many moved into those fields, eventually fulfilling economic functions that gave them a protected political status even as they were restricted in their rights.

By the fifth century, centralized Roman authority was in decline, the political map of Christendom destabilized. It is impossible, therefore, to make statements that apply to Jewish life without exception, but until the eleventh century Jews and Christians coexisted without much change under terms we have been describing. A major turning point occurred in 1096 when crusading Christian fervor to recapture holy places from Islamic forces took its toll on the Jews as well. Massacres followed as Christians also sought to purify their European territory. Following on the heels of those bloodbaths, Jews were obliged by the Lateran Council of 1215 to wear specially marked clothing. Different styles developed, but in France the insignia was a yellow patch, the precursor of the yellow star later decreed by the Nazis. In the popular imagination they became increasingly identified with Satan. Both cause and effect of that pernicious belief was the "blood libel," which alleged that Jews murdered Christian children for religious purposes, a charge that periodically rears its ugly head even today. Jews were also falsely accused of poisoning wells and, worse still, of desecrating the body of Christ by despoiling the bread and wine that Christians took to become Christ himself in the sacrament of the mass. Jews were held responsible, too, for the plagues and famines that ravaged Europe in the fourteenth and fifteenth centuries. Pogroms exacted payment in blood for these "crimes." Outright expulsion occurred as well—from England in 1290, from France beginning in 1306, and from Spain in 1492. The reasons for these and related departures, however, were more complex than appeals to irrational Jew-hatred and random violence suggest. They often hinged decisively on economics.

For centuries most European Jews had lived in western and central Europe, but that pattern shifted as Jews were increasingly forced east. Why they headed in that direction is clarified by recalling that Europe's medieval economy was precapitalist. Far more agrarian than urban, it aimed much less toward investment for industrial production and profit-making than toward subsistence. The avenues open to Jews were not those of farming and ownership of land. Instead they tended to work in certain commercial and professional roles that were needed but not filled by the dominant majority, often because ecclesiastical law and tradition restricted financial dealings. As merchants, traders, and moneylenders, their marketplace activities rarely won them esteem, but at least the Jews had a place because they served a complementary economic function. In a word, however, the Jewish situation in western and central Europe began to deteriorate as the subsistence economy of the feudal period was displaced by nascent forms of capitalism and industrialization, for this transformation led to the emergence of an indigenous commercial class. As it competed with Jews who occupied similar roles, predictably the "outsiders" lost more often than they won.

Shunted into marginal enterprises—peddling and pawnbroking, for example—the Jews in western and central Europe were squeezed economically to such an extent that most of them found it necessary to seek their livelihood elsewhere. The economically backward regions of eastern Europe provided a safety valve. There they could once again make a decent living by filling needed commercial roles in an economy still largely agrarian and subsistence-oriented. Yet, if Jews were once again an economically complementary population, that status still left them vulnerable. In fifteenth-century Poland, to cite one case, Jewish life achieved remarkable autonomy, prestige, and influence. But a century later, when that country was ravaged by Cossacks, Russians, and Swedes, the Jews paid double. They were decimated by Poland's enemies and then by the Poles themselves on the grounds that they had aided the invaders. Nonetheless, the number of Jews in eastern Europe continued to grow, albeit not indefinitely. The modernizing trends that took over in western Europe also worked their way east. Those developments helped to render millions of Polish and Russian Jews redundant, eventually setting them up for the Nazi Final Solution.

Martin Luther, the Protestant Reformation, and the Enlightenment

As the sixteenth century dawned, a definite pattern of migration began of Jews from the western regions of Europe that were more developed to those in the East that were less so. Erasmus (ca. 1466–1536) spoke perceptively for Europe generally when he observed that "if it is the part of a good Christian to detest the Jews, then we are all good Christians."[3] By then anti-Jewish feeling had diversified and intensified as economic and broadly cultural prejudice supplemented its basically religious beginnings in Christendom. All of these forces, plus others of a particular political significance, would conspire to make the Reformation a crucial era in Jewish destiny.

Protestant rebellion produced two main branches. Though not the first, one was inspired by Geneva's John Calvin (1509–64). His version of the Reformation flourished in areas from which Jews had already emigrated in large numbers. That fact may help to account for the relatively low degree of anti-Jewish sentiment in his outlook. In any case, with motives that were political and economic as well as religious, the Christians who followed Calvin not only emphasized individual responsibility and energetic political action, but they also identified their struggle and mission with that of the biblical Jews. Their outlook tended to be pro-Jewish to a much greater extent than was the case with Martin Luther and his German followers. One result was that when the Low Countries came under Calvinist control in the late sixteenth century, they, and particularly Holland, became a refuge for some Jews.

Luther's theology emphasized justification by faith in Christ, not by works. This position led him to criticize a Roman church that seemed to have incorporated a "works righteousness" into its piety, replete with an emphasis on penance, pilgrimages, and indulgences that might win one favor in heaven. The challenge to Rome made by Luther was combined with a fear of political anarchy and an awareness that the triumph of his religious reform depended on political power. Thus, although Luther wrote treatises about the limitation of such power and about the need for rulers to be in harmony with God's will, he also sided with political might that was friendly to his cause and urged obedience to it. Add to those facts the realization that Luther's political consciousness included seeds that would later flower into German nationalism, and it is not hard to see that his legacy is mixed in the light of Auschwitz.

On the Jewish question, Luther's attitudes were first ambivalent and then overtly hostile. In the 1520s Luther primarily wanted to convert Jews. Indeed part of his attack on papal Catholicism was precisely that it had treated Jews wrongly, so much so that Luther could write: "If I had been a Jew, I should have preferred to turn pig before I became a Christian, seeing how these imbeciles and ignorant louts govern and teach the Christian faith." He could add that "the Jews are the blood relatives, the cousins and brothers of Our Lord. . . . Hence I beg my dear papists to call me a Jew, when they are tired of calling me a heretic."[4] By 1543, however, Luther's mood was different. His work "On the Jews and Their Lies" advocated the burning of synagogues and the expulsion of Jews, feelings that were incited by Jewish refusal to see the light and embrace the Christian faith. At the time his writings on the subject were not widely circulated, but his views were symptomatic of the climate of opinion. Four centuries later the Nazis would make public Luther's largely forgotten text, capitalizing on it in ways that Luther could not have anticipated or even imagined; yet those ways probably would not have surprised him altogether either.[5]

The five hundredth anniversary of the birth of Martin Luther was observed in 1983. Luther was nine years old when Columbus discovered the New World, but Luther did as much to discover the new world of the spirit as Columbus did to discover the territorial New World. If, as many historians and sociologists of religion maintain, the modern world is in large measure an unintended consequence of religious and cultural forces arising out of the Protestant Reformation, Luther can be seen as one of its seminal creators. Consider further, then, the extent to which the great Reformer contributed to one of the darker aspects of modernity, antisemitic genocide.

According to Ernst Troeltsch (1865–1923), the new element in the Protestant theology initiated by Luther was "the special content of the conception of grace."[6] Before Luther, grace had normally been regarded as a mystical reality imparted through the sacraments. Protestantism came to regard grace as "a Divine temper of faith, conviction, spirit, knowledge, and trust . . . discerned as the loving will of God which brings with it the forgiveness of sins."[7]

As a consequence, according to Troeltsch, religion became primarily a matter of faith and conviction. This development was, as we shall see, of enormous importance in shaping Luther's attitude toward the Jews. By putting the whole weight of his religious commitment on faith, it became supremely important for Luther to discredit any group that might challenge his belief system. Jews had the unfortunate destiny of challenging, simply by fidelity to their own tradition, what was absolutely fundamental to Luther: his reading of Scripture.

Troeltsch pointed out that the Reformation involved a "reduction of the whole of religion to that which alone can be an object of faith and trust, that is, to that idea of God . . . which represents Him as a gracious Will, holy, forgiving sins."[8] Thus, a crucial element in the Protestant Reformation was the truncation of religion from an all-embracing system of rite, belief, and culture to a system of faith and conviction. More than any of his predecessors, Luther placed the whole weight of his religious commitment on what he held by faith. Troeltsch has commented that Luther's concentration on faith as the decisive element in religion constituted "an immense simplification in doctrine."[9]

Luther was convinced that no institution or body of ritual could enable sinful human beings to ascend to the supernatural. Without extranatural intervention, no human institution, even the church, could rescue humanity from the fate that awaits all creatures. Persons in their ordinary sinful state without God are hopelessly lost. No atheistic existentialist ever held a bleaker image of the human condition than Luther's image of humankind without God. Luther once commented that he would rather be a sow than be a person without Christ, because a sow does not have the fear and the anxiety to which humanity is condemned after the Fall.

Luther's unique contribution to the religious thought of his time was to insist that, though humanity's fallen nature is hopelessly cut off from God, nevertheless the graciousness and righteousness of God are such that sinful persons can be reconciled to God. However, such a reconciliation is entirely dependent on what God, not a person, does. Moreover, the good news whereby we learn of this reconciliation is to be found solely in Scriptures, whose central message and true meaning is God's justification of humanity in and through Christ.

Notice what transpired: Luther abandoned the medieval hope that persons can rise from a natural to a supernatural state through this-worldly means, whether of religion or reason. Everything now depends upon the truth of Scripture's account of God's promises. Luther tells us that Christians are assured that Christ is the "ruling Messiah." He then adds, "If this were not so, then God's word and promise would be a lie."[10] For Luther and those who follow him, if his reading of Scripture is without foundation, then there is no hope of salvation for any human being. Yet, it was precisely his reading of Scripture that was challenged not only by Jews but by many Christians as well. Some way had to be found to meet the challenge.

Luther's "immense simplification in doctrine," to use Troeltsch's phrase, significantly aggravated the hazard of Jews living in regions subject to Lutheran influence. Perhaps we can understand this better if we imagine that in the year 1540, three years before Luther wrote "On the Jews and Their Lies," a delegation of Chinese had been living in Saxony and entered into dialogue with the great Reformer. If Luther had told this imaginary delegation of his faith in redemption through Christ as revealed in the Gospels, they might have responded: "Dr. Luther, we really do not know what you are talking about. We know about Enlightenment and we know about the cycle of dependent causation, but we do not know about your Christ, nor do we know anything about the God you say speaks to people through your holy books."

Without doubt Luther would have been disturbed and annoyed, but it is unlikely that his annoyance would have been remotely as strong as was his annoyance with the Jews. Luther published "On the Jews and Their Lies" in response to a Jewish challenge to his interpretation of Scripture.[11] Luther was moved to write the treatise as a result of a letter he received from Count Wolf Schlick zu Falkenau in which the Count enclosed a polemical treatise by a rabbi against Luther's earlier work, "Against the Sabbatarians" (1538). The Count requested that Luther answer the rabbi's treatise, which is no longer extant.[12] Thus, Luther's most important and most hostile anti-Jewish document was a response to a Jewish challenge to, and a defense of, his own reading of Scripture.

There is, of course, a very important reason why Luther was far more hostile to the Jews than he would have been to the Chinese. Unlike the Chinese, the Jews agreed with Luther that God was the ultimate ground of Scripture's authority. Both Luther and the Jews regarded the human condition as fallen and in need of divine redemption. However, an unbridgeable gap existed in their understanding of how redemption was to take place. For the Jews, redemption would ultimately come about through compliance with the will of God as revealed in Scripture and as interpreted by the rabbis. For Luther, the Jewish belief was not only mistaken but perverse and demonic. To rely upon human works, such as the corpus of Jewish religious practice, was to make precisely the kind of spiritual error that had been fostered by the Roman Catholic Church in its insistence that the sacraments were the path to salvation. Moreover, the Jewish error was compounded by rejection of Christ as the Redeemer. Thus, the Jews were far more offensive to Luther than any other religious community. Having reduced all of Christian hope to a scripturally based faith in Jesus Christ, Luther could hardly have been expected to look kindly upon exponents of a tradition that used Scripture itself to deny what for Luther had become his sole assurance of salvation. If the Jews were right, Luther had nothing to hope for save the sow's fate absent the sow's blessed ignorance.

By contrast, Judaism constituted far less of a challenge to Roman Catholicism than it did to Luther, because of the totality of religion, culture, and tradition which served to undergird the medieval church. Jews may have challenged some aspects of Catholic belief in the Middle Ages, but they were in no position to challenge the imposing edifice of medieval Christian civilization as a whole. Ironically, when Luther reduced the religious foundations of Christianity to faith in Christ as revealed in Scripture, he added greater weight to the Jewish challenge and thus to the Jewish danger. Not only had Luther reduced religious hope to a single source, the Bible, but he had chosen the one source the Jews were best able to challenge. Jewish scholars were at home in their ancestral language, the first language of Scripture, and they were the people into whose midst Jesus of Nazareth had been born.

Luther began his response in "On the Jews and Their Lies" by stating that the interpretation of Scripture was the fundamental area of conflict between him and the Jews. "I have received a treatise in which a Jew engages in dialog with a Christian," he wrote. Luther complained that the Jew "dares to pervert the

scriptural passages which we cite in testimony to our faith, concerning our Lord
Christ and Mary his mother, and to interpret them quite differently. With this
argument he thinks he can destroy the basis of our faith.''[13]

A very large part of "On the Jews and Their Lies" is given to Luther's refutation of the Jewish interpretation of Scripture. Moreover, Luther was altogether
clear concerning what was at stake in this dispute: if the Jewish interpretation is
correct, Christian faith in Christ's redemption is without foundation. Luther's
fundamental motive for his attack was thus the defense of his reading of Christian faith.

In the treatise, Luther asserts that he is neither interested in quarreling with
the Jews nor in attempting to convert them. Whatever hopes he may have had at
an earlier period for their conversion have long since been abandoned. "They
have," he writes, "failed to learn any lesson from the terrible distress that has
been theirs for over fourteen hundred years in exile."[14] Nevertheless, Luther
counseled those Christians who have reason to enter into dialogue with Jews to
offer their religious rivals the following proof of their errors:

> But if you have to or want to talk with them, do not say any more than this:
> "Listen, Jew, are you aware that Jerusalem and your sovereignty, together with
> your temple and priesthood, have been destroyed for over 1,460 years?" . . . Let
> the Jews bite on this nut and dispute this question as long as they wish.
> For such ruthless wrath of God is sufficient evidence that they assuredly have
> gone astray. . . . For one dare not regard God as so cruel that he would punish his
> own people so long, so terribly, so unmercifully, and in addition keep silent,
> comforting them neither with words nor with deeds, and fixing no time limit and
> no end to it. Who would have faith, hope, or love toward such a God? Therefore
> this work of wrath is proof that the Jews, surely rejected by God, are no longer
> his people, and neither is he any longer their God. . . .
> In short, as has already been said, do not engage much in debate with Jews
> about the articles of our faith. . . . there is no hope until they reach the point
> where their misery finally makes them pliable and they are forced to confess that
> the Messiah has come, and that he is our Jesus.[15]

For Luther as for so many Christian thinkers both ancient and modern, the
best refutation of the Jewish reading of Scripture is Jewish misfortune. Luther's
argument was not unlike that of the prophets, save that the prophets were lovingly admonishing their own community, whereas there was no love in Luther's
description of those he regarded as enemies and strangers. Had the Jews understood God's revelation and conformed to the divine will, none of their terrible
sufferings would have taken place. Luther argued that a just God would never
have visited so horrible a fate on those who are truly God's people. Hence, Luther saw only one hope for the Jews: their fate would become so replete with
misery that a few would see the light and accept Christ as their Savior.

There is little doubt how Luther would have interpreted the Holocaust: he
would have seen it as decisive proof of God's rejection of the Jews. Nor is it

surprising that, when the theologians of the German Lutheran Church met in Darmstadt in 1948, three years after the Holocaust, they proclaimed that the Holocaust was a divine punishment and called upon the Jews to halt their rejection and ongoing crucifixion of Christ.[16] Whatever the motives of the theologians in releasing this document, they were undoubtedly speaking in the spirit of the founder of their church.

Although Luther's arguments were harsh and although contemporary Lutherans, at least in North America, have tended to dissociate themselves from the overtly antisemitic aspects of his writings, it must be recognized that this position vis-à-vis Judaism conforms to the classical position of Christendom. Luther explicitly derived his position that Jewish misfortune is proof of Christian truth and Jewish error from Scripture:

> Well, let the Jews regard our Lord Jesus as they will. We behold the fulfillment of the words spoken by him in Luke 21[:20, 22f.]:
> "But when you see Jerusalem surrounded by armies, then know that its desolation has come near . . . for these are days of vengeance. For great distress shall be upon the earth and wrath upon this people."[17]

Moreover, one must sadly observe that Luther's polemical use of history to discredit the Jewish interpretation of Scripture was by no means without a measure of methodological justification. Both Judaism and Christianity have traditionally claimed exclusive knowledge of God's revelation. The Jewish-Christian controversy was fundamentally concerned with the historical question of what God had actually done in relation to Israel and, through Israel, to all of humanity. Jews could hardly have expected that their rabbis could publicly reject the Christian view of God's action in history without a Christian response. This was especially true in the case of Martin Luther. In view of the overwhelming weight he placed upon Scripture as the sole source of revealed truth, it was inevitable that he would attempt to argue from history to discredit Judaism. For Luther to have taken the secular view that honorable people can sincerely disagree on ultimate questions would have been to render doubtful the sole foundation for his hope of redemption.

Unfortunately, Luther's theologically inevitable polemic led him, as well as other great Christian spiritual leaders, to defame Judaism in terms more radical than those with which any other religious community had ever attempted to discredit a rival. The Jews and their religion are, for Luther, the very incarnation of radical evil. Put differently, for Luther the Jews are of the devil. And the devil was a real rather than metaphorical power for Luther. Here are some characteristic expressions of the Reformer's opinions on the subject:

> I advise you not to enter their synagogues; all devils might dismember and devour you there. . . . For he who cannot hear or bear to hear God's word is not of God's people. And if they are not God's people, then they are the devil's people.[18]

You cannot learn anything from them except how to misunderstand the divine commandments.

. . . Therefore be on your guard against the Jews, knowing that wherever they have their synagogues, nothing is found but a den of devils in which . . . blasphemy, and defaming of God and men are practiced most maliciously.[19]

Elsewhere, Luther expressed himself in a similar vein:

They are real liars and bloodhounds. . . . Their heart's most ardent . . . yearning . . . is set on the day on which they can deal with us Gentiles as they did with the Gentiles in Persia at the time of Esther. . . . The sun has never shone on a more bloodthirsty and vengeful people than they are who imagine that they are God's people who have been commissioned and commanded to murder and to slay the Gentiles. In fact, the most important thing that they expect of their Messiah is that he will murder and kill the entire world with their sword.[20]

In the late nineteenth and early twentieth centuries, a forged document entitled *The Protocols of the Elders of Zion* was widely circulated and accorded credibility. In it the leaders of the Jewish community were depicted as secretly plotting world domination. Historians of the Holocaust have maintained that this document provided antisemites with a "warrant for genocide."[21] The *Protocols* was widely disseminated throughout Europe between the end of World War I and the beginning of World War II. Its distribution contributed to creating a climate of opinion in which the extermination of the Jews was held by large sectors of Europe's population to be a benefit. Nevertheless, even the *Protocols* did not go as far as did Luther, who accused the Jews of plotting genocide against the Gentile world. Moreover, Luther was not content with verbal aggression. He actively sought the expulsion of the Jews from Saxony, an effort which succeeded in 1536. When the edict was partly rescinded two years later, Luther was vehement in his opposition. In his very last sermon, preached on 15 February 1546, he demanded the expulsion of the Jews from Germany.[22]

Nor had Luther refrained from advocating overt violence against the Jews and their institutions:

We are at fault in not slaying them. Rather we allow them to live freely in our midst despite all their murdering, cursing, blaspheming, lying, and defaming. . . .

What shall we Christians do with this rejected and condemned people, the Jews? Since they live among us, we dare not tolerate their conduct, now that we are aware of their lying and reviling and blaspheming. . . .

First, to set fire to their synagogues or schools and to bury and cover with dirt whatever will not burn, so that no man will ever again see a stone or a cinder of them. This is to be done in honor of our Lord and of Christendom, so that God might see that we are Christians, and do not condone or knowingly tolerate such public lying, cursing, and blaspheming of his Son and of his Christians. . . .

In Deuteronomy 13[:12ff.] Moses writes that any city that is given to idolatry shall be totally destroyed by fire, and nothing of it shall be preserved. If he were alive today, he would be the first to set fire to the synagogues and houses of the Jews. . . .

Second, I advise that their houses also be razed and destroyed. For they pursue in them the same aims as in their synagogues.[23]

Luther continues at length in much the same spirit, but we have little need to follow him any further. It is, however, interesting to note the comment of the Lutheran editor of the American translation of Luther's works on this passage:

It is impossible to publish Luther's treatise today . . . without noting how similar to his proposals were the actions of the National Socialist regime in Germany in the 1930's and 1940's. On the night of November 9–10, 1938, the so-called *Kristallnacht*, for example, 119 synagogues in all parts of Germany, together with many Jewish homes and shops, were burned to the ground. . . . In subsequently undertaking the physical annihilation of the Jews, however, the Nazis surpassed even Luther's severity.[24]

While the editor's embarrassment at Luther's call to overt violence is obvious, especially in view of the events of World War II, he has apparently overlooked the fact that at the beginning of this passage Luther had written, "We are at fault in not slaying them."

What shall we make of this religiously legitimated incitement to homicidal violence? For many Jews, passages such as this are evidence of a certain moral flaw in the very nature of Christianity and most especially in the stature of Luther himself. For many post-Holocaust Christians, including members and leaders of Lutheran churches, the passages are an embarrassment. We must, however, recall that in the 1930s "On the Jews and Their Lies" occasioned little embarrassment in German Lutheran circles. When the treatise was published in the Munich edition of 1936, the editor claimed approvingly that "On the Jews and Their Lies" was the arsenal from which antisemitism had drawn its weapons.[25] Other leading German Lutherans of the period, including Bishop Otto Dibelius (1880–1967) who was to serve as president of the World Council of Churches in 1965, saw the National Socialist policies toward the Jews as the fulfillment of Luther's program.[26] Of all of the churches of Europe during the period 1933–45, none was as silent or as indifferent to the known fate of the Jews, when it did not actively support National Socialist antisemitic politics, as was the German Lutheran Church.

However one views Luther's writings on the Jews, he was without doubt one of the most influential religious leaders of all times. The sheer violence of the position taken by so dominant a figure points to an important, though often neglected, aspect of Christian anti-Judaism: the crucial question is not why mean-spirited or malicious people were so violently anti-Jewish but why some of the greatest thinkers and most pious saints within Christianity adopted that posture.

Briefly stated, the answer would appear to be that Luther, and others like him, felt compelled to negate and discredit the disconfirming other in order to

maintain the credibility of those religious beliefs and values that were of absolutely fundamental importance to him. Because Judaism and Christianity have a
common scriptural inheritance, the Jew can be, for Christianity the disconfirming
other par excellence, as indeed the Christian can be the disconfirming other par
excellence for Judaism. The related problems of dissonance reduction and the
disconfirming other had an especial urgency for Luther because of the overwhelming importance of his distinctive reading of Scripture for his whole religious system. If that reading proved mistaken, he had nothing left. Luther thus
had little option but to attempt to convince, discredit, or eliminate the Jew as
disconfirming other. To convince meant to seek to convert; to discredit involved
religious defamation such as the canard that the Jews were incarnations of the
devil; to eliminate meant expulsion or mass murder. At the very least, Luther
was compelled to defame the Jews and Judaism in order to minimize the credibility of their reading of Scripture and for their failure to accept Jesus as the
Messiah. A practical consequence of the need to discredit or eliminate the disconfirming other is that, in the process, the other is always in danger of becoming wholly alien, that is, wholly outside of the universe of moral obligation of
those whose values he challenges. This is especially true when, as in the case of
the Jews, the other is identified with the devil. Such an identification can have
the effect of religiously legitimating any conceivable violence, even extermination camps.

It is, however, important to keep in mind that Luther's attack on the Jews is
not an isolated phenomenon but arises out of the monotheistic exclusivism common to all of the religious traditions rooted in the Bible. For practical reasons,
the exclusivism can be softened and played down, but each of the biblical traditions contains the seeds of a resurgence of exclusivistic intolerance and violence
on the part of those who claim that they are defending the true meaning of their
tradition. The exclusivism is grounded in Scripture. Admittedly, Scripture can
be read so as to minimize the problem, but there does not seem to be any way to
eliminate the exclusivistic component altogether. Neither Protestantism, Roman
Catholicism, Judaism, nor Islam appears able wholly to abandon the claim that
it alone is the true faith.

In a complex, interdependent world, there are, hopefully, better solutions to
the problem of the disconfirming other than Luther's. Yet, we had best be
warned by Luther's example. In times of minimal social stress, exclusivistic religions can normally live in relative peace with each other, especially when the
power relations between them are clearly defined. Unfortunately, we have all
too many examples of periods of heightened social stress in which religious and
communal strife have been intensified to the point of large-scale intergroup violence. The Reformation was such a time; so too was World War II. Moreover,
intergroup violence has all too frequently received religious legitimation. Luther's sixteenth-century demonization of the Jews and Judaism, which was in

turn a reiteration of the view of the Jews to be found in the Gospels, gave sacred sanction in the twentieth century to a view of the Jews as enemies wholly outside of any conceivable German universe of moral obligation. Thus, it is hardly surprising that not a single German church group explicitly protested against the stripping of Jewish citizenship rights, the forcible deportation to the east of Jews whose families had lived in Germany for centuries, or the widely known, state-sponsored, systematic extermination of Europe's Jews. Germany was by no means the only country without effective religious protest against the extermination project, and Luther was hardly original in his virulent demonization. Nevertheless, Luther made the Bible available to the Germans in their native tongue and did more to shape the religious life of his nation than any other figure in German history. He did not create the gas chambers. He did, however, contribute significantly to their indispensable precondition, the denial of the Jews' humanity and their transformation into Satan's spawn. What makes his contribution to the Holocaust especially ironic was the nature of his motives. Luther's fundamental interest was the defense of Christian faith. It was the historic misfortune of the Jews that their religious civilization challenged that faith. This did not automatically make them candidates for the gas chambers. It did, however, result in the legitimation of their treatment as satanic nonpersons to whom German Christians felt themselves bound by no moral obligation whatsoever.

The date when Hitler gave public notice of his intention to exterminate the Jews remains a matter of scholarly debate. In any event, it probably was no later than his Reichstag speech of 30 January 1939 in which he proclaimed to the whole world: "If international finance Jewry within Europe and abroad should succeed once more in plunging the peoples into a world war, then the consequence will be not the Bolshevization of the world and therewith a victory of Jewry, but on the contrary, the destruction of the Jewish race in Europe." In the winter of 1939 only Hitler and the National Socialists wanted war and were preparing to go to war. Translated into the language of the real world, Hitler was in effect saying: "I intend to go to war and, before it is over, I intend to exterminate the Jews in Europe." As it became apparent that this was one promise Hitler intended to keep, German Lutheranism was neither able nor, apparently, much interested in defining the mass destructiveness as morally out of bounds. Even three years after the war, German Lutheran theologians could keep silent in the face of the monumental tragedy but felt compelled to proclaim the Holocaust as God's punishment of the people who continued to crucify Christ.

The full danger inherent in the Jewish challenge to Luther's Protestant interpretation of Scripture did not become apparent until World War II. More immediately, however, the Reformation also put at risk those Jews who resided in the Catholic strongholds of Europe. For example, among the Catholic responses to Luther and Calvin was a determination that church law be strictly applied. As that policy was implemented, the Jewish ghetto became more common, especially in Italy and in the Austrian Empire. In Spain another twist was added, this time directed at Jews who had recently converted to Christianity. Those Jews who refused conversion had already been expelled, but discrimination remained for those who had become Christian. Some Jews had converted on an external basis only; they continued their Jewish ways in secret. These "Marranos" (pigs), as they came to be known, were ferreted out by the Inquisition. Its measures, however, were judged insufficient to guarantee the cultural and religious homogeneity that Spain sought, and so a "test of blood" was implemented as well. The implication was that the Jews, even if converted, remained marked by an ineradicable stain. That stain became the pretext for excluding "new Christians" from certain guilds and from some military and educational roles. This Spanish example was not yet one of a full-blown, free-standing antisemitic racism, since the concern about Jewish blood was more the effect of a suspicion about religious impurity than a cause of discrimination in its own right, but certainly these "tests of blood" represented an important advance in the logic of hatred directed against the Jews.

The Reformation fragmented Christian authority in Europe. For Jews it was never more than a mixed blessing, although the Reformation did nurture some forces that would *apparently*—and that term must be underscored—make their lot vastly better. Depressed by the continuous warfare between Catholics and Protestants and between the rapidly multiplying Protestant sects, but greatly impressed both by the power of human reason reflected in the mathematical and scientific advances of the time and by the economic possibilities that they might produce, a new class of bourgeois intellectuals became openly critical of Christianity and of the old order in general. In tandem with the economic developments discussed earlier, their Enlightenment outlook made its initial and most forceful impact in western and central Europe—especially in England and France and to a lesser extent in German and Italian regions. Only later did it find its way east. Not entirely welcome because its ways tended to undermine tradition and long-established social structures, the Enlightenment's optimistic promises to liberate people from fear, superstition, and the dead hand of the past nonetheless made a powerfully winning appeal.

However, to conclude that such a perspective was simply a reaction against Western religion would be mistaken. A more adequate interpretation is that these Enlightenment sentiments were the logical outcome of fundamental motifs in both Judaism and Christianity. Indeed if one wishes to find the beginnings of the modern secular world, they are located here. Only those who believe in God's unique sovereignty could abandon belief in magic, spirits, and powers, and begin rationally to construct a world almost as subject to humanity's sovereign mastery as people were to God's. The paradoxical precondition of the rationalizing and secularized attitude that has effectively eliminated religious and ethical values from so many of the economic and productive processes of the modern world was a religious revolution. The biblical accounts of creation, for example, describe a world devoid of independent divine or magical forces that people must appease. One must stand on proper terms with God, it is true, but in the world itself the forces of nature are ones over which humanity can have dominion even if they cannot be subdued completely. Worldly principalities and political authorities have no divinity. Kings are only men; divinity is God's alone.

The Christian teaching of incarnation established a distinctive link between God and the world, one which the Catholic mass and its doctrine of transubstantiation underwrote, but the emphasis remained on the difference between God and the world. At the same time, although both Jewish and Christian traditions have stressed that men and women sin against God, both religions also incorporate strands that strongly urge the use of the human mind to reason and resolve, to produce and progress, to criticize and calculate. Western religion, therefore, and the secularizing drive of the Enlightenment are more like two sides of one coin than they are simple opposites. Together they yielded—sometimes by design, sometimes inadvertently—a marked emphasis on knowledge as power, which, in turn, placed a premium on instrumental, problem-solving rationality. Because knowledge *is* power, the irony was that the advances of practical rationality could be used for any ends determined by those intelligent enough to master its methods and wily enough to succeed in the struggle to control its direction. Thus, as the cunning of history has unfolded, human reason is less the queen who rules economic and political might and more their handmaiden instead. Among the sacrifices resulting from the legacy of Western religion and the Enlightenment were the European Jews consumed in the Holocaust by National Socialism's Final Solution.

Meanwhile, one of the Enlightenment's major themes was the conviction that Christians and Jews share a common humanity and basic human rights. This idea lent force to the view that citizenship should belong to all inhabitants of a certain territory regardless of their class or religion. In some places Jews found the restrictions of ghetto life relaxed, partly because the nascent capitalist revolution was opening up an economic system in which usury was permissible, international connections indispensable, and concern to maximize profits so intense as to transcend some of the animosity of ethnic prejudice and religious difference. Emancipation was not unthinkable in some Jewish quarters. Assimilation without discarding Jewish identity, if one chose to keep it, no longer seemed impossible. But once again it must be emphasized that the state of the Jewish question in Europe was anything but uniform. As the eve of the French Revolution approached, the seventeenth and eighteenth centuries contained pogroms as well as pro-Jewish *philosophes*. Jewish emancipation was never welcomed universally, and it was resisted with devastating success, as the Holocaust eventually showed. Even some of the secular intellectuals during the Enlightenment used their pro-Jewish pronouncements more as a means to embarrass and discredit Christian authority than honestly to advance the Jewish cause. Others were openly antisemitic, too, sharing Voltaire's outspoken opinion that Jews remained a threat to European culture or suspecting that Jews would actually be subversive elements in the new nation-states. Such suspicions about the ultimately alien status of Jews could diversify and intensify antisemitism yet again by putting it on a secular footing of its own. From that base antisemitism could gnaw away at emancipation, permitting it to exist in letter but not necessarily in spirit. Hostility toward Jews could also dictate the responses to their efforts at assimilation, and ultimately do so in ways that would make those efforts count against Jewish acceptance rather than for it. In a word, the prospect of emancipation was not offered without strings attached. To Jews as individuals it meant everything; to Jews as a nation, nothing. Such was common sentiment. Emancipated Jews would be expected to set aside their peculiar ways and be different no longer. But if they did so, they might still be suspect even so. Once more, Jews would pay double. They would be damned if they did assimilate and damned if they did not.[27]

Later on we shall see in greater detail how these possibilities became approaches to Auschwitz. For now let us conclude by taking stock of some major points highlighted in this survey of historical background for the Holocaust. First, Jewish history is the story of a people who chose to be different and, usually to their disadvantage, were stamped as such by the majority populations around them. As an alien people in Christendom, European Jews possessed little power. Although commonly under duress, Jewish culture and religious life endured there nonetheless. Indeed, far from succumbing to pressures from the Gentile majority, Jewish life proved amazingly resilient and energetic.[28] While preserving Jewish uniqueness, this vitality made Jews readily identifiable. It also made them vulnerable just to the degree that they were politically powerless. Too foreign from the majority, they were destined to become a surplus population ruthlessly targeted for elimination. That fact should stand as a warning to any who take cultural pluralism for granted or who glibly think that separation from the majority ethos may not exact a heavy cost.

Second, although Jews were persecuted and massacred during the period under examination in this chapter, they were not singled out by systematic, state-sponsored programs that aimed at their total extermination. The reasons why include the fact the the Jewish religion gave birth to a rival Christian faith whose power in the West depended not only on repressing Jewish existence but also on sustaining it for spiritual and economic purposes. Thus, Jews were vilified and separated from the powerful privileges of Christendom, but these steps were not sufficient to eventuate in the total annihilation of Jewish life. However, if Christianity had an interest in keeping Jews alive, it must be added that its powers in that regard proved unable, if not unwilling, to prevent the Nazi state from determining that European Jewry should perish.

Finally, anti-Jewish feeling waxed and waned over the centuries, but in Christendom it diversified, too. Economic and cultural elements were incorporated in addition to the religious. Racial overtones and aspects of suspicion that were primarily nationalistic and secular began to intrude as well. So long as Jews could be seen as potential Christian converts and/or as a complementary economic population, their vulnerability was at least reduced. Conversely, as the former consideration became less important in a West secularized by forces latent in its own religious traditions and by the accompanying Enlightenment, the latter status took on greater import. Unfortunately, the chances for Jews to occupy an economically complementary status also diminished as Europe's economy modernized and as political nationalism flourished. Still, as we leave this chapter, it could be argued that things were looking up for the 2.5 million European Jews. That appraisal, sadly, would prove to be an illusion within the lull before the storm. Why that storm broke out in all its twentieth-century fury should be clearer now, but the list of reasons awaits further additions. Probably it always shall.

Chapter 3

~~~~~~

The Irony of Emancipation:
A French Connection

It took Nazi Germany to bring about the Holocaust. Yet without decisive contributions by pre-twentieth-century France, Auschwitz would have been unlikely. Those contributions, ironically, pertain specifically to Jewish
emancipation. France was in the vanguard of that movement, which brought
legal and civic equality to Jews. Significantly, equal citizenship for German
Jews was first proclaimed in 1808 when French forces conquered western regions of that land. When Napoleon was defeated, the German emancipation was
largely rescinded. Further attempts to emancipate German Jews in 1848 did not
last either. Only in 1871, under Bismarck and Wilhelm I, did the Jews of Germany acquire close to full emancipation. As this chapter shows, France's example, including the reactions against emancipation that it spawned, did much,
albeit unintentionally, to set the stage for Hitler's destruction of European Jews.

The political status of Jews first became a matter of public controversy during
the French Revolution, which erupted in 1789. Before the Revolution Europeans generally agreed that Jews were to be treated as a distinctive community of
religious and cultural outsiders. In those places where Jews were permitted the
right of domicile, they were subject to strict constraints on the ways in which
they might earn a living and conduct their affairs. Nowhere in Europe did they
have a voice in public affairs outside of their own community. The decision to
grant them civic equality was radical, and it took an economic, social, and political revolution to bring it about.

At the time of the Revolution, fewer than fifty thousand Jews lived in France,
only five hundred of whom resided in Paris.[1] Some eight thousand Jews of Mar-
rano extraction lived in the south of France. They were descendants of Spanish
Jews who had outwardly converted to Christianity in the 1490s when all openly
believing Jews were expelled from Spain. Most of the "New Christians," as
they were called, remained secretly Jewish. As soon as they reached France,

they reverted to open practice of their ancestral faith. They were, however, far better adjusted to the society and culture of their neighbors than were the forty thousand French Jews who lived in the Rhineland province of Alsace. Alsace had been part of the Germanic Holy Roman Empire until it was annexed to France by King Louis XIV in 1648. The language of Alsace's Jewish population was a local variation of Yiddish, the Judeo-German dialect spoken throughout central and eastern Europe, rather than French.

As we have noted, during the Middle Ages the economy of Europe was predominantly agrarian and feudal. In many locations nonagrarian pursuits, such as trade and money lending, were carried on by Jews. The economic role of the Jews thus complemented that of the non-Jewish population. However, as western Europe began its long process of tranformation to an urbanized, money economy in which even agriculture was industrialized and rationalized, non-Jews began to compete with Jews in those areas of economic activity in which Jews had previously played an important role.

Because of the greater power of Christian competitors, most Jews were forced to leave the increasingly modern economies of western Europe and seek their livelihood in eastern Europe. There, a relatively primitive, subsistence agrarian economy persisted until the nineteenth century. As long as this condition continued, Jews remained an economically complementary class within the larger eastern European population. Because they were needed, political authorities were less likely to seek their elimination than was the case when the economy began to modernize and large numbers of non-Jewish competitors made their appearance.[2]

While the transition to an impersonal money economy enlarged the area of economic conflict between Jews and the increasing number of urbanized, middle-class non-Jews, it also lessened the importance of *inherited status* as a determinant of social and economic rank. In a money economy an individual's background tends to be less important than his or her financial resources. The diminishing practical value of inherited status helped to incite the French Revolution whose motto, "Liberty, Equality, and Fraternity," was rooted in the realities of the new economy.

The Rationalization of Politics

The eighteenth-century cultural movement known as the Enlightenment also fostered the emancipation of the Jews. An important aim of the Enlightenment was the rationalization of politics. In general, Enlightenment philosophers were hostile to religion, which they tended to see as a vestige of a superstitious past. They were also hostile to religion because of the support given by the church to the old royalist order, known after the Revolution as *l'ancien régime*. Throughout French history relations between the throne and the altar have been marked by periods of tension and conflict. Nevertheless, both institutions shared a common view of France as a Christian commonwealth. By contrast, a strong anti-Christian bias was evident in the writings of many of the Enlightenment thinkers, the most important of whom was François-Marie Arouet de Voltaire (1694–1778). This bias did not, however, result in greater sympathy for Judaism. Voltaire, for example, despised Judaism as the source of Christianity and for its polemic attitude toward Greco-Roman paganism. He regarded the Jews as a community alienated from the rest of humankind and practicing a primitive, superstitious religion.[3] Nevertheless, the Enlightenment had the practical effect of fostering Jewish emancipation because it advocated the elimination of religion from the political sphere. Ironically, Enlightenment rationality had the further consequence of fostering the growth of racism. Before the Enlightenment, opposition to the Jews was religiously motivated. By relegating religion to the private sphere, the Enlightenment did not eliminate public hostility. On the contrary, it encouraged the growth of nonreligious reasons for antisemitism, the most important eventually being race.

When the question of Jewish emancipation was brought before the *Assemblée Nationale* during the Revolution, the majority of the *philosophes* favored Jewish emancipation. Simultaneously, they expected the emancipated Jews to divest themselves of their inherited "superstitions" and become more like their fellow citizens in language, culture, and vocational distribution. Thus, acceptance of the Jews as French citizens was conditional on their becoming "new people." Unfortunately, the expectation carried with it the seeds of future mischief. Because of the extreme diversity of social, political, and religious values held by the French, no Jewish cultural transformation could satisfy more than a fraction of the French populace. Indeed, for many French citizens nothing the Jews could do would make a difference. One historian has aptly described the dilemma faced by emancipated French Jews:

> This "new Jew" had been born into a society which asked him to keep proving that he was worthy of belonging to it. Unfortunately, this "new Jew" was never quite told exactly what he had to prove and before which tribunal. Franz Kafka has described this phenomenon in his novel *The Trial*. The hero, and the victim, of this tale is K., who feels burdened by crimes which he wished he knew how to define and who keeps hoping to find the judges who would read him the charges, or at least accept his pleas of guilt.[4]

Another important motive for Jewish emancipation was the conviction that rational economic growth would be seriously impeded were France's widely divergent regions and classes to retain their own distinctive laws and standards. Before the Revolution, France had neither a common system of weights and measures nor a common currency. Internal tariffs between provinces imposed stringent limitations on commercial development. Economic rationalization required a measure of economic, political, social, and even linguistic *homogenization*, such as the introduction of a single system of weights and measures (the metric system), a universal system of education controlled from Paris, and a common currency for all of France. In the political sphere, homogenization was a consequence of the Revolution's assertion of the equality of all citizens. The Revolution discarded as irrelevant, at least before the law, all of the differences of culture, ethnicity, religion, and class that had been decisive in determining a person's status in *l'ancien régime*. All French people became *citizens* rather than members of different estates. The destruction of the traditional social hierarchy, a process which had begun even before the Revolution, contributed greatly toward the eventual creation of mass society.

As soon as the leveling of status was seriously underway, it was almost inevitable that the special status of the Jews would be abolished, albeit reluctantly, and Jews declared free and equal citizens of the French Republic. The more assimilated Jews of the south were granted French citizenship on 28 January 1790. The vote in the *Assemblée Nationale* was quite close, 374-280. Moreover, the vote was taken at a moment when most of the clergy in the *Assemblée*, who were known to be opposed, had left the chamber. Emancipation of the Jews of the north was opposed with great vehemence in Alsace where hostility to the Jews as petty traders, moneylenders, and aliens was especially virulent. Nevertheless, this second emancipation passed on 27 September 1791.

In spite of emancipation, serious religious, social, and cultural differences remained between the Jews and their fellow citizens. Jews and non-Jews had different historical memories, vocational distributions, and religious backgrounds. Of great importance was the fact the the vast majority of the French population was of peasant and Roman Catholic origin. Insofar as the equality and fraternity of French citizens was based upon some measure of homogeneity of origin and outlook, the Jews did not share in that homogeneity.

Opposition to Emancipation

For an understanding of the Holocaust, it is important to note that Jewish emancipation in France was bitterly fought by the Roman Catholic Church and by those royalist circles opposed to the breakdown of traditional society. The church emphatically rejected a conception of secular society in which Jews and Protestants could enjoy the same political rights as Catholics. With some notable exceptions, the Roman Catholic Church actively supported the antisemitic movements in France from the time of the French Revolution until the beginning of World War II.

In fairness, however, it must be stated that the church never advocated a policy of extermination as did the National Socialists. Unfortunately, under twentieth-century conditions, exclusion of a group from membership in the community in which it lives can be functionally equivalent to a death sentence. As long as the earth contained relatively open territories to which people could migrate, group expulsion constituted a harsh way of dealing with an unwanted community, but it did not involve the threat of extermination. Unfortunately, that is no longer the case. It is one of the supreme ironies of the progress of "civilization" that there are no longer relatively open territories. Every corner of the earth is controlled by a political state capable of limiting the right of permanent residence to those whom political authorities deem acceptable. When France's Catholic Church initiated a campaign aimed at denying the right of citizenship to France's Jews, it played an important part in a process whose deathly consequences could only be fully understood in the aftermath of the Holocaust.

Although the nineteenth-century French Catholic Church was normally allied to right-wing political movements, French antisemitism was as much a phenomenon of the left as of the right. In spite of the shortcomings of the old order, every person had a fixed and relatively secure place within it. Although personal status was caste determined, cooperation rather than individualistic competition was the predominant social value especially among peasants and artisans. The communitarian values of the old order were destroyed by the Revolution. Although the Revolution ended the caste system, it brought into being a radically new attitude toward political and social morality which can best be characterized as *possessive individualism*.[5] In place of the old cooperative spirit, people found themselves in competition with their peers. Although far fewer peasants left the land for the city in nineteenth-century France than in England, fierce competition for jobs often had the effect of driving down urban wages to the barest subsistence level. As wealth increased, so too did social misery.

Initially, the new spirit of competition suited the interests of France's commercial and professional classes. Before the Revolution an archaic socio-economic system prevented the bourgeoisie, a class possessed of talent, ambition, and energy, from creating a modern economy for France. With the triumph of the Revolution, this class was free to make full use of its talents. The triumph of the bourgeoisie can also be described as the victory of the city over the countryside or the victory of the world of human artifice over nature. Indeed, according to the *Oxford English Dictionary*, the word "bourgeois" originally denoted " a citizen of a city or burgh, as distinguished from a peasant on the one hand and a nobleman on the other." The Jews had no option but to concentrate in the cities and pursue professional or bourgeois occupations. Even after the Revolution removed their civic disabilities, the French Jews had neither the experience nor the social connections with which to enter agriculture. Nor were the Jews welcomed into the ranks of French labor. They were an urbanized people whose experience had been in trade, commerce, and finance. Moreover, the extreme marginality of their situation compelled them to become individualistic competitors in those fields that were open to them.

When the Jews in France entered upon urban, middle-class occupations, they gained a new enemy, the French left, in addition to their old enemies: the nobility, clergy, and peasantry.[6] Charles Fourier (1772–1837) was one of the earliest of a long line of French socialist antisemites.[7] His hostility to the Jews had something of a time-bomb effect. France was the original homeland of socialist thought and, hence, of socialist antisemitism. For example, until the twentieth century, French socialists were generally hostile to Marxism on the twin grounds that Karl Marx was a German and, although baptized, of Jewish origin. Incidentally, Marx's Jewish origin did not prevent him from adopting an attitude of extreme hostility to Jews and Judaism either. His views were based on economic and religio-cultural rather than racial grounds.[8]

Rejecting the individualism fostered by the Revolution, Fourier advocated organizing society into a system of utopian communities known as "phalansteries." Because these communities were to be agrarian and self-sufficient, they were not expected to need trade, finance, or commerce, the principal areas of Jewish economic activity. However, unlike later antisemites who favored violent measures, Fourier proposed that Jews be forced to engage in agriculture and other forms of "productive"activity. Toward the end of his career, he took a somewhat milder view, advocating the return of the Jews to Palestine where, with Rothschild help, he thought they might create their own "phalansteries."

In the next generation, Fourier's antisemitism was intensified by another of France's leading socialist thinkers, Pierre-Joseph Proudhon (1809–65), who was one of Karl Marx's most important critics. His publicly expressed anti-Jewish sentiments were relatively mild, but his private sentiments were violent. In 1961 Proudhon's notebooks were finally published. Here are some of the entries about Jews:

> *Jews*—Write an article about this race which poisons everything by meddling everywhere without ever joining itself to another people.—Demand their expulsion from France, with the exception of individuals married to Frenchwomen.—Abolish the synagogues; don't admit them to any kind of employment; pursue finally the abolition of this cult.
> It is not for nothing that the Christians call them deicides. The Jew is the enemy of the human race. One must send this race back to Asia or exterminate it.
> . . . by fire or fusion, or by expulsion the Jew must disappear. . . . Tolerate the aged who are no longer able to give birth to offspring.
> *Work to be done*—What the peoples of the Middle Ages hated by instinct, I hate upon reflection and irrevocably.[9]

In the nineteenth century, Proudhon kept his thoughts about extermination to himself. In World War II such thoughts were to become public policy.

According to one historian of socialism, "Proudhon had the countryman's dislike and distrust for that side of modern civilization which rests upon the subjugation of nature."[10] Socialists like Fourier who advocated that Jews be compelled to engage in agriculture ignored the obvious fact that every year more and more peasants were unable to sustain themselves and were forced to migrate to the cities. Moreover, those who found work in the cities were as likely to be engaged in trade, finance, commerce, the professions, and public administration as in what antiurban romantics regarded as "productive" labor. The demand that Jews seek work in the countryside was clearly counter to the basic trends of modern civilization which fostered ever greater urbanization.

Moreover, the universal tendency toward urbanization which characterizes modern civilization had a distinctive character in France. For a young person of ambition, especially in literature, the arts, and journalism, France had and still has only one city, Paris. To be successful meant success in Paris. Jews participated in the gravitation of talent to the capital city. At the time of the Revolution, Paris's Jewish population numbered about five hundred. Twenty years later there were nearly three thousand. By 1869, the year before the Franco-Prussian War, there were approximately thirty thousand. After the war, many Jewish families chose to leave Alsace and settle in the capital. By 1871, of the sixty thousand Jews in France, two-thirds lived in Paris.[11]

Because of their urban concentration, Jews were more visible to France's opinion makers and decision makers than their miniscule numbers would otherwise have warranted. The proportion of Jews to the total population was only one in six hundred. Nevertheless, their presence in the cities, especially Paris, was noted and usually resented by many of the non-Jewish immigrants from the countryside who tended to regard the Jews as an unwelcome, alien presence.

Before 1870 most urban Jews were quite poor, but there were important exceptions, the most important being banking families like the Rothschilds and the Foulds. Jews also prospered in the theater, literature, journalism, law, medicine, and after 1870, in Republican politics. Unfortunately, between 1870 and 1900 France experienced a serious "over-production of intellectuals."[12] Ironically, the "overproduction" was caused in large measure by the democratization of higher education under the Third French Republic, the government that came to power after 1870. Universities were free and overcrowded, especially after 1891 when the length of compulsory military service was reduced for students in graduate and professional schools. Moreover, in addition to the "overproduction of intellectuals," an analogous "overproduction" of doctors, lawyers, engineers, and commercial artists developed. The situation was further exacerbated by the fact that the surplus professionals and intellectuals were predominantly lower middle-class in origin. Lacking sufficient capital to start their own businesses, their training constituted their only hope of attaining a secure and comfortable livelihood. The extraordinary oversupply of trained people was especially evident in journalism. In 1900 the newspapers of Paris employed more than one hundred twenty-five thousand people.[13] With so great a surplus, wages tended to be exceptionally low and the opportunity for advancement almost nil. The situation was no better in the other professions. Less than half of the doctors, lawyers, and engineers could be considered even moderately prosperous. Army officers received salaries wholly inadequate for the style of life they were supposed to maintain. Competition for promotion was bitter. Pensions were low. Widows of officers were left with little protection. Even priests were hard pressed, especially in the rural areas. Such problems, however, were hardly unique to France.

Growing Resentment

Every developing country has experienced the migration of dislocated peasants to urban areas, the rapid expansion of the proletariat, the development of an unpredictable and impersonal labor market, the expansion of the educated and professional classes beyond the nation's absorptive capacity, and the expansion of the capital requirements necessary for business success beyond the resources of the average small business person. In almost every developing country, conditions such as these have yielded a large number of articulate, educated men and women who have become deeply resentful at a society in which they can find no meaningful place. Moreover, transition to a modern economy has been almost universally attended by such grave injustices as exploitative child labor, mass unemployment, and vast urban slums, with all of their accompanying social pathology. In France, those whose frustrated careers made them resentful had only to look around them to conclude that theirs was a hopelessly corrupt society. France's small Jewish population was blamed as the source of the corruption. This pattern, and many others we are noting, would repeat itself in Germany, particularly after World War I.

Middle-class French resentment was intensified by the fact that the French were less inclined to emigrate than were the British, Germans, Norwegians, Swedes, Italians, and many other Europeans. France thus lacked the population safety valve possessed by almost every other European nation. Between 1846 and 1932, 18 million people emigrated from Great Britain and Ireland; 14.2 million people left their homes in Russia, many to colonize Siberia; 5.2 million left Austria-Hungary; and about 5 million emigrated from Germany. Many of these came to the United States. By contrast, only 520,000 left France during this period.[14]

Other elements tended to embitter the French. France became a republic for the third time in 1870. Nevertheless, a very important segment of the French people did not regard the republican government as legitimate. In most countries conservatives tend to be a force for stability. This was not the case in France after her defeat by Germany in 1870 or in Germany after her defeat of 1918. In France the officer corps, the church, and the upper bourgeoisie were composed of people who despised the Republic and were vehemently antisemitic. Nor were these sentiments restricted to the upper strata of French society. They were shared by almost everyone who felt he or she had been injured by the new capitalist order.

Anticipating what would happen in Germany during the post-World War I

Weimar era, those who rejected the legitimacy of the Republic tended to depict the Jews as its principal beneficiaries. Indeed, French Jews perceived themselves as having benefited from the Revolution insofar as they had been granted full citizenship. The Jews were also perceived as having prospered at the expense of other groups in society. Jews had little choice but to pursue careers in those fields which opened up as France modernized. Ironically, these fields tended to offer the greatest rewards for success. In addition to trade, Jews were found in industry, the professions, banking and finance, where successful members of their community were highly visible even when numbers were small. Thus, those who saw themselves as injured by modernization tended to see the Jews as both responsible for and profiting from what they regarded as an illegitimate social order.

The situation in France was in strong contrast to that of England. In spite of the harsh social abuses that attended the industrial revolution in Great Britain, that development took place under a government that was almost universally regarded as legitimate. Moreover, the Church of England, the aristocracy, and the armed forces saw themselves as the leaders of the established order rather than its enemies. There was a poisonous element in French politics that grew stronger as the nineteenth century drew to a close.

The identification of the Jews with the hated world of modernity was evident in the themes of many of France's antisemitic writers. Alphonse Toussenel's book, *Les Juifs rois de l'Epoque* (1845), depicted the miniscule Jewish community as an alien presence controlling France. Toussenel was especially bitter about "Rothschild's railroads," a response to the fact that the Rothschild banking house had provided much of the investment capital for the building of France's railroads. Henri Gougenot des Mousseaux wrote a book entitled *Le Juif, le judaisme, et le judaisation des peuple chrétiens* (1869). Where Toussenel saw Jewish commerce and finance controlling France, Mousseaux claimed that the Jews had successfully used the ideals of the Enlightenment to overthrow Catholic France. The Jews were thus blamed for the French Revolution in spite of the fact that there were no more than five hundred Jews in Paris in 1789.

Blaming the Jews for the fall of *l'ancien régime* was a continuation of an earlier complaint by Catholic leaders who had depicted the Revolution as the consequence of a secret conspiracy of anti-Catholic Freemasons. According to historian Robert F. Byrnes, from 1865 on there was a tendency on the part of the French right to ascribe the French Revolution to the workings of occult forces.[15] Pope Leo XIII, usually a force for moderation, saw the Masons as an anti-Christian force. On 20 August 1884 he issued a decree of the Inquisition identifying the Oddfellows, the Knights of Pythias, and the Sons of Temperance as "the synagogue of Satan."[16]

It was natural for those who wanted to restore some, if not all, of the features of *l'ancien régime* to resort to a conspiracy theory to explain both its fall and the onset of the modern period. To have admitted that *l'ancien régime* could not have survived the challenge of modernization would have been an act of self-criticism opponents of the Republic were not prepared to make. Once the conspiracy theory gained acceptance in Catholic circles, it was to assert that the Jews controlled the Masons and finally to blame the Revolution on the Jews, who were accused by French antisemites of being "kings" of the new epoch.

The defeat of France by Germany in 1870 and the subsequent annexation of Alsace-Lorraine added to French bitterness. Like the Weimar Republic which preceded Hitler's rule in Germany, the Third French Republic was born in military defeat. Moreover, the defeat of 1870 was followed by some of the worst civil violence in Europe's history up to that date. Infuriated by the surrender of the French government to the Germans, thousands of Parisian workers set up the Paris commune, a move that so enraged and frightened the promonarchist government of Adolphe Thiers, which had succeeded Emperor Louis Napoleon, that in the week of 21–28 May 1871, more than twenty thousand Parisians who had fought for the commune were put to death by government troops. Another fifty thousand were arrested. The hatreds thus engendered were to poison the Third French Republic from its inception in military defeat to its demise in 1940.

It was only a matter of time before the Jews were blamed for the defeat of 1870. Before this happened a new Roman Catholic bank, the *Union Générale*, failed in 1882. The bank had been founded in 1878 by Eugene Bontoux, formerly a Rothschild employee. Many of France's leading banks were under Protestant control. Bontoux promised to break what he called the banking monopoly of Jews and Protestants. He received the enthusiastic support of Catholics of every station. For four years the bank was very successful. However, in 1882 it failed as a result of Bontoux' ill-advised attempts to support the price of the stock of the Suez Canal Company in a rapidly declining market. The failure caused great hardship to both its Catholic depositors and investors. Bontoux fled to Spain, where he blamed the Rothschilds in particular and the Jews in general for the failure. Catholic circles were all too ready to believe him.

French antisemitism was greatly strengthened with the publication on 14 April 1886 of a two-volume work, *La France Juive*, by Edouard Drumont. The book was praised in the Catholic press and quickly went through many editions. As was more or less typical with professional antisemites, Drumont was of lower middle-class origins. Born in Paris in 1844, Drumont was the son of a petty bureaucrat. His father died when he was seventeen. Drumont did not go to university but gained employment in the Paris City Hall. After six months he quit and tried journalism. From 1869 to 1885, underpaid and unrecognized, Drumont worked for *Chronique Illustrée*, a left-of-center paper owned by a Jewish family. He also shared with many of his fellow antisemites a yearning for "the old France." Where Toussenel saw the new railroads as a monumental scar on the face of his beloved France, Drumont hated both electric lighting and the new Eiffel Tower, which he regarded as defacing Paris.

The success of Drumont's book encouraged the appearance of many others. Within a short time, the Jews became the scapegoat for all of France's many ills. But in the case of Drumont, there was a modern element to his antisemitism. Where previously antisemites had been either socialist or Christian, Drumont tried to unite conservative Christians and left-wing socialists in a single movement. This was, however, a precarious alliance. As long as attention was focused on what the antisemites were against, unity was a possibility, but neither Drumont nor his allies could agree on a program to cope with the problems of a France that was now beginning to industrialize at a slow but accelerating pace.

Another important development was the founding in 1883 of a new Catholic newspaper, *La Croix*, sponsored by the Assumptionist Fathers, a new French order which was especially devoted to the Sacred Heart of Jesus. The order was responsible for the construction of the world-famous Basilica of Sacre Coeur on Montmartre. *La Croix* was the first newspaper to praise Drumont's book. The paper's antisemitism intensified as its circulation rose. In 1889 its circulation was eleven thousand. By 1893 it had reached one hundred eighty thousand. In addition, it published various Sunday and weekly editions which had a total circulation of two million in 1894.

When we discuss Catholic antisemitism in the period following the Franco-Prussian War, it is important to note a further source of bitterness for French Catholics: the unification of Italy and the destruction of the temporal power of the Pope. In 1867 the Italian patriot Giuseppe Garibaldi (1807–82) led a march on Rome, hoping to wrest control of the city from the Pope. Emperor Napoleon III of France sent an expeditionary force that successfully defended the Papal State. However, after the Prussians defeated Napoleon III in 1870, the Italians seized control of Rome with only token resistance. The Pope became the "prisoner of the Vatican," refusing to leave this very small enclave or to recognize Rome as the capital of united Italy.

French Catholics had seen themselves as the traditional protectors of the Pope. As long as Napoleon III was emperor, the new Italian state was prevented from seizing Rome. After defeat by the Germans, the French were incapable of protecting the Pope. The situation was aggravated by the fact that the Kingdom of Italy enjoyed the protection of Bismarck's Protestant German Empire. French Catholics thus tended to equate their own defeat with the Pope's and to see both as the result of the triumph of godless modernism and Protestantism over Catholic Christianity.

Another element in Catholic antisemitism from 1789 to 1945 was the fact that the church regarded itself, with considerable justice, as the most important institutional victim of the French Revolution. The church viewed the Revolution as an unmitigated social and political catastrophe. It could not accept a secular political order in which Judaism and Protestantism enjoyed a legal status equal to its own. Viewing itself as the one true church, it felt obligated to work to undo what it regarded as the damage done by the Revolution. It sought to restore a Roman Catholic commonwealth in which Jews and Protestants would be relegated to inferior status. Nevertheless, it would be inaccurate to see the church's hostility toward the Jew as motivated by gratuitous malice. The church's Jewish policy was consistent with its vision of the good society, which could only be Roman Catholic. In some, though not all, parts of Europe, the church was prepared to suffer the Jews to live as protected pariahs. Nevertheless, the church was not prepared to grant those who had no stake in the maintenance of a Christian commonwealth the right to a political voice.

It is also important to keep in mind that the nineteenth-century church's antisemitic policy did not have extermination as its objective. The church was attempting to restore the *status quo ante*, that is the hierarchically-ordered Christian society which preceded the French Revolution. In such a world, it was possible to condemn the Jews to pariah status, since the fundamental principle of society was legalized stratification. It was also possible to encourage the emigration of the Jews. Migration always involved hardship, but there were places to which the Jew could migrate. When Hitler came to power in 1933, migration was no longer such a viable option. There was simply no place in the world to which Europe's Jewish masses could go. Nevertheless, in spite of the altered situation, most leading church people failed to understand that the *status quo ante* could not be restored and that, under twentieth-century conditions, to strip a group of political rights could easily result in something far worse than forced emigration or pariah status. Nor was the church alone in failing to comprehend the changed conditions. Most of the leaders of the Jewish community in both eastern and western Europe were equally incapable of discerning the changes.

The Jew as Judas

The Jewish question finally became a decisive political issue for France in 1894 with the arrest and trial of Captain Alfred Dreyfus (1859–1935) for treason.[17] Dreyfus was a member of a wealthy Jewish textile manufacturing family from Mulhouse in Alsace that had opted for French citizenship when Alsace was ceded to Germany in 1871. He was the only Jewish member of the French General Staff at a time when almost every officer of consequence in the French Army was antirepublican and antisemitic. Moreover, the French officer corps had its own "old-boy network" consisting of officers who prepared for the École Polytechnique at a Jesuit preparatory school on the Rue des Postes in Paris. Known as "Postards," they controlled advancement within the officer corps. Non-Postards could advance on the basis of superior scholarship and behavior, but they could never hope to be part of the army's inner circle.[18]

Dreyfus's original appointment to the General Staff in January 1893 elicited strong protests in *La Croix* and *La Libre Parole*, a new antisemitic daily newspaper founded by Drumont in 1892. Drumont's paper also conducted an abusive campaign against Jewish army officers. In one issue he published the names of Jewish officers claiming that they were potential traitors.

There was at least one real traitor among the French officer corps, but it took several years before a significant sector of the French public realized that the traitor was not Jewish. On 15 August 1894, the traitor delivered to Colonel Maximillian von Schwartzkoppen, the German military attaché in Paris, a number of documents containing French military secrets. He also prepared a handwritten *bordereau* or memorandum itemizing the documents. Several weeks later a shady character, who sold foreign secrets to French intelligence, stole the *bordereau* from Colonel Schwartzkoppen's mailbox in the German Embassy and gave it over to the Statistical Section of the General Staff's Deuxième Bureau. The Bureau was the Army's intelligence agency; the Statistical Section was its counterespionage arm.

For some time French intelligence had been aware that a French officer was selling secrets to the Germans. In an attempt to discover the culprit, the Bureau had intercepted a note written by Colonel Schwartzkoppen to the Italian military attaché, Lieutentant Colonel Count Alessandro Panizzardi, which referred to twelve maps of Nice which "the Scoundrel D" (*canaille de D*) had left with Schwartzkoppen for Panizzardi. In spite of the fact that intelligence agencies generally do not give obvious clues to the identity of their contacts, Colonel Jean Sandherr, head of the Deuxième Bureau, decided unhesitatingly that "D," the author of the *bordereau*, and Dreyfus were one and the same person. Sandherr, an Alsatian, was known to be bitterly antisemitic.

Of the three experts who compared Dreyfus's handwriting with that of the *bordereau*, only one declared without reservation that the same hand wrote both samples. Attempts were made to get Dreyfus to confess or kill himself, but to no avail. After several weeks of inquiry, no futher evidence was turned up. Had the story of Dreyfus's arrest not been leaked to the press, Dreyfus might have been released.

There was a leak. Major Hubert Henry, head of the counterespionage section of the Deuxième Bureau, gave the story to his friend Drumont, who used *La Libre Parole* to accuse the army of covering up Dreyfus's "treason" in response to Jewish pressure. The entire press joined in the attack. A court-martial could no longer be avoided. It began on 19 December 1894. The court was composed of a Postard network that was strongly inclined to find the Jew guilty in any event. However, at the end of the first day, both Dreyfus's demeanor and the lack of any supporting evidence began to raise doubts about his alleged guilt. That evening General Auguste Mercier, the minister of war, and Colonel Sandherr put together a file containing "evidence" previously fabricated by

Major Henry and an associate, Major Marquis Mercier du Paty de Clam, as well as a damning commentary by Mercier. The file was given to the judges *without the knowledge of the defense attorney*, Edgar Demange, a prominent Roman Catholic lawyer who firmly believed in Dreyfus's innocence. Much of the material was forged, and it was contrary to French law to withhold evidence from the accused. Nevertheless, on that basis Dreyfus was sentenced to life imprisonment.

On 4 January 1895, on the Champs de Mars, the parade ground of Paris' École Militaire, in the presence of a large number of dignitaries including the papal nuncio to France, Dreyfus was stripped of his rank and publicly degraded before a crowd which shouted "Death to the Jews!" At the end of the ordeal, Dreyfus declared, "I am innocent. Long live France!" In the aftermath, the press magnified the crowd's death curses. Drumont's *La Libre Parole* declared: "It was not an individual who was degraded here for an individual crime. The shame of an entire race was bared in its nakedness." *La Croix* declared, "His cry of 'Long live France!' was the kiss of Judas Iscariot."[19] The Dreyfus trial had become the trial of all of France's Jews. Nor was *La Croix* alone in identifying Dreyfus with Judas. As Colonel Sandherr watched Dreyfus's degradation, he said to a young French diplomat, "That race has done . . . nothing but betray. Remember, that they have betrayed Christ!"[20]

La Croix's identification of Dreyfus with Judas linked the affair with one of the deepest sources of antisemitism in the Western world. Judas betrayed Jesus his Master, for *money*, thirty pieces of silver, and did so with a *kiss*, an act of love and affection. The moral of the identification is clear: like Judas, Jews can never be trusted even when they appear trustworthy.[21] Thus, the condemnation of Dreyfus as a traitor released powerful mythic themes that had always stood barely beneath the surface of the Christian image of the Jew. Undoubtedly, Colonel Sandherr's readiness to believe in Dreyfus's guilt was due in some measure to the power of the Judas image. Unfortunately, Dreyfus's illegal conviction on the basis of fabricated evidence had the effect of reinforcing that image.

The identification of the Jew with Judas was to have an even greater influence on German politics after Germany's defeat in World War I than it did on French politics in the 1890s. Both the Third Republic and the German Weimar Republic were born in military defeat, and defeated nations often find it easier to believe that they were betrayed than defeated by the enemy. It was the Jewish misfortune that the Judas myth served to convince many of the French that the Jews had betrayed them to the Germans, while convincing the Germans that the Jews had betrayed them to the French.

Students of the Dreyfus case have come to the conclusion that, before Henry leaked the story to the press, Sandherr and most of his colleagues were strongly inclined to believe the worst of Dreyfus but there was no conspiracy to incriminate him. After Drumont made an issue of Dreyfus's secret incarceration in *La*

Libre Parole, the army had the strongest motive for incriminating him. The army's inner circle would not be blemished if the officer who had sold secrets to the Germans turned out to be a Jewish outsider. Dreyfus's guilt could only reinforce the position of those officers who believed that France was a Roman Catholic country and that it was a mistake to grant French citizenship to Jews. Moreover, the army could not afford to lend credibility to Drumont's accusation that the army had been bribed by Jewish money to let a traitor go free. Nothing less than a conviction would put that accusation to rest.

If the army had reason to ensure Dreyfus's conviction, Dreyfus had every motive for loyalty. The psychological impossibility of Dreyfus's having betrayed his trust was spelled out by Theodor Herzl (1860–1904), the founder of modern Zionism, in a conversation with the Italian military attaché, Colonel Alessandro Panizzardi. Herzl said, "A Jew who has opened a career of honor as a general staff officer cannot commit such a crime. . . . As a consequence of their long civic dishonor, Jews have an often pathological desire for honor; and a Jewish officer is in this respect a Jew to the *n*th power."[22] As we have seen, Panizzardi worked closely with Colonel Schwartzkoppen, the German military attaché, and knew far more about the facts of the case than he could reveal to Herzl.

Fifteen months after the court-martial, there was a change of government in France. General Mercier was no longer minister of war. Lieutenant Colonel Georges Picquart, another Alsatian, succeeded Sandherr as Head of the Deuxième Bureau. Picquart soon became aware of the fact that Major Count Ferdinand Walsin-Esterhazy, a debt-ridden officer of dubious reputation and morals who was related to one of Hungary's greatest families, was in frequent and suspicious contact with the German military attaché.[23] In June 1896 Esterhazy submitted a handwritten application for a position on the General Staff. When Picquart saw Esterhazy's handwriting, it seemed familiar. Comparing it with the *bordereau* in the Dreyfus file, he concluded that Esterhazy had written the *bordereau* and that Dreyfus was innocent. Although Picquart disliked Dreyfus and was personally antisemitic, he immediately went to his superiors with the discovery.

Picquart was told to forget the whole affair, but he refused. At the same time, in order to revive interest in the case Mathieu Dreyfus, Alfred's brother, decided to publish a false report in a Welsh newspaper, *The South Wales Argus*, that Alfred had escaped from Devil's Island. The hoax succeeded. The antisemitic press claimed that a secret Jewish "syndicate" had conspired to buy off Dreyfus's guards. The case was once again front-page news.

Picquart was of the opinion that the least damage to the army would result from an admission of error in the Dreyfus case. His colleagues and superiors did not agree. Some remained honestly convinced that Dreyfus was guilty, perhaps in collaboration with Esterhazy. However, those who had fabricated evidence had passed the point of no return. Their strategy was to admit nothing, fabricate new "evidence," and leak it to friendly journalists. One such leak appeared in *L'Éclair*, a newspaper which frequently reflected army opinion. Through the article in *L'Éclair*, the army let it be known that Dreyfus had not been convicted on the slender evidence of the *bordereau* but on the basis of evidence "secretly handed to the judges of the court" without the knowledge of the defense attorney. Among the "evidence" cited was a letter allegedly sent by Schwartzkoppen to Panizzardi referring to the demands of "this beast of a Dreyfus." Since no one engaged in espionage would have identified so valuable an asset as a General Staff officer by name, it was immediately apparent that the "evidence" was a crude forgery. Moreover, the army had unwittingly admitted that the trial had been conducted illegally. Lucie Dreyfus, the prisoner's wife, petitioned for a new trial but was ignored. Nevertheless, public interest in the case continued to grow.

Major Henry decided that further forgery was necessary to strengthen the case against Dreyfus. With the help of an underworld character, Henry attached matching stationery to a piece of Italian embassy stationery on which Panizzardi had extended a dinner invitation to Schwartzkoppen. He then caused to be forged Panizzardi's "assurances" that he would deny all knowledge of Dreyfus if asked. This particular forgery became known as the *faux Henry* or false Henry document. As a further precaution, General Charles-Arthur Gonse ordered Picquart sent on a tour of inspection of the Italian frontier, to Algiers, and finally to a dangerous war zone in Tunis, where it was apparently hoped that a Tunisian bullet would silence him. Having filled Dreyfus's file with incriminating forgeries, Henry took advantages of Picquart's absence to do the same to him.

When Picquart realized what was happening, he wrote to Louis Leblois, a lawyer friend, detailing the evidence for Dreyfus's innocence and Esterhazy's guilt. He asked the lawyer to keep the contents of the letter secret, but to reveal them to the president of France should he, Picquart, die. Leblois could not contain himself. He told the vice-president of the French Senate, Auguste Scheurer-Kestner, a respected Alsatian, what he had learned from Picquart, pledging him to secrecy concerning the latter's involvment. Scheurer-Kestner privately let some of his political friends know he believed in Dreyfus's innocence. When news of Scheurer-Kestner's conversations came back to Henry, he decided on more fabrications not only against Dreyfus but to compromise Picquart.

Among the army's many mistakes was the publication of a photographic facsimile of the *bordereau* in *Le Matin*. Esterhazy's handwriting was recognized by a stock broker named Castro, one of a host of people who had had unpleasant dealings with him. The broker sent Esterhazy's letters to Mathieu Dreyfus, Alfred's brother, who formally denounced Esterhazy to the minister of war as the author of the *bordereau*.

Esterhazy suffered further embarrassment when a discarded mistress made public letters he sent her in which he expressed his hatred and contempt for the

French. In one of the letters he wrote, "I would kill 100,000 Frenchmen with pleasure." In spite of the revelations, the newpapers were filled with further "proofs" of Dreyfus's guilt and of the existence of a secret Jewish "syndicate" whose objective was to free Dreyfus, to degrade the Christian Esterhazy, and finally to destroy France.

The Myth of Conspiracy

Reports of a secret Jewish "syndicate" appeared in the mainstream newspapers of the French capital as well as the usual extremist journals. The reports were a variant of the myth of a Jewish conspiracy to dominate the world that had been depicted in another forgery, *The Protocols of the Elders of Zion*. The idea of a secret Jewish conspiracy was, of course, related to the identification of the Jew with Judas. By accusing the Jews of being a group secretly conspiring to conquer the world, it became possible to see any atrocity committed against them as an act of self-defense. The myth thus helped to create the moral and psychological climate in which genocide became an acceptable political policy.

The conspiracy theory of politics, the idea that behind the public facade of politics a determined minority has conspired secretly to control the political order, was applied to the Freemasons, who were held responsible for the French Revolution, before it was applied to the Jews. In an earlier period, witches were alleged to be in league with the devil to destroy Christian society. French Protestants were also the object of such theories. Although a numerically small community, they controlled much of France's banking system and were sometimes accused of seeking to control all of France by means of their capital. Moreover, the left was just as capable of using the theory as the right. Toward the end of the nineteenth century, it was widely held in left-wing and even moderate Republican circles that the Jesuits were seeking to control France and much of Europe through the confessional and their influence on education.

Although men and women have engaged in conspiracies since the beginning of recorded history, the use of the conspiracy theory in mass politics can be seen as related to the bureaucratic centralization of government in which unknown, anonymous bureaucrats have the power to make decisions affecting the lives and property of millions of their fellow citizens. Sociologists and political theorists have commented on the tendency of bureaucrats to insist on the secret nature of their work.[24] Moreover, nowhere is bureaucratic secrecy more important than in the workings of intelligence agencies such as France's nineteenth-century Deuxième Bureau or the CIA and KGB of our own era. In many situations, there are perfectly valid reasons for bureaucratic secrecy. Nevertheless, the claim of executive privilege has been frequently abused to cover up administrative mistakes, cost overruns, and even crimes. An important consequence of bureaucratic secrecy and anonymity is a widespread feeling among ordinary citizens that they are governed by unseen forces beyond their control. In the premodern period, the relations between those who govern and the governed usually had a personal element. People owed their allegiance to a *person*, the local lord and his agents in the first instance, the king at the highest level. In the modern period, political loyalty took on an abstract and impersonal character. Loyalty was due to the *nation*, the *state*, or the *constitution* instead of a person. This was especially the case in bureaucracies. The bureaucrat's fundamental responsibility is to carry out his or her assigned tasks without regard to the personalities of superiors, the nature of the task, or those affected for better or for worse by its implementation. Sociologists have argued that well-functioning bureaucracies constitute an advance in administrative rationality in complex mass societies. While this is undoubtedly true, as with so many other advances in functional rationality, bureaucratic rationality has had ironic, irrational consequences. Since few citizens can discern who really governs beneath the public facade of politics, all sorts of myths concerning invisible political conspiracies can find believers. In the case of the Jews, their concentration in the capital city, their strangeness, their command of financial resources, and the distrust in which they were held resulted in the accusation that they were conspiring to control Christian France. As noted, the consequences of the conspiracy theory were deadly for the Jews. Having been effectively depicted as a menace to public order and security, their elimination from the body politic was widely accepted as a public benefit. Ironically, far from being conspiratorial, most French Jews, like their German co-religionists, were apolitical. Most Jews were more interested in full acceptance as Frenchmen than in politics. The majority of those active in the Jewish community were too frightened by the Dreyfus affair to take an active role in securing justice.

When Mathieu Dreyfus denounced Esterhazy, some sort of official investigation became necessary. The army would have been content with a private investigation and quietly retiring Esterhazy. Esterhazy, who was hardly the model of prudence, insisted upon nothing less than complete vindication. It became impossible to avoid a court-martial. By this time, however, the army was too deeply implicated in the forgeries for the question of his guilt or innocence to be judged on merit alone. As the institution that guaranteed the security of the state against foreign enemies, the army had a claim on the loyalty and trust of all French citizens. Some believed that the fate of a single officer was less important than maintaining the respect of the army. Some indeed held that it was Dreyfus's duty to accept the verdict of the court-martial as a good soldier in the service of France. Thus, even Dreyfus's insistence on his innocence was taken as proof that he was not a true Frenchman. A similar argument was used in the Soviet Union in the 1930s by Stalin's secret police to persuade faithful Communists to confess to crimes they did not commit. Many people prefer order above justice.

Esterhazy was acquitted on 11 January 1898. Too much was at stake to permit any other verdict. The next day Picquart, the faithful soldier, was arrested.

The acquittal moved Émile Zola, France's most widely read author, to publish an open letter entitled *J'Accuse!*, to the president of the Republic in *L'Aurore*, a Parisian newspaper. The letter appeared on 13 January. Its title was emblazoned across the front page in a bold black headline.[25] Zola accused the army of having deliberately falsified evidence, of having willfully perpetrated a miscarriage of justice, and of having committed a judicial crime by convicting Dreyfus contrary to French law. Zola challenged the authorities to try him, which they did. A crucial moment in the trial came when Brigadier General Georges de Pellieux insisted that, in addition to the *bordereau* the evidence against Dreyfus included a letter allegedly written by Panizzardi to Schwartzkoppen assuring the German that, if asked, he would deny all knowledge of Dreyfus. This was the *faux Henry* document. When called as a witness, Picquart declared the document to be a forgery. Zola was nonetheless found guilty. Shortly thereafter, Picquart was dishonorably discharged from the army. Picquart had become a "whistle blower" in the eyes of his brother officers.

A National Obsession

The Dreyfus case now became a national obsession. One French diplomat wrote, "Whatever you may say or do, you are classed as a friend or enemy of the Jews and the Army."[26] Hostesses wrote on their invitations that the affair was not to be discussed. Antisemitism was on the increase. On 5 February 1898 *Civilita Cattolica*, the official organ of the Jesuit order in Rome, expressed the opinion that: "The Jew was created by God to serve as a spy wherever treason is in preparation." The journal saw only one cure for the situation, the victory of antisemitism:

> Thus, anti-Semitism will become, as it should, economic, political, and national. The Jews allege an error of justice. The true error was, however, that of the *Constituante* which accorded them French nationality. That law has to be revoked. . . . Not only in France, but in Germany, Austria, and Italy as well, the Jews are to be excluded from the nation.
>
> Then the old harmony will be re-established and the peoples will again find their lost happiness.[27]

The Vatican secretary of state, Cardinal Rampolla, expressed the opinion that every French citizen was duty-bound to stand by Premier Méline "in his anti-Semitic endeavors."[28] In France itself, the antisemitic campaign was led by Drumont and the Assumptionist Fathers who published *La Croix*. There were riots; Jewish stores were plundered in a number of French cities.

The turning point in the case came with appointment of Godefroy Cavaignac as minister of war in June 1898. Cavaignac came to the Chamber of Deputies on 7 July with three of Henry's cruder forgeries, including the *faux Henry* document, all of which he believed to be genuine. He announced to the Chamber that he was certain of Dreyfus's guilt. Cavaignac admitted that Esterhazy had written the *bordereau*. He assured the deputies that Esterhazy would be dealt with. Then Cavaignac declared that Dreyfus's guilt rested on other evidence, citing the *faux Henry* document and a confession Dreyfus was falsely alleged to have made. When news of Cavaignac's speech reached Picquart, he wrote a letter to the premier of France specifically characterizing the *faux Henry* document as a forgery. Infuriated, Cavaignac was determined to punish Picquart, but called upon a trusted aide to examine the Dreyfus file in order to assure himself of the authenticity of its documents. The aide reported back that the *faux Henry* document was a crudely pasted forgery. Cavaignac, who had acted in good faith, was understandably furious. On 30 August Henry was brought to Cavaignac and admitted the forgery. His arrest followed. A brief communiqué was issued stating that Henry had confessed to writing the letter in which Dreyfus had been named. The next day Henry was found dead in his prison cell. He had apparently cut his own throat.

The news created a sensation. Dreyfus's retrial was now inevitable, The anti-Dreyfusards were momentarily in disarray but quickly regrouped, largely as a result of an extraordinary posthumous defense of Henry by a young royalist, Charles Maurras.[29] Maurras praised Henry for having had the force and initiative to do what was required even if it meant falsifying documents. He praised Henry's suicide as a sacrifice for a noble cause, pledging himself and his friends to avenge his blood.

As we have seen, the mythic identification of Dreyfus with Judas Iscariot was never far from the surface in the Dreyfus affair. Maurras's tribute to Henry completed the myth. By characterizing Henry's suicide as a sacrificial death and by pledging vengeance for Henry's blood, Maurras brought the emotional power of the image of Christ crucified into the affair. With Henry's death, the affair gained a strange sort of a Christ figure in addition to its Judas. Moreover, the implicit identification of Henry with the crucified Christ reflected the sense of victimization the French felt after their defeat and the loss of Alsace-Lorraine in 1871. French Catholics also strongly identified with the pope, who had been stripped of his temporal possessions because of the unification of Italy and was now known as "the prisoner of the Vatican." Dreyfus was thus cast as the Judas who betrayed France to the Germans and whose followers were determined further to weaken an already assaulted church.

In the initial stages of the Dreyfus affair, Maurras had entertained the possibilty that Dreyfus might be innocent. He nevertheless faulted Dreyfus and his family for putting the individual well-being of the accused over the honor and reputation of the army. According to Maurras, even if innocent, Dreyfus should have endured his degradation for the sake of the institution to which France had entrusted her security. But, in Maurras's eyes, nothing could make Dreyfus a Frenchman. At best, Dreyfus, the Jews, Protestants, and Freemasons, were *metics*, resident aliens, owing France no permanent allegiance and only domiciled in

France because of the lure of commerce. By contrast, Henry was depicted as a true soldier of France who was prepared to shed his blood for the earth that bore him.

For Maurras, the Revolution of 1789 and the emancipation of the Jews were profound mistakes which he proposed to correct. He became a leader of a new right-wing movement, *Action Française*, which played an important role in French life from 1900 to 1944.[30] Maurras's distinction between the alleged selfish individualism of Dreyfus and the sacrificial selflessness of Henry was consistent with his indictment of the values of modern France. For Maurras, only a Catholic France ruled by a hereditary monarch could end the warring conflict of selfishness that beset modern France. Maurras also distinguished between what he called the *pays légal*, the legal country, and the *pays réal*, the real France. Maurras held that while the Revolution had mistakenly granted the Jews legal rights, no law could transform a people of alien origin and religion into true French persons. The question that Maurras was unprepared to deal with was the one which had initially prompted the emancipation of the Jews in 1789: in order to create a modern state, the French had abolished separate legal status for distinct groups within the population. In the case of the Jews, the only alternative to granting them equality was to eliminate them from the population altogether. This would have meant either expulsion or extermination. In 1789 extermination of an entire community was not a serious political alternative. Even in 1900 French antisemitism was more interested in controlling Jewish access to political office, social rank, and economic and professional activity than it was in more radical measures, although voices were being raised both in mob demonstrations and by well-placed antisemites calling for the death of Jews.

The call for a massacre of the Jews was frequently expressed in the pages of *La Libre Parole* after Henry's death. Drumont established a Henry Memorial Fund to support the widow and children of the deceased. The names of the contributors were listed daily. Some donors gave their reasons for contributing. A number of priests and army officers called for a massacre of the Jews, recalling the massacre of French Huguenots, instigated by Catherine de Medici, which began on St. Bartholomew's night, 24 August 1572. The massacres, which Catherine justified as being in the interest of public safety, continued until 3 October in the provinces. It is estimated that more than fifty thousand Protestants were slaughtered. Whether those who called for the elimination of the Jews were fully conscious of the consequences of their politics, they were in fact preparing the basis for collaboration in, if not actual implementation of, the extermination of the Jews. Moreover, those who called for the slaughter of the Jews at the time of the Dreyfus affair were doing more than indulging in homicidal fantasies. Their program had as its model a concrete event in French history.

By his literary transformation of a forger into a sacrificial victim, Maurras succeeded in creating a viable myth that enabled the army to maintain intact its sense of honor. He was also able to reinforce the antisemitism of both the army and that section of the clergy which was susceptible. It is important, however, to note that, although the French church was the strongest supporter of the anti-Dreyfusards, Pope Leo XIII did not share the extreme antisemitism or antirepublicanism then prevalent in the French church.

The Dreyfus case dragged on after Henry's suicide, but the issues had been clarified. On the one side were those who fought against what they regarded as an intolerable miscarriage of justice. On the other side were those who were convinced that the legacy of 1789 had been a catastrophic mistake and who insisted that nothing must be done to harm the two institutions that embodied the true spirit of France, the army and the church. Initially, the Socialists were either indifferent or hostile to Dreyfus, partly in keeping with the traditional antisemitism of the French left. However, led by Jean Jaurès, most eventually came to see that what was really at stake was the survival of the legacy of the French Revolution. Dreyfus was brought back from Devil's Island and forced to submit to a second court-martial, which was held in the military-base town of Rennes in September 1899.

There was, however, no possibility that a military court would reverse the first court-martial. Had it done so it would have found one man innocent but, by implication, General Auguste Mercier, minister of war at the beginning of the affair, and a goodly number of General Staff officers guilty. This the court would not do. On 9 September 1899, by a vote of five to two, Dreyfus was again found guilty of high treason. However, it was obvious that the verdict had less to do with Dreyfus's guilt or innocence than with the political impossibility of going against the army high command. Because of "extenuating circumstances," his sentence was reduced to ten years, five of which he had already served. The verdict represented an impossible compromise. Ten years' imprisonment is too light a sentence for a traitor and too severe for an innocent man.

The trial itself attracted worldwide attention, and the verdict was almost universally condemned. The nineteenth century was drawing to a close, although the twentieth century can be said to have begun in France with the Dreyfus trial. Prime Minister René Waldeck-Rousseau had let it be known that he would not let a guilty verdict stand. There was also fear that the Paris Exposition scheduled for 1900 would be widely boycotted. On 19 September 1899, the president of France, Émile Loubet, pardoned Dreyfus. Shortly thereafter, a general amnesty was declared for all those involved.

Some of the most important Dreyfusards were vehemently opposed to Dreyfus's accepting a pardon. One pardons a guilty person; an innocent person needs no pardon. Ironically, Dreyfus had never been a Dreyfusard. He did not understand the political implications of the controversy which had engulfed his life. He had only one desire, to establish his innocence and rehabilitate his career. In any event, a return to the hell of Devil's Island was more than this prematurely aged man could endure. Dreyfus had had enough. The generals also had had enough. They were willing to accept the amnesty. The files on the embarrassing case could be closed, and the army could go about its business.

Only Picquart was embittered by the amnesty. It placed him beyond the reach of his enemies on the General Staff, but he could not accept the permanent blemish on his honor that anything less than complete vindication could bring. He demanded justice, but to no avail. Mathieu Dreyfus would not let matters rest either. He wanted to know why the judges at Rennes had voted as they did. By dogged persistence, he discovered that General Mercier had used the same trick to secure conviction at the second trial that he had employed at the first. He had secretly passed forged documents to the judges which the defendant had no opportunity to see. This made the second trial as illegal as the first. The minister of war conducted a further investigation, but this time no attempt was made at a cover-up. Finally, the case was referred to the High Court of Appeals. Strictly speaking, the case should have been referred to a third court-martial, but there was apprehension lest there be a third conviction. On 12 October 1906 the High Court set aside Dreyfus's conviction, holding that there never had been any evidence against Dreyfus and that the guilty verdict had been in error. Both Dreyfus and Picquart were rehabilitated. Dreyfus was promoted to the rank of major and made a member of the Legion of Honor. Picquart was promoted to brigadier general, the rank he normally would have had. In October 1906 Georges Clemenceau, who had been the editor of *L'Aurore* when Zola published *J'Accuse* in it, became premier of France. While premier he appointed Picquart, now a general, minister of war.

Anticipations of Auschwitz

The Dreyfus trial, coming at the turn of the century, can be seen as a curtain raiser for the far more destructive acts of antisemitism that were to take place in the twentieth century. In the years that followed the trial, the aim of the French right was to put an end to the society created by the French Revolution. In 1936 Charles Maurras was elected to the *Académie Française*. Election carried with it national recognition as one of France's "immortals." Maurras's election also represented the stamp of approval of France's most illustrious group of literary and intellectual leaders. When the Germans defeated France in 1940, Marshall Henri Philippe Pétain, an old Postard who had been a young officer at the time of the Dreyfus affair, became the head of the Vichy-based French state. According to one authority, for the first two years "Pétain's policy seemed to reflect ideas that Maurras had spent his life trying to teach the French."[31] Without much prompting from the Germans, Pétain's regime enthusiastically initiated the kind of antisemitic legislation the French right had sought for decades.[32] When the Germans found the time to implement the Final Solution in France, almost all of the work of rounding up Jews for deportation to the death camps was done by the obliging French bureaucracy and police force. Nevertheless, as we shall see, when the full extent of the extermination program became known, there were limits to French cooperation. In the end, Maurras's antisemitism led him to collaborate with the Germans in World War II. When, as an old man, he was convicted of high treason in 1944 by the Free French, he cried out in the court room, *"C'est la revanche de Dreyfus,"* "This is the revenge of Dreyfus."

It is one of the ironies of history that two journalists with very different loyalties who observed the Dreyfus affair both concluded that the French Revolution's emancipation of the Jews was unworkable. Charles Maurras was one of the journalists. The other was Theodor Herzl, the founder of modern political Zionism. As the Paris correspondent of the Viennese newspaper *Neue Freie Presse*, Herzl had followed the Dreyfus case and had witnessed Dreyfus's degradation on the Champs de Mars. He heard the mob shout "Death to the Jews." Originally an assimilated Jew who believed in the viability of emancipation, Herzl reversed his opinion. The Dreyfus case reinforced Herzl's rejection of emancipation and assimilation as solutions to Europe's Jewish problem. Maurras wanted forcibly to eliminate the Jews from Europe; Herzl believed that it was imperative for the Jews voluntarily to eliminate themselves through the creation of their own state.

On 17 January 1896, a year after Dreyfus's official degradation, Herzl offered a succinct analysis of the causes of modern antisemitism and the difference between modern and traditional antisemitism:

> The Jewish Question still exists. . . . It exists wherever Jews live in perceptible numbers. Where it does not yet exist, it will be brought by Jews in the course of their migrations. . . .
> Only an ignorant man would mistake modern anti-Semitism for an exact repetition of the Jew-baiting of the past. . . . In the principal countries where anti-Semitism prevails, it does so as a result of the emancipation of the Jews. When civilized nations awoke to the inhumanity of exclusive legislation, and enfranchised us—our enfranchisement came too late. For we had, curiously enough, developed while in the Ghetto into a bourgeois people, and we stepped out of it only to enter into fierce competition with the middle classes.[33]

As the twentieth century began, Herzl's view of the prospects of Europe's Jews was one of considerable pessimism. If they prospered, they would arouse envy and hatred; if they sank into poverty, they would be regarded with contempt as utterly useless. If they fled to a new land with little antisemitism, their increasing numbers would create in the new land the very affliction from which they had fled. Herzl believed that there was hope for the Jews but only in a state of their own.

Herzl was undoubtedly a prophet. Nevertheless, as farseeing as his grim analysis proved to be, it erred on the side of optimism. The final catastrophe was unthinkable even to him.

PART TWO

THE NAZIS IN POWER

A CHRONOLOGY OF CRUCIAL HOLOCAUST-RELATED EVENTS
1933–1945

1933

January 30	Adolf Hitler becomes Reich Chancellor
March 22	Heinrich Himmler establishes the concentration camp at Dachau
March 23	Reichstag passes the Enabling Act
May 10	Public book-burnings in Germany targeted at Jewish books and works by opponents of Nazism
July 14	Nazi party established by law as the one and only legal political party in Germany

1934

June 30—July 2	Hitler's purge of Ernst Roehm and the S.A.

1935

September 15	Sweeping anti-Jewish racist legislation passed at Nuremberg

1937

July 16	Buchenwald concentration camp opened

1938

March 13	Austria annexed to the Third Reich
July 6–15	Evian Conference held
September 29–30	Munich Conference agrees to the German annexation of part of Czechoslovakia
October	"Aryanization" of the property of German Jews begins
October 28	Expulsion of some 17,000 Polish Jews from Germany to Zbaszyn on the Polish border
November 7	Herschel Grynszpan assassinates Ernst vom Rath in Paris
November 9–10	*Kristallnacht*

1939

August 23	Soviet-German Pact signed by Molotov and Ribbentrop
September 1	World War II begins with the German invasion of Poland
September 3	Britain and France declare war on Germany
September 17	Red Army invades eastern Poland
September 21	Heydrich decrees the establishment of Jewish ghettos and councils in occupied Poland

1940

January–February	Jewish youth movements organize underground resistance in Poland
April 27	Himmler orders the establishment of a concentration camp at Auschwitz
June 4	British evacuation from Dunkirk completed
November 15	Warsaw ghetto sealed off

1941

June 22	Germany attacks the Soviet Union

July 31	Goering appoints Heydrich to implement the "Final Solution"
December 8	Chelmno extermination camp opened in Poland near Lodz
December 11	Germany declares war on the United States

1942

January	Jewish resistance and partisan groups organized in Vilna and Kovno
January 20	Wannsee Conference plans how to exterminate 11 million European Jews
March 17	Extermination begins at Belzec
May	Killing operations get under way at Sobibor
July	Treblinka death camp opens
July 22	First large-scale deportation of Jews from Warsaw to Treblinka
July 28	"Jewish Fighting Organization" (ZOB) established in the Warsaw ghetto
September	Armed Jewish resistance against Nazis throughout Poland
November 19	Red Army counterattacks at Stalingrad
December 17	The Allies resolve to punish Nazis responsible for the mass murder of Jews

1943

January 18–21	Mordecai Anielewicz leads first armed resistance in the Warsaw ghetto
April 19	Bermuda Conference produces fruitless discussion about how to rescue Jewish victims of Nazism
April 19	Liquidation of the Warsaw ghetto begins; Anielewicz leads the Warsaw ghetto revolt
May 16	Liquidation of the Warsaw ghetto completed
June	Himmler orders liquidation of all ghettos in Poland and the Soviet Union
August 2	Treblinka prisoners revolt
October 2	Danes rescue Danish Jews from the Nazis

1944

January 22	President Roosevelt establishes the War Refugee Board
March 19	Hungary occupied by the Germans
May 15	Deportation of Hungarian Jews to Auschwitz begins
June 6	Allies invade Normandy
July	Majdanek liberated by Russian troops
July 20	German officers attempt to assassinate Hitler
October 7	*Sonderkommando* uprising at Auschwitz

1945

January 18	Auschwitz evacuated; prisoners' "Death March" begins
January 27	Russian troops capture Auschwitz
April 11–May 3	The Allies liberate concentration camps at Buchenwald, Bergen-Belsen, Dachau, and Mauthausen
April 30	Hitler commits suicide
May 7	Nazi Germany surrenders unconditionally to Allies

Chapter 4

Toward Total Domination

Approaches to Auschwitz were not confined to German soil. In the late nineteenth century, they included avenues of military intrigue in Paris. They would also involve provincial streets of Austrian towns and vast expanses of Russian-dominated eastern Europe. The Dreyfus affair drew Theodor Herzl, the founder of modern Zionism, west from Vienna. In France he witnessed a reaction against the emancipation of Jews spawned by the Enlightenment. That reaction would spread with many lethal consequences for the Jews. Indeed, the Dreyfus affair was only one of several decisive indications that the twentieth century would take a greater proportionate toll on Jewish life than any other. Unfortunately, these signs could not be read with complete clarity at the time. They were nonetheless forerunners of the Holocaust.

The Russian Solution to the Jewish Problem

From the beginning of the sixteenth century a definite pattern of Jewish migration developed from west to east throughout Europe. This movement from regions that were more highly developed economically to those that were less so came about because of the rise of an indigenous commercial class that was capable of assuming roles previously filled by Jews. Thus, population estimates for 1825 show that of the 2,730,000 Jews in Europe, about 460,000 lived in western and central Europe, the remainder in eastern and southeastern areas of the continent. In 1900, European Jews numbered nearly nine million. By that time, only about 15% of them lived in Europe's western and central regions.

The economic necessity that drove Jews into the Russian-dominated east was not complemented by opportunities that would last indefinitely. The economy of eastern Europe was to witness development roughly comparable to that of the west. A pattern of displacement of the Jews by the dominant majority repeated itself, but with the added difficulty that fewer readily accessible havens were available. Crucial to this process was the land reform that came to Poland and Russia in 1846 and 1861 respectively. These steps emancipated some forty-eight million serfs. Their freedom, however, proved to be a mixed blessing. The division of the land could not produce a livelihood for all of the growing population. Millions of peasants turned to the towns and cities in the hope of maintaining themselves, but the industrial base was not sufficient to provide them with work. Unemployment was rife. In Russia and even more so in Poland, it affected Jews in multiple ways. The rationalization of agriculture into large, cost-effective units, for example, displaced many Jews from the land. Others found themselves competing with non-Jews in trade and commerce. Still others found themselves thrust into urban centers with an equally desperate non-Jewish proletariat. All the while, Jewish numbers were growing, too. Add in a strong dose of antisemitism, which was always an important factor in these parts, and it becomes apparent that pressures were mounting to explosive levels.

A watershed year for Jewish fate was 1881. On 13 March (new calendar), Czar Alexander II was assassinated by revolutionary terrorists. Influential government circles blamed the Jews. The first of a three-year wave of murderous pogroms ensued on 27 April. The violence recurred from 1903 to 1906 and again between 1917 and 1921 during the Russian civil war. Significantly, the pogroms of 1881–84 can be called state-sponsored. Mobs acted with impunity. The target population did not receive the normal protection of the law until the Russian intention was unmistakable: Jews should go elsewhere. By the tens of thousands, Jews got the message, and a westward exodus began. Discriminatory laws affected those who stayed behind. Particularly noteworthy were the "May Laws" of 1882, which severely restricted Jewish movement and opportunity within areas under Russian jurisdiction. The intent of these measures was to make life so uncomfortable for the Jews that they would leave—voluntarily if not because the law required them to do so.

In sum, by laying the groundwork for the capitalist transformation of eastern European agriculture, emancipation created the conditions for the beginnings of a small but growing indigenous middle class. As this class developed, the Russian government, traditionally hostile to the Jews, had even less reason to tolerate a minority that was seen as foreign to the nation's ethnic and religious consensus. The ultimate aim of Russian policy in the aftermath of the events of 1881 was the total disappearance of Jewish life from Russia.

No one understood that aim better than Konstantin Petrovich Pobedonostsev, a highly influential bureaucrat who zealously advocated the Russification of all non-Russian minorities. Responding to a group of Jewish petitioners in 1898, he stated succinctly the Russian solution to the Jewish problem: "One third will die out, one third will leave the country, and one third will be completely dissolved in the surrounding population."[1] Thus, decades before World War II, Russian policymakers articulated essentially the same goal with respect to the Jews as did the early National Socialists. There was, of course, an important difference between the means even a modernizing bureaucrat like Pobedonostsev was prepared to use before World War I and those the Nazis would employ during World War II. Even as Pobedonostsev propounded his Russian solution, however, events destined to close the gap between means and ends were underway.[2]

Hitler, Germans, and the Jewish Question

When Pobedonostsev set forth his Russian solution, Adolf Hitler (1889–1945) was a nine-year-old schoolboy in the obscure Austrian village of Lambach. Little did anyone know that he would become a dominant world figure, let alone that his infamy would have so much to do with the Jews. Biographies of Hitler abound.[3] So in lieu of summarizing his life, let us note some salient details that put him on the way to Auschwitz. Consider first that Bismarck's creation of a unified German empire in 1870 was followed by a decade of economic depression. Already those conditions exacerbated tensions in Germany and Austria between Jews and non-Jews. To make matters worse, large numbers of Jews from the East immigrated to Berlin, Vienna, and other major population centers. In 1846, for example, 3,739 Jews lived in Vienna; in 1900 there were 176,000. In 1852, 11,840 Jews lived in Berlin; by 1890 there were 108,044, some 5% of the city's population. Concurrent with the Jewish influx, which heightened tensions, another emigration was afoot. Between 1871 and 1885, 1,678,202 Germans, approximately 3.5% of the entire population, migrated to the United States. The peak of this *Auswanderung*—250,000 persons—occurred in the crucial year of 1881–82.

In 1891, ten years after the beginning of the decisive Russian pogroms, Leo von Caprivi, the chancellor of the German Reich, observed that "Germany must export goods or people."[4] Caprivi understood the classic dilemma of production and consumption that besets every modern technological society. Germany's ability to produce exceeded her capacity to consume. Without foreign markets, Germany would be faced with an unacceptable level of mass unemployment at home. Over the long run such destabilization could not be tolerated.

For a time, emigration of its native population was considered the normal, acceptable method of population elimination in Germany. Reliable estimates show that about 6 million people left Germany in the nineteenth and early twentieth centuries.[5] Specifically for the period 1846–1932, we find 4.9 million departures from Germany, another 5.2 million from Austria-Hungary.[6]

Amidst these massive population movements, Hitler, 18, headed for Vienna to find his way in the world. His hopes did not pan out. Denied admission to the Vienna Academy of Fine Arts, he also lost his beloved mother, who had been attended by a Jewish physician, to cancer in December 1908. Five years of embittered Viennese wandering ensued. Hitler observed the Jewish population, now full of unassimilated eastern arrivals. They struck him as alien in every way. Later he would identify their presence as a major factor in forcing Germans out of a place that was rightfully theirs. For the present, intent German nationalist that he was, the young Hitler could no longer abide Vienna and the polyglot Hapsburg Empire it epitomized. In May 1913 he left for Munich.

Recalled to Austria in February 1914 to be examined for military service, Hitler was rejected as too weak and unfit. But when war broke out in August, he volunteered and was accepted for service in a Bavarian infantry regiment. Wounded twice, he served with distinction, winning the Iron Cross (First and Second Class), although he was never promoted beyond the rank of lance corporal. In October 1918 Hitler was badly gassed. By the time he recovered, Germany had surrendered. Along with many other Germans, Hitler was stunned by the capitulation. The intensity of his belief that the nation had been "stabbed in the back," betrayed specifically by Jewish interests from within, was matched only by the fervor of his disdain for the conditions imposed on Germany by the Treaty of Versailles.

The war had given Hitler's life a purpose. Its ending seemed once more to leave his hopes in ruin, but it did nothing to lessen his antisemitism.[7] On the contrary, Hitler's Jew-hatred intensified in postwar Munich, the city that did more than any other to give birth to National Socialism. There, for example, Hitler witnessed a series of politically naïve, left-wing Jewish attempts to bring about an enduring socialist revolution in Catholic, conservative Bavaria. They failed but not without leaving a lasting impression on Hitler. At the same time, Munich was a principal gathering place for White Russian refugees who brought with them *The Protocols of the Elders of Zion* with its myth of a Jewish conspiracy to rule the world. The book was speedily translated into German and English and then given worldwide dissemination. When the White Russians depicted bolshevism as an assault by alien Jews on the essence of European Christian civilization, the very conspiracy to which the *Protocols* referred, the visibility of Jewish leadership in the short-lived Bavarian Republic and the even briefer Soviet Republics lent credibility to the accusations. The impact of these events should not be overlooked in accounting for Hitler's linking of antisemitism and anti-Marxism.

It must also be underscored that World War I was a struggle different from any ever fought before on the European continent. Specifically, it was a war of mass death—ten million soldiers and civilians fell in the conflict. In Germany there was regret, not so much that so many lives had been lost, but that the sacrifice had been in vain. No sooner had the guns fallen silent than various German groups resolved that the enormous blood sacrifice would somehow be made good in the future. In some of these groups antisemitism figured prominently. A case in point was an obscure group called the *Deutsche Arbeiterpartei* (German Workers' party), which was founded in January 1919. Still in the army, Adolf Hitler was assigned—ironically, as it turned out—to investigate radical political activity. His orders put him in contact with the DAP in September 1919. Finding that its ideas coincided with many of his own, Hitler became member Number 55. Later, he became member Number 7 of the executive committee. Within two years, Hitler was leading the fragile organization. Capitalizing on his powerful rhetorical talents, the renamed National Socialist German Workers' party, which now contained some forty-five hundred members, gradually made Munich take notice. Wishfully believing the Weimar Republic was near collapse, on 8 November 1923 Hitler half persuaded and half forced influential political and military leaders in Munich to back his attempt to seize power in Germany. This plan was a disaster but only in the short run. Sentenced to five years in prison, Hitler was back on the streets by Christmas 1924. In the meanwhile he had used his time in jail to write *Mein Kampf*. It became one of the most influential books of our century.

In *Mein Kampf*, Hitler reckoned that nature's basic law is that of eternal struggle in which conflict is the means to greatness.[8] In addition, Hitler found two other natural laws that he regarded as vitally important. These he called the laws of heredity and self-preservation. Nature, contended Hitler, balks at the mixing of species in reproduction. It also preserves the strongest while eliminating the weakest. Human life is not exempt from nature's ruthless process, which always takes the shortest, most efficient path in selections that destine the strongest for life. The crucial difference, however, is that human beings can know—indeed they must know—that their individual and social existence unfolds in an arena of unending mortal struggle. The strong, therefore, will not flinch from embracing a principle that was self-evident to Hitler, namely, that national survival may well depend on aggression and violence. Crucial in those considerations, Hitler urged, is the additional fact that a people's survival and movement toward excellence depend on geography. Sufficient land (*Lebensraum*) is essential for a vital people and for the purity of its way of life.[9] To achieve greatness and the space it requires, brutal means may be necessary. A people's spirit is tested as it is required to apply maximum force in subduing its enemies.

The links between these dimensions of Hitler's world view and his virulent antisemitism are not far to find. In fact, the two components were interfused. Nature and history, thought Hitler, are of one piece. Early on he was driven by the conviction that human existence and the racially superior German people in particular were threatened by racial pollution. Thus, Poles, Russians, Ukrainians, and other Slavic peoples, as well as "defective" Germans or "asocials" (for example, the mentally retarded, the physically handicapped, homosexuals, and criminals), would become Hitler's targets. Topping this list, however, was the racial enemy Hitler regarded as the most unrelenting of all: the Jews. In a word, *Mein Kampf* testifies that wherever Hitler saw a threat to the ethnic and national survival he prized, wherever he sensed an obstacle to the geographical expansion he craved, he ultimately found the Jews. Following Hitler's lead, propaganda portrayed the Jews in three major ways at once: as international anti-German conspirators, criminals, and life-threatening pestilence. Jews subverted, plundered, and infected the very people who deserved to dominate the world. The German will had to beat back this challenge once and for all. Under his leadership, Hitler believed, the Nazis could and would provide the requisite force.

The reasons why Germans joined the Nazi party or eventually voted for Hitler were diverse. Party members and the Nazi electorate came from varied classes. Nazism attracted them because it took a strong stand against communism, or because other parties did not back their economic and political interests and the Nazis promised to do so. Antisemitism played a part, too, although not necessarily the most decisive one. If antisemitism was not the major factor in accounting for Nazi voter appeal, however, its attraction was unsurpassed for Hitler. This man, it should be remembered, was not a lunatic nor even simply an opportunist. He possessed and could inspire "idealism," which in his case meant that antisemitism was at the core of all of his thought and action. Hitler was no antisemite because he was a racist; rather he was a racist because he was an antisemite. Moreover, his uncanny political intuitions and his antisemitism served each other well. He sensed effectively when and how to stress "the Jewish question" and when and how to downplay it. Never was that question and the intention to answer it decisively far from his mind. Alternately Hitler whipped up and reined back the most predictable and endemic hatred at large in European society. Once he and his like-minded antisemitic colleagues were firmly in the saddle, those idealists spurred Germany to Auschwitz.

The Nazi party contained disputing factions, which included different degrees of antisemitism, but by 1926 Hitler quelled the most contentious of them. Ably assisted by Joseph Goebbels and Hermann Goering, he put behind him the defeat suffered in the Munich *Putsch* and launched campaigns to win broader popular support. He gained followers from diverse sectors of the political spectrum. The Nazis won only twelve seats in the 1928 Reichstag elections, but as the Great Depression engulfed the world, German interest in Hitler's economic proposals accelerated. In response, Hitler did not belabor the Jewish question per se, but Nazi rhetoric skillfully alluded to Jewish contributions to the evils that were of greatest concern to voters, such as the continuing limits imposed on Germany by the Versailles Treaty, communism, international finance capitalism, and the economic instability of the Depression. To Hitler, Jewishness was primarily a racial matter, but he did not confine it strictly to that realm. Non-Jews might also be "spiritual Jews" insofar as they identified with democracy, socialism, and internationalism, which were among the causes Hitler identified as "Jewish." Such people also became his targets. Hitler's popularity, however, did not increase primarily because of his antisemitism. Sarah Gordon puts the point succinctly: "Middle-class and other voters did not vote for Hitler because he promised to exterminate European Jewry. Neither did they vote for him because he promised to tear up the constitution, impose a police state, destroy trade unions, eradicate rival political parties, or cripple the churches."[10] Yet when he got the requisite power, these are precisely the things Hitler went on to do.

Meanwhile, insisting he would only attain power by legal means, a strategy that increased his credibility with Germans who deplored periodic outbursts of Nazi streetfighting, Hitler and his party did much better in 1930, garnering 107 seats in the Reichstag and a popular vote exceeding six million. Not only was Hitler in undisputable control of the Nazi party, he had become a major political figure in Germany at an auspicious moment. For the Weimar regime, which was never greatly loved by large numbers of Germans who regarded it as foisted on them by the victorious Allies after World War I, was becoming wracked by factionalism that weakened it beyond recovery.

Hitler's total domination of Germany was not far off. Before we reach that part of our story, however, it will be well to observe what was happening concurrently in Poland, where so much of Hitler's Final Solution of the Jewish question was enacted, and in the United States as well. In the 1920s, the flood of eastern European immigrants to the United States, the most promising destination, produced an explicitly anti-Jewish response in the United States Congress. The Report of the Congressional Committee on Immigration entitled "Temporary Suspension of Immigration" and dated 6 December 1920 was concerned almost exclusively with bringing Jewish immigration to a halt. The report cites the published statement of a "commissioner of the Hebrew Sheltering and Aid Society of America": "If there were in existence a ship that could hold 3,000,000 human beings, the 3,000,000 Jews of Poland would board it to escape to America."[11] By 1924, the year the membership of the Ku Klux Klan reached an all-time high, Congress passed the Johnson Act, which tightened immigration quotas. As of late April 1938, for example, the Act would have permitted "national origin immigration quotas" to accommodate 27,370 persons from Germany (including Austria); 6,524 from Poland; 2,712 from the Soviet Union; 869 from Hungary; and 377 from Rumania. Doors for Jews were closing on both sides of the Atlantic.

The 1919 statement that all three million Polish Jews would emigrate to America if they could was no doubt an exaggeration. Still, the vast majority did want to leave, for the political and economic situation of the Jews of Poland, the country with by far the largest number of Jews in the period between the wars, deteriorated each year. The restoration of Polish independence in 1918 included a violent wave of antisemitism. Thousands of Jews had fought for Poland's freedom, but typically the Jews were regarded by the Poles as unassimilable foreigners. That hostility was intensified by the fact that the Jewish population was overwhelmingly urban, giving Jews a disproportionate representation in Poland's cities, whereas the Polish population was overwhelmingly rural. In addition to the miserable conditions of the Polish peasants, between seven and eight million Poles were unemployed or woefully underemployed in a country of 32.5 million.[12]

The Polish government reacted to the economic predicament by enacting a series of ever more stringent measures designed to transfer whatever jobs and resources there were from Jewish to Polish hands. The downward mobility of the Jews was immediately evident in government-sponsored agencies. After 1918, Jews were barred from positions in all state bureaus and state-owned enterprises. At no time did the Polish government attempt effectively to expand the economy so that both Jews and Poles might be gainfully employed. In addition, the anti-Jewish measures were actively supported by Poland's Roman Catholic Church, which regarded the Jews as agents of secularization, liberalism, and bolshevism. Roman Catholic faith was regarded as an indispensable component of authentic Polish identity, and religious hatred of the Jews attained a virulence of far greater intensity in Poland than in any other European country, including Nazi Germany.

Without their knowing it, the Jews of eastern Europe were entering an inescapable deathtrap as the 1930s began. Poland was determined to make life as miserable for them as possible as a way of inducing them to leave. Forming at the same time were German forces that would murder them. Emigration had ceased to be a live option for the vast majority. Even Palestine would soon be closed by the British White Paper of May 1939, which ended all legal Jewish immigration save for fifteen thousand a year to be admitted for the next five years.

Nevertheless, while the Polish and the National Socialist governments would share a common aim in their Jewish policy, few Poles in the twenties and thirties seriously entertained the possibility of establishing a system of mass extermination in their country. The Poles were neither modern nor secular enough to plan and execute a systematic program of mass extermination. Under Adolf Hitler and the Nazis, the Germans were.

Although Adolf Hitler had led the Nazi party for almost ten years, he did not become a German citizen until mid-February 1932. At that time the Nazis needed to field a candidate against the Weimar Republic's incumbent president, the eighty-five-year-old Field Marshal Paul von Hindenburg. Hitler, the only Nazi with a chance to win, had to be naturalized before he was eligible to run. In a Germany wracked by economic depression and political chaos—six million Germans were unemployed—Hitler campaigned "For Freedom and Bread," hoping a beleaguered lower middle class and idealistic youth would bring him victory. Hindenburg, perceived by moderate Germans as the last bulwark between communism or Nazism, defeated Hitler by seven million votes. The splintering of the electorate, however, was sufficient to force a runoff, since Hindenburg had not received a majority. The Field Marshal won the second contest, but only after Hitler narrowed the margin by one and a half million votes.

Hindenburg's victory brought Germany neither peace nor unity. The Weimar Republic's parliamentary system, never a tower of strength, had been especially shaky since September 1930 when it became clear that no government could successfully rule Germany without Nazi support. Elections for the Reichstag brought the Nazis nearly fourteen million votes in late July 1932, a total more than half a million higher than the combined results of the Nazis' two closest rivals, the Communists and the Social Democrats. Braced by this showing, Hitler was determined to be chancellor, the chief executive of the German government. But the tide turned against him—momentarily. In elections held on 6 November, the National Socialists received two million votes less than they polled the previous July. Thirty-four Nazis were unseated in the Reichstag. A stunned and discouraged Hitler wrote at the end of 1932: "I have given up all hope. Nothing will ever come of my dreams."[13] Rarely has a self-appraisal been so inaccurate. By 30 January 1933, Hindenberg had been persuaded to invoke emergency dictatorial power granted him under the constitution to prevent an overthrow of democratic order. Ironically, when Hindenburg used his authority to appoint Hitler chancellor, he ensured the very result his action was supposed to forestall.

German industrialists, military leaders, and right-wing politicians had successfully prevailed upon a hestitant Hindenberg to appoint Hitler to the chancellor's post. Their hope was to control Hitler, who in turn would control the labor unions and stem the Communist tide that seemed ready to engulf German society. Once more a self-appraisal backfired; only this time it was not Hitler's. Handed the power he craved, Hitler and the Nazis moved quickly to consolidate their gains. Strides in that direction were made when secretly-inspired Nazi arson at the Reichstag on 27 February 1933—the Communists were blamed—enabled the Nazis to persuade President von Hindenburg to curtail civil rights "for the protection of the People and the State." By 24 March 1933, the Reichstag passed the so-called "Enabling Act," the single law that would provide the constitutional foundation for Hitler's "leaderstate" in which his decisions were law. The Enabling Act modified the Weimar constitution so as to give Hitler direct legislative authority. Although the act expired on 1 April 1937, by that time the Nazi regime had effectively legalized all that it would need to do. On 14 July, for example, the Nazis were established by law as the one legitimate political party in Germany. Three months later, Hitler announced his intention to withdraw Germany from the League of Nations, calling for a plebiscite on the issue to be held on 12 November, the day after the anniversary of the armistice that had ended World War I. With Hindenburg's ambivalent support, Hitler's policy was overwhelmingly endorsed. A few weeks later, another decree made the NSDAP "the representative of the German state idea and indissolubly linked to the state."[14] Hitler could well have imagined that the dissolution of his dreams just a year before had now reversed itself so that the vision of *Mein Kampf* might still come true: "The German Reich as a state must embrace all Germans and has the task, not only of assembling and preserving the most valuable stocks of basic racial elements in this people, but slowly and surely of raising them to a dominant position."[15] Implied by these views was the need for additional territory (*Lebensraum*) in which the enlarged German *Volksgemeinschaft*, an ethnically and culturally homogeneous community devoid of all dissonant others, could flex its muscle with room enough for all who belonged and none for those who did not.

The Twisted Road to Auschwitz

Obviously the Jews were excluded from Hitler's "most valuable stocks of basic racial elements." Instead he took them to be an absolutely unwanted population, thoroughly dissonant biologically, culturally, and not least of all economically. Recall that Hitler grew up in the heyday of a pan-German nationalism fueled by Bismarck's unification of Germany in 1870. Also significant was the depression of 1873–79. Taking a heavy toll, the depression left economic disturbance in its wake. History testifies that ethnic and religious intolerance rises when economic uncertainty advances and leaves its marks. The lower middle class in Germany and Austria had been hit especially hard. Like their counterparts elsewhere, these people were often the victims, not the beneficiaries, of economic modernization. Handicapped in competition with well-financed, large-scale enterprises, they were threatened by proletarianization and in hard times with unemployment. Even the resumption of an upward trend in the business cycle left these artisans, small retail merchants, and farmers disadvantaged in comparison to the owners, managers, and laborers in much bigger financial and industrial concerns. Blame for the disparity was often laid at Jewish doorsteps.[16] The determination of a politically active sector of the indigenous German middle class to eliminate a competing economic population that was regarded as alien to both the national and religious consensus cannot be underestimated. Although it is not the whole story, one must not overlook that the Jews of Europe became a surplus population not so much because they were unemployed but because they were seen as a threat to a group that feared its own downward mobility.

As a young man, Hitler watched thousands of eastern European Jews, driven from Russia and Poland, flood into the urban centers of Germany and Austria. During this same period, record numbers of ethnic Germans, their economic prospects in decline, had to depart from their native lands and emigrate across the Atlantic if they were to find a better life. When Hitler put this equation together, he concluded that, as far as Germans were concerned, the Jews would forever be unwelcome competition, never an economically complementary population. From that perspective, he found the Jews damnable on all sides. It struck him that those who were not squeezing Germans in a power struggle to make ends meet had surely exploited them in achieving financial success. Other Jews, he reasoned, threatened to destabilize traditional German society by their liberal democratic leanings, if not by embracing various forms of Marxist socialism or communism. Hitler was not alone in holding such views. They thrived among his lower-middle-class contemporaries, whose social and economic standing grew still more precarious in the twenties and early thirties.

During this time, Jews understandably identified with the ideas and interests that seemed best to serve their needs. Thus, they tended to equate modern human rationality with pluralism, liberalism, and tolerance. Meanwhile their Gentile counterparts in the German-speaking world were attracted to other forms of modernity that stressed cultural homogeneity, standardization, and centralization. Thus, what the Jews hoped for in the way of a pluralistic community, influential members of the dominant majority took to be no community at all, but a congeries of atomized strangers. These Germans sought to restore older bonds based upon kinship and shared origins. The irony, of course, was that the emancipation of Europe's Jews had appeared to offer them civic equality, but as a leveling measure it did away with official recognition of very real differences in tradition, culture, and function among the varying elements of the population. It was only a question of time before voices were heard demanding the elimination of those whose differences could not be leveled. In spite or even because of their claim to be good Germans, Jews fitted into that category. Racial nationalism offered the lower middle class in particular an appealing political program, for it legitimated hostility toward the hated Jewish competitor while providing an ideological basis for community with the owners of large-scale business and the managers of large-scale government, with whom they were inextricably related in any case. Hence, when the National Socialists proclaimed *"Die Juden sind unser Unglück"* ("The Jews are our misfortune"), the message of unreconcilable differences resonated. In Hitler's cry to create a single Aryan neotribe—a project both elicited and nurtured by such tools of modern technology as high finance, industry, bureaucracy, transportation, and wireless communication— millions found the National Socialists articulating what they had long been feeling. They rallied loyally, for from their perspective National Socialism sought to restore civic unity and altruism. The Nazi appeal was all the stronger because it was not based on an abstract religious or humanitarian ideal of human solidarity in general, but rather on dreams rooted in specifically German blood and soil. As a result, pieces were falling in place to ensure that the situation for European Jewry would prove disastrous.

Economic discontent that deplored Jewish competition and thereby labeled

Jews superfluous did much to lead the way to Auschwitz and other Nazi death factories. Yet that road was anything but straight and narrow. First, it was not easy to remove Jewish life from the German economy. Far from debunking the conviction that Jews were superfluous, however, that problem only meant that policies to confirm what was firmly believed had to be devised. The National Socialists proved equal to that task and many others. Eventually they would have in place the administrative apparatus to manage a thoroughgoing destruction process. That process would define its victims, concentrate them, and then destroy them—expropriating their wealth, energy, and personal effects along the way. Although not always foreseen, the process would exhibit an inherent pattern, a logic of its own, but in the early stages difficulties arose in arriving at a systematic and coherent Jewish policy, and these were exacerbated by volatile factions within the Nazi party itself. During the initial years of Hitler's rule, Karl A. Schleunes believes, "the Nazis stumbled toward something resembling a Final Solution to the Jewish Problem. The Final Solution as it emerged in 1941 and 1942 was not the product of a grand design. In fact, when the Nazis came to power, they had no specific plans for a solution of any sort. They were certain only that a solution was necessary. This commitment carried the Nazi system along the twisted road to Auschwitz."[17]

What Schleunes meant can be illustrated by noting that as far back as 1920 Hitler said, "We will carry on the struggle until the last Jew is removed from the German Reich." He frequently reiterated the fact that such "removal" (*Entfernung*) was one of his top priorities.[18] The precise meaning of these beliefs, however, as well as the means for carrying them out could be defined in various ways. As early as 1918, Hitler may have sensed that killing was the only genuine Final Solution for the Jewish problem. By 1939, and perhaps as early as 1936, mass annihilation was certainly in sharper focus. No formal written order by Hitler is extant, which is not surprising given his basic principle of avoiding signed commands whenever possible, but Hitler's word was law and frequent mention of "*the* Führer order" among Nazi officials indicates that Hitler did overtly decree extermination for the Jews during the summer of 1941. As Sarah Gordon points out, "One cannot climb into Hitler's mind, and he was extremely proud of hiding his true intentions even from his closest associates. But it was entirely consistent with Hitler's style that he formulated a plan, took small steps toward achieving it to 'test the waters,' or, as he put it, used his sixth sense to tell him what he could or could not do, and then pounced upon his enemy to deliver the fatal blow."[19] In sum, despite the lack of written documentation that Hitler ordered the Final Solution, the evidence that Hitler did so is compelling. Such an order was entirely consistent with Hitler's philosophy. Nazi participants who discussed the Holocaust, both during and after the war, reiterated that the killing was ordered by the Führer. Given the magnitude of the Final Solution, plus Hitler's supreme authority in the Third Reich, it is virtually unthinkable that anyone other than Hitler could or would have launched the annihilation of Europe's Jews. The invasion of Russia in 1941 would provide the needed cover for genocide. But in the 1930s, Nazi strategy, consonant with Gordon's appraisal of Hitler's style, was very different. One reason was that Hitler had to contend with many problems all at once. Unification of his own party was among them.

Hitler carried out a revolution in Germany, more through legal channels than through violence. It was in Hitler's long-range interests to continue on that path, for he had come to power with the promise to restore rather than to destroy traditional German society. He attracted industrial and military support for that reason. On the other hand, Hitler's party followers included many who had taken his revolutionary rhetoric, especially the parts about the Jews, with great seriousness. Now that the Nazis were in power those elements had to be placated or at least reckoned with. Of particular importance in this regard was the SA (*Sturmabteilung*).

Under the leadership of Captain Ernst Roehm, described by one commentator as "a curious mixture of military reformer and Bavarian crook, . . . who, more than any other one man, was responsible for launching Hitler . . . into German politics," the SA, which was first organized in August 1921, eventually had a membership of nearly four million men.[20] Swelled by the Depression at the end of the decade, the bulk of its ranks was an uprooted bourgeoisie augmented by a cadre of former professional soldiers. All sought new forms of community for Germany and found their desires best embodied in the Nazi program. Hitler, whose political savvy included the principle that terror and brutality can rally respect, saw the SA as a terrorist organization to assist the party leadership. Roehm's vision was larger. Especially after Hitler's political victories, he expected a freer hand in using the SA for revolutionary conquest within the state. Roehm's vision was considerable, and Hitler was leery of it because Roehm constituted a double threat. On the one hand, he was a competitor in Hitler's desire to dominate his own party completely. On the other, the SA made the industrial and military leadership uneasy about the direction Hitler's revolution would take. It was one thing to battle Communists in the streets, but German industrialists were hardly sympathetic to the socialist tendencies espoused by some elements within the SA. Roughing up Jews might be tolerable, but the German military, whose support Hitler needed, looked askance at the possibility that Roehm's military power might become sufficient to compromise the army's traditional independence from outside influences.

Hitler's promises to the German people included an end to economic and political instability and a restoration of national honor. These aims, including his claims to solve the Jewish problem, implied a series of orderly programs, not the convulsions that the SA's activities might unleash. Continued non-Nazi support, as Hitler understood in these early months of 1933, depended on keeping the SA in check, although without pushing them into total disaffection if that could be avoided. Ultimately, Hitler reckoned, the risks on the latter count were better to take than those of alienating the affection of German industry and military power. Thus, in June 1934 when Hermann Goering and Joseph Goebbels, joined by Heinrich Himmler, all of whom were jealous of Roehm's vast power, convinced Hitler that Roehm was plotting a revolution of his own, Hitler purged the SA. Roehm's murder removed a major threat to Hitler's hegemony. If the purge eliminated some of the NSDAP's most ardent members and disillusioned others who felt that the party had betrayed its own cause by being too cautious and moderate, the net result was a step toward tighter central control for Hitler.

That control became firmer still in the summer of 1934 when word reached Hitler that President von Hindenburg was near death. On August 2, just an hour before he died, the Reichstag passed a law merging the offices of chancellor and president effective upon von Hindenburg's death. This convenient maneuver left Hitler as supreme commander of the armed forces, whose members soon took an unprecedented oath of unconditional obedience to Adolf Hitler, Führer of the Reich and its people. As Hitler received the accolades of the Nazi party congress in Nuremberg that September, he had survived internal challenges to his personal power that would not reach a comparable magnitude until the near-miss assassination attempt in July 1944.

Rational and Irrational Antisemitism

The preceding discussion of the conflict between Hitler and Roehm and of Hitler's care to consolidate his authority necessarily glossed over some of the important details concerning the twisted road to Auschwitz. To fill them in, we need to retrace some steps. First, it bears remembering that as early as 1919, a few days before he joined what would become the National Socialist Party, Hitler distinguished between two kinds of antisemitism, rational and irrational. He wrote:

> Purely emotional antisemitism finds its final expression in the form of progroms [*sic!*]. Rational antisemitism, by contrast, must lead to a systematic and legal struggle against, and eradication of, what privileges the Jews enjoy over other foreigners. . . . Its final objective, however, must be the total removal [*Entfernung*] of all Jews from our midst.[21]

If he was obsessed by that "final objective," Hitler did not forget his distinction between the types of antisemitism either. He also understood the principle that mob violence can serve a rational purpose by putting a target population on notice that they are cast wholly outside a community's social contract. But Hitler also recognized that his war against the Jews could not be won by random violence and hooliganism. Instead it would have to be a campaign deliberate and calculated, organized and sustained. Hitler planned accordingly, although it also took time for the full implications of that vision to dawn in historical practice.

For example, in late 1932, just prior to Hitler's rise to power, plans for implementing the anti-Jewish sentiment that had so long been a Nazi cornerstone were surprisingly modest. If the party received an absolute majority in the forthcoming elections, the main scenario called for depriving Jews of their rights by new legal statutes. But if power depended on a coalition, the Nazi strategy would be to undermine Jewish rights through administrative means. Such caution was not shared by the SA, which by March 1933 had launched an anti-Jewish campaign of its own, replete with boycotts of Jewish businesses and street fighting. These wildcat actions, which lacked central direction even from the SA itself, served to vent some spleen but brought more distress than comfort to a Nazi regime seeking to stabilize its authority over German life.

In Hitler's first months of power, Nazi hooliganism was rife. If it served a useful purpose by intimidating Hitler's nonsupporters, this terrorism also eluded the control that Hitler needed to advance his own aims, not to mention eroding confidence in his promises to maintain law and order. As a step toward rationalizing the terror process, a secret police force, the Gestapo, was organized under Goering's authority in March and April 1933. Meanwhile appeals for discipline went largely unheeded by the SA, prompting Hitler to seek a way to let it flex some muscle but in a way that would not be counterproductive to the Nazi effort to undermine Jewish status administratively. A nationwide boycott against Jews in the business world and the professions appeared to be a way out.

Under the guise of being a defense against anti-German slander in the foreign press, which, according to Nazi propaganda, was being trumped up by Jewish interests, the German boycott of Jewish elements in the economy was to be enforced by the SA and other local party units, who would agitate concurrently for the development of a quota system to restrict the number of Jews permitted in various professions. As the boycott was announced, however, Hitler found himself in a bind. Prices dropped dramatically on the Berlin Stock Exchange, creating troublesome anxiety among his nonparty supporters. At the same time, Hitler could not afford to lose face with the Nazis, and with the SA in particular, by calling off the action. Compromise led to plans for a one-day boycott. Meanwhile Goebbels worked to minimize lost prestige through the means available to him as head of the newly formed Ministry of Public Enlightenment and Propaganda. On Saturday, 1 April 1933, the boycott went into effect, but only in fits and starts and without discipline. It was cancelled before the day was done.

Adverse reaction from foreign governments was substantial. Ironically, however, the failure of this attempt worked to Hitler's advantage. It showed that the party radicals, who had been given responsibility for implementing the boycott, were seriously wanting as formulators and executors of anti-Jewish policies. More importantly, it became clear that the boycott strategy, especially if it had been successful, would have exacted a price far greater than any gains it could have achieved. A systematic boycott of Jewish business would have been so disruptive to the German economy as to be infeasible. The Nazi need was to stabilize and nurture that economy, not to put it under further threat. Thus, greater rational calculation about how to deal with the Jewish question would be required.

Although they targeted Jews as unwanted and in that sense superfluous, neither random violence nor hastily contrived and ill-administered programs provided effective anti-Jewish measures. None of those lessons were lost on Hitler and his closest associates, but it took time to clarify their meanings and to put their implications into practice. One other crucial problem came to light as well. Insofar as the Nazis' propaganda picture of the Jews led them to envision a worldwide economic conspiracy, they also believed that a boycott against German Jews would take foreign heat off of the Nazi regime. When that assumption proved false, some Nazi leaders realized that they might be blinded about Jewish reality by their own propaganda. Henceforth more accurate insight about Jewish life, inside Germany and abroad, would be essential.

Hitler appears moderate on the Jewish question in 1933 when compared to some of his followers in the SA. Nevertheless, it is a mistake to think that his antisemitism was ever less than radical. As Sarah Gordon argues, "Hitler used anti-semitism to establish a new ideology, to create an illusion of consensus on racial issues, to isolate opponents by social atomization, to divert Germans from his failure to fulfill promises, to terrorize the population, to weaken the power of the state relative to the party, and to justify expansion and war."[22] His moderation was rooted in tactical considerations, not in benign intentions, and thus the boycott's failure did nothing to deter him from his aim of "removing" the last Jew from the German Reich. The issue was only how best to define and then to accomplish that goal, given the political circumstances. If direct economic intervention fell short, perhaps a more solid entrenchment of Nazi political power would open the avenue of "paper violence."

As already noted, the passage of the Enabling Act on 23 March 1933 was a decisive breakthrough for Hitler. This action by the Reichstag gave Hitler power to legislate and govern by decree, including the latitude to set aside provisions in the Weimar constitution that guaranteed legal equality for all citizens. It was not left to Hitler alone, however, to use law against the Jews. Advice was forthcoming from all sectors of the Nazi party, and on 7 April the first of eventually some four hundred anti-Jewish measures went into effect. The earliest of these dismissed Jews from civil service positions and restricted Jewish enrollments in educational institutions. Among the host of other restrictions aimed at excluding Jews from public life, government, culture, and the professions were measures prohibiting Jewish farming and ritual slaughter. Significantly, immigrant Jews who had been naturalized found their citizenship revoked, a fate that soon affected all German Jews, leaving them extremely vulnerable.

Early on it was obvious that such legislation would be enforceable only to the extent that there was clarity about who was ruled in or out of the laws' purview. The Nazis wrestled long and hard with this critical problem of definition, never solving it to everyone's full satisfaction. The issue was complicated because Nazi ideology made Jewishness a matter of blood. Paradoxically, however, these racial lines inevitably could be determined only by reference to religious identity. Thus, not only would decisions have to be made concerning the amount of Jewish blood that was sufficient to make one a target of discrimination under the law, but also determinations as to a person's religious heritage would become essential—for Gentiles as well as for Jews—in answering questions about bloodlines.

Early attempts at definition utilized the term "non-Aryan." While intended to target Jews exclusively—the crucial regulation of 11 April 1933 defined a "non-Aryan" as a person who had a Jewish parent or a Jewish grandparent—both the category and its definition were too imprecise. "Jew" was the specific designation that had to be refined, but not until 1935 was the legal definition sharply focused. That definition designated as Jewish anyone having at least three full Jewish grandparents. Also included were persons with two full Jewish grandparents and any of the following features: belonging to the Jewish religious community as of 15 September 1935 or joining thereafter; being married to a Jew at that date or later; being born from a marriage contracted after 15 September 1935 in which at least one partner was a full or three-quarter Jew; or being born after 31 July 1936 as the illegitimate offspring of extramarital relations involving a full or three-quarter Jew. The intent of these decrees was to make unalterable their targets' status and fate. The criteria, however, did not cover everyone who possessed Jewish blood. Thus, further calculations were needed to classify the *Mischlinge*. In sum, *Mischlinge* of the first degree were defined as persons descended from two Jewish grandparents but neither belonging to the Jewish religion nor married to a Jew on 15 September 1935 or thereafter. *Mischlinge* of the second degree were persons who had one Jewish grandparent. With some variation, these basic definitions prevailed in German-occupied countries and Axis states. *Mischlinge* were subject to discrimination, but they were less at risk than those classified as full Jews.

The complexity of these definitions alone, not to mention the range of detail covered by the various anti-Jewish laws, was far removed from the uncoordinated physical violence the SA longed to unleash. What a campaign of "paper violence" required instead was a vast bureaucratic network, a web of offices to plan, interpret, implement, and enforce the required actions. The twisted road to Auschwitz was engineered neither by Hitler alone nor solely by his Nazi party. Its construction enlisted, in the words of Raul Hilberg, "an ever larger number of agencies, party offices, business enterprises, and military commands. . . . The machinery of destruction *was* the organized community in one of its special roles."[23]

Hitler understood intuitively what the German sociologist Max Weber had noted twenty years earlier, namely, that in a modern state the power to achieve political domination rests with the forces that control bureaucracy. As Hitler rose to power, he inherited and directed a sophisticated German civil service that was willing to serve its master and capable of efficient operations on complex problems. Indeed, once nudged into action, in this case dealing with the Jewish problem, it would take the wishes of its leaders to heart and calculate the best ways to realize them. Instead of helping those in peril, the apparatus of government worked to increase their defenselessness and then to get rid of them. In carrying out such steps, the German bureaucracy was not acting atypically when compared to other modern states that have existed before or since. But the skill with which the German system carried out its mandate does reveal the extent to which state power can threaten people for whom it no longer wishes to care. This is not to say that the German bureaucracy was a monolith that worked single-mindedly to rid the Reich of Jews; nor did German bureaucrats unanimously formulate one basic anti-Jewish plan and set it inexorably into motion. The destruction process that culminated in death camps moved step by step. Here it faltered; there it was confused. Sometimes costly unintended consequences emerged, and on a few occasions it was subverted from within by officials such as Bernhard Lösener, who sought to ameliorate Jewish plight by drafting legislation so that it touched fewer Jews rather than more. But the destruction process never relented. As long as Nazi power lasted, the bureaucracy that served it remained in motion, too. Without it there could have been no Final Solution.

Meanwhile, legislative measures against German Jews proved less effective than the Nazis hoped. Those tactics left the more violence-oriented factions of the party unsatisfied, but those who sought a more orderly handling of the problem were also troubled, because the qualifications attached to some of the laws exempted too many Jews. For example, the earliest laws exempted non-Aryan officials who had been employed in the civil service on or before 1 August 1914. Special provisions held for Jewish veterans of World War I as well. Joseph Goebbels effectively regulated cultural activities so that Jews were excluded from film production, literary publication, broadcasting, and the press. Still, as 1933 drew to a close, even Jewish observers could say that, although many German Jews had lost their economic base for existence, a tolerable Jewish future remained possible in Germany. Coupled with the fact that relatively little legislative action was taken against the Jews in 1934, the purging of the Roehm elements in the Nazi party also portended a moderating climate for Jewish life. Indeed several thousand Jews who had fled Germany returned home in early 1935.

The calm was deceptive. In May 1935, Hitler reintroduced general military conscription as part of his rearmament plan. Jews, however, were considered unfit for service. If that decision was a relief to some, it caused profound humiliation for others, and not without reason because especially in Germany, where military service was honored and provided opportunities to enhance one's prestige, this action was a further step toward making Jews second-class citizens. But the most spectacular anti-Jewish legislation was reserved until September when the Nazis held their party rally at Nuremberg. The "Nuremberg Laws," passed unanimously by the Reichstag on 15 September, contained two fundamental provisions. First, the "Reich Citizenship Law" stated that German citizenship belonged only to those of "German or related blood." Henceforth Jews would be guests or subjects only. Moreover, even blood was an insufficient condition for citizenship. It was to be granted by certificate, and that certification was to be functionally controlled by the Nazi party. Receipt and retention of citizenship, then, depended less on an inalienable right and more on approved conduct. Second, the "Law for the Protection of German Blood and Honor" prohibited marriage and sexual intercourse between Jews and persons of "German or related blood." Also outlawed were the employment of German female servants under 45 years of age in Jewish households and display of the Reich flag by Jews. Such decrees put Jews even more at the mercy of the German state, especially when one notes that the previously discussed definition of Jewishness, promulgated two months later, gave all anti-Jewish measures a more precise focus.

The legislative phase of the Nazis' anti-Jewish campaign put German Jews under duress by severing social contacts between Jews and Germans; imposing restrictions on housing, movement, and work; creating identification measures; and establishing Jewish administrative mechanisms for helping to carry out the various decrees. But these steps were not enough to produce the Holocaust. If the Nuremberg Laws were the zenith of the legislative phase, the enforcement of such decrees and the others that came before and after would not have eradicated the ongoing existence of a Jewish community in Germany, second class though it surely would have been. Hitler and the Nazi leadership became aware of that fact, which left them far from their professed goals of making German life *Judenrein*. Thus, as the Nazis used law against the Jews, it proved to be a two-edged sword. If law kept order and spiked the hostility spawned by random violence, it also constrained the Nazis. By itself, law offered no Final Solution.

Wanting to be certain that the 1936 Olympic Games would be on German soil, the National Socialists soft-pedaled their anti-Jewish policies in late 1935 and 1936.[24] But having used the Olympics successfully to showcase the Reich, the Nazis had to do more to satisfy the racial purists. Pressure to stifle Jewish participation in the German economy intensified, and thousands of small Jewish businesses began to be liquidated after harassment by local Nazis. The German economy as a whole, however, was still not vigorous enough to permit tampering with all Jewish businesses, disconcerting though it may have been to the Nazi rank and file to see major Jewish firms continuing to prosper while the "little man" had to battle to make ends meet. Major legislation to excise Jewish economic influence from German life was forthcoming, but it was developed with caution.

Prior to November 1938, the Nazi strategy was to "Aryanize" the German economy. Jewish businesses—so defined if they were owned by or under the dominant influence of Jews—would be sold "voluntarily" to private German corporations. To encourage such sales, three types of pressure were applied. Germans were urged to boycott Jewish firms; Jewish access to raw materials was restricted; and the depressing effects of these measures were psychologically sufficient to nurture Jewish fear that already troubled circumstances could always take a turn for the worse. Nevertheless, the Nazi policies once again were less than optimally effective. In April 1938, for example, some forty-three thousand Jewish firms still did business in Germany. Therefore, additional steps were taken to facilitate compulsory Aryanization, which became effective that autumn. One significant step was a more rigorous definition that identified any business enterprise as Jewish if, to cite only some provisions of the decree, it had a Jewish proprietor, involved a Jewish partner, or included Jews among its board of directors on or after 1 January 1938. Other actions set termination dates for many small Jewish firms. Licenses were taken away from Jewish doctors, and Jewish lawyers were prohibited from practicing after 31 December. In November and December the vise tightened further. Jewish retail establishments were to be dissolved and liquidated by the end of the year, and on 3 December 1938 another decree provided that all Jews could be required to sell or liquidate industrial and real estate holdings within a stated time. By 1939 the German Jews, now numbering about half of the five hundred thousand who resided there prior to Hitler's victory in 1933, were badly impoverished. Jewish professionals and ordinary workers alike found outlets for their labor restricted, and much Jewish capital was now in German hands. Even German Jewish communal organizations could no longer own property, their right to act as legal entities stripped away. And yet despite the Nazi attempts at apartheid and economic discrimination, all of which meant powerlessness for German Jews, the Jewish problem remained. Indeed, two events made it worse for the Nazis, moving them to find new paths for ridding the Reich of Jews.

The Last Year of Peace

Late in the afternoon of 29 September 1938, British Prime Minister Neville Chamberlain received a hero's welcome as he returned to London. Earlier that day he had joined Benito Mussolini, of Italy, Édouard Daladier of France, and Hitler in signing the Munich Agreement, which permitted the Nazis to annex the Czech Sudetenland in exchange for Hitler's promise that no further territorial demands would follow. "I believe," said Chamberlain of his pact with Hitler, "it is peace in our time."

War was never far from Hitler's mind nor from the Nazi program. The fate of the Jews hung in the balance because Hitler believed that Jews must be eliminated from Germany to avoid the repetition of a Jewish "stab in the back" that would thwart the military effort. The Nazi goal of a racial utopia required war both to validate German superiority and to create an empire. From the outset of Hitler's rule in Germany, then, he worked to put the Reich on a war footing, not least because doing so relieved Germany's unemployment problem, which was solved by 1938. Part of the Four-Year Plan that he directed Hermann Goering to implement after the Olympic Games in August 1936 called for taking Czechoslovakia, but that invasion would follow the annexation of his native Austria. Hitler stuck to his timetable. On 12 March 1938, after long months of intimidation and threats supported by Austrian Nazis, Hitler occupied Austria without resistance while the world watched. Two days later Hitler entered Vienna in triumph.

For our purpose perhaps the most significant fact about the *Anschluss* or annexation of Austria is that it brought some two hundred thousand Austrian Jews into the Third Reich. Since 1933, Nazi policies had not succeeded in eliminating that many Jews from Germany itself. Thus, the *Anschluss* considerably increased the magnitude of the Nazis' Jewish problem. National Socialist strategies, of course, had aimed at making life so uncomfortable for German Jews that they would be prompted to get out, but these tactics had not succeeded completely. The dimensions of the Jewish problem created by the *Anschluss* called for more effective measures. Austria became a laboratory to test them. One of those put in charge was a young, recently promoted *Untersturmführer* (second lieutenant) in the SS. This rising expert on Jewish affairs was Adolf Eichmann.

Able to work in a relatively unencumbered fashion, Eichmann initiated an assembly-line technique of forced emigration for the Jews of Austria. Heretofore in Germany, emigration, like "Aryanization," had been "voluntary" although very desirable from the Nazi point of view. Incentives to make that "choice" remained mixed, however, because Nazi policies also levied heavy taxes against Jews who left. In addition, the red tape to be negotiated was considerable, consuming weeks before a Jew could exit. Thus, some German Jews believed the lesser of evils was to stay put and to hope that things would improve or at least not get worse. Under Eichmann's administration, the Central Office for Jewish Emigration got its program under way in Austria during the spring of 1938. Softened up by a reign of terror far greater than any the German Jews had seen, the Austrian Jews were eager to leave. Eichmann's policies were costly for Jewish victims from an economic standpoint, but they speeded up the emigration process immensely. As one Jewish leader, Franz Mayer, recalls Eichmann's technique, "You put in a Jew at one end, with property, a shop, a bank account and legal rights. He passed through the building and came out at the other end without property, without privileges, without rights, with nothing except a passport and order to leave the country within a fortnight; otherwise he would find himself inside a concentration camp."[25] If Mayer's account is oversimplified, still in six months' time Eichmann removed fifty thousand Jews from Austria, twice the number who left Germany in any year since 1933. He demonstrated "that appropriate bureaucratic and organizational measures rendered the Jewish problem amenable to solution."[26] Neither his plans nor his personal administrative skills went unnoticed by the Nazi leadership, for he was eventually put in charge of the deportation that took Jews from every quarter of Europe to the death camps.

We shall return to Eichmann's status in the SS, as well as to some of the problems that were produced by his Austrian policy of forced emigration, but consider first another momentous event, the *Kristallnacht*, which occurred eight months after the *Anschluss*. In addition to the thousands of German Jews who still resided in Germany as late as 1938, the presence of nearly seventy thousand Polish Jews inside German borders remained an embarrassing stain on the Nazi policy of a *Judenrein* Germany. This embarrassment took on even broader implications when the Polish government, fearful that Polish Jews in Vienna and elsewhere under German control might return to Poland, announced on 31 March that all Polish citizens living outside of Poland must have their papers approved by Polish consulates or lose their Polish citizenship. Less modern and secular than the Germans' but hardly less intense, Polish antisemitism was fueled by a religious hatred more virulent than in any other part of Europe. The antisemitism of Polish policy became clear when Polish Jews, upon appearing at Polish consulates, were denied the stamp of approval. The Nazis could also read the handwriting on the wall: Germany would soon be burdened by a large community of Polish Jews rendered stateless by action of the Polish government.[27] Stateless Jews, the Nazis could see, would be wanted by no one. Ridding Germany of them by emigration would be extremely difficult.

The Poles had established 31 October as the last date for Polish nationals to obtain the necessary consular approval. When the Germans learned that Polish policy would indeed exclude reentry into Poland for Polish Jews, who would then be rendered stateless, the Nazi Foreign Ministry decided that expulsion would have to follow. By 28 October Polish Jews, rounded up by the Gestapo, were being shipped to the Polish frontier, but the Poles were not ready to accede to German wishes. Blocked from Poland, unable to return to Germany, detained in hideous conditions, these Jews found themselves in a hapless no-man's land. An uneasy compromise was reached after several days. The Poles accepted most of the refugees; others were allowed to return to Germany. Matters were anything but settled, however, especially when a seventeen-year-old student, living in Paris at the time, learned that his parents were among the Jews who had been expelled from Germany.

Herschel Grynszpan decided to take action, but in his wildest fantasies he could hardly have anticipated what his determination would produce. Apparently Grynszpan's intention was to assassinate the German ambassador to France, but in the early morning of 7 November his bullets found instead Ernst vom Rath, a secretary in the German embassy. The news broke in Germany without any special flourishes—until 9 November, when the press announced that vom Rath had died the previous afternoon. Under Goebbels' direction, the press editorialized that Jews in Germany ought to be identified with the crime and that punishment would follow.

Kristallnacht, a "night of broken glass," ensued. Some three hundred synagogues were torched. Plundering and looting of Jewish shops went unchecked. By the thousands, Jews were placed under arrest and sent off to concentration camps. Property damage totaled hundreds of millions of marks. These actions were carried out primarily by the radical elements in the Nazi party, including the SA. It was turned loose by a Goebbels speech in Munich during the fifteenth anniversary celebration of Hitler's 1923 Beer Hall Putsch after the Führer agreed that "the SA should be allowed to have its final fling."[28]

The "fling" was a multiple disaster. Hard-hit though it left the German Jews, those results proved minor in comparison to the ones that emerged from the renewed power struggle that *Kristallnacht* set off among the Nazi leadership. Nazi officials such as Himmler and Goering were caught off guard by *Kristallnacht*, but in addition to wanting to block a Goebbels power play, they were also convinced that street violence was counterproductive, not least of all economically. The Goering-Himmler argument carried the day. As the influence of Goebbels and the radical wing of the party declined, the need for a decisive, coordinated, and rational anti-Jewish policy became ever clearer. There was never a repetition of *Kristallnacht* in Germany. Renewed emphasis fell on forced emigration, with Reinhard Heydrich directed to implement in Germany a program like the one established by his subordinate Eichmann in Austria. Experts in the controlled use of terror and bureaucratic pressure had finally suppressed the drives that resulted in random violence. The road to Auschwitz had become more open, less twisted.

"The Most Fantastic Association of Men Imaginable"

As the Nazis tightened their grip of total domination on the Jews in 1933–39, men such as Heydrich, Eichmann, and Himmler came increasingly to the fore— along with the organization they represented, the SS (*Schutzstaffel*, Protective Squad). The development of the SS and the emergence of a clearly defined policy toward the Jews were closely linked and warrant attention. For the Holocaust bears the unmistakable mark of this "order of the 'Death's Head,' " which Heinz Höhne identifies without exaggeration as "the most fantastic association of men imaginable."[29]

Called into existence in April 1925, the SS was a select group of SA members armed to protect Hitler, top party leaders, and party meetings. It numbered less than three hundred members in January 1929, compared to some sixty thousand in the SA, when Hitler named Heinrich Himmler *Reichsführer–SS*. Twenty-eight at the time, Himmler was a former school teacher and chicken farmer who had climbed up the Nazi ladder, serving as the NSDAP deputy gauleiter (district leader) of Lower Bavaria for a time and then as deputy leader of the SS. As Himmler began to transform the SS into an elite, racially pure cadre that would take direction solely from Hitler, it became clear that along with his mystical devotion to German blood and soil were the makings of a "cold professional policeman who possessed an almost instinctual understanding of the use of power."[30] Always serving Hitler's desires faithfully, that understanding usually advanced Himmler's ambitions as well.

Fearing the threats posed by the power of the SA and its leader, Ernst Roehm, Hitler counted increasingly on Himmler's help, committing to him and his men—they numbered about three thousand by the end of 1930—the task of carrying out police duties within the party. To help him handle this assignment, Himmler in 1931 turned to Reinhard Heydrich, four years his junior, whose antipathy toward Jews may have been fueled by the desire to disarm the false but persistent allegation that his own family tree contained Jewish blood. Heydrich proceeded to develop a secret security branch, the *Sicherheitsdienst* (SD), within the SS. It became an awesome surveillance system whose network eventually extended to all of Nazi-occupied Europe.

Spurred by economic unrest, SS membership leaped to fifty thousand by the time the Nazis took power in 1933, but only after the purges of 1934 did Himmler and Heydrich secure the independence of the SS from the SA. Meanwhile the first concentration camps appeared in Nazi Germany. One of them, set up by Himmler in March 1933, stood not far from Munich near the town of Dachau. *SS-Oberführer* (Senior Colonel) Theodor Eicke and his *Totenkopfverbände* (death-head units, so named for the skull and crossbones insignia on their tunics) were in charge. Like all institutions of their kind, before and since, these proliferating camps provided a rational way to incarcerate people whom the state wished to eliminate either temporarily or permanently without necessarily killing them, most of whom had committed no crime and could not be confined through the normal workings of the criminal code. Put differently, in contrast to normal prisons, concentration camps tend to be extralegal institutions of incarceration for the guiltless but unwanted. Whoever controlled such a weapon had vast power, but at first there was no central administration for the Nazi camps. Himmler came out on top, however, when the secret police or Gestapo, formed originally by Hermann Goering, came under his authority. Henceforth the camps were in Himmler's jurisdiction as well. Now the inspector for concentration camps, Eicke consolidated them and introduced uniform procedures. After World War II began, Eicke was succeeded by Richard Glücks and then by Oswald Pohl, who presided when the camp apparatus operated at its zenith.

The SS, SD, and Gestapo had overlapping spheres of influence that no organizational chart could map adequately, but the fact was (and it got Hitler's official stamp of approval on 17 June 1936) that Himmler was chief of the German police in addition to being the *Reichsführer–SS*. As the oath taken by every SS man upon induction made plain ("I swear to you, Adolf Hitler, as Führer and Chancellor of the German Reich, loyalty and valor. I pledge to you and to the superiors whom you will appoint obedience unto death, so help me God."), Himmler could unleash means of physical coercion and instruments of terror far more devastating than any that the SA's emotional, *ad hoc* violence could muster.

In the early months of the Nazi reign, Jewish matters were not a priority on the SS agenda. But by the summer of 1936, Himmler and Heydrich having consolidated their authority, an expanded SD bureaucracy developed a special department (Section II–112) on Jewish affairs. Second in command was Adolf Eichmann.[31] Raised in Upper Austria, Eichmann had joined the Nazi party in April 1932, just after his twenty-sixth birthday. When the Nazi party was declared illegal by Austrian Chancellor Engelbert Dollfuss, Eichmann returned to his native Germany and subsequently joined the SS. Learning that a new section of the SS, the *Sicherheitsdienst*, wanted recruits, Eichmann applied and soon found himself assigned to gather information about freemasonry, which leading Nazis, in accord with the teaching of *The Protocols of the Elders of Zion*, suspected was part of an international Jewish conspiracy.

Though bored by these duties, Eichmann was forced to center on the Jewish problem. Studying its various dimensions, he emerged as something of an expert on Jewish affairs, a fact that distinguished him from most National Socialists who actually knew very little about Jewish history and culture. In particular, Eichmann studied Zionism and became convinced that forced emigration was probably the most expedient solution for the Jewish question. As Eichmann's superiors discerned that this young man also had organizational talent, his knowledge, philosophy, and skill would make him a decisive figure in the destruction process.

Eichmann is best known for organizing the transports that took Jews to the death camps, but in 1937 his efforts were directed toward Jewish emigration. As Eichmann perceived the situation, greater pressure had to be brought against Jews to convince them to get out of German territory. Simultaneously conditions that would permit their leaving had to be expedited. The latter factors, in particular, meant that Jews must retain enough financial resources so that other countries would not look completely askance at them, and that consideration, in turn, meant that Nazi antisemitic propaganda might have to be toned down. Neither Eichmann nor the SS alone, however, controlled Jewish policy at this time. Competing Nazi views were still transmitting conflicting signals to German Jews. For example, one important consideration was the matter of what steps the Nazi regime would take to help ensure that Jews had a place to go. Eichmann, for example, spent considerable energy working on Jewish emigration to Palestine. Those efforts, however, were undertaken with misgivings, shared by Hitler, that it might be unwise to allow the concentration of too many Jews in any one place outside of Germany, let alone to enhance the possibility of a Jewish state which might pose threats to Nazi hegemony. Such fears, indeed, promoted suspicion that even forced emigration might not be an adequate solution for the Jewish question. Something more final and permanent would emerge as necessary, but not yet. Eichmann's successful Austrian experiments in this area, coupled with the mixed results of the *Kristallnacht* pogrom, kept alive the basic if unclearly articulated Nazi aims at this time—to eliminate Jews from the German economy and then to drive them out of the Reich—even as they helped to make SS expertise dominant in Jewish affairs.

Not until 31 July 1941 did Heydrich receive orders from Hermann Goering, then Hitler's chief deputy, that he should "make all the preparations in organizational, practical, and material matters necessary for a total solution [*Gesamtlösung*] of the Jewish question in territories under German influence." The master plan for carrying out this "final solution [*Endlösung*] of the Jewish problem" was to be submitted to Goering "in the near future."[32] Although the exact date of Hitler's order to Goering remains unknown, Hitler had been alluding to "the annihilation of the Jewish race in Europe" for many years, at least since his speech to the Reichstag on 30 January 1939. His words are worth quoting once more: "Today I will be a prophet again: If international finance Jewry within Europe and abroad should succeed once more in plunging the peoples into a world war, then the consequence will be not the Bolshevization of the world and therewith a victory of Jewry, but on the contrary, the destruction of the Jewish race in Europe."[33] Rhetoric and actual development and implementation of policy, however, did not yet coincide altogether, even in July 1941, because Goering's earlier orders to Heydrich of 24 January 1939 were still to promote emigration and evacuation of Jews from German territory. Nonetheless those orders were significant. Not only was Eichmann's Austrian model put into effect in Germany, but also a decisive step had been taken to centralize implementation of Jewish policy and to locate responsibility for it within the SS. Eichmann's reward for services already rendered took him first to Prague, where he was to oversee the deportation of some three hundred thousand Jews who had to be dealt with after Hitler gained control of Czechoslovakia, then to Berlin to head the Reich Central Office for Jewish Emigration, and finally in 1941 to section IV–B–4 of the RSHA (*Reichssicherheitshauptamt*, the Reich

Central Security Office), where as head of Jewish Evacuation Affairs he organized transports to the killing centers from all over Europe.

The evolution of Eichmann's career illustrates the SS's role in a destruction process moving toward total domination. As Eichmann first rose to influence, forced emigration and an advance of SS authority in Jewish affairs moved to center stage. But with the expansion of Nazi power—taking in Austria and Czechoslovakia prior to the outbreak of World War II and then encompassing vast areas when the Nazi *Blitzkreig* followed—forced emigration became impossible due to the sheer size of the Nazis' Jewish problem. To illustrate, Poland alone contained more than three million Jews when the Nazis conquered that country. Another 2.7 million Jews eventally came under Nazi jurisdiction after Hitler invaded the Soviet Union. Add to those figures the population of Jews in central and western Europe, and the Nazis had nearly ten million unwanted Jews on their hands.

Eichmann was asked in the summer of 1940 to develop a plan for evacuating four million Jews to Madagascar, but it soon became clear that in wartime such a project would not be realistic. Other methods of population control to assure a *Judenrein* Nazi empire had to be found. Such concern led some SS scientists to experiment with techniques for mass sterilization. Under the cover of war, that same concern led other segments of the SS into Poland and the Soviet Union to enact mass murder.

The Failure of Emigration

None of the National Socialist strategies in the prewar 1930s—boycott, legislation, Aryanization, or emigration—provided a totally satisfactory solution to the Jewish problem, partly because the "problem" itself remained ill-defined. Was the issue one of separating Jews from Germans through apartheid as biological antisemitism insisted and as the pogroms of the SA demanded? Or was it simply to eliminate Jews from economic influence? Or was the only sufficient condition one in which Jews physically left German soil altogether and in ways that would make their return inconceivable?

Movement toward the latter conclusion was steady, but that evolution took time and its direction was not obvious when the Nazis came to power. Moreover, Hitler himself seems not to have played a decisive directing role, waiting instead to see how the struggles would turn out between the competing factors he had helped to create, and commissioning the SS to prepare a coordinated effort against the Jews only after it prevailed late in 1938. At no time, however, did either Hitler or his followers ever consider the possibility that the Jewish problem was no problem at all. In fact, as each measure brought further problems with it, "a more extreme approach appeared to be the only alternative to the less-than-total solutions which had proved unsatisfactory or unworkable."[34] One of the reasons why forced emigration proved to be both unsatisfactory and unworkable, thus necessitating a more extreme approach, was simply that the nations of the world chose not to open their doors to all of the potential Jewish refugees.

In the late 1970s and early 1980s, a number of "boat people," mostly from Southeast Asia and the Caribbean, were driven from their homelands and left to drift and die without a port of entry. These "homeless, tempest-tost" refugees were different from those the Jewish poet Emma Lazarus had in mind when she wrote the poem now etched at the base of the Statue of Liberty in New York Harbor. And yet those Asian and Latino victims were not so different either. The hordes of people who emigrated—some voluntarily, others choicelessly— from Europe to America in the nineteenth century, for example, might have been "boat people," too, had there not been a safety valve, a place to go where they could make a new start. These people, like their more recent peers, were in some sense redundant, surplus people, whose presence in existing states was no longer highly valued or at least did not seem very promising. The great difference is that so many of them found new homes. Some of the Jewish refugees created by Nazi policies in the 1930s did, too. Most did not.

Numerous factors beyond the Nazis' control thwarted their plans for forced emigration. Global economic depression, to cite one factor, persisted well into the 1930s. Many nations did not want to add to their burdens by needlessly enlarging their own populations, especially when doing so entailed acceptance of Jews left impoverished by Nazi acquisition and emigration taxes. Although Zionist agencies worked at occupational retraining for German Jews, their predominantly professional and business skills were disadvantages in a competitive situation where countries often favored immigrants with craft and industrial skills. A rising average age among German Jews was also an impediment, since countries tended to prefer youth and discriminate against the elderly. Most German Jews also thought of themselves as thoroughly German. They were understandably reluctant to leave their homes. On the other hand, antisemitic feeling in other nations clearly stood behind most of the aforementioned impediments to emigration. Thus, even if entry visas were available, the advantages of emigration did not patently outweigh the possibly short-term and perhaps limited liabilities of staying in Germany.

The feasibility of emigration as a solution to the Jewish question depended on the availability and willingness of other nations to take Jews. That fact, in turn, slowed down the process from the Nazi viewpoint because the exit process had to be handled in an ordered and legal manner that would not tax already strained international good will too far. When Eichmann speeded up the process from the German angle with his efforts in Austria, his success also created a critical refugee problem worldwide. Jewish agencies such as the American Joint Distribution Committee and the *Mossad le' Aliyah Beth*, which worked especially to bring Jewish refugees to Palestine, devoted their energies to meeting the need.

Hope that assistance might come from other quarters was prompted by U.S. President Franklin D. Roosevelt's decision to call for an international conference on refugee problems intensified by the *Anschluss*. Such a conference was held in early July 1938 at the French resort town of Evian.

Thirty-two nations sent delegations to Evian. The Nazis permitted representation from the German and Austrian Jewish communities. Upon hearing the Jewish accounts, the nations in attendance quickly discerned that, short of doing nothing at all, their efforts would have to be directed at alleviating conditions within Germany. Otherwise they would have to open their doors to the refugees, which most were unwilling to do. In fact, the American invitation to Evian had included the assumption that non-German governments would not have to foot the bill for any necessary emigration, nor would they have to make any substantial revisions of existing immigration quotas. Thus, an Inter-Governmental Committee on Refugees, headed by George Rublee, one of Roosevelt's troubleshooters, was formed to negotiate with the Nazis.

The Czechoslovakian crisis and *Kristallnacht* both intervened to delay Rublee's arrival in Berlin, but it is doubtful that he would have found the Nazis much more open to negotiate before those events than they proved to be afterward. Working with Hjalmar Schacht, the head of Germany's state bank, Rublee got an agreement that would have ransomed substantial numbers of German Jews. Yet the fact remained that the world was divided into two camps—one that wanted to be rid of Jews and one that would not accept them. As far as concrete results to help Jewish suffering were concerned, the Evian conference and its aftermath amounted to little. An incident on the other side of the ledger, however, is worth mentioning. A Swiss delegate to the conference expressed concern about the threat of a flood of refugees into his country, stemming from the Austrian *Anschluss* and the fact that the Swiss and German governments had no visa requirements between them. Subsequently, after the Swiss applied further pressure during the summer of 1938, the German government specified that all German passports belonging to Jews were to be stamped with a large red J. By the end of the year, every Jew in the Reich was also required to have a special identification card available at all times. Such measures abetted the cause of anti-Jewish discrimination outside of Germany as well as within.

Jewish persecution reached new heights in Germany during the summer of 1938. Meanwhile substantial numbers of Jews did flee. Until the middle of 1938 about a third of the emigrants—some fifty thousand since Hitler's takeover—found their way to Palestine. Most went in accord with the Ha'avara Agreement that had been negotiated between the Nazis and Jewish officials in Palestine in August 1933. Under these arrangements, Jews heading for Palestine left their assets behind in special blocked bank accounts. They would receive half of their holdings back in Palestine currency upon arrival, with the remaining half being credited toward the purchase of German goods by Jewish officials in Palestine.

Even with the Ha'avara Agreement, which was a lucrative boost to the German economy, Jewish emigration to Palestine was not an easy matter. For one thing, the British wanted to stabilize the Middle East to ensure control of the Suez Canal, its passage to India. So British power in the region acceded to Arab pressures restricting Jewish immigration to Palestine in the second half of the 1930s.[35] Specifically, the British issued their White Paper on Palestine on 17 May 1939. Terminating the promise to establish a Jewish National Homeland in Palestine, which had been announced in the Balfour Declaration of 2 November 1917, the White Paper laid plans for a Palestinian state with a permanent Arab majority. Future Jewish immigration to Palestine—without Arab consent, which was unlikely—would end after seventy-five thousand were admitted between 1939 and 1944. Once war began, the possibility of legal immigration constricted even more. Jewish emigration to Palestine did continue. Even when it could be arranged, however, the price of passage on ramshackle vessels was extremely high. Once afloat there was no assurance of a successful arrival. Clandestine night landings along the Mediterranean coast were frequent but increasingly difficult as British patrols tightened a net that either took Jewish refugees into custody or simply turned them back to sea. The British government did not directly murder Jews in the Holocaust, but its actions in the late 1930s and afterward did clarify the redundant status of Europe's Jews. The British government did not want to be inconvenienced by an influx of Jews into the one community where they could have been welcomed unconditionally. Britain's power to back up that attitude politically helped to convince Hitler that the Jews were indeed unwanted refuse. Left in his hands, they were crushed.

The situation in other parts of the world was not much different, as the tragic case of the *St. Louis* illustrates. On 14 May 1939, this German liner left Hamburg for Havana, Cuba. Of the more than nine hundred Jewish refugees aboard more than seven hundred had fulfilled American immigration requirements, which opened the door for them to enter the United States within a matter of months. Meanwhile special Cuban permits were to provide a way station. The purchase of passage and necessary documents had stripped away their few remaining assets. When the *St. Louis* docked in Havana on 30 May, news arrived that the Cuban government had revised its immigration restrictions on 5 May. The Cuban entry papers held by the Jewish refugees were worthless. On 2 June Cuban President Frederico Laredo Bru ordered the *St. Louis* to leave.

Hope that American officials might expedite entry into the United States proved worthless, too. For more than a month the *St. Louis* and her homeless Jewish boat people cruised without a safe place to land. Finally England, France, Holland, and Belgium agreed to divide up the refugees, but with the understanding, supported by the League of Nations, that their actions must not be viewed as setting precedents. Some of those who were rescued from the *St. Louis*, of course, eventually fell again into the Nazi web, a fate that came even sooner for other transports which were ultimately forced to return to Germany when they could find no refuge.

As autumn 1939 approached, pressures within Germany and around the globe increasingly turned the Jews under Nazi domination into a surplus people. Resources were not lacking to meet their subsistence needs, nor did these Jews lack ability, intelligence, or potential social utility. Their gifts and talents were abundant, but Nazi Germany weighed those assets and found them wanting in comparison to the gain that would accrue if the Jewish presence disappeared. That step would be a major stride toward fulfillment of the National Socialists' dream of a *Volksgemeinschaft*. If actions speak louder than words, other nations in the world were not opposed to this Nazi sentiment. Implicit though the conclusion may have been, the plight of the Jews supported a proposition—reiterated again and again of other groups in our recent post-Holocaust world—that "here are people we can best afford to do without."

Implied or stated in enough times and places, that feeling fueled Nazi yearnings for some lasting solution to the Jewish problem and even gave Joseph Goebbels some reason to think that he discerned what Hitler's professed opponents would never admit openly. At bottom, Goebbels would write in his diary entry for 13 December 1942, "I believe that both the English and the Americans are happy that we are exterminating the Jewish riffraff."[36] Goebbels' reasoning cannot have been off the mark entirely. Faced with the prospect that Hitler might flood them with unwanted Jewish refugees, governments around the world were not in a very favorable position to criticize the Nazis for their internal handling of the Jewish question. In effect, Hitler could and did say: "If you don't like the way we treat our minorities, take them yourselves." Few were ready to do so; most kept quiet and let Hitler proceed with the dirty work. Lacking a safety valve, pressure built to move outright extermination of Jews to the top of the Nazi agenda. The cover of war would make that Final Solution possible; the outbreak of war would make it necessary. As Hitler and his armies prepared to invade Poland in 1939, the road to Auschwitz, paved with twists though it still continued to be, had its end in view.

Chapter 5

War and the Final Solution

Prior to the outbreak of World War II, the Nazi handling of "the Jewish question" drew heavily on precedents developed through the centuries by church authorities and secular governments. Precedent was insufficient, however, when the war presented both the opportunity and, from the Nazi perspective, the necessity for a radically different approach. The Germans would call it the Final Solution, an idea that was itself an invitation to inference because its meaning was not crystal clear initially to everyone concerned. As the end in view became that of doing away with the Jews of Europe altogether, the Nazi bureaucracy faced an unprecedented challenge. How should the Jews be destroyed? What could be done with their property and their corpses? How should the whole process be coordinated and, critically important, how could it be kept secret as far as possible, too? No blueprints existed to solve these problems, for no one had faced them before. The Final Solution therefore authorized innovation. Every aspect of the operation required invention, and under the cover of war, invent and innovate the Nazis did.

During World War II Germany fought two wars: the first a relatively conventional war against France, Great Britain, and the United States; the other a war wholly unlike any other in modern history. The war against the West was frightful in the damage done and the lives lost, but it remained relatively conventional. The Geneva Convention concerning the humane treatment of prisoners of war was essentially observed by both sides, although toward the end of the war German General Alfred Jodl toyed with the idea of denouncing the Convention and massacring all Allied prisoners of war as a way of "burning bridges" behind the Germans and spurring them on to desperate efforts in the face of defeat. Still, the basic norms of conventional warfare were more or less observed in the West.

Nothing was conventional about the war Germany waged in the East, an uncompromising, ideologically-motivated war of conquest, colonization, and extermination. The first group targeted for extermination was Europe's Jews, the overwhelming majority of whom lived in eastern Europe. Immediately before the German invasion of Poland on 1 September 1939, approximately 3.3 million Jews lived in Poland out of a total population of 35 million. In the area of the Soviet Union conquered by Germany in the summer of 1941 lived more than 2.7 million Jews. Hitler's eventual plan was to murder every one of them. In the case of the Russians, Hilter regarded them as both racially inferior and dominated by Jews as a result of the Bolshevik Revolution. Since he regarded the Russian Revolution as a victory for Judaism, in spite of communism's profound antipathy toward Judaism, he was determined to uproot both bolshevism and Judaism.

Genocide in the Soviet Theater of Operations

Although the Germans had already ghettoized and killed tens of thousands of Jews in Poland between 1 September 1939, when the war began, and 22 June 1941, when they invaded the Soviet Union, the deliberate, systematic extermination of Europe's Jews did not begin in earnest until the German invasion of Russia. As the *Wehrmacht's* regular army units overwhelmed the surprised Russian forces and drove ever deeper into Russia, they were accompanied by relatively small, highly mobile, units called *Einsatzgruppen* or "Operational Units," whose mission was to round up and murder all Jews found behind German lines. The personnel of the *Einsatzgruppen*, who were among history's worst mass killers, were not members of the *Wehrmacht*. For example, *Einsatzgruppe A* consisted of an amalgam of the *Waffen-SS* (34%), Gestapo (9%), Criminal Police or "Kripo" (4.1%), *Ordnungspolizei* (13.4%), non-German auxiliaries (8.8%), *Sicherheitsdienst* or SS intelligence (3.5%), and technical and administrative personnel (27.2%).[1] The *Einsatzkommandos* were detailed to the *Reichssicherheitshauptamt* (RSHA), the Reich Central Security Office, which had been organized and was led by Reinhard Heydrich.[2] On 24 January 1939, Hermann Goering, then second only to Hitler, commissioned Heydrich to "solve the Jewish question by emigration and evacuation in the way that is most favourable under the conditions prevailing at present."[3] As circumstances changed and extermination replaced emigration as official policy, the means available to Heydrich to implement the Final Solution were enlarged until they included the RSHA, the *Einsatzgruppen*, and the system of death camps which we will discuss later in this chapter.

In May 1941, about a month before the Russian invasion, *Einsatzgruppen* commanders were assembled at an RSHA training center in Pretsch in Saxony and told that they must be prepared to liquidate all those who were even potentially enemies of the Reich. Several dozen RSHA officials were given intensive, secret training, as well as indoctrination about the "Jewish menace." According

to Otto Ohlendorf, one of the *Einsatzgruppe* commanders, Heydrich delivered
to the commanders a Führer order, which in the Third Reich had the force of
law, that "Communist functionaries and activists, Jews, Gypsies, saboteurs and
agents must basically be regarded as persons who, *by their very existence*, endanger the security of the troops and are therefore to be executed without further
ado."[4] There was also a meeting in Berlin shortly before the 22 June invasion of
Russia at which Heydrich stressed the need to murder children.[5]

The *Einsatzgruppen* were divided into four groups consisting of between five
hundred and nine hundred men, led by SS Generals Franz Walter Stahlecker,
Artur Nebe, Max Thomas, and Otto Ohlendorf respectively. Three of the groups
covered Russia from north to south, the fourth was responsible for the Crimea
and the Black Sea region. Each group followed immediately behind the German
army as it invaded Russia. In the beginning, the basic strategy of the *Einsatzgruppen* was to get to Jewish communities and seal their fate before the victims
had any idea of what was happening to them. The Germans also encouraged the
local population to launch pogroms and spontaneous massacres. In Riga, Latvia,
for example, convicts were released from prison, given iron bars, and told to
murder Jews.[6] The results were only partially successful. In spite of the powerful indigenous antisemitism of the region, the local populations did not always
respond with the enthusiasm the Germans expected. Enthusiasm for pogroms
was greater in Lithuania and the Ukraine than in Latvia. In Estonia the population did not oblige the Germans at all, although the Germans were easily able to
destroy the small Jewish population.

Although the pogroms were only partially successful, they did serve at least
two purposes. The Germans were able to implicate others in the slaughter, and
they were able to recruit squads among the Lithuanians, Ukrainians, and Latvians who were later used as auxiliary police in implementing the Final Solution.
Nevertheless, the Germans preferred their own controlled, systematic, less emotional methods to spontaneous massacres. As noted, Heydrich's RSHA consisted of a mixture of government bureaucrats, police, and SS officials, all
of whom preferred order and structure even in mass murder. Moreover, the
Einsatzkommando officers were largely respectable, upper-middle-class professionals and intellectuals, not bloodthirsty killers, career SS men, or the scum of
German society. Some had been deliberately chosen by Heydrich because they
had been members of SS auxiliaries who regarded their SS affiliation as an ef-
fortless, part-time avocation that could help them advance their civilian careers.
Heydrich wanted to teach intellectuals like Otto Ohlendorf that membership in
the SS was no "honorary" sideline. Ohlendorf, the commander of *Einsatzgruppe D*, had been research director of the Institute for World Economy and
Transport in Kiel and a doctor of jurisprudence who had studied at Leipzig, Göt-
tingen, and Pavia. Many *Einsatzgruppe* leaders were lawyers. One, Ernst Biberstein, had been a Lutheran pastor. These white-collar murderers were a

representative cross section of well-educated, respectable Germans in the Third Reich.[7] After the war, they insisted that they were honorable citizens who had only done their duty when the order to exterminate the Jews was the law of the land. Such people had little tolerance for disorder and pogroms. For the sake of efficiency and to bolster their own illusion that they were acting in the service of their nation for a higher ideal, they preferred well-organized murder to uncontrolled killing.

There was a discernible pattern to the German killing operations. When the *Einsatzgruppen* first came into a town or village, they would order the Jews to set up a *Judenrat* or Jewish council, usually headed by the local rabbi. A day or two later the council was informed that the Jewish population was to be registered for transportation to "Jewish territory." The council was then ordered to call all Jews together in some central location, such as the town square. The assembled Jews were then herded into buses, vans, or trains, depending on what was available, and taken a few kilometers out of town to a ravine, ditch, or some other place suitable for mass burial. There they were stripped of their clothes and their money and shot on the spot. Some *Einsatzgruppen* forced the victims to lie down and then fired point blank into the back of their necks. Some commanders preferred the more impersonal method of massed gunfire from a distance. Other Jews were forced down in what was called "the sardine method" *(Ölsardinenmanier)*. The new layer of victims was compelled to lie down with their heads above the previous layer's feet and then they were dispatched. Others were lined up along the edge of a ditch and shot in successive waves. This was considered the most "humane" method of killing. In the region of Odessa one hundred forty-four thousand civilians were killed by the Rumanians, primarily by drowning. In Minsk many victims were burnt alive.[8]

There are many descriptions of the murders. We cite one by a German witness of an "action" that took place outside of Riga, Latvia, on 30 November 1941, because it makes absolutely clear the thoroughly rationalized, assembly-line character of these government-sponsored operations. One ought not, however, to assume that all of the operations went as smoothly. In most, some victims were buried and even burned alive after bullets had failed to finish them off.

> The columns of Jews advancing from Riga, comprising about one thousand persons each, were herded into the cordon, which was formed in such a way that it narrowed greatly as it continued into the woods, where the pits lay. The Jews first of all had to deposit their luggage before they entered the copse; permission to carry these articles had only been granted to give the Jews the impression that they were taking part in a resettlement. As they progressed, they had to deposit their valuables in wooden boxes, and, little by little, their clothing—first overcoats, then suits, dresses, and shoes, down to their underclothes, all placed in distinct piles according to the type of clothing.
> . . . On the previous evening, 29 November 1941, there had been an average

snowfall of seven centimeters. On 30 November between 7:00 A.M. and 9:00
P.M., it did not snow.

   Stripped down to their underclothes, the Jews had to move forward along the
narrow path in a steady flow toward the pits, which they entered by a ramp, in
single file and in groups of ten. Occasionally, the flow would come to a standstill
when someone tarried at one of the undressing points; or else, if the undressing
went faster than expected, or if the columns advanced too quickly from the city,
too many Jews would arrive at the pits at once. In such cases, the supervisors
stepped in to ensure a steady and moderate flow, since it was feared that the Jews
would grow edgy if they had to linger in the immediate vicinity of the pits. . . .
In the pits the Jews had to lie flat, side by side, face down. They were killed with
a single bullet in the neck, the marksmen standing at close range—at the smaller
pits, on the perimeter; at the large pit, inside the pit itself—their semi-automatic
pistols set for single fire. To make the best of available space, and particularly of
the gaps between bodies, the victims next in line had to lie down on top of those
who had been shot immediately before them. The handicapped, the aged, and the
young were helped into the pits by the sturdier Jews, laid by them on top of the
bodies, and then shot by marksmen who in the large pit actually stood on the
dead. In this way the pits gradually filled.[9]

   It would have been impossible for the *Einsatzgruppen* to conduct a monumental killing operation within a war zone without the wholehearted approval and
cooperation of military authorities, especially in the initial stages of a gargantuan, surprise invasion. Negotiations carried on in the spring of 1941 between
the RSHA and the *Wehrmacht* concerning the role of the *Einsatzgruppen* and the
support to be given by the *Wehrmacht* concluded that the military would provide
the *Einsatzgruppen* with quarters, fuel, food, rations, and radio communica-
tions. It was also agreed that any "representative of enemy ideology" who fell
into German hands was to be done away with. This included Communist officials, political commissars, and "all Jews."[10] By this extraordinary agreement,
the German Army ceded to the RSHA the right to commit mass murder of unarmed civilians within its theater of operations. Moreover, the RSHA was the
only nonmilitary agency admitted to the Russian theater during the invasion
campaign. In the words of Raul Hilberg, the RSHA became "the agency that,
for the first time in modern history, was to conduct a massive killing
operation."[11]

   In addition to facilitating the work of the *Einsatzgruppen*, in many instances
the army went out of its way to turn over Jews to the *Einsatzgruppen* and to request their speedy dispatch. Moreover, the army frequently participated in the
killing in order to get the job done quickly. The extermination program was popular with the generals. When Heinrich Himmler addressed three hundred generals, admirals, and general staff officers in Posen, which was then part of the
Reich, on 26 January 1944, he announced that the Führer's orders for the Final
Solution to the Jewish problem had been carried out and "there no longer is a
Jewish question." Save for five officers, all three hundred joined in applause.[12]

The German army's complicity in the extra-combat mass murder of unarmed civilians was further heightened as a consequence of an agreement between Heydrich and General Hermann Reinecke of the General Armed Forces Office signed 16 July 1941 to the effect that the *Wehrmacht* was to "free itself" of all prisoners of war who were "carriers of Bolshevism." Beneath the verbal camouflage, a principal purpose of this agreement was to permit the RSHA to enter prisoner of war camps in order to select and kill Jewish members of the Soviet armed forces. By 21 December 1941, more than sixteen thousand prisoners of war had been murdered. The exact proportion of Jewish victims is not known.[13]

The behavior of the civilian population in the German-conquered regions of the Soviet Union also facilitated the German action. In general, only the ethnic German population actively assisted in the slaughter. The behavior of the non-Germans has been characterized as passive, although in Lithuania Bishop Vincent Brizgys forbade the clergy to help the Jews in any way.[14] However, as Hilberg has observed, the passivity and neutrality of the local population favored the Germans who were able to proceed with their gruesome task without hindrance. Whenever Jews attempted to escape the German net, they were typically refused assistance of any kind by the non-Jewish population.

The Jewish predicament was further complicated by the fact that a large segment of the conquered peoples of Russia, the Ukraine, and the Baltic welcomed the German invaders as liberators from Stalinist terror. They soon discovered, however, that German behavior in the conquered territories was based upon racist contempt for the Slavs as subhuman. Within a year, the majority of the conquered peoples had turned against the Germans. One of the severest criticisms of German policy in Russia came from Alfred E. Frauenfeld, an Austrian Nazi of long standing, who was commissar-general in the Crimea. Frauenfeld described German policy as "a masterpiece of ineptitude; within a year it has achieved the considerable and astonishing feat of turning a completely pro-German people, who welcomed us as liberators, into partisans roaming the forests and marshes. . . ."[15] Unfortunately, by the time the local population grasped the nature of the German enterprise, the majority of the Jews in the conquered territories were dead. Those who still survived were almost entirely beyond help.

Elsewhere we discuss the question of Jewish resistance. Here it is sufficient to note that most of the Jews were overwhelmed before they had any idea of German intentions. The controlled press of the Soviet Union did not publish information concerning German behavior in Poland until the Nazi invasion of Russia negated the Hilter-Stalin Non-Aggression Pact of 23 August 1939. Moreover, the Jews remembered that in World War I German troops in eastern Europe had behaved well and, in many places, had been regarded as liberators. *Lacking any kind of military tradition and initially misreading German intentions, approximately 1.4 million defenseless Jews went to their deaths in Estonia, Latvia, Lithuania, White Russia, and the Ukraine. They took few Germans with them.*

When the German army launched its surprise invasion of Russia, 22 June 1941, it was able to move very rapidly to a line about six hundred miles inside Russia. However, the farther into the interior the Germans penetrated, the fewer Jews they found. The majority of the Jews living under Soviet control were domiciled in the western border regions and in the Baltic states of Lithuania and Latvia. As a result of the speed with which the Germans were able to move initially, many Jewish communities were bypassed in the first sweep of the *Einsatzgruppen*. By September 1941, the Germans realized that, in spite of the huge number of Jews they had murdered, hundreds of thousands still remained alive in the newly conquered regions. At the beginning of the war, 4 million Jews lived in the area in which the *Einsatzgruppen* eventually operated. In the first sweep, 500,000 had been killed, 1.5 million had fled, and 2 million survived. [16] In the meantime, these conquered regions had been divided administratively into a military area under the direct control of the *Wehrmacht*, and several large areas to the west: the *Reichskommissariat Ostland*, which included Estonia, Latvia, Lithuania, and White Russia, and the *Reischskommissariat Ukraine*. In addition, a smaller region around Bialystok was practically incorporated into the Reich.

Following a pattern already in effect in Poland, the Germans decided that the surviving Jews would be concentrated in ghettos where those capable of working for the *Wehrmacht* would be put to work, albeit under abusive conditions calculated to kill off as many as possible through starvation, cold, and disease. Slave labor was always considered a temporary measure by Hitler, who had no intention of permitting any Jew to survive the war.

In the ghettos the Germans set up *Judenräte* or Jewish councils to whom they gave the task of controlling the inner workings of the community. Ghettoization facilitated German control so that they could expropriate at will whatever property remained in Jewish hands, place the Jews on starvation diets, and assure their easy availability when the decision to finish the work of extermination was put into effect. In the meantime, the Germans were determined to profit from Jewish skills. The way the Germans made use of Jewish labor in one city in White Russia is described in the report dated 25 January 1942 by Gert Erren, the German District Commissar, stationed at Slonim:

> When I arrived, there were about 25,000 Jews in the district of Slonim. Of that number, about 16,000 were in the city of Slonim, so that more than two thirds of the city's population were Jews. . . . I . . . made my preparations for a major Action. Expropriation was the first step, and the furniture and supplies that became available were used to equip all German offices here, those of the armed forces included. . . . Stuff that was not fit for Germans was released to the city to be sold to the populace, with the proceeds being added to our official revenues. There followed an exact survey of the Jews according to number, age, and profession, and the segregation of all craftsmen and skilled workers and their being marked by special identifications and separate housing. The Action undertaken by the Se-

cret Police on November 13 freed me from all useless eaters, and the approximately 7,000 Jews who now remain in the city of Slonim all are a part of the labor force. Their permanent fear of death makes them willing workers, and in the spring, they will be examined and sorted out with a view to a further reduction. . . .[17] (From THE NAZI YEARS: A DOCUMENTARY HISTORY, by Joachim Remak, © 1969 Prentice Hall, Inc. Englewood Cliffs, NJ 07632.)

In those parts of eastern Europe with the greatest concentration of Jews, they constituted as much as 90% of the managerial personnel and skilled workers in the armament factories. From the German point of view, it would have been desirable to replace the Jews with Ukrainians, Poles, or White Russians, who would eventually be replaced by Germans. However, there were an insufficient number of trained non-Jewish replacements. At this point, a conflict between ideology and military necessity became unavoidable. On many occasions the *Wehrmacht* and civilian authorities attempted to delay the "deportation" of especially useful Jews. Often, the reprieve was granted temporarily, but Himmler always insisted that economic and military requirements were not to override National Socialist ideology. *Hitler and his inner circle saw the war as a unique and perhaps never-to-be repeated opportunity finally to "solve" the Jewish problem. They were determined to make the most of it.* If the war were to be lost, Hitler was determined that the Jews would go under with him.

The pause between the first wave of *Einsatzgruppen* killings and the final phase did not last long. By the end of 1942 most of the Jews in German-occupied Soviet territory had been killed, although a few larger communities such as Vilna, Lithuania, continued on until late 1943, albeit with ever-diminishing numbers. In the second phase, the *Einsatzgruppen* played a less significant role. Both the police regiments and the SS had expanded greatly. Unlike the *Einsatzgruppen*, they were assisted by auxiliary police recruited from the population of the occupied areas.

In the second wave of killings, the Jewish population was wholly aware of its fate. Unfortunately, when the community's turn came, there was no escape. As in the first wave, the extermination actions began with the digging of mass graves by Jewish labor battalions. Next, the ghetto was surrounded and the Jews moved to a collection point. It was useless to try to hide in one's home. Those who did were usually burned alive. The Jews at the collection point were then brought to a ditch or mass grave outside the town, forced to strip, and murdered in the same manner as in the first sweep. The process was repeated from the Baltic to the Ukraine. Hundreds of thousands perished. The plight of the Jews was made even more difficult by the fact that in June 1943 Himmler ordered the ghettos officially transformed into concentration camps. About one hundred thousand Jews took to the forests where they joined either Soviet or Jewish partisan movements. The majority of those who fled were eventually caught by the Germans, but they at least knew that they had not surrendered to their fate without attempting some kind of resistance. Undoubtedly, the most fortunate were the Jewish partisans who were able to destroy in combat at least a few of those who sought to destroy them. It is estimated that a total of 2,350,000 Jews were murdered by the Germans and their auxiliaries in western Russia.

The executions were carried out openly and were known to both the civil authorities and the *Wehrmacht*. Even some hardened and convinced Nazi ideologues found it difficult to murder masses of helpless men, women, and children. Nevertheless, one German leader was especially enthusiatic about the process. Field Marshal Walter von Reichenau issued an infamous order of the day on 10 October 1941 in which he characterized the murders as "just punishment we must lay on that inferior humanity which is Jewry." Léon Poliakov has summarized the basic fact concerning the killings: "In the immense reaches of Russia some thousands of SS executioners, helped by an international riffraff and also amateur murderers from the *Wehrmacht*, exterminated Jews with complete freedom, 'as if on a stage,' while the *Wehrmacht* staff and the civil authorities turned their eyes the other way." There was some protest concerning *how* things were done but not *that* they were done. The majority of Germans present in the east regretted only the manner of the executions, not the fact that they took place.[18]

Inevitably, the gruesome task took its emotional toll on the perpetrators. Heavy drinking was common among the executioners. In July 1943 Artur Nebe, commander of one of the four *Einsatzgruppen*, was reportedly "a mere shadow of his former self, nerves on edge and depressed."[19] On two occasions he went on sick leave with a nervous breakdown. His driver was reported to have shot himself because of his horror at the mass slaughter.[20] On the other hand, a year later Nebe was offering "asocial gipsy half-breeds" from Auschwitz to be used as human subjects for life-endangering "medical experiments" involving the drinking of sea water.[21] Another *Einsatzgruppe* commander Erich von dem Bach-Zelewski was committed to an SS hospital after suffering from a nervous breakdown and nightmares. The hospital doctor reported that Bach-Zelewski was afflicted with hallucinations connected with the shooting of Jews. When Bach-Zelewski asked Himmler whether the killings might be brought to an end, he was told that the enterprise was a Führer order. Bach-Zelewski was warned of dire personal consequences should he persist in concerning himself about the fate of the Jews.[22]

One of the strangest German responses to the killings was that of General-kommissar Wihelm Kube, *Gauleiter* (district leader) of White Russia. Kube was an old Nazi and a bitter antisemite who was hardly likely to object to the worst kind of treatment meted out to the Jews. Yet he ended up attempting to protect the German Jews in his charge. We have already noted that there was a conflict between ideology and the requirements of Germany's war economy. The conflict was mirrored within the SS itself. In White Russia the second extermination sweep was initiated in February and March 1942. Kube opposed the sweep. He had come to understand that continuation of the slaughter, with its elimination of Jewish industrial workers, would destroy the region's economy. This, however, was of no consequence to *SS-Obersturmbannführer* (Lieutenant Colonel) Eduard Strauch, the commander of the *Sicherheitspolizei* (SS security police) and the "Jewish expert" for White Russia. Strauch was only interested in exterminating Jews, regardless of the economic and military consequences. On 27 October 1941, a liquidation action began against the Jews of Slutsk in spite of the pleas of *Gebietskommissar* (area commissar) Carl, Kube's subordinate, to spare Jewish workers. The action itself was an especially disorderly slaughter which took place all over the town. Bodies were piled up in the streets and many wounded Jews were buried alive.

An outraged Kube filed a complaint against the entire officer corps of the police battalion responsible. He indicated that he had no objection to the "orderly" extermination of Russian Jews, but he objected to the "bottomless infamy" of burying victims alive. In November 1941, seventy-three hundred German Jews from Hamburg, Düsseldorf, Frankfurt, Bremen, Berlin, and Vienna were deported to the concentration camp for German Jews in Minsk, the principal city of White Russia. Kube vehemently protested killing Jews from the German cultural milieu, a number of whom had served Germany in World War I and had received the Iron Cross First Class. Emboldened by the knowledge that his superior, Heinrich Lohse, loathed the economic blindness and barbarity of the killing as much as he did, Kube persisted and continued well into 1943 the protests he had initiated two years earlier. Strauch and Himmler both were relieved when a partisan bomb, planted under his bed by his maid, took Kube's life on 22 September 1943.[23]

Even Himmler found the executions disturbing. Bach-Zelewski reported that on a visit to Minsk, the Reichsführer asked the commander of *Einsatzgruppe B*, Artur Nebe, to kill one hundred people so that he could see what the actions were really like. When the shooting started, Himmler averted his eyes. When two women among the victims did not die, Himmler shouted at the police to end their misery and not to torture them. According to Bach-Zelewski, after the executions a visibly moved Himmler told those assembled that he hated the "bloody business" but that he was obeying "the highest law" by doing his duty.

Hating the "bloody business" did not prevent Himmler from ordering the execution of the inmates of a mental hospital he visited later that day. Himmler then ordered Nebe to see if more "humane" methods of killing might be found. Nebe suggested dynamite and requested permission to try some out on sick people. In spite of protests from Bach-Zelewski and Major General Karl Wolff, chief of Himmler's personal staff, permission was granted. Dynamite was tried but proved worse than useless as a "humane" murder method.[24] Himmler's request did lead to a new method of killing, however: the use of specially constructed vans in which the victims were driven about until the van's carbon monoxide fumes, which had been funneled into the passenger compartment, caused their asphyxiation.

One of the more bizarre aspects of the mass killings was that it was possible for an SS officer to be charged, convicted, and executed for the unauthorized murder of individual Jews at a time when the German state was authorizing the shooting and gassing of thousands of innocent civilians daily. For example, Karl Koch, who served as commandant of Buchenwald before being placed in charge of the killing center at Majdanek, near Lublin, was actually tried and executed for the unauthorized murder of two prisoners at Buchenwald. Koch's prosecution was the result of the diligent efforts made by Konrad Morgen, a lawyer with the SS Financial Crimes Office. In the course of investigating Koch's blackmail and murder activities at Buchenwald, Morgen visited Majdanek and Auschwitz, where he discovered that millions of human beings were being killed by the SS. The discovery did not disturb Morgen. On 11 March 1964, Morgen made a statement to the *Süddeutsche Zeitung* that at the time he distinguished three kinds of murder, two of which were "legal," namely, the extermination of the Jews and the "mercy killing" of infirm Germans. According to Morgen, these had been ordered by the highest authority of government and nothing could be done about them. By contrast, the SS judicial machinery was prepared to take action whenever a member of the organization committed an "unauthorized," private murder.

Morgen's investigations of private crime by SS personnel proved more successful than might have been expected. He secured more than two hundred convictions. In addition to Koch, the concentration camp elite who were sentenced included Hermann Florstedt, commandant at Majdanek, who was executed; Hans Loritz, commandant of Oranienberg; and Adam Grünewald, commandant of Hertogenbosch. In addition, Karl Künstler, commandant at Dachau, was dismissed for drunkenness and debauchery; and Maximilian Grabner, head of the political section at Auschwitz, was accused of murder but not convicted.[25]

As a trained jurist serving as an SS officer, Morgen understood the importance of distinguishing between state-sponsored murder and murder committed by individuals for their private ends. German authorities used such distinctions to diminish whatever scruples the *Einsatzgruppen* personnel might have felt for the killings. The mass deaths were treated as a legitimate action of the state, to which the *Einsatzkommandos* were expected to respond with unquestioning obedience. *Undoubtedly, an important reason for Hitler's insistence before 1933 that he would only come to power by legal means was that he wanted all Germans to accept as legitimate his unlimited authority to command.* In this he was entirely successful. If, as some historians believe, Hitler had determined as early as 16 September 1919 to exterminate all of Europe's Jews, his insistence on possessing legitimate authority can be seen as an indispensable component in the implementation of the most radical program ever proposed by a German politician. Possession of legitimate authority enabled Hitler to become a mass murderer of unarmed civilians with absolute legal impunity. Had he seized power by force, large sectors of the German population might have rejected his authority, especially when confronted with orders to commit acts that even hardened National Socialists found difficult.

One method of limiting emotional stress and maintaining discipline among the killers was to depersonalize the operation. This method was favored by the most intellectual of the *Einsatzgruppen* leaders, Otto Ohlendorf. Ohlendorf made every effort to keep the victims calm until the moment of execution, so that there would be no untoward graveside disturbances. He also prevented personal contact between the executioners and their victims. The executioners were made to feel that they were acting upon superior orders as members of a military unit. Individual shooting was not permitted. Every effort was made to diminish any sense of personal responsibility on the part of the killers. In this way, the SS leadership attempted to remove any burden of guilt the killers felt for their behavior.[26]

Himmler and his commanders also attempted to manage the difficulties experienced by the *Einsatzkommandos* by using those very difficulties as a means of strengthening the resolve of the men to carry out their task. In his speeches to the SS, Himmler praised the executioners for having overcome their natural feelings in order to do the gruesome job. In an oft-quoted speech delivered in Posen on 4 October 1943 to SS leaders, Himmler declared:

> Most of you will know what it means to have seen 100 corpses together, or 500, or 1,000. To have made one's way through that, and—some instances of human weakness aside—to have remained a decent person throughout, that is what has made us hard. That is a page of glory in our history that never has been and never will be written. . . .[27]

Thus, the men were praised for having been "strong" enough to have overcome all normal feelings of human sympathy and compassion. In the same speech, Himmler also declared that no member of the SS had the right to disobey, insisting that the killings were to be regarded as the legally-sanctioned elimination of those who had no right to live. Nevertheless, legal fictions can distort reality only so far. The heavy drinking and the emotional disturbances experienced by many of the men indicate that no amount of legalistic reconstruction of human reality could wholly eradicate the normal human response to grievous human suffering. A "better" way of killing had to be found, not for the sake of the victims, but for the sake of the killers. As we shall see, the "better" way appeared.

Toward the Rationalization of Genocide

As we have seen, the first systematic German attempt to exterminate an entire Jewish population was carried out by the *Einsatzgruppen* in the occupied areas of the Soviet Union. The monumental destruction was wholly unlike any ever before encountered by the Jews of Europe. The Jews had frequently been subject to persecution, ghettoization, and killing. Never before in their history had they been the object of unremitting, state-sponsored, wholesale annihilation.

It is important to understand that the Final Solution was in no sense a large-scale pogrom. The word "pogrom" has been defined as "an attack, accompanied by destruction, the looting of property, murder, and rape, perpetrated by one section of the population against another."[28] Of Russian derivation, it first designated the anti-Jewish attacks that occurred in the Czarist Empire between 1881 and 1921. Before the Russian Revolution, the sympathy of most Czarist officials for the perpetrators of pogroms was open and unambiguous. People were raped and murdered, their property destroyed with little or no interference from the Russian police or armed forces. Indeed, in many instances government officials encouraged the mobs to attack Jews. These attacks killed thousands of Jews and caused the massive destruction of Jewish homes and businesses in the period between 1881 and the beginning of the Russian Revolution in 1917. A far greater loss of life occurred from 1919 to 1921 during the Russian Civil War, a period of unparalleled violence for all of Russia. An estimated sixty thousand Jews were killed and four times that number wounded by the anti-Soviet "White Army" and armed anti-Jewish bands.

The pogroms resulted in the largest mass migration of Jews in history, an outcome welcomed by the Czarist government. Between 1881 and 1921 more than four million Jews, unable to depend on the legal protection of the state, emigrated from the Czarist Empire, the vast majority settling in North America. Nevertheless, the Russian pogroms were very different from the Final Solution. Although both the Russian and the German plans similarly sought to eliminate the Jews as a demographic presence in their respective countries, the Czarist government resorted to murder as a means to encourage the Jews to depart whereas the Germans looked upon extermination as an end in itself and vastly expanded its reach. This is apparent in the list of Jews presented by Reinhard Heydrich on 20 January 1942 to senior officials of the German government at the Wannsee Conference, which Heydrich had called to announce that the Führer had decided upon the "Final Solution of the Jewish problem" and to coordinate the activities of the ministries of the German government, the SS, and the Nazi party in implementing the Final Solution. In addition to listing the number of Jews in the countries occupied by or allied to Germany, Heydrich also listed the Jews in Spain, England, and Switzerland as targeted for extermination. The

Germans were not only interested in getting rid of the Jews in their territory; they sought to destroy them wherever they might be found.

Paradoxically, the *practical* implementation of the Czarist program required far more mass emotion than did the German Final Solution. Hatred was an indispensable component in the Russian pogrom, which can be characterized as "hot" destructiveness. By comparison, although many instances of sadistic Nazi brutality could be cited, the Final Solution was a "cool" method of killing. Admittedly, the German government used all of its resources to stir up the hatred of the Germans against the Jews and, by the time the war was underway, the antisemitic propaganda campaign had proven quite successful. Still, one did not have to hate Jews in order to take an active part in implementing the Final Solution. After the war, a number of the leading perpetrators, including Adolf Eichmann, a principal architect of the process of destruction, and Franz Stangl, the commandant of the Treblinka death camp, claimed that they did not "hate" Jews but were merely doing their duty.[29] These claims were undoubtedly self-serving since they were made after the individuals involved had been captured and imprisoned. Nevertheless, four years before his capture when Eichmann granted an interview in Argentina to Willem Sassen, a Dutch Nazi journalist, he said that while he had no regrets, there was nothing personal in his involvement in the Final Solution, and that he "never had any bad experience with a Jew. . . ."[30] As noted, one of the problems facing the *Einsatzgruppen* commanders was how to cope with the emotional disturbances experienced by their men during and after the mass killings. The aim of most of the commanders was to diminish rather than intensify the emotional component of the killing operation, rendering it as impersonal and as cold-bloodedly systematic as possible.

Yet another *crucial* difference between the Final Solution and the earlier pogroms was the fact that the Czarist regime never claimed that the pogroms were a legitimate act of government. By contrast, the Final Solution was a series of officially sanctioned actions taken by legally empowered agents of the German state. Indeed, the full title of Heinrich Himmler, whose organization had the principal responsibility for exterminating the Jews, was *Reichsführer–SS und Chef der Deutschen Polizei* (the Reich leader of the SS and chief of the German police). The Nazi program of mass murder and abusive slavery was not carried out by criminals but by the so-called forces of law and order in Hitler's Germany. Moreover, Hitler was recognized by the vast majority of Germans as the legitimate head of the German government. Every German in the government and the armed services had to take an unconditional oath of obedience to Hitler. His orders carried with them the full force of law. The program of total extermination was organized and implemented by the German state at the zenith of its power with the full cooperation of every major German political, social, religious, and business institution. No assault of remotely comparable power had ever been inflicted upon the Jews in their entire history. It is hardly surprising that they proved incapable of any viable defense.

Because of its negative effects on the killers, Himmler ordered that a method of killing other than shooting at mass graves be developed. The alternative method was not hard to find. Mass gassings had already been used by the Third Reich to eliminate "undesirables." The first Nazi extermination victims were not Jews but aged, infirm, and mentally-ill Germans who had been certified as "unfit" for life within the Third Reich. They were gassed and cremated in special hospitals by German doctors and nurses who were assisted by SS euthanasia "specialists."

The euthanasia program was of crucial importance in the evolution of the program to exterminate Europe's Jews. Ideologically, the program's roots were to be found in the American eugenics movement of the late nineteenth and early twentieth centuries. Relying heavily on Charles Darwin's theory that the human species has evolved through a process of natural selection involving the *survival of the fittest*, the conviction arose among a number of American physicians, businessmen, and corporate leaders that it would be unwise to permit nature alone to determine the future character of the human species without the guiding control of scientific intelligence.[31] Their fundamental concern was to direct the way Americans were bred so that those afflicted with hereditary, debilitating physical or mental illness did not proliferate and enlarge the proportion of society with such disorders. Considerable racism was involved in the eugenics movement's ideas concerning who would be prevented from breeding. The high incidence of disease, mental disturbance, and asocial behavior among poverty-stricken Blacks, Indians, and Mexican-Americans was attributed to congenital defects in the way these groups had evolved. White Anglo-Saxon Protestants and related Protestants of northern European stock were said to be at the apex of the world's evolutionary hierarchy. Italians, Slavs, and Jews were regarded as considerably lower in evolutionary development. Not surprisingly, the proponents of this theory of inherent, biologically determined WASP racial superiority were themselves of white Anglo-Saxon Protestant background.[32]

Implicit in the theory of the inherited, biological basis of poverty, asocial behavior, and susceptibility to debilitating disease was the conviction that neither education nor economic improvement of the allegedly inferior groups could alter their defects. Moreover, the "inferior" groups were regarded as a long-term danger to American society. Offspring from unions of members of the "higher" and "lower" groups were thought to inherit the undesirable qualities of the "lower" groups which tended to have far more children than WASP high-achievers. Above all, the dependent members of the "lower" groups were considered a hopelessly nonproductive drain on society's resources.

Members of the eugenics movement had a simple solution: compulsory sterilization. They proposed that population growth be "scientifically managed" so that the "desirable" part of the population might increase as the unhealthy portion disappeared. "Scientific selection" would improve on natural selection. In a parallel development, a movement was started to limit immigration to the United States primarily to the Protestant and Germanic countries of northern Europe. The aims of this movement were achieved with Congress's passage of the 1924 Immigration Bill.

In 1904 the Pennsylvania State Legislature passed *An Act for the Prevention of Idiocy* which contained a compulsory sterilization clause. The bill was vetoed by the governor. However, between 1907 and 1928 twenty-one states passed sterilization laws aimed at controlling the reproduction of socially deviant individuals. *The United States was thus the first country to pass laws calling for compulsory sterilization in the name of racial purification.*

As so frequently happens when well-meaning individuals use government to "improve" society, the American eugenics laws were to have unforeseen and unintended consequences. The American attempt to unite science and law in the quest for a "healthy" society had a greater impact on Germany than on the United States. As early as 1904 Ernst Haeckel (1834-1919), a German physician, zoologist, and philosopher who taught at the University of Jena, called for the elimination by "mercy death" of Germany's "unfit" as a means of "saving useless expenses for family and state."[33] Such thinking did not make much headway until Germany's defeat in World War I when some highly influential German scientists began to search for ways to restore the "healthy" portion of the German people. In 1920 Karl Binding, a jurist, and Alfred Hoche, a psychiatrist, wrote a book entitled *The Release and Destruction of Lives Devoid of Value.* Binding and Hoche advocated the state-sponsored killing of "worthless" people. Among those whom they targeted for elimination were those who were "mentally completely dead" and those who *"represent a foreign body in human society,"* a foretaste of things to come. Moreover, in his capacity as director of the psychiatric clinic at the University of Freiburg, Hoche cautioned against feeling any sympathy for "lives devoid of value."[34]

Hoche and Binding planted a fertile seed, but public officials were not yet prepared to act upon their proposals. They were, however, interested in compulsory sterilization of the hopelessly infirm, the feeble-minded, unwed mothers, and criminals eligible for parole. In August 1923 the director of health institutions in the district of Zwickau in Saxony wrote to the Ministry of the Interior, pointing out that there was nothing especially radical about compulsory sterilization: ". . . what we racial hygienists promote is not at all new or unheard of. In a cultured nation of the first order, in the United States of America, that which we strive toward was introduced and tested long ago."[35] The ministry then sought the help of the foreign office to ascertain American practice in compulsory sterilization. After contacting American penal and mental institutions, the German embassy in Washington reported to Berlin that twenty-four states had compulsory sterilization legislation on their books.[36] The example of the United States thus facilitated a favorable reception for compulsory eugenic sterilization in Germany.

On 25 July 1933, less than six months after Hitler came to power, the new regime published a decree providing for the compulsory sterilization of men and women suffering from "hereditary diseases." However, the compulsory sterilization law was only a prelude. According to the Nuremberg trial testimony of Dr. Karl Brandt, the National Socialist Reichskommissar for Health, in 1935 Hitler had told Reich medical leader Gerhard Wagner that, if war came, he would initiate a program of euthanasia. As in so many of his other promises to murder and destroy, Hitler proved true to his word. Toward the end of October 1939 Hitler sent a handwritten note, dated 1 September 1939, to Philip Bouhler of the Führer Chancellery which read: "Reichsleiter Bouhler and Dr. Brandt are authorized to extend the responsibilities of physicians still to be named in such a manner that patients whose illness, according to the most critical application of human judgment, is incurable, can be granted release by euthanasia."[37]

The Führer Chancellery was a special department established by Hitler to administer his private affairs. It was ideally suited to administer a secret program such as mercy-killing. By his handwritten note, Hitler empowered his subordinates to exercise the power of life and death over tens of thousands of suffering Germans who had been innocently entrusted by their families to Germany's health care institutions. The program itself was the product of a vicious union of scientific arrogance and political power by men who were under no illusion concerning the negative public reaction that would ensue were the program ever to become known. It was for that reason that the killing institutions were camouflaged as healing agencies.[38] Authority for the project was shared by Philip Bouhler and Dr. Leonardo Conti, head of the health department of the Ministry of the Interior. The agency responsible for the project, euphemistically called *Die Gemeinnützige Stiftung für Heil und Anstaltspflege* (General Foundation for Welfare and Institutional Care), came to be known as "T-4," because its headquarters were located at Tiergartenstrasse 4 in Berlin. The staff of T-4 included a number of the more prominent medical doctors and psychiatrists of the Third Reich, including Professor Werner Heyde, Dr. Fritz Mennecke, and Dr. Hermann Pfannmüller. Everything about the project had the surface aura of medicine; yet between January 1940 and August 1941, when the program was officially terminated, no fewer than seventy thousand men, women, and children were killed. Moreover, while the program was underway, one prominent scientist, a Professor Kranz, wrote an article in the April 1940 issue of National Socialist journal, *N.S. Volksdienst*, in which he estimated that there were one million Germans whose "removal" would be desirable.[39] In view of the fact that Kranz's opinion was published in a party newspaper in wartime, when censorship was at its most stringent, his views cannot be dismissed as the private excess of an idiosyncratic imagination. *Clearly, if National Socialist ideologues were willing to contemplate the murder of one million of their fellow Germans, many of whom were merely handicapped, they would be entirely free of scruples when it came to murdering Jews and non-Germans.*

When the project was initiated, questionnaires for each patient were sent to all German mental hospitals and psychiatric clinics. The questionnaire asked the name, age, and illness of the patient. On the basis of the responses, a committee of three T-4 medical bureaucrats decided whether the patient was a candidate for a "mercy death" (*Gnadentod*). A blue pencil was used to mark the questionnaire with a " + " if the patient was to die; a red pencil marked "-" for the few patients permitted to live. If the diagnosis was unfavorable, the patient was sent to an "observation station" for a few weeks. Absent a more favorable diagnosis while under observation, the victim was transferred to a euthanasia center and killed immediately. According to Brandt's testimony, about 95 % of those under observation were sent to a euthanasia center. These life-and-death decisions were made without consulting either the victims or their families, who first learned of the fate of their loved ones by a duplicitous form letter. The letter informed the next of kin that the victim had died of heart attack, pneumonia, or some other fictitious ailment and that the police had ordered the immediate cremation of the body because of "danger of contagious disease" at the institution. The letter further stated that visits to the institution had been prohibited by the police for the same reason.[40] Cremation precluded all possibility of autopsy.

It is now believed that a program for putting children "to sleep" with injections was already underway in the summer of 1939 before the war started. There were eleven special centers for killing children and six for adults. The first adult euthanasia center was established in an abandoned prison in Brandenberg and was administered by *Kriminaloberkommissar* (Criminal Police Inspector) Christian Wirth.

Although the killings were called "mercy deaths," they had nothing to do with euthanasia as that term had previously been understood. Traditionally, euthanasia was the act of releasing a terminally-ill patient from unbearable pain, usually with consent. To the extent that it had ever been considered justified, euthanasia had been an effort on the *patient's* behalf, not the state's. Moreover, there was no mercy in these Nazi "mercy" killings. In the project's initial stages, there was confusion concerning the best murder method. Calculated starvation was one of the first employed. We have the text of a report dated 7 September 1940 by Pastor Paul Gerhard Braune addressed to members of the Ministry of Justice. This courageous pastor was an administrator of Lutheran mental institutions and one of the first of the clergy actively to oppose the project. In his innocence, however, Braune mistakenly thought the authorities would put a stop to what he regarded as an indefensible abuse:

... Visits to the institutions in Saxony plainly show that the mortality rate is being increased by withholding food. The daily subsistence rate ... is being reduced to the equivalent of RM 0.22 to 0.24 [nine cents]. Since the patients cannot possibly survive on that, they are made to take a drug (paraldehyde) which renders them apathetic. ... the patients time and again call out "hunger, hunger.". ... Hundreds have died a quick death in the last few months as a result of these measures.

Nor are just those patients involved here who are absolutely beyond feeling. On the contrary, these are patients who know quite well what is happening, and are watching how many funerals are taking place each day. One report describes the mortal fear of a patient who had an exact presentiment of the fate that is to meet him and his fellow sufferers.[41]

Employment of starvation as a killing agent was a logical extension of the National Socialist idea that the hopelessly ill and infirm were "useless mouths." Had the program continued without interference, it is very likely that old age alone would have merited eligibility for a "mercy death."

Efficient Death

Starvation of "useless mouths" was also practiced in Poland. While active, systematic murder of the Jews in Poland did not begin in earnest until December 1941 when the extermination center at Chelmno began operation, the Jews had already been forced into ghettos and placed on a starvation diet during the first year of the war. During that period starvation was the method of extermination preferred by German bureaucrats.[42] Starvation was an ideal form of "clean," cool bureaucratic violence in which government officials, comfortably installed in offices hundreds of miles distant, were able to decide on the survival or extinction of whole communities with no contact with the human consequences of their paper calculations.

The deliberate starvation of mental patients reported by Pastor Braune did not take place at euthanasia centers where the killing normally happened but at ordinary German mental institutions. In the euthanasia centers killing was more efficient. At the Brandenberg euthanasia center, the first to be established, *Kriminaloberkommissar* Christian Wirth deemed it sufficient to have the patients shot in the back of the neck, a method, which, as we have seen, was widely used by the *Einsatzgruppen* in the Soviet territories. Wirth was also the first to experiment with gassing, and when responsibility for the centers was transferred to doctors, asphyxiation became the preferred procedure. In each of the centers a gas chamber disguised as a shower was constructed. The killing agent was carbon monoxide gas, generated by engines and poured into the chambers by pipes. Each center also contained a crematorium for speedy corpse disposal. On the occasion of the ten-thousandth "mercy killing" at Hadamar, the personnel celebrated with a party. As drinks were served, one staff member supplied the humor by dressing up and playing the part of a Roman Catholic priest.[43]

It was impossible to cover up so many murders, especially since the killing centers were located in Germany and Austria rather than in the conquered territories to the east. Effective secrecy was dependent upon officially-sanctioned duplicity, but some of the lying was transparent. For example, one family was told that a victim had died as the result of an infected appendix. His appendix had been removed ten years earlier. By 1941 protests were heard from some highly influential German church leaders, the most important being a sermon preached by Clemens August Graf von Galen, Roman Catholic bishop of Münster, on 3 August 1941.[44] Another important opponent of the program was Theophil Wurm, the Lutheran bishop of Württemberg. There were, incidentally, no such overt protests by German church officials concerning the Final Solution. The response of the Vatican was more muted. The only public protest to come from the Vatican was a brief statement by the Holy Office that "the extinction of unworthy life by public mandate [is] imcompatible with natural and divine law." The statement was not printed in the official Vatican newspaper, *Osservatore Romano*. The statement was mentioned once, *in Latin*, over Vatican radio on 2 December 1940, hardly an energetic way of stating public disapproval.[45]

Recent historical scholarship has uncovered the fact that highly placed Roman Catholic leaders were aware of Hitler's plan to initiate a euthanasia project at least a year before the war began.[46] In 1938 a Catholic professor of moral theology at the University of Paderborn, Josef Mayer, was commissioned to write an opinion for Hitler on the subject of the church's attitude toward euthanasia. The substance of Mayer's one-hundred-page response was that, since there were both reasonable grounds pro and con as well as Catholic authorities on both sides, euthanasia of the mentally incompetent could be considered "defensible." According to Gitta Sereny, a well-known British journalist of Austro-Hungarian background, the real purpose of commissioning Mayer's research was to determine how the church would respond to such a program. Hitler understood that the church would be opposed in principle to euthanasia. *The question that really interested him was whether the church would actively oppose the program.* When the text of Mayer's opinion was presented to the papal nuncio (ambassador) to Germany, Cesare Orsenigo, for transmission to the Vatican, the nuncio withheld all comment, save to remark that he took "informal cognizance of the information." This was a diplomatic way of telling the Germans that he did not consider the matter sufficiently important to transmit to the Vatican. Without officially approving the killing operation, the nuncio signaled that there would be no serious Vatican opposition. He was correct. Orsenigo was a prelate of great authority who fully represented the viewpoint of Pope Pius XII, who in turn had been in charge of the Vatican's foreign relations as papal secretary of state until 1939. Before assuming that office he himself had been papal nuncio to Germany. Hitler had the information he wanted.[47]

In spite of the Vatican's passivity, Hitler could not ignore the growing discontent with the program in Germany, especially after von Galen's sermon. The sermon infuriated Hitler, but he decided that wartime was inopportune to begin a struggle with an important leader of Germany's Roman Catholic Church. Vowing to his inner circle that he would settle his score with von Galen after the expected National Socialist victory, Hitler ordered the program "officially" terminated on 23 August 1941. In reality, the program was never entirely terminated. Children continued to be "granted a mercy death" throughout the war, and Schloss Hartheim was used to gas prisoners from the nearby Mauthausen concentration camp until the end of the war. Incredibly, according to the *Times* of London, 3 July 1945, mentally infirm children were still being exterminated at Kaufbeuren in Bavaria even after the American occupation had begun.[48]

Although T-4 originally sought candidates for elimination solely from German health institutions, selections were soon made from concentration camp inmates as well. Actually, this use of the program may have been foreseen from the beginning, as most of the euthanasia centers were located near the camps.[49] In order to understand how T-4 came to be used to kill concentration camp inmates, it is important that we do not make the very common mistake of equating concentration camps with extermination camps. Although thousands of concentration camp prisoners were tortured, forced to become subjects of mutilating medical experiments, and killed, the fundamental purpose of these camps was different from that of the extermination camps. Originally, concentration camps, such as Dachau and Buchenwald, were institutions of incarceration for opponents of the National Socialist regime who had committed no offense punishable in the traditional German courts. Until November 1938 the camps contained few Jews. In the aftermath of *Kristallnacht*, 9–10 November 1938, thousands of Jews who had committed no crime were thrown into the camps. Most were released after paying a ransom or proving that they were about to emigrate.

During the war the system was vastly expanded so that a network of concentration camps was established throughout all of German-occupied Europe.[50] In addition to holding opponents of the regime, the camps served as mammoth slave labor depots. Because the labor of non-German slaves was regarded as an expendable commodity, the death rate in the camps was extremely high. Nevertheless, unlike the extermination camps, incarceration in a concentration camp was not tantamount to a death sentence. However slim the odds, some wartime inmates could hope for eventual release, provided they were not Jewish.

Dante's *Inferno* suggests that the entrance to Hell bears the inscription, "Abandon all hope ye who enter here." The same inscription would have been appropriate at the gateways to every German death camp. These installations were situated in Poland nearby the largest concentrations of Jews in Europe, in close proximity to railroads, and yet sufficiently remote from widespread public view so as to minimize publicity about them elsewhere, including Germany. The first to be put into operation was Chelmno or Kulmhof in December 1941. It was followed by Belzec (March 1942), Sobibor (May 1942), and Treblinka (July 1942). Every human being condemned to a death camp was under an ir- revocable sentence. These camps had a single reason for being: the extermina- tion of Jews and Gypsies. Working efficiently and quickly in ways that resembled factory methods of mass production, the operations of these killing centers were unprecedented. Concentration camps and gas chambers had existed before, but innovative Nazi specialists brought the components together to do something novel: kill on an assembly-line basis. Built at a time of extensive concentration camp expansion, these killing center sites were chosen to empha- size seclusion and rail access. Similar in design and area—a few hundred square yards in size—they were set up to persuade the arrivals that they had reached a transit camp. But hardly any found a way out. When today we speak of Holo- caust survivors, we refer almost entirely to those who were ''fortunate'' enough, if indeed such words are applicable, to have been slave laborers in con- centration camps. According to the very conservative Polish estimate, only eighty-two Jews survived the camps at Chelmno, Belzec, Sobibor, and Tre- blinka. More than 1.5 million Jews and some 50,000 Gypsies were murdered in those places. The survivors were ''work-Jews'' whom the Germans kept alive to help operate the camps.

At Auschwitz, which became the largest killing center, the magnitude of death was the equivalent of one death per minute, day and night, for a period of three years. More Jews were murdered there than at any other camp. Yet Au- schwitz was not exclusively a death camp. In addition to its main extermination center, Auschwitz-Birkenau, it included, for example, Auschwitz-Monowitz, an industrial installation operated by slave labor working in the synthetic rubber manufacturing works of I. G. Farben, the huge German petrochemical conglom- erate. The conditions under which the inmates were kept at Auschwitz- Monowitz were calculated to kill most of the slaves within three months while extracting their last measure of energy.[51] Death through labor was the official policy. Nevertheless, a few exceptionally hardy or lucky prisoners were able to survive, especially if they arrived toward the end of the war.

Chelmno, the first death camp, did not begin operation until 8 December 1941. However, as soon as gas chambers to dispatch Germany's ''useless mouths'' were in place in such euthanasia centers as Grafeneck, Sonnenstein, Schloss Hartheim, Bernberg, and Hadamar, it was obvious that the same instal- lations could be used to get rid of other ''useless mouths.'' In early 1941 a pro- gram known as *Aktion 14f13* was begun in which the facilities and personnel of the euthanasia centers were employed to weed out concentration camp inmates regarded as physically or socially undesirable—homosexuals were thus labeled—in the Third Reich. This selection process was initially administered by T-4 doctors. At least twenty thousand people are estimated to have been sent to the euthanasia centers under *Aktion 14f13*. This program also continued after the euthanasia program came to an "official" halt on 23 August 1941.

In August 1941, Karl Koch, the commandant of Buchenwald, told the camp doctor that all Jews in the camp could be sent to Bernberg, a nearby euthanasia center. The transition from the "mercy killing" program to the initial stages of a program for the extermination of the Jews can be discerned in the following letter written by a T-4 physician, Fritz Mennecke, to his wife. Mennecke was responsible for the selections at Buchenwald:

> . . . I examined 105 patients, Müller 78, so that 183 questionnaires were filled out. Our second batch consisted of 1,200 Jews who do not have to be "examined"; for them it was enough to pull from their files (very voluminous!) the reason for their arrest and write them down on the questionnaires. . . .
>
> We shall continue with the same program and the same work. After the Jews will come 300 Aryans who have to be "examined." We shall be busy up to the end of next week. Then we shall go home.[52]

By the time the euthanasia program was officially terminated, a trained team of four hundred had been assembled. They had acquired a considerable measure of expertise in the efficient and economical extermination of any category of persons so targeted by the German state. For the Third Reich, this resource was too valuable to disband, especially in view of the fact that Hitler fully expected to resume the project after the war. As circumstances developed, there was no need to disband. Much work awaited the doctors, nurses, orderlies, and SS personnel in Russia and Poland, for those regions contained vast numbers of Jews and non-Jews who, according to Nazi ideology, were truly surplus because their very existence threatened the predominance of the Aryan race whose superior value and purity had to prevail at all costs.

The Chelmno death camp was located about fifty miles northwest of Lodz, the second largest city in Poland. After the German invasion, the region around Lodz was incorporated into the Reich and called Warthegau. The name of Lodz was changed to Litzmannstadt. As part of the Reich, Warthegau was not supposed to contain any Jews. In the summer of 1941, SS Gruppenführer and Gauleiter Arthur Greiser requested of Himmler and Heydrich the services of experts who could clear his region of Jews. Himmler obliged by appointing Hauptsturmführer (Captain) Herman Lange. Three gas vans, which had already been used by the *Einsatzgruppen* in Russia, were sent to Chelmno where an old mansion isolated in the woods was transformed into the "first murder factory in human history."[53]

Killing operations began at Chelmno on 8 December 1941. Jews arrived by railroad from Lodz and were then taken to the mansion where they were told they would be put to work in factories. The operation was camouflaged with signs reading "To the Showers" and "To the Doctor." Told that they were going to the showers, the unsuspecting Jews were commanded to strip and then driven into the rear compartment of a large truck which was positioned at the end of a dark corridor. When the compartment's capacity was reached, its doors were locked, the truck's motor started, and the carbon monoxide exhaust gas piped in. As in all of the later killing centers, nothing was wasted—except human beings. When the doors of the death truck were opened, a special group of Jews called *Sonderkommandos* removed gold from the teeth of the dead, searched the cavities of the bodies for any remaining valuables, and then disposed of the remains in mass graves. These special Jews were usually able to survive for a few weeks before their turn came for extermination. Chelmno operated until the spring of 1943. It reopened for a brief period in June and July 1944. Estimates vary concerning the number killed at the camp. According to a low postwar German estimate, 170,000 persons were killed there, of whom 152,000 were Jewish. According to the more realistic estimate of the Polish Commission on War Crimes, 356,000 persons were killed there, 90% of them Jews.[54]

As in Russia so in Poland, gassing in vans by exhaust fumes proved to be undependable and "inefficient." Sometimes it would take hours to kill the victims. Occasionally, they were still alive when the doors were opened. Sometimes wounded and even unhurt victims were able to flee the grave sites and get word to Jewish communities that deportation meant extermination. Given the German penchant for order, such chaos was intolerable. An "expert" better than Lange had to be found to set things right. *Kriminaloberkommissar* Christian Wirth, whom we have encountered as the head of the first euthanasia center, was available. On the recommendation of Dr. Ernst Grawitz, the SS medical officer-in-chief, Himmler ordered the gassing expert Wirth transferred to Lublin to work under *SS-Gruppenführer* (Major General) Odilo Globocnik, who had been placed in charge of the project of exterminating the Jews in Poland. Globocnik was in turn responsible to Reinhard Heydrich, who had overall responsibility. After Heydrich's death by assassination on 4 June 1942, Globocnik named the extermination operation *Aktion Reinhard* in his honor. Although Heydrich was assassinated by members of the Czech underground, it was widely believed among members of the Nazi elite that the killing was a Jewish undertaking. Globocnik thus injected the element of revenge into the list of rationalizations for the Final Solution.

As head of the extermination project in Poland, Globocnik worked in close collaboration with Viktor Brack of the Führer Chancellery, who had been in charge of the euthanasia project. Wirth also retained his connection with the project. While at work in the death camps, he would often refer to himself as "we in the Institute . . . ," thereby indicating that he saw his new assignment as an extension of his T-4 responsibilities.

With his T-4 experience, Wirth regarded the Chelmno operation, especially its mobile gas vans, as the work of an amateur. He decided to rationalize the procedure. In order to minimize the possibility of panic among the victims, Wirth designed disguised buildings that contained several gas chambers. It was impossible for new arrivals to discern the sinister character of the site from the outside. We have a description of one of Wirth's creations, an installation in the Belzec extermination camp, by Kurt Gerstein, an enigmatic anti-Nazi German Christian who served in the SS:

> Alongside the station there was a "dressing" hut with a window for "valuables." Further on, a room with a hundred chairs [designated as] "the barber." Then a corridor 150 meters long in the open air, barbed wire on both sides, with signs: "To the baths and inhalants." In front of us a building like a bath house; to the left and right, large concrete pots of geraniums or other flowers. On the roof, the Star of David."[55]

The first Wirth-designed gas chambers were installed in the Belzec extermination camp, which commenced operation 17 March 1942. With its six gas chambers, it had a capacity of fifteen thousand people a day. In May, Sobibor was ready. It had a capacity of twenty thousand. Two months later, Treblinka was opened sixty-two miles from Warsaw. It was the largest of these camps and was the one where most of the Jews from the Warsaw ghetto were murdered. In addition, Majdanek was constructed near Lublin. Like Auschwitz, Majdanek was a multipurpose camp, though on a smaller scale.

Actually two camps were at Treblinka. Treblinka I was a concentration camp for Jews and Polish dissidents. It was possible for a Pole to survive Treblinka I; very few Jews did; they were invariably transferred to Treblinka II, an extermination camp. Treblinka II covered an area of almost fifty acres, divided into two sections. New victims were received in the first section. A small number of physically fit young Jews stood a chance of being selected to work in the camp. The rest were doomed to follow the same procedure that had proven successful at Chelmno. They were sent to an undressing barracks where they were forced to strip completely. Women went to a mass "beauty parlor" where their hair was shorn and then sent to Germany where it was used in insulation and upholstery fabrics. The women were also subject to internal search for hidden valuables. Nothing of possible use to the Germans was discarded, except human beings. Next came the *Himmelfahrt* or "ascent to heaven," a camouflaged path about ten feet wide and three hundred feet long through which the naked men and women, segregated by sex, were forced to run in rows of five, goaded on by the whips of the Ukrainian auxiliaries and the SS. At the end of the path, the prisoners came to the gas chambers. The men entered first; the women were last. Frequently, the gassing installations broke down, leaving the prisoners waiting naked for death in all kinds of weather. Undoubtedly, many of the victims mistakenly thought that the gas chamber would prove to be a refuge from the whippings and the harsh weather. It was the practice to fill the gas chambers to capacity, another expression of the German attempt at efficiency and resource conservation. SS personnel watched the executions through peepholes. In their death agony, the victims stood pressed together with expressions of utter horror on their faces. Most defecated involuntarily as they perished. Reality exceeded the worst premodern, nightmare fantasies of hell.

When movement ceased in the gas chamber, there was a macabre division of labor. One group of *Arbeitsjuden* or "work-Jews" separated the bodies, hosed down the blood, pus, and excrement, cleansed the chamber, and hauled the remains toward mass graves. Another group known as the "dentists" removed gold fillings and dentures from the mouths of the dead. Yet another group searched rectums and vaginas for gold and diamonds. Himmler and Heydrich were concerned that there remain behind no traces of the murders, especially after the Russian army began to move westward. Thus in February 1943 a new project was started in the camps. The remains of the dead interred in the mass graves were dug up by a special group of prisoners who served *Kommando 1005*. The disinterred remains were burned on huge pyres of iron grates and wood.

The head of the *Kommando 1005* operation was *SS-Standartenführer* (Colonel) Paul Blobel, an alcoholic architect from Düsseldorf. Blobel had been in charge of the *Einsatzkommando* that murdered and buried thirty-four thousand Jews in a ravine at Babi Yar outside of Kiev. In June 1942 Himmler ordered Blobel to "erase the traces of *Einsatzgruppen* executions in the East."[56] Blobel worked on his grisly assignment throughout the eastern occupied territories. In the late summer of 1942, he moved on to Chelmno where his methods of mass human waste disposal included dynamiting the corpses. However, the preferred method remained burning. Not surprisingly, Blobel failed in his cover-up mission. It was impossible to eliminate all traces of the murder of millions of human beings. Once again, a better method had to be found.

Before we turn to the refinements in human waste disposal achieved by the SS, we should note the fate of the "work-Jews." With the exception of some specialized personnel, such as goldsmiths and doctors, the *Arbeitsjuden* did not last long. They were the object of incredibly sadistic "sport" on the part of the SS including random executions and boxing matches which continued until one of the two fighters died. Those *Arbeitsjuden* who did survive were periodically exterminated to make way for their fresher and healthier counterparts. As a rule, the *Kommandos 1005* lasted much longer. Unlike the skilled Jewish workers who were sent from *Wehrmacht* munitions factories to death camps, those Jews who had mastered the skills involved in exhumation and mass open-air cremation were too valuable to kill quickly. Incidentally, at times Treblinka's scenes from hell were enacted with the musical accompaniment of an orchestra made up of prisoners. The basic operation at Belzec and Sobibor was quite similar to Treblinka. All the execution operations at these camps were technically under Christian Wirth's control.

Destination Auschwitz

The Final Solution did not follow a blueprint. Detailed steps were often fixed through an invitation to invent that became part of the destruction process. Thus, in comparison with the killing methods Wirth found at Chelmno, his were an "improvement." However, as the transports rolled into Poland from all over Europe, it was obvious that further "improvements" were desirable. Many were made under the supervision of Rudolf Franz Ferdinand Höss, commandant of Auschwitz.[57] Unlike the leaders of the *Einsatzgruppen*, who tended to come from respectable, middle-class professions, Höss was a prison professional who had spent most of his adult life as either a prisoner or a jailer. Born in 1900, he received a ten-year prison sentence in 1924 for his part in the killing of Walter Kadow, a German who had denounced a Nazi to the French forces then occupying the Rhineland. At the time of the crime, Höss was a bookkeeper, a profession that was to serve him well as commandant of Auschwitz. While in prison, he was befriended by Martin Bormann who, by the end of World War II, was the second most powerful man in Germany because of his position as head of the National Socialist Party Chancellery. At the end of 1934 Höss was released from prison and in April 1935 made a "block leader" at Dachau. His rise within the SS hierarchy was rapid thereafter.[58] By June 1936 he had been commissioned an *SS–Untersturmführer* (second lieutenant), having gone through the noncommissioned ranks in a little more than a year. Höss apparently had a talent for prison work.

Auschwitz, the Polish town of Oświęcim, is about an hour's drive from Krakow. Before World War I it had been the site of an Austrian army barracks. Technically, the town had been "restored" to the Reich during the war as a consequence of the conquest of Poland. By order of Himmler, the barracks site was established as a concentration camp on 27 April 1940. Thirty German criminals were brought to Auschwitz to serve as camp officials and Höss, himself a criminal-turned-official, was appointed commandant in May 1940.

As the camp grew, the first part, known as Auschwitz I, served as both the administrative center and a concentration camp. Among the first prisoners were Polish political offenders—including some Jews—and hundreds of Roman Catholic priests.[59] Auschwitz I was never a death camp. Nevertheless, the rations distributed to the Poles were far more adequate than those given the Jews, and in all such camps the mortality rate was exceedingly high. In October 1941, after the *Einsatzgruppen* had made their first sweep through Soviet territory, a second, larger camp, Auschwitz-Birkenau, was established to house Russian prisoners of war, almost all of whom died or were killed shortly after arrival. Birkenau was to become the death camp at Auschwitz.

A third branch of the camp was constructed at Monowitz (Monowice) to provide slave labor for the huge synthetic rubber or Buna plant constructed by I. G. Farben at Auschwitz. We shall need to elaborate this part of the story in Chapter 8, but here it must be noted that I. G. Farben was the most important corporate employer at Auschwitz and I. G. Auschwitz, as it was named, was its newest subsidiary.[60] In 1940, faced with a rubber shortage, the government encouraged I. G. Farben to build a Buna factory at Auschwitz, where the corporation could take advantage of the plentiful coal, water, and concentration-camp labor. The labor was very cheap. It consisted of slaves who were worked to death. Abusive labor was added to starving, shooting, and gassing as methods of extermination. Such labor was designed to serve the objectives of two institutions at the same time. I. G. Farben was interested in securing labor at minimal expense. The SS was interested in killing Jews. Both objectives were easily met at Auschwitz.

I. G. Farben's interest in Auschwitz was an expression of the corporation's forward-looking, entrepreneurial spirit. It invested in I. G. Auschwitz, with its seeming guarantee of an endless stream of expendable slaves, as a long-term, profit-making business venture. In accordance with Hitler's dreams of *Lebensraum*, the corporation's directors saw Germany's postwar economic future as lying in the conquered territories to the east. They wanted to guarantee I. G. Farben a head start in the business world which, they believed, would arise in the wake of Germany's conquests. I. G. Auschwitz was not meant to be a temporary, wartime speculation. It was for that reason that the directors of the corporation, all of whom were respectable German businessmen with excellent international connections, decided that the corporation would assume the entire risk of the huge investment. They did not want to share this unique business opportunity even with the German government. They committed RM 900,000,000 to the project. In terms of 1985 purchasing power their investment came to approximately $2 billion, making I. G. Auschwitz the largest single project of the huge I. G. Farben petrochemical empire. Moreover, by virtue of their own on-site visits, as well as the on-site administration of Walter Dürrfeld, director of I. G. Auschwitz and a trusted, cultivated, senior executive of I. G. Farben, the corporation's directors were fully informed concerning the character of their venture. The involvement of the corporation in mass murder at their Auschwitz installation is succinctly detailed in the indictment of their leading executives during the Military Tribunal at Nuremberg:

> Farben, in complete defiance of all decency and human considerations, abused its slave workers by subjecting them, among other things, to excessively long, arduous, and exhausting work, utterly disregarding their health or physical condition. The sole criterion of the right to live or die was the production efficiency of said inmates. By virtue of inadequate rest, inadequate food. . . . and because of

inadequate quarters (which consisted of a bed of polluted straw, shared by from two to four inmates), many died at their work or collapsed from serious illness there contracted. With the first signs of a decline in the production of any such workers, although caused by illness or exhaustion, such workers would be subjected to the well-known "Selektion." "Selektion," in its simplest definition, meant that if, upon a cursory examination, it appeared that the inmate would not be restored within a few days to full productive capacity, he was considered expendable and was sent to the "Birkenau" camp of Auschwitz for the customary extermination. The meaning of "Selektion" and "Birkenau" was known to everyone at Auschwitz. . . .

The working conditions at the Farben Buna plant were so severe and unendurable that very often inmates were driven to suicide by either dashing through the guards and provoking death by rifle shot, or hurling themselves into the high-tension electrically-charged barbed wire fences. As a result of these conditions, the labor turnover in the Buna plant in one year amounted to at least 300 percent. Besides those who were exterminated and committed suicide, up to and sometimes over 100 persons died at their work every day from sheer exhaustion. All depletions . . . were balanced by replacement with new inmates. Thus, Farben secured a continuous supply of fresh inmates in order to maintain full production.[61]

The spirit of I. G. Auschwitz was perhaps best exemplified by one SS officer who was reported to have said to the prisoners, "You are all condemned to die, but the execution of your sentence will take a little while."[62]

When the war crimes trial of the Farben executives was over, five of the defendants—Otto Ambros, who visited Auschwitz eighteen times; Walter Dürrfeld, who was in charge of I. G. Auschwitz; Fritz Ter Meer; Karl Krauch; and Heinrich Bütefisch—were convicted of "slavery and mass murder." The maximum sentence meted out was eight years. Because of the politics of the cold war, none of these men served his full sentence. Instead, the I. G. Farben executives went on to highly successful careers. For example, Fritz Ter Meer was elected chairman of the supervisory board of Bayer, A. G., one of the world's largest pharmaceutical companies, and Dürrfeld became the director of the supervisory board of Scholven-Chemie, A. G., of Gelsenkirchen.[63]

In June 1941 Himmler ordered Höss to prepare to use Auschwitz for the Final Solution of the Jewish problem. Instead of inefficient carbon monoxide, Höss introduced a pesticide known as Zyklon B, which was made under license from I. G. Farben by two German firms, Tesch und Stabenow of Hamburg and DEGESCH of Dessau, an I. G. Farben affiliate. On 3 September 1941, the gas was first tried out on nine hundred prisoners, most of whom were Russian prisoners of war. The experiment proved to be a "success." Thereafter Zyklon B was used to kill Jews for a period of thirty-four months. Estimates concerning the number of Jews killed at Auschwitz vary from 1 million to 2.5 million, with the lower figure being the more likely.[64]

Transports were organized from all over Europe to bring Jews to Auschwitz.

The first killings took place in January 1942 in a transformed farm house at Birkenau. Thereafter, new gas chambers disguised as shower rooms were installed as were crematoria, an innovation reminiscent of the euthanasia centers but initially absent from the other death camps. The crematoria were built by thousands of prisoners who were themselves cremated in their own creations once the work was completed.[65] There is considerable disagreement concerning the capacity of the four crematoria, which contained forty-six ovens in all. The best estimates suggest a capacity of less than five thousand a day. When the Jews of Hungary were brought to Auschwitz in May and June of 1944, the crematoria were incapable of handling six thousand bodies a day.[66] From time to time the crematoria would break down and the bodies were burned in huge open pits. In August 1944 the crematoria were extensively supplemented by these pits, which proved more economical, a quality undoubtedly appealing to the Nazi managers.

The first Jewish victims came from Poland. They were all killed. On 30 March 1942, the first French Jews arrived. Unlike the Polish Jews, they were subjected to a *Selektion* in which the healthy and physically fit became slaves and the others were sent to the gas chambers. As the boxcars laden with victims arrived, those selected for slave labor were sent to the right side, the others to the left, traditionally the "sinister" side. The selection usually took half an hour, during which time the crematorium motors brought the ovens up to the right temperature for incinerating bodies. Those on the left side were then driven to the crematoria gate which was three hundred yards from the railroad ramp. At the gate a sign read "Entrance Forbidden to All Who Have No Business Here Including SS." The prisoners were then taken to a huge underground room two hundred yards long with a large sign reading "Bath and Disinfectant Room."

Dr. Miklós Nyiszli, a physician at Auschwitz, witnessed the extermination of one convoy of three thousand men, women, and children.[67] According to Dr. Nyiszli, soldiers announced to the prisoners that everyone must be completely undressed in ten minutes. At the end of ten minutes they were all completely naked. An important German motive for the undressing was economic efficiency. The victims' clothes were to be sent to Germany, and it was necessary to remove them before the gassing lest they be soiled in the victims' death agonies. Undoubtedly, there were other motives for beating the prisoners and stripping them of all human dignity. In her prison interviews with Franz Stangl, former commandant of Treblinka, Gitta Sereny asked him: "Why if they were going to kill them anyway, what was the point of all the humiliation, why the cruelty?" Stangl replied: "To condition those who actually carried out the policies. To make it possible for them to do what they did."[68] By stripping the victims of all human dignity and subjecting them to maximum humiliation and cruelty, it was easier for the Germans to murder the Jews as subhuman vermin.

After the disrobing, the prisoners were then directed into another room of similar size. In this room at thirty-yard intervals were columns of sheet iron pipes with many perforations. The purpose of the columns was to serve as a conduit for the poisoned gas. When everybody was inside, someone called out, "SS and *Sonderkommando*, leave the room." As the doors were locked and the lights turned off, a luxury car furnished by the International Red Cross arrived outside of the building housing the underground gas chamber. An SS officer and a deputy health service officer (*Sanitätsdienstgefreiter*) got out of the car. The health officer put on a gas mask and poured four cannisters of Zyklon B granulated crystals into the top of the pipes. As the crystals descended into the chamber they became poison gas. Within ten minutes, three thousand people were dead. Twenty minutes later the ventilators had evacuated the gas. The *Sonderkommando* first loaded the unsoiled clothing on trucks. They then entered the gas chamber where the victims' bodies were piled from the floor to the ceiling. In their panic the victims had trampled each other in the hope of reaching the top of the room and escaping the gas which began its deadly work at the floor level. The bodies were bloated, bruised, disfigured, and soiled. After hosing down and separating the bodies, which were knotted to each other, the *Sonderkommando* dragged the dead to an elevator in an adjoining room. Between twenty and twenty-four bodies were loaded on the elevator at a time. From the elevators they were taken to the ovens. Before cremation, hair was removed as was gold from the victims' teeth. The yield in gold was between eighteen and twenty pounds a day.

Not all of the victims were gassed. There was a location known as the "pyre" in the village of Birkenau. Only one building in the village was left standing, a country house which was used as an undressing room for those destined for the pyre. Nyiszli describes one action in which five thousand people were led three hundred to four hundred at a time to be undressed. They were then forced to run for fifty yards between two columns of SS, who beat them with truncheons. The pyre at the end of the course was hidden from view. It was a ditch fifty yards long and six yards wide containing burning bodies. As the victims arrived at the pyre, they were grabbed by two members of the *Sonderkommando* and dragged to SS marksmen who shot them in the back of the head. Dead or still alive, the victims were then thrown on the burning pyre. The majority of the victims were in fact burned alive. More than five thousand victims a day were put to death in this fashion.[69]

In addition to gassing, shooting, burning, and murderously abusive labor, mutilating medical experiments, carried out by German doctors and reported without protest in German medical societies and journals, must be mentioned in listing the methods of extermination. From the German point of view, since every Jew was deservedly condemned to death, the Germans felt entirely free to dispose of them as they wished. The Germans had created a society of total domination in which there were absolutely no moral limits to the uses to which the dominators could put the dominated. When German doctors realized that they had an almost unlimited supply of unwanted human beings at their disposal, some very important medical school professors, research scientists, and pharmaceutical companies made the most of their opportunity.[70] Many of the experiments involved attempts to discover cost-effective methods of mass sterilization. Some involved castration and uterine mutilation. Other experiments were motivated by Nazi ideology. Professor August Hirt of the Reich University of Strasbourg wanted to study the skulls of "Jewish-Bolshevik subhumanity." He requested that his subjects be kept alive until proper measurements were taken and then killed. The bodies of seventy-nine freshly killed and scientifically measured Jewish men, thirty Jewish women, four central Asians, and two Poles were delivered to the professor, thereby assuring him of a plentiful supply of skulls.[71]

The End of Killing

On 2 November 1944, seeing the handwriting of defeat on the wall, Himmler ordered an end to the gassing of Jews on arrival at Auschwitz. Himmler had already ordered the cessation of deportations of Hungarian Jews to Auschwitz on 25 August 1944. On 26 November 1944 he ordered the dismantling of the gas chambers and the crematoria. By taking these steps, the Reichsführer SS acted contrary to the wishes of Hitler, the leader to whom he had pledged unconditional obedience. As Germany's defeat became ever more certain, Himmler became possessed of the illusion that he might position himself to succeed Hitler as a leader acceptable to the victorious allies. Himmler forbade Ernst Kaltenbrunner, who had succeeded Heydrich as head of the RSHA, to continue extermination of the Jews. He further commanded Kaltenbrunner to care for "weak and sick persons."[72] Although the gas chambers at Auschwitz were dismantled, Himmler's orders were sabotaged by Kaltenbrunner, Eichmann, and the chief of the Gestapo, Heinrich Müller, wherever possible. Thus, as late as 27 April 1945, less than two weeks before the war's end, Kaltenbrunner ordered the commandant of Mauthausen concentration camp in Austria to kill at least one thousand men a day.[73]

The dismantling of the death camps was not the end of the Jewish ordeal. As the German army retreated westward, the surviving Jews were forced on foot toward what remained of the Reich. On 17 January 1945, as the Red Army approached, fifty-eight thousand prisoners headed west from Auschwitz. Too infirm to be moved, six thousand prisoners were left behind. In the bitter cold of the Polish winter, the westward trek of the ill-clad, lice-ridden Auschwitz inmates became a death march. Those who reached Germany became a new source of slave labor for German industry.

Even before the Soviet seizure of Auschwitz, significant numbers of Jews were once again to be found in what remained of the Reich. Between May 1944 and March 1945, for example, twenty thousand Jews were brought to Buchenwald.[74] Buchenwald and the other regular concentration camps in Germany soon became hopelessly overcrowded even by National Socialist standards. In February and March 1945 prisoners too frail to work were brought to Bergen-Belsen which had been a *Wehrmacht* "convalescent camp" for wounded prisoners of war.

In March 1945 there were 41,520 inmates at Bergen-Belsen. Most of these prisoners, who included 26,723 women, were Jewish. On 15 April there were sixty thousand inmates. During the previous week alone, twenty-eight thousand had been dumped on the camp. The food supply was cut off and a devastating typhus epidemic broke out. Left to their own devices, some of the surviving prisoners ate the dead as thousands of unburied corpses piled up and rotted away. A total of thirty-seven thousand prisoners died in the "convalescent camp" before liberation by the British army; fourteen thousand died afterward. Even so, it was a miracle that there were any survivors. Kaltenbrunner, Eichmann, and other die-hard Nazis wanted to kill all of the prisoners. Himmler wanted some alive as pawns in his unsuccessful negotiations with the Allies. He ordered that the concentration camps be handed over intact to the Allies. It was largely for that reason that there were any survivors from Buchenwald, Bergen-Belsen, and Ravensbrück, a women's concentration camp.

There can be no fully accurate estimate of Jewish losses in the Holocaust. Hilberg puts the figure at 5.1 million, Bauer at 5.8 million, and Dawidowicz at 5.9 million.[75] Whatever the differences, the basic facts of this sad chapter of human history remain: nearly two-thirds of the European Jews—and one-third of the Jews in the world—lost their lives to Nazi Germany and its allies.

Chapter 6

Victims and Survivors

Abba Kovner, a prize-winning poet, led the first Jewish resistance organization in the ghettos of eastern Europe. Some sixty thousand Jews, about 30% of the population, lived in his home city, Vilna, which often was called the Jerusalem of Lithuania. Engulfed by the Nazi advance eastward in the summer of 1941, Vilna was occupied on 24 June and soon scourged by squads from *Einsatzgruppe A*. Assisted by Lithuanian police, the Nazis did away with twenty thousand Jews prior to ghettoizing the remainder on 6 September 1941. Most of the dead had been murdered at Ponary, six miles distant from the city, but Nazi precautions to make the mass killings inaccessible to public view did not prevent a few stunned survivors from returning to Vilna early that September. Their reports met disbelief. By midmonth another ten thousand Jews had vanished. Two weeks later on Yom Kippur, 1 October 1941, another massive *Aktion* condemned thousands more. Yet for those who remained behind, just as for those who did not envision their fate until too late, the picture remained unclear. As Kovner suggests, Vilna's survivors could see that "they were doomed to a life of suffering, trouble, and persecution. But that the slaughter of millions was a possibility—no; that was something the darkest imagination could not conceive, something no one wanted to believe."[1]

Life seemed to hinge upon possession of a precious yellow work permit that also entitled its holder "to protect his family, which, under German ground rules, was limited to husband, wife, and two children under sixteen."[2] The strategy of population elimination entailed that there were never enough permits to go around. Nor did every family fit within the German boundaries. The Nazis' calculating rationality intended that Jews themselves should have to make fateful decisions concerning which members of their own families would be most vulnerable. Those who lacked or could not be covered by these tickets for life continued to be prey for Ponary. The *Aktionen* continued until 21 December 1941. Thereafter the Vilna ghetto, reduced to some 12,500 Jews, would continue struggling for life until it was liquidated in September 1943. Pivotal in that struggle were the 150 young Zionists who gathered in a soup kitchen at 2 Strashun Street in early January 1942 to hear Kovner read a call for resistance. Adopting a biblical image (Ps. 44:11), it insisted: "We will not be led like sheep to the slaughter!"

Thanks to Kovner there was armed resistance in the Vilna ghetto, but at the outset of this chapter it is crucial to note his later testimony, namely, that his phrase "like sheep to the slaughter" continues more than forty years later to be one that "haunts me now wherever I go." What haunts Kovner is that his own words, ironically and inadvertently, have been stripped from their context and have come to undergird the impression that the Jews were ultimately the ideal victims for Hitler because they were so utterly passive in receiving the Nazis' crushing blows. It is not Kovner's point that Jewish behavior against the Nazis was characterized by armed resistance. Nor is it to deny that there was Jewish passivity. But he is haunted by the fact that the phrase has become a code word. It designates a stereotype containing a lack of understanding no less real than that which prevented the Jews of Vilna from recognizing, as Kovner proclaimed in 1942, that "Hitler plans to destroy all the Jews of Europe, and the Jews of Lithuania have been chosen as the first in line."[3]

Kovner prefaced his first call for resistance by urging Jewish youth not to trust "those who are trying to deceive you." First and foremost, he had the Germans in mind. But the sources of deception were not restricted to them alone. They were present within the ghetto, too. Disbelief and even hope could be deceptive, but beyond those personal and psychological dimensions, some interpreters have argued that a crucial source of deception could be found in much of the Jewish leadership during the Holocaust. Especially in the internal administration of the Jewish ghettos, it has been asserted, Jewish leaders themselves played vital if not collaborating roles in leading their own people to the slaughter by complying with the Germans.[4] In her book *Eichmann in Jerusalem* (1963), Hannah Arendt took Raul Hilberg's appraisal one step further:

> Wherever Jews lived, there were recognized Jewish leaders, and this leadership, almost without exception, cooperated in one way or another, for one reason or another, with the Nazis. The whole truth was that if the Jewish people had really been unorganized and leaderless, there would have been chaos and plenty of misery but the total number of victims would hardly have been between four and a half and six million people.[5]

Arendt's allegations might have taken the Vilna ghetto as a case in point. For example, when the Germans prepared the work permits that enabled some Jews to survive there, the distribution of those yellow tickets was handled not by the Germans themselves but by the Jewish council (*Judenrat*) which was charged with internal governance of the ghetto. Jewish leadership had to decide what to do with the work permits. The German instructions established quotas for skilled workers required by the wartime economy. Beyond those boundaries, the *Judenrat* had to handle the matter for itself, and this it did by distributing the tickets. As events unfolded, the distribution process involved the Vilna *Judenrat* in a selection process that determined who might live and who would die. If that fact was not apparent at first, it soon became unmistakable. For it was not long until the Jewish police, empowered to maintain law and order inside the ghetto, found themselves required, under SS supervision, to ferret out those without the work permits. They were subsequently killed at Ponary.

The man in charge of the Jewish police in Vilna was Jacob Gens. He not only participated in the roundups but gradually became the dominant Jewish leader inside the ghetto. One of Gens's biographers finds that "to the Germans he presented the image of a good and faithful servant." Some of Vilna's rabbis reminded Gens of Maimonides's teaching, namely, that even if only a single Jew's life were demanded, then all should be killed rather than give up that person. Gens found a different justification more fitting for Vilna's circumstances: "I cast my accounts with Jewish blood and not with Jewish respect. If they ask me for a thousand Jews, I give them because if the Germans themselves came, they would take with violence not a thousand but thousands and thousands and the whole ghetto would be finished. With a hundred I save a thousand; with a thousand I save ten thousand." Gens believed that he would eventually stand vindicated "at the bar of judgment before Jews," though he also admitted that "many Jews regard me as a traitor."[6] Arendt found the latter part of Gens's self-estimate far more apt than the former.

Arendt's appraisal unleashed a storm of controversy, not least because this highly respected political philosopher happened to be Jewish. Although few scholars are prepared to follow her in thinking that an unorganized and leaderless Jewish people would have suffered less devastation during the Holocaust, there is little doubt that her proposition sparked a profound concern to determine in a systematic way what were the Jewish responses to Nazi persecution. Personal testimonies and individual eyewitness accounts proved invaluable in this regard. In the process, as Hilberg points out, it also became clear that "not only was German destructive activity bureaucratic, but so also was Jewish dying. . . . There was a Jewish history which was not merely personal but also organizational, having to do not only with the way people felt, with their attitudes and reactions individual by individual, but also a very voluminous, complex and difficult subject matter, namely, the organization of Jewish life under the Nazis during the thirties and early forties."[7] These documents, hundreds of thousands of them, are still being researched; interpretations are still being formed, debated, and tested. When Hilberg calls that subject matter complex and difficult, he does not exaggerate. Situations and reactions were not identical, nor were the individuals involved. Enough exceptions are available to make

almost every generalization questionable. All can agree that the victims as well
as the killers had much to do with making the death count what it was. But how
are the victims' roles to be described and how are their responses to be ap-
praised? Those unsettled questions must be addressed if we are not to be
haunted by stereotypes or deceived by false impressions about the Holocaust.

An Impulse Toward Community

Against Hannah Arendt's claim that an unorganized, leaderless band of Jews
stood a better chance against the Nazis, it can be argued that her proposition is
beside the point because such community dissolution was not more than remotely possible. Centuries of adversity taught Jews to cope not by heading off
in separate directions but by coming together to meet shared needs and to find
ways to carry on their cultural, educational, economic, and religious lives. That
same experience also vindicated the wisdom of developing leadership that could
find favor with Gentile authority or at least ease the burdens that might be
placed upon Jews. It was rarely the case, however, that widespread Jewish unity
was easily achieved, as the situation in Germany during the 1930s illustrates.

About five hundred thousand Jews lived in Germany in 1933. Insofar as Ger-
man Jews could be classified into coherent groups, their diversity and divi-
sions—the latter partly caused by the increased immigration of eastern European
Jews—were still considerable. There were, for instance, traditional Orthodox
Jews who would see Hitler's oppression as a judgment or test befalling them as
God's chosen people. At a distance from them were various Zionist factions, but
their interests could also interpret Nazi oppression as instrumental in building
Jewish nationalism and spurring emigration to Palestine. Still other Jews were
members of internationally oriented Marxist organizations, Socialist or Communist. Their outlooks intensified opposition to Hitler but not necessarily along
specifically Jewish lines. Perhaps the largest segment of German Jewry, however, was a highly assimilated middle- and upper-middle-class group. If not
very religious, they still retained a primary identity as Jews but also thought of
themselves very much as Germans. Concentrated in large cities, their visibility
and eventually their vulnerability were enhanced because they were over-
represented in business, commerce, the professions, and university life. Though
not captains of industry, their educational and entrepreneurial skills did give
them higher average incomes than those of most non-Jewish Germans. All of
these factors helped make them a target population. Other Jewish groups represented regional concerns. The point to underscore is that as Hitler came to
power in 1933 German Jews lacked an effectively unified organizational or ideological base for blunting, let alone physically resisting, the Nazis' antisemitic
campaigns.

Yet, as Hitler coalesced his power in 1933, many German Jews sensed that
they must unify. Specifically it struck them that a single organization with a

strong central leadership was needed. Enough consensus was achieved to launch the *Reichsvertretung der deutschen Juden* (Federal Representation of German Jews) on 17 September 1933, with Berlin's Rabbi Leo Baeck, Germany's most prestigious Jew, as its head. The solidarity reflected by this organization, however, was fragile and superficial. For if German Jews talked about unity, their practices continued to be oriented toward factional differences. Simultaneously structured and fragmented by a multitude of diverse organizations, Germany's Jews were both more and less than a single community.

Raul Hilberg suggests that there are five main reactions that may be made against force of the kind that the Nazis brought to bear against German Jews in the 1930s: armed resistance, alleviation, evasion, paralysis, and compliance.[8] Armed resistance was not the *Reichsvertretung*'s way but neither was paralysis. Trying to represent all German Jews, it worked to expand economic possibilities, to facilitate emigration, and to defend Jews against defamation and violence. Early on, the *Reichsvertretung* frequently sent protesting memoranda to Nazi officials. As it petitioned the Nazi regime, it also advised German Jews about stances to take toward Nazi measures and worked to implement programs of education and culture, relief and welfare. Its tactics were primarily those of alleviation, predicated on the conviction that Jews could outlast and even discredit Hitler's antisemitism.

If alleviation tactics often led the *Reichsvertretung* to encourage evasion via emigration, on other occasions they required numerous acts of compliance. One ironic example involved a plebiscite held on 12 November 1933. Hitler wanted a vote of approval for his domestic and foreign policies. Still possessing the right to vote, what were Jews to do? The *Reichsvertretung* petitioned the government for clarification, reminding the officials that the Jews would be suspect if they failed to vote and even more so if they voted "Nein." Yet how could they possibly vote "Ja" in their circumstances? Having to settle for explanations that an affirmative vote was needed to ensure Germany's international status and world peace, the *Reichsvertretung* counseled that "the vote of the German Jews can be only Yes."

Tactics of alleviation and compliance perhaps helped to make Nazi oppression bearable. It could not be self-evident, moreover, except to those blessed with twenty-twenty hindsight, that a genocidal catastrophe was in store for German let alone European Jewry, for in the early months the restrictions placed on German Jews, oppressive as they were, did not stand out as unusually cruel in the light of previous history. But a catastrophe was in the making; nor would its course be reversed by alleviation or compliance. With the enactment of the Nuremberg Laws of 1935, any hint of Jewish criticism brought severe reprisals. Hope that the Nazi dictatorship would be brief, or even that tolerable accommodations with it could be made, began to dwindle. By 1938 even Heinrich Stahl, Baeck's deputy chair in the *Reichsvertretung*, would say that there was no future for Jews in Germany. His forecast was grimly corroborated by *Kristallnacht*. In the wake of shattering glass, twenty-five thousand Jews were imprisoned in concentration camps. For several months, suicides accounted for more than 50% of Germany's Jewish burials.

An event less spectacular but perhaps of even greater significance occurred a short while later. By a state decree of 4 July 1939, the *Reichsvertretung* became the *Reichsvereinigung der Juden in Deutschland*. Under this decree, relief efforts and the upkeep of Jewish schools remained within the purview of the organization, but other functions changed considerably as the name was altered. No longer was the emphasis to fall on the representation of Jewish interests, but rather the *Reichsvereinigung* would be an "association" including all persons classified as Jews by Nazi definitions. It would, moreover, be responsible for handling tasks assigned to it by the Interior Ministry, among them providing the Gestapo with information, communicating governmental decrees to the Jews, and helping to enforce those measures. Without changing personnel, the Jewish communal organization had been taken over by the Nazis. It would become instrumental in the forthcoming destruction process.

The Germans' experience with the *Reichsvertretung*-transformed-into-*Reichsvereinigung* provided a model that could be adapted to fit conditions created by the outbreak of war in September. Hence, three weeks after the invasion of Poland, Reinhard Heydrich, head of the security police, supplemented a crucial order. Not only would all Jewish communities of less than five hundred members be dissolved and transferred to concentration centers, but additionally "in each Jewish community, a Council of Jewish Elders is to be set up which, as far as possible, is to be composed of the remaining influential personalities and rabbis. . . . It is to be made *fully responsible* (in the literal sense of the word) for the exact execution according to terms of all instructions released or yet to be released."[9] Owing to their historic tradition of internal communal autonomy and responsibility, the beleaguered Jews initially regarded these Jewish councils (*Judenräte*) as legitimate mediating institutions between themselves and the German authorities. But the *Judenrat* was not the *Kehilla* of old. It would become, however involuntarily, a functioning adjunct of the SS bureaucracy. Its responsibilities included the maintenance of tolerated social services, rationing and food distribution, the collection of demographic information, administration of labor permits, manpower allocation, and finally, the rounding up of Jews to be sent to slave labor and extermination centers. Compliance with German orders did not cease even when the Germans demanded the rounding up of thousands of Jews daily for deportation. The success of the Germans in incorporating the *Judenräte* into the SS bureaucracy suggests that the capacities of a modern government even include the organization of an entire people to facilitate their own elimination.

Under Nazi domination, the *Judenräte*'s first duty was to communicate or to carry out Nazi orders, regulations, and wishes. Within those boundaries, they had to cope with Jewish communal needs as best they could. Increasingly these restrictions included the fences and walls of ghettos, especially in the east, where in 1941, for example, three million Polish Jews would be concentrated in Warsaw, Vilna, Bialystok, Krakow, and Lodz. From those locations, journeys to the death camps did not take long. The *Judenräte* would help see to that, just as the *Reichsvereinigung* did in Germany proper when deportations began there. By 10 June 1943, the Nazis could dissolve the *Reichsvereinigung*, for Germany was virtually *Judenrein*. Of the approximately five hundred thousand Jews living in Germany in 1933, about three hundred thousand emigrated during the Hitler era. Between 1940 and 1944, nearly 135,000 were sent to labor and death camps. Only about five thousand survived. Another thirty thousand who had emigrated to other European countries also lost their lives at the killing centers. Within Germany, five thousand Jews hid successfully, while another twelve thousand who were partners in mixed marriages escaped destruction. By any reckoning very few Jews were left in Germany at the end of the war. Nor are there many today.

Only two members of the *Reichsvereinigung* survived. One was Leo Baeck. Deported to Theresienstadt, he became an honorary member of the *Judenrat* in that ghetto. Even after he became convinced that rumors about gas chambers at Auschwitz were true, he decided to tell no one, reasoning that "living in the expectation of death by gassing would only be the harder."[10] His decision was not unlike that of other Jewish leaders. Baeck spoke of his decision as grave. We can assume that he did what he thought was best, surmising that to publicize death by gassing would lower morale, increase despair, and make foregone a conclusion that might somehow be forestalled for those still in the ghetto. He continued to pursue tactics of alleviation until the end, thinking they were the best resistance against the Nazis. Inclinations to think that he was wrong, however well-intentioned, should be held in abeyance until additional alternatives are considered.

Dilemmas and Alternatives in the Ghettos

Ghettoization of Jews was a crucial step in the Nazi destruction process. It was in the ghettos, especially those in eastern Europe, that the Jews were concentrated, thus making other areas *Judenrein*. They were then dispatched to die in the killing centers when attrition from starvation and disease did not happen fast enough. Every ghetto was different, not only in terms of its leadership, inhabitants, and the precise policies dictated by the local Nazi officials in charge but also in physical location and design. The largest, Warsaw, was eventually surrounded by a high brick wall. Situated in the *Generalgouvernement*, a portion of Poland that the Nazis treated as a conquered province, it still afforded more opportunity for Jewish escape than did the ghetto in Lodz. The latter appeared to be more open, surrounded only by barbed wire and a board fence, but it was situated in the Wartheland, a part of Poland annexed into the Reich and populated by ethnic Germans whose enthusiasm for Nazi antisemitism was strong. The smaller Vilna ghetto stood in the middle of the city. Access in and out was perhaps easier than in Lodz or Warsaw, and the surrounding territory afforded more options owing to the forests nearby and to the diverse Gentile population in a region that had once been Polish, then Lithuanian, and most recently a Soviet Republic.

Variety in the ghettos spread across Europe from east to west, however, does not eliminate the fact that those places, which could be defined as captive city-states linking territorial confinement with complete subjugation to German domination, also shared much in common. First, they were all political entities, characterized by enforced segregation of their inhabitants from the surrounding population. The Nazis brought them into existence to control and thin Jewish life, and the Nazis required a Jewish leadership to implement their decrees. Second, each ghetto was a socioeconomic organization. Many inhabitants worked for the Germans. Indeed, most of the *Judenräte* perceived that it was only by maximizing those opportunities and by laboring diligently that their ghettos had a chance to survive. The ghettoized Jews often proved amazingly resourceful in making themselves economically valuable to the Germans. Makeshift factories purchased time for thousands of Jews. Smuggling, bribery, and other clandestine operations supplemented the precarious and ever-dwindling food supply. Yet the final outcome remained primarily under German control. That power dictated when Jews, working or not, were superfluous; it could also enlist the *Judenräte* and their Jewish police forces to curtail the illegal activities that became indispensable for sustaining ghetto life. Meanwhile the *Judenräte* and their offices were not the only centers of activity in a complicated community network of social-welfare organizations, cultural associations, religious and ideological collectives. With or without a *Judenrat*'s blessing, these self-help institutions, voluntary and largely autonomous, did much to sustain the ghetto. Supplementing whatever a *Judenrat* might do directly, they collected and distributed food, found people shelter, and organized other necessities. Under their encouragement, artists created, historians recorded, physicians practiced, and scientists did research as best they could. They were instrumental in seeing that outlawed schools functioned secretly. They supported theaters, orphanages, hospitals, and child-care centers. Without their auspices, banned religious observances could not have been so widely held.

Believing the Nazis would lose the war, the *Judenräte* and the diverse self-help agencies acted as though the ghetto had a future. If they had no alternative, the fact remained that the ghetto was a German creation, which at best was a way station for Jews between prewar freedom and wartime annihilation. Ironically, by making life more bearable even the best accomplishments of the

Judenräte and other relief groups could be used to the Germans' own advantage, for every success encouraged the hope that things were not as bad as they always turned out to be. Signs that the vise was closing were available, too. Preeminently, the ghetto economy, chronically wracked by unemployment and faced with constantly dwindling assets to procure the food needed for subsistence, was incompatible with long-term survival. Yet only rarely did strategies of physical resistance meet with *Judenräte* approval. Instead the policy of rescue-through-work was upheld, and the meager resources available to the *Judenräte* were stretched to meet communal needs. Considering the duress, it is no surprise to learn that social equality and economic justice did not always prevail. As in all other human societies, those with greater power, status, and needed skills commanded more of the scarce resources. The weak got less. In December 1941, for example, Warsaw's "Council functionaries were getting the largest food allocations, 1,665 calories a day, compared to an average of 1,125 calories allocated to the general population."[11] Even those who got more, however, were hardly immune to violent death.

The fundamental dilemma for the *Judenräte* was that "they could not serve the Jews indefinitely while simultaneously obeying the Germans."[12] That squeeze could be unbearable. To illustrate, consider the fact that Adam Czerniakow kept a diary. Its entry for 29 April 1942 observes that the Nazis wanted ten maps and population figures for the Warsaw ghetto. That demand came to Czerniakow as chairman of that community's *Judenrat*. A balding engineer in his sixties, Czerniakow served in this position for nearly three years. Like the other statements in his diary, this one does not make forecasts or reflect on long-range plans. It records reports and rumors, many of them ominous, in subdued tones and without elaboration. If Czerniakow could sense that those orders to produce population data and maps might foreshadow deportations that would end in the gas chambers at Treblinka, those intuitions did not betray him. Less than three months later, his diary's last notation states: "It is 3 o'clock. So far 4,000 are ready to go. The orders are that there must be 9,000 by 4 o'clock."[13] The numbers cited by Czerniakow refer to the quota of Jewish life the Nazis expected the Warsaw *Judenrat* to help them "resettle." By the end of World War II, 99% of the half-million Jews who had occupied the Warsaw ghetto were dead, a majority of them slain at Treblinka after deportation. Czerniakow did not live to see this destruction process unfold to its bitter conclusion. Not long after finishing the last entry in his diary, he swallowed the cyanide tablet hidden in his desk.

Opinion about Czerniakow is divided. One Warsaw survivor, Alexander Donat, believes that if suicide bore witness to Czerniakow's personal integrity, it did not attest to his greatness, for he spread no alarm about the imminent deportations. Yet Czerniakow had worked day after day to alleviate Jewish need within the ghetto. Permitted to deal directly only with low-ranking Nazi officials, he nevertheless met with them time and again to solicit relief for his people. Unfortunately, the results were paltry. Never could he obtain the food, space, or security the Jews so desperately needed. Periodically he might secure the release of a prisoner, get better conditions for Jewish children, or locate a little more to eat. What such victories meant, ironically, is part of Czerniakow's tragedy. They were seized upon as testimony that survival in the ghetto might be possible. In fact, the unrelenting Nazi aim was to rid Warsaw of Jews completely and permanently.

Judenräte officials, however, were not privy to Nazi plans. They did not know exactly what ultimate fate the Nazis had in store for the Jewish ghettos. Nor did those officials ever volunteer to help deport Jews, even when Nazi assurances about "resettlement" might have been tempting. To think that they *collaborated* with the Germans would be a perverse distortion, and even to say that they *cooperated* with them blurs the fact that these men were impelled by terror to comply. Noncompliance was an alternative, but it was a ticket for immediate deportation if not summary execution. Czerniakow's path of suicide was another way out, one taken by several others in authority, but it offered little hope for the ghetto population as a whole, which the *Judenräte* were committed to save in the best ways they knew how. Hence, they tended to be leery of armed uprisings, too, fearing these would bring severe Nazi reprisals that would doom the entire community. In fact, the variety of *Judenräte* responses ranged widely. Jewish leaders in the Polish cities of Lublin and Krakow, for example, tended to obey every Nazi order exactly and without diversionary tactics. Similar situations existed in Vienna and throughout the Netherlands. Even late in the war, when Nazi intentions were at least an open secret, on the eve of the deportation of the Hungarian Jews, 3 May 1944, the *Judenrat* in Budapest petitioned the Hungarian interior minister: "We emphatically declare that we do not seek this audience to lodge complaints about the merit of the measures adopted, but merely ask that they be carried out in a humane spirit."[14] In places such as Minsk and Kovno, on the other hand, the *Judenräte* were actively involved in organizing or assisting armed resistance groups. Similar situations existed in Slovakia and Belgium. Recalcitrance to compliance, it should be added, also tended to be greater during the period 1939–41 than afterward, owing to the fact that many of the early *Judenräte* members were experienced, responsible prewar leaders as well. Their stubbornness was thinned out by Nazi executions, and replacements less likely to frustrate German expectations were found.[15]

If a majority of *Judenräte* did not exhibit determined resistance to Nazi orders, neither did most comply helplessly. In a broad middle range, where the strategy of rescue through work was the governing policy, there was still fairly often genuine *Judenräte* resistance to the Nazi threat. At least that case can be made if the meaning of "resistance" encompasses "all active and conscious organized action against Nazi commands, policies, or wishes, by whatever means:

social organization, morale-building operations, underground political work, active unarmed resistance or, finally, armed resistance.''[16] In reckoning with the ghettos and concentration camps erected by the Nazis, such a way of construing resistance is not out of place; for in any way that Jews refused to give up and disappear, it could be said that they thwarted the Nazi aim. Hence when the *Judenräte* supported schools and cultural activities, when they worked to organize food supplies, when they tried to negotiate for Jewish lives or facilitate escape efforts, as some did from time to time, their resistance was real. In this light, even the strategy of rescue through work may be construed as a resistance tactic. And when Jewish leaders cautioned against armed uprisings or even took steps to quash them, which was not always the case, the line to draw is not necessarily one between resisters and nonresisters but rather between different philosophies of resistance. For not only was the possibility of armed resistance within the ghettos hamstrung by a lack of weapons, resistance groups themselves also had to weigh if and when to strike. They could never be unaware of the devastating reprisals that the Nazi policy of collective responsibility would visit on the entire community.

As head of the *Judenrat* in Lodz, Mordecai Chaim Rumkowski, a childless widower who had formerly been a businessman and the director of an orphanage, ruled that ghetto dictatorially "by force of personality, tenacity of purpose, organizational intelligence, and political shrewdness, even outwitting the SS in its attempt to displace him."[17] Mocked and despised both for his pretentious airs and his nearly fanatical belief that work would save the Jews of Lodz, he was nonetheless obeyed because his strategy seemed credible. By the summer of 1944, however, the snare and delusion were apparent. Indeed, as early as 16 December 1941, the Germans told Rumkowski that twenty thousand Jews must leave Lodz. When he announced this order to the ghetto four days later, Rumkowski claimed that he had persuaded the Nazis to take only half that number. The Jewish leadership itself, moreover, could determine those to be relocated. However inadvertently or unwillingly, Jews were taking an active role in the very process of population elimination that the National Socialists desired. The selectees, Rumkowski suggested, would probably move to smaller towns where food was more plentiful. The Resettlement Commission established by Rumkowski—it included representatives from the ghetto's police force, judicial and penal agencies, and office of vital statistics—determined that the first to go should be recent arrivals in the ghetto and persons convicted of crimes. The families of these "undesirables" were included. The Jewish bureaucracy in the ghetto did its work, enforcing the deportation orders by refusing food rations to those who declined to leave. Within a month, the first group went off, not to small towns but to the killing center at Chelmno. In a speech to vindicate his action, Rumkowski argued that he had received a ruthless order. He had carried it out to prevent the Germans from doing so even more violently, and he had also been able to reduce the numbers required. In fact, by removing part of the ghetto population, which he referred to as a "suppurating abscess," he implied that his action ensured safety for those who remained.

A lull of several weeks followed the last of the initial deportations. Then, in late February, new orders resumed them. During the next six weeks, one thousand persons had to leave daily. The Resettlement Commission kept making the selections. When the supply of lawbreakers diminished, the unemployed and recipients of ghetto welfare came next. A strategy of thinning out first the harmful and then the unproductive elements in the ghetto repeated itself in numerous places. Through the spring and on into the summer, the Nazis' calculated pattern of respite from and then resumption of the deportations continued, too. Increasingly corroborated, rumors about Chelmno multiplied. Rumkowski had this information as new orders demanded deportation of the sick, adults over sixty-five, and children under ten. Amidst escalating terror and panic, these orders were also carried out in Lodz by Rumkowski's forces and the Germans. Rumkowski pleaded with the Germans to exempt the nine-year-olds. The petition refused, his conclusion was that "we can't go against the order, only lighten its execution. Do you think the Germans will be so gentle and kind if they carry out the order themselves?"[18]

As 1942 began, about one hundred sixty thousand Jews lived in the Lodz ghetto. The unforgiving deportations spared only sixty thousand by August 1944. Now, under penalty of death, they were also ordered to the trains. The implications of deportation were no longer mysterious. Still, compliance followed initial refusal to obey, for there could be no doubt that the Nazis would ravage the ghetto and glimmers of hope remained that movement from Lodz would not be disastrous. Rumkowski urged the people to go peacefully. He could have stayed behind with the few hundred men and women assigned to clean out the ghetto, but he elected to join the last train with his brother and his family. When it departed on 30 August 1944, Chelmno was no longer operating, but Auschwitz was. Permitted by the Germans to watch the last of the Lodz Jews walk to their deaths, Rumkowski entered the gas chamber at the end of the line.

Unarmed, weak, and often starving, the Jews in Lodz lacked the resources to mount an effective resistance against the Germans or even against Rumkowski. But especially as the war wore on, whatever inclination may have existed to do so was reduced by hope that Germany's defeat might come in time. Russian troops were not far away in the summer of 1944. Had they not stalled their own advance, tens of thousands of Jews might have survived, and Rumkowski's policy of salvation through work would have had a better outcome. That scenario did not unfold; work brought no salvation to Lodz. Rumkowski was no willful accomplice of the Germans. Nonetheless his ghetto remained so vulnerable to German domination that it became a self-destructive machine, even paying the one-way train fares charged by the German railways for transportation from Lodz to the death camps.

The tragedy is that, short of reversing and radically altering a two-thousand-year-old pattern of Jewish-Gentile relationships, it is hard to imagine that the Lodz ghetto, once established by the Nazis, could realistically have been anything else than a death trap. For the long-standing Jewish strategy of coping with Gentile threats had been that of alleviation and compliance. But the Nazis were playing a new game with different rules. When their objective became a Final Solution, alleviation was at best momentary; compliance at worst meant self-destruction. To mount a more effective resistance would have taken years, even generations, of groundwork that reevaluated the basic assumptions of individual and communal Jewish life in Europe. Some movement in that direction had occurred—various Zionist impulses, for example, come to mind—but not even these envisioned what finally happened under Hitler. Until too late, there was simply no compelling logic to convince Europe's Jews that there would be a Holocaust. After it was too late, Jewish responses were characterized much less by violent resistance than by the rationalization that sacrifice of the few might save the many—especially if the latter worked hard. Where obedience to Nazi orders could not be construed as a life-saving strategy, there were still Jewish arguments for compliance on the grounds that suffering could thereby be reduced. Along with these justifications for Jewish responses, the victims' vocabulary came to include counterparts to Nazi euphemisms that repressed the deadly nature of the circumstances.

However the ghettos are differentiated, notes Lucy S. Dawidowicz, "for the most part, caution and prudence guided the ghetto populace with regard to the danger of German reprisals. On this matter, in contrast to others, a general consensus existed between them and the Judenrat."[19] Hence, when Abba Kovner's speech in the Vilna ghetto promoted the formation of the United Partisans Organization (*Fareinikte Partisaner Organizatzie,* FPO), consisting largely of Zionist and Communist youth, eventual public knowledge of its existence created tensions that nearly resulted in internal ghetto violence and certainly showed the lengths to which Jacob Gens would go in carrying out his version of the policy of alleviation and compliance. Clandestinely organized in early 1942, the FPO aimed at sabotage and armed revolt against further German deportations. Flight to the surrounding forests would be attempted only when action in the ghetto became untenable. There were no illusions about defeating the Germans, but it was hoped that an uprising in the ghetto might spark rebellion outside by Lithuanians and Poles. Though he knew of the FPO's existence, Gens at first looked the other way and even offered some assistance. At the same time, he insisted ever more firmly on "law and order" within the ghetto so as not to provoke the Germans. By early summer the FPO's hopes of obtaining Gens's full support were crushed.

Yitzhak Witenberg, a Communist, was the FPO's commander. His identity revealed by a Lithuanian Communist who had been arrested and tortured by the Gestapo, Witenberg became a wanted man. He was drawn out of hiding on 15 July, when Gens called an important meeting with the FPO leadership, having assured them that the Gestapo had been bribed to forget their commander. Searching for Witenberg, two Lithuanian policemen interrupted the meeting, accompanied by Gens's chief of the Jewish police force (*Ordnungsdienst*). Kovner denied that Witenberg was present, but Gens identified him, and the Lithuanians placed Witenberg under arrest. Suspicious that something might be amiss, an FPO unit in the neighborhood was able to free Witenberg, who returned to hiding. Ordered to turn Witenberg over to the Gestapo, Gens the next evening appealed to the ghetto as a whole, warning that unless the Germans were obeyed, the ghetto would be savaged. Though ready to defend their leader, the FPO soon observed that civil war would be a more likely outcome than the appearance of public solidarity. Finally, the Communists in the ghetto insisted that Witenberg be surrendered. He was taken away in a Gestapo car, which had been waiting at Gens's office, and killed the next day. The FPO never mounted a significant armed uprising within the ghetto, although some of their number did escape to partisan groups in the forests and others battled the Germans during the ghetto's final days. The Vilna ghetto was liquidated on 23 September 1943. Nine days before, Jacob Gens had willingly reported to Gestapo headquarters where, accused with unintended irony of helping the partisans, he was shot to death.

The story of Vilna is not the same as that of any other Jewish ghetto in Europe, and yet it is, too, because the outcome was virtually always similar. The *Judenräte* frequently helped to register and concentrate the Jews, thus aiding Nazi deportations. They often underwrote Nazi cover stories about "resettlement" and denied rumors of atrocity. They hindered counteraction additionally by harassing potential armed resistance movements. If outright collaboration was rare among the Jewish police, it could doubtlessly be found in certain elements of that group. As for the *Judenräte* some interpreters have judged that "unfortunately, as the war dragged on and killings increased, reluctant compromise became little more than a euphemism for reluctant collaboration."[20] But that judgment will seem too harsh to others. The *Judenräte* simply lacked the knowledge and the power to compete with the Nazis on anything approximating equal terms. Even if they did not always do the best that was within their severely limited power, they deserve no general indictment of even reluctant collaboration. Nor did the people in the ghettos go like sheep to the slaughter. They did what they could and had to do to survive. No less than their leaders, however, they were simply unable to stem the tide that carried them away.

No amount of new evidence is likely to settle debate about the Jewish councils to everyone's satisfaction. The problem is that *intention, function,* and *result* in the cases of the *Judenräte* were intertwined and snarled with such complexity that it is extremely difficult to find precise language to describe the actions that the councils took. In order to save Jews, they had to participate in the destruction of Jews. If the emphasis falls on intention, the *Judenräte* appear in a more favorable light than if one stresses results. But evaluations that tip the scales by weighing one or the other of those elements must still reckon with the *Judenräte*'s functional status and its context of possibilities. The inescapable core of their function was to facilitate implementation of Nazi decrees. The ways to avoid doing so were limited. Hence the intentions of the *Judenräte* might be good enough, in spite of the results, and yet the results, which make the functional status plain, show that even the best intentions may play into the hands of power that is utterly opposed to them. Success in showing that the *Judenräte*'s intentions were, generally speaking, not blameworthy makes the Holocaust less painful for Jews than it would be if the Jewish cause had been rife with overt collaboration. But the most important outcome of that achievement may be to stress what powerlessness means. For whatever their intentions, the *Judenräte* were not effective life-saving agencies. They never could have been; they lacked the power requisite for such work. That condition was not their fault. Credit for it belongs to the Germans and to centuries of Gentile domination of a Jewish minority. To belabor the point of whether the *Judenräte* were blameworthy is an issue less important than that of who holds power and how a relatively powerless group can best defend its interests.

Fighting Resistance

Photographs of Jews lined up for the *Einsatzgruppen*, boarding Nazi transports, or filing toward the gas chambers may give the impression of obedient passivity. What those pictures do not show is that a lack of physical resistance at the time of mass murder is not something peculiar to Jews. Faced with imminent execution by the Nazis, French Maquisards, Russian prisoners of war, and Czechs at Lidice did not resist physically. Nor did the Poles deported from Warsaw after their abortive uprising in 1944, months after the Jewish ghetto fighters there had battled the forces of General Jürgen Stroop for weeks. More recently, Southeast Asian refugees seldom resisted when attacked by Thai pirates or slaughtered by the Khmer Rouge. They calculated that more of their numbers were likely to escape if they submitted passively than if they offered physical resistance.

The pictures mentioned above, moreover, do not show the conditions prior to their being taken. Neither can they fully portray the experience of victims such as those described in Hermann Graebe's eyewitness account of what preceded one *Einsatzgruppe* action: "The father was holding the hand of a boy about ten years old and was speaking to him softly; the boy was fighting his tears. The father pointed to the sky, stroked his head, and seemed to explain something to him. . . ."[21] As for the prior conditions, Jews who had attempted to elude roundups had usually paid with their lives. Once caught, those who did not remain calm could anticipate being shot summarily, too. Families wanted to stay together as long as possible, and some individuals looked on their deaths as religious martyrdom. Nor, as Isaiah Trunk has argued, can the following be discounted:

> There is perhaps a further moral and psychological element explaining why most of the victims went quietly and passively to their death: a possible refusal to show the murderers any panic or hysteria that might have given additional pleasure to the sadists among them. The victims preferred dying with dignity and with scorn toward the killers. The Jews might also have actually wondered whether it was worth fighting for one's life in a world where the human beast could rule undisturbed amid the passive silence of the entire civilized world.[22]

Not all Jews, of course, shared this outlook concerning death with dignity. They affirmed another instead, namely, that a physically armed, fighting resistance was essential, not because it would save lives but because it would show a scorn toward the killers, a refusal to let Jewish life be taken with impunity.

Armed resistance must be understood realistically, not romantically. It does not materialize spontaneously as an inescapable demand felt by heroic victims under intolerable oppression, especially when the oppressed are weakened by hunger and disease and are woefully armed as well. It is mustered only against great odds—internal as well as external—and the impetus behind it takes time to develop just as the execution of effective acts of armed resistance requires careful preparation and judgment. The extent of armed resistance within Jewish ghettos, inside the Nazi concentration camps, among Jewish partisan units (it is estimated there were at least twenty-eight of them in Poland alone) and in underground groups across the European continent is now known to have been much greater than the stereotype of "sheep to the slaughter" implies. Insight about how this resistance emerged and what it accomplished is important for grasping further the odds that the Jews faced in combatting the Nazi effort to annihilate them.

One can speak of *dissent* against a regime in situations where the possibility of significant legal opposition remains. For Jews, dissent against the Nazis was impossible; there were no significant legal channels within the German power structure that could be utilized. All opposition, therefore, was resistance, whose nucleus can be defined as "challenging the intrinsic right of authority to select and implement policy."[23] In varied forms, Jewish resistance to Nazism emerged early on and continued until the Nazi cause was crushed. But this resistance was not primarily one of physical force. Neither the realities of Jewish political status in Europe, nor the tradition of Jewish responses to adversity, nor the lack of material support from other resistance groups during World War II provided European Jewry the wherewithal to launch effective armed uprisings. A more compelling logic was that it was better not to take the risks of violent resistance, which might provoke even worse repression, than to endure existing conditions, however minimally bearable they might be.

Particularly in the ghettos and camps, hope for survival made it harder, not easier, to organize armed resistance. Moreover, as the hope for survival became sufficiently dimmed to remove it as an impediment to physical resistance, the odds against anything more than some sort of a moral victory rose immensely. That realization, too, could impede violent rebellion, for one might feel that it is better to die with others than to resist absurdly, futilely, with no hope of winning and with the very real possibility that one's agony might only increase. For others, however, it was precisely the hopelessness of their situations that led them to take action. They thought in terms neither of military victory nor of personal survival. They were determined to do what they could to stop the Nazis. Particularly in the ghetto uprisings, a sense of Jewish honor and identity came to the fore along with ideological commitments—Zionism, socialism, or communism were the most typical—that emphasized a historical sense of struggle, group loyalty, and a cause that transcended personal survival in importance.

Organized armed resistance by Jews occurred throughout Europe, although its presence in the West has been overlooked owing to the fact that it often functioned as "a kind of underground within the underground."[24] Jewish resistance in eastern Europe was at once more identifiable and more problematic, as some examples involving Jewish partisans illustrate. Unlike most partisan fighters who can at least count on passive support in their locale, Jewish partisan units in eastern Europe usually encountered as much hostility from local populations as they did from the Germans. In addition, although the Allied forces parachuted arms and material to Polish partisans, similar assistance was consistently withheld from Jewish resistance units, ostensibly because Jews were not a clearly defined national group. In eastern Europe, moreover, Jewish partisans had the best chance of survival if they were able to join a Soviet partisan group. Once accepted, however, they ceased to fight directly for their own people. Although Soviet policy opposed putting Jews in special jeopardy, some Soviet partisans were antisemitic. Under the best of circumstances, service in a Soviet unit involved subordinating direct action for one's fellow Jews to purely Russian war aims.

Within the ghettos, Jewish resistance had problematic aspects not only because of extreme difficulties in obtaining arms but even more fundamentally because Jewish opinion was divided religiously and politically. Even among the mostly young Zionist, Socialist, and Communist groups, who eventually sparked the armed fighting, there was early on no unanimity of opinion. Furthermore, each group had its individual organizational problems, not the least of which was communication from place to place in areas under severe Nazi restrictions. Prior to the first reports of mass murder, which began to circulate in the ghettos during the summer of 1941, the underground Zionist and left-wing political groups worked primarily to make ghetto life more bearable. Those concerns included clandestine journalism to expose *Judenräte* corruption. Although these groups were stunned by the incredible nature of the first reports, they responded differently from most, including many *Judenräte* officials, by investigating further. A majority of these leaders found their worst suspicions confirmed: Jews were facing an unprecedented genocide. Diverse ideological views and local conditions, however, meant that even then there was no single, agreed-upon strategy but instead a series of quandaries to be faced. Even among those groups who agreed that it was essential to form combat groups and to accumulate an arsenal, there was a question whether to maintain their own cadre, escaping from the ghettos to fight with partisans in the forests, or to remain inside the ghetto walls to attempt protection of the entire community, a task that would entail a virtually suicidal encounter with Nazi troops even if it allowed release for feelings of hatred and revenge. These questions were answered differently, but in nearly all the large ghettos armed resistance developed, some of it as early as spring 1942. In Bialystok some fighters joined partisan groups; others stayed inside the ghetto to resist the German liquidation in August 1943. Urban guerrilla units hindered the Nazi deportation efforts in Krakow; some fought on until this ghetto succumbed in March 1943. The Nazis met armed force in Vilna, too. Even in Lodz, where German domination and *Judenrat* control were extremely strong, raids and sabotage operations occurred. None of the ghetto resistance efforts, though, is more celebrated than the one in Warsaw.

In the Warsaw ghetto, it is noteworthy that the first shots fired by the resistance movement were directed not at Germans but at Jews. The initial target was the chief of the Jewish police. Others belonging to the Nazi-controlled Jewish bureaucracy were also assassinated with the result that the Warsaw *Judenrat* lost much of its power. These events occurred in the late summer and early autumn of 1942. Only about seventy thousand Jews then remained in the ghetto, less than 20% of those who had once been there. Death in the gas at Treblinka had taken those who survived starvation and disease. Defense measures proceeded as the Jews awaited the next blow. Coming in January 1943, it caught the fighters by surprise, but the Germans drew fire, and Jews had the unaccustomed thrill of seeing them "retreat in fright from a handful of young Jews equipped only with a few pistols and hand grenades."[25]

In response Himmler ordered the total dissolution of the ghetto. That task began on 19 April 1943, at 3:00 A.M. Under the leadership of Mordecai Anielewicz, 24, some fifteen thousand Jews armed with makeshift weapons sought to hold out as long as possible against a Nazi force twice that size and vastly better armed. Their assignment was to clear the ghetto in three days. It took them four weeks instead. The first Jewish counterattack drove the German force out of the ghetto. The result, however, was never in doubt. In a matter of days, Jews were caught and killed increasingly. The ghetto was in flames when

May arrived. Some fighters, Anielewicz among them, took their own lives rather than fall into Nazi hands. A few escaped through the sewers. Thousands of unarmed Jews perished in the fighting; more than fifty thousand others were captured and dispatched to killing centers and labor camps. Perhaps another five or six thousand got out of the ghetto during the confusion of the fighting, but most of them were tracked down later, thanks to Polish gangs who abetted the Nazi search. German casualties, on the other hand, amounted to no more than a few hundred.

Armed resistance in the ghettos was no more effective as a life-saving device than the accommodating policies of the *Judenräte*, but the difference was that the resistance groups never rationalized their existence along those lines. Resistance was more an end in itself for them. Their model was the Zealot defense of Masada during the ancient Judeo-Roman war. These Jewish resisters had no illusions about their situation during World War II. Nevertheless, they were determined to fight to the bitter end. If their efforts were unable materially to affect the execution of the Final Solution, they perceived correctly that to attempt resistance against hopeless odds would prove symbolically important, as it obviously has in Israel especially. The ghetto fighters simply wanted to do what they could to stop the Nazis, and for that reason Jews will always honor Mordecai Anielewicz and Zivia Lubetkin in ways that no *Judenräte* member will ever be honored.

Jewish partisan activity was a thorn in the Nazis' flesh, no doubt winning life for numerous Jews, but the ghetto fighter, the partisan, and the Jewish member of other underground networks were never positioned to determine decisively the fate of their fellow Jews, let alone the destruction of the Third Reich. Even less could those Jews do so who mustered armed resistance in the camps. Besides small-scale fighting escapes from various labor camps and brigades, there were armed uprisings in Sobibor, Treblinka, and Auschwitz. Resources to carry out such activity were so scant, the odds against its accomplishing anything of material importance so great, that armed resistance in these places was rare. The astonishing thing is that it happened at all.

Armed revolts in the death camps were instigated primarily by veteran prisoners, who, in adapting to the most extreme conditions, had moved beyond confusion or despair but still recognized that they were as good as dead. If they no longer had the ideological zeal of some of the ghetto fighters, their experience taught them the ways of conspiracy and deception. Violence was not ruled out when rebellion became literally their only alternative. In Auschwitz, for example, it was chiefly Greek Jews assigned to work in crematoria who succeeded in blowing up one of those ovens on 7 October 1944. Knowing that SS policy would consign them to death in a matter of months, these men, some of them formerly resistance and army personnel, worked with determination and with the cooperation of resistance movements all through the Auschwitz camp to accumulate the devices needed for their sabotage. Interestingly enough, at the last minute the resistance leadership in Auschwitz, echoing arguments used by the *Judenräte* in some ghettos, urged the *Sonderkommandos* not to proceed because doing so might result in the murder of the entire camp population. The revolt was not aborted, but the SS did crush it in two hours and eventually killed nearly all the crematoria workers involved. At Sobibor, sixty men and women survived the revolt, but only twelve out of nearly two hundred made good their escape from Treblinka.

The known samples suggest that thousands of other acts of violent Jewish resistance occurred during the Holocaust, many of them motivated by a desire to get word to other Jews and to the outside world about what the Nazis were doing. Nor were these efforts typically the work of individuals acting in isolation. Friendship and cooperation were essential. So were individual initiative and determination, commitment to a cause or at least the willingness to risk everything rather than to accept defenselessly an inevitable death. Given the odds, the importance of such actions lies less in their objective success than in what they reveal about the range of human responses to extreme conditions of domination and about the costs of powerlessness. Far from being nonexistent, Jewish armed resistance was remarkable during the Holocaust. But its impressive quality derives largely from the fact that it came from a people facing hopeless odds. Whatever glory it contains, the price for it was too high. Not that the cost would have been reduced if the armed resistance had failed to materialize—that argument by some of the *Judenräte* lost its compelling power after 1943, and it will not convert many now. What remains persuasive, though, is that the tribute paid to a tragic Jewish resistance would be unnecessary if Europe's Jews had not been so defenseless.

The Chances of Survival

For those who did not take flight or perish before reaching a ghetto or camp, the Nazi plan finally called for eliminating the Jews by working them to death or by murdering them outright. Jewish resistance to those intentions was not limited to *Judenräte* policies of salvation through work or of giving up some to save others; nor was it limited to desperate acts of armed resistance. In between were countless other personal and collective responses aimed at thwarting the Nazi goal. These included rescue efforts where the difference between life and death might be determined by whether Jews could muster help to get their brothers and sisters across a border or into a safer region of the same country. These actions were directly aimed at saving Jewish lives. Unfortunately, they often depended for their success on Gentile contacts who were frequently unreliable. For the most part, when Jewish flight was easiest it also seemed less necessary. Hence, it did not occur in time. In general, whatever escape routes remained open, the great majority of European Jews who did not elude Hitler's reach before the war did not escape at all. As the war wore on, the Nazis showed an inclination to accept payment in war matériel or cash for Jewish lives.[26] But these opportunities dwindled away when the necessary support could not be amassed in time, again owing largely to the fact that when the victims had been rendered powerless to act on their own behalf, too few others—Jewish or Gentile—outside the zones of Nazi influence would do so promptly either. Powerlessness made Jews superfluous and destined them for Auschwitz.

Between five and six million Jews—about 3.8 million in 1941–42 alone—perished in National Socialism's program of population elimination via ghettoization, slave labor, concentration camps, and killing squads and centers that implemented mass murder under the cover of war. The total more than doubles when one notes non-Jewish statistics such as the following: 3.3 million Soviet POW's perished in Nazi captivity; more than 4 million Soviet civilians, over 2.5 million Polish civilians, and 1.5 million Yugoslav civilians met similar fates. It should also be noted that up to five hundred thousand of Europe's large population of Gypsies were slaughtered. In addition to German citizens who lost their lives in the euthanasia campaign, another thirty-two thousand were executed between 1933 and 1945 for political crimes. Thousands of homosexuals, singled out as "defectives," were eradicated, too. With a vengeance, the Nazi ideology of racial purity rendered people unwanted.[27]

As with the Jewish losses, no exact count of the non-Jewish victims of Nazi murder will ever exist, but it remains true that Hitler targeted Jews alone for extinction, and the largest group of people murdered by the Nazis were European Jews. Country-by-country statistics will vary depending on the year used to determine borderlines and on how refugees are counted, but following Raul Hilberg's conservative calculations, based on 1937 borders and including refugees with their countries of origin, the following picture emerges.[28]

Including what started with the ghettos and the *Einsatzgruppen,* the labor and death camps killed nearly three million Polish Jews (90% of that population). A similar percentage was also dispatched in the Baltic states of Lithuania, Latvia, and Estonia. In those regions, which the Soviet Union incorporated in July 1940, more than two hundred thousand Jews lost their lives. As for the rest of the USSR, close to another million Jews were killed. Nearly two hundred thousand from Germany and Austria—again close to 90%—also died, along with three-quarters of the Jews (one hundred thousand) from the Netherlands. Jewish losses in Hungary and Rumania combined to total about four hundred and fifty thousand, more than half of the Jewish population in those areas, with most of the deaths coming in 1944, well after it was clear that Germany would lose the war. The Czechoslovakian percentage was even higher; two hundred and sixty thousand from that territory lost their lives. About seventy-five thousand French Jews were killed, and continuing to the bitter end, sixty thousand Greek Jews and a like number from Yugoslavia—more than two-thirds in both of the latter cases—were eliminated. The Nazis called all of these Jewish victims not people but *figuren*—numbers or figures—and if the statistics get smaller as one considers Belgium, at least twenty-four thousand dead, or Bulgaria, which lost fourteen thousand, or Italy, where the total was about nine thousand, the final reckoning is still devastating, especially when it is remembered that 25% of the dead were children not yet in their teens. Moreover, 80% of the Jewish scholars, rabbis, and full-time teachers of Torah alive in 1939 perished during the Holocaust. The cultural and religious life of eastern Europe's Jews became virtually extinct.

"Through the fumes I saw the vague outline of huge ovens. We were in the cremation room of the Auschwitz crematorium."[29] By the hundreds of thousands, Jews entered that room, though hardly any of them knew it, let alone lived to write about it after the war was over. Filip Müller, a Czech Jew who entered Auschwitz in April 1942, was an exception. From May 1942 until the gassings stopped in November 1944, he was one of the *Sonderkommandos* who had to burn the Jewish corpses produced by this Nazi death factory. He tells how the demand for body disposal always exceeded the camp's capacity, even though thousands of bodies were cremated daily. He reports how the camp's officials experimented with the most efficient ways of cremation, expending the least amount of fuel to obtain the most ashes. Forced to be part of the worst, Müller knew that he, too, would eventually be killed, but before that time, the burden of his work overwhelmed him. On 8 March 1944 he tried to take his own life by joining a group of Czech Jews in the gas chambers. The gas chamber was not yet full or sealed off. More arrivals were awaited. During this interlude Müller was recognized by some of the victims. No exit was available to them, but they insisted that Müller must not die. He must remain alive to testify. They pushed him out of the gas chamber; and the SS sent him back to work the ovens. Müller writes that he had not previously thought of suicide, nor did he do so again. Instead he did what he could to resist.

A month later, when two young Slovak Jews, Alfred Wetzler and Rudolf Vrba, escaped from Auschwitz with help from the camp's underground, they carried the names of SS officials, accounts of various transports, a label from a tin of Zyklon B gas pellets, and Filip Müller's map of the gas chambers and crematoria. That October, Müller participated in the *Sonderkommando* uprising; he escaped death by hiding in a crematorium chimney, which on this occasion was uncharacteristically free of smoke owing to a reduced number of transports, which had also signaled the *Sonderkommando* "selection" that had provoked the uprising. Müller's luck held. He lived to help dismantle Auschwitz and then in January 1945 was evacuated to Austria, where American troops liberated him.

Müller was one of thousands of Jews who survived the Nazi concentration camps. Thousands more had managed to hide or flee. In all, approximately one third of Europe's nine million Jews remained alive, but if the Nazi destruction process could not claim complete success, its impact was still devastating. A burgeoning literature of social-psychological research indicates that, while many survivors have exhibited an amazing resilience to make new lives, some excelling in their chosen careers and dedicating themselves to educate people about the Holocaust, most also must cope with "chronic or recurrent depressive reactions often accompanied by states of anxiety, phobic fears, nightmares, somatic equivalents, and brooding ruminations about the past and lost love objects."[30] However unjustified the feeling may be, deep guilt at having survived, when so many perished, is reported by some. Understandably, the children of survivors have their special difficulties in relating to their parents' experience and in securing their own identities.

The toll on Jewish children during the Holocaust itself was severe. From the Nazi perspective, their die was cast by the faith of those children's great-grandparents. No mercy could be shown to boys and girls thus targeted; they were the next generation of the population that genocide must eliminate. Thus, "Jewish children had to fend for themselves in a world so base no prior experience could have prepared them for it. . . . The percentage of Jewish children who survived this German infanticide is the lowest of any age group to have come out of the Holocaust alive."[31] One and a half million Jewish children under the age of thirteen lost their lives to the Nazis in the major killing centers at Chelmno, Belzec, Sobibor, Treblinka, Majdanek, and Auschwitz, and in the hundreds of labor camps that pocked the Nazi map of Europe.

What survival chances existed for those who entered the Nazi camps? Only a handful of Jews escaped death at Chelmno, Belzec, Sobibor, and Treblinka. These places were almost exclusively killing centers; they spared but a few Jews for work in running the camp. At Auschwitz and Majdanek, which had large industrial satellites, survival was possible only for those prisoners who had successfully passed an initial inspection. Overall, only about 10% of the arrivals, the most able-bodied men and women, were "selected" for labor instead of for immediate death. Jews sent directly to other labor camps could not expect much better odds. Typically, Jewish slaves endured for little more than three months before disease, starvation, random violence, or "selection" claimed them. What did make one's chances for survival better or worse were one's country of origin and when during the war one became a Nazi target. For those caught in the Nazi machinery, physical resistance never was a substantial impediment to death, quite the contrary, but beyond the requisite minimum of physical strength and health, certain qualities of spirit and character that enabled people to cope with extreme stress were also a factor.

Before focusing further on those personal dimensions, however, it should be underscored that the Holocaust required considerable support from the governments and peoples allied with or occupied by the Germans.[32] In no two countries were the responses of the non-Jewish populations to the Holocaust identical. Those differences materially affected Jewish fate. Where the Germans were effectively resisted, for example, the SS had neither the personnel nor the resources to eliminate the Jews by themselves. The greatest Nazi success in bringing about the extermination of the Jews occurred in Poland, Lithuania, Latvia, and the Ukraine. In these countries popular sympathy for the Final Solution was widespread; after the German invasion, moreover, no indigenous governments were permitted even a collaborationist role by the conquerors. That outcome precluded the official resistance that was attempted in countries where the Germans did not dismantle the indigenous governments.

Far removed from the 90% death rate, among Jews in eastern Europe was the fate of Jews under the Italian Fascists. Although allied with the Third Reich, Benito Mussolini's regime generally remained unresponsive to Nazi insistence that Italy deport its Jews. Only after Italy's surrender to the Western powers on 8 September 1943 and the subsequent Nazi occupation, which swiftly reinstated Mussolini as a Nazi puppet, were the Italian Jews placed in extreme jeopardy. Similarly, Nazi extermination plans met genuine resistance in France. Although the policies of the Vichy government—the puppet regime tolerated by the Nazis in an unoccupied zone of France—were openly antisemitic, its antisemitism was largely religious and "medieval" rather than racial and "modern." That regime relinquished foreign Jews but opposed handing over French Jews to the Germans. Moreover, once it became clear that all deported Jews were slated for extermination and that Germany had lost the war, the Vichy authorities began to sabotage the deportation of foreign as well as French Jews.[33] In Denmark, which had the advantages of advance warning of deportation roundups (the news was leaked by a high German official) and a receptive haven across the water in neutral Sweden, resistance ensured the survival of nearly all Danish Jews. In addition to Sweden, Spain and Switzerland were the other major European neutrals. Their political motives were not identical, ebbing and flowing with the tides of war. Neither were their policies about Jews consistent. Sweden tended to grant them sanctuary and even publicized the fact. Spain did not extradite Jews who entered illegally, but it did not offer sanctuary openly either. Although Switzerland was strategically situated to help Jews and actually contained the largest population of Jewish refugees among the three neutral states, its anti-Jewish policies were the most rigorous. In short, the willingness to receive Jews in these neutral countries was inversely related to the likelihood that large numbers of them would cross their borders.

Significant numbers of German and Austrian Jews survived because they had emigrated prior to the Final Solution. Those who remained were at severe risk precisely because they were under immediate Nazi jurisdiction. By contrast, though many perished in slave labor, Greek Jews were not deported until March 1943 when SS control became direct. The SS killing apparatus turned to Bulgaria in the following month. But that country, sensing a forthcoming German defeat, proved reluctant to turn its native Jews over to the Nazis. Antisemitism was rife in Rumania, where it took a heavy Jewish toll. Yet the Nazis never got full cooperation in organizing deportations from that country either. As the war began to turn against Germany in 1943, support waned among the Nazis' collaborators. The nature of the Final Solution was better known, which also reduced support for the Nazi dream of a *Judenrein* Europe, and pressures mounted to save healthy Jews for work.

The destruction of some four hundred thousand Jews living in wartime Hungary proved to be a tragic exception, but one that in no way contradicts the judgment that direct Nazi control was the most decisive factor in influencing Jewish chances for survival. The antisemitic Hungarians were willing to disenfranchise and pauperize the Jews and to permit pogroms. They also conscripted Jews into labor brigades and were willing to surrender foreign Jews to the Nazis. However, they were reluctant to participate directly in the outright extermination of their own Jewish populations. Thus, the decimation of Hungarian Jewry happened only after the Germans occupied that satellite in March 1944, when much Hungarian loyalty to Germany crumbled as Russian troops advanced westward. The degrees of local antisemitism and of governmental cooperation with the Germans were vital factors in determining Jewish survival. Most important, however, was the degree of direct Nazi power and in particular SS authority present in a given place. A German general might have enough clout to oppose SS deportation efforts, as happened in Belgium; but as the Dutch situation illustrates, mass populations of occupied territories, however much their decency might aid individual Jews, lacked the power to block Nazi objectives. Nor were those designs effectively hindered by the British, Soviet, or American governments, none of which "showed any pronounced interest in the fate of the Jews." Truly they had become a surplus people.

Sometimes regarded as fabricated atrocity stories, early reports reaching the West were often met with skepticism, downplayed, suppressed, ignored, or simply disbelieved. Nonetheless the Allies possessed trustworthy information about the destruction process months before they publicly acknowledged in December 1942 that the Jews were being slaughtered en masse. At that time, the Allies were preoccupied with the invasion of North Africa, and the Americans in particular had to rally their forces after a series of military disasters in the Pacific. But even after those mitigating circumstances are taken into account, the abandonment of the Jews remains. Some Russians would have had no regrets about Auschwitz; others were too preoccupied with their nation's own survival to care. As for the British and the Americans, "publicity about the mass murder seemed undesirable, for it was bound to generate demands to help the Jews and this was thought to be detrimental to the war effort."[34] Thus, these governments adhered to a policy that the war against Germany must be their top priority. A corollary to that point was that any special missions on behalf of the Jews would be a diversion from the most critical goal and would even weaken solidarity at home by creating suspicion that somehow this was a "Jewish war." Thus, when Joel Brand, a leader of the Jewish rescue committee in Hungary, obtained an agreement from Eichmann and Himmler in the late spring of 1944 to exchange a million Jews for ten thousand trucks, Allied pressure subverted the deal on the grounds that such negotiations would strengthen the enemy.

The American record in rescuing Jews surpassed that of England, the Soviet Union, and the other Allies. That result depended largely on the War Refugee Board, established by President Franklin D. Roosevelt on 22 January 1944, which helped save approximately two hundred thousand Jews. It also must be said, however, that concerted American efforts early on could have rescued thousands more. That possibility was thwarted by widespread antisemitism and anti-immigration sentiment in American society, as well as by the indifference of political leaders and in particular the refusal of the President to speak out. Bowing to political pressures generated by government officials John W. Pehle, Raymond Paul, and Josiah E. DuBois, Jr., who had documented a State Department record of distorted messages, sabotaged proposals, and general procrastination where Jewish plight was concerned, Roosevelt finally brought the WRB into existence. Even then, the board was underfinanced. Ninety percent of its costs had to be covered by Jewish contributions. Incidentally, less than a thousand Jewish refugees were actually brought to the United States by the WRB. They were long detained under less than desirable conditions at a camp near Syracuse, New York, on the shore of Lake Ontario.[35]

Meanwhile, the first of several American air reconnaissance missions over the Auschwitz area occurred on 4 April 1944. Some of these aerial photographs showed lines of naked Auschwitz prisoners waiting their turn to enter the gas chambers, but military attention riveted on the more central points of interest: German industrial plants under construction at Auschwitz's Monowitz component. Later that year—on 20 August, 13 September, and 18 and 26 December—hundreds of five-hundred-pound bombs were dropped there by American bombers of the 15th Air Force. Acting on the Vrba-Wetzler report, there had been repeated pleas during the spring and summer of 1944 from persons such as Dr. Gerhart Riegner, who represented the World Jewish Congress in neutral Switzerland, that the rail routes to Auschwitz and the gas chambers and crematoria themselves should be targeted. Many of these pleas reached the Allied governments. Logistical problems in undertaking such missions, moreover, were not insurmountable. The Allies now had air supremacy over Europe. Hungary was being bombed almost daily. Although the Allies fire-bombed Dresden, annihilating more than one hundred thousand civilians to no military purpose, they decided to leave Auschwitz alone. A few well-placed bombs would have disrupted normal operations there and bolstered prisoner morale, but this was not the first time during the war that the Allies rebuffed Jewish pleas.[36]

On 12 May 1943, for example, Shmuel Zygielbojm took his own life in London. Shortly after the Nazi occupation of Poland in 1939, this Socialist member of Warsaw's first *Judenrat* proposed that a labor pool be organized so that when the Nazis requisitioned workers, the quota could be supplied with a minimum of chaos and violence. By November, he may have reconsidered the wisdom of his proposal, for he argued that new Nazi orders to form a ghetto in Warsaw should be resisted. Unable to win support, he fled Poland two months later as the Gestapo tried to track him down. Finding his way to London, he became in early 1942 one of the Jewish members of the Polish government-in-exile. There he sought Allied military support for the ghetto uprising in April 1943. Getting none, he elected to join his fallen Warsaw friends and to leave behind a farewell letter which concluded: "By my death I wish to make my final protest against the passivity with which the world is looking on and permitting the extermination of the Jewish people."[37]

The degree to which that passivity even extended to the non-European Jewish world, it should be added, remains a controversial subject on which the last word has yet to be declared. Even the 1984 report of the American Jewish Commission on the Holocaust, a panel of distinguished American Jews, chaired by former U.S. Supreme Court Justice Arthur J. Goldberg, debates about which Jewish groups were most active and effective on the American scene, and what they did or failed to do about the Holocaust. In summarizing the commission's report, however, Goldberg and Arthur Hertzberg did make an observation on which all parties could agree: "No matter how able the leaders of a small people may be in calling attention to its danger, there has to be someone out there willing to listen, who has the power to act. The human tragedy in the twentieth century, and in those before, is that moral altruism is rare among the wielders of power."[38]

The indifference encountered by Shmuel Zygielbojm helped to keep the transports rolling to the labor and death camps. Once selected to work inside them, Jews had to bank on their own resources, however meager those might be. A more individualized account of what they experienced follows in the discussion of Holocaust literature (Chapter 9), but some general conditions were common to all those who struggled to endure the camps. By Nazi design, few of these, unfortunately, were matters over which any individual had autonomy. Age, sex, health, and profession, for example, could all make a difference. Reprieve from immediate death came most often to healthy males between the ages of sixteen and fifty. If one could lie successfully about one's age, that might help. More decisive was something harder to control, namely, did one look strong, able, and relatively young? Special skills could be advantageous, permitting one to do less physically draining work. Here, too, an ability to bluff was helpful. Yet even if one had special skills, they gave no assurance of safety. Work assignments were often completely arbitrary. Prior to any of these considerations, of course, would be the issue of the type of camp to which one was sent. Deportation to Auschwitz meant better odds of survival than assignment to Treblinka. Better still was to be sent to a camp outside Poland altogether. Such judgments are relative, of course, because much also depended on when a person arrived; whether work was indoors or outdoors, heavy or light; how benign or brutal the *Kapos* (prisoner-overseers) might be; whether one had opportunities to "organize" (steal) extra food or goods that could be traded; whether one could fight off debilitating disease or pass the periodic selections that kept the death count rising. All along the line—though never more than in the type of camp to which one was sent and in the initial decisions of the SS slave labor selectors—life and death depended on matters of chance.

Eyewitness testimony and later research both indicate that a primordial instinct for life—the will to live—was also a vital factor in survival. Like resistance, it is easy to romanticize this quality by assuming that all people will fight for their lives no matter what. Such is not the case, however. Nor will it do to qualify survival of the Holocaust by adding a prefatory "mere." In a situation where the willful destruction of life is the norm, the grandeur of death dissolves. Dying was no triumph in Auschwitz but to survive was virtually miraculous, not only because the chances against survival were so great but also because survival depended on a yearning for life, intensified by despair, that was transformed into determination. Apparently survivors rarely think of themselves as heroes. More than one has observed that the best people in the camps did not survive, a view supported by Salmen Lewental, who was a member of the last Jewish *Sonderkommando* in the gas chambers at Auschwitz. Among the comments found in a manuscript he buried—it was unearthed in 1962—are these: "There was a time in this camp, in the years 1941–42, when each man, really each one who lived longer than two weeks, lived at the cost of lives of other people or on what they had taken from them."[39] The survivors passed through hell. Saying that they "merely" survived implies a moral objection but one dysfunctional in Auschwitz because it would hand the Nazis an even greater victory. Those who forestalled that outcome by surviving achieved something irreplaceable and indispensable: they refused to let the killers have the final word.

Life can become unbearable, emotionally disengaged, so that one no longer can or cares to struggle. Withdrawn and detached from their own lives, those referred to in the camps as *Musselmänner* went through the motions of living until their weak, emaciated bodies ceased functioning altogether or until they were selected for the gas. Prisoners learned to discern the look of those who had in effect passed beyond and given up struggling to live on. Those who retained that drive could never be sure that experience would not push them to the breaking point. Even less could they count on their will to live as an insurance policy to guarantee survival. The functional significance of this trait meant an unusual sensitivity and constant alertness to capitalize on any opportunity that might better one's chance for life. Adherence to the codes of conventional morality was a luxury that camp life did not usually afford. Prisoners sometimes stole from each other as well as from Nazi storehouses. At times they killed each other and collaborated with their captors. There are some reports of cannibalism, too. The Nazis intended camp life to be degrading, and it was. Yet the camps were not simply jungles in which might made right. Within the camps, for example, the inmates devised their own system of survivor justice. If many acts normally prohibited were tolerated, prisoners who spied for the Germans or stole food from other prisoners were not likely to survive the discovery of such deeds. Individuals were sustained by family members who lived on, by friends—both old and newly made—by relationships based on nationality, religious or political persuasion, and even by the occasional good will of an SS guard or a member of the surrounding native population. Determination to remember or to avenge the dead and refusal to forsake the living clearly made a difference. Indeed one Jewish survivor-psychiatrist holds that "it was those people who were capable of showing interest in others who, mentally, had the best chance of retaining their individuality—and perhaps also of surviving as integrated persons."[40]

If a person did not go straight to the gas chamber, survival in Auschwitz and other camps was possible only if one could adapt—physically, psychologically, and above all quickly—to rationally organized savagery. Overwork, malnutrition, and despair often took their heaviest toll during the first few weeks. The first reaction to the camps upon arrival has been described as one of extreme fright. At the initial selection, more than 80% of the new arrivals at Auschwitz were driven to the gas chambers. Thus, in addition to the necessity of adjusting to a radically dehumanized environment, the surviving inmates were usually compelled to cope with the sudden loss of all family members. The trauma of arrival was commonly followed by a state of acute detachment in which the prisoners saw themselves as disinterested observers in a terrible drama over which they had little control. This detachment can be seen as a defensive mechanism by which the individual sought to master the initial fright. For those "condemned to life," the next stage involved an almost total withdrawal of affect from those areas of human activity that were not absolutely indispensable to survival. Feelings such as compassion for others, concern for personal appearance, and sex commonly gave way to a solipsistic concern for sheer survival. Yet another element in successful adaptation was the inmates' capacity to adapt to total degradation without personal disintegration, and in this dimension interpersonal relationships often made the difference.

The prisoners were not bound together by common loyalty to an ideal or to a leader. Each seeking to live, they were less a cohesive group than a crowd. Cooperation and comradely feelings were not precluded, indeed they were often essential for life, but the most fundamental fact was that the SS had absolute power of life and death over the inmates. It is no surprise that in extremity the inmates' responses were typically individualistic. Stripped of so much personal autonomy—even defecation required permission—prisoners not only underwent a radical narrowing of feeling but frequently regressed from a higher to a lower stage of personality development. Some tended toward identification with the SS, imitating their modes of behavior and values. In its more extreme forms, this tendency was found among some *Kapos* who had "adjusted" so totally to camp life that its ways were the only reality that remained for them. Their horizons became limited to making their "real life" more bearable. Such total resignation to camp life, however, was not the typical response among those who survived. While making the adjustments that were necessary for life at all, they resisted equating reality with the camp alone.

Those lucky enough to pass the first selection and subsequently strong enough to endure their initial disorientation and debilitation often gathered new wits about them. They learned to understand the camp's routines and to anticipate its dangers. A favorable work assignment and friendly contact with older prisoners—not easily achieved because the arrival of new inmates often preceded selections from among the old prisoners—seemed to reduce the likelihood of death for several months, provided always that chance was on one's side. But then the mortality rate soared again. The long-term effects of gradual starvation plus the accumulated effect of an experience that was never free from brutality, filth, disease, suffering, and selection—except perhaps for moments of sleep—made it seem that rescue would never be in time if it would come at all. Physical strength and psychic energy waned together. No one could be sure that theirs would be sufficient to endure indefinitely the crushing Nazi regimen, which was intended to produce despair. The Nazis envisioned no emancipation for these Jewish slaves. All of them were to become corpses. Yet these doomed men and women still held out. "They might make it, they probably won't, but they will not stop trying"—that attitude, along with good luck, made it possible for liberating armies to find the living among the dead.[41]

The Role of the Survivor

Hitler succeeded in destroying prewar Jewish life in Europe. His killers laid their hands on Jews of every type and from every region: unskilled laborers from Lithuania and craftworkers from Greece; doctors from Paris, lawyers from Berlin, writers from Vienna; shopkeepers from Holland and farmers from Poland; from Hungary and Rumania, from everywhere, Jews of all ages, of diverse political outlooks and religious persuasions. The toll did not cease as the camps in eastern Europe were closed down by advancing Soviet troops. Hundreds of thousands lost their lives during forced marches into German territory. Even after the camps at Buchenwald and Bergen-Belsen were liberated in April 1945, indeed after Germany's surrender, the Holocaust continued.[42] Too weakened to reclaim their freedom, former prisoners died in "displaced person camps" after being liberated from the Nazi concentration camps.[43] Others could not outlast the British blockades that prevented their entry into Palestine. Some perished in a postwar pogrom in Poland when the ancient charge of ritual murder unleashed anti-Jewish violence in Kielce during July 1946. Still others doubtlessly have had their lives shortened because neither body nor spirit can recover unscathed from the deprivation, disease, and despair produced by those earlier years.

The figures are imprecise, but an estimated two hundred thousand Jews were liberated from the Nazi camps in 1945. Thousands of other survivors who had been in forced labor, with partisan groups, or in hiding were also freed from Nazi power. If most of them tried at first to return to their former homes, typically little was left to find. Thus, many of the survivors headed for Palestine. Entry was difficult everywhere, but large numbers also found their way to the United States and Canada. Each one has had to cope with the past; none has done so in exactly the same way.[44] Initially many remained mute about the Holocaust. and some still are. Yet persistently and even increasingly many others have agreed that the role of the survivor is to testify. Early on, some of this testimony was critical in legal proceedings against Nazi leaders, including Nuremberg and the controversial Eichmann trial in Jerusalem. On other occasions, and perhaps even more painfully, Jewish survivors have witnessed for and against each other in adjudicating charges of collaboration brought against members of the *Judenräte*, ghetto police, and other Jewish leaders.[45]

Reluctance to speak about the Holocaust diminished among survivors after Israel's Six-Day War in June 1967. Once more extermination threatened Jewish life. That threat, plus the ensuing Israeli triumph, seemed to have a cathartic, therapeutic effect in releasing many survivors from silence. As a result, testimony takes on greater urgency as the time approaches when the last eyewitness of the Holocaust will be a survivor no longer. In recent years the urgency to testify has also been intensified by a proliferation of writings and conferences purporting to show that the Holocaust never happened. Antisemitism remains alive and well, and one of its more recent wrinkles is the allegation that talk about the Holocaust is part of a Jewish-Zionist plot, deviously designed to win sympathy and support that will enhance Jewish domination of the world. The Holocaust began with similar words, and words can kill. Painful though it may be to dignify such charges by responding to them, perceptive survivors know that they cannot allow denials of the Holocaust to be uttered without rebuttal.

One of them, Elie Wiesel, the 1986 Nobel Peace Prize winner, has written an eloquent, impassioned "Plea for the Survivors." Again and again, he points out, survivors have had to testify because "they were placed in the position of having to defend their honor and that of the dead." This predicament arose not because of extreme revisionist denials of the Holocaust, but rather because of more ordinary insinuations: "Why did the victims march to the slaughterhouse like cattle? . . . Why did *you* remain alive, *you* and not another?" If one was not there, contends Wiesel, one cannot fully understand what happened. At the very least, therefore, he asks for some humility from those who at a distance try to analyze and appraise what the survivors did or did not do. The Holocaust, he thinks, must be "studied more and more, in all its forms and all its expressions." No important question should go unasked, but his point is that unless honesty and sensitivity infuse each other the hope of even partial understanding dissolves. More than a few survivors make that plea their own. Wiesel, it should be added, does not claim that being a survivor confers complete understanding of the Holocaust either, for survivors confront a special enigma, namely, not being able to account fully for why they were spared:

> They knew they had had nothing to do with it. The choice had not been theirs. Intelligence, education, intuition, experience, courage—nothing had counted. Everything had been arranged by chance, only chance. A step toward the right or the left, a movement begun too early or too late, a change in mood of a particular overseer, and their fate would have been different.[46]

Along with the millions who did not escape, their fate would also have been different if non-Jewish resistance to National Socialism's antisemitism and policies of population elimination had been more effective. So in concluding our reflections on the Holocaust's victims and survivors, let us think again about power and powerlessness.

Remorse, Guilt, and the Victim as Nonperson

At the end of World War II, the National Socialist state collapsed. Survivors of a very different kind, many of those directly involved in subjecting the Jews and other victims to abusive slave labor and extermination, were captured and brought to trial. It is not surprising that former SS officers expressed no remorse. In general, they claimed that they had merely obeyed orders. The only crime they could envisage would have been disobedience, not mass murder. However, in addition to SS personnel, some of the most important and respected German industrial leaders were brought to trial for knowingly and voluntarily employing death-camp slave labor under conditions which were so abusive that the average victim died within three months. Utilization of slave labor was no isolated phenomenon. It involved many of Germany's most important corporations, such as I. G. Farben, Krupp, Bayer, Allgemeine Elektrizitäts-Gesellschaft (AEG), Siemens, and Telefunken. After the war, some of the business leaders were sentenced to long prison terms for "crimes against humanity." Nevertheless, within five years not a single convicted industrialist remained in prison. They were released and restored to their positions of leadership in German industry.

If the convicted industrialists had any sense of regret, there was a simple but concrete way they could have expressed it. Thousands of former slaves had survived the war. Some had sought token compensation from the corporations that had enslaved them. Invariably, the corporations refused to pay any compensation whatsoever. The victims then turned to the courts. Many of the proceedings dragged on into the 1960s. Some of the corporations finally agreed to token payments. For example, former slaves at the Auschwitz plant of I. G. Farben received no more than $1,700 for their ordeal. Most former slaves received far less. One world-class billionaire, Friedrich Flick, whose industrial empire included the Mercedes automobile corporation, adamantly refused any payment until the day he died in his ninetieth year.[47]

Even when payments were finally made, the corporations invariably insisted that the settlement include the statement that the corporation acknowledged no legal responsibility. Perhaps the most depressing aspect of the entire story is that even after their restoration to positions of leadership and prosperity, the German industrialists expressed little regret for what they had done, even though they were directly and knowingly involved in the deaths of tens of thousands of concentration camp inmates. In their attitudes, if not in their party affiliations, these men proved themselves to be unrepentant National Socialists into the eighth and ninth decades of this century.

How shall we understand these men who in their daily lives were not sadistic brutes but respected business leaders of their community during the period of National Socialism and afterward? There is no evidence that in their personal lives they were men of exceptional evil. On the contrary, within their own community, they were obviously capable of winning enduring respect and loyalty.

It would appear that these men felt no remorse because they regarded their victims as wholly outside of their universe of moral obligation. This was the condition of all of Germany's wartime enemies to some degree, but no group was more remote from any conceivable German universe of obligation than the Jews. Even before the modern period, Jews were regarded as aliens who were outside of Europe's "sanctified universe of moral obligation." This type of moral universe has been defined by sociologist Helen Fein as "that circle of people with reciprocal obligations to protect each other whose bonds arose from their relation to a deity or sacred source of authority." According to Fein, a necessary though not a sufficient condition for genocide is the definition of the victim as outside of a dominant group's universe of obligation.[48] Whatever residual sense of shared humanity linked the Jews to their neighbors before World War II tended to disappear under the murderous pressures of that war. During the war, Europe's Jews were considered alien to the universe of obligation not only of the National Socialists but of almost all peoples of the earth. This was evident in the refusal of all countries to give even temporary shelter to more than a token number of those whom Hitler had condemned to death. Put differently, *during World War II Europe's Jewish victims were considered "nonpersons."*[49]

Originally, the *persona* was the mask worn by actors in the ancient theater. Without a *persona* one could not play a part in the theater's highly artificial environment. Eventually, the *persona* took on political meaning and became the mask one wore in the artificially constructed environment of the theater of politics. A person was a being possessed of legal rights, hence a juridical person. Slaves and women were not regarded as full persons because they had no right to a voice in the life of the community.[50] Aristotle, for example, characterized the slave as an "animate tool."[51] It was, of course, clearly understood that slaves were biologically human, a fact dramatized in the frequent sexual encounters between masters and slaves. Nevertheless, whether human beings are regarded fully as persons has less to do with biological than with political and legal conditions. Individuals who belong to no community willing or able to protect their rights may be biologically human but politically they are nonpersons. Similarly, members of every group that has endured genocide in the twentieth century were effectively stigmatized as nonpersons before their final travail. Before or concurrent with their travail, they were deprived of their political and legal status as members of the community in which they lived.[52] This was as true of the Armenians in Turkey during World War I as it was of the Jews of German-occupied Europe during World War II and the Vietnamese boatpeople after the Vietnam War.

Although more innocent victims have been legally murdered in the twentieth century than any century before, the phenomenon of the innocent victim has a long and bloody history. Human sacrifice is an important manifestation of this phenomenon. One American demographer, Woodrow Borah, recently calculated that the Aztecs sacrificed about two hundred and fifty thousand human beings or about one percent of their total population every year.[53] Practical as well as religious motives explain this gargantuan slaughter. The Aztec Empire was a cannibal empire whose elite made up for their protein deficiencies with the flesh of human victims after the completion of the sacrificial ritual. Commoners were prohibited from eating the flesh of human sacrifices. Nevertheless, it was not the Aztec custom to offer up members of their own polity as sacrifices. The victims had to be strangers taken in war. Aztec warriors who captured enemy prisoners were given permission to consume sacrificial flesh even if they were commoners. This privilege served as an obvious incentive to effective military performance.

After a successful war, the Aztecs tended to withdraw from enemy territory instead of incorporating it into their own empire. For example, the Aztecs frequently made war on the Tlaxcalans, whose territory was wholly surrounded by the Aztec empire. Nevertheless, the Aztecs made no move to conquer the Tlaxcalans. Cortes, the conqueror of Mexico, was puzzled by this behavior and asked Montezuma why he refused to consolidate his empire. The Aztec ruler replied that, since the Aztecs did not normally eat their own people, they required nearby populations upon whom they could prey. The Tlaxcalans thus provided the Aztecs with a veritable human stockyard from which they could obtain both their flesh and their sacrificial offerings.

Given the cannibalistic nature of the Aztec system, it would have been impractical for the Aztecs to incorporate the Tlaxcalans. Had they done so, they would have had to make some arrangement guaranteeing the Tlaxcalans the minimal human rights enjoyed by subject peoples. Pariah status is one such arrangement. Slavery is another. The Aztec system required a steady supply of human beings who were regarded as entitled to no human rights. The problem was solved by preying upon rather than conquering the Tlaxcalans and other weak neighbors. The Tlaxcalan captives shared a fate common to almost all innocent victims: in the Aztec world they were nonpersons.

There is a resemblance between the attitude of the German business leaders toward the Jewish captives whom they worked to death in their factories and the Aztec attitude toward the captives they utilized as sacrificial victims and as a mass source of protein. In both cases the captives were regarded as a human stockyard wholly at the disposal of their captors. This is illusrated in an incident recounted by Primo Levi, an Italian Jewish chemist who was enslaved by the Germans at the Auschwitz factory of I. G. Farben. As a dazed, thirsty, and confused new slave at I. G. Auschwitz, Levi reached out a window to slake his painful thirst with an icicle. An SS guard immediately snatched away the icicle. Levi then made the mistake of asking the guard *"Warum?"* "Why?" *"Hier ist kein warum!"* "There is no why here!" answered the guard.[54] In a society of total domination, no explanations are due nonpersons. Such individuals are kept alive only as long as they are deemed useful; their elimination is not considered murder.

George M. Kren and Leon Rappoport have written extensively on the subject of the victim as nonperson. They have observed that when a victim is targeted for destruction, as were the Jews in World War II, the fact that she or he is objectively innocent of wrongdoing can actually put that person at an enormous psychological disadvantage. The victim's first response is likely to be a futile attempt to prove innocence. Seldom does the victim comprehend that *justice is a political category before it can become an effective moral category*. There is no justice in the state of nature where life incessantly preys upon life. Only as a member of a humanly constructed, political community—that is, only as a full person—is it normally, but by no means always, possible to find some measure of justice.

When victims experience the shock of discovering that, whatever their ability, training, or previous status, they have been stripped of normal human status and have become nonpersons, they are unlikely to understand the most salient fact about their condition: Absent some means of altering their political status, nothing they say or do is likely to be of any consequence. *"Hier ist kein warum!"* As Kren and Rappoport point out, the predicament of the nonperson was prophetically dramatized in Franz Kafka's novel *The Trial* more than a decade before the National Socialists came to power. In the novel, "K," the protagonist, is arrested without cause, accused of an unspecified crime by unknown accusers, and judged guilty by an unseen judge. When executed, his last words are "Like a dog," signifying his total loss of human status and the meaninglessness of his death.

Religion has attempted to overcome the contradiction between the biological and political definitions of being human by asserting that all human beings are equally beloved by their Creator. While in theory all persons are regarded by the biblical religions as children of a divine Creator, in reality no religion has been effectively capable of extending its universe of obligation beyond its own believers, at least in times of extreme stress. Thus, Jews were never full persons in Christian Europe. Baptism was Christendom's ritual of entry into full personhood. The literature of Christianity vacillated between seeing the Jews as destined to become full persons when they finally converted and seeing them as incarnations of the devil. What this literature could not accord Jews was the status of full persons. Moreover, Christianity was not alone in this denial. By ascribing to themselves the role of an elect nation, chosen by God for a biblically certified eschatological mission, by rejecting connubium with those among whom they lived, and by refusing to share common food at a common table, the Jews rejected the role of actors in the theater of politics among the peoples of Christendom. Let us remember that what is at issue in our discussion is not biological but political status. One cannot, after all, be a full participant in a political life of a community while refusing to partake of a common table or to offer one's sons and daughters in marital union with one's fellow citizens. Moreover, the Jewish liturgy contained a profound rejection of political community. One cannot fully participate in the life of a community while praying that the time may come when God will take one to one's proper home elsewhere.

The above is said without any ascription of blame to either Judaism or Christianity. Actually, the Jewish yearning to return to their ancestral homeland, expressed throughout the prayer book, and the doctrine of *Galut*, which held that Israel was in exile among the nations, probably constituted the only appropriate response to a situation in which Jews could cease to be alien only by ceasing to be Jews. Nevertheless, the doctrines of both Judaism and Christianity had the practical effect of denying to Jews the status of full persons in political life. What was not understood until World War II was that the price of this denial could be mass extermination.

Confronted with the threat of extermination, the most fortunate potential victims are those with the material and psychological resources to become full persons somewhere. Status can be changed by flight to another community in which the potential victims have the possibility of being treated politically as persons. This option was successfully taken by those German Jewish refugees who emigrated to the United States in the 1930s and eventually became American citizens. People can also become full persons by the intelligent and successful use of political and military force. Apart from those who are able to emigrate to a community in which they can become citizens, only those nonpersons who have the power to create a political community in which they can *effectively define themselves as persons* can hope to overcome their negative status.

A state is, above all, that institution which possesses a monopoly of force within a given territory.[55] Normally, a group can only establish a state and achieve such a monopoly by the use of force and violence to eliminate competitors. Thus, only after Algerian violence compelled the French to withdraw from their land were the Algerians able to create their own state and become full political persons. Similarly, only after the Israelis defeated the Arab armies that sought to deny them statehood in 1948 did they cease to be potential victims and become full persons in the political sense of that term. The 1982 massacre of the Palestinians in the Sabra and Shatilla refugee camps after the PLO armed forces had withdrawn from Beirut was evidence that the Palestinians had ceased to be full persons in Lebanon. Lacking a community prepared to defend them, they immediately became prey to those who sought totally to eliminate the Palestinian presence there. It is a doleful fact of human existence that personhood, functionally defined as the right to play a role in the theater of politics, cannot be divorced from considerations of power. It is normally the fate of human nonpersons to be powerless in the face of those who would use or eliminate them.

In the final analysis, human beings are reduced to the status of nonpersons by a want of power. Typically only those nonpersons who can somehow acquire power have any hope of extricating themselves from their negative condition. This can best be understood by concentrating on the humanly constructed nature of political order. If the ultimate foundation of any political order is the possession of a monopoly of force within a given territory, then membership in a political community implies having a share in that force, either by directly wielding it or by having an undoubted claim on its protection. Lacking such shares of power, people easily become vulnerable targets—functionally speaking, they became nonpersons. For example, as the American frontier moved westward, even the weakest white settlers had a share in the power of the United States that no Indian tribe could match. Indian resistance proved insufficient to prevent the United States government from dealing with that population as it willed. Likewise, although it was of enormous symbolic consequence for the future, Jewish retaliatory violence in wartime Europe offered little hope of practical success. Only after the war did the surviving Jewish victims have the hope of establishing themselves as full political persons by creating, through the use of force, their own state.

The lack of remorse on the part of Germany's business leaders, and a very large number of other Germans and Austrians, after World War II can thus be seen as part of a larger phenomenon. Feelings of guilt and remorse are as much political and social as they are psychological. Especially in times of threat and danger, they are likely to be experienced only if one harms those who are part of one's own universe of obligation. No such feelings are likely to arise if one harms those for whom one feels no obligation. On the contrary, one is more likely to feel gratification for damage done to an enemy.

The late Benjamin Nelson succinctly described the evolution of modern civilization as a moral journey from "tribal brotherhood to universal otherhood." Inherent in the modern predicament is the attrition of the sense of mutual obligation even among members of the same community. Put differently, the progress of modern life has involved the progressive depersonalization of human relationships. Insofar as the religions of the West have taught that all men and women are the children of one sovereign Creator, they have sought to reverse the process of depersonalization and to enlarge the human universe of moral obligation so that it includes all of humanity. The experience of the Holocaust and of its victims and survivors in particular is one more reminder that the ideal remains unrealized. In reality, the practical consequence of the Holocaust and the other manifestations of large-scale demographic violence in our era has probably been to make its realization both more urgent and, at the same time, more problematic.

PART THREE

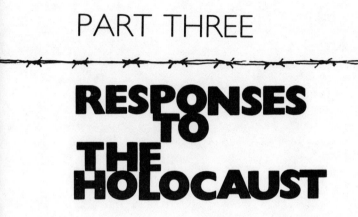

RESPONSES
TO
THE
HOLOCAUST

Chapter 7

Their Brothers' Keepers? Christians, Churches, and Jews

Cain quizzed God: " 'Am I my brother's keeper?' " According to the biblical story (Gen. 4:1–16), this firstborn of Adam and Eve did so in reply to God's inquiry concerning the whereabouts of Abel. Despite the ignorance implied by Cain's response, Abel's location was well known to them both. His blood crying to God from the ground, Abel was dead, murdered by his brother out of envy because he found favor not granted to Cain. God cursed Cain: " 'When you till the ground, it shall no longer yield to you its strength; you shall be a fugitive and a wanderer on the earth' " (v. 12). Then God marked Cain for life so no one would kill him, and Cain departed to the east of Eden. Jewish and Christian histories repeat that sibling rivalry, typically inverting the relation of elder to younger brother so that most often Christian Cains have slaughtered Jewish Abels. Thus it was during the Holocaust when Cain's question tested every Christian. Its indelible mark remains, and not least because the Holocaust provides a test case for contemplating what religious persuasions are likely or unlikely to accomplish when state power is bent on implementing programs to eliminate surplus people.

"If we claim to be Christians there is no room for expediency. Hitler is the Anti-Christ. Therefore we must go on with our work and eliminate him whether he is successful or not."[1] Implicated in the July 1944 plot against Hitler, the author of those words, long a dissenter against National Socialism, was hanged by the SS at Flossenbürg on 9 April 1945 only days before Germany surrendered. Dietrich Bonhoeffer is frequently named to show that within Germany there was Christian resistance to the Third Reich. That resistance was not only individual but also institutional, for Bonhoeffer helped to lead the Confessing Church (*Bekennende Kirche*) that battled the Nazis and the accommodation of German Christianity to their policies. Among its membership, and in other segments of the German population as well, courageous men and women made strenuous efforts to stem the tide of antisemitism, to save Jewish families, and to strive for amicable relations between Gentiles and Jews, even if such efforts cost their lives. Once entrenched, however, Nazi totalitarianism was extremely hard to dislodge from within. It was easier to "go along." Most Germans did. The courage of dissenters in the churches, schools, and universities, and in the circles of business and government itself—this chapter and succeeding ones will contain numerous illustrative examples—stands out as all the more remarkable. By reminding people of the difficulty of stopping state-sponsored population extermination once it is underway, their witness invites reflection that drives home anew how imperative it is that people care for one another.

The German people were not uniformly rabid Jew-haters. Nor did Hitler come to power primarily because he advocated making Germany *Judenrein*—least of all by using gas chambers and crematoria. Hitler and his cohorts, obsessed with racial hatred and a murderous historical mission, nevertheless found the support they needed to assume dictatorial control of the German state and its population. Approaches to Auschwitz followed. They did so partly because most Germans were normal people. Unfortunately, normal people are not particularly heroic. Imperfect, they usually worry about themselves and their families first and about others—especially if the others seem alien—last if at all. The compliance of normal Germans therefore helped Hitler target and dispatch defenseless persons by the millions. By contrast, opposition to Nazism by Bonhoeffer and other Germans was indeed heroic, all the more so as one recognizes that theirs was a minority example.

As a Christian, Bonhoeffer did not stand alone. In Germany a chorus of Christian dissent could be heard. Yet it was comparatively small, its timing off, its voice on "the Jewish question" erratic or faint. As Hitler rose to power, an overwhelming majority of Germans could be called baptized Christians. Not all were practicing believers, let alone authentic followers of Jesus, but Germany was at the heart of Christian civilization. Only a small percentage of Germans would have denied a Christian identity. Indeed, despite Protestant-Catholic tensions, that identity did much to foster the sense of German community. Far from opposing Hitler, most German Christians welcomed and trusted him. Their allegiance, moreover, was not offered in spite of his Jew-hatred but at times even because of it. Probably because they thought the claim incredibly exaggerated, their fidelity to the Reich was not shaken when leading Nazis such as Martin Bormann, Hitler's closest associate, paraded openly what Hitler believed but prudently downplayed, namely, that "National Socialism and Christianity are irreconcilable."[2]

Christian resistance to the Reich was excised by Nazi persecution. That generalization is valid, but more accurate, claims one Christian scholar, is the acknowledgment that "*apostasy* not *persecution* is the key word" in assessing why German Christians did not resist Hitler more effectively.[3] Religiously equivalent to treason, apostasy occurs when people forsake their "loyalty to a community and its beliefs."[4] That definition admits that not all baptized Christians are necessarily authentic Christians. To say or do some things and not to say or do others is to renounce a religious identity even if one still claims to possess it. Such distinctions, however, depend on norms that legitimize differentiations between genuine believers and apostates. Rarely are those standards simply agreed upon or easily enforced. Certainly they were much disputed within Hitler's Germany. Yet today the consensus is that apostasy was rife among baptized Christians in Germany and elsewhere during the Nazi era. For example, anti-Jewish legislation, *Kristallnacht*, and the methodical *Einsatzgruppen*, not to mention Treblinka and Auschwitz, demonstrated that in Germany Christian obedience to the state usually transcended loyalty to God, faith in Hitler commonly superseded dedication to Jesus, and true worship typically lost out to unrepentant idolatry as masses turned to the false gods of pure blood, race, and culture. Not only in Germany, but elsewhere also millions of Christians did too little to thwart and too much to support a regime that would have sent Peter, Paul, Mary, and even Jesus to the gas chambers. Whether through failure to take Christian identity seriously, zealous commitment to a religion identified as Christian but fundamentally antithetical to Jesus' teachings, or some disposition in between, apostasy abounded in Christian civilization from 1933 to 1945.

Typically this indictment assumes that the rise of the Third Reich and the fall of European Jewry could have been averted if only Germany's baptized Christians had acted differently. To that "if only," others are commonly added: if only the Pope had responded differently, if only the Christians and churches in Nazi-dominated territories had reacted differently, if only Christian influence in the Allied nations had mobilized differently. Often inflected indignantly, these hypothetical, counterfactual quandaries deepen guilt feelings as they enlarge the scope of apostasy. But most of these impassioned "if onlys" allow observers to remain, ironically, on the surface. If Christian apostasy characterized much of the Hitler era, shock and outrage must not becloud how and why it happened.

"You Can't Be Both"

Hardly less than the nation as a whole, Germany's churches were demoralized by their country's defeat in World War I. Guided by a Lutheran theology that stressed obedience to legitimate political authority, the major Protestant communities had embraced the Kaiser's nationalistic war aims. Their members found an unanticipated surrender, its attendant economic upheavals, the Versailles Treaty, and the Weimar Republic, which was more imposed upon than welcomed by the people, difficult to reconcile with the messages they had heard from their religious leaders about God's will for Germany. The past troubled Germany's Roman Catholics, too.[5] Concentrated in Bavaria and the Rhineland, they comprised one third of the German population in World War I. Yet, in a land where nationalism emerged from Martin Luther's Reformation, this minority found themselves suspect. Allegiance to the Pope might compromise Catholic loyalty to the fatherland. In fact, their wartime dedication had been unswerving, but in addition to the religious disillusionment brought on by the Kaiser's loss, Catholics still had to deal with Protestant discrimination.

Mainstream German churches faced a credibility problem. As perceptive as it was conservative, the dominant Christian leadership understood that nothing can be resurrected quite so well as a lost cause. The solution, therefore, was not far to find. It consisted of preaching a new version of an old gospel: nationalism. Germany had not been wrong. The justice of its cause, the appeal went on, was being vindicated in retrospect by the irreligious materialism and liberalism—often attributed to "Bolshevik" (i.e., Jewish) influences—that were poisoning the defeated nation. Christians should restore German purity and strength; hence Christian leaders emphasized devotion to the welfare of the German people, *das Volk*, and nationalistic aversion to Versailles, Weimar, and communism. One additional target helped the churches to recoup: Jews. Forms of the Christian religion, then, reasserted an ancient role. Joining with nationalism, economic pressures, and political yearning, they helped to build the attitudes that rendered Jews irreversibly redundant.

Although they uttered the obligatory warning that it was un-Christian to hate, during the Weimar period German church officials often stated that Jews disrupted the nation and threatened Christian civilization generally. Undergirded by claims that God's judgment was upon the Jews, such pronouncements did little to discourage the conviction that a Christian could be an antisemite without pangs of conscience. Nor did they curb violent outbursts of anti-Jewish racism. But some knew apostasy when they heard it. Witness one protest from 1928: "We are persuaded that the anti-Semitic movement, which in the aftermath of the World War has had so mighty a boom, is irreconcilable with the Christian point of view and is incompatible with our debt of gratitude to the cradle of Christianity."[6] Two of the twentieth century's leading theologians, Karl Barth and Paul Tillich, put their hands to that statement. Voices like theirs were too few, however.[7] Dismissed from the University of Frankfurt am Main in 1933 for opposing Nazi regulation, Tillich emigrated to the United States. Two years later Barth took refuge in Switzerland. Their departures punctuated what would become increasingly obvious. Most Christians and churches in Germany were on a course parallel if not identical to Hitler's. Racialized and radicalized though they might be, Hitler's anti-Jewish measures had roots in traditional Christian antisemitism. Hence the Nazis and many of Germany's Christians would hold common aims: to segregate the Jews from the rest of the population; to eliminate them from positions of influence in business, the arts, and the professions; to make them emigrate or, failing that, to subject them to involuntary apartheid through enforced ghettoization. Even after the facts were generally known, the Final Solution would stand above reproach by the silence that characterized nearly all of Germany's official church bodies.

Before 1930 most German church leaders paid little attention to Hitler. Even when events required sober recognition of his movement, few Christian leaders saw him as a serious threat. True, his speeches and methods were at times extreme; much of *Mein Kampf* was at odds with Christian teachings, too. But his party platform endorsed "positive Christianity" and "freedom for all religious denominations in the State so far as they are not a danger to it and do not militate against the customs and morality of the German race."[8] Ambiguities in those declarations were downplayed, for Hitler was known to be a Roman Catholic. If he lacked enthusiasm for the churches, neither did he assault them publicly. Evidently supporting their concern for *das Volk*, he professed need for help from Bavarian Catholics and Prussian Protestants to rejuvenate Germany. His nationalism and anticommunism, both inseparable from his antisemitism, persuaded more and more of Germany's Christians.

In the early thirties some Catholic leaders spoke openly about the incompatibility between Hitlerism and Christianity. Others explicitly instructed their followers not to join Hitler's party. If some welcomed his emphasis on racial purity, insisting only that it be achieved without use of immoral procedures, others were more skeptical, and at least one bishop refused the sacraments to known Nazis. This opposition nonetheless left the official Catholic stance as no more than one of reserve when Hitler became chancellor on 30 January 1933. Barely scathed by Catholic dissent, Hitler received an even friendlier welcome from the Protestants. Notably, it came less from small sects than from the Evangelical churches to which most German Protestants belonged.[9] The Jehovah's Witnesses, in particular, stubbornly refused to bow to Hitler; in return, the Nazis persecuted them ruthlessly. In contrast, the mainline Protestant churches not only sympathized with Hitler's political aims but at times also rewrote church doctrines to benefit Hitler still more, a step far beyond any taken by German Catholics. Among the "German Christians," as his most devout Protestant disciples came to be known, the Führer's program was a holy crusade. Hitler was God's man for Germany, the savior himself. Carefully avoiding religious entanglements that might prove embarrassing, however, Hitler withheld his full blessing from the "German Christians." By his reckoning, no Christian denomination had a future. "One is either a Christian or a German," he said. "You can't be both."[10] In due time he wanted to eradicate them all, but presently Christian support was useful. Although Hitler did not restrain completely the anti-Christian eruptions of Nazi extremists, at this stage he appeased Germany's Christians wherever possible.

Split into more than twenty independent regional organizations, including Lutheran and Reformed denominations, the Evangelical churches had been moving toward unification since January 1933. Abetted by Nazi manipulations, the "German Christians" controlled the church elections that July, and one of them, Ludwig Müller, became the first bishop of the Evangelical Reich Church. Their plan was to impose an "Aryan paragraph" without delay. Paralleling the anti-Jewish actions taken by the state in April, it would severely limit how Christians of Jewish descent could participate in church life. Led by Berlin pastor Martin Niemöller (who eventually spent years in concentration camps at Sachsenhausen and Dachau), opposition rallied. Fearful of dividing the church, the Nazi-controlled authorities could not enforce this aim. Recognizing that a church struggle would jeopardize national unity, Hitler further distanced himself from the "German Christians" by warning them that no religious group could presume to call on the state's support.

The opposition's victory was based not on an unequivocal rejection of antisemitism but on a defense of other Christians. Still, a line had been drawn. Soon a dissenting minority called the Confessing Church, including more than five thousand—about one-third—of the Protestant clergy at its peak in 1934, challenged the Nazi order. Although vacillation and political pressure reduced that figure, this Christian group significantly energized such German resistance to Hitler as there was inside the Reich. Its best known public testimony, the Barmen Declaration (May 1934), condemned "the false doctrine that the State, over and above its special commission, should and could become the single and totalitarian order of human life." Nor, the Declaration added, could the church become "an organ of the State."[11] Its implications were far-reaching, for the heresy of the "German Christians," against which the Declaration protested, was their embracing of Nazi antisemitism. Still, the Jewish question was not explicitly addressed. Practically speaking, the Declaration's major impact was to insist on confessional purity and to defend the church against state interference. For even in the Confessing Church there was mixed opinion about the Reich. By no means were all of its leaders thoroughly opposed to Nazi ways.

Thorough opposition to Nazism was characteristic of Karl Barth, major author of the Barmen Declaration and by any measure one of the first and most outspoken dissenters in Germany. The greatest Christian theologian of the twentieth century, he defined the meaning of Christianity in the tumultuous period that included two world wars. Although a Swiss national, Barth served as a professor in Germany from 1921 to 1935. In 1930, he accepted the chair of systematic theology at the University of Bonn. There he witnessed the closing years of the Weimar Republic and Hitler's assumption of power on 30 January 1933.

Unlike the vast majority of Germany's great religious leaders and theological minds, from the start Barth had no illusions about the pagan, anti-Christian nature of National Socialism and of the impossibility of any compromise with it. About his feelings on the day Hitler came to power Barth wrote: "[I] knew where I stood and what I could not do. In the last resort, this was because I saw

my dear German people beginning to worship a false God.'' With great pre-
science, Barth predicted that National Socialism would aim at the complete
eradication of Christian belief and expression, but that ''it could only move towards this goal . . . step by step, indirectly and in a variety of guises.''[12]

Barth was also unlike the vast majority of his theological colleagues for having publicly opposed the persecution of the Jews. On 10 December 1933, he
preached a sermon on the subject, ''Jesus Christ Was a Jew.'' In the hate-ridden
atmosphere of the time, Barth's simple act of reminding his church that Jesus
Christ was a Jew showed great courage. A number of the congregation's members left the church in protest against the sermon. Shortly thereafter Barth wrote
to a woman who was a church member that ''anyone who believes in Christ,
who was himself a Jew, and died for Gentiles and Jews, *simply cannot* be involved in the contempt for Jews and ill-treatment of them which is now the order of the day.''[13] Barth took part in the formulation of the Barmen Declaration
by which members of the Confessing Church insisted on the lordship of Jesus
Christ and, in so doing, placed important limits on the degree to which Adolf
Hitler could claim their loyalty. Later, in May 1967, Barth wrote to Eberhard
Bethge, a German clergyman and biographer of Dietrich Bonhoeffer:

> I myself have long felt guilty that I did not make [the Jewish] problem central,
> at least public, in the two Barmen declarations of 1934 which I had composed. In
> 1934, certainly, a text in which I said a word to that effect would not have found
> agreement either in the Reformed Synod of January 1934 or in the General Synod
> of May at Barmen—if one considers the state of mind of the confessors of faith in
> those days. But that I was caught up in my own affairs somewhere else is no ex-
> cuse for my not having properly fought for this cause.[14]

With the Nazi rise to power, all professors were required to open their lectures with the Nazi salute. This Barth refused to do. After the death of Paul von
Hindenberg on 2 August 1934, Hitler combined the offices of chancellor and
president. As a university professor, Barth was now required to take an unconditional oath of loyalty to the Führer. When Hans Naumann, rector of the University of Bonn, invited Barth to take the oath, Barth did not refuse but he
stipulated that he could be loyal to the Führer only within the limits of his responsibilities as a Christian. The National Socialist state was unwilling to accept
any limitation on the oath. Even so distinguished a Christian as Rudolf
Bultmann urged Barth to take it, but he would not. On 26 November 1934,
Barth was suddenly suspended from his university duties. The reason given was
that ''by his behaviour in office he has shown himself unworthy of the recognition, the respect and the trust which his calling requires.''[15]

During the rest of the academic year, Barth was subject to legal harassment
by the Nazis. The following academic year he accepted the position at the University of Basel which he held for the rest of his professional career. In Basel,
Barth became the chair of the Basel Committee of Swiss Aid for [Exiled] Ger-

man Scholars. He endeavored to facilitate the reception of Jewish refugee and other anti-Nazi scholars in other countries.

This Christian's record remained consistent. On 5 December 1938, for example, he responded to *Kristallnacht* by lecturing in Zurich on "The Church and Today's Political Questions," declaring that "anyone who is in principle hostile to the Jews must also be seen as in principle an enemy of Jesus Christ. Antisemitism is a sin against the Holy Spirit."[16] During World War II, Barth protested the German campaign against the Jews. On one occasion he visited Heinrich Rothmund, chief of the foreign division of the Swiss police, in Berne to appeal on behalf of a number of immigrant Jews. Rothmund was hostile to the admission of Jews even temporarily. Later, on the basis of information given him by Chaim Zvi Taubes, the rabbi of Zurich, Barth organized a petition to the federal councilor Ernst Nobs, pleading that the Swiss government take prompt action on behalf of Hungarian Jews who were in immediate danger of extermination.

Barth's courageous stand is noteworthy because of his role as the greatest Christian theologian of the twentieth century. From start to finish he understood the real nature of National Socialism and tolerated no compromise with it. If his was also a minority example, there were other members of the Confessing Church who tried to emulate him. Acting on their own on 4 June 1936, the ten members of the provisional board and council of the Confessing Church—Martin Niemöller among them—addressed a lengthy memorandum to Hitler. It tackled the issues of blood and race more explicitly than the Barmen Declaration had done. It stated that "when, within the compass of the National Socialist view of life, an anti-Semitism is forced on the Christian that binds him to hatred of the Jew, the Christian injunction to love one's neighbor still stands, for him, opposed to it."[17] It also protested against concentration camps, secret police methods, and other Nazi abuses. These protests were sufficient to endanger the lives of all who signed them.

It must also be said, however, that if the memorandum clarified how Christian conscience ought to resolve competing claims for obedience, it stopped short of disavowing antisemitism altogether. Moreover, the memorandum was not intended to be a public document. Only three copies of the final version were made. One was kept by Friedrich Weissler, a Jewish convert who served as a legal adviser for the Confessing Church. He gave his copy to Ernst Tillich to read. Meaning well, Tillich copied it, and, with Werner Koch, shared it with the foreign press. After the leak, the Confessing Church did publicly embrace the memorandum's contents. About a million copies of a pulpit declaration, summarizing the memorandum, were circulated. Shortly thereafter, Tillich, Koch, and Weissler were arrested and sent to concentration camps. Tillich and Koch were eventually freed, but Weissler's brutal treatment led to his death at Sachsenhausen on 19 February 1937, the Confessing Church's first martyr.

In the Protestant and Catholic communities alike there was concern about the increasing apartheid in German society, especially as it affected converted Jews and the partners in mixed marriages. But even this minority concern did not strike the core of Nazi antisemitism, which was actually strengthened when many church officials readily opened their baptismal registers to meet Nazi demands for proof of Aryan descent. Anyone who could not provide the necessary documentation was suspect. By participating in the crucial step of defining who was or was not an Aryan, the churches made the eventual destruction of the Jews easier.

What would have happened if the churches had not complied? Any study of the Nazi era poses that question repeatedly. A stand here, a refusal there—Hitler was alert to public feeling, and if there had been more small acts of Christian courage, large ones might have followed to prevent the Final Solution. The small acts were too few; big ones happened rarely. Unable to transcend their differences—some would rationalize the forthcoming extermination as divine punishment against the Jews for rejecting Jesus, others would regard it as doing the unpleasant but necessary dirty work that would make possible a purely Christian Europe—Christian leaders in Germany or elsewhere never rallied their congregations to make a unified, principled protest against the Nazis' fundamental Jew-hatred. Nor did decent rank-and-file Christians muster such dissent on their own. Hitler watched how Christians responded to his policies and tactics of terror. He learned that there was no need to fear them unduly.

Hindsight makes it easy, too easy, to denounce Christian apostasy in Germany. Indeed, such denunciation tends to say too much and too little. As Barth's testimony shows, for example, during the 1930s even the best Christian leadership in Germany usually felt no necessity to oppose Hitler's antisemitism in an uncompromising manner. In a word, most German Christians at the time felt no sense of apostasy because Jews were not considered as existing within the Christian universe of moral obligation. On the contrary, as alien outsiders of a special kind, Jews were not really the "neighbors" Christians ought to love. A barrage of Nazi propaganda and astute political maneuvers by Hitler did somewhat obscure the state's full intentions, but in addition Protestant leaders in Germany were neither theologically nor sociologically disposed to become prophetic critics of their state. Nor did their action or inaction appear in a vacuum, for these Christians were raised and trained in a milieu not entirely of their own making. To speak of the mass apostasy of baptized Christians in the Third Reich says too much and too little unless their conduct is seen on a continuum that stretches far back into the past. Barth, Bonhoeffer, and other clear-sighted Protestants knew that the churches had to draw a line somewhere with National Socialism, which was far more than a majority of Germans ever saw. But during the thirties few of them saw that the crucial line ought to be drawn over Nazi treatment of Jews. Not enough in their Christian heritage or individual thinking equipped them to make that judgment. In 1933, for example, even Bonhoeffer had observed: "Now the measures of the state towards Judaism in addition stand in a quite special context for the church. The church of Christ has never lost sight of the thought that the 'chosen people,' who nailed the redeemer of the world to the cross, must bear the curse for its action through a long history of suffering."[18] For all his efforts opposing Nazism and working to save Jewish lives, it is not clear that even Bonhoeffer himself totally rejected this anti-Jewish Christian tradition of the curse. Eventually Barth may have done so more clearly, but in 1942 he wrote, "There is no doubt that Israel hears; now less than ever can it shelter behind the pretext of ignorance and inability to understand. But Israel hears—and does not believe." In 1949, four years after the Nazi surrender, Barth continued to suggest that the evil that came to the Jewish people was "a result of their unfaithfulness," that the Jew "pays for the fact that he is the elect of God," and that the Jewish people are "no more than the shadow of a nation, the reluctant witnesses of the Son of God and the Son of Man."[19] Such testimony, which could be found even among the German Christian leaders who opposed Hitler most decisively, indicates that within Germany accommodation to Hitler was no weird, isolated aberration that could have been easily avoided. It was rooted in Christian and Jewish beliefs about covenant and divine election that had helped make Jews vulnerable for centuries. Failure is not thereby condoned, nor responsibility dissolved. Instead their webs extend and complicate.

Despite opposition by the Confessing Church, Hitler could increasingly control the Protestant churches. This he did through administrative shackles, intimidation, and violence. Thousands of Protestants were imprisoned during the 1930s, many in concentration camps. More than a few lost their lives. If such measures periodically discomfited even the "German Christians," by and large their enthusiasm for Hitler was unabating while the Confessing Church was driven more and more underground.

Meanwhile Hitler's relation to the Roman Catholic Church, potentially the more troublesome because it possessed an international structure that might resist Nazi nationalism, had been solidified by an early diplomatic triumph which solved that problem. Realizing that official recognition of Nazi authority by the Vatican could be politically valuable abroad as well as at home, Hitler also sensed correctly that the papacy would deem it wise to safeguard the church's status in Germany. In the spring of 1933, Nazi overtures were favorably received by the Vatican's secretary of state, Eugenio Cardinal Pacelli, a former papal diplomat to Berlin who was destined to become Pope Pius XII. The concordat signed that July accorded legal status and protection to the German Catholic Church and its organizations if—but only if—they were dedicated to purely religious activities. Neither before nor after the signing did the Nazis refrain from anti-Catholic pressure, and Cardinal Pacelli would soon claim that "a pistol had been pointed at his head.'' His alternatives had been either to come to terms with Hitler or to risk "the virtual elimination of the Catholic Church in the Reich.''[20] Allowing for rationalization by Pacelli, a mounting list of falsely arrested nuns and priests, closed convents and monasteries, and harassed parochial schools did move Pope Pius XI to issue a 1937 encyclical *Mit brennender Sorge*, which protested the church's difficulties and accused the Nazi government of violating its word, but overlooked the wrongs being done to the Jews. The Vatican never renounced the treaty, which is to say it never revoked its stamp of legitimacy on the Reich.

If Catholic policy did not facilitate the emergence of an equivalent to the Protestants' Confessing Church, nonetheless there was resistance to Hitler among German Catholics, much of it against Nazi attempts to isolate young people from the church's influence. Though the church spoke out here and elsewhere, it rarely criticized Hitler directly. Constantly on the defensive, Catholic power within Germany was no match for his in the ensuing battle. Some reasons why can be seen by studying the career of Munich's Michael Cardinal von Faulhaber. One of the better Christian leaders of the day, he attacked the Nazi glorification of race and was persistently and publicly condemned by the National Socialists for refusing to ratify their programs. Even so he did not disavow Hitler; nor was he primarily concerned with defending the Jews. The Nazis capitalized on his ambivalence.

Ardent nationalist, defender of Germany's cause in World War I, Faulhaber received his red hat in 1921. Never enthusiastic about the Weimar Republic, he was also uneasy about Hitler's growing power. Even if the Cardinal was pleased by the concordat of 1933, he quickly realized that Hitler would obey it only as seemed expedient. Yet, while speaking against Nazi persecution of his church, Faulhaber found Hitler credible when the Führer stressed the shared concern of the Reich and the church to overcome communism. The Nazis benefited again when the prelate instructed his bishops to congratulate Hitler for safeguarding international peace by signing the Munich Agreement. Though not the most outspoken cleric, Faulhaber complained about the Nazi euthanasia program in 1940, but four years later he deplored the attempt on Hitler's life and reaffirmed his personal loyalty to him. As for his relationships with the Jews, Faulhaber's theological training made him an expert on Jewish Scripture, and he publicly denounced Aryanized Christianity as intolerable. Still, his theology contained elements of the "teaching of contempt." and it cannot be said that he vigorously defended Jewish rights and lives against the Nazi onslaught.

Catholic leaders with different insights and greater courage did exist. One was Father Bernhard Lichtenberg. He prayed openly for Jews at his Berlin cathedral, which made him a marked man, and he joined Bishop Clemens August Graf von Galen to lead the anti-euthanasia campaign. Lichtenberg perished en route to Dachau. His fellow priest, Alfred Delp, was hanged for his resistance.

Bishop Galen became one of hundreds of Catholic clerics among the half million Germans who found themselves imprisoned. That company included Catholic laypeople such as Gertrud Luckner and Grete Wunsch, arrested for spearheading Caritas Catholica, an organization that distinguished itself by helping Jews in many countries. Rarely, however, could German Catholics of any kind say that they were threatened primarily because they made Jewish need their chief concern.

On the Protestant side, some clergy helped Jews flee, most notably Berlin's Dean Heinrich Grüber, who was sent into Dachau when such assistance was banned in 1940.[21] But overall the Protestant and Catholic records in this area were the same. Lutheran Bishop Theophil Wurm defended Jews in letter after protesting letter to leading Nazis, including Goebbels, Himmler, and Hitler himself. Bonhoeffer, too, continued to speak for Jews. Yet even within the Confessing Church there were relatively few public outcries in support of them. Vilified by Nazi propaganda, fearful of reprisals, at times traumatized by the violence—paper and physical—that swept from the Nuremberg Laws to *Kristallnacht* and beyond, forthright dissenters against antisemitism and indifference to Jewish peril became understandably fewer and farther between. Other concerns had priority. Once the nation went to war, pressure mounted to avoid national disunity. If anything, that pressure became even stronger as the tide turned and the German homeland was ravaged.

Contrary to some expressions of righteous indignation, from a purely historical perspective it is neither shocking nor even puzzling that in Germany "nothing was done by either church, except on a purely fortuitous and individual and clandestine basis, on the greatest crime of all: the setting up of Death Camps and the murder of six million Jews."[22] Yet that judgment cannot be the last word. Clearly, for example, pressure brought to bear by Christian leaders did influence Hitler to curtail his euthanasia program, albeit not before he had executed thousands of "defective" persons. Clearly, too, early Christian resistance to Hitler was sufficient to signal that serious doubts about Nazism were in order. More than one choice was open to Christians who gave Hitler their support. They were not inexorably compelled to follow him. No doubt some swore loyalty to Hitler knowing they had forsaken Christian principles, but the tragedy beyond is that, in spite of Protestant and Catholic dissent, so many did so without the slightest feeling that they had betrayed their religious identity. On the eve of World War II, "95 percent of the eighty million people of the greater German Reich were still registered as members of the Catholic or Evangelical churches, and even the majority of the three million Nazi party members still paid the church taxes and registered themselves as Christians."[23] Clearly, had German Protestants and Catholics rallied together against Hitler in the thirties, Auschwitz would have remained inconceivable. But most of these folk were of no mind to hinder Hitler. Even when he battered Christians and churches, most

German Christians still obeyed him. Why would one expect them to do otherwise when his primary targets were Jewish outsiders?

The best time to oppose Hitler decisively was in the first half of the thirties. Disastrously, those years were also the most ambiguous ones for discerning what his power would bring. Hitler himself did issue warnings to Christians—his hatred toward the Jews was already on record—but the signs of the times were blurred. Not well read, they were even less heeded. Before the best leadership realized it, events had gone too far.

After the collapse of the Third Reich, Martin Niemöller observed that German Christians had "let God wait ten years." His famous personal statement does much to sum up why Nazism got its way so long.

> First they came for the socialists, and I did not speak out—
>   because I was not a socialist.
> Then they came for the trade unionists, and I did not speak out—
>   because I was not a trade unionist.
> Then they came for the Jews, and I did not speak out—
>   because I was not a Jew.
> Then they came for me—and there was no one left to speak for me.[24]

Germany's baptized Christians could and should have behaved differently. Still, the charge of apostasy that rightly follows ought to stand in perspective. Given the German economic and political situation plus that nation's Christian tradition, teaching, and current leadership, the allegiance that Germany's Christians gave to the Third Reich, far from being unthinkable, was rather natural. What ought to be surprising is not that so few of them came to the Jews' defense but that some did. If that assessment is valid for the thirties, it is even more so in the context of World War II. Once war began, the possibility remained that Christians in Germany could avert the Holocaust. Unfortunately, that possibility was far more theoretical than practical. Sound appraisals of other Christian communities that witnessed the Holocaust can be no different.

Politics in the Vatican

Germany's Christian opposition to the Reich and its anti-Jewish policies was muted by a religious tradition that stressed obedience to political authority, a devoutly nationalistic spirit, a typically human proclivity to conform rather than to risk trouble from the state, and a widespread attraction to the anti-Jewish course that Hitler set for the nation. Hence the German churches remained largely compliant to Hitler's wartime aims. What about Christian dissent against Nazism elsewhere, specifically dissent against the destruction of the European Jews? That question swirls controversy around the Vatican, center of the Roman Catholic world. One reason is that Catholic more than Protestant Christianity involves a hierarchical organization culminating in a single leader, the Pope. It is tempting, therefore, to assume the following: if only the Pope had emphatically condemned the Final Solution, Catholic obedience would have derailed the approaches to Auschwitz; and because this scenario never materialized, apostasy is obvious, especially since Roman Catholic power overall was far less Hitler's captive than that of the churches within the Reich itself. Closer inspection reveals greater complexity than this facile reasoning acknowledges. That complexity does not eliminate apostasy. Yet it would have been highly unusual if either the Pope personally or the Vatican as a whole had performed differently during World War II.

Note initially that the Pope's place is unique in Christendom, for he heads both a church and a state. Once the papacy dominated politics as well as piety. Though small today, its earthly domain still symbolizes that the Pope's spiritual authority has standing in worldly matters, too. But ironically, far from enhancing papal inclinations to speak and act boldly, the pontiff's political role compromises them. For example, the Lateran Treaty (1929), which established the present Vatican City, recognized the papacy's right to exercise moral influence. It also specified that the Vatican, a collective term designating the church's official leadership as it is embodied in the papacy and the hierarchy centered in Vatican City, "remains and shall remain outside all temporal rivalries between other States . . . unless the partisans in dispute make jointly appeal to its missions of peace." The Pope's problem, then and now, is that in wearing two-hats-in-one he must assess the political status of the moral and spiritual pronouncements made by himself directly or by his official Vatican representative. How scrupulously any given Pope adheres to the constraints of political neutrality varies with circumstances and personality. Yet the Pope's dilemma exists: his authority is not as a single individual but as the head of a church. Power is conferred by that position, but its trappings make the Pope less than free.

Furthermore, recall some additional features of the prewar situation. The Vatican signed a treaty with Hitler early on; then found to its dismay, though not to its total surprise, that the agreement would not be honored; offered protests about the violation of the concordat but let the pact stand and with it the legitimacy of the Nazi state. That legitimacy was endorsed, moreover, because Hitler successfully portrayed the Reich as a bulwark against communism, which the Vatican feared much more than Nazism. Nurtured by and presiding over a church in which antisemitism had been endemic for centuries, neither Pope Pius XI nor certainly Pope Pius XII, the two pontiffs who witnessed the Holocaust's onset and fury, represented a version of Christianity that would have inclined them naturally to make defense of Jews a top priority. Their most trusted advisors in the Vatican or elsewhere were products and representatives of the same teachings. Collectively these religious officials were primarily concerned about the welfare of their Catholic followers. They believed that direct, thoroughgoing opposition to Hitler and his anti-Jewish policies would not serve those interests well. Available in its entirety only recently, the record of wartime diplomatic exchanges between the Vatican and the Pope's emissaries in various European capitals between 1939 and 1943 shows that this conviction did not change fundamentally during the Holocaust.[25]

Pius XII reigned throughout World War II. Believing that diplomacy was the papacy's best way to exert influence, he also interpreted the Lateran Treaty conservatively. Under his rule, political neutrality characterized the Vatican even as it employed diplomatic channels to advance moral and spiritual aims. The delegates of Pius XII, then, were to foster relations between recognized governments and the church, to report on the church's condition in those regimes, and to facilitate the church's work. The latter task can be interpreted to imply that Vatican diplomats were to work in a spirit of Christian service to meet as far as possible the just needs of all people in their host countries. Everything depended, though, on what was perceived as possible.

During the war, the Vatican retained diplomatic posts in European capitals such as Berlin, Rome, Bratislava, Budapest, and Bucharest. Although they performed many of their tasks well, it can be said that "the Vatican diplomats only rarely acted on behalf of Jews as Jews, and this usually only for specific individuals. They sometimes had words of sympathy for the Jews, but little action followed from these words."[26] The diplomats faithfully reported discrimination against Jews to their superiors in Rome. They also protested racial laws if those decrees harmed Jewish converts or violated the church's prerogatives. Nazi prohibitions on intermarriage, for example, drew opposition, though less for their racist quality than for the church's desire to fend off governmental interference. Additionally, the church frequently sponsored emigration for converted Jews. By defending the rights of baptized Jews, Catholic authorities implicitly rejected the Nazi ideology that labeled Jews sub- or nonhuman. In few cases, however, did the implicit become explicit. No evidence indicates that Vatican diplomats protested the fundamentally racist nature of the Nazi decrees. Instead, more than one Catholic diplomat saw providence in the Nazi onslaught, for it led some Jews to save their lives by conversion. Others saw racial legislation as reducing Jewish influence that could be detrimental to Christian society. In short, Vatican diplomats were not immune to antisemitism.

Deportations of Jews were also reported to the Vatican, the diplomats' reactions to their own testimony varying with situation and disposition. Some intervention occurred nearly everywhere but sporadically, apologetically, and even reluctantly. Nowhere was the diplomats' condemnation greater than where Nazis invaded church rights. On the whole these men were well-intentioned, not malevolent. Nor should one suppose that their efforts alone could have stopped the deportations or changed the fate awaiting Jews in death camps. Yet they did far less than was possible, not nearly as much as one's ideal image of a papal diplomat might require. That evaluation, however, cannot stand without qualification. For like all diplomats, these men were to serve their superiors.

The wartime Vatican diplomats reported to Luigi Cardinal Maglione, who served as the Vatican's secretary of state until he died on 22 August 1944. Afterward Pius XII acted as his own foreign minister, which fits with other evidence suggesting that the Pope ultimately controlled the Vatican's war policies. Maglione's diplomats followed his lead. He defended church rights and Jewish converts, at times intervening personally on behalf of the latter and showing thereby that he implicitly rejected the principles of Nazi racism. Yet nothing in the diplomats' lack of protest about the basic injustice of racial laws contradicted Maglione's position either.

A similar pattern existed where Jewish deportation was concerned. Here Maglione dictated no overall strategy. The varied behavior of his diplomatic corps reflected the mixture of instructions he sent out. Directions to intervene were issued from the secretary's office, but they were not motivated primarily by the conviction that Jews themselves were being fundamentally wronged. Maglione's chief concerns were to protect baptized Jews, to denounce the immoral purposes (mainly prostitution) for which he feared the Jewish deportees might be used, or to avoid embarrassment for the church.

The destruction of the Jewish people got little of Maglione's attention, though not for lack of information about it. Already by the summer of 1941 he had reports about mass murder. Flooding in from many places, they became better documented as months passed. Nonetheless, Maglione, who was long known for his caution, stated as late as December 1942 that the testimony could not be verified. It might be Allied propaganda. When appeals still poured in, Maglione's personal response and his instruction to the diplomats were to emphasize that "the Holy See has done and will continue to do all possible for the Jews."[27]

Maglione did not do all that was possible. But to clarify that judgment, the unused options available to him as Vatican secretary of state must be measured. Short of resigning in protest, a gesture probably as futile as it was unlikely, essentially there were two: he could have delivered a strong, unambiguous condemnation of the crimes against the Jews, doing so within the context of established diplomatic relations; or, he could have underscored his denunciation by breaking diplomatic relationships with the offending powers. Moral denunciation would not have diverted the Nazis from Auschwitz for long if at all, but the breaking of diplomatic relations would have reduced somewhat the respectability Hitler received from their continuation. Yet every sign indicates that the Vatican considered representation in the Axis bloc so important that it never seriously entertained the option of using a diplomatic break to express moral protest. Short of severing diplomatic relations, Maglione could have used his diplomatic corps to make a more resounding protest against Nazi policies, but in assessing that option, some additional points must be made.

In several areas where vast numbers of Jews were destroyed—Poland, Lithuania, Russia, for example—the Vatican had no diplomats. Prior to the mass murder of the Jews, either the Nazis or the Soviets had expelled the Vatican's emissaries. Even more telling, it is unlikely that Maglione would have taken strong actions on behalf of the Jews without explicit instructions to do so from his superior, Pius XII. The soundest inference is that such instructions were not given. It is hard to imagine, however, that the Pope's silence worried his secretary. To illustrate, in the late summer of 1943 Maglione declared that the fate of Christian Europe hung in the balance of the struggle the Nazis were waging against Communists in the east. Receiving the German ambassador a few weeks later, he stressed that the Vatican had acted "so as not to give to the German people the impression that it has done or wished to do the least thing against Germany during this terrible war."[28] At worst, Maglione thought that stopping communism was worth the price of Jewish annihilation; at best, he placed a higher priority on diplomatic relations with Germany than on Jewish survival. When he opposed Zionism and yet was miffed that Jews were not more appreciative of the Vatican's efforts on their behalf, his actions were not out of character.

Pope Pius XII left little in writing about the duress of the Jews under Hitler. In tone, however, the typically brief and scattered references in his speeches and letters do reflect the man: formal, restrained, dispassionate. If he wanted the church's local representatives to use their own discretion in responding to the Nazis, the Pope's instructions to that effect usually counseled prudence not boldness. Asserting that everything permitted and indicated by the circumstances had been and would be done, he urged that a lack of restraint would invite further evils. For the most part silent personally, this Pope preferred diplomatic channels for handling "the Jewish question." He and his secretary of state were in contact daily, and Maglione's diplomatic records reveal that their contents were discussed with the Pope. There can be little doubt that the policies of the secretary of state toward the Jews bore the stamp of Pius XII. He set the course of speaking out when the church's interests were at stake and of holding back when the fundamental injustice to Jews was the issue. He placed a premium on reserve, caution, and maintenance of diplomatic relations with the powers that sought to obliterate the Jews. To do otherwise—especially to lift his own voice to impose ecclesiastical sanctions on the oppressors, to excommunicate Hitler, or even to incite Catholic disobedience to the Führer—would neither have been in character nor have struck him as expedient, let alone right.

Before becoming Pius XII, Eugenio Pacelli spent twelve years in Germany, a time he called the best of his life. Significantly, his duties stationed him in Munich during a critical period, the year after World War I ended. In the chaos of that era, a series of left-wing Jewish leaders attempted ineffectually to bring about an enduring socialist revolution in conservative, Catholic Bavaria. The brief episode ended in a right-wing bloodbath, the effects of which were unfortunately enduring. Pacelli himself had been harassed by troops of the Munich Soviet, and Cardinal Faulhaber was detained by the leftist regime, too. One is tempted to speculate that Pacelli's Munich experience helped to shape his wartime view that National Socialist Germany was Europe's bulwark against godless bolshevism. His experience may also help to explain his wartime silence on the extermination of Europe's Jews, a program about which the pontiff had excellent information. In any case, Pacelli's love for Germany never made it easy for him to criticize that nation bluntly. Unemotional, at home in the language of diplomatic ambiguity, Pacelli ascended to the papacy as an inheritor of problems and attitudes that did little to make him a crusader for Jews. At least since the French Revolution, for example, the Catholic hierarchy felt its authority threatened by various liberal, anticlerical movements—communism was only the most recent—and the fires of its theological antisemitism were stoked by perceptions that Jewish influence in these movements was considerable. Always concerned to protect its own influence, the Vatican could hardly find it religiously, and certainly not politically, natural to make protection of Jews a top agenda item, least of all when its own sense of geographical isolation was exacerbated by the Fascist regimes of Mussolini and Hitler, whose treaties with the Vatican appeared to count for little.

Survival seemed to dictate a prudent form of dissent. Nor was silence, however pained, unthinkable. Far from assuming that he could speak from strength, Pius XII accented the liabilities of protest, the dangers of letting neutrality be damned. Even had he been by nature more disposed to redress Jewish suffering, those impulses would have succumbed to worry. Personal denunciations might not deter the Nazis but impel them further and faster toward their murderous aims. Church members, especially those under Hitler, might disobey the Vatican if pressed too far, thus weakening instead of strengthening the church. Any aid for the Jews might be rendered more difficult, not easier, if he broke his own silence. Pius XII could not dismiss any of these worries as obviously lacking foundation. Thus unfolded politics in the Vatican during the Holocaust. The record still cannot quash indictments of apostasy, for as Christ's deputies, Pius XII and his prelates were on the whole too timid, too worried, too little like their Savior not to betray him and his Jewish people. Yet their performance invites another response, one less judgmental but equally profound. It is sadness—sadness that those with religious power were not bolder, that political circumstances did not permit more room to maneuver, and that a long history, not an accident, granted just those persons authority and those circumstances existence so that catastrophe could strike.

The Boundaries of Obligation

As Jews were "defined, labeled, stripped, isolated, stored, shipped," they were increasingly excluded—intentionally by the Nazis and their collaborators and at least functionally by most other communities—from circles in which people honor reciprocal responsibilities to protect each other.[29] As far as Germany's churches and the Vatican's policies were concerned, such an exclusion was illustrated by the fact the Christians did protest Nazi encroachments when Christian lives were at stake, though imperfectly even then, but threats to Jews tended to be observed silently. Determination to care for one's own and to ignore or even to harm others in the process is natural, but other forces work within human existence, too. Among them are moral and religious traditions that raise questions about the boundaries of obligation. "Am I my brother's keeper?" is one of those questions. "Who is my neighbor?" is another.

Jesus explained that his Jewish way had two essential elements: to love God and to love one's neighbor as oneself (Luke 10:26–28). For anyone who claims to be a Christian, a follower of Jesus, loving one's neighbor as oneself defines the boundaries of obligation. Hence it is critical to know how to answer the question, who is one's neighbor? Jesus deftly turned that question back on its asker with a parable about a Good Samaritan who cared for a defenseless victim who had been robbed, beaten, ignored by religious leaders, and left to die. Jesus' implication was that the Good Samaritan "proved neighbor to the man who fell among the robbers" (Luke 10:36) because he let *need*—not race, nationality, class, or creed—define his universe of obligation. A Christian is to emulate the Good Samaritan's compassionate service. True Christians will never say that they do so completely. They confess shortcomings, even willful failures, which is why they ask God to strengthen their resolve to keep trying. So it bears repeating: not all Christians are Christian. Authentic ones try persistently to be the Good Samaritan. Many others call themselves Christian, but that identification is inauthentic to the extent that they ignore the expanded boundaries of obligation suggested by Jesus. Of such narrowness apostasy is made.

It is fantasy to presume, however, that fully authentic Christians and churches could have prevented Auschwitz. Their numbers have always been too few. Numerous, however, were the less than authentic Christians who made possible the establishment of a powerful Christian culture hostile to Jews. They could have prevented the Holocaust, for in reality they were indispensable in bringing it about.

Sociology confirms these suspicions.[30] Both in percentages and in gross numbers, the degree of Jewish victimization in various European states correlates directly with the prevalence of prewar antisemitism in those places. Where antisemitism was intense, public cooperation in targeting Jews was easier, help for Jews scarcer, and Jewish evasion more difficult than in states with lower levels of anti-Jewish feeling. Yet there are problems in assuming that those correlations imply cause and effect. In virtually every case it is equally clear that whenever the Nazis chose to maximize their efforts, the Jewish death rate was staggering. Consider Poland: of its 3.3 million Jews, 90 percent perished. Add in Germany and Austria, the Ukraine and other Russian territories where the *Einsatzgruppen* roamed at will, Hungary after the Nazi occupation in 1944: there are more than another 1.5 million Jewish deaths. Whatever inferences one draws about the levels of antisemitism in those areas, the Nazis had vast power to enforce boundaries of obligation that excluded Jews totally. That authority crumbled only as military might intervened from the outside. In only a few European countries did more than 50% of the Jewish population escape. Most of the two million Soviet Jews who survived were in areas not conquered by the Nazis. In the other cases, church-supported resistance played a part. Denmark and Bulgaria provide the two most striking examples, but their peculiarities make generalizations problematic.[31]

Less than 1% of the total population, Denmark's eight thousand Jews were thoroughly integrated into that nation's life. Nothing would convince the Danes that their Jews were an undesirable, alien presence. The predominant Lutheran Church made it clear that Jews and Christians were members of a single religious family; it was incumbent upon Christians to include Jews in their universe of obligation. Thus, just as Denmark's churches castigated Hitler's antisemitism in the thirties, when the Nazi roundups got under way in the forties, Danish Christians made good their solidarity with Jews by helping to ferry them to Sweden where nearly all found refuge. The Danes' performance is undimmed by the fact that demography and geography aided them in resisting the Final Solution effectively. But those favorable circumstances do invite pause before one jumps to conclusions about the degree to which similar wartime determination, even if practically conceivable, would have been successful in other locales.

With fifty thousand Jews inside its immediate prewar border (among a population of more than six million), Bulgaria had been relatively free of anti-Jewish discrimination during the early decades of the twentieth century. Neutral at first, this Balkan state became a Nazi satellite primarily to regain territory lost after World War I. Soon Bulgaria felt pressure to legislate against and then to deport its Jews. In response, the head of the dominant Bulgarian Orthodox Church rejected Nazi racism, underscored that God alone had the right to punish Jews, and intervened personally to bolster Bulgarian reluctance to deport them. This action came too late to save fourteen thousand Jews living in territory newly annexed by Bulgaria, but most of the Jews in "Old Bulgaria" survived. Unlike those in Denmark, the Bulgarian Jews were not highly assimilated. Yet in both cases cultural, religious, and political solidarity existed between Christians and Jews. Resistance to deportation worked. That it did so in Bulgaria's case, however, cannot be divorced from recognition that the Nazis never took full control of the government as they did in Hungary, whereupon 70% of a huge Jewish population was destroyed in less than twelve months. One can ask: what would have happened after the Nazi occupation if Hungarian attitudes toward Jews had been more like those of the Bulgarians? One can also ask: how sustained or effective would Christian solidarity with Jews have been if the Nazis had brought their full force to bear in Bulgaria?

Correlating high ecclesiastical influence and low percentages of Jewish victimization, Denmark and Bulgaria were the brightest spots, but in neither situation is it easy to determine how far Christian conviction to help Jews stimulated similar cultural convictions or vice versa. What is clear is that in other places where Christian commitment motivated relief for Jews, the overall performance warrants mixed reviews. To illustrate, consider responses from the preeminent churches in some other European states. In western Europe, the Dutch Reformed Church as a whole remained passive while fierce Nazi pressure eliminated 75% of Holland's Jews. In Norway the Lutheran Church refused to pledge loyalty to the Nazi puppet, Vidkun Quisling, and although unable to stop deportation of Norwegian Jews to Auschwitz, it issued an open protest against that action. If those steps alerted some Jews and encouraged the Norwegian resistance to aid them, still only half of Norway's eighteen hundred Jewish people escaped. The Nazis were less successful percentage-wise in France and Italy, but in France the Roman Catholic hierarchy was certainly not unified in opposition to the elimination of Jews, while in Italy a more consistent Catholic distaste for Hitler's genocidal campaign probably reflected anti-German cultural convictions more than pro-Jewish religious ones.

Further east, the archbishop of the Greek Orthodox Church supplemented his petitionary appeals with liberal distributions of baptismal certificates to fleeing Jews and with instructions to priests and people to assist Jews when the Nazis hit Athens. Such measures were impotent to save even one quarter of the Greek Jews. The head of the Rumanian Orthodox Church spoke out against deportation in a country riddled with antisemitism, but if that effort helped to arrest the death rate, still three hundred thousand Jews perished, mainly at the hands of the Nazis' Rumanian allies. If many Hungarian Jews remained alive as late as 1944, that outcome was due less to the charitable power of the dominant Roman Catholic Church than to Hungarian officials' calculation that the outright annihilation of their Jews would bring no appreciable gain. From distant Turkey, apostolic delegate Angelo Roncalli, who would later become the much-loved Pope John XXIII, provided baptismal certificates to rescue some Hungarian Jews, but when the Germans occupied Hungary, the hierarchy there said even less than the Vatican instructed in protesting the ensuing deportations. With few exceptions, the record was hardly better elsewhere, and in some cases it was much worse. A Nazi satellite created in March 1939, Slovakia, for example, was ruled by a Roman Catholic priest and political party. Under them, Slovakia deported some sixty thousand Jews. The Vatican did protest, but no sanctions were threatened against the priestly leadership of the state. Nor did Pius XII ever make explicit that it was a sin for a Catholic priest to cooperate in delivering Jews to the Nazis. "The misfortune," lamented another Vatican official, "is that the President of Slovakia is a priest. That the Holy See cannot bring Hitler in line all can understand. But that [the Pope] cannot curb a priest, who can understand that?"[32] Less that 20% of Slovakian Jews survived.

Antisemitism abounded, and where it did not, Nazi violence impeded public opposition by the major churches. Nevertheless, some correlations still hold. Where the churches resisted there were fewer Jewish victims. Where church officials spoke out against Nazi policies, Jews had more success in evading their enemies. Where significant church protest was found, state collaboration with the Nazis was checked. Likewise, when church protests were minimal or absent, such collaboration went unarrested. When both church and state maintained solidarity with Jews, the yield of victims was lowest of all. Had these correlations been more widespread, Nazi success would have been far less. Realistically, however, there is not much reason to think that the churches involved were likely to act differently than they did.

So far, this analysis of Christian responses to the Holocaust has focused on Europe. What was the reaction of churches in the United States? Typical accounts of American reaction acknowledge that silence prevailed. Then they go on to explain that trustworthy information was lacking and that the geographical regions involved were sufficiently remote to situate Holocaust rumors far from the center of American consciousness. Auschwitz, after all, was an out-of-the-way place in eastern Europe, obscured by global combat that took heavy American casualties in the Pacific as well as in western Europe.

Recent scholarship does little to change the view that silence prevailed in the United States, but it also makes clear that one loophole, a simple appeal to ignorance, must be closed. That judgment holds not only for the American government but also for American Christianity. Important studies done by Robert W. Ross and David S. Wyman use the activity of the Protestant press as a point of reference. Their findings disagree. Ross contends that "the whole story" of the Holocaust appeared "extensively, continuously, and often comprehensively in the American Protestant press."[33] Challenging Ross's handling of the data, Wyman contends that the coverage was "hardly extensive." A more apt judgment, he believes, is that "the bulk of the Protestant press was silent, or nearly so."[34] The collision of these analyses, however, gives little comfort to those who would simply plead ignorance where the Holocaust was concerned. Degrees of awareness no doubt varied considerably, and ignorance may have been a legitimate claim in many individual cases, but in general American Protestants—especially those in leadership positions—were not uninformed. Although not always on the front pages, reports about Nazi treatment of the Jews had been carried in the American press from the beginning of the Third Reich. By November 1942, and regularly thereafter, authenticated information about the Nazi extermination of the Jews was made public in the United States. One way or another, silence prevailed in spite of knowledge, a proposition valid for American Catholics as well.

If silence and accompanying inaction, but not sheer ignorance, were the norms for American Protestants where the Holocaust was concerned, it is also true that some Protestant leaders and groups, frequently sustained by support from American Jewish agencies, worked hard to arouse a meaningful response. Their achievements, however, make it possible to list shortcomings that warrant consideration, for each failure debunks the ease with which one can speak of "massive actions or interventions" to obstruct the Final Solution and punctuates the difficulty of actually launching them.[35]

What Ross regards as a failure to persuade is at the heart of the matter. It involved the issue of getting Christians who knew what was happening to give the Jewish plight priority in their concerns. Usually their priorities fell elsewhere: early on to the persecution of the churches and later on to the war effort overall. In themselves, Hitler's constant anti-Jewish pressure and his eventual annihilation of the Jews never became even a third or fourth order of business for American Protestants generally. The extent to which one interprets that outcome as a "failure," however, depends on several variables. They include an appraisal of what people, Christian or not, are most likely to do; an assessment of what they ought to do; and particularly in this case a reaction to the Christian understanding that sin is commonplace. Uncontestably, even when people believe that God's will enjoins them to love their neighbors as themselves, precious few do so persistently; and even when they do, their neighbors rarely seem to be among those they are prejudiced against. That such circumstances ought not to exist is a truth matched only by the fact that what is and what should be are usually far apart. There was a failure to persuade when American Protestant leaders confronted their fellow Christians with the Holocaust. To hold that such failure differed from what could be reasonably expected is to entertain a view of human nature and of Christian anthropology far more optimistic than any reading of history, politics, or the Bible's unstinting exhortations against sin can sustain.

The point is not to condone a performance that could have been better than it was. It is to say that moral judgment demands historical perspective. For only if we understand how natural it was for Christians to forsake Jews during the Holocaust can we grasp the magnitude of the gap that needs to be closed between them and the enormity of the indifference that always underwrites powers that will harm defenseless persons. So it is important to add that a failure to persuade spawned a failure of concerted effort. Such as they were, Protestant responses were less than coordinated. Their organizers were diverse, the motives and aims of the groups varied, even the church communities that protested most did not speak with one voice. That outcome was nothing new. American Protestants have never been characterized by unified efforts on social issues. More distinctive have been their multiple and even conflicting responses, a quality ensured by the pluralism in their forms of governance, their teachings, their insistence on local autonomy, and their suspicion of hierarchical authority. Certainly they have never spoken with a single, harmonious voice concerning Jews—before, during, or after Auschwitz. To speak of a failure of concerted effort to save Jews under Hitler is to speak of a real failure. To do so meaningfully also requires one to comprehend the odds that any greater success would have had to surmount.

Failures to persuade and to organize concerted action were compounded by the failure of even modest action. Relief funds were raised and aid dispersed. Rallies were held, petitions signed, statements issued, and committees formed, some bringing Christians and Jews together. Additional ways of protesting the Nazis' anti-Jewish measures included sending representatives to Hitler and to other Reich officials during the 1930s, and then after the onset of war, directing delegates to President Roosevelt and other governmental officials in the United States. That more could have been done in these areas is unquestionable. Imagination may have failed to envision other potent measures, too, but realistically to conceive of American Protestantism's doing anything that would decisively have blocked Hitler's genocidal plans for the Jews is wishful thinking. In theory the disposition, the groundwork, and the power to muster such a campaign might have been available, but not in practice.

American Protestants did concur with the United States government that the only way to stop Hitler and to close the death camps was to crush his Reich militarily. Here, too, a failure shadowed the eventual Allied victory. It can be said, for instance, that "leaflets, broadcasts, and bombings of rail lines, the barracks of the SS, even the camps themselves would have been a welcome sign that the Allies knew what was going on and that they cared."[36] Such morale-raising and life-saving acts were not carried out for the Jews, but they might have been, and perhaps Protestant influence could have encouraged those missions.

A fifth failure is alleged, one of moral passion and confession after the full reality of Majdanek and Treblinka became known. In contrast to the vigorous reaction of the American Protestant press to the atomic bombing of Hiroshima and Nagasaki, the Holocaust's greater devastation elicited little more than stunned silence. To bring an indictment of failure in this instance may seem inconsequential if not misguided and hypocritical. Americans did annihilate Japanese cities; they did not create Nazi death camps. Nor can moral outrage reverse the clock. Even confession for things done or undone, whatever its healing effect, will not resurrect the Holocaust's victims. Stunned silence has greater integrity than the silence of indifference or forgetfulness, and yet there is a need for moral passion and confession after Auschwitz. Christians—Protestant and Catholic, American and European—could have prevented Hitler's destruction of the Jews. No one individual or group could have done it singlehandedly, but if there had been more effort by Christians and churches, the acts of resistance could have multiplied. An accumulative effect might have taken hold far in advance of 1945. Such points must be underscored emphatically after all the forceful reasons have been analyzed to show why it was natural for Christians to fail as they did. What happened never had to be. To say otherwise encourages indifference and forgetfulness toward Hitler's victims. It also dishonors those who did work to save the Jews, some at the risk of their own lives.

The Avenue of the Righteous

In the spring of 1942, SS officer Ernst Biberstein went east. He had already been involved in deporting Jews to killing centers, but his new assignment would take him from an administrative post into the field to relieve an officer in *Einsatzgruppe C*. One of four squadrons charged with eliminating Jews behind the lines of the German advance into Russia, *Einsatzgruppe C* policed the Ukraine. Among its credits was the murder of more than thirty-three thousand Jews at Babi Yar the previous September, a task accomplished in only two days. Biberstein missed Babi Yar, but he did nothing to diminish the record of his unit once he assumed command. It was unnecessary to deport thousands of Jews because Biberstein and his men worked efficiently. Before joining the SS in 1936, Biberstein had been a Protestant pastor. He was not bloodthirsty. No evidence shows that he sought to lead a crew of killers. Yet when one speaks about the murder of six million Jews by baptized Christians, Biberstein's case makes a point. His is only one example, admittedly extreme, within a spectrum of activity that included not only direct participation in murder but also the many sorts of complicity required to make a process of destruction happen.

As Biberstein moved from killing by administrative decision to killing by ordering executioners to fire machine guns, a young German soldier reached Munich, following orders that transferred him to the university there for training as a medic. Earlier, his letters alluded to events that had shaken him to the core. "I can't begin to give you the details," he wrote. "It is simply unthinkable that such things exist. . . . The war here in the East leads to things so terrible I would never have thought them possible."[37] Willi Graf referred not to combat against Russian troops but to slaughter by the *Einsatzgruppen*.

In Munich two of Graf's closest friends were Hans and Sophie Scholl, both in their early twenties. Motivated by an understanding of Christianity and a love for Germany that were at odds with Hitler's, the Scholls were determined to do more than ask haplessly, "What can we do?" With Hans in charge, their public dissent began. Although they possessed abundant courage, ingenuity, and high ideals, their power was scant. Nonetheless, along with their philosophy professor Kurt Huber, 51, and fellow students Alex Schmorell, Christoph Probst, and Willi Graf, leaflets from their resistance movement, "The White Rose," attacked Nazism.

German resistance to Hitler remained scattered. It did not land many telling blows, as the Scholls' effort seems to demonstrate. Their group operated for less than a year, its output restricted to several thousand copies of seven different flyers. The war and the death camps churned on for more than two years after the White Rose was crushed. The results seem paltry, but a second glance is in order. The war was still in Hitler's favor when the students' protest began in 1942. By the time the Scholls were caught, that tide had turned at Stalingrad. The White Rose could assume no credit for this reversal, but the Nazis did take its activity seriously, all the more so as Hitler's war plans began to collapse. Nazi justice proceeded quickly. On 22 February 1943, only four days after their arrest, the Scholls and Christoph Probst stood trial. Eight hours later they were beheaded.

"Somebody, after all," testified Sophie Scholl, "had to make a start."[38] Where intervention on behalf of Jews was concerned, not enough Christians did. Yet criss-crossing the many thoroughfares to Auschwitz, making them less direct and more twisting, was another route that could mean survival. When documentation shows that they saved Jewish lives for unselfish reasons, non-Jews are honored at the Avenue of the Righteous of Nations, which is part of the Israeli Holocaust Memorial, Yad Vashem, in Jerusalem. Although most of these "Righteous Gentiles" were baptized Christians, not all were practicing believers. Fewer were church leaders. Authentic Christians, however, are visible at Yad Vashem, and their numbers grow. The Avenue of the Righteous is formed by commemorative trees, the first ones planted in the 1950s.[39] They stand in double rows along the walk that slopes upward to the memorial buildings. Too numerous to be placed along the original route, recent additions make a grove on a scenic knoll nearby. One wishes for forests of trees and for countless avenues, but at least some Christians made a start.

One-third of Europe's Jews were not killed by the Nazis. Jewish endurance, ingenuity, and resistance alone account for much of that fact. Yet it is not uncommon for survivors to stress that they would not have lived unless non-Jews helped them. For example, a Lithuanian librarian, Anna Shimaite, delivered dozens of Jewish children from the Vilna ghetto. A Czech-German industrialist, Oskar Schindler, spent a fortune to rescue from SS selections some twelve hundred Jews working under his supervision in Poland. Swedish diplomat, Raoul Wallenberg, used his political authority, plus financial support from the American War Refugee Board, to shelter thousands of Hungarian Jews before disappearing inside the Soviet Union.[40] Beyond the publicized cases are many other courageous acts of mercy and resistance. No isolated person could do very much to save Jewish lives during the Holocaust. Rescue depended not only on individuals but on groups of people working together. Networks of assistance, which involved communities and institutions at least to some extent, were critical. It is vital to remember those facts in assessing the performance of Christians. Some Christian communities and institutions, as well as individuals, served better than others. If the admirable cases originated more at the local level than through the energy of national or international ecclesiastical bureaucracies, that result suggests what might have been accomplished if maximum Christian power had benefited the Jews.

Magda Trocmé was invited to plant a tree at Yad Vashem in 1972. Dedicated to her late husband, André, it branches out to remember more than a solitary Protestant minister. Along with a more recent tree in her honor, its roots and foliage represent their children, the members of their church, and nearly all the citizens of Le Chambon-sur-Lignon.[41] It was late September 1934 when the Trocmés began their work in the small Protestant church at that unremarkable village in the Cévennes mountains of southeastern France. Descendants of a Huguenot religious minority, violently persecuted in earlier French history, the congregation responded to the new pastor and his wife as their helpfulness and practical version of Christianity enlivened its conventional if sturdy faith.

During World War I, André Trocmé had lived in a part of France occupied by the Germans. As he saw the devastation of war, André also made friends with one of the enemy, a German medic. He was a Christian who happened to believe that a follower of Jesus ought not to kill. Permanently influenced by the German's example, Trocmé gradually forged a theology that stressed nonviolent resistance to evil. Evil he interpreted rather simply as harmdoing to human life, and André's emphasis was on resistance to it as much as on nonviolence. The negative injunction—"Do not kill"—was insufficient. It had to be supplemented by positive action to relieve suffering and to stop harmdoing. The Christian's responsibility was to be vigilant for ways to move against destructiveness. Such was André Trocmé's interpretation of Jesus' commandments to love God and one's neighbor as oneself. The Chambonnais would practice remarkably well what their Protestant preacher taught them.

Life's quality in Le Chambon had been rejuvenated by the Cévenol School, a private academy envisioned by Trocmé and administered by Édouard Theis, who doubled as André's assistant, plus Roger Darcissac, another close friend. Along with Magda Trocmé, they led Le Chambon to seize the special opportunities to resist which came that way after France fell to Hitler on 22 June 1940. Geography placed Le Chambon in Vichy, that unoccupied region south of the Loire River which the Nazis permitted their puppet, Marshal Philippe Pétain, to govern. Within four months, the Vichy regime enacted major anti-Jewish legislation and authorized the internment of foreign Jews. Measures in the occupied zone were even more punitive and swiftly applied. On 27 March 1942, the first deportation to Auschwitz left the Drancy transit camp. In Paris that July, another roundup netted thirteen thousand non-French Jews. Awaiting deportation, nine thousand of these victims were hideously imprisoned in a sports stadium, the Vélodrome d'Hiver. Half were children under sixteen. None of them survived. Pétain's government prepared to follow suit. Fifteen thousand foreign

Jews were handed over to the Nazis for deportation in August 1942, and three months later, when the Germans occupied Vichy, there were few havens of any kind for Jews on French soil. Le Chambon remained one of them.

During the winter of 1940–41, Magda Trocmé had answered an evening knock at her door. There stood a frightened woman who identified herself as a German Jew. In northern France, she had heard that there might be help in Le Chambon. Could she come in? Magda Trocmé's answer was, "Naturally." That single word says a lot. From then on Jewish refugees arrived almost daily. None were turned away. They were fed, hidden, and whenever possible spirited across the Swiss border by cooperating Christians, some devout and some not, who were convinced that it is simply wrong to leave anyone in harm's way. Why these acts did not bring full Nazi retribution to Le Chambon has not been fully explained, for the activities there were less than completely secret. But one crucial reason has been identified: Major Julius Schmäling, a Nazi who had governmental responsibilities for two years when the Germans occupied this region of France. He knew what the people of Le Chambon were doing and let it happen. Likewise, André Trocmé and his followers knew that they had some protection, and they did not let their opportunity slip away.[42]

Aiding endangered Jews was not something the unpretentious Chambonnais Christians regarded as heroic or as unusually good. It was only the natural fulfillment of their commitment. Not that they overlooked the danger or the need for care. Organization, trust, and planning were essential to their success, just as it had been indispensable for a groundwork of teaching and learning to be laid for them to root their commitment in solid ground. The Chambonnais did not save everyone. They were not, after all, professional rescue specialists but only ordinary folk who had to improvise their resistance against trained killers.

Ninety thousand Jews in France lost their lives to those professionals. The amateur lifeguards of Le Chambon rescued only a few hundred. If that contrast does not overwhelm their achievement and drive it toward triviality, then one might point out that their relative isolation in an inconsequential town may have kept them out of the spotlight because the French police and the Gestapo had more important prey to nab. The Chambonnais had the luxury of room to maneuver, moreover, because they lived at first in Vichy France and because later, during the Nazi occupation, they got help from Major Schmäling. Or if those mitigating circumstances are insufficient to place Le Chambon in a context that diminishes its brilliance, then it can be argued that nonviolent resistance could hardly provide a model for bringing down the Third Reich, not to mention the fact that the Chambonnais' conduct was, above all, imprudent. On the latter count, for instance, note what happened to André Trocmé's young cousin Daniel.

A slender teacher with a heart ailment, Daniel Trocmé had accepted André's invitation to come to Le Chambon to help coordinate rescue efforts on behalf of refugee children. If the police raided Le Chambon looking for Jews—and they did so with increasing frequency as the war went on—warnings usually came in time to enable the refugees to hide in the surrounding countryside. Once the warning came too late; the Gestapo caught Daniel and his children. Though he could have found a way to save himself, Trocmé refused to leave the young deportees. He never returned to Le Chambon. It was learned later that he died at Majdanek. Confirmed, too, was the fact that even after his death the Gestapo kept trying to verify what Daniel Trocmé's compassion for Jews mistakenly led them to suspect, namely, that he himself was Jewish. If Daniel Trocmé was imprudent to get involved, it is also true that a tree in his honor lives today at Yad Vashem. It questions prudence, especially from a Christian point of view, just as it also warns that no life is trivial, no circumstance inconsequential, and no model of resistance without cost.

How goodness happened at Le Chambon suggests why it did not happen in too many other communities of baptized Christians. Le Chambon had leaders who self-critically evaluated what it means to follow Jesus. They took the parable of the Good Samaritan as normative, which meant that their universe of obligation broke the boundaries of racism, nationalism, and antisemitism. This leadership prepared its followers to look for opportunities to resist harmdoing. The preparation included awareness that it is critical to act *in time*. The Chambonnais were receptive. Without that disposition, André Trocmé would have been a forgotten voice in the wilderness, and he would have no tree along the Avenue of the Righteous. Perhaps those French men and women were responsive because they were the inheritors of a minority status that had brought suffering to their ancestors. Outside the establishment, perhaps they were more naturally inclined to help others in similar positions. Or perhaps because they encountered refugees not en masse but as individuals, the Chambonnais could recognize human hurt in ways that touched their better natures and did not overwhelm them with the hopelessness of meeting a need so vast that nothing one could do would make much difference. It would be wrong to discount such possibilities. It would also be wrong to overlook that these people chose to help when needy Jews stood before them.

The Chambonnais could have done otherwise, just as those who failed to do nearly as much could have acted differently. Yet in the case of the latter's failure, the factors that saved Le Chambon from apostasy were largely missing, which is to say that the links of Christian responsibility form a chain reaching far back in time. Those who were in a position to give a better account of themselves as Christians stand guilty of making less than a fully authentic Christian witness. The factors that led them to those fateful choices included the lack of self-critical leadership with an awareness akin to André Trocmé's, the absence of preparation that would have purged the antisemitism in Christianity, and too little stress on the significance of *acting in time* to prevent harmdoing. Instead of working to make their followers receptive to messages of that kind, Christian leadership itself took familiar lessons to heart, ones that their followers could accept more comfortably. Hence nationalism, racism, antisemitism, prudence that disarmed protest, and caution that urged too few to start resisting—those cultural teachings were baptized as Christian. Nothing new had happened, however, for such is the stuff that has typically entrenched the nominal but culturally dominant forms of Christianity. Sadly, the Holocaust demonstrates how much harder it is to convert baptized Christians into authentic Christians than to make them antisemitic killers, accomplices to murder, and indifferent bystanders. "Am I my brother's keeper?" Cain's natural way is crowded. The rugged Avenue of the Righteous is not. Unless Christians join those who took the road not taken, they betray the one they claim to follow and crucify the ones they should embrace.

Chapter 8

Business as Usual?
Professions and Industries
During the Holocaust

Arbeit Macht Frei. Work makes one free. Those words arched the entry to Nazi slave labor and death camps. Attention usually focuses on the principal extermination centers—Auschwitz-Birkenau, Belzec, Chelmno, Majdanek, Sobibor, and Treblinka—where upon arrival millions of Jews were hastily dispatched. Although it is less well known, the Nazis also managed some sixteen hundred forced labor camps. During the twelve years of the Hitler regime, millions slaved within them. They knew the irony in the Nazi slogan, for *Vernichtung durch Arbeit*—annihilation by work—was the reality.

Under Nazi jurisdiction, Jews became superfluous partly because they provided unwelcome economic competition for the Germans who feared downward mobility and unemployment. Hence, this redundant population was eventually stripped of more than political rights. They lost long-term economic value, too. During the scarcities of wartime, of course, their labor was certainly useful, even essential. Nevertheless, only irregularly and periodically did considerations of economic utility take precedence over intentions that Jews should disappear. Hitler's war, after all, was a race war. It was fought largely to fulfill his ethnic theory. Hence, periodic exemptions for Jews never lasted. For even if momentarily the Jews were economically useful, they remained superfluous because of the ideal of *Volksgemeinschaft*. This fact reminds us once again that people who have been rendered surplus often possess advanced education, talent, and skills. It is as easy for talented people to lose their place in the world as it is for those who cannot cope with the complexities of technological civilization. Thus, once war began, if Jews were spared at all, they would be worked to death. True, psychologically as well as economically, Germany paid a staggering bill for the Holocaust. Does it follow, then, that genocide serves nobody well and that the Nazis would have advanced even their self-interest had they made more sensible use of the Jews? To say yes simply takes too lightly the fact that relatively few Germans, civilian or military, judged any cost sufficiently compelling to make them intervene decisively against the destruction process.

Within the Third Reich, ridding German culture of Jews was a fixed, predetermined end that governed other policies. The issue was not this aim's validity but how the goal could most practically be attained. The drive behind this objective, however, did not rest solely on ideological or patriotic beliefs. Beyond concerns about security and survival, factors that can never be taken lightly in a police state governed by terror, there were careers to advance, honors to win, and profits to extract. In such circumstances, it was business as usual and then some. For example, German corporations invested huge sums to construct factories that could capitalize on slaves provided by the SS. Already intertwined extensively, both the private and governmental sectors found such arrangements more than acceptable. By consuming Jewish labor, German industry got cheap energy. The by-products partly assuaged Heinrich Himmler's insatiable hunger for Jewish corpses. Genocide had something in it for everyone. Thus rationalized, Nazi slavery created nothing less than a new form of human society, one predicated—neither figuratively nor randomly but literally and systematically—on working certain people to death for political gain and economic profit. The care with which estimates were made is documented by records from the SS Economic-Administrative Central Office, or *Wirtschafts-Verwaltungshauptamt* (WVHA). Calculating that a concentration camp inmate could be expected to work for nine months—a figure that turned out to be too high—SS economists reckoned that a total profit of 1631 Reichsmarks could be forecast for an inmate's labor. This calculation figured the cost precisely: food, clothing, and RM2 for burning the corpse. Included on the profit side of the ledger were the benefits of an efficient use of the inmate's effects: gold from teeth, clothes, valuables, money. Though no cash figure was mentioned, this report noted that additional income could be realized from utilization of the corpse's bones and ashes.[1]

Other illustrations from medicine, law, education, science, and the civil service will clarify another crucial point: the Holocaust could not have occurred without help from countless professionally skilled civilians and the institutions they represented. As the implications of that claim are drawn out, the most important one will *not* be that Germans of the Hitler era were a special breed, a people unnaturally irresponsible and cruel. On the contrary, this German case is better regarded as symptomatic of potentialities that are widespread in every modernized society. With that proposition in mind, one more fact with ominous possibilities for the future bears underscoring, too. Typically, the professions and their institutions, at least as they existed in Germany during the 1930s and 1940s, proved incapable of thwarting state-sponsored policies of population elimination. Quite the contrary, those professions and their institutions moved genocide along until it could only be stopped by superior military force from the outside.

Ordinary Officials, Extraordinary Tasks

People often assume that a society's well-educated elite will lead a nation not into temptation but will instead deliver it from evil. Even after the benefit of the doubt is given, the Holocaust casts doubt on such optimism.[2] More than once, Hitler rightly feared assassination. From beginning to end, the Reich kept an entire nation under surveillance, watching for every sign of resistance. Nazi suspicion resulted in thousands of arrests, concentration camp sentences, and executions. Much of this paranoia was unfounded but by no means all of it. Though constantly restrained by state terror, circles of resistance existed throughout Germany. People from all walks of life were involved—heroically and sacrificially. Yet Jewish misfortune was not decisive in motivating either the leadership or the rank and file of German resistance to Hitler.[3] To annihilate the Jews, as well as to run the government and wage war, the Third Reich required brain power that only the educated classes could provide. Hitler got that help without much difficulty. That fact, in turn, gives pause concerning other assumptions one might make.

If the well-educated are thought to provide the leadership a society needs, that premise is usually connected to the belief that members of professional elites, individually and collectively, exercise independent, self-critical judgment. Their "objectivity," in short, saves everyone from the error of self-indulgence and ideological blindness. The case under scrutiny here, unfortunately, does not validate that hope. Speaking generally, German doctors and lawyers, for instance, were hardly bastions of independence. Rather, they were quite prepared to advance Hitler's authority. The same holds for German educators from the kindergarten to the university. As for scientists and bureaucrats, their dispositions may not have been so ideologically committed as those of many German teachers or as financially motivated as those of the captains of German industry, but these professionals also joined their peers in medicine and law to salute the Führer. They did so not always by flocking eagerly to the swastika. Indeed they sometimes resented and even resisted attempts to Nazify their professions. Yet by sticking to the practical, problem-solving rationality that their professional training emphasized, they remained both sufficiently apolitical and nationalistic to suit Hitler's purposes. The following question, therefore, suggests itself: are professional elites more likely to side with or against the reigning political establishment? The German case is instructive not merely because it helps to corroborate the former position but also because it makes clear that the genocidal intentions of an established regime, far from having to beg or coerce support from the professions, may prove so tempting that an elite eagerly delivers its society further into evil. With those possibilities in mind, let us look more closely at some details.

In the Holocaust's lore, few names are more infamous than Josef Mengele's.

Long thought to be hiding somewhere in South America, this man was the target of an extensive international manhunt. Huge rewards were offered for information leading to his capture. A thousand questions about Mengele remain, including how he escaped American custody and found his way to Paraguay, an issue that became the subject of a United States Department of Justice investigation in 1985. But one question has presumably been laid to rest. Acting on a tip on 31 May 1985, West German police raided the home of Hans Sedlmeier, an employee of the Mengele family business. Letters were discovered, some of them apparently written by Mengele himself. Their trail led to Sao Paulo, Brazil. The ensuing investigation revealed that Mengele had lived in the vicinity for some thirteen years until he drowned in 1979. Early in the summer of 1985, forensic experts testified that the remains of a man thought to be Wolfgang Gerhard were actually Mengele's. In March 1986, Mengele's death was corroborated further when X-rays of his teeth were shown to match those of the skeleton experts had previously identified as that of Mengele.

Born in 1911, the "Angel of Death," as he came to be known, was especially loathsome because he was a doctor, a healer-turned-exterminator. Son of a prominent German family, handsome and elegant, Mengele was bright and studied hard. He enjoyed philosophy and earned two doctorates, a Ph.D. in anthropology as well as an M.D. He was a competent, qualified researcher with a special interest in genetics. Before arriving at Auschwitz by choice on 30 May 1943, *SS-Hauptsturmführer* (Captain) Mengele had served three years with a *Waffen-SS* unit in the east. There he had been wounded and declared unfit for combat. His numerous military decorations included the Iron Cross First and Second Class. As an SS doctor at Auschwitz, he would send some four hundred thousand concentration-camp prisoners to their deaths.

Mengele met the transports arriving at Auschwitz. Directing a cacophony of life and death, his baton pointed left or right, selecting who should go directly to the gas and who should be saved for work. Meeting trains, however, was not the only activity to fill Dr. Mengele's time and that of his medical associates at Auschwitz.[4] Mengele, for example, specialized in experiments on children— twins whenever possible—to find ways to increase the birthrate of German women. He experimented by surgery or syringe on several hundred pairs of children. Very few of these girls and boys survived. Other physicians also certified prisoners to be fit for torture, injected drugs to obtain confessions, and practiced surgery on death camp inmates. They regularly monitored the gas chambers as well. Ostensibly acting as scientists, Nazi doctors also joined Mengele in research.

Human beings are often the most suitable subjects for medical experiments. Nazi doctors did not have to settle for dogs or monkeys. Their guinea pigs were human, although Nazi research aimed to exclude Jews from that species. In Auschwitz's society of total domination, the experimentation process could be streamlined. No informed consent from the subjects was necessary, nor was any compensation owed them. Inhibiting moral restraints took a back seat to practical and ideological passions for knowledge. In the name of Nazi science and cost-effective rationality, anything and everything could be done to these prisoners—and was. Nor was the work done solely by individual researchers. German pharmaceutical firms took advantage of opportunities to test their new products on prisoners. Except as data to be studied, no one had much regard for the victims of these experiments. Exposure to low pressure, cold, and sea water; deliberate infection of specifically inflicted wounds to produce gangrene; injection of caustic chemicals into women's uteri; mutilation and grafting of limbs; detailed study of skulls removed from Jewish bodies with proper scientific care—extraordinary research of this kind was done by respectable professionals who reported their findings at medical meetings where no protests were recorded. Although some of the research, had it involved the willing participation of the subjects, might have constituted normal attempts to extend medical knowledge, most was as scientifically unproductive as it was demented. The point, however, is not that only German doctors under a dictator like Hitler are capable of utilizing defenseless human beings as the unwilling or unwitting subjects in such projects. That potential knows no national boundaries. Likewise, German medicine has not been the only group interested in demographic and genetic engineering.

In at least three ways, German physicians tried to assure that a particular kind of human being would rule Europe, if not the world, forever. Their pioneering precedents will always provide a tempting model for governments that contend with redundant people. First on the physicians' list of experiments were attempts to perfect techniques of mass sterilization, a project in which German doctors had been enlisted since 1933. Some explored novel methods of surgical castration; others worked to show that X-rays were a better method. In every case, the point behind the ever-increasing number of mutilated bodies was the same: total security against the Jews—or against any target population—could not be obtained simply by defeating them, for they might reproduce and avenge themselves. Logic required total annihilation. By perfecting sterilization, even the traces of Jewish blood in *Mischlinge* exempted from the gas could eventually be eliminated.

At the other end of the life cycle, German doctors implemented Hitler's campaign for euthanasia. As early as 1939, he ordered the "mercy killing" of German citizens suffering from "incurable" disorders, including mental illness and birth defects. The sacrifice of classes and whole peoples for the sake of "improvement" does not stop with admission to the culture of modernity. Indeed, the fact that National Socialism would unleash a euthanasia campaign against German citizens suggests how even fewer moral compunctions existed to prevent the destruction of alien Jews. Whenever a government is willing to destroy its own people, it is unlikely to be very concerned about destroying those who are outside the bonds of community, especially if those outside are regarded as a threat. By the end of 1939, then, the first of five euthanasia centers were operating, their victims eventually numbering nearly one hundred thousand Germans whose flaws made them a liability economically and genetically. The man in charge of the program overall was Christian Wirth. Having initiated the use of gas to destroy superfluous Germans, Wirth reappeared in Poland after the euthanasia campaign was brought to an end by protests late in the summer of 1941. There he helped to implement the Final Solution.

Third, there was the *Lebensborn* (Spring of Life) scheme. Established by Himmler in 1936, this program gave governmental encouragement and support for unmarried women of sound Aryan stock to be impregnated by virile SS men. The offspring were praised as a gift of pure life for the nation. Continued throughout the war, this aspect of the *Lebensborn* movement was supplemented by Slavic children whose Nordic appearance qualified them for removal—sometimes voluntary, more often forcible—from the east and resettlement in German homes, thus replenishing a population being undesirably depleted by the war. Without allies from German medicine, none of these programs would have achieved their considerable success.

Nazism was largely a racist ideology that relied on biological and medical metaphors. Jews, in particular, were likened to vermin, parasites, or to gangrenous appendages. German health required their removal. Thus, German physicians blurred the difference between healing and killing to the extent that they accepted the mandate Hitler gave them, namely, that their Faustian task was to master the evolution of a superior human breed. In the Third Reich, the physician's primary responsibility was not to heal sick individuals but to fulfill the state's wishes. Such practices did not cease with the demise of Nazi Germany. Today in various countries around the world doctors obediently diagnose political dissidents as mentally ill; they refine exquisite forms of medicalized torture; they work for intelligence agencies. Medicine, no less than war, can be politics carried out by other means.

Germany's medicine had long been preeminent in the world, and by no means were all German doctors like Mengele. Most accepted only fragments of the Nazi ideology or were simply professionally indifferent to it. Probably less than four hundred of the ninety thousand German doctors actively took part in experiments such as those conducted at Auschwitz. Yet the medical profession as a whole did practically nothing to call such activity into question. Nor had it raised any protest in 1933 when Jewish doctors were restricted from practicing. Silence obtained in this latter case partly because Gentile physicians benefited economically from a reduction of competition for positions and patients. Throughout the Nazi era, the potential for dissent was also minimized because the German medical profession had no tradition of overt political involvement.

If German doctors typically regarded themselves as apolitical, it is also note-worthy that between 1933 and 1945 more than 30% were members of the Reich's Physicians' League, an adjunct to the Nazi party. They were well-repre-sented professionally in the SS as well. That ought not to be surprising, how-ever, for physicians from Nazi Germany or anywhere else have a basically conservative profile. Despite the healing oaths they swear, doctors are ordinary men and women who will abet state policies of population elimination when they find it expedient to do so.

Patterns in other German professions were not much different. If the majority of German lawyers, for example, neither held Nazi beliefs before Hitler took power nor were converted wholeheartedly to them afterward, most were civil servants, including judges, whose actions corroborated the thesis that modern bureaucracies will serve any master with the power to control them.[5] Long ac-customed to an authoritarian jurisprudence, the bench and the bar found the Weimar Republic more anomalous than the Third Reich, largely because so lit-tle in the German legal profession changed during that democratic interlude. Nor were Hitler's nationalism and antisemitism a liability as far as most lawyers were concerned. On the contrary, German lawyers overwhelmingly backed the revitalization of Germany that Hitler promised, and the Gentile majority wel-comed ways to curtail the competition brought about by the disproportionate number of Jews in this profession. Thus, laws, decrees, decisions, and sen-tences were handed down in accord with Hitler's wishes by men disciplined in German legal training. Add to these considerations the fact that German lawyers never had the social status enjoyed by leaders in business or the military and the following conclusion rings true: if one were seeking effective opposition to Hitler within the professions, the bench and the bar would have been nearly the last places to look. Risking their careers, if not their families and their lives, heroic individual exceptions could be found in this case, as in all the others dis-cussed in this chapter, but more than anything else they would only prove the rule that professional expertise in Germany sided far more with Hitler than against him. In the lawyer's case, moreover, that rule contains a telling re-minder. A society's legal experts may not outlaw genocide but legitimate and even legalize it instead.

German school teachers and university professors were not Hitler's adversa-ries either. Quite the opposite; the teaching profession proved one of the most reliable segments of the population as far as National Socialism was concerned. Throughout the Weimar era, Germany's educational establishment, continuing its long authoritarian tradition, remained unreconciled to democracy and nation-alism.[6] Once in power, the Nazis expunged dissenting instructors, but there were not many. On the other hand, at least two leading Nazis, the rabid an-tisemites Heinrich Himmler and Julius Streicher, had formerly been teachers. Eventually more than 30% of the top Nazi party leadership came from that background. Teachers, especially from elementary schools, were by far the largest professional group represented in the party. Altogether almost 97% of them belonged to the Nazi Teachers' Association, and more than 30% of that number were members of the Nazi party itself. From such instructors, German boys and girls learned what the Nazis wanted them to know. Hatred of Jews was central in that curriculum.[7]

If Hitler's German contemporaries gave him strong support, even more loyal were the children of that generation, the young men and women born during or shortly after World War I. Indeed, to a large degree the Nazi effort was a youth movement, led mainly by men in their mid-forties to early fifties who could count on young people growing up deprived in a defeated Germany and thus wanting something more. In 1931 antisemitic riots broke out in universities throughout Germany and Austria. They were inspired by the Nazi Student Organization, which counted some 60% of all German undergraduates in its ranks, then a figure about twice the level of Nazi support among the population as a whole. Far from decrying their students' pro-Nazi actions, many German professors were themselves moving into Hitler's orbit. Some three hundred of the nation's most illustrious scholars, for example, signed a declaration urging votes for Hitler just before the decisive election in March 1933.

On the eve of Hitler's rise to power, more than 10% of Germany's professors were Jewish, as were a quarter of her Nobel laureates. German intellectual and scientific life was drastically diminished as most of them fled the country. Among the remaining professors, disillusionment with Nazi ways became increasingly common, stimulated partly by an anti-intellectual streak among Nazi leaders who always considered this university elite suspect. Nonetheless, whether through a widespread disdain for politics in general, or from a mixture of sympathy, indifference, and fear—if not outright backing—generated by the Third Reich in particular, the German academic community continued to teach and to do research in ways that made it much more Hitler's friend than foe. If educational institutions and leaders are rightly regarded as bulwarks against prejudice, totalitarianism, and mass death, the Holocaust counsels that educational professions can serve very different ends. The teaching and scholarship done ordinarily in German schools and universities helped to transmute Auschwitz from an extraordinary possibility into an acceptable routine.

Professions define people. One tragic legacy of the Holocaust is that there can no longer be total innocence in such identifications. For what profession was not implicated in making the Holocaust happen? If attempts to displace Albert Einstein's "Jewish" physics with a superior "Aryan" version constituted utter folly, nevertheless Germany's professional scientific societies allowed themselves to be Nazified.[8] That step helped to make it impossible for many of the nation's best scientists to work there because they were Jewish. Through 1935, nearly 20% of the natural science faculties in Germany were dismissed for that reason. Some twenty contemporary or future Nobel prize winners were among them. This lost scientific expertise returned to haunt Hitler with a vengeance, but the Holocaust shows again that no profession is intrinsically safe from culpability in mass death.

Engineering reveals a similar story.[9] Like the German scientific community, these technocrats were content to leave the affairs of state to Nazi politicians as long as their own departments and careers advanced. By rising to the challenge of an abundance of Nazi projects, the engineers served themselves on both counts while meeting Hitler's aims as well. German engineers posed few questions about the ends their efforts achieved, particularly insofar as the Holocaust was concerned, but they handled with distinction their job of calculating precisely the most efficient ways to reach the goals set by their Führer.

An army of professional civil servants expedited the Final Solution, too.[10] Conveniently, Hitler found at his disposal the expertise of an already existing bureaucracy, which for the most part consisted of decent, hard-working, incorruptible men. True, new offices such as Goering's Air Ministry and Goebbels's Ministry of Propaganda had to be established after the Nazi victory. Nazis especially committed to handling the Jewish question were also put into influential new slots. Yet the party never had to restructure or permeate extensively an institution that would do its bidding without protest. Some officials were dismissed; others were pressured to conform. But most German civil servants toed the line without dissent, and many joined the Nazi party eagerly. Sincerely believing that carrying out their state duties was the right thing, they would help to annihilate millions of human beings with an undisturbed conscience. Their activity in this regard, unfortunately, has not been uncharacteristic of modern bureaucracies before or since.

As Hitler came to power, the established state secretaries and their long-time subordinates were motivated primarily by yearnings for a national revival. Antisemitism was strong among them, too, and while these men initiated little in the way of anti-Jewish campaigns, they hardly flinched when Hitler put such plans in motion. Those directives made the German bureaucracy grow, for nearly every branch of the civil service soon needed its so-called "Jewish experts." Mostly these desks were filled by ordinary, if ambitious, university graduates who had specialized in law and were intent on successful administrative careers. Personally, these younger men may not have been zealously antisemitic, but they understood that power and influence were at stake in managing well the Jewish affairs that fell to them. They did not run the Final Solution, but often they worked hard to please their superiors, the party members who infiltrated the civil service at higher levels and made sure the bureaucracy facilitated the evolving stages of population elimination that hit the Jews. Antisemitism, nationalism, political calculation, personal ambition: with few individual exceptions—and given the circumstances they belong in the category of the unexpected—those factors were enough to ensure that the German civil service—old guard, young men on the rise, or party infiltrators—would make the Final Solution work. Granted, there were rivalries among these offices. The spoils went to those who could extend furthest their offices' influence in deciding the Jewish question. Yet even if competition often exceeded cooperation, the new results still meant death for the Jews.

State-sponsored programs of population elimination require attention to a thousand details. Among the most important were those involving the *Deutsche Reichsbahn*, as the German railroad system was known during the Hitler era.[11] This institution's role is often bypassed, but without it European Jewry could not have been destroyed. Operating within the German bureaucracy as a part of the Transportation Ministry, the *Reichsbahn* was one of the largest organizations in the Third Reich, including in 1942 about half a million civil servants and nine hundred thousand workers. German military conquests, not to mention the demands of war itself, enlarged and complicated the rail system, but the people who ordinarily staffed it proved capable of handling the extraordinary tasks assigned them. Essentially the same personnel who ran the *Reichsbahn* before the war did so between 1939 and 1945 and afterward as well. During the war they simply adjusted to the needs at hand. These included moving troops, industrial cargo, and Jews from all over Europe.

The destruction of the European Jews was not supported by a special Nazi budget. The *Reichsbahn* had bills to pay; it could not transport Jews for free. In this case, its paying customer was the SS, which used the proceeds from confiscated Jewish property to make many of the payments. The SS also had to compete with other agencies for allocation of rail space. This competition, however, was not too severe. The pull of the SS meant that it was common for death camp transports to win priority over the *Wehrmacht*'s requisitions for reinforcements and munitions. No European Jew was left alive for lack of transportation. The volume of Jewish traffic even justified special rates for the trains that rolled constantly to killing centers strategically located near heavily traveled trunk lines. Hilberg sums up the basic procedure as follows:

> Even though Jews were carried in freight cars, they were booked by the Reichbahn's financial specialists as passengers. In principle, any group of travelers was accepted for payment. The basic charge was the third-class fare: 4 pfennig per track kilometer. Children under ten were transported for half this amount; those under four went free. Group fare (half of the third-class rate) was available if at least 400 persons were transported.[12]

These fares, of course, were all one-way.

The *Reichsbahn*'s personnel were respectable citizens. No experts in Jewish affairs, they were merely decent people doing their jobs. Yet what they did could have been neither a mystery nor a secret to most of them. If only a handful of Germans knew all about the destruction of the Jews, very few knew nothing about the Final Solution. The professionals who kept the stock rolling on time had to know that they managed death trains. Even so, their business went forward as usual, showing that even the most common enterprises can and do turn out to be vital elements in destroying the defenseless.

"The Problem ... Can Now Be Regarded as Definitely Solved"

Between October 1941 and October 1944, the German railroads delivered some 2.5 million Jews to their deaths. The transportation network also benefited from forced Jewish labor. But how the allocation of that resource worked, and what follows from those labor policies, can best be grasped by taking note of some other German industries and their leaders. Among them were unusually competent men such as Dr. Carl Krauch, chair of the supervisory board of I. G. Farben; Alfried Krupp, chair of the Krupp empire of coal and steel; and Friedrich Flick, head of the Mitteldeutsche Stahlwerke. These executives and their peers had vast scientific knowledge and managerial skill. Their business acumen was high, their loyalty to Germany indisputable, and their innovative ability to solve problems unsurpassed. Before most people could say "transnational corporation," these industrialists ran such enterprises. Hitler and his policies struck them as good for business, and without their support Hitler never could have gotten very far. If the German industrialists overestimated their ability to control Hitler and underestimated the degree and kind of power he came to wield, nevertheless, as long as it lasted, the marriage between them was more than convenient.

Consider, for example, that in 1935 one of the problems confronting Hitler was production of a synthetic rubber known as Buna. At the seventh Nazi party congress in Nuremberg on 11 September, Hitler claimed that this problem could "now be regarded as definitely solved."[13] His boast was a propagandistic exaggeration but not by much. German scientists did know how to produce synthetic rubber, just as they also knew how to convert coal into synthetic fuels that could power Nazi tanks and planes. The difficulties of mass production, however, were substantial—especially so once World War II was under way. Attempts to cope with them would take I. G. Farben to Auschwitz. Buna was never produced there, but a factory and its supporting operations were well along. The energy that built them, however, was not synthetic. It came from Jewish slaves. That path took this world-leading firm into the most grisly depths of the Holocaust, into the dock at Nuremberg, and then well beyond.

Defeat in World War I came to Germany substantially because the country was deficient in natural raw materials. British blockades eventually took a heavy toll on German efforts to import required resources for fuel, gunpowder, and rubber. This lesson was not lost on Hitler. Determined that history would not repeat itself, he successfully wooed I. G. Farben, which wanted governmental support to turn abundant German coal into gasoline by hydrogenation. On 14

December 1933, a bargain was struck. In return for his governmental support, Hitler would not have to worry about oil until Allied bombing raids in May 1944 razed I. G. Farben's synthetic oil operations.

The prelude to this mutual interest is intriguing. At the turn of the century, several German companies—BASF, Bayer, Hoechst, Cassella, and Kalle—had cornered the world market for synthetic dyestuffs. Still they battled each other viciously, which discouraged Carl Duisberg, the general manager of Bayer. Then, on a trip to the United States in 1903, he became aware of the trust movement that was booming in spite of the Sherman Antitrust Act. Duisberg was especially captivated by the example of John D. Rockefeller and Standard Oil. Although war was required to bring it off, Duisberg would eventually win favor for a similar plan of organization among German chemical plants.

German strategy in World War I called for a short struggle and a swift victory. Care to provide a sound industrial base for a war of attrition was minimal. When it became clear that a long war of attrition was precisely what was in store, the most critical need was to develop German self-sufficiency in the production of gunpowder. Steps in that direction had been taken as early as 1913 when a major breakthrough by Fritz Haber and Carl Bosch resulted in a process to produce ammonia synthetically. Within a year, large quantities of ammonia were available, most of it used in fertilizer. At the same time, however, Bosch was experimentally producing small amounts of saltpeter, the basic raw material for gunpowder, by oxidizing the synthetic ammonia. Little was made of this development until it became apparent in 1915 that Germany would have great difficulty importing the raw materials it needed to produce gunpowder for the war effort.

Now German leadership turned to Bosch, but he needed time to gear up for full production. In the meantime development of another decisive weapon seemed imperative. As military liaisons discussed the options with German industrialists, it became clear that poisonous chemicals were among the byproducts of German dyestuffs. These chemicals could become devastating instruments of war. Thus, on the afternoon of 22 April, cannisters of chlorine gas were opened at Ypres, Belgium. By day's end, fifteen thousand soldiers lay on the battlefield, five thousand of them dead.[14]

Production of the poisonous gas required several steps. They were divided up rationally among the best-suited firms. Meanwhile Bosch's gunpowder project moved ahead, vastly enriched by government support. All was not well, however. With the Battle of the Somme in July 1916, Germans found it thinkable that they might lose the war. Taking that eventuality into account, the chemical magnates believed that they would more likely hang separately than together. Thus, Duisberg's dream of a unified dyestuff conglomerate was realized: I. G. Farben—*Die Interessen Gemeinschaft der Deutschen Teerfarbenindustrie*—was born in August.

Although Duisberg's intuitions about the future would prove correct, the immediate future of I. G. Farben was rocky. Not only did the victorious Allies bring sanctions against the companies that had armed German forces, but postwar economic uncertainties also made things shaky. Carl Bosch, whose star was rising, decided that a more decisive step must be taken. Heretofore I. G. Farben had been a federation of cooperating units, but by 9 December 1925, Bosch succeeded in welding them into a single corporation, *I. G. Farbenindustrie Aktiengesellschaft*, the largest company in Europe and the biggest chemical firm in the world.

The company's expansionist ambitions were unslacking. Increasingly I. G. Farben took control of Germany's munitions industry, and Bosch's dream of German self-sufficiency in oil also kept the hydrogenation project alive. Ever mindful of new sources of capital, Bosch hoped to bring Standard Oil of New Jersey into the operation. In all likelihood he would have achieved that goal had not the Great Depression and the discovery of vast petroleum reserves in Texas dropped the price of oil so low that Standard lost interest in further development of the process to convert coal.

Meanwhile Hitler and the Nazi party were asserting themselves. Indeed for a time I. G. Farben was a Nazi target, owing to the fact that Jews were centrally involved with the firm. Bosch defended the Jews in I. G. Farben, and thus his personal relationship with Hitler was never very good, but the two men and their constituents had too many overlapping interests to be seriously at odds for long. Military preparation was Hitler's goal. I. G. Farben could facilitate that aim. Bosch and his associates knew a good deal when they saw one.

By 1937 the company had been Nazified: all members of the managing board were party members, Jewish leadership had been removed, and Hermann Goering had put Carl Krauch in charge of fulfilling all Nazi needs in the chemical field. As Germany invaded Poland on 1 September 1939, I. G. Farben's interests were flourishing. Indeed Nazi victories in the East were creating attractive possibilities for industrial expansion. Sensing the importance of such options, I. G. Farben successfully courted the Nazi leader most likely to have decisive influence in that area, Heinrich Himmler, head of the SS.

These gains were not without problems. The war, for example, might create a labor shortage for German factories. That fact was instrumental in a report filed by Otto Ambros, who was to determine for I. G. Farben the best location for a new plant to produce Buna. The spot Ambros favored had numerous assets: ample coal and water, plus ready access to good highway and rail facilities. In addition, a supply of labor would not be in doubt. The place to build the factory, Ambros argued, was near the Polish town of Oświęcim (Auschwitz).

I. G. Farben, of course, was not the only enterprise planning expansion at Auschwitz in 1941. The SS had similar intentions, only its goal was to manufacture corpses. As events unfolded, these objectives proved very compatible. In any case, I. G. Farben was so optimistic about the possibilities in Poland that it was willing to use its own funds to build a new, privately owned firm called I. G. Auschwitz. With a capital investment totaling nearly $2 billion in today's money, it would be the largest single project in the I. G. Farben system. All that the firm asked from the government was help in procuring the necessary labor at reasonable rates.

Himmler and his commandant at Auschwitz, Rudolf Höss, were willing to cooperate. The mutually beneficial agreement was made, and I. G. Farben began to supplement the gas chambers of Birkenau with death by work and starvation. However, if cost-effective efficiency was the goal, the first year at I. G. Auschwitz was a mixed success. Prices for inmate labor were cheap enough, but the workers—already less than energetic because of their meager diet—were further weakened by the long daily trek to the factory site. With valuable time and energy lost, it was not a rational way to run a business, but the situation could be improved if the laborers were closer at hand. Thus, in July 1942, I. G. Farben obtained permission to build its own concentration camp called Monowitz.

This camp had a rational division of labor: I. G. Farben fed and housed the slave laborers; the SS handled security, discipline, and the supply of workers. If no Buna materialized from this process, its efficiency was remarkable on other counts. One could calculate quite precisely that the vast majority of workers at I. G. Auschwitz would be dead within three or four months of their initial stint. Poor food, inadequate sanitation, brutal guards, periodic selections to weed out the unfit—these realities combined with draining physical labor to make I. G. Auschwitz's most important product: death.

Consider two items more. First, among the firms dominated by I. G. Farben was *Die Deutsche Gesellschaft für Schädlingsbekämpfung* (the German Corporation for Pest Control), better known as DEGESCH. Among its products were amethyst-blue crystals of hydrogen cyanide, which on contact with air created a deadly gas—one milligram per kilo of body weight was lethal. Marketed as an effective pesticide under the trademark Zyklon B, it worked wonders for genocide. As SS purchases of this product increased, DEGESCH did its part by removing a special indicating odor normally used to warn human beings of the gas's deadly presence. DEGESCH took this step with some reluctance, though, not because Zyklon B was being used to kill human beings, but because the corporation feared that production of the gas without its telltale odor might jeopardize their monopoly patent.

"The supply," notes Raul Hilberg, "was kept up to the very end. The SS did not run out of gas,"[15] though Auschwitz officials feared they might. In storage Zyklon B deteriorated within three months. It could not be stockpiled. Thus the necessity of killing ten thousand Hungarian Jews a day during the summer of 1944 depleted the reserves. A decision followed to cut by half the twelve boxes of pellets ordinarily used each time a gas chamber was filled to capacity with fifteen hundred Jews. Zyklon B kills by internal asphyxiation. Its damage to the respiratory system is accompanied by dizziness, fear, and vomiting. Ordinarily, it took about fifteen minutes in the gas chambers to dispatch a load of life. Cutting back on the volume of gas meant that the death throes of the victims would be agonizingly prolonged. But that result was much less important than the fact that the reduced dosage was cheaper. How little it was cheaper, though, says much about what Jewish life was worth. At the exchange rates then in effect, the SS's economy measure produced a savings of less than $10 per chamber load. An individual's life was worth less than one cent; but even that was too much for some Nazis to spend. During the summer of 1944, they found it more cost-effective not to gas Jewish children at all. Instead they were burned alive. Meanwhile DEGESCH's investors suffered much less. Business returned them dividends of 100 to 200% from 1940 to 1943.[16]

What should one conclude? Does anything guarantee that it is not good business, rational business, to kill—unless it is a collective will that says "No!" with force sufficient to command respect? *Arbeit Macht Frei*? Those words mock the dead. They also mock the living who think that Holocaust business is vanquished from the earth.

"I Have Lived Only for My Work"

The most familiar eyewitness accounts of the Holocaust are by Jewish survivors. The Nazi mind is less inclined to remember things past, but the autobiography of Rudolf Höss is one telling exception. Among its noteworthy insights is Höss's confession that he lived only for his work.[17] What was Höss's work? What relation did it bear to *Arbeit Macht Frei*?

One historian calls Höss "the man from the crowd."[18] Another commentator describes him as a "very ordinary little man."[19] Such observations are true. Höss was a functionary, a cog in a huge machine, and he was not widely known—except perhaps indirectly by prisoners under his authority—outside of a restricted circle within the SS. Yet to encounter Rudolf Höss is to meet an unusual individual, for he was the best at what he did. What he did was no trivial undertaking. In Höss's case, working one's way to the top meant becoming the commandant of Auschwitz. It could be true that anyone might fill that role, if we mean that the propensity to unleash mass death is something from which no person is immune. On the other hand, to think that just anybody could manage Auschwitz is to underestimate Höss's ability.

We have met Höss before, but recall some of the highlights of his career. Höss was raised in a devout Roman Catholic home. Obedience to authority was emphasized along with the plan that Rudolf would become a priest. An introverted boy who loved horses and the out-of-doors, Höss found himself attracted to the army instead. Secretly joining a regiment in 1915, he fought with such distinction on the Turkish front that he not only received the Iron Cross First and Second Class but also at the age of seventeen became the youngest noncommissioned officer in the German army. In 1924, Höss was sentenced to ten years imprisonment for his part in the murder of Walter Kadow, who allegedly had denounced a German terrorist, Leo Schlageter, to the French. Describing himself as a prisoner more obedient than embittered, Höss was amnestied in the summer of 1928 after serving one half of his sentence. Although he had been a Nazi since 1922, Höss could not be persuaded to take any party office after his release; instead he hoped to become a farmer and a family man. Höss did decide to join the SS in 1933, but his agrarian dreams lingered on even after 1934 when Himmler urged him to take up full-time duty at a concentration camp. Höss followed Himmler's direction and went to Dachau where he worked his way up through the ranks, entering the SS officer corps with promotion to *SS-Untersturmführer* (second lieutenant) on 13 September 1936.

Early in 1940 Nazi officials decided that a new concentration camp should be built in Poland. The site was Auschwitz. Assignment as commandant was hardly a plum, and Höss got the post mainly because his superior at Sachsenhausen disliked him and was only too glad to recommend Höss for the position. Strict discipline and obedience did not save the SS from personal rivalries, and Höss's narrative complains repeatedly that they thwarted his conscientious attempts to do the best job possible at Auschwitz. Nevertheless, "every fresh difficulty only increased my zeal," Höss reports, and despite the obstacles he encountered, Höss did work remarkably well. His camp grew; it also diminished. If Höss rejected a figure of 2.5 million dead as "far too high" because "even Auschwitz had limits to its destructive possibilities,"[20] that total cannot be far from the mark Höss achieved before he was through.

Höss's was not a pedestrian performance. He worked hard because he believed his tasks were important, meaningful, rational, even good. Not that he took pleasure, least of all sadistic pleasure, in killing. On the contrary, there simply was a problem to be solved. Part of the problem, of course, was solved before it came to Höss's obedient hands. Convinced that the Nazi cause was right and therefore that the orders he received were to be followed without skepticism, Höss's dilemma was to make the Final Solution proceed as smoothly as possible. It was also to enable German industry to meet its labor need. Höss's ingenuity with Zyklon B went far toward handling the first assignment. Little fault could be found with his cooperation on the second count either.

Prior to his arrival at Auschwitz, Höss knew a good deal about forced labor. Prisoners work—Höss had learned that principle first-hand while he was himself an inmate, and it was a cornerstone of his administrative policy, too. In Höss's early experience, work meant rehabilitation. Working hard and well meant that one was learning a lesson, paying for wrongdoing in a way that would change consciousness for the better, not to mention breaking the monotony of imprisonment itself. Meanings of this kind, Höss relates, were behind the sign *Arbeit Macht Frei*, which he first saw at Dachau. True, he notes, such a philosophy could apply completely only "where the conditions are normal."[21] If the conditions were less than that when he took over at Auschwitz, neither was Höss quite expecting that his new camp would become a full-fledged *Vernichtungslager*. Thus, *Arbeit Macht Frei* went up there as well and stayed to deceive those who would die.

On 1 March 1941, according to Höss, Heinrich Himmler paid him a visit at Auschwitz. Accompanying Himmler were high executives of I. G. Farben. Plans to make Auschwitz an industrial center were well along, and Himmler instructed that prison labor would be made available as required. Indeed Himmler's proposals reached far into the future. He envisioned a postwar, peacetime operation of some thirty thousand inmates, presumably available to work for major branches of the German armaments industry that would be transferred there after the war.

In the summer of 1942 Himmler visited Auschwitz one last time. Meanwhile he had summoned Höss to Berlin a year earlier. In effect, the purpose of that meeting was to inform Höss that Auschwitz would become "the largest human slaughter house that history had ever known."[22] Höss was to be in charge. During the subsequent review of Auschwitz, Himmler observed the extermination process without comment, and then went on to inspect the Buna operation. His main concern was to increase worker efficiency. Höss tried to impress Himmler with the administrative difficulties, but at the end of the inspection tour, Höss was told that he would have to manage as best he could. Himmler then promoted Höss to lieutenant-colonel and left.

Original plans called for all Jewish arrivals at Auschwitz to be destroyed without exception. However, as the first transports of German Jews arrived, a different order stated that able-bodied men and women would be segregated and formed into labor brigades. Höss's difficulties compounded. Not only was Auschwitz two camps in one, but he had to cope with competing interests among the groups concerned with the labor pool. How many Jews should be selected for work? Which were fit? How would the logistics of security best be handled? In spite of these tough questions, in spite of the smoke and stench from bodies burning in the crematoria under his administration, Höss claimed that he still hoped to make Auschwitz "a clean and healthy place." Höss could say that "in Auschwitz everything was possible,"[23] but he was wrong. "Everything" made no room for hopes like those.

A Polish court condemned Höss to death on 2 April 1947. Two weeks later he was hanged at Auschwitz. The point, however, is not that the criminal always returns to the scene of the crime and even less that justice prevails. It may be discovered in a very different place by considering the following question: how cynical was Höss when he put up his sign, *Arbeit Macht Frei*, at the entrance to Auschwitz and kept it there until the end?

Any reading of Höss's narrative must allow for his desire to put himself in the best light. Still, at least at the outset of Höss's tenure at Auschwitz, there is not much reason to suppose that he callously intended *Arbeit Macht Frei* to have the mocking effect that certainly resulted. That adage, after all, contained a grain of truth. If—and it was a very big if—one got the chance to work, and if—once again a very big word—that work did not kill, then being able to work might keep one alive until rescue from outside arrived.

I. G. Farben, the SS, and Rudolf Höss controlled social reality at Auschwitz. They imposed *Arbeit Macht Frei* as a categorical imperative. It can be argued that their use of power was wrong, and theory after theory tries to back up that judgment. Good, but not good enough because when Rudolf Höss says that he lived only for his work, he also testifies that the decisive factor in life is who holds power over it.

Ethical reflection makes it crucial to ask: who ought to have power, and what should be the case? Rudolf Höss makes it clear that it is equally crucial for ethical reflection to ask: who is and will be in power, and what is going to happen in those cases? Granted, responses to the latter questions alone may not tell us what ought to be done. In that sense the traditional notion that ethics is logically prior to politics still rings true. Such priority, however, guarantees nothing. The human will to power—individual or collective—does not do so either, but in this world's history nothing goes further to determine what shall be.

At the end of his autobiography, Höss does say that "the extermination of the Jews was fundamentally wrong," but basically, Höss explains, the extermination was wrong because it failed: "It in no way served the cause of anti-Semitism, but on the contrary brought the Jews far closer to their ultimate objective." This unrepentant Höss was a good soldier to the end, and thus he also admits matter-of-factly: "I am responsible." True, Höss restricts that admission to those decisions that were in his sphere, reserving to others the responsibility for orders he received. Difficult though it may be, Höss also wants his readers to try to understand that "he, too, had a heart and that he was not evil."[24] If moral sensitivity finds that plea less than credible, a fundamental point is nonetheless well taken from the commandant of Auschwitz. In this world theoretical good counts for very little, but what shall in fact count for good matters very much. That determination belongs to people who take responsibility and hold it.

No Sign of Remorse

The Universal Declaration of Human Rights adopted by the General Assembly of the United Nations on 10 December 1948 proclaims that "recognition of the inherent dignity and of the equal and inalienable rights of all members of the

human family is the foundation of freedom, justice and peace in the world."
Such language has a long history, but it is not accidental that the United Nations
spoke out in the aftermath of Holocaust business. Aroused by the postwar trials
that condemned some Nazi leaders to death, protesters decried "crimes against
humanity." Moral pronouncements abounded. Who could oppose "human
rights" after Auschwitz? Indeed nowadays everyone defends them, verbally at
least. Yet how much justice is done remains a question.

As an American prosecutor at the Nuremberg trials, Benjamin B. Ferencz became concerned about restitution for Jewish survivors who had labored in the
Nazi camps. His book, *Less than Slaves*, testifies that too many German industrialists showed no sign of remorse. With the outbreak of World War II, the Nazis made labor conscription commonplace. The treatment accorded such
workers depended on their classification in a Nazi racial hierarchy that relegated
Slavs and Gypsies to subhuman status along with Jews. Germans were affected,
too. Political and religious dissidents, criminals, homosexuals—all who ran
afoul of Nazi law could find themselves imprisoned and enslaved. Jews fared
worst. If they were allowed to live at all, theirs was the most strenuous and dangerous work. Nevertheless, some of these men and women not only survived
but also went on to seek compensation from their captors. Their cases were
heard in courts of law as well as in settings aimed at moral persuasion. Ferencz's report is that power—economic and political but not ethical—determined
the verdicts: "Of the hundreds of German firms that used concentration camp
inmates, the number that paid anything to camp survivors could be counted on
the fingers of one hand. . . . Even the severe hardship cases of those who had
survived work for I. G. Farben at Auschwitz got no more than $1,700 each."[25]

Well, one might ask, should anything different have been expected? From an
ethical perspective, righteous indignation over such trivial individual recom-
pense for wasted lives comes easily. But Ferencz outlines the successful defense
mustered by those with a different perspective. War was the excuse; Germany
was fighting for her life. Labor was essential, and nobody could expect favors,
least of all Jews whom Nazi propaganda had successfully portrayed as a major
cause of the global conflict. Indeed, the industrialists went on to say, German
industry was under the gun. Disobedience of Nazi commands would have been
dealt with summarily. Practically speaking, German companies had to accept
the reality of forced labor. Otherwise their firms were in jeopardy and with them
Germany as well.

Most ethical perspectives find such defenses lacking, especially so in the light
of documents and oral testimony by former SS leaders which it make plain that
German businesses could obtain concentration camp labor only by requisition-
ing it. True, other options available were probably scant, but the fact remains
that industry decided to utilize slaves. That reality becomes all the more clear
when one recalls the treatment received by these workers—starvation diets, vir-

tual absence of health care, and, in the case of I. G. Auschwitz, imprisonment in a camp built specifically by and for the industry itself.

But could it not be argued that these labor policies saved lives? Without them, after all, Jews would have been gassed without further ado. German industry tried that argument. Not without validity, neither will it ring true completely. Had Germany won the war, the fate of those workers was sealed. Of course, Ferencz argues, there were exceptions. Some German businessmen took remarkable steps to alleviate the Jewish plight and to save threatened lives. Industrialists such as Hermann Graebe and Oskar Schindler are examples, along with lawyers such as Otto Küster and Walter Schmidt, who spoke out on behalf of the survivors after the war. It should also be mentioned that some German courts did not hesitate to find in the survivors' favor. These exceptions, however, tended to prove the rule: both during the war and afterward "it was only those who had nothing to be ashamed of who expressed a sense of guilt and culpability."[26] Failure to speak out is understandable, even from a moral point of view, under the duress of war in a Nazi state. After the war was over, it became less so. Or perhaps it is even more understandable because practical rationality requires that business must get back to normal. Business did so.

Consider, for example, the trials that ensued at the end of World War II. The most famous were thirteen held in Nuremberg between 1945 and 1949. Significantly, no representative of heavy German industry was among the twenty-two officials who stood before the International Military Tribunal (including judges and prosecutors from the United States, Great Britain, France, and Russia) that conducted the first trial where Nazi leaders such as Hermann Goering, Julius Streicher, and Albert Speer were in the dock. The first trial lasted from November 1945 until October 1946. Subsequent tribunals convened in the occupation zones of the four Allied powers. In the American zone, German industrialists were prosecuted in three of the Nuremberg trials.

The International Tribunal indicted the first Nuremberg defendants for conspiring to commit and for committing crimes against peace, war crimes, and crimes against humanity. Those charges were repeatedly brought against defendants in other courtrooms, too. Most of the German actions against the Jews were punishable under the traditional laws of war. Such laws, however, did not automatically pertain to anti-Jewish measures executed entirely within Axis territory. Nor were the Nazis' prewar anti-Jewish actions covered under that jurisdiction. Count Four, "Crimes Against Humanity," was conceived to handle "murder, extermination, and 'persecution on political, racial or religious grounds,' whether committed 'before or during the war,' just so long as such acts were undertaken or executed in connection with other acts 'under the jurisdiction of the Tribunal.' "[27] The prosecution of prewar and wartime acts under this count, however, never quite lost an ex post facto quality, for the defendants were not obviously subject to any "international agreement in existence in

1933, 1939, or even 1944 that made it illegal to persecute religions or to exterminate populations."[28]

Understandably necessary though the postwar trials may have been from psychological and even moral points of view, the legal structures available at the time were not fully adequate to handle the unprecedented results of the Holocaust. The ensuing justice nevertheless decreed prison sentences for numerous leaders of German industry: Alfried Krupp, twelve years; Walter Dürrfeld and Otto Ambros of I. G. Auschwitz, eight years; and Carl Krauch, six years. No defendants related to I. G. Farben were found guilty for supplying poisonous gas to the concentration camps.[29] Nor were any of these civilian industrialists in prison for long. By the end of the 1950s, the Western Allies had released those for whom they were responsible. For the most part, a similar pattern held in the Soviet Union and other eastern European countries formerly occupied by the Nazis.

The cases of two are especially instructive. First, conviction at Nuremberg for the enslavement and mass murder of two hundred thousand inmates at Auschwitz did not bar Otto Ambros from later employment as a high-level technical advisor to a major American corporation, W. R. Grace and Company, and as a consultant to the United States Department of Energy. When queried about Ambros in March 1982, a representative of W. R. Grace Company was quoted as follows: "We do not feel there was anything wrong in employing this man in a technical position years after whatever he did." The spokesperson added that J. Peter Grace, chairman of the board, "is extremely proud" of his relationship to Ambros and did not find the appointment "embarrassing in any sense." James W. Nance, a special assistant to President Ronald Reagan for national security, confirmed with apparent approval that Ambros had "recently" served as a consultant to the Department of Energy. A White House spokesperson declared that Ambros, who served only three years for his crimes, "had paid his debt to society."[30] If nothing else, Ambros's welcome in the highest levels of American business and government after conviction for Holocaust-related crimes demonstrates the degree to which technical and administrative competence have been divorced from moral values in contemporary society. Moral values remain in question in other respects as well, for Ambros was only one of thousands of Nazi war criminals who found a haven in the United States after World War II. Allan A. Ryan, director of the Office of Special Investigations from 1980 to 1983, which was formed within the United States Department of Justice in 1979 to identify and prosecute Nazi war criminals in America, puts the point this way: "The record is clear that preventing the entry of Nazi criminals to the United States was not a high priority, and was not taken seriously." He expressed hope that "our record in dealing with Nazi criminals is not entirely beyond salvage."[31]

The second case is that of Friedrich Flick, who received a Nuremberg sentence of seven years in prison for his support of the SS and for the use of slave labor in his vast industrial empire, Mitteldeutsche Stahlwerke, which "controlled over three hundred companies . . . [and] manufactured everything from toilet paper to dynamite."[32] Many of Flick's colleagues were acquitted altogether, but some of them joined their leader in jail. By January 1951, however, the American official in charge of such matters, John J. McCloy, had released them all. Good behavior figured into that decision, but of greater importance was the Cold War. American political policy needed German industrial leadership. Quickly German industry was back at work rebuilding its forces and its bank accounts. When Friedrich Flick died in 1972, he was the richest man in Germany and among the wealthiest in the world. He paid nothing at all to his former Jewish slaves in spite of persistent efforts on their behalf. A fitting epitaph might be the pronouncement he made in self-defense at Nuremberg: "Nothing will convince us that we are war criminals."[33] Flick's fate and disposition are not an isolated case, thus leading one to ask: what happened to justice? what does "human rights" mean? if people search for "some credible set of theonomous or autonomous moral norms governing the conduct of men and nations," where are they left?[34]

Can Right Make Might?

"The philosophers," asserted Karl Marx, "have only *interpreted* the world, in various ways; the point, however, is to *change* it."[35] Auschwitz did so. I. G. Farben, Friedrich Flick, and Rudolf Höss contributed to that end as well. And Marx was not completely correct because even thinking fostered by philosophical and religious minds advanced civilization, however unintentionally, toward the Final Solution. Such factors show how the world works, namely, that without *might* there seems to be little hope that theoretical *right* can prevail. In that case, is there any place left to stand and say that *right* makes *might*?

Holocaust business contains few surprises for anyone who studies history, which G. F. W. Hegel so aptly called a slaughter-bench. At the same time, such realities provoke strong feelings of protest and rebellion against what occurs. Senses of right and wrong are real, and the Holocaust helps to focus them. Even Heinrich Himmler knew as much. He and the other perpetrators of the Holocaust were aware of the psychological turmoil created by their orders to kill. They did their best to make those tasks easier, more "humane," by distancing the killers from their victims. Thus they substituted mass gassings for the shootings of the *Einsatzgruppen*. Beyond such administrative decisions, however, the Nazis could rely on an ally of vast authority: human consciousness itself. Humanity's capacity to think is amazingly pliable, especially so in its ability to justify whatever the powers that be want done. The explanations offered by German industrialists to warrant their use of slave labor were only one strand in a web of rationalization and repression that did much to ensure that dissenting moral scruples would be subordinated to higher necessities or even that the dictates of morality and mass murder would coincide.[36] The Nazis were not totally successful in this regard. But when one remembers that the persons responsible for the Holocaust were a cross-section from virtually every profession, skill, and social class, then the persistence with which the Final Solution went forward without effective moral dissent is the more striking.

One effective way for the Nazi machine to bridge the gap between traditional moral inhibitions and the destruction of so many human lives was to mask what was going on. Thus, instead of parading Auschwitz openly, steps were taken to shut off information from those who did not have to know. The Nazis skillfully used censorship in the press and other media to conceal actual details of the Final Solution. On the other hand, it was important to be sure that people who did know were involved in making the Final Solution happen. Within this circle, discussion of the killing was discouraged; criticism of it was taboo. Repeated use of euphemisms in memos and reports made everything easier, too. Where conscience still created dissonance, other remedies were available. Nazi propaganda never relented in its insistence that Germany must be rid of the Jews. They were portrayed simultaneously as conspirators who would destroy the nation, as criminals who would greedily seize what was not theirs, as vermin who plagued superior human life. In short, their elimination was promoted at once as a preventative war, a meting out of economic and social justice, and a health-restoring purge. This persuasion, however, still might not dispel entirely an individual's uneasiness about his or her involvement in the anti-Jewish campaigns.

Whether a person was part of the relatively small cadre who killed first-hand or one of the huge network of desk-bound personnel who destroyed people by composing memoranda, drafting blueprints, signing correspondence, and making telephone calls, he or she frequently took comfort from referring to orders from superiors and the necessity to obey. Indeed, at times orders were created after the fact to help people reconcile what had already taken place without explicit directives. Separation of duty from personal feeling was also important; life was compartmentalized into public affairs and private relations. One could organize transports to Auschwitz during the day and then embrace spouse and children in the evening. Denial of personal vindictiveness or pleasure in doing one's duty was essential, too. Thus recognizing the unpleasantness of certain tasks, far from making them impossible, could support the conviction that they must, after all, be done.

Still other defense mechanisms included role distinctions. A Friedrich Flick, for example, might employ slaves, but he could tell himself that he would never become a Rudolf Höss. Perhaps even a Höss could compare himself favorably to persons with hands dirtier than his and be convinced that he would never go that far. Such boundaries were frequently crossed, of course, but even if they were not, such comparative thinking enabled people to keep doing the jobs that were already theirs. That outcome was sufficient to keep the Holocaust going. Emphasis on group responsibility could also neutralize individual pangs of conscience. Since so many were involved in carrying out the Final Solution, one could argue that no individual's part could be too reprehensible. No matter how much one might wish or try to make things different, the vastness of the operation rendered one powerless to intervene effectively. That line of thought probably did as much as anything to ensure that the Holocaust could only be stopped by superior military force from the outside. Prevalent especially in the upper echelons of power, one more justification is worth noting: the view that life unfolds in a jungle of power struggles. If one does not keep winning, which to the Nazis entailed killing, then one loses. The latter can be a fate worse than death. That vision energized Hitler and his key aides. It ensnared a group of people who worked until most of European Jewry perished, Germany lay in ruins, and much of Western civilization became a wasteland.

"The owl of Minerva," wrote Hegel, "spreads it wings only with the falling of the dusk." He meant that human reason and philosophy in particular achieve understanding only in retrospect; they are hard pressed to give "instruction as to what the world ought to be."[37] If Hegel is correct, the tools of moral philosophy and religious ethics are meager. Still, they have a role to play that nothing else can duplicate. Moral reflection, for example, can clarify and intensify feelings of wrong prompted by Holocaust business. Such thinking can show the importance of those feelings by revealing what happens when they fail to work their way into practice. Yet that understanding alone does little to change the world as long as societies concretely reward activities that kill and take punitive action toward those who refuse to cooperate.

If one wants to affirm the United Nations' declaration that "everyone has the right to life, liberty, and security of person," one must realize that such claims are as fragile as they are abstract. The same is true of the Genocide Convention submitted by the United Nations to its members in 1948 as a reaction to Nazi efforts to destroy European Jewry. The United States became the ninety-seventh nation to approve the treaty when the Senate ratified the pact on 19 February 1986. The long delay was occasioned by fears that if the United States agreed to the treaty that makes genocide a crime the nation might be indicted by its adversaries. That fear can be found in other countries as well, for the United States is not alone in reserving the right to exempt itself from World Court jurisdiction in genocide cases that might be brought against it. In truth, however, the practical effects of the Genocide Convention are limited, for power, not pacts, is what breaks or makes mass killing. Rights, liberty, and security of person are real only in specific times and places, only in actual political circumstances. Apart from such concrete settings those ideals are only that. Granted, they are ideals that attract. They can bring out the best in people. They can even rally powerful forces behind them. They may even have a transcendent status ordained by God. To assume, however, that they are more than ideals until men and women take responsibility to make them a concrete reality may well be an illusion.

By itself, moral indignation is largely irrelevant when the powers that be determine that the disappearance of defenseless persons and the prosperity of their persecutors constitute business as usual. Yet the question remains: can right make might? The answer is: it all depends. The crucial variable in that response is the human *will*. How will people respond to the feelings and thoughts that condemn Holocaust business? Still marked so much by concentration camps of labor and death, this post-Holocaust world deserves an entry sign. Let it read *Arbeit Macht Frei*. Shall those words provoke the good work that justly sets people free, or will they merely mock us all?

Chapter 9

What Can—and Cannot—Be Said? Literary Responses to the Holocaust

A teacher of Hebrew, Chaim Kaplan, kept a journal in the Warsaw ghetto. Dated 4 August 1942, the final line in its last entry asks a question: "If my life ends—what will become of my diary?"[1] Kaplan sensed there was nothing hypothetical about the first part of his uncertainty. No "if" existed; it was only a matter of "when." And "when" was soon. By the end of that month, Kaplan had perished in the gas chambers at Treblinka. The only open part of his question was "what will become of my diary?"

That issue was not on Kaplan's mind alone. Diaries, thousands of them, were kept by men, women, and children wherever the Nazi scourge targeted Jews. Nor was an intense desire to record and remember reflected only in written words. As circumstances permitted in the ghettos and camps, artists sketched and painted, musicians composed and played.[2] Much of this activity occurred in the Theresienstadt ghetto. Situated near the Czech city of Prague, it served a dual function. An assembly center for transports of Czech Jews to Auschwitz, Theresienstadt also was a "model" to reassure foreign governments and international welfare agencies that Jews, especially elderly ones from Germany, were living in a decent place. Hence artists and musicians were selected for Theresienstadt. Most were eventually deported and murdered.

Although their sounds are forever silenced, concerts were held and operas were performed in Theresienstadt, sometimes at the Nazis' behest but also at the Jews' own initiative. Rarely did an ensemble or cast stay intact for long, however, their ranks depleted by unrelenting departures for the gas. A few musical compositions survived, but most perished along with a host of musical talent. In other places, too, many far less amenable to beauty than Theresienstadt, musical expression, whether in folk, liturgical, classical, or even jazz forms, helped some people to endure and many others to find some moments of dignity and sanity amidst overwhelming horror and degradation.

Jewish artists were decimated, too. More of their works survived, however; some thirty thousand of them are now catalogued. At Theresienstadt, Jewish painters often had to do work for the Nazis, but they also risked their lives to depict secretly the actual conditions in their camp. In every ghetto or camp where such work was done, it had to be hidden to survive. Some artists buried their pictures in jugs, bricked them into walls, even taped them to their bodies during forced marches. Materials were easier to get in Theresienstadt than in many other places. Bread was often the price for pencils and paints. Paper might be scrounged from any scraps that came to hand. Flour sacks and burlap bags became improvised canvas. All across Europe artist-victims created. Putting art in the service of history, they left behind glimpses of the Final Solution. Perhaps even more importantly these works themselves are documents whose sheer existence tells what no words could ever say. Art historians and critics discern differences in the training, technique, and talent of these artists, but few will deny that the mixture of passion and detachment reflected in their works, individually and collectively, have exceptional power to transmute aesthetic debates and disagreements into respectful appreciation.

A picture is worth a thousand words. Yet neither the haunting silence of melodies that have disappeared nor the speechless power of line and color substitute for words. Especially during the Holocaust, words were the most available resources for recording what had to be remembered. Whether spoken or written, they could give the dying a lasting voice.[3] Focusing on the written testimony, no one knows how many eyewitness accounts have been lost forever. Like the paintings of an Aizik Feder or a Malvina Schalkova, or the musical scores of a Viktor Ullmann and a Pavel Haas, how they survived makes one wonder. Smuggled, buried, occasionally just left behind—some of these scrolls of agony have resurfaced. Speaking with authority, they include the hopes and fears of young people such as Mary Berg in Warsaw, Etty Hillesum in Amsterdam, Moshe Flinker in Brussels, and Eva Heyman in Nagyvarad; the testimonies of Janusz Korczak, who accompanied the children of his orphanage to their deaths, and Emmanuel Ringelblum, who coordinated a historical archive in Warsaw; and even the tragic witness of *Sonderkommandos* who had to burn the bodies of their fellow Jews before their own lives were consumed.

Artists such as Charlotte Buresova, David Olere, and Lea Lilienblum lived to create after the Holocaust. Linked with that company are other survivors—Jean Améry, Primo Levi, and Leon Wells; Zivia Lubetkin, Donia Rosen, and Nechama Tec, to mention only a few—who have groped for words to make memories that might tell as directly as possible what happened, disappeared, and remained. In addition, there are other writers—some of them survivors, others who were not in the Holocaust, still others who were and did not survive—who have enlisted the characters of story and the images of verse to reveal and to respond to the catastrophe that engulfed European Jewry. A representative sample of these authors and their works by no means exhausts what has come to be known as Holocaust literature.[4] That category includes essays—historical, philosophical, and religious—as well as diaries and autobiographical accounts of eyewitnesses in addition to those works of poetry and prose fiction that are substantively governed by the Jewish plight under Hitler. As this chapter seeks to illustrate, however, the best of the latter reveals especially well a set of issues and themes that are fundamental for anyone who approaches Auschwitz.

Just as Holocaust literature includes diverse genres, its authors represent varied nationalities and write in different languages. Most, though not all, are Jewish, but even that shared identity promotes a broad stylistic spectrum. Permeating the diversity, however, are issues that these writers confront in common. They invite their readers to wrestle with them, too. Despite their remarkable literary gifts, nearly all of these authors feel a profound ambivalence. It is impossible to write adequately about the Holocaust; yet that task must be attempted. They regard themselves as unequipped to do such work; yet they are compelled to try. The corresponding tension for a reader, at least for one who was not "there," is between an effort to understand and an awareness that the Holocaust eludes full comprehension. These dilemmas have multiple dimensions. The Holocaust, for example, outstrips imagination. It is one thing to be creative when the possibilities open to imagination exceed what has become real. It is quite another to find that reality has already given birth to persons, places, and events that defy imagining. "Normal men," observed one survivor, "do not know that everything is possible."[5]

Perhaps history prepares post-Holocaust minds to be more accepting of the idea that "everything is possible." Nonetheless how is one to comprehend that the Nazi way included "idealism" that did not merely permit torture and murder but commanded that they occur day and night? So a problem remains: can poetry and prose fiction help one to know what happened and to cope with its impact? There are no metaphors or adequate analogies for the Holocaust. Nor can Auschwitz be a metaphor or an analogy for anything else. If those realizations inform the ambivalence of those who write poetry or prose fiction about the Holocaust, still they must feel that their expressions are at least potentially capable of communicating something urgent that can be said in no other way. But that conviction makes their task no easier, and when a reader works to grasp what the best of the Holocaust writers say, he or she will sense how the Holocaust makes those writers struggle with words. How can words tell the truth, describe what must be portrayed, convey and yet control emotion so that clear insights will emerge? Every imaginative author faces such questions, but they become unusually demanding when one encounters the Holocaust. Now words and art forms must be used against themselves, since they are unable to say all that is required, and yet no other resources are available.

When writers emphasize the impossibilty of communicating the realities of the Holocaust via words, they are sometimes accused of mystifying that event. They either make the Holocaust so exceptional that it loses contact with the rest of human history, the argument goes, or they obscure and becloud it in rhetoric that invests Auschwitz with a mythical or mystical aura that opposes lucid, rational analysis. Critical opinion may reach varied verdicts on those charges where different authors and works are concerned, but the representatives examined here—all of whom do see the Holocaust as unprecedented and fraught with dimensions and implications that go beyond the realms of politics, economics, and history—are not guilty of culling the Holocaust out of worldly reality. Nor have they obscured or beclouded the past. On the contrary, their efforts complement, and are complemented by, all sound historical analysis. They are rooted both in the enormity of human loss brought about by the Holocaust and in the need to retrieve whatever can be left of a human future after Auschwitz has exposed the illusory quality of so many cherished assumptions. Consider, then, the efforts of Yitzhak Katzenelson, André Schwarz-Bart, Ka-tzetnik 135633, Charlotte Delbo, Tadeusz Borowski, William Styron, and Elie Wiesel. The themes they emphasize—lamentation, resistance, endurance, survival, honesty, choice-making, protest—reveal what the creative imagination can communicate about the Holocaust and the human future.

Lamentation

Born in Russia in 1886, Yitzhak Katzenelson nearly survived. His *Song of the Murdered Jewish People*, a poem unsurpassed in Holocaust literature, mourns its author, too. Katzenelson's poetic talents first flourished in Warsaw, winning him critical acclaim and widespread popularity. He traveled extensively in Europe, visited the United States, and went twice to Palestine. Ardent Zionist though he was, Katzenelson was always lured back to Poland. Thus, eight days after the Nazi invasion, he was trapped with his wife Hannah and their three children in Lodz, which had been his home for thirty-five years. Some three months later, at his wife's urging, Katzenelson journeyed to Warsaw to find better circumstances. The situation there was worse, as his family, now expelled from Lodz, learned when they reached Katzenelson.

Three years passed. Katzenelson was still in Warsaw, barely hanging on with his eldest son, Zvi, in the final days of the Jewish ghetto. He had seen the wall go up, the sadism of German soldiers, and the deportation of thousands of Jews. He had been helpless to prevent his wife and two of his children, Yomele and Benzikl, from being among them. Despite his despair and grief, Katzenelson continued to teach. He wrote, too—plays that were performed, poems and prose works that were read. He became friends with the young men and women in the Jewish Fighting Organization (ZOB), which would lead the Warsaw ghetto uprising. Katzenelson took heart from them. They were inspired by him as well.

Katzenelson's friends smuggled him out of the ghetto just a few days before the uprising began on 19 April 1943. When he and his son obtained forged Honduran passports that permitted him to become part of a planned prisoner exchange between the Nazis and the Allies, it seemed he might survive. Thus, in May 1943 Katzenelson waited in a German camp at Vittel, France. If Katzenelson's personal condition seemed to be improved, he knew the fate of his people was not. Realizing that he had indeed witnessed the murder of the Jewish people, he finally brought his poetic power to bear on that reality. So, on 3 October 1943, two days after Rosh Hashanah, this poet who would have preferred to compose light, melodious love poems, began a three-and-a-half-month labor that gave birth to his most important work. Like so many Jews who wrote during the Holocaust, Katzenelson understood that his poem must go into hiding. With the help of another prisoner, Miriam Novitch, it was buried beneath the roots of a pine tree near a soccer field at the camp's edge. Miriam Novitch would recover the poem. Meanwhile, Yitzhak Katzenelson had been deported to Auschwitz. Something had gone awry with the exchange of prisoners—it is still unclear what—but two weeks later, on 31 May 1944, the Nazis recognized the kind of passport Katzenelson had held. Death ironically echoed his repeated lamentation: ''It was too late.''[6]

Penned in Yiddish on sheets of lined paper, *The Song of the Murdered Jewish People* consists of fifteen cantos. Each has fifteen stanzas, each stanza four lines. Neat, symmetrical, ordered, this structure conveys agony and loss that no form can contain. Choosing not to follow a strictly chronological ordering of the events he witnessed, Katzenelson focused instead on moments in the process of destruction. The chronology is not the memory of linear sequence but of particular experiences that epitomize the catastrophe Katzenelson endured. The moments all fit together, and as the poem builds its bridges, the lines cover the full range of Jewish suffering, including Katzenelson's special burden of feeling both the necessity and the impossibility, the obligation and the inability, to denounce and to lament what happened.

''Sing!'' is the poem's first word. It is a command, but by whom? It challenges, pleads, protests, and mocks ironically, all at once. For how can anyone ''sit on the ruins of the murdered people and sing?'' The poet invokes the dead to lift the only appropriate song: ''Scream, scream aloud!'' But the dead are nowhere to be found, though they are also everywhere. ''Emerge,'' Katzenelson writes, ''reveal yourselves to me.'' And as they do, their commanding ''soundless scream'' shall be obeyed: ''Yes . . . Hand me the harp . . . I will play!''[7]

Katzenelson's voice says: ''I play.'' But what can and cannot, must and must not, be played? Those are searing questions. One cannot sing ''of trust and hope, / As in bygone days,'' for "No bone is left for new flesh, new skin, / For a new spirit of life." Hannah, Benzikl, Yomele—all are gone. Their voices heard and smiles seen in memory, such recollection only adds to "my misfortune, that I am still alive. . . ."[8] The pain is all there is to play.

The poet makes pain his song. Of all the agonies, few tortured more than his witnessing how "Jews were being used, ah, to destroy my Jews!" Jewish police do the Nazis' will; they fill the deportation quotas, the "wagons of pain, laden with the living carried to death." If the horses only knew, they would wring their "front legs, / Like human hands, in despair. . . ."[9] If the wheels only knew, but "they go on" dumbly, indifferent like the sun and the sky and the God who is—or is not—there. The train is waiting.

The train is gone and then back too soon: its "wagons have returned! Only yesterday at dusk they left." As though possessed by empty bellies that crave starving Jews, the wagons are oblivious to the suffocating scenes inside "their gaping mouths." There living Jews speak to dead ones unaware that they are clutched by death. A few jump out; others confess; none escape. Only the train returns—empty. "O tell me you empty train cars," insists the poet, "tell me where you have been!" Lamentation and rage blend together, for the poet knows. They have been to "the other world." Katzenelson presses further his one-way dialogue with the train: even though you are made of iron and wood, how can you endure it? The image goes too far: "It's not your fault, they load you, tell you: Go."[10] Yet tears would be easier to shed if the rolling wheels would say a word about the end.

The end cannot be told, and yet it can because "I know how it began." The Nazis demanded; the Jewish Council complied. One day the train deported six thousand Jews from Warsaw. That was not enough; a new day's order is for ten. Chairman Czerniakow agreed to six. But what are four more? Too many, and "you take poison" before the council convenes. The order is for ten, and Katzenelson writes: "Someone spoke. His tongue shook like a leaf. / All of them listened. . . . As if the dead chairman conducted the meeting."[11] Czerniakow's death had greater meaning than his life, suggests the poet, and ten thousand turned out not to be too many.

Those in the transports were not the first ones. "The first to perish were the children, abandoned orphans." Katzenelson saw "the two-year-old grandmother" who witnessed what "her grandmother could not dream." He wondered at "the five-year-old mother" feeding "her younger, crying brother," talking him "into joy" with imagination that, Katzenelson writes, his own mother could not have mustered. He watched, listened, felt, "wept and said to myself: Don't cry, grief disappears, seriousness remains."[12] And that seriousness means refusing to forget what "eighty million criminals" have done in making Jewish childhood impossible.

"O why such punishment?" Such a serious question intensifies the pain because "we all knew, . . . we hid it from ourselves" until it was too late. Memory turns back time. "A day before yesterday, yesterday, even this morning / You could still reach a frontier by bus, train, freight."[13] But when was yesterday? How long ago was this morning? Was it Wednesday, the day Poland was invaded and the exits shut? Fleeing Jews with nowhere to go, they might as well go home, but where is home? It has become a ruin of burned synagogues, desecrated scrolls, and tortured rabbis.

The heavens saw it begin. Sun, moon, and stars continued on their way. No longer can they inspire; no more must they bring forth psalms of awe and praise. Impassive, their distance soils them like the earth. The heavens stand accused: "There is no God in you!" The Jews of Poland are no worse than any who have lived before, but surely they have suffered more: "In every one of them / A Jeremiah wails, a tormented Job cries, and a disillusioned king intones Ecclesiastes." Will the heavens stay unmoved? "May a fire from earth ascend to you and fire from you descend upon earth."[14]

Together with his family, Katzenelson saw "the beginning of the end." A blond German looked at Yitzhak and Hannah and then killed someone else, someone more distinctly Jewish. It could have been them, and in the end it was, except "I remained alone with my oldest, watching the end of us all in fire and flames. . . ." And then the poet sings a love song of remembrance to his wife. The love and the remembrance, however, temper tenderness like steel: "Don't let oblivion heal our eternal wound," implores Katzenelson. "In our terrible agony, in this void," he continues, "I charge you with my wrath, / Bear it, as you bore my sons. . . ." And then he specifies, carefully and passionately, what she must help him remember: small coats never again to be worn by the departed child-actors who would have performed his play in the ghetto, and how all that remained for him to bring away from the orphanage was "a segment of my play, a dwarf—with no beginning or end."[15]

His ability to sing transmuted into lamentation, his grief turned into protesting rage, now Katzenelson warns: "Plug your ears. Don't listen—be deaf! I'm going to tell about Mila Street." The great deportation of Jews from the Warsaw ghetto began on 22 July 1942. At first there were exemptions, but Katzenelson describes Mila Street six weeks later. All exemptions are void; all remaining Jews must undergo "selection" for "resettlement." If there is to be no remnant, then there must be no God, "but if He existed it would be even worse! Both God and Mila Street . . . What a combination! . . . There is a God! Yet such injustice, such mockery, and such terrible shame!"[16] And then Katzenelson reports an incident on Mila Street, on the way to the *Umschlag-platz*, Treblinka, and nothingness. A minor occurrence from a macrocosmic perspective, this moment on Mila Street is a microcosm of the Holocaust's destructiveness:

I watched and saw: They removed a sack from the skinny back of a Jew,
The sack began to cry. . . . A child! A Jewish child! The gendarme is furious:
He looks for the father. . . . Yells to the child: "Identify him!" The child
    stares at his father,
He looks at him and doesn't cry. . . . He looks at his father but doesn't iden-
    tify him!

The little boy! The German hauled out another Jew, an "innocent one." You!
Placed them both with the thousands condemned to die—such a joke!
I saw it—O leave me alone. Don't question. Don't ask—what? when? where?
I warned you not to probe and never to ask about Mila Street.[17]

There was no escaping Mila Street, yet momentarily a remnant did remain,
rebellious and resisting. Katzenelson encouraged those young fighters. *The
Song of the Murdered Jewish People* is full of respect, pride, and love for most
of the Jews who endured and perished in Warsaw, but on only one occasion
does this poem sing with anything like joy. Such a note is unmistakable when
Katzenelson records an amazed German scream—"The Jews are shooting!"—
and when a few more arms are obtained to supplement the sparse arsenal of the
Jewish Fighting Organization. But too soon "it's all over."[18]

Biblical accounts of the Exodus say that a pillar of cloud by day and a pillar
of fire by night led Jews to new life in the Promised Land. During the Holocaust cloud and fire signified something else, and thus the poet questions:
"Why? No human being in the world asks why, yet all things do: Why?" Expressing much more than incomprehension, that question encompasses a
profound sadness and also a refusal to accept that "we may be killed and murdered with impunity." A way of life has disappeared, and in murdering the
Jewish people, the rest of humanity has been grievously wounded, too. Hence
the poem ends with a cry of judgment, at once thunderously determined, quietly
vehement, and forcefully restrained: "O distant sky, wide earth, vast seas; Do
not crush and don't destroy the wicked. Let them destroy themselves!"[19] Could
that cry hint, ever so faintly, at redemption?

On 18 January 1943, just before Yitzhak Katzenelson heard a dying German
scream "the Jews are shooting," he spoke to a group of young ghetto fighters.
One of them recalls his words: "The Germans have murdered millions of us,
but they will not prevail. The Jewish people lives, and so will it continue to
live. Our eyes will not see it, but they will pay dearly. After we die, our deeds
will be remembered forever. . . ."[20] About a year later Katzenelson completed
The Song of the Murdered Jewish People. It displays none of the confident hope
of his earlier speech. Its song is persistently in the minor key of lamentation,
mourning profoundly through its tones of protest, rage, and yearning for vindication. Through the compression of verse and the compactness of image, he
gives magnificent voice to those feelings, thereby accomplishing one of the
tasks that nothing other than Holocaust literature can do quite so well: to focus

our passion and our thoughts together on the sheer human loss that the Holocaust brought about. Mourning that loss does not ensure that the killers of defenseless people will not prevail, but failure to share Katzenelson's grief
removes one critical obstacle in their path. Without a sorrow that knows what
no words can ever say eloquently or powerfully enough, namely, how wrong it
is to let human lives be wasted, the future projects us toward mass murder all
over again.

Resistance

André Schwarz-Bart resisted the Nazis. Though very differently, so did
Ernie Levy, the chief character in Schwarz-Bart's prize-winning novel, *The
Last of the Just* (1959). Born in 1924, the author, a French Jew of Polish descent, lost his parents to the Nazis and found his way into the Resistance. Arrested, he escaped to do battle against the Nazis again, and then after the war he
continued the struggle against antisemitism and population elimination by becoming a writer. *The Last of the Just* is rooted in an ancient Jewish legend.
Different versions exist—Schwarz-Bart has deviated from them all by creating
a family line of "just men"—but each suggests that the world continues to exist only because of a few genuinely righteous persons. For their sake, God
withholds destructive wrath, and the rest of humankind is reprieved. In some
accounts there must be thirty-six who are just; in others, even one is enough.
Usually the just are not obvious. They may be unknown even to themselves. In
this novel, Ernie Levy becomes a just man, a *Lamed-Vovnik*. He is aware of
this role, too, though he may not understand, as Schwarz-Bart's readers do,
that he is the last.

What would it mean if Ernie Levy, or someone like him, were really the last
of the just—not just the last in the Levy line of just men that Schwarz-Bart has
posited but the last of the just, period? It might mean that the legend is false.
The world's existence does not depend on just people and maybe not on God
either. Or, alternatively, perhaps there continue to be other just people; Ernie
was not the last. Or perhaps the world, or at least *a* world, *did* come to an end
when Ernie perished. Or, yet again, maybe there are grains of truth in all three
of those options and more. Schwarz-Bart leaves such questions open. They invite the reader's reflection as the author explores the heritage, manifestation,
and outcome of Ernie Levy's resistance to National Socialism's destruction of
the European Jews.

Schwarz-Bart's novel, which ends in an Auschwitz gas chamber, begins a
millennium before. The English town of York was ravaged by a pogrom in
1185. Under the leadership of Rabbi Yom Tom Levy, a group of Jews refused
to convert to Christianity, though failure to do so meant death. Besieged in a
tower, possessing but a single weapon, they resisted by dying willingly at the
rabbi's hand instead. He finished this work by plunging the dagger into his own

throat. The narrator remarks that this incident was not remarkable but "only a minor episode in a history overstocked with martyrs." Nevertheless a legend grew up around this rabbi from York, namely, that his youngest son had somehow survived the pogrom and been told in a dream that the action of his father had moved God: " 'And therefore to all his line, and for all the centuries, is given the grace of one Lamed-Vovnik to each generation. You are the first, you are of them, you are holy.' "[21]

Later the identity of the *Lamed-Vovnik* in the Levy line became obscure, but the fate of that family became a microcosm of the history of the European Jews. Harried and driven from west to east, Ernie's branch of the family tree reached Poland, Russia, and then in the late eighteenth century the obscure town of Zemyock near Bialystok. Ernie's father was born there but decided to leave when the turbulence of the Russian Revolution during World War I decimated the Jews of Zemyock in yet another pogrom. The most promising land of exile, surmised Benjamin Levy, was neither the United States nor France but Germany. Greater civility, warmth, and gentleness could be expected from the German character. Berlin proved disappointing, but the town of Stillenstadt became a home. There, eventually joined by his parents who had lost other children to the Cossacks, Benjamin married and became Ernie's father. A schoolboy when Hitler came to power in 1933, Ernie was beaten senseless in that same year by Christian playmates who forced him to represent Jews crying for Jesus' death during his trial before Pilate.

Stillenstadt was home no longer. Fleeing with his family to France after *Kristallnacht*, Ernie enlists in the French army but learns that his family has been interned because they are *German* Jews. After France falls, he learns additionally that they have been deported east. His father's judgment seems bitterly vindicated: *"To be a Jew is impossible."*[22] Ernie tries to make his Jewish identity disappear, but the destiny of the *Lamed-Vovnik* is inescapable. Drawn back into a Jewish community in occupied Paris, he befriends and falls in love with Golda. When she is caught in a roundup, Ernie goes to the Drancy concentration camp to find her. He succeeds but only to discover that Golda will be deported along with hundreds of orphaned children. Once again, Ernie volunteers "to go in and not come out."[23] At night the transport gets under way, jammed with children. They are distraught, crying, panicked. Ernie comforts them by telling stories. The stories do not tell the truth, or at least they mask it, because they describe the train's destination as the Kingdom of Israel. A woman, a doctor, overhears. " 'How can you tell them it's only a dream?' she breathed, hate in her voice. Rocking the child mechanically, Ernie gave way to dry sobs. 'Madame,' he said finally, 'there is no room for truth here.' " The child Ernie held did not hear this exchange, for "Ernie looked down and discovered that the living corpse he was rocking had become a dead corpse." In this place, what else is there room for, the woman started to protest, and then she glimpsed Ernie's face more closely: " 'Then you don't believe what you're saying at all? Not at all?' " Ernie heard the woman's bitter weeping, her "terrified, demented laugh." He did not reply.[24]

The train arrives. Ernie refuses separation from Golda and the children, but there is no silver lining in the clouds of smoke emitted by the chimneys of Auschwitz. "This story," writes Schwarz-Bart, "will not finish with some tomb to be visited in memoriam. For the smoke that rises from crematoriums obeys physical laws like any other: the particles come together and disperse according to the wind that propels them. The only pilgrimage . . . would be to look with sadness at a stormy sky now and then." Such awareness wears heavily on the narrator-author, who interrupts himself at the end to say: "I am so weary that my pen can no longer write." Near collapse under the burden of what it tries to describe, Schwarz-Bart's prose resists that fate. Drawing together powerfully, it takes the reader, at least evocatively, into the gas chamber where Ernie Levy, father to Jewish children and husband to Golda, gives up his life: "The dying children had already dug their nails into Ernie's thighs, and Golda's embrace was already weaker, her kisses were blurred when, clinging fiercely to her beloved's neck, she exhaled a harsh sigh: 'Then I'll never see you again? Never again?' Ernie managed to spit up the needle of fire jabbing at his throat, and as the woman's body slumped against him, its eyes wide in the opaque night, he shouted against the unconscious Golda's ear, 'In a little while, *I swear it!*' "[25]

Schwarz-Bart places words of affirmation—"Hear, O Israel, the Lord is our God, the Lord is One"—on the lips of Jews dying at Auschwitz. To them he adds some of his own: "And praised. *Auschwitz*. Be. *Maidanek*. The Lord. *Treblinka*. And praised. . . ." He also notes that Ernie Levy's presence seems to linger on, but the reader is left to conclude what such an ending might mean. For Ernie was the last of the just. Schwarz-Bart has portrayed the Holocaust as the culmination of a long history of anti-Jewish violence in Europe. Moreover, as he has traced that history, his novel provides a picture of Jewish responses to their minority status, a spectrum that ranges from martyrdom and exile to evasion and a naive, compliant accommodation. There are incidents of physical resistance, too, but Schwarz-Bart stresses the fundamental defenselessness of the Jews, "who for two thousand years did not bear arms and who never had either missionary empires nor colored slaves."[26] The novel's sadness is not predicated on the conviction that the opposite of those realities would have been better. On the contrary, this novel excels in honoring spiritual resistance and the extent to which courage, dignity, grace, and compassion can find expressions in the midst of ultimately tragic and hopeless situations. Resistance before inevitable death includes choosing how to die. To die on one's own terms, not to be terrorized and victimized by the slaughter nor to succumb to meanness and viciousness, is to die at the height of spiritual resistance to oppression. Ernie

Levy does so, and in addition he enables others to die with dignity and some modicum of peace. At times this compassion requires him not to tell the truth, or at least to mask it, but Ernie stands for a compassionate solidarity with his people.

Responding to the story he has written, Schwarz-Bart says, "At times one's heart could break in sorrow." This saga of spiritual resistance seems to enjoin exactly that reaction. For grand as Ernie's actions are, he and Golda and those children perished. Ashes, scattered and lost, may be all that remains of them— except for memories. The memories, however, are left to wonder whether the world that destroyed "the last of the just" is worthy any longer of Ernie's gentleness and warmth. Or is his way only one more vestige of innocence that went up the chimneys and disappeared? Schwarz-Bart subtitles the final part of *The Last of the Just*: "Never Again." He colors the meaning of those words by quoting from Katzenelson's *Song of the Murdered Jewish People*: ". . . The sun, rising over a town in Poland, in Lithuania, will never again greet an old Jew murmuring psalms at the window or another on his way to the synagogue. . . ."[27] It may never greet another Ernie Levy either, because the world has no room for him any longer.

That judgment, however, may be too simple. For one thing, recall that "Never Again" also signifies determination that there must be not another Auschwitz for Jews or for any other people. That outcome is unlikely unless there are compassion and solidarity such as Ernie Levy's. Caught in circumstances where he was largely powerless, Ernie did what he could to keep the defenseless from being abandoned altogether. There is the grandeur of his character, there is also the tragedy. Powerlessness invites catastrophe. Power may do so, too, but both of those facts together underscore what may be the most crucial implication that emerges from Schwarz-Bart's novel: Ernie Levy must not be the last of the just. His particular model is not necessarily the one to welcome or to encourage, because to do so would also be to legitimize the conditions of oppression that made him a volunteer for Drancy and Auschwitz, a volunteer who could not afford the luxury of telling the truth if children were to be spared the worst. Yet there is no subsitute for his fidelity, compassion, and courage on behalf of defenseless victims. This means, in turn, that there is a sense in which Ernie Levy must be the last of the just, for no one should ever again have to volunteer as he did. That truth is also matched by another: such a need will disappear only to the extent that there is power to defend those who cannot protect themselves.

The Last of the Just is an extended meditation on resistance. Like Katzenelson's poem, it makes plain the enormity of loss that the Holocaust created. Lamenting that loss, it questions the future, thereby urging us to retrieve and renew the forces that insist no human being ought to be considered surplus. Although a world ended at Auschwitz, another one very different and yet much the same still exists. The legend of the just has not been falsified, but it has not been verified either. Its validity remains in suspense, leaving those who live after Auschwitz to decide whether being just is impossible.

Endurance

The best Holocaust literature makes visible the invisible dimensions of history. Moving beyond the analysis of cause and effect, penetrating subjective experience deeper than any science can, it strives to reveal what cannot be seen because once-existing eyes have been glazed by death. Auschwitz was full of eyes. Some watched them and survived, including those of Ka-tzetnik 135633. That is not Yehiel Dinur's real name. Yet it is because the young reporter in prewar Poland saw those figures etched into the flesh of his left arm at Auschwitz. There he became "Ka-tzet." So were all the inmates in every *Konzentrationslager*—KZ for short, pronounced "*Ka-tzet*" *auf Deutsch* with the prisoners themselves adding the Russian suffix *nik* for good measure. Dinur lived to write. His most widely read work is a novel, *House of Dolls*. Based on a Holocaust diary, it tells the story of Daniella Preleshnik, a teenaged Jewish girl whose life the Nazis prostituted in a labor camp. Even more powerful, however, is *Star Eternal*. The prose poems in that slender volume—"Phases" as the author calls them—are among the unrivaled gems of Holocaust literature. Published first in Hebrew, its original title *Star of Ashes* tells better what the eyes of Auschwitz saw. For ashes filled the heavens, and this poet's history testifies that anyone who looks skyward without seeing ash eternal is blind.

Ka-tzetnik's eyes open with dawn in an Auschwitz without beginning or end. They behold a galaxy of camps. They scan "ten thousand pairs of eyes" spilling out of the blocks. They will see again life pouring from "the railroad platform to the crematorium," its "drops ever changing," the stream "ever the same." These mostly Jewish eyes are old and young but not too young, not too old. Eyes of science, trade, art, common labor—all of these are here and more besides. These eyes wonder; they question. But Ka-tzetnik sees that all issues are reduced to one for which they beg an answer: "*When will the soup ration ever be handed out?*" An SS sentry descends a watchtower. His replacement takes over. Every Auschwitz dawn begins the same: with eyes that open hungry if at all.[28]

"Before"—how much a single word can come to mean. Life *before* must have been on another planet. Ka-tzetnik does not mystify. How else could one begin to envision the contrast between the highway to the crematorium and Park Street? The same eyes have seen both, just as the same eyes can read of both. They are all in the same world, but the same world is not the same. On Park Street of Metropoli, writes Ka-tzetnik, "all the people set their watches by the 'Electra' clock."[29] They did before; they do after. The sunshine has not changed either. But Park Street will not be the same as Park Street on 1 September 1939, for it is the first Polish street seized by the invading Germans.

A boy takes a final ride on a bicycle. His school starts in two days; but it will not begin. The men of Metropoli go to work. Some used shovels before; they do again. Although digging is always the same, today it unearths a pit that changes everything. Eyes in the hole see German boots and machine gun muzzles. Soon they cover other eyes that watched a grave take shape until they filled it. The digging eyes "weren't buried in the pit."[30] But they are not free. Still able to wonder why, they have seen the Holocaust's "first common grave." It is important to see what they could not know, because without the first common grave, the others could not have been.

Now the earth is white with frosty breath. Winter comes every year. Bundled people walk the streets: "Couples . . . He and she . . . She and he. . . ." They are old. This season their footsteps in the snow are different. They are boarding trains for Auschwitz. Silver flakes erase the prints, and then the people, too, are gone. Seasons change and next the *Aktion* corners children. Not all are taken, but when the Nazis leave the ghetto: "Suddenly, the children in the hovels burst out sobbing. Fathers turn prosaic eyes to them: What in the world are the left-over children crying for?"[31] Did any eyes really flicker with that question? Eyes must have probed those invisible dimensions of history. They were human. Not to see with them as far as possible is to leave too invisible what cannot be seen.

Years pass. Little is new except that one day the last transport approaches Auschwitz. Last victims from the last ghetto, they know too much, but they shall learn even more because their eyes will know what has been seen a million times before. The last transport does not mean death in every sense. For there was also the last transport that contained some who were selected to live and work a while. They went inside the Auschwitz "Bath House." Soon drenched, they later understood that "truly happy were those who got, not water out of sprinklers, but Zyklon cans jetting blue gas into their lungs, instead." Survivors had to be lucky to live, but Holocaust literature like Ka-tzetnik's reveals invisible memories that show how unlucky they are. They must live with what they saw, and those visions include: "staring at the planks above. Bare, unplaned planks. Twenty inches from the eyes."[32]

Block curfew has been called. "Inside"—another ordinary word that now must convey extraordinary meaning—men are confined to the triple-tiered hutches, ten to a hutch. Hours pass inside. Somebody must piss. How ordinary, but during block curfew that urge can be a matter of life and death, for "every one in Auschwitz knows what a prisoner gets for pissing in the block." Nine pairs of eyes watch a tenth in agony because there is nothing he can do. They want him to start so they can let go, too, and put the blame on him. It happens, and then one sees again what the "stove" is for. Made of brick, "thirty-two inches high, twenty inches wide," it runs end to end down the center of the block. Never fired, it is for heat of a different kind. Quickly it is draped with a man. "From here you see only his naked underpart," but the Block Chief's view is better as he beats to death a prisoner who pissed. Who was the man lying on the brick stove? As Ka-tzetnik asks: "Life! Life! Who are you?"[33]

Words must mean more after Auschwitz than they did before. So must things: for example, bowls, pots, and prayers. Inside, life depends on soup. It must not be lost or wasted, and so life also depends on a bowl or pot. It depends, too, on the size of that container, not because the Block Chief ladles unfairly but because it is essential to spill nothing. History has little to say about bowls, nor does political science countenance pots of soup. But eyes watched them both intently, religiously. Sociologists and psychologists rarely contemplate the difficulty or the significance of handling a portion of soup, let alone when the soup is scalding and one's bowl is shallow and somebody jostles you. Gut-level prayer, suggests Ka-tzetnik, was less of "the life of your wife, of your child, the life of a world that was—all those you've forgotten ages ago" and more for "a deep bowl, with wide rims."[34] Bowls, pots, and prayers are among the invisible dimensions of history that no understanding of the Holocaust can be without. Literature that considers them, meditates upon them, performs its unmatched service by struggling to show what can no more be seen.

Evening comes. At this hour, says Ka-tzetnik, "strange longings sometimes stir. . . . What is it, my soul, you yearn for at evening rollcall in Auschwitz?" Ka-tzetnik does not spell out those longings, explain the feelings; they are too private, too personal to be reported, and yet the surrounding scene suggests their form. Barbed wire and the setting sun beyond: could there be a world somewhere with freedom? Far off a returning women's labor commando: mother? sister? A comrade who can stand no more, the sound of the brass-band of Auschwitz struck up as a new transport arrives: will there be anyone left to love if the killing ever stops? Despair comes closer when darkness falls. As night comes over Auschwitz, the mind's eye sees a face: "Where are you now, beloved? . . . From my bread ration today I saved a crumb for you."[35]

Auschwitz eyes see others but not themselves. Stripped naked, hope demands it, for a selection to winnow out the weak is underway. How does one look? So much depends on the answer. All eyes ask. All eyes reassure. But they know better even as they accept the reassurance sent their way. No matter what the language, the deception is the same. Yet the only real question is: who will be chosen? Numbers have been recorded by the camp doctor; some standing, though alive, are already dead. Numbers are called. This is Auschwitz death— knowing you are dead while still alive. But who can say what Auschwitz death is like? Not the dead or the living, yet Ka-tzetnik saw terror, fear, and pain as the eyes of the living and the dead gazed into each other for the last times: "Why don't they scream?! Why don't they weep?! Why is it so quiet here?!"[36]

Things were not completely quiet, however, because "there's a bottleneck at the crematorium.'' Death's chosen must wait to die. Forced into the Isolation Block, they scream for their bread ration. If they are to live another day, the ration is owed them. This argument seems futile, but it is not the last. Quietly, two of the condemned—Ferber, a young Zionist, and the rabbi of Shilev—conclude a debate started before they entered Auschwitz and continued inside, too. The rabbi was wrong, says Ferber: Jewish fate is sealed because there was too little resistance against the Germans. The rabbi will not agree: Israel will be brought forth " 'from the very blackness of this night.' "[37] And then, suggests Ka-tzetnik, as the bread ration din went on, Ferber's weeping eyes made him see that the argument had to end with the rabbi's words. Not because they were his, but because they were so human, so Jewish, in their refusal to despair. Screams for bread can be heard, but who knows what people say quietly in the Isolation Block before they die? No documents record exchanges in that place. Yet one must try to hear what has been silenced, or the Holocaust's history will be written without its heart.

Liberation turned ''Planet Auschwitz,'' as Ka-tzetnik calls it, into an abandoned relic. It brought a mocking irony, too, for on ''which side of the open gate'' was freedom to be found? Not outside because too many remained within, but not inside either because there they would remain a ''mound of ash.'' So, if not liberation, then what? The survivor knew: ''locked in the pupils of his eyes was the planet Auschwitz before it had turned to stone. And only he, of all in this place, can take these pupils out with him.''[38] In lieu of liberation, then, a vow: the voiceless mound of ash shall have a voice.

Park Street looks the same. People still set their watches by the Electra clock. Thus one discovers how hard, how lonely, it is to be the voice for a voiceless mound of ash. Time is the problem. Now it is ''after''—another of those words that can never be the same—but for Metropoli that means time to look ahead, time to forget. For a Ka-tzetnik that can never be the rhythm of ''after.'' It means time to look back, time to remember. And so on Park Street one sees people who disappeared, things that were taken, and strangers in familiar places. They do not welcome Auschwitz eyes. They do not wish to be disturbed in their time without Jews. Park Street is his, but it is not-his, too. Nothing is left here anymore, which is not easy to say, because ''this is where your cradle stood—.''[39]

The cradle is gone. So is the mother who rocked it. She used to plait her daughter's hair. Now only the golden hair remains—seventeen years long. It is somewhere in Germany woven into a blanket, a piece of upholstery, who knows? Instead of ten thousand pairs of eyes, there are now ten thousand pairs of shoes—piles of them, all kinds, without end. One pair is Father's. His ''heels were never crooked'' because his ''step was always straight.'' A son would recognize those shoes anywhere, and yet they are not to be seen either. Hair, shoes, mother, sister, father—more words that can never be the same.

Wiedergutmachung—the German term for "reparation"—does not exist, though the word does. Yet one longs for something. Not money, but maybe a strand of hair or a shoe would help, or even "a broken wheel from my little brother's skates; and a mote of dust that on my mother rested—."[40]

Ka-tzetnik's *Star Eternal* ends with a mote of dust. Some Holocaust literature concludes on a more affirmative note. Amidst the devastation there are glimpses of redemption. That motif has not been absent here. Ferber and the rabbi of Shilev took Israel's star to be eternal. And yet *Star Eternal* shines more in spite of despair than because of optimistic confidence, for all the stars, Israel's included, are stars of ashes, motes of dust. Yet, they smoulder with memory, ignite with passion, blaze with the demand that their light must endure and not go out. To see stars like that, eyes must be trained. They must not be mystified but crystal clear, and that is why a Ka-tzetnik's vision is so vital. It shows what to look for and how to see what cannot be seen.

Survival

Everything stops when the sirens scream at eight o'clock. Two minutes later an Israeli morning goes on as usual. But not entirely, for it is Yom Hashoah, the spring day that annually commemorates the Holocaust. Observances are also held in other countries now; in France, for example, where a woman named Charlotte Delbo was deported to Auschwitz in January 1943. She survived to write *Auschwitz et après*, a trilogy of prose and poetry about Auschwitz and "after." Reminding us of the thousands of women annihilated by National Socialism at Auschwitz—"for the women and children always go first"— Delbo's reflections share Katzenelson's sense of loss, Schwartz-Bart's sensitivity about resistance, and Ka-tzetnik's revelations of the unseen dimensions of endurance. As she revisions her persistent contact with mass death, the emphasis falls on what it means to survive. Words do not make that easy to express, for "I am no longer sure that what I have written is true," says Delbo, "but I am sure that it happened."[41]

The first volume of Delbo's trilogy suggests that survival is impossible, for it is titled *Aucun de nous ne reviendra* (*None of Us Will Return*). At Auschwitz, "the station is not a station. It is the end of a line." Contemplating those who arrive there, at "a station without a name, . . . which for them will never have a name," she notes that "they do not expect the unthinkable."[42] Nor do her readers. But the unthinkable, which Delbo never mystifies, the sheer unending grind of death—unredeeming and unredeemable—became so pervasive that it was beyond transfiguration. If gas, disease, starvation did not waste one away, survival after Auschwitz did not mean so much a return to life but only, in Lawrence Langer's words, *death-with-life*. What that condition entails, why it is a factor to be contended with not only by literal survivors but also, in some sense, by all who live after Auschwitz—those are two of the questions that govern Delbo's Holocaust literature.

Disjunction characterizes death-with-life. Delbo writes of "a skeleton of a woman" whose remaining life is a "mechanical dance" of death. And then she breaks off, for "now I am sitting in a café writing this story—for this is turning into a story."[43] What her mind's eye sees did happen, but when a woman is reduced to the mechanical movements of a skeleton, mere narrative cannot describe such horror, and the search for terms graphic enough to depict the reality turns what happened into a story. So the words must be broken off. Only then is it possible that they may succeed in coming close to saying what needs to be said. Yet the disjunction is more than that, for there sits Delbo in the café, writing, while her life is with the death of a naked skeleton. The disjunction is not limited to the breaking off of words or to the chasm between "then" and "now," "here" and "there," which are, after all, disjunctions bridged by a single person's experience. A more radical disjunction is that between those who think they know and those who really do. This is a gap that words reveal more than bridge. For example, living can be so reduced to a bodily endurance that "one can see one's mother dead and not cry."[44] And then the disjunction doubles back again: a writer sitting in a café, perhaps able to cry again, must reckon with a knowledge that makes her wonder whether, or at least in what sense, she is the same person "before" and "after."

Delbo wants her readers to see bodies. That is what survivors, direct and indirect, must contend with. Unmistakably the bodies are human, and yet in what sense? Beautiful, resilient, and strong—these are not apt terms to describe the last vestiges of a human being, whose existence is better portrayed by focusing on a hand, an elbow, a neck, whose life has been reduced to physical exertion, and even that energy is so drained and waning that when "the dog pounces on the woman, sinks its teeth into her throat . . . we do not move, stuck in a viscous substance that prevents us from making even a gesture—as in a dream."[45]

In Auschwitz, writes Delbo, "No ones says: 'I am thirsty. I am cold.' " There such things go without saying. Indeed to utter them would be an absurdity unthinkable. To contend with death-in-life is to recognize that one group of human beings can create an environment, not just for scattered individuals here and there but for masses of men and women, calculated to induce hunger, thirst, and frigidness so that the most common expressions of need are reduced to silence. Sound does break the silence in Auschwitz, however, often in screams. They reach the blue of an indifferent sky more than ears. And so little remains: a discarded wooden leg survives its owner, reappearing out of mud and snow long after the flesh it supported has rotted. There is no reverence for life, nor for death, though to die might bring a giddy instant in which one knows "the end of suffering and struggling, . . . a bliss that we did not know existed." The very lack of reverence for death, however, brings Delbo back to life: "I want to die but not to be carried out on that little stretcher. Not to be carried out on that little stretcher with my feet dangling and my head dangling, naked under the ragged blanket. I do not want to be carried out on that little stretcher." But if Auschwitz reduces the reasons for living to that extent, the narrator concludes that "none of us should have returned."[46]

Part II of *Auschwitz and After* is *Une Connaissance inutile*, which can mean either a knowledge or an acquaintance, both useless. Once more a firsthand acquaintance with and a knowledge about the human body loom large, and the issue is this: what is one to do with the awareness that Auschwitz creates? Delbo's narrator describes a thirst-quenching drink. So deprived that she plunged her face horse-like into a water bucket, she realized, "Saliva returned to my mouth. The burning in my eyelids abated. Your eyes burn when your tear ducts are dried up. My ears heard again. I was alive." She experienced some physical restoration and learned how much one can stand. The chance to bathe in a stream, for example, prompted her to observe that "I took off my underpants stiffened by the remnants of dried diarrhea . . . and I was not sickened by the odor." But what is such knowledge worth? As the narrator reflects, survival confers little dignity or pride. Instead particular memories may be degradingly useless because meaningful communication about them is so nearly impossible. In a post-Holocaust world, when most people say "I am thirsty," they just "go into a café and order a beer."[47]

As for love, it is no longer so tragically triumphant as conventional wisdom—better to have loved and lost than never to have loved at all—would have it. To an overwhelming degree, Delbo suggests, the Holocaust defeated love. Her own husband was executed by the Gestapo shortly before she was transported to Auschwitz. Granted a last meeting, they found their impending separation compounded by the only act of love that seemed possible: mutual deception, men and women pretending to each other not to know the fate awaiting them. Ending that way, love is not triumphal. In Auschwitz love could not even be remembered well. Memory itself was a luxury that energy did not permit. It added pain too great for those already living beyond their means.

Auschwitz did not exist without respite. Some camp jobs were better than others, transfers to less lethal sites occurred, and for some liberation eventually beckoned. Delbo went through those phases. As she did so, other forms of useless knowledge became apparent. They involved things known "before": the taste of a cup of coffee, " 'getting up late, going here and there, doing what I please.' "[48] Such things, once taken for granted, were so well known that they ought to come back quickly. But they do not. They must be relearned, and even then none is possible as before, at least not unless one becomes oblivious. Liberation pushes one toward oblivion, even in terms of memory, but whatever consolation that might contain is mocked by the fact that it will compound the uselessness of being there. If Charlotte Delbo is correct, survival after Auschwitz brings with it alienation and sadness more than a return of normality, especially for those who were "there" but also in part for any who will open themselves to the "useless knowledge" of that experience.

For centuries philosophers and poets have urged, "Know thyself." Delbo is ambivalent: "I've spoken with death / so / I know / that so many things we learned were useless / but I learned that at the price of suffering / so great / I wonder / if it was worth it." Experience broadened her horizons only to shrink her sense of wonder and possibility. She does not feel herself to be a better person for what she has endured, though some effort to justify her living seems imperative: otherwise "it would be too stupid / finally / for so many to have died." To survive in that way, however, she will "need to unlearn / otherwise it's clear / I couldn't go on living." And the poet's voice even cautions that for those who were not there perhaps it is "better not to believe / all these stories / of people returning."[49]

Mesure de nos jours (*Measure of Our Days*), the trilogy's final volume, utilizes a series of monologues by Delbo's narrator and some of her friends to underscore how reentry into "normal" life is fraught with difficulties. As for herself, the narrator says: "I was in despair at having lost all capacity for illusion or dream, all resilience to imagine or explain things. That's the part of me that died in Auschwitz."[50] That adds up to death-with-life, but this transformation has not changed very much. The world remains full of illusion, dream, resilience, imagination, and explanation. Mado, the survivor who thought "if we return, nothing will be the same," was wrong. Yet how is one to respond to simple, perennial questions, such as "Where are you from?" "Auschwitz" is not the answer expected, but "Bordeaux" does not say what must be said. Mado was not wrong: nothing is the same. Yet that truth is allowed to slip away and not without reason, for "to live in the past is not to live. . . . I died at Auschwitz."[51]

Other of Delbo's women do "return." For Poupette, who wanted so much to survive, sadness continues to accumulate as a present and a future shadowed by an Auschwitz past lead to a marriage that does not work, problems over children, and other tribulations for which there might be consolation if one had not already suffered too much. Marie-Louise apparently has done much better. Now a wife and a mother, well-situated in a country estate, she talks freely about the camp, reads about the Holocaust extensively, and has even returned to visit Auschwitz. "You see," she explains, "I have everything I want. I'm happy." If things are that simple, Delbo suggests, then Marie-Louise's reentry is as truncated as that of the others. For if they cannot master the unlearning required for happiness, Marie-Louise's achievements in that regard have reduced the past to a superficiality that betrays it. Marceline's problem is different. Her husband offers encouragement: you cannot let bad memories crush you; human nature has uncanny ways of adapting and readapting. Nonetheless, about the same time each year, Marceline falls sick. The cause of her illness is medically unclear, but she calls it her "typhus anniversary."[52] Auschwitz is in her blood. Adaptability has limits more severe than her husband's optimism knows.

Near the end of the book, several of the surviving women attend the funeral of a comrade. One remarks that she never weeps at funerals now because one is lucky to have one. None of them could even dream of a funeral in Auschwitz, but now they have other dreams about that place. The narrator reports hers, a recurrent one, "inexplicable" like Marceline's fever. It is the nightmare of being paroled from prison, trying hard to run away or to forget the way back, but then returning as she had promised to do. As she returns, her cries awaken her at the moment of seeing "the barbed wire, the watchtowers, the outline of the chimneys. I never see anything else. I always cry out before seeing more." Fevers and nightmares reveal dislocated selves. "Have I several faces too?" asks Delbo's narrator. She envisions three: one intelligent and mobile; a second covering the first, "tired, worn, concealed"; and the third a veneered "mask of courtesy." It "serves as a pass key to use when we leave the house, go out into life, approach people, take part in all the things that are happening around us."[53]

The chapter fades before the funeral. Instead of ending the *Measure of Our Days* with a ceremony for a single death, a gesture singularly inappropriate for a meditation on the unnoticed slaughter of millions, Delbo focuses on Françoise, another woman who saw her husband before he was shot and she was deported. Looking back on all that has been lost, on the many invisible dimensions of history, the issue remains: how to live with what one knows. Remaking life, renewing it—those concepts are too optimistic for survivors like Delbo. At best their survival seems to be a reprieve. Thus, Delbo's austere trio ends with no chorus of hope, without moral exhortation. Yet grief or rage is not its final mood. Instead she asks for acceptance, understanding, and help: "I don't know / if you can still make / anything of me / But if you have the courage to try. . . ."[54] Perhaps among those who were "there" and those who are "here"—survivors both direct and indirect—a determination to try can be forged into a survival that refuses to let desolation be the only measure of our days.

Honesty

Like Ka-tzetnik 135633, Tadeusz Borowski was numbered. His tattoo made him Ka-tzetnik 119198. Although quite close to Yehiel Dinur's, Borowski's number was different because he was not Jewish. Also, he arrived at Auschwitz in late April 1943, three weeks after the Nazis, apart from special cases, stopped gassing Aryans. Borowski might have escaped selection anyway. This Polish man was healthy, strong, and only in his early twenties when the police nabbed him. Borowski had finished his university degree "underground," because the

Germans prohibited such training for Poles. Completing his last examinations just as major roundups began in Warsaw during the spring of 1940, Borowski found work that kept him from being conscripted for labor in Germany. He wrote, too, his poetry and prose appearing in Warsaw's clandestine press. Eventually arrested and jailed for his underground activities, he spent two months in Pawiak, the notorious prison that stood adjacent to the Warsaw ghetto. From his cell, he saw the Jewish uprising and the German retaliation. At Auschwitz he nearly died from pneumonia, but luck was with him, and he found himself assigned to relatively light work, ultimately serving as a medic. Evacuated from Auschwitz in the late summer of 1944, Borowski was liberated at Dachau the next May. In time, he returned to Poland. He seemed destined to be an important voice in the Communist press. This future, however, was cut short on 1 July 1951. Borowski opened a gas valve and took his own life.

This Way for the Gas, Ladies and Gentlemen is the series of remarkable short stories that Borowski left behind. They are all about Auschwitz, about Borowski himself. Written shortly after his release, authored in the first person, the narrator in several of the stories is one Vorarbeiter Tadeusz, a deputy kapo. This perspective gives Borowski's stories uncompromising realism, bitter irony, and humane feeling all at once, each of these qualities complicated by Borowski's experience that some boundaries between victim and executioner are blurred. Toward the end of Borowski's compact volume, there is a brief meditation. Less than a thousand words long, it is called "A Visit." The narrator sits at a writing desk after Auschwitz. He looks out a window. He sees and recollects: men working, weeping, gathering fortunes, killing; women doing the same. He also recalls those on their way to the gas who "begged the orderlies loading them into the crematorium trucks to remember what they saw. And to tell the truth about mankind to those who do not know it."[55] The author ponders the many men and women he saw in Auschwitz. He will write about them, but he wonders "which one of them I should visit today." His selection is complicated, he notes, because "I am troubled by one persistent thought—that I have never been able to look also at myself." In his stories, Borowski looked at himself, perhaps so much so that the looking drove him to the gas. "I do not know," he wrote, "whether we shall survive, but I like to think that one day we shall have the courage to tell the world the whole truth and call it by its proper name."[56] Borowski's "whole truth" fosters disillusionment. No less than his stories, the outcome of his life enjoins Borowski's readers to be troubled, persistently, about what to make of the disillusionment that an honest encounter with the Holocaust creates unavoidably.

In *This Way for the Gas, Ladies and Gentlemen*, disillusionment begins with the statement that "all of us walk around naked." While waiting for a new transport to arrive, Vorarbeiter Tadeusz and his fellow inmates are deloused. Their nakedness, however, turns out to be more than physical. In this Auschwitz block dwell prisoners with privileges. They have enough to eat. Though "a bit coarse to the taste," their bread is "crisp, crunchy." There is bacon, milk, even French wine, because after these laborers unload the trains of people destined for death, they can take some of the food left behind. Other items required to enhance life in Auschwitz can be "organized" later from the huge storage area known as "Canada." Concern mounts when transports do not arrive. Work is hard when the cars roll in, but as Henri says, "They can't run out of people, or we'll starve to death in this blasted camp. All of us live on what they bring."[57]

Henri's friend, the narrator of this story, does other work. He has not been on the ramp before, that place where the new arrivals undergo selection. Having cleared things with the kapo, Henri invites him along. Off they go to meet the Polish Jews from Sosnowiec-Będzin. On this bright, hot day, the first cars reach Auschwitz shortly after noon. The unloading begins. Ironically, "a Red Cross van drives back and forth, back and forth, incessantly: it transports the gas that will kill these people." Darkness brings no relief—until the last of the fifteen thousand have been dispatched. Even Henri, who can claim that "since Christmas, at least a million people have passed through my hands," is exhausted. He and his comrades, however, have their reward. For several days the entire camp will be sustained by the Sosnowiec-Będzin Jews, who are already burning. Everyone will agree that "Sosnowiec-Będzin was a good, rich transport."[58]

The Auschwitz described in Borowski's stories is filled with reports of mass murder, sadistic violence, filth, disease, and starvation. His point is that in this world of human domination such happenings have been so commonplace that it is possible to add, "Work is not unpleasant when one has eaten a breakfast of smoked bacon with bread and garlic and washed it down with a tin of evaporated milk." Auschwitz is a new form of human society where living depends on dying; living well depends on access to power that condemns others. Not that the appalling quality of such relationships goes unnoticed—the brutality is not disguised or rationalized—but Borowski's narrator frames matter-of-factly events that seem poles apart and yet are part of the same time and space at Auschwitz. In the spring of 1943, for example, the medical orderlies got to build a soccer field near the hospital barracks. One Sunday, as the narrator reports in "The People Who Walked On," "I was goalkeeper." Although the selection ramp could be viewed from the playing field, the goalkeeper's back was to it when a train arrived. Retrieving a ball that had gone out of bounds, he noticed the arrivals. A short while later, the ball again went astray. A second time the goalkeeper's attention was drawn to the ramp. It stood empty; the train was gone, too. Virtually unnoticed—perhaps because the process was so routine, or because the goalkeeper's attention was so much on the game, or both—"between two throw-ins in a soccer game, right behind my back, three thousand people had been put to death."[59]

Borowski's narrator is no unfeeling brute. If he smiles "condescendingly when people speak to me of morality, of law, of tradition, of obligation," he also feels revulsion, outrage, over the absurd juxtaposition of events and believes that evil " 'ought to be punished. No question about it.' " Witnessing the incongruity of an infant in Auschwitz, he feels that he would also "like to have a child with rose-colored cheeks and light blond hair."[60] And though he would dismiss that vision as a "ridiculous notion," he also wrote love letters to his fiancée, an inmate in Auschwitz's FKL (*Frauen Konzentration Lager*). *This Way for the Gas* collects them in a segment called "Auschwitz, Our Home."

These letters speak honestly, without illusion and yet not without tenderness. There is nothing cloying or sentimental when Borowski writes: "One human being must always be discovering another—through love. . . . This is the most important thing on earth, and the most lasting." The reasons those words ring true is that they are uttered against a backdrop of lucidity about the propensities men and women have to dehumanize each other and themselves as well. He ascribes no heroism to his remaining alive. He is only one of the ten lucky souls plucked from labor in the killing center at Birkenau and assigned to the Auschwitz hospital for medical training. His absurd "mission" will be "to lower the camp's mortality rate and to raise the prisoners' morale," but he does not deny that it may keep him alive, and he can even speak of certain days as "delightful." Life in these quarters, with its library, museum, its view "almost pastoral—not one cremo in sight"—seems almost a haven.[61]

No "philosophic formula" can grasp all that happens at Auschwitz, partly because what seems inexplicable and abnormal has become totally familiar. Without "hocus pocus" or "hypnosis," mass murder happens, and "we have now become a part of it. . . ." This, too, is reported matter-of-factly, without self-loathing or righteous indignation. Yet the letter-writer quietly urges an outlook less resigned: "Look carefully at everything around you, and conserve your strength. For a day may come when it will be up to us to give an account of the fraud and mockery to the living—to speak up for the dead."[62]

When it comes to revealing how the Holocaust mocked human life, nothing is more important than to testify that human domination can become so oppressive that it turns hope, that most natural and irrepressible emotion, into a trap. "We were never taught how to give up hope," wrote Borowski, "and this is why today we perish in gas chambers." He means that, apart from our own power, there is nothing in existence to guarantee that cost-effective human domination will not reduce a person's life to "a body that has been exploited to the utmost: with a number tattooed on it to save on dog tags, with just enough sleep at night to work during the day, and just enough time to eat. And just enough food so it will not die wastefully. . . . If you die—your gold teeth, already recorded in the camp inventory, are extracted. Your body is burned and your ashes are used to fertilize the fields or fill in the ponds." Borowski's disillusionment does not stop with the realization that victims fitting those descriptions are real. It also announces honestly how widespread the complicity can be. Disillusionments about safety and immunity must be accompanied by those that unmask pretense about virtue and innocence. Borowski said of the camp, indeed of the whole world, "this is a monstrous lie, a grotesque lie."[63] Hope, too, will be deceptively false unless it can be forged out of disillusionment's truth.

Where disillusionment's truth will lead, especially when hope is involved, is uncertain, as a few final glimpses of Borowski's work make clear. In "Silence," a group of released prisoners are about to lynch an SS guard. Unwittingly, a young American officer intervenes when he enters the newly liberated barracks to urge respect for law and to assure the men that the guilty will be brought to justice. Feigning approval, waiting until the officer had stopped at all the blocks and returned to his headquarters, the exprisoners drag the SS man to the floor, "where the entire block, grunting and growling with hatred, trampled him to death." In "The January Offensive," Borowski recounts a postwar discussion in which some former inmates of concentration camps insist that "morality, national solidarity, patriotism and the ideals of freedom, justice and human dignity had all slid off man like a rotten rag." Listening to them was a Polish poet who responded with an incident that reputedly occurred in January 1945. After fierce fighting, Russian troops had freed a Polish city from German control and were advancing west. Among the Russian soldiers, needing attention at the hospital in that place, was a young woman. Though unwounded, she was pregnant and in labor. Her healthy child born, they stayed at the hospital only a single day. Baby tied to her back, automatic rifle in hand, she resumed her way to Berlin. The former inmates were skeptical. If the poet's story was not made up, it certainly suggested that the Russian woman had not been humane, for she had needlessly endangered the life of her own child. The discussion ended, but in a postscript Borowski adds that one of the Auschwitz comrades eventually received a letter from a woman "whom he had left pregnant in the gypsy camp when in October '44 he was taken in a transport from Birkenau to Gross-Rosen, Flossenbürg and Dachau."[64] Along with hundreds of other sick and pregnant women, that mother and her child had been liberated by the Russians' January offensive.

Back in Warsaw, Borowski's narrating writer notes that the world has for some time seemed to be "inflating at incredible speed, like some ridiculous soap bubble" which "will dissolve forever into emptiness, as though it were made not of solid matter but only of fleeting sounds." He describes his feelings in his new-old postwar city, noting the crumb-dry dust of the ruins, the newly installed windows and freshly painted walls of restored buildings, whose rooms are occupied by people of importance. He goes there to ask "perhaps a trifle too politely, for things that are perhaps too trivial, but to which nevertheless I am entitled—but which, of course, cannot keep the world from swelling and bursting like an over-ripe pomegranate, leaving behind but a handful of grey, dry ashes." The crowds of people he sees on the streets during the day seem to him to make a weird snarl, a gigantic stew, flowing "along the streets, down the gutter," and seeping "into space with a loud gurgle, like water into a sewer."[65]

As darkness falls, he looks out a window, then pushes himself away and heads for his writing desk, engulfed by a feeling that he has lost valuable time. The world still exists. He will try to muster "a tender feeling" for those who remain in it, and "attempt to grasp the true significance of the events, things and people I have seen. For I intend to write a great, immortal epic, worthy of this unchanging, difficult world chiselled out of stone."[66]

Is this ending ironic, perhaps made all the more so by Borowski's suicide, or did he accomplish what he intended to do? The answer depends on what can—and cannot—be said. It also depends on how one answers this question: where does the disillusionment of Holocaust literature lead? In Borowski's case the answer remains ambiguous and ambivalent, because the truth he could discern did not point in a single, clear-cut direction, least of all to optimism. Unmistakably, though, Borowski placed a premium on exposing illusion. In that respect the words of his living and the silence of his dying are of one piece. Both resound with the insistence we have heard from him before: "It will be up to us to give an account of the fraud and mockery to the living—to speak up for the dead."[67]

Choice-making

William Styron's historical novel *Sophie's Choice* has been acclaimed for its brilliance and bitterly attacked for misappropriating and exploiting the Holocaust and for perversely promoting "an Erotics of Auschwitz."[68] The novel's importance stems from its sustained reflection on the significance of choosing in a context of human domination. For if some Holocaust literature disillusions us about what is possible, Styron's story shows how victims themselves can be put in a position of participating, not willingly but still actively, in their own demise. This they do by making choices, a reality that subverts the optimistic assumption that choice makes life worth living and substitutes instead the realization that choices may make life unbearable. Under Nazi pressure, Jews and other victims still had to decide what to do. If those choices rarely permitted more than opting only between evils, which were not even clearly differentiated between "lesser" or "greater," the choices were no less real, and the Nazi scheme of destruction entailed that their victims had to make them. Styron explores these dynamics of choice-making in the Holocaust by unraveling the story of a resident of Brooklyn, Sophie Zawistowska, a fictional Polish Catholic who survived.

Sophie had a hand in the Holocaust. She had helped her father, an influential

Polish professor, by typing a pamphlet in which he advocated the elimination of the Jews. Neither that contribution nor her regret over it, however, would spare her from being swept into Auschwitz after committing a theft. While incarcerated, her considerable linguistic and secretarial skills won her an assignment to work for Rudolf Höss, the commandant of Auschwitz. Urged to use her position to assist the underground resistance movement, Sophie planned to steal a radio from Höss's house. She knew where one could be found, a small portable that belonged to Höss's daughter, Emmi. Passing the girl's room every day on her way upstairs to the office where Höss did his work, once she tried for the radio, but Emmi caught her. Sophie was nearly undone. Her sense of failure ran deep, only less so than the realization that she would never regain her courage to steal the radio.

She understood the frailty of freedom, not simply because of the incident with the radio, but because of the setting in which that event took place. Nothing was more important in that setting than her children, Jan and Eva. Jan was alive somewhere in Auschwitz. Höss had promised that Sophie could see him, and her attempted theft took place with the knowledge that she would jeopardize her chance to embrace the boy whose life gave hers a reason for going on. Sophie was not without courage, but once was enough. She could not put the radio ahead of her need for Jan. Nor could Sophie be blamed, especially when she remembered Eva. Eva had disappeared because Sophie chose.

Tadeusz Borowski noted his luck in arriving at Auschwitz in April 1943 just three weeks after a directive to spare non-Jews from the gas went into effect. Sophie Zawistowska arrived at the death camp on April Fool's Day, 1943, just before Rudolf Höss implemented the life-saving orders from his superiors. As she was prodded from the stifling train that brought her and the children from Auschwitz, the customary selection took place. An SS doctor—Styron calls him Jemand von Niemand, which makes him "Anybody"—decided to make choice real, dreadfully so. Instead of losing both Jan and Eva to the gas, Sophie could pick one to live. " '*Ich kann nicht wählen!*' she screamed."[69] " 'I cannot choose.' " And then so as not to lose them both by choosing not to choose, Sophie let Eva go. Limited, choiceless, though it was, Sophie's choice was real. So was her sense of guilt, however undeserved. Set free in 1945, she came to the United States. Liberation, however, left her imprisoned. Sophie found inescapable the conclusion that her own life, even in America where she hoped to start anew, was not worth living. In 1947 she also let it go—by choice.

Some human suffering may be viewed as instrumental or redemptive. The Holocaust defies such hope. No imaginable good-to-come will make up completely for what was lost in the Nazi era, and a case like Sophie's proves the point. The power of Styron's story lies in its impact on those who do survive. Stingo—the white boy, a Presbyterian from the South, who narrates the novel—cannot prevent Sophie's suicide or that of Nathan, her American-Jewish lover.

But Stingo endures, and he has learned about himself. Although he trashed most of the journal he kept in 1947, three fragments remain. They form the novel's conclusion. *"Someday I will understand Auschwitz"*—that vow, Stingo reflects years later, is "innocently absurd." *"Let your love flow out on all living things"*—that one is worth saving "as a reminder of some fragile yet perdurable hope." Last is some poetry: " *'Neath cold sand I dreamed of death / but woke at dawn to see / in glory, the bright, the morning star.'*"[70] Sophie's life was over; Stingo's is not. If choice destroyed hers, he will resist a similar fate only by using the power to decide in a struggle to make life more worth living, not less so.

Although criticized for being preoccupied with sex, unscrupulously mixing fact and fiction, and substituting caricatures for characters, suffice it to say here that *Sophie's Choice* rises far above such objections. For our purposes two other criticisms are more important because they illuminate so effectively problems that a writer faces in speaking about the Holocaust. The first of these charges is that Styron's novel is a "prominent example of the tendency to universalize Auschwitz as a murderous threat against 'mankind.' " Styron, it is alleged, places Auschwitz too much "within a generalized history of evil"[71] That claim leads to a second objection, namely, that Styron stresses other themes at the expense of the particularity of the predominantly Jewish victims and their predominantly German executioners. For example, Styron emphasizes that it is wrong to damn Germany as a whole for the Holocaust; he interprets antisemitism as only one factor among many that are crucial for comprehending the Nazi policies of population elimination; and he insists that vast numbers of Gentiles suffered and died as well as Jews, underscoring that many Germans martyred themselves in opposition to the Nazis. The effect, it is argued, goes beyond apologetics to the creation of a misleading Holocaust mythology.

In response to the charge that Styron has universalized the Holocaust too much, at least this much is clear: Styron does not see in the Holocaust simply an unprecedented and unique event but also a symptom of something pervasive in human life as it evolved into the late twentieth century. So here the issue is joined: to what extent should one see the Holocaust as a catastrophe in the history of one people, the Jews, and to what extent should it be seen as a catastrophe in the history of humankind, a catastrophe that may be the prelude to something more to come? A fitting answer would seem to be that it should be seen as fully as possible in both ways. Styron made his choice, namely, to emphasize the latter perspective, an outcome that may have much to do with the fact that he is not Jewish but instead, like Stingo whose prototype he is, a white American Gentile whose origins are in the Protestant South. That fact may also suggest why Stingo's loss of innocence—historical, psychological, and sexual all at once—is brought about by Sophie, the Polish Catholic, not by a Jewish survivor.

Styron writes of Sophie that, "although she was not Jewish, she had suffered as much as any Jew who had suffered the same afflictions, and . . . had in certain profound ways suffered more than most."[72] He needs no reminding that Auschwitz was above all a killing center for Jews. Nor does he need to be told that if Sophie had been Jewish, in all likelihood she would have had no choice. He knows those things just as well as he understands the risks he took in making a Gentile the focal point of his Holocaust novel. Styron could not claim first-hand acquaintance with experience like Sophie's, which is one of the chief points he makes in describing Stingo's voyage of discovery, but perhaps he could feel more responsible in writing about a Gentile Sophie than about one of her Jewish counterparts. Another alternative, of course, would have been not to write at all. The merits of Styron's work are sufficiently obvious to make plain that such a choice would have been unfortunate.

As for the charge that Styron diffuses responsibility for the Holocaust, ignoring the particularity of the victims and the executioners, it is true that Styron is attracted to the complexity, ambiguity, and subtlety that human destructiveness and responsibility for it so often reflect. Again, Styron's experience was not that of Auschwitz, but his reflection is informed by encounters with racism, domination, and violence that a sensitive American Southerner can bring to the Holocaust. Although the American experience with black slavery and the European experience of Jewish genocide are anything but identical, they are part of a human experience that does reveal again and again the depths of complexity, ambiguity, and subtlety that Styron chose to plumb. Killing at Auschwitz was straightforward, crystal clear, and impossible to miss—without hocus-pocus or hypnosis, as Borowski said—but it could be that way in part because of opposite factors. To focus them is indispensable if the particularity of the Holocaust is to be understood and the responsibility for it accurately apportioned.

Stingo is this novel's subject at least as much as Sophie. When he decides that his vow to understand Auschwitz was "a brave statement but innocently absurd," his realization is not simply owing to the incomprehensible magnitude of the Holocaust, but also to the awareness that it did involve specific persons—Germans, Jews, Poles, even Americans—and particular times and places, each with separate complexities, ambiguities, and subtleties. Stingo comments, for example, on his reaction to hearing Sophie tell of her arrival day at Auschwitz: "I was eating bananas in Raleigh, North Carolina, I thought, thinking this not for the first time since I had known Sophie, yet perhaps for the first time in my life aware of the meaning of the Absurd, and its conclusive, unrevocable horror."[73] The novel's importance lies not only in its being about Auschwitz and all it signifies. It resides also in its tracking of Stingo's discovery of that place. Most Americans who approach Auschwitz, especially but not exclusively non-Jews, will find much of Stingo in themselves. Led by Styron's narrator to encounter the Holocaust via *Sophie's Choice*, they will also encounter themselves and each other. For them, few works in Holocaust literature will be more effective in enabling them to do what Tadeusz Borowski urged, namely, to look at themselves in the light of Auschwitz. When they do, the importance of reevaluating what freedom and choice-making mean should be unavoidable.

Protest

A transport arrives at Birkenau. Bewildered Jews from Sighet and other Hungarian towns emerge from train-car prisons into midnight air fouled by burning flesh. Elie Wiesel, his father, mother, and little sister are among them. Separated by the SS, the boy loses sight of his mother and sister, not fully aware that the parting is forever. Father and son stick together. In the commotion, they hear one of the kapos exclaim, "What have you come here for, you sons of bitches? What are you doing here? . . . You'd have done better to have hanged yourselves where you were than to come here. Didn't you know what was in store for you at Auschwitz? Haven't you heard about it? In 1944?"[74]

Wiesel and his father learned soon enough what was in store for them. They were sent "left" by Dr. Mengele, the SS doctor whose baton determined life and death. Their line marched directly toward a pit of flaming bodies. Steps from the edge, they were ordered toward the barracks. The fire, however, had left its mark: "Never shall I forget those flames which consumed my faith forever." Wiesel's father perished, but the son survived. For more than ten years he published nothing, and then *Night* appeared. Unsurpassed, this memoir, lean and spare, describes his death camp experiences in 1944–45. It begins with a boy who "believed profoundly." It ends with this reflection: "From the depths of the mirror, a corpse gazed back at me. The look in his eyes, as they stared into mine, has never left me."[75]

Since the publication of *Night*, Wiesel has authored more than twenty books—novels, plays, dialogues, reflections on biblical characters, and meditations on contemporary Jewish life, to note only some of the versatile forms of his writing. Rarely do these works speak so explicitly about Auschwitz as *Night* does, but never is the Holocaust absent from his writings, which collectively form the most impressive contribution to Holocaust literature made by any single author.[76] "I knew the story had to be told. Not to transmit an experience is to betray it. . . . But how to do this?"[77] Words, Wiesel reports, had to be searing, but they all seemed "inadequate, worn, foolish, lifeless." The effort to transform them had to be made—perhaps so he would not go mad, but certainly because doing so might wrench the victims from oblivion and keep death from having the final say. Writing, in short, is a way to remain faithful, provided a Holocaust author writes "certain things rather than others" and takes responsibility "not only for what he says, but also for what he does not say."[78]

The words needed to tell the story faithfully must share Katzenelson's sense of loss, Schwarz-Bart's emphasis on resistance and compassion, Ka-tzetniks's power to remember and to seize on small detail, Delbo's grappling with survival, Borowski's disillusioning honesty, and Styron's sensitivity about dominating power and choice-making. Nor do those qualities exhaust the list. At the very least, protest against despair needs to be pronounced. In Wiesel's writings, that quality is salient.

"At Auschwitz," Wiesel declares, "not only man died, but also the idea of man. . . . It was its own heart the world incinerated at Auschwitz."[79] Along with his sense that God needlessly permitted the Holocaust, an event that no good-to-come could possibly justify, these experiences of loss produce despair, which means to lose or to give up hope. Nonetheless, Wiesel asserts, to be Jewish is "never to give up—never to yield to despair."[80] This is easier said than done, as Wiesel shows in some of the masterful dialogues, simple and complex at once, that appear in his works from time to time. Most of these make no explicit reference to the Holocaust. Yet that catastrophe is their setting. One in *A Jew Today* is between "A Father and His Son."

The father is concerned. "How," he asks his son, "are you able to resist despair?" Not so difficult, comes the reply, because memory puts things in perspective. If something seems good now, admittedly it turns out to be less so against the backdrop of what happened "thirty years ago." But when things seem terrible in the present, they are also less terrible by contrast. This answer is not convincing. It shows, in fact, that resistance to despair is exceedingly difficult, for what happened "thirty years ago" shrouds all remaining life. What he feels, the son goes on to tell his father, is "sadness, Father. Nothing but sadness." He confesses not to be seeking happiness; it is too simple to be real in a survivor's history. Nor is love what he looks for; it is a gift bestowed and received, not something one can go out and find. Power is not the goal either. Neither is knowledge; it is to be feared, not because it is inessential to keep learning about what happened but because such awareness may be taken as a substitute for understanding. The two—knowing and understanding—are not identical where Auschwitz is concerned, at least not for Wiesel, and indeed the father's son wants "only one thing: to understand, that is all."[81] The problem is that understanding is even more difficult to obtain than happiness, love, power, or knowledge. In fact, it is impossible to understand the Holocaust; it *must be* impossible to understand it, for to understand it would be to have an acceptable answer to why it happened. Answers of that kind do not, must not, exist. But if that outcome is not the worst one imaginable, it still does little to drive despair away.

Before he died, the father asked his son to remember and to tell everything. The son said he would, then qualified his answer honestly: he would try his best. The father believed him then and still does now, and yet the father is concerned. The dead have heard the son's testimony, but what about the living? "If we have not succeeded in changing mankind,'' the father wonders, ''who can ever succeed? Tell me, son: Who will change man? Who will save him from himself? Tell me, son: Who will speak on his behalf? Who will speak for me?''[82] Committed to say what the dead cannot, survivors still try. But, the son admits, they are weary. No, despair does not give up easily.

This dialogue never happened. It could not have happened. And yet it did. Wiesel tells a tale about meeting an old teacher who had known Wiesel's grandfather. The teacher wanted to know what his friend's grandson was doing. When Wiesel answered that he was a writer of stories, the teacher asked, ''What kind?'' Specifically, he wanted to know, were these stories about things that happened or could have happened? Yes, replied Wiesel, his stories were of that kind, but the old teacher, sensing ambiguity in the response, pressed on: well, did the stories happen or didn't they? No, Wiesel admitted, not all of the things in his stories did happen; in fact, some of them were invented from start to finish. Disappointment came over the old man. That means, he said, that you are writing lies. Taken aback, Wiesel paused, then responded: ''Things are not that simple, Rebbe. Some events do take place but are not true; others are—although they never occurred.''[83] Wiesel adds that he does not know whether his answer was sufficient, but it is also true that he has not stopped telling and writing ''legends of our time.''

Separated from husband and son, father and brother, a mother and her daughter walk together, and they, too, have a dialogue.[84] The little girl, eight years old, wonders where they are going. Their destination, says the mother, is ''the end of the world.'' Her daughter asks if that stopping point is far, for she is tired. So is everyone, her mother replies, and the little girl responds: ''Even God?'' Her mother does not know, but she adds: ''You will ask Him yourself.'' What might God say to an eight-year-old girl who would like to see ''the peddlers, the acrobats, the tame bears,'' but who instead sees the chimneys and flames of a factory that makes and destroys history by consuming ''the innocence of the world''?[85] Perhaps nothing at all, which would not be good even though silence might be better than some of the words that God could speak or that human voices have offered apologetically on God's behalf.

One reason why despair is not easy to dispel is that the Holocaust is inexplicable with God but also cannot be understood without God. In *Night* Wiesel spoke of the flames that destroyed his faith forever. That is not inconsistent with his continuing dialogue with God. For if Auschwitz made it no longer possible to trust God's goodness simply, it made questions about God and wrestling with God all the more important. Wiesel has been heard to say: ''If I told you I believed in God, I would be lying; if I told you I did not believe in God, I would be lying.'' This survivor refuses to let God go, because that act may be one way to testify that the human heart was not completely incinerated at Auschwitz. Yet Wiesel remains at odds with God, because the only way he can be for God after

Auschwitz is by being against God, too. To accept God without protest would both vindicate God and legitimize evil too much. Nowhere does Wiesel argue for that point more effectively than in his drama, *The Trial of God*, whose stage instructions indicate that it should be played as a tragic farce.

The play is set in the village of Shamgorod at the season of Purim, a joyous festival replete with masks and reenactments that celebrate a moment in Jewish history when oppressors were outmaneuvered and Jews were saved. Three Jewish actors have lost their way, and they arrive at the village. Here they discover that Shamgorod is hardly a place for festivity. Two years before, a murderous pogrom ravaged this town. Only two Jews survived. Berish the innkeeper escaped, but he had to watch while his daughter was unspeakably abused on her wedding night. She now lives mercifully out of touch with the world.

In the region of Shamgorod, anti-Jewish hatred festers once again, and it is not unthinkable that a new pogrom may break out and finish the work left undone. Purim, however, cannot be Purim without a play, and so a *Purimspiel* will be given, but with a difference urged by Berish. This time the play will enact the trial of God. As the characters in Wiesel's drama begin to organize their play-within-a-play, one problem looms large. The Defendant, God, is silent, and on this Purim night no one in Shamgorod wants to speak for God. Unnoticed, however, a stranger has entered the inn, and just when it seems that the defense attorney's role will go unfilled, the newcomer—his name is Sam—volunteers to act the part. Apparently Berish's Gentile housekeeper Maria has seen this man before. Have nothing to do with him, she warns, but the show begins.

Berish prosecutes. God, he contends, "could use His might to save the victims, but He doesn't! So—on whose side is He? Could the killer kill without His blessing—without His complicity?"[86] Apologies for God do not sit well with this Jewish patriarch. "If I am given the choice of feeling sorry for Him or for human beings," he exclaims, "I choose the latter anytime. He is big enough, strong enough to take care of Himself; man is not."[87] Still, Berish will not let God go. His protest is as real as his despair. Neither deny God's reality; both affirm it by calling God to account.

Sam's style is different. He has an answer for every charge, and he cautions that emotion is no substitute for evidence. In short, he defends God brilliantly. Sam's performance dazzles the visiting actors who have formed the court. Who is he, they wonder. Sam will not say, but his identity and the verdict implicit in *The Trial of God* do not remain moot. As the play's final scene unfolds, a mob approaches to pillage the inn at Shamgorod once more. Sensing that the end is near, the Jewish actors choose to die with their Purim masks in place. Sam dons one, too, and as he does so, Maria's premonitions are corroborated. Sam's mask is worthy of his namesake, Samael. Both signify Satan. As a final candle is extinguished and the inn's door opens to the sound of deafening and murderous roars, Satan's laughter is among them.

Set three centuries before, this play is not about the Holocaust. Yet it is, because Wiesel introduces the script by reporting that he witnessed a trial of God in Auschwitz. What he does not mention in that foreword, but has indicated on another occasion, is that when the three rabbis who conducted the Auschwitz trial had finished and found God guilty, those men noted that it was time for their customary religious observances, and so they bowed their heads and prayed.[88] Why they did so may be related to a story Wiesel tells about a Jewish family long ago expelled from Spain. Plagued at every turn, they could find no refuge, except that sleep turned into death for them, one by one. At last only the father was left, and he spoke to God:

> "Master of the Universe, I know what You want—I understand what You are doing. You want despair to overwhelm me. You want me to cease believing in You, to cease praying to You, to cease invoking Your name to glorify and sanctify it. Well, I tell you: No, no—a thousand times no! You shall not succeed! In spite of me and in spite of You, I shall shout the Kaddish, which is a song of faith, for You and against You. This song You shall not still, God of Israel."[89]

The little girl who asked a question about God as she moved toward the end of the world, also had one for her older brother: "Will you remember me too?" He tells her that he has "forgotten nothing." He will tell that she was only eight, that she had never seen the sea or been to a real wedding, and that she never hurt anyone. She wants him to remember how she loved her new winter coat, Shabbat, and God. He shall; he will speak, too. The little sister worries about her brother, now a man so alone and cold. She grieves for herself, for him, for them all. She also asks two more questions and her brother answers.

> "When you speak of your little sister leaving you like that, without a hug, without a goodbye, without wishing you a good journey, will you say that it was not her fault?"
> "*It was not your fault.*"
> "Then whose fault was it?"
> "*I shall find out. And I shall tell. I swear it to you, little sister. I shall.*"[90]

The Nazis found Jews guilty of being Jewish. They were rendered superfluous and sentenced to death. Some interpreters have argued that various Jewish failures contributed to their own demise. But the Holocaust was not the fault of eight-year-old sisters, nor of any of the victims or survivors—at least not first and foremost. Yet some do blame the victim, which compounds despair and undercuts some of the hopes that the liberated survivors held. As Wiesel tells that story, he stresses that many of those freed from the Nazi camps believed that the world must not have known about their fate. Disabused of that naïveté, they still clung to the idea that if they told what had happened to them, the effect would be sobering and transforming. That hope, too, proved illusory, for the story has been told, responsibility has been assessed, and if anything the Holocaust is more widely a part of human memory today than at any time before. The labor, however, has not been sufficient to check the violence, suffering, and indifference that waste life away. Instead the threats of population riddance and of nuclear holocaust persist. Not even antisemitism has been eclipsed. Perhaps eventual self-destruction is the price humankind must pay for Auschwitz, but that counsel of despair is not Wiesel's last word. In stating his case for-and-against-God, against-and-for-humanity, he identifies more with the movement of one more ageless dialogue. God's creation is at stake. It is far from perfect, and thus,

> "Could you have done better?"
> *"Yes, I think so."*
> "You could have done better? Then what are you waiting for? You don't have a minute to waste, go ahead, start working."[91]

Those lines are unambiguous, predicated on an undeniable truth of a Holocaust century, namely, that unless people take a stand against mass death, its toll will be taken more easily. Yet a question remains: have things gone so far that memory and protest rooted in the Holocaust are essentially futile?

In 1981 Wiesel published a novel entitled *The Testament*. It traces the odyssey of Paltiel Kossover, a character who represents hundreds of Jewish intellectuals condemned to death in 1952 by Stalin, a man whose contributions to mass death exceed Hitler's by millions. In this novel the Holocaust stands not center stage but, as usual in Wiesel's works, casts its shadows before and after all the action. Moreover, this book contains Wiesel's most fundamental answer to the question about futility. Arrested, interrogated, Kossover expects to disappear without a trace. Encouraged by his interrogator to write an autobiography—in it, the official hopes, the prisoner will confess more than he does by direct questioning—Kossover has no reason to think that it will ever reach anyone he loves. Even less can he assume that by telling the tale of his own experience, he will in any way influence history. Still, he tries his best, and what his best amounts to is summarized in an ancient story—often repeated by Wiesel—that serves as *The Testament*'s prologue.

It speaks of a Just Man who came to Sodom to save that place from sin and destruction. Observing the Just Man's care, a child approached him compassionately:

> "Poor stranger, you shout, you scream, don't you see it's hopeless."
> "Yes, I see."
> "Then why do you go on?"
> "I'll tell you why. In the beginning, I thought I could change man. Today, I know I cannot. If I still shout today, if I still scream, it is to prevent man from ultimately changing me."[92]

The stranger did everything he could—to no avail except that he remained faithful.

The Holocaust changed the world. Holocaust literature changes those who write it and those who read it. All the writers we have encountered in this chapter share Wiesel's hope that their struggles with words will help to make just men and women, who will keep the hunger and thirst for righteousness alive and insist that no human being ought to be considered surplus. In Wiesel's novel, Kossover's testament does find its way out of a Soviet prison. It reaches and touches the poet's son. Stranger things have happened in our day, and there are testaments aplenty. If they reach and touch us, then a chance remains that protest will survive to keep despair at bay. If that happens, the enormous loss signified by the Holocaust is not all that remains. A future, stripped of illusions, still awaits our determination.

Chapter 10

The Silence of God: Philosophical and Religious Reflection on the Holocaust

"As a Jew," Elie Wiesel has written, "you will sooner or later be confronted with the enigma of God's action in history."[1] Religion was not a sufficient condition for the Holocaust, but it was a necessary one. What happened at Auschwitz is inconceivable without beliefs about God held first by Jews and then by Christians. For many who live after Auschwitz, however, it is God, not genocide, that is inconceivable. At the very least, the Holocaust makes both Jewish and Christian religious affirmations more difficult and problematic than they were before.

In an earlier day instances of natural destruction occupied much of the attention of philosophers and theologians. Considering, for example, the great earthquake that devastated Lisbon in the mideighteenth century, they argued whether such events could be reconciled with the claim that we live in the best of all possible worlds or whether God could be regarded as both omnipotent and totally good. The Lisbon earthquake caused fires and floods. It killed thousands of people. It was also beyond human control. In centuries past, philosophers were well aware that some catastrophes are produced by human action, but their analyses often pivoted around natural disasters—"acts of God" as they were called—that human might could not prevent.

Nature's fury still demonstrates how fragile our lives can be. But today two factors stand out in bold relief. First, human beings do have considerable ability to control some of nature's destructive might. Death still claims everybody, but it need not come so quickly or painfully as in earlier times. If those results leave one to wonder why natural devastation has been so prevalent, they also testify that suffering can be reduced, that human life is not completely in the grip of necessities and inevitabilities which cannot be broken, and that affirmations about life's goodness can be underwritten by successes which make human existence more secure.

The second point, unfortunately, is less a cause for celebration. For if headway has been made against natural destruction that threatens human life, the problem of human destructiveness seems greater than ever. Ours is an age of redundant populations, refugees, concentration camps, and mass murder. It is capped by the ultimate dehumanizing threat: nuclear war. Violent deaths, caused by human catastrophes not by natural disasters, number over one hundred million in the twentieth century alone. The scale of human-made death demonstrates conclusively that ours is not the best of all possible worlds.

The Holocaust is paradigmatic. It was not the result of sporadic, random violence carried out by hooligans. Driven by a zealous antisemitism, which seemed totally rational to those who used it as a springboard to power, the Holocaust was a state-sponsored program of population elimination, a destruction process that could successfully target the Jews only because it received cooperation from every sector of German society. Why was this permitted to happen? That question indicts men and women, but since they did not begin history by themselves, the issue becomes a religious one as well. What or who started history is a question without a definitive answer. It is not, however, a question without answers. People have formed innumerable convictions, all of them fallible and possibly even false, to fathom their individual and collective experience. Weighing evidence differently, some of these beliefs are less affirmations in their own right and more rejections of claims held by others—as in atheism, for example. Or, they are manifestations of a refusal to affirm or reject—as in agnosticism—because too much knowledge is lacking. Over time many of a person's responses to religious questions and to questions about God in particular will change both in substance and in certitude. Others will stay remarkably the same in spite of traumatic events that create massive dissonance between what was believed before and what could possibly be accepted after.

The Holocaust certainly qualifies as a watershed event. A typical reaction is to feel that Auschwitz seriously impugns the credibility of many, if not all, the claims about God that Jews or Christians have usually made. Indeed the Holocaust appears to call the very existence of God into serious doubt, if it does not make God's nonexistence perfectly clear. Some would argue that the Holocaust was not required to do these things. Previous human history contained far more than enough senseless injustice to demonstrate that trust in God was a delusion. Such appraisals, however, do not give the Holocaust its due. Both in its own right and in the impact of its massive addition to history's accumulated waste, the Holocaust can shatter belief that had been able to endure more or less intact everything else that went before. Theologians and philosophers who wish to defend Jewish or Christian views about God have always had a formidable task to show that God is not buried beneath history's debris. Few who encounter the Holocaust with seriousness would deny that Auschwitz makes their interpretive efforts more problematic than does any other reality.

Philosophers and theologians usually claim to ground their arguments in appeals to actual human experience. Unavoidably these appeals go beyond direct knowledge of individual cases or the statistically documented studies of human behavior and belief carried out by social scientists. Philosophers and theologians draw on such material, and on historical studies as well, but their efforts often require them to raise and reflect on questions that exceed immediate experience. The facts, it is often said, speak for themselves. They do not always speak clearly, however; nor are they self-interpreting. Philosophy and theology are disciplines that seek to interpret experience so that its most basic features—structural and normative—are clarified.

"Unique" and "unprecedented" are two descriptive terms often applied to the Holocaust. Jews in particular are likely to insist on using them, along with an emphasis on the particularistic nature of Nazi genocide, which specifically targeted Jews for total extermination root and branch simply because the Jews were Jews. Such emphases have validity because they help to demonstrate that the Holocaust was a boundary-crossing event, one of those moments in history which changes everything before and after, even if the substance and direction of the change take time to dawn on human consciousness. As philosophers and theologians probe the religious impact of the Holocaust, they can help to bring that dawning to fullness. They can also explore and indicate how that dawning might be shaped, since its course, like all human experience, remains subject to variation.

The Religious Testimony of Survivors

The first to probe the religious impact of the Holocaust were not philosophers and theologians who thought about the Nazi onslaught after it ceased. Men and women who lived and died and in some cases survived the hiding places, the ghettos, and the camps already carried on that activity as their circumstances, energy, and inclination permitted. Their observations and feelings, expressed in diaries and eyewitness accounts, provide some of the most important experiental data for philosophers and theologians to encounter. Such testimony has an irreplaceable significance because it represents those who had to cope with the Holocaust firsthand. To make pronouncements or even suggestions about what can or cannot, must or must not, be credible religiously after Auschwitz without knowing what the survivors think about their own experiences would be to develop one's philosophy or theology in a considerable vacuum.

Until recently knowledge about the faith and doubt of Holocaust survivors had to rest largely on inferences drawn from oral and written testimony that remained scattered and unsystematically analyzed. There is still much to do in collecting this testimony, but thanks to the cooperation of hundreds of survivors, a major social scientific study is now available. During the 1970s, Reeve Robert Brenner polled a thousand Israeli survivors to ascertain the religious change, re-

jection, reaffirmation, doubt, and despair that the Holocaust brought them. Selecting the subjects at random from survivor rosters, especially from those
carefully maintained at Yad Vashem, Israel's national Holocaust memorial, he
received more than seven hundred responses to a lengthy questionnaire. Of
those who responded, one hundred were interviewed personally, the remainder
by mail. The data gathered is rich, the testimony moving. Much of it speaks
about the silence of God, which is one way to designate what may be the most
crucial religious problem posed by the Holocaust. How survivors have coped
with that silence is instructive for the interpretive work that falls to philosophers
and theologians today. Also challenging are some of Brenner's conclusions.

When Brenner speaks of "Holocaust survivors," he means Jews who successfully endured "various types of Nazi concentration camps, including deten-
tion or internment camps, transit and exchange camps, and annihilation or death
camps where crematoria were installed." Within his random and representative
sample, one of the most fundamental findings is that 53% "consciously and specifically asserted that the Holocaust affected or, to a certain extent, modified
their faith in God." The other 47% "averred that the Holocaust had no influence on their beliefs about God." Considering the cataclysmic qualities of the
Holocaust, plus the fact that 69% of the surveyed survivors held that they had
believed in God prior to the Holocaust, a figure that would have been another
10% higher for eastern European Jews, the size of the 47% category may seem
surprising. Brenner has no doubts that the survivors explored their religious histories profoundly and honestly in answering the wide-ranging and disturbing
questions he raised about religious behavior and belief before, during, and immediately after the Holocaust, and in the present as well. Nor does he regard the
significant numbers of people—approximately one in three—who remained un-
wavering in their belief in the existence of God, personal or impersonal, as sufficient to modify his judgment that for those caught in the Holocaust "a radical
transformation of faith took place." The most salient feature of this transformation is that of the 55% who before the Holocaust believed in "a personal God"
who is involved in humanity's daily life, more than one in four rejected that belief either during or immediately after the war. Nor have they reclaimed it since.
At the heart of this rejection stands a fundamental premise, namely, that if there
were a personal God who is involved in humanity's daily life, that God would
surely not cause or even permit an Auschwitz to exist.[2]

Stubbornly powerful though it is, that assumption has not governed all theological reflection either during or after the Holocaust. In fact, Brenner's research found a vast array of religious responses among the survivors who
responded. They included Orthodox Jews who say the Holocaust was God's
punishment for Jewish refusal to honor their historic covenant with the God who
made them a chosen people. Others affirmed God as One who is impersonal,
uninvolved in human history generally or in the Holocaust specifically. And if

nearly three out of four of the 53% who found their faith affected or modified by the Holocaust underwent "either a complete loss or an attenuation of religious faith," the remainder reported that the Holocaust made them more religious. Overall about 5% of Brenner's sample were transformed from atheists into believers. If that figure seems insignificant, Brenner puts it in a different light by noting that "nearly one of every four religiously transformed survivors began to believe in God because of the Holocaust."[3] That is, of those who moved from the basic position of affirming or denying the existence of God, the shifting was not exclusively in one direction. Twenty-five percent of that group found themselves moved to affirm the existence of God when they had not done so before, and the impetus for the movement was the Holocaust itself. In all, Brenner observes, the total loss of faith in the existence of God among his sample of Holocaust survivors came to 11%.

Faith in God after Auschwitz is not easy for Holocaust survivors, for questions about God's silence quickly lead to another question: how can one believe in God at all after Auschwitz? Brenner found, however, that the believers' perplexity and discontent with their own beliefs had parallels in the experiences of those who professed atheism. Granted, those who sustained or arrived at atheism during the Holocaust were spared the frequently agonizing questions posed for those who affirmed God's reality. In some cases this atheism was strident, maintaining not merely that the existence of God, especially of the omnipotent God of Israel, is incredible but also that no theologian could possibly be qualified to controvert, let alone refute, that conclusion unless he or she had been through the "selection" itself. On the other hand, Brenner found the atheism of others less self-assured. For some survivors, Brenner is convinced, profession of atheism is less a simple theological posture and more an emotional reaction, an expression of deep hurt and anger against God for leaving Jews so radically abandoned. Others found their atheism producing a sense of guilt. This was not guilt over having survived (Brenner's findings turned up very little of that syndrome), but rather a sense that one's atheism betrays too many of those who perished and even entails disloyalty to the Jewish tradition itself. At least for Jewish survivors, atheism after Auschwitz, however natural a response it may be, is rarely easy or comfortable.

If it is ironic that "those Holocaust survivors who became non-believers appear to feel the urgent need to explain and justify their non-belief to a far greater extent than believers seem to feel the need to justify *their* belief,"[4] still the believers are left to contend with demanding questions about the kind of God they affirm. Again, the variety of outlook is the most striking feature in Brenner's sample. Far from irresistibly driving survivors away from belief in God, the Holocaust draws out many different views, thus suggesting that post-Holocaust religious options are not simply reducible to affirmation of one God or of none at all. The sheer diversity of affirmative views underscores that no single idea about God will ever be acceptable to all. That same pluralism, however, means that the spectrum of what one may find religiously credible after Auschwitz remains open wide. One survivor's religious convictions do not necessarily speak for anyone else. Nor do those of philosophers or theologians who declaim for or against God in the Holocaust's aftermath. What such reflection can do is to help people confront the options so they can consider what honestly makes the most good sense to them. Survivors do this by showing how they personally have coped with massive destruction. Philosophers and theologians can share in the quest by developing various options in greater detail; by testing the alternatives critically as to their assumptions and implications; and by bringing imagination to bear to reinterpret religious traditions and to break new ground that reveals the significance of the Holocaust and the resources we need to reduce the waste that human power can spew out.

Survivors do not provide ultimate, final answers to complex questions raised by the Holocaust. No one can. The survivors' religious disagreement is substantial, but it is also worth noting that those who affirmed God's reality tended toward a consensus about views they *rejected*. None, for instance, regarded the Holocaust as evil that might really be good in disguise if viewed from a proper perspective. Nor did it seem to them that the Holocaust was a device used by God to refine or to purify moral character through suffering. Also unrepresented was the suggestion that there is an ultimate source of evil, a devil, who coexists with God: God may be the source of evil as well as of good, but God has no peers. At no time, moreover, did the survivors believe that Jews would finally disappear from the earth, and they welcomed the state of Israel as vindication of that trust. But likewise, when questioned whether Israel was worth the Holocaust, their collective response was "if not a resounding and thunderous no, then certainly an emphatic no, a declination with little hesitation or uncertainty." Indeed if the state of Israel was insufficient to justify the Holocaust, not one "among these 708 twentieth-century Jewish victims . . . thought the world-to-come—whether as afterlife, heaven, messianic future, resurrection, or whatever a survivor may conceive—was sufficient alone to make sense out of the Holocaust" either.[5]

Although it does not follow that the survivors were equally unanimous in rejecting all affirmations of a world-to-come, large numbers—but not all—denied the theory that those who perished in the Holocaust were being punished by God for their own sinfulness. More than 70% of those who responded to that issue set aside any interpretation that linked the Holocaust to God's wrath or judgment in response to human sin. The Holocaust, they stressed, was humanity's doing, not God's. In emphasizing that point, however, the survivors recognized that the issue of God's relation to the Holocaust is not set aside. Their response to the following question, which merits quotation in full from Brenner's study, made that fact plain:

With regard to the destruction of the Six Million which one of these responses is the most acceptable to you?

 a. It is inappropriate to blame God for the acts of man (man may decide to kill or not to kill).
 b. It is not for us to judge the ways of God.
 c. God was unable to prevent the destruction.
 d. The Holocaust was the will of God (it was part of His divine plan).
 e. Nothing can excuse God for not having saved them.[6]

Of the 26% in Brenner's survey who chose not to answer this question, virtually all were non-believers. Among the remainder, the response most frequently chosen first (34%) was *b*. This option was followed closely (27%) by *a*. One out of four chose *e*. Overall only 9% of the survivors picked *d*. Fewer still checked *c*. The configuration of choices suggests that Holocaust survivors who believe in God take seriously the reality of human freedom and responsibility. Nonetheless, far from removing puzzles about God, that emphasis on freedom stands by another, namely that it is not for us to judge the ways of God. The latter response implies ambivalence as much as piety. In spite of humanity's freedom, or even because of it, the ways of God remain puzzling in light of the Holocaust, an intimation that is reinforced by the fact that hardly any of the survivors decided theologically that God was unable to prevent the destruction.

The opinions of Holocaust survivors are not necessarily normative theologically, but neither are they without significance and interest when compared with some of the theological interpretations of the Holocaust that both Christians and Jews have offered recently. For as we shall see in what follows, many of those interpretations in one way or another emphasize the very point that the survivors find immensely difficult to accept, namely, that God was somehow unable to prevent the destruction.

A Christian Response

Slowly and painfully Christians are discovering the Holocaust's impact on their tradition. The awareness that Christian anti-Judaism contributed much to the destruction of European Jewry requires them no less than Jews to reconsider the most fundamental aspects of their faith. Although Christian theology in America has usually played second fiddle to European and specifically German theological work, when it comes to responses to the Holocaust, American thinkers are more in the vanguard. Significantly, there are more Jews in the United States than in any other country. Not only does that fact warrant special American ties to the state of Israel, but also it makes Holocaust reflection by American Christians all the more important.

As American Christian responses to the Holocaust developed until recently, study concentrated on two main areas: appraisal of church life in the Third Reich and inquiry about the Christian roots of antisemitism. These analyses

were largely historical. Now a movement is under way to go beyond that neces-
sary beginning and toward substantial theological revision. Seriously studying
what Jewish thinkers have to say, Christian writers such as Robert McAfee
Brown, Harry James Cargas, A. Roy and Alice Eckardt, Eva Fleischner, Franklin Littell, John T. Pawlikowski, and John K. Roth contribute to this process.
The most significant current example, however, is provided by Paul M. van
Buren, who is completing a systematic Christian theological response to the
Holocaust. In a projected four-volume work that assesses Christian thought in
light of the Holocaust—including the sensitive question of how Christians
should regard Jesus after Auschwitz, the vigor of Jewish religious life throughout the centuries, and the reemergence of the state of Israel—van Buren does
much to overcome Christian triumphalism and the notion that Christianity has
superseded or negated Jewish faith.[7] Unfortunately, his suggestions about God's
relation to Auschwitz are far less credible than his estimates about how to recon-
ceive the relations between Christians and Jews so that anti-Jewish sentiment in
Christianity is laid to rest forever.

Van Buren's theology stresses that Christians worship the God of the Jews,
the same God presumably who is the God of the survivors polled in Brenner's
survey. Although he underscores the difficulties of speaking about God at all
after Auschwitz, van Buren joins the survivors in stressing that God has created
us free and responsible. To bestow us with those qualities, he believes, is a loving thing for God to do. It also entails that God has "to sit still and to suffer in
agony as His children move so slowly to exercise in a personal and loving way
the freedom which He has willed for them to have and exercise."[8] Confronted
by the question, "Where was God at Auschwitz?" van Buren believes that God
was in the midst of that destruction, suffering "in solidarity with His people."
The objectives of this suffering God, he surmises, might have included "trying
to awaken His creatures to their irresponsibility. Perhaps He was trying, by simply suffering with His people, to awaken His church to a new understanding of
love and respect for them." Obviously uneasy about those answers, van Buren
adds: "The cost seems out of all proportion to the possible gain, so silence may
be the wiser choice."[9] If so, van Buren eschews it and goes on to elaborate his
views about God's suffering.

Those views amount to an apologetic defense of God predicated on the principle that God's creation of human freedom "constitutes a divine self-determi-
nation. . . . Having made this decision and taken this step, there are some
things which God cannot be and some choices that are no longer open to Him.
. . . "[10] Specifically, God could not intervene to stop the Holocaust, asserts van
Buren, "without ceasing to be the God of love and freedom who has . . . conferred responsibility and free creative power on His creatures."[11] Here van
Buren begs the question twice over. Responsibility and free creative power are
not incompatible with Holocaust interventions by God unless God or van Buren

defines them that way. Moreover, if van Buren or God does define them that way, then one might wonder how that decision is supposed to embody love, seeing that its outworkings in history led to unremitting slaughter in the Holocaust. Van Buren pleads that, if we are to think of God as a parental figure—the imagery is common to both Judaism and Christianity—"then this must surely be an agonizing period in God's life."[12] Well it might be, though less because of van Buren's emphasis that God is so explicitly bound by the existence of human freedom and more by second thoughts about what God did in creating a world of freedom in which irresponsible destructiveness destroys more than love appears to save.

About one matter van Buren is perfectly credible: "God is not a God who does it all for His creatures." He may even be correct that if more Christians had acknowledged that fact earlier, millions murdered by Hitler might have been rescued. But if we are to go on to suggest, as van Buren does, that the Holocaust becomes divine revelation, informing us "that God requires that we take unqualified responsibility before Him for His history with us,"[13] then at the very least common decency would seem to enjoin us to ask God, or at least van Buren, whether there were not a more effective, less wasteful, way for God to get that message across. Van Buren reads the emergence of the state of Israel in a similar light. That development did occur because of human initiative, but to speak of such effort as containing revelation from God concerning human responsibility should raise still more questions about what God is doing. For however wonderful the state of Israel may be, the Holocaust survivors speak convincingly when they emphasize that in no way is it worth the price of the Holocaust, which has played such an unmistakable role in establishing and in sustaining Israel.

Van Buren's Christian theology tries to retain a God whose goodness is as great as God's suffering and whose love is as vast as God's freedom. As far as history is concerned, however, his account suggests that God's power recedes as humanity's emerges. Van Buren believes that Christians take "the crucifixion to be God's greatest act," the very essence of suffering love.[14] But van Buren's perspective underplays the fact that the crucifixion would have been just another Roman execution had it not been succeeded by what certain Jews took to be a substantial intervention in human affairs, namely, the resurrection of Jesus from death itself. At the very core of Christianity—and it poses a serious inconvenience for van Buren's Holocaust theology—is the assertion that God's divine power far exceeds anything that human beings can do. God is not bound by human freedom unless God chooses to be. And if God wants to be, so that the divine presence at Auschwitz is that of suffering with the victims and not interceding on their behalf, then that is a problem for us all—God, Christians, Jews, and everybody else.

A credible Christian theology in a post-Holocaust world neither can nor will want to take God off the hook quite so easily as van Buren does, unless it is true that Christians are simply unwilling to confront the awesome and dreadful possibility that their God of love is at times needlessly and even wantonly involved with evil that did not have to be. "If we are to speak of ourselves as being responsible for history," writes van Buren, "then we shall have to find a way to speak of God that corresponds."[15] True, people are responsible for history, but humanity's responsibility cannot be the whole story. It is irresponsible, not to say unchristian, to assign responsibility inequitably. If God exists, God must bear a fair share. God's responsibility would be located in the fact that God is the One who ultimately sets the boundaries in which we live and move and have our being. Granted, since we are thrown into history at our birth, we appear in social settings made by human hands. But ultimately those hands cannot account for themselves. To the extent that they were born with the potential and the power to be dirty, credit for the fact belongs elsewhere. "Elsewhere" is God's address. Stendhal, the French novelist, need not have been correct when he remarked that God's only excuse is that God does not exist. Still, to use human freedom and responsibility as a defense for God does not ring true as we now ought to be mature enough to see. God's establishment of that very freedom and responsibility, at least given the precise forms it has taken in history, rightly puts God on trial.

Van Buren remains hopeful about human existence after the Holocaust. Having stressed God's limited intervening role in history, he asserts that history shall be redeemed. To transform history into something very different from the slaughter-bench Hegel envisioned it to be, radical changes are required. The issue is who will carry them out? By van Buren's reckoning, the burden of freedom places overwhelming responsibility on human shoulders, unless God changes and suddenly falls back on a more dramatic divine intervention within history than van Buren's discerning of the ways of God provides a basis for expecting. Where is the evidence to suggest that, in a post-Holocaust world, human beings have made or are likely to make substantial progress in redeeming history? Who, in short, is going to do the redeeming? Van Buren holds little stock in secular humanity; its ways did too much to pave the way to Auschwitz. Christians, he notes, are declining in absolute numbers in the world. Perhaps, then, the task falls to the Jews. If it does, it is not likely that their human power alone will succeed in turning the world's swords into plowshares and its spears into pruning hooks. If lions and lambs are to lie down together in peace on this earth, nothing less than a massive intervention in history by God appears to be necessary. Given God's continued policy of nonintervention, the historical order will probably remain less than redeemed. Meanwhile, Jews and Christians alike are left to await the fulfillment of God's promises, even as they try themselves to make the world less destructive.

Reeve Robert Brenner reminds us that "nearly three of every four survivors

were of the conviction that the Six Million were destroyed only as a consequence of man's inhumanity to man and with no connection whatever to God.''
Though in one way or another the Holocaust has diminished our sense of God's
presence in history, the fact remains that human existence does not account for
itself. The fact is enough to keep at least the question of God in our midst. Insofar as the question of God remains alive in the survivor community polled by
Brenner, it bears remembering that only 5% ''were of the conviction that 'God
could not have prevented the Holocaust.'. . . For most other survivors, 'a God
who is not all-powerful is no God at all.' ''[16] The views of these survivors suggest that religious questions about the Holocaust concern power. As Jewish and
Christian theologians continue to wrestle with the silence of God, the survivors'
testimony is a reminder that the power equation between God and humanity remains at issue.

Covenant and Election

Central to van Buren's *A Christian Theology of the People Israel* is the conviction that ''the Jews are the chosen people, and chosen as a people, they are
not a people consisting of individually chosen persons.'' This theology of covenant and election, van Buren continues, led Israel to take ''its historical experience to be evidence of how things stood between itself and God. Defeat by
enemies and natural disasters were evidence of divine displeasure over Israel's
infidelity.'' Acknowledging with Brenner the current difficulties of such a view,
van Buren notes that there has nonetheless been a paucity of ''Jewish explora-
tion of the appropriateness to the Holocaust of the rabbinic response to the destruction of the Temple—that it happened 'for *our* sins.' '' He properly
acknowledges that for Christians the issue of sin and the Holocaust should point
to ''centuries of Christian teaching of anti-Judaism.'' As to the Jewish dimensions of this issue, van Buren concedes that ''this is hardly a subject on which a
Gentile can speak.''[17]

The Holocaust has bequeathed to the post-war Jewish religious community
extraordinarily painful questions as to whether and to what extent God, as traditionally understood in Judaism, was involved. To understand these problems, it
is important to distinguish between *religious* and *philosophical* problems. For
philosophers, the Holocaust raises the age-old question: how can a God who is
thought to be omnipotent, omniscient, and omnibenevolent permit such evil to
occur? The evil of the Holocaust—in which thousands of human beings were
exterminated daily—was undoubtedly of far greater magnitude than the examples which usually elicit the question of the apparent contradiction between
God's power and goodness. For example, in Dostoevski's novel *The Brothers
Karamazov*, Ivan Karamazov argues that he cannot reconcile the suffering
of even a single innocent child with the claim that God is both good and all-
powerful. The Holocaust poses the philosophical question with especial ur-

gency. Nevertheless, the question remains in many ways the same whether the contradiction involves a single instance or a multitude.

When we turn to the religious problem posed by the Holocaust, numbers do make a crucial difference. In confronting the Holocaust, both Judaism and Christianity must show that its occurrence is consistent with a biblical understanding of God. For Judaism, this means the view of God received from Jewish Scripture as interpreted by the rabbis. Although the book of Job raises the question of the innocent individual sufferer, Jewish Scripture does not depict God as promising that the innocent *individual* will be exempt from suffering in this world. The Bible does, however, depict God as choosing a particular community as the object of special divine concern; promising to protect that community if they were faithful to divine Law; and warning of dire *group catastrophes* which God will inflict if the community ignores divine commandments.

If God is in fact especially concerned with what happens to God's chosen people in history, then the Holocaust is more than a particularly gruesome example of the age-old philosophical contradiction between an all-powerful, infinitely good God and human evil. From the perspectives of both Judaism and Christianity, the Holocaust can hardly be considered a random occurrence since it was inflicted upon that community which the Bible asserts to be God's chosen people.

In the past, whenever the community of Israel experienced a major disaster, her religious teachers interpreted the event as divine punishment inflicted upon the nation because of its failure to fulfill the biblical covenant. Christian teachers offered a similar interpretation. Jewish and Christian authorities agreed that God was the ultimate Author of Israel's misfortunes. They disagreed only in identifying the nature of the sin for which Israel was punished. Invariably, Jewish authorities identified the offense as some want of conformity to God's Law. By contrast, Christian authorities saw the same misfortunes as due to Israel's rejection of Christ as the Messiah.

Thus, given the classical theological positions of both Judaism and Christianity, the fundamental question posed by the Holocaust is not only "why was God silent (or absent) during the Holocaust?" but also "did God use Adolf Hitler to inflict terrible sufferings upon six million Jews, including more than one million children, plus more than six million others who perished in Nazi murders of defenseless people?" It should be recognized, however, that even if God were the ultimate Author of the death camps, it does not follow that those divine actions were necessarily punitive. Both Judaism and Christianity allow for the possibility that the innocent may be called upon to suffer sacrificially for the guilty. Neither Jewish nor Christian Scripture interprets every misfortune as divine punishment. For example, Job is depicted as having experienced great misfortune without having offended God. Similarly, the "Suffering Servant" of Isaiah 53 appears to have been an innocent sacrificial victim whose death atones for humanity's sins.

Nevertheless, whenever Israel experienced *radical communal misfortune*, her religious teachers almost always interpreted the event as divine punishment. This was the case in 586 B.C.E. when Jeremiah prophesied concerning the impending fate of Jerusalem which was then threatened by Nebuchadrezzar, king of Babylon:

> The word of the LORD came to Jeremiah: "Behold, I am the LORD, the God of all flesh; is anything too hard for me? Therefore, thus says the LORD: Behold, I am giving this city into the hands of the Chaldeans and into the hands of Nebuchadrezzar king of Babylon, and he shall take it. The Chaldeans who are fighting against this city shall come and set this city on fire, and burn it, with the houses on whose roofs incense has been offered to Baal and drink offerings that have been poured out to other gods, to provoke me to anger. For the sons of Israel and the sons of Judah have done nothing but evil in my sight from their youth; the sons of Israel have done nothing but provoke me to anger by the work of their hands," says the LORD. (Jer. 32:26–30)

Given Jeremiah's belief in Israel as God's chosen people, it was impossible for him to view the fall of Jerusalem as an event devoid of religious significance. The prophet understood that divine election places an awesome responsibility on Israel. Undoubtedly, he was mindful of the terrible warning the prophet Amos had pronounced upon his own people at an earlier time:

> Hear this word that the LORD has spoken against you, O people of Israel, against the whole family which I brought up out of the land of Egypt:
> *"You only have I known*
> *of all the families of the earth;*
> *therefore I will punish you*
> *for all your iniquities."* (Amos 3:1–2, italics added)

Jerusalem was destined to fall yet again at the end of the Judeo-Roman War of 66–70 C.E. At the time, the rabbis, who had succeeded both the prophets and priests as the religious authorities within Judaism, interpreted their people's misfortunes as had their predecessors. A characteristic example of the rabbinic response is to be found in the liturgy for the Holy Days and Festivals which is still used by traditional Jews:

> Thou has chosen us from all peoples; thou hast loved us and taken pleasure in us, and hast exalted us above all tongues; thou hast hallowed us by thy commandments, and brought us near unto thy service, O our King, and hast called us by thy great and holy Name. . . .
> *But on account of our sins we were exiled from our land, and removed far from our country.*[18]

We have noted in Chapter 2 that the young Christian church also interpreted the fall of Jerusalem as divine punishment. Given the fact that both the classical

Jewish and Christian authorities have consistently interpreted major Jewish communal disaster as divine punishment, it is impossible to avoid the following questions: is the Holocaust to be considered yet another example of God's punishment of the Jews for failing to remain steadfast to the covenant? if we cannot understand the Holocaust in this way, does this significantly affect our religious belief?

In the history of the Jews, there have been many group tragedies. Nevertheless, only three major communal disasters have irrevocably altered the character of the Jewish world: Nebuchadrezzar's defeat of Judea in 586 B.C.E., the fall of Jerusalem to the Romans in 70 C.E., and the extermination of six million European Jews during World War II. Not since 70 have the Jews of the world experienced a catastrophe remotely like that which they endured between 1939 and 1945. In reality, never before in their long history have the Jews experienced so overwhelming a disaster.

Given the doctrines of covenant and election, it has been impossible for Jewish thinkers to ignore the religious implications of so overwhelming a catastrophe. In reality, no subject has so dominated the concerns of Jewish thinkers, at least since the mid-1960s when two radically different theological interpretations of the Holocaust first appeared: *The Face of God after Auschwitz* by Ignaz Maybaum and *After Auschwitz* by Richard L. Rubenstein, the co-author of this book. Rubenstein's volume has received far more attention both from scholars and the media. There is general agreement that the Holocaust became a predominant subject within Jewish theology after its publication. Although Maybaum's book was written in English, it was published in the Netherlands, and for many years remained almost totally unknown in the United States. No two works of Holocaust theology are in such total disagreement. Precisely for that reason, they ought to be considered together. Their disagreement illuminates many of the crucial issues confronting religious faith after Auschwitz.

Maybaum, a Viennese-born Reform rabbi, served congregations in Germany until 1939 when he emigrated to England and served for many years as a liberal rabbi and theologian. In his book Maybaum affirms the continuing validity of God's covenant with Israel. He further insists without qualification that God continues to intervene in history, especially the history of the chosen people, the Holocaust being one of God's most important interventions. Maybaum also holds that Israel has a divinely ordained mission to bring knowledge of the true God and divine Law to the nations of the world. This idea was strongly affirmed in the nineteenth century by Reform Jewish thinkers in both Germany and the United States. It never met with favor among traditional Jews or Zionists. The ideal of the ''mission of Israel'' is important for Maybaum's understanding of the Holocaust.

Although Maybaum sees the Holocaust as God's deliberate intervention, he rejects the idea that it was in any sense a divine punishment. Maybaum uses the crucifixion of Jesus as his model for interpreting the Holocaust. Just as Jesus was the innocent victim whose death made possible the salvation of humanity, the millions of Holocaust victims are divinely chosen sacrificial offerings.

The use of the crucifixion as a theological model by a rabbi may seem strange, but Maybaum argues that God's purposes can only be understood if God addresses the nations of the world in the language they understand. It is Maybaum's view that the nations of the world can only hear and respond to God's call when it is expressed in the language of death and destruction. Hence, the importance of the crucifixion, which is the only model by which the Christian world can comprehend God's activity. According to Maybaum, it was the awesome fate of six million Jews, *precisely because they were God's chosen people*, to become sacrificial victims in the death camps so that God's purposes for the modern world might be understood and fulfilled: "The Golgotha of modern mankind is Auschwitz. The cross, the Roman gallows, was replaced by the gas chamber."[19]

Maybaum concurs in the view that the Jewish world has experienced three overwhelming communal disasters in its long history. He uses the Hebrew term *Churban* (destruction) to characterize these events. The Holocaust is Judaism's third *Churban*. According to Maybaum, a *Churban* is an event of utter destruction which is world-historical in its scope and significance. It is a divine intervention which has as its purpose a decisive alteration of the course of history. Nevertheless, there is a creative element in this floodtide of destructiveness. A *Churban* marks the end of one era and the beginning of a new and better one, both for the Jews and the world as a whole. Unfortunately, the new era can only come into being if the old is destroyed. Maybaum holds that the destruction of Jerusalem in 586 B.C.E., which initiated the Diaspora of the Jews, was the first *Churban*. It can be argued that the uprooting of a population from its native soil, such as took place when Nebuchadrezzar exiled a large part of Judea's population to Babylon, is an unmitigated disaster. However, in keeping with the idea of "the mission of Israel," Maybaum holds that the first *Churban* had the fortunate consequence of enabling the Jews to bring knowledge of the true God and divine Law to the pagan nations beyond Judea's borders. Had not Israel suffered the pain of exile, knowledge of God's word might have remained confined to one small community. Thus, the first *Churban* was an example of God's "creative destructiveness."

The second *Churban*, the Roman destruction of Judea and Jerusalem, is also seen by Maybaum as progressive. With the destruction of the Jerusalem Temple, the synagogue became the predominant Jewish religious institution. Unlike the Temple, the synagogue is an institution in which God is worshiped through prayer and study rather than animal sacrifices. Maybaum regards this new type of worship as spiritually "higher" than the old type. Only by means of the destruction of the older, more "primitive" religious life could the newer, more "spiritual" type come to predominate. It should, however, be noted that not all Jews or Christians regard the displacement of sacrificial forms of worship as progress. To this day, Orthodox Jews pray for the restoration of the Jerusalem Temple and its biblically ordained sacrifices. Roman Catholics participate in sacrificial worship whenever the Mass is celebrated, and all Christians regard Jesus as the supreme sacrifice. In *After Auschwitz*, Rubenstein explicitly rejects the idea that prayer is a higher mode of religious life than sacrifice.[20] Maybaum's idea of religious "progress" would thus appear to be dependent upon an unexamined affirmation of the values of nineteenth-century Reform Judaism that are by no means universally accepted in the late twentieth century.

Maybaum also sees the dispersion of the Jews among the nations of the Roman world as progressive. Although the Jews lost their political independence, they were, in Maybaum's view, enabled to fulfill their mission by spreading the knowledge of God throughout the Roman empire. By contrast, most religious Jews have never regarded the Diaspora as progressive. Traditional Jews saw the Diaspora as divine punishment, and many Christians have believed that the Jews were doomed by God to wander homelessly because of their denial of Jesus as the Messiah.

Maybaum argues that the third *Churban*, the Holocaust, was yet another example of God's use of the Jewish people as sacrificial victims in an act of creative destruction. According to Maybaum, God used the Holocaust to accomplish the final overcoming of the Middle Ages and the full transition of the peoples of the world into the modern world. Humanity's "sin" for which the Jews had to die in the Holocaust was the retention by Europe of the old remnants of the medieval feudal world in an age in which they were no longer appropriate. It is Maybaum's view that after World War I the West could have brought "freedom, land reform and the blessings of the industrial revolution to the east European countries."[21] Instead, it did nothing. As a result, the slaughter of that war was in vain and Hitler was sent by God to do what "the progressives" should have done but failed to do. This meant that the work of creative destruction had to be carried out at an infinitely greater cost in human suffering.

For Maybaum, the Holocaust was God's terrible means of bringing the world fully into the modern age. This transition could not have occurred without the destruction of all that was medieval in Europe. Maybaum points out that the vast majority of the Jews who perished in the Holocaust were eastern European Jews who still lived in a medieval, feudal way more or less as their ancestors had, ritually and culturally isolated from their neighbors. In spite of the fact that it took a Hitler to destroy this outmoded way of life, Maybaum interprets the extermination of eastern European Jews as an act of creative destruction. Unfortunately, so too did the National Socialists, though obviously for very different reasons. With the passing of the community, which had been the most faithful to the ancient beliefs and traditions of rabbinic Judaism, the world's Jews were concentrated in the United States, western Europe, Russia, and Israel. There they were free to participate fully in an enlightened era of progress, rationality, and modernity.

In discussing Maybaum's ideas concerning God's reasons for destroying the Jews of eastern Europe, we feel constrained to point out that he appears uninformed concerning the actual character of the east European Jewish community in the years immediately before World War II. While it is true that many of eastern Europe's Jews lived self-contained, ghettoized lives, Maybaum ignores the fact that a very large proportion of the Jews of Poland, Lithuania, and Rumania had fully entered the modern world, as indeed had many Orthodox Jews. Maybaum appears to equate religious traditionalism with medievalism. If that identification were valid, we would have to regard millions of Orthodox Jews, conservative Christians, and Moslems as somehow not a part of the modern world. In reality, there have been many legitimate ways of responding to modernity, among which participation in or return to traditional religion is by no means the least important.

Maybaum also expresses a quasimessianic enthusiasm for the place and role of the Jews in the post-Holocaust world. His enthusiasm for the destruction of the medieval elements in Jewish life is such that he can equate the modernized, post-Holocaust Judaism of the "enlightened" Western world with the "first fruits" of redemption: "The Jewish people is, here and now, mankind at its goal. We have arrived. We are the first fruits of God's harvest."[22]

Nor does Maybaum flinch from carrying his theological argument to its bitter, logical conclusion. When Nebuchadrezzar sought to destroy Jerusalem, the prophet Jeremiah referred to him as "Nebuchadrezzar, the king of Babylon, my servant" (Jer. 27.6). Jeremiah had no doubt that, however terrible Nebuchadrezzar's deeds, the Babylonian conqueror was only the instrument of the sovereign Lord of history. In a deliberate allusion to Jeremiah, Maybaum depicts God as declaring "Hitler, My Servant!" Insisting that Hitler was God's instrument, Maybaum continues: "God used this instrument to cleanse, to purify, to punish a sinful world; the six million Jews, they died an innocent death; they died because of the sins of others."[23]

There are obviously enormous problems with Maybaum's defense of the biblical God of history and the election of Israel. No matter what "higher" purposes were, in Maybaum's view, served by the Holocaust, he regards God as One who was quite willing to subject millions of innocent people to the most degrading and obscene suffering and death ever experienced by a human group. Moreover, we are compelled to ask whether the "higher purpose," namely, the definitive onset of modernity, for which the victims were alleged to have been sacrificed, was worth even a single life. In the nineteenth century, German and American Reform Jews greeted the onset of the modern world, with its removal of ghetto restrictions, as a divinely bestowed, proto-messianic redemption. It is not difficult to understand why those who for centuries had been restricted to a ghettoized existence were filled with enthusiasm for the Enlightenment and its promise of civic emancipation. It is, however, difficult to understand how an intelligent thinker can retain that kind of optimism now that the night side of modernity stands fully revealed. This is not the occasion to detail the horrors the world has experienced precisely because we have entered into the age of modernity. Nor do we suggest that we could or should abandon modernity. Nevertheless, when we turn to the problems of environmental pollution, the threat of nuclear annihilation, the world-wide phenomenon of technologically-induced mass unemployment and poverty, we see that there is reason for skepticism concerning Maybaum's unreserved enthusiasm for modernity.

Nor, as Steven T. Katz has argued, can the crucifixion be used by Maybaum as an appropriate model for the Holocaust. In the crucifixion, God descends to the world, takes human form, and voluntarily gives up human life to save a world of undeserving sinners. In the crucifixion, God causes God to suffer for the sake of others. In Maybaum's version of the Holocaust, God inflicts hideous suffering upon millions of frail, frightened, and undeserving human beings.

In fairness, it must be said that Maybaum's interpretation of the Holocaust is motivated by a desire to defend the classical Reform Jewish version of the biblical image of God and the biblical doctrines of covenant and election. Maybaum fully understands the logical entailments of the faith he defends. Unlike Maybaum, most religious thinkers tend to affirm the God-who-acts-in-history while hedging that God acted in history at Auschwitz. By asserting that God's ways are "mysterious" such thinkers seek to affirm traditional faith while avoiding the negative consequences of doing so. Put differently, they seek to avoid the horns of a very unpleasant religious dilemma: absent the affirmation of some version of the traditional biblical view of God, believers may ask whether there is sufficient reason for participation in a religious community; yet if God is depicted as ultimately responsible for Auschwitz, some believers may ask themselves whether such a God is worthy of their love, trust, and loyalty.

Thus it is not surprising that many religious thinkers and clergy have tended to gloss over the whole question of God and the Holocaust. To his credit, Maybaum has refused to do this. His position indicates the kinds of affirmations that are logically required to defend the biblical image of God in the light of the Holocaust. This does not mean that Maybaum has provided the *only* logical defense of the biblical-rabbinic view of God. Nevertheless, he does show that it is impossible to affirm the existence of the biblical God of covenant and election, who is also the God-who-acts-in-history, without in some way affirming divine action at Auschwitz. Usually, such a position involves affirming God's omnipotence at the cost of compromising divine love and mercy. Maybaum himself attempts to avoid this split by insisting that Auschwitz does not constitute evidence of the absence of God's love and mercy since two-thirds of the world's

Jews survived, the Holocaust was of brief duration, and it was followed by the "Promised Land" of the fully realized modern age. Maybaum cites the prophet Isaiah to make his point:

> "For a brief moment I forsook you,
>   but with great compassion I will gather you.
> In overflowing wrath for a moment
>   I hid my face from you,
> but with everlasting love I will have compassion on you,
>   says the LORD, your Redeemer" (Isa. 54:7–8).

Nevertheless, we question whether many will follow Maybaum in regarding the events of 1933–45 as "a small moment" or the contemporary world as an example of God's "everlasting kindness." In the opinion of many scholars, including us, the so-called Final Solution was a consequence rather than a cause of the modernization of Europe's economy and society. In contrast to Maybaum, who interpreted the Holocaust as the last gasp of medievalism, they have maintained that it was a thoroughly modern enterprise in its methods and spirit. It is thus possible to credit Maybaum with the courage involved in following his theological position to its logical conclusion without finding his position credible.

Richard L. Rubenstein had not heard of Maybaum until many years after the 1966 publication of *After Auschwitz*. Had he read Maybaum before writing *After Auschwitz*, Rubenstein would certainly have referred to his writings as shedding light on why he was compelled to reject the traditional biblical God of covenant and election. As we shall see, there has been considerable development in Rubenstein's theological position, especially since 1976. Rubenstein's theologically controversial stand in 1966 was triggered not by intellectual speculation but by a crucial encounter with a German clergyman. In August 1961 Rubenstein had scheduled a research trip to West Germany to begin on Sunday, 13 August. He was spending that summer in the Netherlands. On 13 August the wall was hastily erected between East and West Berlin creating a major international crisis. Rubenstein decided to postpone the trip until Tuesday, 15 August. When he arrived in Bonn, the West German capital, he was invited by his hosts, the *Bundespresseamt*, the Press and Information Office of the Federal Republic, to fly immediately to Berlin to view the crisis firsthand. He accepted.

When Rubenstein arrived in Berlin, many people there were fearful that the Third World War was about to erupt. Rubenstein attended a mass rally of two hundred and fifty thousand West Berliners in the Rathaus (City Hall) Square which was addressed by Willy Brandt, then mayor of West Berlin and later chancellor of the German Federal Republic. He also spent a day in East Berlin and observed a tense, fearful city on military alert. Wherever he went in East or West Berlin, the atmosphere was apocalyptic in the true sense of the word. People were afraid that nuclear war might break out, bringing the world to an end.

In that atmosphere, Rubenstein was invited to interview Heinrich Grüber, dean of the Evangelical Church in East and West Berlin, at his home in the West Berlin suburb of Dahlem. The meeting was set for 4:30 P.M. on Thursday, 17 August. As Rubenstein entered Grüber's home, a column of American tanks noisily rumbled by on the street outside. Rubenstein and Grüber discussed many issues. Inevitably, the conversation turned to the Holocaust. During World War II, Grüber had attempted to rescue baptized Jews whose treatment by the Nazis was no different than that meted out to other Jews. He also opposed the antisemitic program of the Nazis and was incarcerated for three years in Sachsenhausen concentration camp. In the spring of 1961, Grüber was the only German to testify at the Jerusalem trial of Adolf Eichmann, one of the leading National Socialist architects of the Holocaust.

In his conversation with Rubenstein, Grüber affirmed a biblical faith in the God-who-acts-in-history and in the covenant between God and Israel. Like Maybaum, Grüber believed that the Holocaust was God's doing. He, too, likened Hitler to Nebuchadrezzar as one of the "rods of God's anger." When Grüber asserted that Israel was God's chosen people and that nothing could happen to the Jews save that which God intended, Rubenstein asked him: "Was it God's will that Hitler destroyed the Jews?" Grüber replied by quoting from the Psalms: "For thy sake are we slain all the day long" (Ps. 44:22). He then continued: "For some reason, it was part of God's plan that the Jews died. God demands our death daily. He is the Lord. He is the Master; all is in His keeping and ordering."

Grüber had no doubt that Hitler's actions were immoral and that Hitler would be punished. He also had no doubt that those actions ceased to be immoral when God was the perpetrator: "At different times God uses different people as His whip against His own people, the Jews, but those whom He uses will be punished far worse than the people of the Lord."[24] Rubenstein did not have time to ask Grüber to specify why the Jews were being punished, but there is no reason to doubt that Grüber regarded Jewish misfortune as Christian thinkers have throughout most of the history of that tradition. In fact, Grüber's colleagues in the German Evangelical Church meeting in Darmstadt in 1948 asserted that the Holocaust was a divine punishment visited upon the Jews and called upon the Jews to cease their rejection and continuing crucifixion of Jesus Christ.[25] If such pronouncements are heard no longer, it remains significant that, three years after the end of World War II, the leaders of the Evangelical Church were telling the Jews that they had nobody to blame but themselves for the Holocaust and that their only possible hope was to cease to be Jews and become Christians.

Rubenstein has since wondered whether his own views on God and the Holocaust would have changed as much as they did as a result of meeting Grüber had a non-German member of the clergy, speaking in a less crisis-ridden moment and in a less apocalyptic setting than the divided former capital of the Third

Reich, offered him the same interpretation of the Holocaust. He has concluded that dramatic circumstances surrounding his encounter with Grüber and the fact that Grüber was a clergyman, albeit one who had endured great hardship because of his opposition to National Socialism, were important components in changing his opinions on the subject. Above all, the Berlin setting reminded Rubenstein that the question was more than an abstract speculation with little practical consequence in people's lives.

Rubenstein has since referred to Grüber as a "straight arrow," by which he sought to convey his impression that Grüber was a man with an uncompromising sense of religious vocation. When the German theologians met at Darmstadt in 1948, some may have been motivated by anti-Jewish hostility and residual sympathy for National Socialism. That was not the case with Grüber. Like Maybaum, he took his faith in the God-who-acts-in-history with utmost seriousness. He knew what such a faith entailed. He did not attempt to avoid its logical consequences. If God acts in history, it was clear to Grüber that God alone was the ultimate Author of the Holocaust. Grüber had the courage of his convictions, whether he was expressing his opposition to National Socialism during the Third Reich or affirming his belief in the God of the Bible.

There was, however, an important difference between Grüber and Maybaum. Ironically, the rabbi had used the crucifixion as his model for understanding the Holocaust whereas Grüber has used the prophetic-Deuteronomic model of the God of the covenant as his model. Grüber saw the Jews as *guilty* offenders against God's Law. In fairness to him, he had a similar view of his own people. Maybaum could neither challenge God's sovereignty nor imagine any crime which would justify extermination at the hands of the Nazis, yet he had no doubt about the innocence of the victims. This compelled him to turn either to the model of the Suffering Servant or to the crucifixion. Maybaum regarded the Jews as innocent sacrificial victims.

When Rubenstein left Grüber's home, something in him had changed permanently and decisively. Undoubtedly, the change had been gestating for a very long time. Nevertheless, the encounter with Grüber convinced him that he could no longer avoid the issue of God and the Holocaust. There was little Grüber had said about Jewish misfortune that had not been spoken by the prophets and rabbis in the past. Rubenstein understood that Grüber was a man of courage and good will who, because of his beliefs, could not have offered any other opinion. Since Grüber's position was essentially in harmony with Scripture, Rubenstein was convinced that an inescapable difficulty was involved in the position of both Grüber and traditional Judaism. In 1966 he expressed his new convictions:

> I believe the greatest single challenge to modern Judaism arises out of the question of God and the death camps. I am amazed at the silence of contemporary Jewish theologians on this most crucial and agonizing of all Jewish issues. How can Jews believe in an omnipotent, beneficent God after Auschwitz? Traditional

Jewish theology maintains that God is the ultimate, omnipotent actor in historical drama. It has interpreted every major catastrophe in Jewish history as God's punishment of a sinful Israel. I fail to see how this position can be maintained without regarding Hitler and the SS as instruments of God's will. The agony of European Jewry cannot be likened to the testing of Job. To see any purpose in the death camps, the traditional believer is forced to regard the most demonic, anti-human explosion of all history as a meaningful expression of God's purposes. The idea is simply too obscene for me to accept. I do not think that the full impact of Auschwitz has yet been felt in Jewish theology or Jewish life. Great religious revolutions have their own period of gestation. No man knows when the full impact of Auschwitz will be felt, but no religious community can endure so hideous a wounding without undergoing vast inner disorders.[26]

Because of his position, Rubenstein has often been accused of atheism. It is important to note that on no occasion has he denied the existence of God, although he has rejected the image of God presented in the Old and New Testaments, and he has insisted that ''we live in the time of the death of God.'' What he meant is succinctly stated in the following passage:

No man can really say that God is dead. How can we know that? Nevertheless, I am compelled to say that we live in the time of the ''death of God.'' *This is more a statement about man and his culture than about God.* The death of God is a cultural fact. Buber felt this. He spoke of the eclipse of God. I can understand his reluctance to use the more explicitly Christian terminology. I am compelled to utilize it because of my conviction that the time which Nietzsche's madman said was too far off has come upon us. There is no way around Nietzsche. Had I lived in another time or another culture, I might have found some other vocabulary to express my meanings. I am, however, a religious existentialist after Nietzsche and after Auschwitz. When I say we live in the time of the death of God, I mean that the thread uniting God and man, heaven and earth, has been broken. We stand in a cold, silent, unfeeling cosmos, unaided by any purposeful power beyond our own resources. After Auschwitz, what else can a Jew say about God?[27]

Today, Rubenstein considers his position more akin to mystical religion, both Eastern and Western, than to existentialism. Moreover, he no longer regards the cosmos as ''cold, silent, unfeeling.'' At the very least, insofar as humanity is a part of the cosmos and is capable of love as well as hate, it cannot be said that the cosmos is entirely cold and silent. Rubenstein's response in *After Auschwitz* must be seen as the expression of a highly assimilated Jew who, because of the Holocaust, had committed himself to the defense of his inherited religious tradition and then, triggered by his Berlin encounter with Grüber, found that he could no longer believe either in the God of that tradition or in the tradition's crucial doctrines of covenant and election. Given both his loss of faith and the events of World War II which brought it about, his view of existence was understandably bleak at the time. Today, Rubenstein would balance the elements of creativeness and love in the cosmos somewhat more evenly with those of destruction and hate than he was prepared to do in 1966. What has not changed is his affirmation of a view of God quite different from the mainstream view of biblical and rabbinic Judaism and his rejection of the notion that the Jews are in any sense a people either chosen or rejected by God. On the contrary, he holds that the Jews are a people like any other whose religion and culture were shaped so as to make it possible for them to cope with their very distinctive history and location among the peoples of the world. Put differently, Rubenstein has consistently denied that the existence of the Jewish people has any divinely bestowed superordinate significance whatsoever.

Rubenstein's unqualified rejection of the biblical God and the doctrine of the chosen people was a step of extraordinary seriousness for a Jewish theologian. Later his critics were to ask whether anyone who accepted Rubenstein's views had any reason for remaining Jewish. For millennia the literature and the liturgy of normative Judaism have been saturated with the idea that God had chosen Israel from among all the nations of the world and that Jews were under a divinely sanctioned obligation to obey the divinely ordained laws and traditions of the Torah. Why, it was asked, should anyone keep the Sabbath, circumcise male offspring, marry within the Jewish community, or obey the dietary laws if the God of the Bible did not exist?

Briefly stated, Rubenstein's early response was that the demise of Judaism's theological validation did not entail an end to the psychological or sociological functions the religion fulfilled. He relied heavily on the fact that, save for the case of conversion, entrance into Judaism is a matter of birth rather than choice and that even conversion to Christianity does not cancel Jewish identity. There is an ethnic component to Jewish identity which persists long after the loss of Jewish faith. Rubenstein was aware of the fact that many Jews had in fact experienced their own loss of faith but remained Jews nevertheless. He argued that religion is not only a system of belief but a system of shared rituals, customs, and memories by which members of a community cope with or celebrate the moments of crisis in their own lives or the life of the community. He thus maintained that religion is not so much dependent upon belief as upon practices related to the life cycle. For example, no matter how tenuous the faith of the average Jew or Christian, he or she would normally find their inherited traditions the most suitable vehicles for consecrating such events as the birth of a child or a marriage. In a crisis such as the death of a parent, spouse, or child, the need to turn to the religious ways of one's inherited tradition would be even more urgent. Rubenstein wrote:

> Though I believe that a void stands where once we experienced God's presence, I do not think Judaism has lost its meaning or its power. I do not believe that a theistic God is necessary for Jewish religious life. Dietrich Bonhoeffer has written that our problem is how to speak of God in an age of no religion. I believe that our problem is how to speak of religion in an age of no God. I have suggested that Judaism is the way in which we share the decisive times and crises of life

through the traditions of our inherited community. The need for that sharing is not diminished in the time of the death of God. We no longer believe in the God who has the power to annul the tragic necessities of existence; the need religiously to share that existence remains.[28]

In rejecting the biblical image of God, Rubenstein expressed his belief in the immanence rather than the transcendence of Deity. The Bible depicts God as transcending the created world. But there is another view of God, one in which God is thought to be immanent in the cosmos, which in turn is regarded as alive and capable of thought, reflection, and feeling. In this view, the cosmos in all its multiplicity is none other than the expression of the single unified and unifying Source and Ground we name as God. Moreover, if human beings are an integral part of the cosmos, which in turn is an expression of the Divine Ground, then Deity is capable of thought, reflection, and feeling, at least in its human manifestation. This view affirms that human thought and feeling are expressions of divine thought and feeling. We cannot enter into details on this complicated subject. It is, however, relevant to note that this view of God has been expressed in at least two major modes of religious sensibility in the West, the nature paganism of the prebiblical world and religious mysticism. Having rejected the biblical God and not God in essence, largely because of his profound disagreement with the doctrine of the chosen people, it is not surprising that Rubenstein turned to both paganism and mysticism in order to find an alternative basis for religious life.

Rubenstein's turn to nature paganism paralleled the return of the remnant of the Jewish people that survived the Holocaust to their ancestral homeland, and the rebirth of an independent Jewish state for the first time since the Judeo-Roman wars of the first and second centuries. A people who are at home, argued Rubenstein, live a very different kind of life than does a band of wandering strangers. Citing the traditional Jewish liturgy, he pointed out that during the whole period of their wanderings, the vast majority of the Jewish people had prayed that they might be restored to the land of their origin. Wherever they dwelt in the Diaspora, their lives and their safety were wholly dependent upon the tolerance of others. During the two thousand years of the Diaspora, Jewish history always had a goal: to return to the homeland from which the Jews had been exiled. That goal was given expression in prayers, originally written in the aftermath of the Judeo-Roman Wars, and still recited three times daily in the traditional liturgy:

> Sound the great horn for our freedom; raise the ensign to gather our exiles, and gather us from the four corners of the earth. Blessed art thou, O Lord, who gatherest the dispersed of thy people. . . .
>
> And to Jerusalem, thy city, return in mercy, and dwell therein as thou hast spoken; rebuild it soon in our days as an everlasting building, and speedily set up therein the throne of David. Blessed art thou, O Lord, who rebuildest Jerusalem.[29]

With his nineteenth-century Reform Jewish ideas about the "mission of Israel," Maybaum rejected the spirit of these prayers and argued that the Diaspora was "progress" and an integral part of God's plan for humanity. Rubenstein was closer to Jewish tradition in identifying the Diaspora as a form of communal alienation. He further pointed out that the Holocaust had demonstrated how hazardous it was for any people to be utterly dependent for their security on a majority that regarded them as religiously and culturally alien, especially in times of stress.

If Jewish history had as its goal return to the land of Israel, Rubenstein maintained that Jewish history had, at least in principle, come to an end when that goal was attained and a Jewish state was established in Israel. It may have made sense, Rubenstein argued, to worship a God of history while Jewish history was still unfulfilled, that is, while Jews still envisioned the goal of their history as a return to Israel in the distant future. The Jewish situation changed radically when the goal was reached. Not only had Jewish history come to an end, but after Auschwitz the God of history was no longer credible. Rubenstein further argued that, whenever in the biblical period the Jewish people had felt at home in their land, they turned to the earth gods of Canaan. Since Rubenstein was not a polytheist, he argued that after Auschwitz and the return to Israel, the God of nature, or more precisely the God manifested in and through nature was the God to whom the Jews would turn in place of the God of history, especially in Israel. This was consistent with his view that religion was essentially the way we share the crisis moments, that is, the turning points, of both the life cycle and the calendar. Having rejected the biblical God of history, Rubenstein turned to a modified form of Canaanite nature paganism.

Another strand in Rubenstein's post-Holocaust view of God was mystical religion. As the years passed, it became predominant. His earlier paganism, which was inextricably linked to the land of Israel, receded in importance even as Israel itself became less important in his own thinking. He had argued that when the Jewish people were at home in their own land, they had turned to the nature gods of the land. He came to see that the majority of the world's Jews were not "at home" in Israel. Even those who lived there were constantly mindful that the fragile state and its people could be annihilated were the Arabs to win a single decisive wartime victory. The majority of those outside of Israel had no desire to settle there. Clearly, the "goal" of Jewish history had not been reached, and Jewish history was not at an end. Although he remained unable to accept the biblical version of the God of history, he became convinced that most religious Jews eventually would, *even if that meant regarding Auschwitz as divine punishment.*

He also saw that the Jewish people in Israel had little interest in nature paganism. To the extent that they ceased to accept the biblical God of history, they became *secular* Jews rather than pagan. That distinction is fundamental. Secularism is a dialectical outcome of the negation of biblical religion. By asserting that God is the only sacred reality and that both the human and the natural orders are dependent creations, biblical religion fostered a development sociologists have called *Entzauberung der Welt* (disenchantment of the world). Whereas the ancient nature pagans saw divinity/ies immanent in both the natural and human orders, biblical religion ascribed divinity to God alone. When faith in the biblical God was lost, men and women were left to dwell in a wholly godless universe. It was that phenomenon rather than nature paganism to which Rubenstein was giving expression when he wrote that "we stand in a cold, silent, unfeeling cosmos." For the pagan, and for Rubenstein at a later period, the cosmos is neither cold nor unfeeling. On the contrary, it is full of life. Moreover, the source of that life is Divine Life. Rubenstein's earlier emphasis on the coldness and silence of the cosmos had been partly a response to the fate of the victims of the Holocaust. It was also an expression of the secular view of the nature of things, which is a likely consequence of rejecting the biblical view. Still, the mystical view of God was already present in *After Auschwitz*. It was to deepen as Rubenstein's life experiences deepened and most especially as he came into contact with the civilizations of Asia and their religions. Indeed, today Rubenstein's mystical theology has certain affinities with Buddhism as well as with elements in Hegel, although the germ of his current position was already present in his earlier writings:

> I believe there is a conception of God . . . which remains meaningful after the death of the God-who-acts-in-history. It is a very old conception of God with deep roots in both Western and Oriental mysticism. According to this conception, God is spoken of as the *Holy Nothingness*. When God is thus designated, he is conceived of as the ground and source of all existence. To speak of God as the *Holy Nothingness* is not to suggest that he is a void. On the contrary, he is an indivisible *plenum* so rich that all existence derives from his very essence. God as the *Nothing* is not absence of being but superfluity of being.
>
> Why then use the term *Nothingness*? Use of the term rests in part upon a very ancient observation that all definition of finite entities involves negation. The infinite God, the ground of all finite beings, cannot be defined. The infinite God is therefore in no sense a thing bearing any resemblance to the finite beings of the empirical world. The infinite God is nothing. At times, mystics also spoke of God in similar terms as the *Urgrund*, the primary ground, the dark unnameable abyss out of which the empirical world has come.
>
> At first glance, these ideas may seem like little more than word play. Nevertheless, wise men of all the major religious traditions have expressed themselves in almost identical images when they have attempted to communicate the mystery of divinity. It is also helpful to note that whoever believes God is the source or ground of being usually believes that human personality is coterminous with the life of the human body. Death may be entrance into eternal life, the perfect life of God; death may also end pain, craving, and suffering, but it involves the dissolution and disappearance of individual identity. . . .
>
> Perhaps the best available metaphor for the conception of God as the Holy

> Nothingness is that God is the ocean and we are the waves. In some sense each
> wave has its moment in which it is distinguishable as a somewhat separate entity.
> Nevertheless, no wave is entirely distinct from the ocean which is its substantial
> ground.[30]

In mysticism Rubenstein had found the God whom he could affirm after
Auschwitz, yet as critics pointed out, there was little that is distinctively Jewish
in Rubenstein's view. This did not trouble Rubenstein. As he matured, he was
willing to accept the role of outsider to his own inherited tradition. He was unwilling either to reject the inheritance or to affirm its truth. He did insist that in
the past it had enabled most Jews to cope with their very difficult life situation
as eternal strangers in the Christian and Moslem worlds. Yet, he also saw the
Jewish community in America rapidly diminishing in number as a result of intermarriage. He suspected that the unprecedented rate of intermarriage was in
fact a delayed response to the Holocaust of those who no longer believed, as
Jews once had, that Judaism was worth dying for.

Recently, Rubenstein wrote that, outside of Israel, the Jewish religious mainstream will consist primarily of that relatively small remnant of the Jewish people who continue to affirm faith in the God of history and the election of Israel.
He agreed with his critics that without such a faith there is simply no reason for
Jews to remain eternal strangers in the predominantly Christian world in which
they live.[31] In his lectures, he has also observed that while relatively few Jews
join that world through baptism, many Jews facilitate their children's entry into
the Christian world by marrying Christian partners. This, too, can be seen as an
important Jewish response to the Holocaust. The Holocaust had finally revealed
the full dimensions of hazard involved in being permanent strangers in the modern world. In the long run, only those who firmly believe that in remaining
strangers in a Christian world they have been chosen by God to serve God are
likely to have the courage to remain Jewish.

Mending the World

The first theological response to the Holocaust to be received with widespread
favor within the Jewish community was that of Emil L. Fackenheim, a Reform
rabbi and distinguished philosopher who left his native Germany in 1939 after
imprisonment in the Nazi concentration camp at Sachsenhausen and who has
spent the major portion of his career as a professor at the University of Toronto.
Fackenheim's thinking about God and the Holocaust must be seen against the
background of his fundamental religious position. Fackenheim's conviction is
that both Judaism and Christianity affirm an "actual Divine Presence" that can
and does manifest itself in the real world. This Presence is neither an intellectual
hypothesis about God nor merely a subjective feeling on the part of the believer.
It is the Presence *par excellence*, a Presence which is revealed in Scripture but
which is not confined to it. Fackenheim has written that "in a genuine divine-

human encounter—if and when it occurs—Divinity is immediately present to the believer."[32] Fackenheim also denied that the social sciences have any constructive role in comprehending the Presence. The Presence is a real, not an imaginary or projected, datum of the believer. The Presence can be met; it cannot be argued into or out of existence. Fackenheim's religious thought, including his reflections on the Holocaust, can thus be seen as an attempt to spell out the consequences for contemporary religious faith of the experience of the Divine Presence.

In any discussion of Fackenheim's thinking about the Holocaust, it is important to keep in mind that his position has evolved considerably as his own reflections on and knowledge of the Holocaust have deepened. Fackenheim has written that for more than twenty years he was convinced that the Holocaust was not a theological problem for Judaism. Judaism, he argued, was subject to no historical refutation until the time of the Messiah.[33] In the late sixties, he changed his mind: "Doubtless the greatest doctrinal change in my whole career came with the view that at least *Jewish* faith is, after all, *not absolutely* immune to *all* empirical events."[34] In a more recent book, Fackenheim elaborated on that change. He expressed agreement with Rabbi Irving Greenberg's observation that:

> "The Holocaust poses the most radical counter-testimony to both Judaism and Christianity. . . . The cruelty and the killing raise the question whether even those who believe after such an event dare to talk about God who loves and cares without making a mockery of those who suffered."[35]

Although there has been a tendency to view Fackenheim and Rubenstein as opposites, both men emphatically reject the idea that the Holocaust was a divine punishment. Moreover, Fackenheim is no more able to accept the doctrine of covenant and election as it is understood by Orthodox Jews or Christian fundamentalists than is Rubenstein. Fackenheim's affirmation of the Divine Presence is by no means identical to the traditional biblical-rabbinic God who rewards obedience to divine commandments and punishes disobedience. Like Rubenstein, Fackenheim has also rejected the idea that the victims were sacrificial offerings required by God, as Ignaz Maybaum has suggested. Additionally, Fackenheim's view of revelation is quite different from the traditional view. As early as 1951, Fackenheim distinguished the *presence* of Divinity from the explicit *content* of the covenant:

> Revelation thus remains a mystery even while it is revealed; and every single word spoken by any prophet is inexorably shot through with human interpretation. Franz Rosenzweig observed: "Revelation is not identical with legislation; it is, in itself, nothing but the act of revelation itself. Immediately, it is its own sole content; properly speaking, it is completed with the word *vayyered* ('and He descended'); even *vayyadabber* ('and He spoke') is already human interpretation."

... Orthodoxy identifies the human—if ancient—interpretation of the revelation with the revelation itself; ... All interpretation of revelation is human.[36]

The above passage does point to a fundamental difference between Fackenheim and Rubenstein. Rubenstein is a native-born American who has been more deeply and persistently influenced by conservative American Protestantism than Fackenheim. While in no sense rejecting the idea that the text of Scripture requires interpretation, Rubenstein does insist that when one is confronted with doctrinal issues as fundamental as God's relation to Israel, something close to the "plain meaning of Scripture" must be taken very seriously. If Scripture depicts God as demanding obedience from Israel on pain of dire punishment for disobedience, Rubenstein insists that the intent of the text cannot be softened because we are embarrassed by its modern application, for example, that Hitler is to be seen as a modern Nebuchadrezzar. Rubenstein would insist that we are faced with a choice that can neither be evaded nor glossed over: either the scriptural account of the covenant is accurate or, however we understand God, Divinity is not the God-who-acts-in-history-and-chooses-Israel. Rubenstein's Berlin meeting with Grüber was decisive because both men took the plain meaning of Scripture seriously. Grüber accepted its meaning. Rubenstein had too much respect for the integrity of the text to water down its meaning. Since he could not accept Hitler as a modern "rod of God's anger," he had no choice but to reject the biblical doctrine of covenant and election.

In reality, Fackenheim rejects the *literal* biblical doctrine no less than does Rubenstein, although he continues to employ scriptural imagery as if he were within the old tradition. This is neither dishonesty nor evasion on Fackenheim's part. It represents an honorable and creative but very different approach to religious faith, an approach that holds that all revelation is mediated by believers who stand in a particular historical context and who reflect that context in the way they understand and testify to their encounter with Divinity. As we shall see, for Fackenheim the context in which Jewish people experience the Divine Presence after Auschwitz is radically different than it was before.

In the past Fackenheim has maintained that God was present during the Holocaust, as indeed the Divine Presence had been encountered in all of the decisive moments of Israel's history. According to Fackenheim, God has been revealed in Jewish history through a series of "root experiences," events of such decisive character that they have influenced all subsequent periods of Jewish life. These "root experiences" include the Exodus from Egypt and the giving of the Torah at Sinai. Both at the Red Sea and at Sinai, Israel experienced the saving activity of God which shaped Jewish character ever after. At Sinai the saving God was also experienced as a commanding God. Moreover, in every age Israel has recollected these "root experiences" not as events of a long-vanished past but as present assurances that "the past saving God saves still."[37]

In addition to "root experiences," Fackenheim held that Israel experienced "epochmaking events" which have tested and challenged the "root experiences" with new and terrible situations. The destruction of Jerusalem, first by the Babylonians and then by the Romans, constituted such epochmaking events. In both cases, the test was met. In spite of the overwhelming nature of the tragedies, first the prophets and then the rabbis taught their community to hold fast to their faith in God's presence in history and to their faith that God would redeem Israel in the future as God had in the past. These were by no means the only epochmaking events. Throughout the long night of the Diaspora, Israel's "root experiences" were tested over and over again. In every instance, Israel reaffirmed its commitment to the "saving and commanding" God of the Exodus and Sinai.

The Holocaust was the most radically disorienting "epochmaking event" in all of Jewish history. Fackenheim insisted that the Jewish people must respond to this shattering challenge with a reaffirmation of God's presence in history. Fackenheim acknowledged that it is impossible to affirm God's saving presence at Auschwitz, but he did insist that while no "redeeming Voice" was heard at Auschwitz, a "commanding Voice" was heard and that the "commanding Voice" enunciated a "614th commandment." The new commandment is said to be that "the authentic Jew of today is forbidden to hand Hitler yet another posthumous victory." Fackenheim has spelled out the content of the 614th commandment:

> We are, first, commanded to survive as Jews, lest the Jewish people perish. We are commanded, second, to remember in our very guts and bones the martyrs of the holocaust, lest their memory perish. We are forbidden, thirdly, to deny or despair of God, however much we may have to contend with Him or with belief in Him, lest Judaism perish. We are forbidden, finally, to despair of the world as the place which is to become the kingdom of God lest we help make it a meaningless place in which God is dead or irrelevant and everything is permitted. To abandon any of these imperatives, in response to Hitler's victory at Auschwitz, would be to hand him yet other posthumous victories.[38]

Probably no passage written by a contemporary Jewish thinker has become as well known as this. It struck a deep chord in Jews of every social level and religious commitment. Most of Fackenheim's writing is on a philosophic and theological level beyond the competence of the ordinary layperson. Not so this passage, which is largely responsible for the fact that Fackenheim's interpretation of the Holocaust has become the most influential within the Jewish community. A people that has endured catastrophic defeat is likely to see the survival of their community and its traditions as a supreme priority. Fackenheim gave expression to this aspiration, and he gave it the status of a divine command. Instead of questioning whether the traditional Jewish understanding of God could be maintained after Auschwitz, Fackenheim insisted that God's Presence to Israel, *even in the death camps*, was not to be challenged on pain of being considered a posthumous accomplice of the worst destroyer the Jews have ever known. The passion and the psychological power of this position are undeniable.

There are however, unfortunate consequences of Fackenheim's position. Those Jews "who denied or despaired" of the scriptural God have been cast in the role of accomplices of Hitler. Given the influence of Fackenheim's ideas within the Jewish community, that is a matter of considerable seriousness. Moreover, Fackenheim went so far as to suggest that those who did not hear the "commanding Voice" at Auschwitz were *willfully* rejecting God: "In my view, nothing less will do than to say that a commanding Voice speaks from Auschwitz, and that there are Jews who hear it and Jews who *stop their ears.*"[39] Fackenheim either excluded or ignored the possibility that some Jews might honestly be unable to believe that God was in any way present at Auschwitz, no matter how metaphorically that idea was presented. To stop one's ears is, after all, a voluntary act. The practical consequence of Fackenheim's insistence that the "commanding Voice" had prohibited Jews to deny or despair of God has been to limit meaningful theological debate on the Holocaust within the Jewish community to those who could affirm, as did Fackenheim, that the God of Israel was somehow present at Auschwitz. Instead of seeing the Holocaust as the shared trauma which had shaken every Jew, and certainly every Jewish theologian, to the core of his or her being, the Jewish community has, following Fackenheim's lead, often treated theological dissenters as if they had handed Hitler "yet other posthumous victories." Fackenheim is not responsible for this development. Fackenheim's description of the commanding Voice gave expression to a deep-seated Jewish response to the Holocaust and defined the limits beyond which the Jewish community was apparently unwilling to tolerate theological debate.

In spite of its power, Fackenheim's position was not without difficulty even for the tradition he sought to defend. Given Fackenheim's conviction that revelation was inseparable from interpretation, it was not clear whether the commanding Voice was a real or a metaphorical event. There is now reason to believe that Fackenheim would reject both alternatives and would hold that the commandment would have been unreal without an affirmative Jewish response. It was, however, possible to inquire of those who took it as a real event whether anyone had actually heard the commanding Voice enunciate the 614th commandment during the Holocaust years. If language is to have any reliable meaning, *something* resembling the content described by Fackenheim had to be communicated to somebody who thereafter testified to his or her experience. Taken literally, there does not appear to be any credible evidence that anybody heard the 614th commandment, as indeed Fackenheim's recent description of how he came to write the passage would indicate. In *To Mend the World* (1982),

Fackenheim told his readers that after he had come to the conclusion that the Holocaust was a radical challenge to Jewish faith, "my first response was to formulate a '614th commandment.'"[40] Fackenheim may have been like a prophet of old in receiving a "word" that insisted on communication, but the status of his commandment as commandment remains—perhaps unavoidably—ambiguous.

Fackenheim's critics also found considerable difficulty with his assertion that the commanding Voice had enjoined Jews to "survive as Jews." In the case of traditional Jews, no such commandment was necessary. They have always believed that Jewish religious survival was a divine imperative. They had no need of an Auschwitz to receive such an injunction. In the case of secularized Jews, the commandment appeared to be a case of pedagogic overkill. It hardly seemed likely that even a jealous God would require the annihilation of six million Jews as the occasion for a commandment forbidding Jews to permit the demise of their tradition.

Perhaps the most questionable aspect of the "614th commandment" was the injunction not to deny or despair of God lest Hitler be given "yet other posthumous victories." Here Fackenheim confronted the fundamental issue of Holocaust theology, but whereas other theologians attempted, each in his or her own way, to offer a view of God that was not at odds with the empirical evidence of history, Fackenheim told his readers what God has commanded.

Does this mean that Fackenheim perpetrated a fiction in order to maintain the theological integrity of his reading of Judaism? Given Fackenheim's faith in the Divine Presence, there was simply no way he could have thought of God as absent from Auschwitz. It was impossible to speak of a saving Presence at Auschwitz. Yet, utter defeat and annihilation could not be the last word. A way out of the ashes had to be found. The "614th commandment" expressed what most religious Jews regard as their sacred obligation in response to the Holocaust. In the language of Jewish faith that response could most appropriately be communicated in the imagery of the commandments. Fackenheim's 614th commandment is religiously and existentially problematic. That, however, is beside the point. *It is perhaps best to see Fackenheim's 614th commandment as a* cri de coeur *transmuted into the language of the sacred.* That would at least help to explain why it has touched so many Jews so deeply.

In *To Mend the World*, Fackenheim returned to the problem of the Holocaust as a radical "counter-testimony" to religious faith. Although he did not reject the notion of a commanding Voice at Auschwitz, his response to the Holocaust had lost the dogmatic edge it seemed to have a decade earlier. More than ever he emphasized the fact that in every major institution and in every dimension of human experience, the Holocaust was not a "relapse into barbarism" but "a total rupture" with the previously accepted values of Judaism, Christianity, and Western philosophy. His view is largely in accord with that of George M. Kren and Leon Rappoport, who have written that the Holocaust is a crisis in human behavior of such dimensions that all of the guidance mechanisms of Western society, "institutions of law and religion and education," proved impotent in meeting it.[41] Fackenheim has added that not only did these institutions fail to respond to the crisis but in the ensuing years they have largely taken the path of escapism in treating the Holocaust as if it were an unfortunate incident which requires neither self-examination nor serious inquiry into how to prevent its repetition. Fackenheim insisted that there cannot be even the beginning of a mending of the rupture unless the full measure of the catastrophe is understood.

Fackenheim therefore turned his attention to the question of how the mending and healing process could begin. He used a term taken from the tradition of Jewish mysticism, *Tikkun*, to mend or restore, to denote the process. In the beginning of his book Fackenheim stated the nature of his quest: "But if the Holocaust is a *unique* and *radical* 'counter-testimony' to Judaism and Christianity . . . how can there be a "commandment" to resist its destructive implications, to say nothing of the will and the strength to obey it?"[42] In no case could the mending take place solely in the "sphere of thought." The rupture took place in the sphere of life, and it is in that sphere that *Tikkun* was necessary. Fackenheim did not regard thought and life as opposed. He did, however, regard life as the prior category in the present crisis.

In the case of Jews and Judaism, the creation of the state of Israel "on the heels of the Holocaust" was the most authentic Jewish response to the National Socialist "logic of destruction" that came to full expression in the Holocaust. That "logic of destruction" was totally different from all previous attempts of one people to exterminate another. Following Hitler's lead, the National Socialists regarded the Jews as vermin and bacilli, rather than human beings, and were determined to murder them, wherever in the world they were to be found. They were not, however, content with murder. They created a "logic of destruction" in which technical intelligence, planning, and rationality were employed in the death-camp universe to bring about, first, the most extreme form of Jewish self-loathing and then mass Jewish *self-destruction*.

Terrence Des Pres has identified this process as "excremental assault."[43] For example, with their penchant for order, the Germans insisted on severely restricting the time and the place at which the prisoners could eliminate their waste. Going to the toilet at any other time was punished by vicious beatings and death. At the same time, the available toilet facilities were hopelessly inadequate. One camp section at Auschwitz had only a single latrine for more than thirty thousand female prisoners.[44] In addition, the soup that was the prisoners' principal fare made many ill with severe diarrhea and dysentery. Unable to control their bowels, they were compelled to risk severe beatings or death by "illegally" going to the toilet. Alternatively, they evacuated in their own utensils or clothing. The "excremental assault" actually began when the Jews were first herded like animals into cattle cars and transported to the camps. Forced to stand during the seemingly endless journey, it was often impossible for the victims to avoid vomiting, defecating, or urinating where they stood.

As Des Pres and others have pointed out, the whole system had the deliberate purpose of filling prisoners with such deep self-contempt that they no longer had any wish to survive. As a result, many of the victims were transformed into a new kind of being, the *Muselmann*. Fackenheim cites Primo Levi's description of the process:

> On their entry into the camp, through basic incapacity, or by misfortune, or through some banal incident, they are overcome before they can adapt themselves; they are beaten by time, they do not begin to learn German, to disentangle the infernal knot of laws and prohibitions until their body is already in decay, and nothing can save them from selection or from death by exhaustion. Their life is short, but their number is endless; they, the *Muselmänner*, the drowned, form the backbone of the camp, an anonymous mass, continuously renewed and always identical, of non-men who march and labour in silence, the divine spark dead within them, already too empty really to suffer. One hesitates to call them living; one hesitates to call their death death.[45]

According to Fackenheim, the most original and characteristic product of the Third Reich was the *Muselmann*, the person who is dead while alive and whose death is no longer a human death. The "destructive logic" of the system operated inexorably to mass produce those worked to death into *Muselmänner* before they expired. Moreover, the power equation was such that no victim stood much chance of successfully resisting the National Socialist machine, which aimed to rule the world and did in fact rule Europe during the war.

Amazingly, there was resistance, and it is in that resistance that Fackenheim finds both the Jewish religious response to Auschwitz and the beginning of the Jewish *Tikkun*. The first response occurred when some camp inmates resisted the "logic of destruction" and prevented themselves from becoming *Muselmänner*. Resistance also took the form of pregnant mothers in the camps refusing to abort their pregnancies, hoping against hope that their children would survive and frustrate the National Socialist plan to eradicate every last Jew. It took other forms as well: Jewish partisans took to the woods to fight the Nazis in spite of the fact that Polish partisans were often as determined to destroy them as were the Germans; Hasidic Jews prayed when forbidden to pray; young Jews who could have fled to the woods elected instead to remain in the ghettos with their families in the hope of giving them some protection. Fackenheim acknowledges that, when measured against the success of the machine of destruction, the number who resisted was small. That, however, was not the fundamental issue. What was decisive was that there were some who did resist against hopeless odds. By their acts they demonstrated that the "logic of destruction" could be overcome.

Fackenheim argues that it is not enough to grasp the Holocaust universe conceptually. As a trained philosopher, he understands that when thought completes its work of philosophic comprehension, the thinker is left with a peculiar sense of tranquillity not unlike that felt by an audience after witnessing a Greek tragedy. For example, after contemplating the whole course of human history, with its record of crime, slaughter, and horror, Hegel was able to write in utter calm and philosophical detachment: "The wounds of the spirit heal and leave no scars behind."[46] Hegel exhibits a similar tranquillity when contemplating the presence of evil in history:

> In order to justify the course of history, we must try to understand the role of evil in the light of the absolute sovereignty of reason. We are dealing here with the category of the negative, as already mentioned, and we cannot fail to notice how all that is finest and noblest in history is immolated upon its altar. Reason cannot stop to consider the injuries sustained by single individuals, for particular ends are submerged in the universal ends.[47]

For such philosophers, to comprehend is both to transcend in thought and to forgive. Like the audience at a Greek tragedy, they contemplate the tale of strife secure in the knowledge that it was right that things were the way they were.

Contemplation of the Holocaust leaves us with no comparable tranquillity. The Holocaust cannot be transcended in thought. A universe that systematically aims to create *Muselmänner* is radically different from that of the tragic hero. Fackenheim therefore insists that it is not enough to understand the Holocaust intellectually, theologically, philosophically, or historically. Instead, the Holocaust universe must be *resisted* in "flesh-and-blood-action and life." Moreover, once an enterprise like the Holocaust has proven its success, everything that follows is changed. State power becomes infinitely more threatening. Antisemitism takes on a permanently genocidal character. Civilization itself now includes death camps and *Muselmänner* among its material and spiritual products. Those who understand something of what took place in the Holocaust are no longer able to view European civilization without seeing rationally organized, systematized "excremental assault" as one of its components. It is, for example, difficult for a knowledgeable visitor to look at the handsome uniform of a Paris policeman without recalling that it was men wearing the same uniform, not the SS, who rounded up Paris's Jews to form the cattle car trip to Auschwitz that started on the French National Railroads. Nor can one forget that papers on sadistically abusive experiments on death camp victims were read without protest at meetings of German medical societies during the war. The Holocaust has revealed new dimensions in the practice of medicine. As a result, resistance to the Holocaust universe and *Tikkun* become never-ending imperatives. It is in that sense that Fackenheim can still speak of a commanding voice at Auschwitz.

Fackenheim stresses that it is only as a consequence of the *deed* of resistance that resisting *thought* can come to have any meaning. Such resistance is an "ontological category." The Holocaust, he argues, was both an ordered and disordering universe designed to leave its victims with no possibility of re-orientation so that they might escape the fate of becoming *Muselmänner* and passing from the world of the living dead to death itself. The first act of resistance was the simple decision, against all odds, to survive and, if the worst came, to die the death of a human being. The second was to grasp the nature of the "logic of destruction." This is a difficult enterprise because there is always the danger, as we have seen with Hegel, that what is understood will be accepted, at least in thought. Fackenheim therefore insists that such thought must be accompanied by active resistance.

In the case of those victims who found the courage to resist, thought and action were intertwined. As Fackenheim has stated, "Their *recognition* of the Nazi logic of destruction *helped produce resistance to* it—a life-and-death struggle that went on day and night."[48] In addition, more was involved than mere self-protection. As the Holocaust was a *novum* in human history, *this* resistance was also a *novum*. It was both a way of being and a way of thought. During the Holocaust, Fackenheim asserts, authentic thought was to be found neither in the greatest of philosophers, who neither understood Nazism nor were troubled by the death camps, nor within the circles of Europe's religious leaders. Authentic thought was actual only among the resisting victims.

One of those resisting victims was a Polish Catholic noblewoman, Pelagia Lewinska, who was an Auschwitz inmate. Fackenheim cites her memoir in which she told of her resistance:

> At the outset the living places, the ditches, the mud, the piles of excrement behind the blocks, had appalled me with their horrible filth. . . . And then I saw the light! I saw that it was not a question of disorder or lack of organization but that, on the contrary, a very thoroughly considered conscious idea was in the back of the camp's existence. They had condemned us to die in our own filth, to drown in mud, in our own excrement. They wished to abase us, to destroy our human dignity, to efface every vestige of humanity . . . to fill us with horror and contempt toward ourselves and our fellows.
>
> . . . From the instant when I grasped the motivating principle . . . it was as if I had been awakened from a dream. . . . *I felt under orders to live.* . . . And if I did die in Auschwitz, it would be as a human being, I would hold on to my dignity. I was not going to become the contemptible, disgusting brute my enemy wished me to be. . . . And a terrible struggle began which went on day and night.[49]

This testimony is of great importance to Fackenheim. Lewinska felt under orders to resist and to survive. Fackenheim interprets her experience as evidence of the ontological dimension of resistance and of the "commanding Voice." He acknowledges that Lewinska does not tell us who gave her the orders. He does, however, tell of other victims, religious Jews, who felt they were under the same orders and had no doubt that the orders came from God.

In previous eras, the ultimate testimony of fidelity a Jew could offer was *kid-*

dush ha-Shem, the sanctification of God's Holy Name that took place when he or she willingly accepted martyrdom rather than betray his or her religion. Fackenheim points out that such martyrdom no longer made sense in the Holocaust. There was no such sanctification in the pathetic death of *Muselmänner*. To die under any circumstance was to give the German death machine what it sought of all Jews. Thus, resistance embodied a new kind of sanctification, *kiddush ha-hayyim*, the sanctification of life. Any refusal to die and outlive the infernal process became holy, not only for the individual survivors who were saved but for the religious tradition National Socialism sought to destroy.

Fackenheim's answer to the question, "Who heard the commanding Voice at Auschwitz?" is this: all who felt "under orders" to survive, resist, and overcome the "logic of destruction." Nevertheless, in *To Mend the World* he does not seek to defend the traditional Judaism of covenant and election, reward and punishment. He is no longer interested in reducing the dissonance between the "countertestimony" of the Holocaust and the teachings of Judaism as was, for example, Ignaz Maybaum. On the contrary, he emphasizes the rupture between the pre-Holocaust and the post-Holocaust world. He insists that the Holocaust is not a "relapse into barbarism" but a "total rupture." Citing Martin Buber, Fackenheim frankly acknowledges, that in the aftermath of the Holocaust "our 'estrangement from God' has become so 'cruel' that, even if He were to speak to us, we have no way of understanding how to 'recognize' him."[50]

Fackenheim offers a number of examples of the rupture. We cite two. Even after abandoning his earlier enthusiasm for National Socialism, Martin Heidegger, arguably the greatest philosopher of the twentieth century, was unable to be seriously concerned with the fact that *his* nation had introduced those prototypically modern phenomena, the death camps and the *Musselmänner*, into the heart of Europe. Similarly, although the Vatican was undoubtedly one of the world's best informed institutions during the war, the Pope was unable to utter a single word *explicitly* condemning the destruction process or warning Catholics of the danger to their souls of participation in the process.

Nevertheless, Fackenheim argues, the rupture cannot, must not be the last word. What has been broken must be mended by acts of *Tikkun*. In the past Jewish mysticism audaciously described the disasters experienced by the Jewish people as catastrophes within the very substance of Divinity. Thus, when the Jewish people were driven into exile in consequence of the Judeo-Roman Wars of ancient times, the Kabbalistic tradition described God's Holy Presence, the *Shekhinah*, as also going into exile. The seventeenth-century mystic, Isaac Luria, described the creation of the universe as a consequence of a cosmic rupture in the Divine Ground which he called the "breaking of the vessels." This was a Kabbalistic metaphor for the Jewish experience of being out of place and homeless at a particularly dark hour in Israel's history.

The mystics sought to mend the earthly rupture which had rendered the Jew homeless and the heavenly rupture which, so to speak, had made God a stranger to God's self. They did so by special prayers and rituals, which they regarded as mystical acts of *Tikkun*. Today, Fackenheim contends, new acts of *Tikkun* are necessary to mend the ruptured world. Such acts may prove impossible. Under the best circumstances, they are likely to be only fragmentary. Still, we have reason to hope in their partial success because contemporary acts of *Tikkun* were already accomplished during the Holocaust years. Fackenheim cites the example of Dr. Kurt Huber, the Munich professor of philosophy who publicly protested the acts of the National Socialist regime as a member of the "White Rose" and, as a result, was sentenced to death on 19 April 1943 by the court of Roland Freisler, Germany's most notorious Nazi judge. Huber could easily have enjoyed the relatively comfortable life of a philosophy professor. All he had to do was to keep his opinions to himself. Instead, invoking the ideals of Kant and Fichte, he willingly took upon himself the role of philosophic martyr. Huber refused to restrict his opposition to the realm of thought. He chose to unite thought and action. While Martin Heidegger was Germany's greatest "thinker," Huber took the path of Socrates and became a martyr.

Fackenheim cites another act of *Tikkun*, that of Bernhard Lichtenberg, canon of Berlin's St. Hedwig's Cathedral. On 10 November 1938, the day of *Kristallnacht*, Canon Lichtenberg beheld the monumental pogrom initiated by the Nazis, went to his church, and prayed publicly for the Jews and concentration camp prisoners. He continued to do so daily until he was arrested on 23 October 1941. When brought to trial, he testified that he was scandalized by the vandalism in an ordered state and felt that the only thing that he could do to help would be to pray for the Jews. He said that, if freed, he would continue to do so. While in prison he resolved upon release to join Berlin's Jews, who had been shipped to the Polish city of Lodz. He never got the chance. He died on the way to Dachau. Fackenheim compares the public prayer and martyrdom of Canon Lichtenberg with the silence of Pope Pius XII. He sees Lichtenberg's martyrdom as an act of *Tikkun*. As with Huber, all that Lichtenberg required for safety was silence. In both instances, the "logic of destruction" was resisted not by theory but by utterly selfless action.

Among the first Jewish acts of *Tikkun* were the astonishing acts of resistance to total excremental assault during the Holocaust. The most profound response to the Holocaust was the collective decision of the survivors to make their way from the graveyard of Europe to the one place where Jews could be at home. Fackenheim sees the establishment of the state of Israel as the fundamental Jewish act of *Tikkun*. It is, he admits, an incomplete and an endangered *Tikkun*. Nevertheless, it constitutes a profound attempt to overcome the Holocaust, not in theory or by a return to the grudging sufferance of the Christian world, but by the creation of conditions in which, for the first time in two thousand years, Jews have assumed responsibility for their own future, both biologically and spiritually. Moreover, Fackenheim argues, the emergence of the state of Israel is the indispensable precondition of a "post-Holocaust *Tikkun* of Jewish-Gentile relations." During the Holocaust, Jewish powerlessness was such that their survival was wholly dependent upon non-Jews. According to Fackenheim, "After the Holocaust, the Jewish people owe the whole world the duty of not encouraging its vices—in the case of the wicked, murderous instincts, in the case of the good people, indifference mixed with hypocrisy—by continuing to tolerate powerlessness."[51]

Implicit in Fackenheim's conception of the post-Holocaust Jewish *Tikkun* is a rejection of the Judaism of the Diaspora, if for no other reason than the obvious fact that in the Diaspora Jews remain dependent upon others for their survival. Only in Israel are they in control of a state possessed of the weapons with which they can defend themselves. Mindful of the total character of the rupture created by the Holocaust, Fackenheim declares that, although Jews continue to live in the *Galut*, the Diaspora, *Galut* Judaism may have been destroyed by the Holocaust, an opinion incidentally shared by Rubenstein. For both Fackenheim and Rubenstein, if the broken threads of Judaism are to be mended—and at this writing it is not clear that they can be—the mending can only take place in Israel. Moreover, this *Tikkun* will involve both religious and secular Jews, who are bound together by a common inheritance that includes not only the Holocaust but the Bible. Neither the secular nor the religious Jew would have found a home in Israel were it not for the Bible. The Holocaust may have driven them to the eastern shores of the Mediterranean. Only the Bible has the power to keep them there. Thus, in Israel and probably in Israel alone is there hope for the beginnings of a Jewish *Tikkun*.

It is noteworthy that the subtitle of *To Mend the World* is "Foundations of Future Jewish Thought." Fackenheim does not offer a complete theological response to the Holocaust or a new dogmatic foundation for post-Holocaust Judaism. He merely points the way and suggests the dimensions of the task. Fackenheim's religious journey has thus taken him from his personal encounter with the National Socialist "logic of destruction" in the land of his birth, including his own incarceration in Sachsenhausen, to a period in which he reacted to the total rupture of his world by attempting to find security in a posture of dogmatic and fideistic neo-Orthodoxy and then to his present position of openness, tentativeness, and awareness of how profound the rupture has been and how fragile and beset are our post-Holocaust resources for *Tikkun*. As most people mature, they tend to lose something of their physical and intellectual flexibility. That has not happened to Fackenheim, who has manifested an extraordinary capacity for self-criticism, insight, and growth in his awesome vocation.

A final word must be said about the richness of Fackenheim's thought. Because of our concern with the Holocaust, we have focused our attention on a single thread in his work, his explicit response to the Holocaust. We have been unable to do justice to the richness of Fackenheim's thought which encompasses, among other disciplines, an authoritative knowledge of Western philosophy, especially German philosophy in the modern period, Jewish religious thought and philosophy, and modern European history. His knowledge has enabled him to examine with great lucidity the profound character of the modern crisis. Above all, it has enabled him to move reflection concerning the Holocaust and its aftermath beyond the parochial and to demonstrate its universal significance.

The Religious Future

Finally, we consider the work of the late Arthur A. Cohen, one of the first Jewish thinkers of his generation to publish a major theological work, *The Natural and the Supernatural Jew* (1962).[52] Like Fackenheim, however, Cohen was initially silent on the problem of God and the Holocaust. He did not address that problem in a book-length publication until the appearance of a more recent work, *The Tremendum* (1981). There Cohen explained his silence, suggesting that he, like many of his peers, "had no language with which to speak of evil (other than by exhibition and denunciation)." This left him deeply moved by the Holocaust but unable to speak of it. Cohen admitted he "had constructed a modern theology without dealing with evil, either in itself or in its horrific manifestation as *tremendum*."[53]

In *After Auschwitz* (1966) Rubenstein criticized Cohen for writing a Jewish theology without confronting the question of God and the death camps. Nevertheless, Rubenstein recognized that in the aftermath of a trauma as radical as the Holocaust, it was not surprising that Jewish thinkers waited a whole generation before turning to the question. The shock was simply too great. In 1966 Rubenstein wrote:

> A religious community has some resemblance to a living organism. It is impossible savagely to rip out half of its substance without drastically affecting the surviving remnant. The first reaction to such a wounding must be shock and numbness. I do not believe the period of shock has entirely spent itself. It is only now that a tentative attempt can be made to assess the religious meaning of the events.[54]

Cohen later acknowledged Rubenstein's criticism:

> Richard Rubenstein was right. I had ignored Auschwitz, imagining that somehow I had escaped. But he was not right in that imputation. I did not imagine that I had escaped (or that any Jew of the non-European Diaspora had escaped). But I was struck dumb and I turned aside . . . and that amounts to the same thing: avoidance. The *tremendum* cannot be avoided.[55]

Writing about the Holocaust, Cohen uses *tremendum* to denote the event. He has said that he was mindful of Rudolf Otto's characterization of God's holiness as *mysterium tremendum* when he chose his term. According to Cohen, both *mysterium tremendum* and *tremendum* convey "the aspect of vastness" and "the resonance of terror." Nevertheless, the two terms refer to utterly disparate realities. In contrast to God's awesome holiness, Cohen sees the Holocaust as:

> . . . the human *tremendum*, the enormity of an infinitized man, who no longer seems to fear death or, perhaps more to the point, fears it so completely, denies death so mightily, that the only patent of his refutation and denial is to build a mountain of corpses to the divinity of the dead, to placate death by the magic of endless murder.

Cohen offers a further explanation of his use of *tremendum* in connection with the Holocaust: "I call the death camps the *tremendum*, for it is the monument of a meaningless inversion of life to an orgiastic celebration of death, to a psychosexual and pathological degeneracy unparalleled and unfathomable to any person bonded to life."[56]

Like Otto's *mysterium tremendum*, Cohen's *tremendum* is intended to convey a sense of unfathomable mystery. Cohen writes of the "palpable irrationality" of the Holocaust, an event which he regards as surpassing all others in its extremity and its uniqueness. He questions the possibility that the conceptual and intellectual tools normally used by historians and political and social scientists to comprehend war, religious and social conflict, and mass slaughter are appropriate to understanding the Holocaust.

Like Rubenstein and Fackenheim, Cohen eventually came to see that the Holocaust had rendered problematic faith in the biblical God of covenant and election. Nevertheless, when Cohen formulated his theological response, he was more explicit in addressing the difficulties the Holocaust poses for classical theism than in confronting the specific problems it raises for the normative biblical-rabbinic view of God's relation to Israel. In regard to the perennial question of the contradiction between an omnipotent and omnibenevolent God and the existence of even a single case of innocent suffering, Cohen argues that a constructive theology after the Holocaust must have at least three characteristics: (1) God must abide in a universe in which neither evil nor God's presence is accounted unreal; (2) the relation of God to *all* of creation, including demonic elements and events, must be seen as meaningful and valuable; (3) the reality of God can no longer be isolated from God's real involvement in the life of creation. If any of the three characteristics is without foundation, asserts Cohen, God ceases to be anything other than a "metaphor for the inexplicable."

In attempting to satisfy these criteria, Cohen, like Rubenstein, leans heavily on the Kabbalistic theology of Isaac Luria (1534–72). He also acknowledges his indebtedness to philosophical traditions appropriated for Jewish thought by the German-Jewish thinker Franz Rosenzweig (1886–1929). This tradition was spelled out most completely by Hegel's contemporary, the German philosopher

Friedrich Wilhelm Joseph von Schelling (1775–1854). Schelling in turn was strongly indebted to the medieval Rhineland mystic Jakob Böhme (1575–1624) and to the first words of the Fourth Gospel, "In the beginning was the Word."

The idea of human freedom is crucial to Cohen's Holocaust theology. Relying heavily on the aforementioned sources, Cohen holds that in the beginning the divine *Urgrund* (Primal Ground of all reality) overflowed its original and absolute self-containment in a movement of love. As long as God was all-in-all and there was nothing beside God, there could be neither manifestation of divine love nor personality, both of which require a nondivine otherness, such as a created world and creatures capable of responding to God. Thus, the world is, for Cohen and his theological predecessors, God's created other, lovingly formed by the Divine Word. Nevertheless, without the presence of humanity, the world would be devoid of freedom and incapable of responding to God's love or personality. It is humankind who, partaking of God's speech and divine freedom, is alone capable of responding to God. According to Cohen, freedom was originally intended by God to be tempered by reason, thereby preventing it from becoming willful caprice. Unfortunately, this did not happen, and human freedom, without which we could not be human or respond to God, eventually became the willful caprice of the Holocaust.

Cohen is especially concerned with responding to those who complain of the silence of God during the Holocaust. He argues that this complaint is in reality a mistaken yearning for a nonexistent, interruptive God who is expected magically to intervene in human affairs. According to Cohen, if there were such a God and if God were capable of interfering in history, creation would be an extension of God rather than an independent domain brought into being by God's creative love. Freedom, the essence of humanity, would be nonexistent and human beings would be mere automatons. Put differently, if humanity is free, God cannot intervene in human affairs no matter how depraved they become. Cohen's position is summarized in the following statement:

> . . . what is taken as God's speech is really always man's hearing. . . . God is not the strategist of our particularities or of our historical condition, but rather *the mystery of our futurity*, always our *posse*, never our acts. If we can begin to see God less as the interferer whose insertion is welcome (when it accords with our needs) and more as the immensity whose reality is our prefiguration . . . whose plentitude and unfolding are the *hope of our futurity*, we shall have won a sense of God whom we may love and honor, but whom we no longer fear and from whom we no longer demand.[57]

Clearly, Cohen does not see God as having a concrete role in history. Cohen thus rejects the idea that God was ultimately responsible for the Holocaust. Instead, Cohen relegates God's active role in history to the future. This is a theological strategy not unlike that of the German Christian theologian Jürgen Moltmann. It is, however, subject to much the same criticism: by denying

God's role in contemporary history and by relegating decisive divine activity to the future, Cohen, like Fackenheim in his earlier period, consigns God's activity to a domain wholly inaccessible to empirical confirmation and hence subject to every conceivable flight of fancy. One can say almost anything about God's future activity because there are no hard facts against which such claims can be measured. Although powerfully evocative, one wonders what actual content can be legitimately be assigned to words such as "the hope of our futurity."

Nevertheless, Cohen does not see God's presence in history as limited to the indefinite future. Cohen describes the divine life as "a filament within the historical, but never the filament that we can identify and ignite according to our requirements." Cohen holds that humankind has the power to "obscure, eclipse, burn out the divine filament,"[58] but it is not in God's power to limit human freedom. Insofar as God takes an active role in human affairs, it is as Teacher *par excellence*. The speech of God offers humanity a teaching with which to limit the destructive and capricious elements in human freedom. According to Cohen, that teaching is to be found in the *Halakha*, the corpus of rabbinic law. Beyond the role of Teacher, God exercises no direct interference with human freedom.

There is, of course, a very powerful reason why Cohen refrains from seeing God as playing a greater part in history than that of "divine filament." Were Cohen to do so, he would be confronted with all of the difficulties that flow from seeing God as the ultimate Author of the Holocaust. Nevertheless, one can ask whether the problem of God and the Holocaust has been solved by limiting God's role to that of "divine filament" and Teacher of essentially free agents. By this limitation, Cohen may have portrayed God as functionally irrelevant. A human being who is prepared to accept the consequences of his or her actions will have no reason to take God-as-filament into account. As long as such a person is prepared to accept the costs as well as the benefits of his or her behavior, there will be no reason to be concerned with a God who places no restraint on human freedom.

There are other difficulties that confront Cohen and all those who attempt to extricate post-Holocaust Judaism from the dilemma of having to choose between a view of God that renders God functionally irrelevant and one which sees God as using Hitler and Auschwitz as instruments of divine punishment. Although we do not here consider in depth the thought of the Orthodox Jewish thinker, Eliezer Berkovits, he has sought to defend the traditional Jewish belief by adopting a position on God and human freedom similar to Cohen's.[59] According to Berkovits, God created free persons not automatons. This has had the paradoxical consequence that "while he [God] shows forebearance with the wicked, he must turn a deaf ear to the anguished cries of the violated."[60] Thus, for both Cohen and Berkovits, the Holocaust is not the work of a punishing God but of men and women who have obscenely used their freedom for mass destruction.

Another traditional doctrine Cohen seeks to defend by a nontraditional reformulation is that of the election of Israel. Thus, Cohen argues: "The death camps ended forever one argument of history—whether the Jews are a chosen people. They are chosen, unmistakably, extremely, utterly."[61]

In actuality, unless one sees the Holocaust as divine punishment, the Holocaust is more likely to raise doubts about than to serve as proof of Israel's election. Moreover, it is possible to ask whether Cohen has confused being targeted for annihilation by human beings with being chosen by God. The Holocaust simply reveals the obvious fact that the Jews were targeted for annihilation. The fate of Europe's Jews demonstrates, if indeed demonstration be needed, that in times of acute stress Jews are in danger of becoming the target *par excellence* of the nations of the world. This is hardly identical with being chosen by God.

Like Rubenstein and Fackenheim, Cohen recognizes that the Holocaust has resulted in a Jewish return to history, by which all three men mean a return to a situation in which, at least in the state of Israel, Jews are dependent upon themselves rather than host peoples for their survival. As noted, Fackenheim regards the return as the beginning of a Jewish *Tikkun*. Cohen's assessment is less positive. He suggests that the return to history may prove "more threatening even than genocide has been, for in no way is the Jew allowed any longer . . . to repeat his exile amid the nations, to disperse himself in order to survive." In a similar vein, Cohen comments that immersion in a history without transcendent meaning may lead to a modern form of paganism: "History without a capstone, time without eternity, the present moment without the inbreeding of the *eschaton* leaves us, as Jews, with little more than the chthonic vitalities of our blood as shield and buckler."[62]

The Greek word *chthonos* means "earth." Cohen thus concludes that, absent faith in some version of the God of history, the Jewish return to history is likely to be a return to a modernized version of a very ancient earth paganism. Rubenstein had come to a similar conclusion two decades earlier. Cohen, however, is unwilling to rest content with a Jewish people enmeshed in the powers of earth. Having failed to find a "beyond" for the individual, he refuses to abandon hope in the immortality of the Jewish people as a sacred collectivity.

Given this hope, Cohen sees the state of Israel as a far less significant response to the Holocaust than does either Rubenstein or Fackenheim. According to Cohen, political states are a part of the incessant rhythm of history's rise and fall. A Jewish state is no exception. Hence, the eternity of this people cannot take a political form. Cohen writes that he stands outside the wall of the Jewish state as well as any other state. Nevertheless, he does not stand outside the Jewish people which, he asserts, constitutes "the eternal speaking of revelation to the Jew of history." In view of the twentieth-century experience of the Jews, Cohen understands his position to be problematic. *If the Holocaust has a single overriding lesson, it is that there is absolutely no limit to the obscenities a deter-*

mined and powerful aggressor can freely visit upon stateless, powerless victims. In the aftermath of the Holocaust, the survivors could no longer trust their safety to anyone but themselves. They risked their lives to create a Jewish state in the full knowledge that it might be destroyed by its enemies. If the state survived, they would enjoy normal human dignity; if it perished, they would at least die honorably, defending themselves rather than as pathetically impotent victims of some future excremental assault.

Cohen's critics have found much to praise in *The Tremendum*. They have, however, tended to find his attempt at a constructive theology after Auschwitz to be the weakest part of the book. Nevertheless, if Cohen has failed to offer a credible post-Holocaust theology, his failure probably tells us more about the inevitable difficulties confronting Jewish theology after Auschwitz than about any lack of ability or brilliance on his part. Put simply, it may be impossible to affirm the traditional Jewish God without also affirming the one idea that nearly every post-Holocaust Jewish thinker, save Maybaum, has rejected, namely, that the Holocaust was an integral part of God's action in history. Cohen himself has apparently recognized the limitations inherent in any attempt to write Jewish theology after the Holocaust. He writes: "I have promised only to cross the abyss. I have not promised to explain it. I would not dare."[63] Yet, if Cohen has failed to offer a credible post-Holocaust theology, his failure can, with justice, be described as tragic rather than personal. Let us recall that the tragic is not so much the story of human error or folly as it is the inexorable unfolding of a destiny wholly resistant to human intention. When Oedipus learned that he was destined to kill his father and marry his mother, he did everything he could to evade that destiny. Nevertheless, every evasive measure only brought him closer to the fated denouement. For the best and certainly the most understandable of reasons, Cohen may simply have attempted the impossible.

Does that mean that the ancient and hallowed faith in the biblical God of covenant and election has no future among religious Jews? On the contrary, it is probably the theological option most likely to have a future. Whatever doubts secularized Jews may currently entertain, that faith has been the hallowed, authoritative faith of the community of Israel from time immemorial until the modern period. It has given the Jewish people two supremely important gifts, the gifts of meaning and hope. Instead of viewing their experiences as a series of unfortunate and essentially meaningless events, biblical-rabbinic faith has enabled the Jewish people to see their history as a meaningful expression of their relations with their God. Moreover, no matter how desperate their situation became, their faith enabled them to hope that, sooner or later, "those who sow in tears will reap in joy." The old biblical-rabbinic view that God is the ultimate Actor in history and that the Jewish people are bound to God by an eternal covenant remains the most coherent, logically consistent way of understanding Jewish experience and history that is acceptable to the Jewish people. Rubenstein has pointed out the bitter, yet inescapable, consequences of holding this faith after Auschwitz. Nevertheless, no credible theological alternative has emerged that does not deny the very foundations of normative Judaism.

Faith in covenant and election appears to be indispensable to the Jewish religious mainstream. One does not have to be a Jew to be a monotheist. What distinguishes Judaism is the faith that God has chosen the Jewish people to serve and obey God by fulfilling the divine commandments revealed in Scripture and authoritatively interpreted by the rabbis. Moreover, it can be argued that the Christian world *expects* Jews to affirm faith in the biblical God of covenant and election for a simple but compelling reason: from an evangelical perspective, the Jews were the chosen people to whom God sent the Son as humanity's redeemer. The Jews have, of course, failed to recognize the true nature of Jesus Christ. Hence, God's election passed from the Israel "according to the flesh" to the Israel "according to the spirit," namely, to all those who have recognized Christ's true nature. Nevertheless, most believing Christians still have no doubt that, sooner or later, at least a "saving remnant" of Israel will finally see the light.[64] Like Judaism, Christianity cannot abandon the doctrines of covenant and election.

Christian influence on Jews and Judaism is far greater than is commonly recognized. By virtue of the fact that both Christians and Jews regard the Bible as of divine inspiration, Christians give Jews a context of plausibility for their most deeply held beliefs. If Jews lived in a culture in which the majority accorded the Bible no greater respect than we accord the Greek myths, Jews might still hold fast to their beliefs but they would receive no external reinforcement. Even the fact that Jews and Christians disagree about the true nature of Jesus reinforces the context of plausibility, for the disagreement is about the true meaning of the Book both regard as divinely inspired.

The profound influence of American Christianity on American Judaism, even on Orthodox Judaism, ought not to be underestimated. The world's largest Jewish community lives in and is ultimately dependent for its security and the security of the state of Israel on the world's largest Christian community. The state of Israel's strongest American Christian supporters are Fundamentalists who believe in the inerrancy of scriptural revelation. As conservative Christian influence continues to grow within the United States, it will encourage Jews to affirm a faith rooted in biblical revelation.

Thus, both external and internal influences foster a renewed Jewish affirmation of covenant and election. Even those Jews whose reasons for remaining in the synagogue are primarily ethnic rather than religious are likely to convince themselves that the principal beliefs of the Jewish mainstream are true. To do otherwise would be to create too great a dissonance between belief and practice. If the survival of the Jews as a group outside of Israel is perceived to depend upon religious affiliation and some measure of Jewish religious practice, which in turn are thought to be legitimated by faith in the God of covenant and election, even those whose basic commitment is ethnic are likely to find some way to affirm *the only system of religious belief that legitimates Jewish survival.* The alternative is to abandon Jewish identification altogether.

That alternative is actually being taken by the unprecedented number of young Jews who marry non-Jews and whose children or grandchildren are raised as Christian. While this is not the context in which to discuss the widespread phenomenon of intermarriage among contemporary Jews, that phenomenon must also be seen as a powerful response to the Holocaust on the part of those Jews who may have asked themselves Fackenheim's question concerning the morality of exposing distant descendants to antisemitic indignities. Those Jews who believe that in preserving Judaism they are fulfilling God's will have no difficulty in exposing their descendants to the potential hazards of a future catastrophe. Those who have lost that faith have no reason for doing so.

For those who have questioned the coherence of their post-Holocaust belief structure and who nevertheless elect to remain Jews, religious belief and practice will be in tension as long as the traditional legitimations of Jewish religious practice cannot be affirmed. Traditionally, the entire body of Jewish religious practice was founded upon belief in God's revelations to Moses, the patriarchs, and the prophets. As long as this fundamental belief is not affirmed, there will be a painful dissonance within Jewish religious practice and belief. As the horror of the Holocaust recedes in time, religious Jews, although greatly reduced in number, may once again find themselves reducing the dissonance by declaring with the traditional Prayer Book that "because of our sins all this has come upon us." That time has not yet come, but it may be on its way.

PART FOUR

THE
AFTERMATH
AND
THE
FUTURE

Chapter 11

~~~~~~

The Legacy of the Holocaust

The Holocaust is still news. Hardly a week passes without the breaking of a story that again rivets attention on that event. In the spring of 1986, for example, Pope John Paul II visited the main Jewish synagogue in Rome. No pontiff since St. Peter had been known to make such a gesture. Although John Paul deplored not only the centuries of oppression suffered by the Jewish people but also the Holocaust in particular, he stopped short of a full apology for almost two thousand years of official Roman Catholic prejudice against the Jews. As of this writing, the Vatican had not yet recognized the modern state of Israel either.

About the time of the Pope's synagogue visit, Kurt Waldheim, whose distinguished post-World War II diplomatic career included a decade as Secretary General of the United Nations, faced charges of participation in war crimes—complicity in the deportation of Greek Jews to death camps among them—while he served in the German army. Amidst these well-founded accusations, Waldheim was elected president of Austria. The controversy swirling around his case attracted international attention. Neal Sher, head of the United States Justice Department's Office of Special Investigations, recommended that Waldheim be banned from entry to the United States. Meanwhile Austria had to reconsider a past that involves not only the *Anschluss* of 1938 but also a long history of deepseated antisemitism, the fact that Hitler, Eichmann, and other notorious SS men were Austrians, and considerable enthusiasm for the Nazi cause during the years that this staunchly Roman Catholic country was an important part of the Third Reich.

Such accounts are more than ephemeral press releases. As part of the legacy of the Holocaust, they help to testify how deeply Auschwitz continues to wound human life. Even if, to use Emil Fackenheim's words, we can "mend the world," the Holocaust will still scar the earth.

A Historical Crisis

For those who were trained to believe that the traditions of Western civilization constitute both a defense against and an overcoming of obscene barbarism, the Holocaust constitutes an unprecedented historical crisis. The Holocaust was a new kind of *civilized*, legalized, state-sponsored destructiveness for which there is no historical precedent, although, alas, there are anticipations.[1] In the past, soldiers have spontaneously pillaged, raped, and murdered members of defeated communities. Political leaders have subjected their enemies to calculated mass violence, such as the extermination of the Melians by the ancient Athenians and the fire bombing of Hamburg and Dresden during World War II. Nevertheless, the Holocaust was different from these. The Holocaust can be seen as perhaps the most "successful," but by no means the only, program in which a modern, legally empowered government deliberately and cold-bloodedly targeted a portion of its own citizens and/or populations in occupied nations for extermination. Never before in history had depersonalized, bureaucratized mass death been carried out on so vast a scale against unarmed civilians or as a function of a government recognized as legitimate by the overwhelming majority of its citizens.

According to historian George M. Kren and social psychologist Leon Rappoport, a historical crisis may be said to occur ". . . when events make such a profound impact on the way people think about themselves and the world around them that the apparent continuity of their history seems drastically and permanently changed."[2] Among the more important symptoms of the historical crisis is the undeniable fact that the principal institutions, which in the past have protected human beings against unwarranted assault and destruction, proved virtually impotent in the case of the Holocaust. On the contrary, religious and legal institutions played a significant role in facilitating the state's program of extermination. Consider once again the part played by religious institutions. Although Hitler was ideologically committed to a euthanasia program, he called it off when religious leaders of the stature of Roman Catholic Bishop Clemens August Graf von Galen and Lutheran Bishop Theophil Wurm publicly protested. By contrast, no German church leader of any stature raised a comparable protest against the Final Solution. Moreover, the silence was not a consequence of ignorance. Although the German government attempted to camouflage the extermination process, the slaughter was on so vast a scale that the fact that the Jews were being exterminated was widely known in Germany.[3]

Nor was the situation very different in Poland. During the war the Polish church leaders were hardly in a position to influence German behavior. After the war, some of Poland's most important religious leaders found little reason to moderate their hostility toward the few Jews who remained alive in their country. In 1946 after the Germans had killed more than three million Polish Jews,

Poles murdered seventy Holocaust survivors in Kielce on the basis of the false rumor that the Jews had kidnapped a Christian boy and killed him in a "ritual murder." When asked to stem the violence by condemning the Kielce massacre, Bishop Wyszynski of Lublin not only refused but added that he was not altogether convinced that the Jews did not commit ritual murder! Shortly thereafter Bishop Wyszynski became a cardinal and primate of Poland. Cardinal Wyszynski's successor, Jozef Cardinal Glemp, has attempted to discredit the Solidarity movement by accusing it of having been infiltrated by Trotskyites, a code word for "Jews" in contemporary Poland. Glemp has also expressed publicly his sympathy for *Endecja*, Poland's prewar, ultra rightwing, antisemitic National Democratic Party.[4] A principal component of *Endecja's* political program was the total elimination of the Jews from Polish life. For our purposes, the attitudes of Cardinals Wyszynski and Glemp are important because they come *after* the Holocaust. Neither prelate was in ignorance of the facts.[5]

In the case of the German church leaders, their refusal to oppose the Final Solution must be seen in historical context. Between 1933 and 1939, the National Socialist antisemitic policies met with substantial official Catholic and Protestant approval, although there were some protests and acts of kindness by individual German Christians to Jews.[6] Until the actual implementation of the wartime extermination program, many leaders in both the Protestant and Catholic churches of Germany openly sympathized with the National Socialist aim of eliminating the Jews as a religious, cultural, and demographic presence in Germany. Hitler's antisemitism was often seen as fostering a genuinely Christian Germany.

There was, however, a very important difference between Hitler's approach to the elimination of the Jews and that of church leaders in both Germany and Poland. From 1919 on Hitler gave much thought not only to the *objective* of eliminating the Jews but to the *method* by which they were to be eliminated. The Jews were a community with a continuity of domicile in German lands extending back to the Roman era. It would not have been easy to uproot such a community in the best of times. However, the years between 1933 and 1939 witnessed the greatest worldwide economic depression of modernity. In a period of global mass unemployment, few governments anywhere were willing to accept more than a token number of Jewish immigrants. After May 1939 the British government prevented more than a trickle of Jews from entering Palestine. Thus, emigration had ceased to be a viable method of population elimination. Hitler understood this and did not flinch from employing the most extreme methods of elimination when the war provided an opportunity.

In Germany both the Protestant and Catholic churches favored a nation that was wholly Christian and Germanic. In Poland the Catholic Church wanted a Poland that was wholly Roman Catholic. Unlike Hitler, few, if any, of the church leaders faced the all-important question of implementation, at least not openly. During the war, when German church leaders became privy to the secret that was no secret, namely, that the Jews were being murdered in the east, they were caught between their desire for a wholly Christian and Germanic Fatherland and the fact, clearly understood by Hitler, that this could only be accomplished by genocide. In modern times, when emigration is impossible, those who seek cultural, religious, or ethnic homogeneity are likely to find that their objective can only be achieved by mass murder. After the war, when the German method of eliminating the Jews became public knowledge, there were expressions of regret on the part of some church leaders concerning *how* the Jews were eliminated. Few Germans expressed pride in the extermination camps. Even neo-Nazis have tried to invent a myth that the Holocaust never happened. Nevertheless, one may ask whether there was much genuine regret about *what* the camps accomplished. Germany was finally free of Jews. For all practical purposes, there were no longer any demographic impediments to a Christian and Germanic Fatherland.

The situation was not very different in Poland. Before the war, both the government and the Polish church regarded Poland's three million two hundred and fifty thousand Jews as an unwanted "surplus population."[7] In 1939 both institutions sought its total elimination. They thus shared a common political objective with the National Socialists. That objective was not achieved by emigration but by extermination. It cannot be denied that the Germans gave the Polish church what it wanted.

Under the circumstances we must ask whether either the Polish or German churches can entirely wash their hands, Pilate-like, of responsibility for fostering a political objective that could *only* be achieved by genocide. What, moreover, is the moral status of an institution that fosters a political objective without considering the question of implementation? An alternative is the possibility that responsible elements within the German and Polish churches fully understood the requirements of implementation and deemed it unnecessary or unwise to specify the method required since they would not be required to carry out the dirty work of extermination. In either case, the leaders of both the German and Polish churches were unwilling or unable to do much to prevent genocide.

When we turn from the German and Polish churches to the world center of the Roman Catholic Church, the most important single institution for the fostering of religious and moral values in the Western world, we find the same wartime silence. With its tens of thousands of priests and its religious and academic institutions throughout Europe, the Vatican had one of the best intelligence networks in the world. The Vatican was in a position to know more and to know it earlier than any other non-German institution. Yet in spite of that knowledge, on no occasion during the war did Pope Pius XII utter an *unambiguous, explicit, public* condemnation of the extermination process or the death camps. (In fairness to the Catholic Church, thousands of Jews did survive in Hungary and elsewhere because of other protests emanating from the Vatican.)

Whatever the reasons for the silence, the historical record is clear. The government of Europe's most powerful nation during World War II employed its agencies of law and order systematically to enslave, gas, burn alive, and shoot to death tens of thousands of men, women, and children daily without any effective, public protest by the churches. If the churches did not wholly approve of the dirty work of National Socialism, there was always some reason why silence was more important than protest. Thus, religion was neither able to prevent nor even to express verbal opposition to the rise of a wholly novel state-sponsored institution in the heart of Christian Europe: the industrialized, assembly-line, depersonalized, mass extermination camp.

By the same token, legal institutions failed completely to provide any protection for the victims. On the contrary, some of Germany's best legal minds accepted the task of creating the legal basis for depriving millions of citizens of Germany and the occupied lands of their rights, their jobs, their property, and finally their lives. Put differently, the law became a singularly effective device for transforming citizens with political rights into "nonpersons" devoid of the most elemental human rights. As early as September 1919 Hitler called for the "removal," *Entfernung*, of Germany's Jews by legal means. When one compares the destructiveness inflicted by German officers of the law on human beings who had committed no crime with the violence inflicted upon Jews by outright criminals, it is painfully obvious that the legally empowered officers of the state were the infinitely greater danger. Before Hitler, Germany prided itself on being a *Rechtsstadt*, a community governed by laws. Ironically, Germany retained the semblance of being a *Rechtsstadt* even under Hitler. Everything done to the Jews was in accordance with the law. The laws had, of course, changed drastically. A *Führerbefehl*, a Hitler order, had the force of law. Any action, no matter how vicious or obscene, could be taken as long as it was consonant with Hitler's decrees.

In the past the social contract between rulers and ruled carried with it the implicit understanding that, if the ruled were reasonably law-abiding, they could normally expect at least minimum protection of life and property. Normally, sovereignty did not include the right to mete out punishment in the form of abusive incarceration, torture, and death without cause. By contrast, in the Third Reich even wounded war veterans who had risked their lives in World War I and had been awarded the Iron Cross were burned alive or sent to the gas chambers with their fellow Jews. In the Third Reich, the social contract proved null and void, not only for Jews but for any group targeted as victims by state authorities. Nor has this been true of Germany alone. It has also been the situation in the Soviet Union, Kampuchea, Vietnam, and many other countries.

In *The Cunning of History*, Richard L. Rubenstein argued that the fate of Europe's Jews demonstrated that rights do not belong to persons by nature, that people only have rights insofar as they are legally certified members of a political community willing and able to defend their rights.[8] *The Cunning of History* was published in 1975. On 17 April 1975, the Communist Pol Pot regime conquered Phnom Penh, capital of what was then known as Cambodia and now is known as Kampuchea. Within one week the entire population of that city was forcibly evacuated and deposited in the jungle regions where the majority perished. Out of a population of seven million, the Vietnamese Communists estimate that the new regime was responsible for the death of three million persons. American authorities estimate that the new government was responsible for the death of two million. In either case, the proportion of human beings put to death by their own government staggers the imagination.

Like National Socialist Germany, the Pol Pot regime was determined to use state terror and mass murder to restructure society so as to achieve a fully homogenous community. The Nazis aimed at "racial" homogeneity; the Pol Pot regime aimed at class homogeneity. It sought to create a self-subsistent, agrarian Communist state. Its leaders were convinced that the population of Kampuchea's cities had been too corrupted by capitalist ideas and foreign influences ever to be integrated into the community they proposed to create. As in National Socialist Germany, any citizen whom the government regarded as unassimilable automatically became a rightless nonperson. The Pol Pot regime resorted to the same methods against its unwanted citizens as did Hitler.[9] Once again, it became painfully apparent that, if there is an uncontested right, it is no longer the "inalienable" right of the citizen to "life, liberty, and the pursuit of happiness," but the Godlike right of the state to do anything it wishes with its citizens, provided they are incapable of effective resistance.

The terrible right of a modern state to exercise genocidal sovereignty was implicitly confirmed in September 1979 when the United States, Great Britain, Australia, and Canada joined the majority of seventy-one nations that voted to recognize the Pol Pot regime's right to membership in the United Nations as the *legitimate* government of Kampuchea. Only thirty-five nations were opposed; thirty-four abstained.[10] The regime's seat had been challenged by the Vietnamese-dominated puppet regime which had dislodged Pol Pot from Phnom Penh. At the time of the U.N. vote, the facts of the Pol Pot program of extermination were known to the governments of the world. When the United States supported Pol Pot's bid to retain U.N. membership, its intention was not to approve of genocide but to prevent Kampuchea's U.N. seat from going to the puppet government sponsored by Vietnam. Nevertheless, the U.N. vote did show that the practice of genocide does not disqualify a sovereign state from recognition as a legitimate member of the family of nations. We do not point to this dreary example because we feel the government of the United States had a reasonable alternative. We do regard it as yet another example of the failure of the time-honored categories of politics and law to provide a defense against genocide.

The philosopher Thomas Hobbes distinguished between the state of nature in which the human condition was one of "war of all against all" and that of civil society in which persons banded together and submitted to the authority of a sovereign in order to put an end to the radical insecurity of the same state of nature. We have now learned that life in civil society can be far more dangerous than life in the state of nature for groups targeted for elimination. At least in the primitive state of nature each person had some chance to defend himself against potentially predatory neighbors.

Persons born into civil society are educated to believe in the implied social contract between the state and its citizens, between the ruler and the ruled. If they keep their part of the social contract, they do not expect to be the prey of an adversary infinitely more dangerous than a predatory neighbor, the organizational and technological power of the modern state. Confronted by its power, individuals or groups targeted for elimination find themselves in a far more hopeless condition than they would have been in the state of nature. Under modern conditions, both flight and self-defense on the part of the victim are likely to prove useless. If the victims are unwanted by the state in which they are domiciled, there is a very good chance that they will not be wanted anywhere, no matter what their talents may be, as indeed was the fate of the Jews during World War II. Such victims find themselves in a novel form of the state of nature, the state to which those cast out of civil society are condemned.

Thomas Hobbes's state of nature *preceded* the formation of civil society. The Holocaust has revealed a vision of the state of nature which *follows* civil society. The Nazis characterized their victims as subhuman, using the German word *Tiermenschen*, literally animal people, as a way of so degrading them that no guilt would be felt for any violence done to them. Perhaps intuitively, the Nazis understood that their victims had been condemned to the very modern form of the state of nature which they had created, namely, a condition in which civilized human beings are expelled from civil society and denied all traditional human rights. Given the Nazi penchant for saving everything but the victims' lives, even the stripping naked of the victims before killing them had an economic purpose, since it cost less to launder and recycle clothes unsoiled by involuntary defecation. Yet there may perhaps have been another reason for the stripping, as indeed Franz Stangl, the former commandant of Treblinka, suggested to journalist Gitta Sereny: there is something artificial about membership in civil society. If Hobbes is correct, symbolically if not historically, the creation of the social contract is an act of artifice designed to protect people from amoral nature. By stripping the victims of their clothes and by searching the orifices of their bodies, thereby denying them any remnant of privacy or dignity, the Nazis emphasized how completely they had rendered their victims *Tiermen-*

schen. In any event, traditional legal institutions offer no remedy for people in such a condition. The few victims who survived were only saved by the *destruction* of the National Socialist legal system and the passing of sovereignty from the Third Reich, a state that sought to destroy them, to states that permitted them to return to normal civil society.

In addition to the failure of religious and legal institutions to prevent mass murder, a failure partly due to the role of science in reducing the credibility of religion with its assertion of a universally binding moral standard, Kren and Rappoport regard the Holocaust as evidence of ''the failure of science.'' They argue that ''the scientific mode of thought and the methodology attached to it were intrinsic to the mass killings.''[11] Not only was industrialized mass murder facilitated by scientific methods of research, organization, and implementation, but ''the rational-abstract forms of conceptual thought required and promulgated by science provided the basis for systematic and efficient identification of people by race, transportation of large numbers to concentration points, killing, and body disposal.'' Moreover, science provided both ''the inspiration and justification for these technical activities.''[12] This was especially true of the way Charles Darwin's theory of evolution, with its conception of the ''survival of the fittest,'' was used to legitimate both racist ideology and mass extermination.

In addition, science fosters an emotionally detached, depersonalized professionalism in which technical expertise comes to be wholly divorced from moral values. This attitude was especially in evidence among the SS personnel responsible for the killings. After the war, these men insisted that they were under no obligation to evaluate the rightness of their behavior, but they did have an unconditional obligation to carry out the responsibilities delegated to them by their superiors. Value-free, scientific professionalism took on a new meaning when the daily destruction of tens of thousands of human beings became no more than a task to be carried out as efficiently, impersonally, and unemotionally as possible.

Nor, when we consider the role of science in the Holocaust, can we ignore the importance of the eugenics movement and the T-4 medical professionals to the implementation of the Final Solution. As we have seen, the role of the eugenics movement was crucial. It provided scientific legitimation for mass murder. Trusted medical symbols took on a new meaning. What began as medical advocacy of eliminating ''unworthy lives,'' ended with the delivery of Zyklon B gas to the death chambers in vehicles carrying the insignia of the International Red Cross and the pouring of the gas crystals into the chambers by a ''sanitation officer.'' In the Third Reich, medical science fostered the idea that the killings were nothing more than a health measure. Moreover, the national committee of the German Red Cross was headed by such SS medical luminaries as Dr. Ernst Grawitz and Professor Dr. Karl Gebhardt. Gebhardt was condemned to death by the U.S. Military Tribunal and executed in 1948 for his part in medical ''experiments'' which included using female prisoners at Ravensbrück concentration camp as human guinea pigs and deliberately infecting them with gas gangrene. Grawitz committed suicide in 1945.

One way of confronting the historical crisis is to deny its relevance to more fortunately situated human beings. The simplest expression of such denial is to say to oneself, ''It happened to them, not to us.'' This is especially tempting if one does not share the religious or cultural background of the victims. The National Socialists encouraged denial both in Germany and in occupied Europe. Before and during World War II, *German propaganda used every conceivable device to convince the peoples of Europe of the wholly alien character of all their victims.* In the case of the Jews, the German government flooded the world with all manner of antisemitic propaganda. The Jews were not alone. German propaganda stressed that the Russians were ''truly subhuman.'' The SS publication house even published a propaganda magazine entitled *Untermensch*, ''Subhuman,'' which was filled with pictures of Soviet prisoners of war in the most pathetic condition as proof of their want of humanity.[13]

The propaganda succeeded. When the killing time came, with few exceptions, the best the Jews could hope for from the majority of the peoples of Germany and occupied Europe was indifference. Nevertheless, denial is not an entirely functional response. When the government of perhaps the best-educated people in the heart of Christian Europe created as a new state institution the industrialized death camp and successfully introduced mass extermination as a legitimate state function, the entire human moral and political universe was irrevocably altered.

International Dilemmas

Nazi Germany surrendered to the Allies on 7 May 1945. During the first week of May 1985, President Ronald Reagan visited the Federal Republic of Germany to commemorate the fortieth anniversary of the end of World War II in Europe. His goal was to strike notes of amity with the Germans. Thus, at Chancellor Helmut Kohl's invitation, the President agreed to visit the German military cemetery at Bitburg. Controversy erupted, however, when it was learned that Bitburg's graves included forty-nine members of the *Waffen-SS*. Although that branch of the SS had not run the death camps, ample evidence exists to show that members of the *Waffen-SS* and indeed the *Wehrmacht* in general did play essential roles in the destruction of the European Jews, especially in collaboration with the mobile killing units that followed the German advance into the Soviet Union.[14] In any case, the SS identification proved explosive and helped to show that the German extermination programs continue to influence international political relations more than forty years after the killing stopped.

The Holocaust was an intrinsic part of a larger program of governmental destructiveness. Had Hitler won the war, the euthanasia program would have been officially resumed and greatly expanded. We have noted that a leading German physician, Professor Kranz, publicly estimated that at least one million Germans were candidates for "mercy" deaths.[15] Of overwhelming importance in the larger program of destruction was the war against Russia. Hitler assembled 250 senior officers of all branches of the armed services on 30 March 1941 to inform them of the utterly novel character of the forthcoming war, a war unlike any ever fought in Christian Europe. General Franz Halder, chief of the Wehrmacht general staff, took notes on Hitler's two-and-one-half-hour speech on that occasion. One sentence from Hitler's speech epitomizes the character of the war he and his generals were about to fight: "What is involved is a struggle of annihilation."[16] Never before in the history of Christian Europe did a major power aim at the utter enslavement and ultimate annihilation of another. The war in the east was so different from the Second World War in the west that one German writer, Joachim C. Fest, has written concerning the Russian campaign: "And for all that the campaign was strategically linked with the war as a whole, in its nature and in its morality it signified something else entirely. It was, so to speak, the Third World War."[17]

It is not our purpose to begin another detailed discussion of that war save to stress the intrinsic relationship between the extermination of infirm Germans, the slaughter of the Jews, and the war of annihilation against the Russians and other Slavs and to point out some of the ways the German program has irrevocably changed the human condition. Writing in *Foreign Affairs*, the influential quarterly of the Council on Foreign Relations, concerning the possible effect on contemporary Germany of a conflict between the United States and the Soviet Union, Richard Lowenthal, professor emeritus from the University of Berlin, has observed: "For with the newly deployed missiles before their eyes, the crucial common factor in the minds of Germans in West and East is the certainty that *they, at any rate, will not survive a nuclear war*" (emphasis added).[18] If a conventional war breaks out in Europe, the most likely theater of operations will be Germany. In such a war it is highly likely that Germany will be laid waste no matter what the outcome. However, should the Russians see themselves beginning to lose the war or if nuclear war were to break out, it is unthinkable that the Russians would tolerate a situation in which the Germans might once again possess the capacity to launch a future war of annihilation in the East. And, no matter what the outcome of an East-West conflict, for the foreseeable future the Russians will have the nuclear capacity to annihilate Germany.

It can, of course, be argued that such a scenario is so extreme as to border on nightmare fantasy. Unfortunately, the twentieth century has witnessed realization of all too many nightmare fantasies. Moreover, we would be well-advised to consider such a scenario from the Russian point of view. They have never forgotten how close the Germans came to winning their war of annihilation and enslavement. Nor has the Soviet ruling elite forgotten that millions of Russians,

Ukrainians, and other Slavs at first regarded the invading Germans as liberators because of their hatred of Stalin and his bloody rule. Had the Germans fought a conventional war and treated the enemy population as human beings, their chances of victory would have been greatly enhanced. It was only because they treated the Slavs as subhuman racial inferiors that the vast majority of even the anti-Communist Slavs rallied to Stalin. As bloody as Stalin had been, the Slavs quickly learned that they were faced with a force far more terrible and destructive.

One could cite all too many examples of the combination of brutishness and folly that characterized German behavior in occupied Russia. We cite but one. The *Allgemeines Wehrmachtsamt* (AWA) was the department of the German army charged with responsibility for Russian prisoners of war. It kept meticulous records. According to the AWA, 1,981,000 Russian prisoners of war died in German camps. In addition, the AWA listed 1,308,000 as having perished as a result of "Exterminations," "Not Accounted For," and "Deaths and Disappearances in Transit" (the categories are those of the AWA). To this must be added the uncounted number of prisoners who were shot on the spot and never taken prisoner. At one point, Himmler suggested murdering two million Russian prisoners as a convenient method of doubling the ration of the remainder so that the Germans might extract "real labor" from the surviving prisoners. In many of the camps the Soviet prisoners were simply locked up and denied all food and water. The Germans only entered these camps to incinerate with flame throwers the stinking mountains of unburied dead.[19] In all, more than twenty million Soviet citizens died in what has come to be known in the Soviet Union as the Great Patriotic War.

Under the circumstances, even were communism to cease to be the Russian political system, no responsible Russian leader will ever again tolerate a situation in which the Germans are in a position to threaten the security of their country. At present, the division of Germany and the Soviet occupation of the theoretically independent German Democratic Republic prevents the Germans from constituting such a threat. As long as the *status quo* continues, the Russians have no reason to fear a German attack. However, were any kind of East-West war, conventional or nuclear, to break out, the power relations between all of the combatant nations would immediately be changed and become unpredictable. In such a circumstance, it is inconceivable that any Russian leader would trust the survival of his nation to the uncertain fortunes of war. Under the murderous pressures of war, it is hard to believe that the Russian elite would not consider a Final Solution to their German problem. Moreover, as General Charles de Gaulle understood, no American president is likely to put at risk millions of inhabitants of American cities to avenge the destruction of European cities, especially if the Russians refrained from carrying the missile attack to the cities of North America.

An important objection to our scenario is the fact that the Federal Republic of Germany gives no evidence of behaving as did the Third Reich. We concur in that judgment. Nevertheless, we do not believe the responsible leaders of any country, Communist or non-Communist, can ignore the worst possible case in formulating long-term national strategy. By fighting a war of extermination, Hitler added an entirely new dimension both to the Russian perception of the worst possible case and what may have to be done in wartime to prevent its realization.

Moreover, Russian fear of Germany affects her relations with the United States. World War II ended with Germany both defeated and divided. To this day both the United States and Russia remain fearful lest the other power gain control of all of Germany. Such control would obviously alter the world balance of power. Similarly, *both* the Russians and the West fear a reunified Germany. Save for the Soviet Union, a reunified Germany would speedily become the dominant European power, both economically and militarily. To this must be added the Russian fear that an anti-Communist United States might look with favor upon an attack by a reunified Germany on Communist Russia.

The Russian strategy for preventing the Americans from altering the balance of power in Europe is to build an ever-more-potent nuclear weapons system. The Americans have no choice but to do the same. Currently, the cost to the American people of this peace of mutual terror is a swollen defense budget which has created unprecedented budget deficits and a national economy radically distorted by military requirements. Thus, whatever its real justification, Russian fear of a second German war of extermination has led to the spreading threat of global extermination. With their nuclear weapons the Russians threaten the United States with extermination should it attempt to alter the European power balance; with their weapons the Americans threaten the Russians in a like manner. Furthermore, both sides are the prisoners of technological improvement. Each side must constantly upgrade its weapons systems at ever-escalating costs lest it fall behind its rival. The superpowers are thus trapped in a spiraling posture of mutual nuclear threat from which no one has found a credible exit.

It is not our intention to suggest that the Russians are destined to exterminate the Germans. It is our intention to demonstrate how the introduction of annihilation as a political objective in the relations between peoples has permanently altered the world's moral and political landscape. Similarly, without in any sense entering into the merits of the issues dividing Israel and her Arab neighbors, it should be obvious that the politics of extermination have tragically but irrevocably shaped the character of the ongoing conflict in the Middle East. For many years the publicly stated objective of Israel's neighbors was to drive the Jews into the sea. That is still the publicly stated objective of radical Islamic states such as Libya, Syria, and, recently, Iran. Moreover, to this day calls for such a "solution" to the Arab-Israeli conflict are still issued in the Arab language even in the so-called "moderate" Arab states.

Under the circumstances, the Israelis perceive the Arabs as seeking the same kind of Final Solution as did Hitler. This does not mean that the Israelis fear that Arab *methods* would be the same as those of Hitler. Were the Arabs to win a war against the Israelis, they would have other means of effectively eliminating the Jews from the Middle East. Instead of using gas, the Arabs could, for example, imitate the Turks in their massacre of the Armenians. The Turks simply marched large numbers of Armenians without food or water into the desert and left them there. Should it be argued that a scenario in which the Arabs destroy Israel lacks credibility because no combination of Arab states currently has the military capability, Israeli commanders might respond that it is their duty to prevent this from ever happening. After the Holocaust, no responsible Jewish leader can ever again ignore an extermination threat when such a threat is uttered by a public person with access to instruments of state power.

From time to time it is suggested that the Israelis might achieve peace with their neighbors by trading the territory they control on the West Bank for credible guarantees of peace. Unfortunately, like the Russians, the Israelis must always assume the worst possible case, namely, that their neighbors will exterminate them if they ever gain the power so to do. In any peace negotiations, the Israelis must always ask themselves whether concessions might hasten the day when the Arabs would have the power to exterminate them.

Even if no one outside of Israel knows with certainty whether the Israelis possess nuclear weapons, it is difficult to believe that the Israelis would not make every effort to possess and, if necessary, to use whatever weapons of destruction they are capable of building or acquiring. Were the Arabs ever decisively victorious in a war against Israel, it is hard to imagine that the Israelis would submit to a second Holocaust without unleashing their most destructive weapons on their enemies.

Thus, the legacy of the German programs of extermination lives on and poisons the relations between nations, as indeed that legacy is likely to do for countless generations to come. Four decades after the end of World War II, every major nation is trapped by the politics of extermination in international affairs. That is perhaps the sorriest legacy bequeathed to the world by Adolf Hitler.

Surplus People

There are yet other ways in which the twentieth-century politics of systematized extermination have permanently altered the human condition. As obscene as the Holocaust was, from the point of view of its perpetrators it was an almost totally successful program of population elimination. From the point of view of the leaders of the Third Reich the Jews were a *surplus people*. The concept of a surplus people is neither absolute nor merely quantitative. Regardless of talent or ability, a group becomes "surplus" if, for any reason, it has no viable economic or political role in the community in which it lives. Before Hitler the Jews had a role in Germany. Undoubtedly, many Germans saw them as competitors. Nevertheless, they were not a surplus population. Their situation changed for the worse when Hitler became chancellor. His government embarked upon a program aimed at progressively denying Jews any role in either Germany or German-occupied Europe. Thus the Jews were stripped of their jobs, their property, and their status as citizens. Having been deprived of their place in German society, the Jews became a surplus people. All that remained was for the German government to inflict the final blow.

The Jews became surplus because the Nazis had the power to define social reality in Germany from 1933 to 1945 and in occupied Europe from 1939 to 1945. In the modern era, other groups have become surplus by the action of the market place as well as by government fiat. Among the most important factors leading to the rise of a surplus population of significant size are the following:

(1) An unprecedented increase in population without a comparable increase in resources capable of sustaining the population growth.

(2) Rationalization of the means of agricultural and industrial production with the result that ever fewer workers are capable of producing an ever-expanding volume of goods.

(3) Radical alterations in demand patterns of a market economy that render millions of workers economically redundant. This condition was especially prevalent during the Great Depression of the 1930s which led to the rise of Hitler.

(4) The vocation displacement of a powerless minority community by unemployed members of an indigenous majority community. This indeed was the plight of the Jews in many parts of Europe under Hitler. This has also been the plight of other minorities in recent years, such as the ethnic Chinese in Southeast Asia and the Indians and Pakistanis in Uganda.

(5) The appearance of famine or other types of large-scale material scarcity in which too many people compete for too few goods. This indeed is the plight of millions of human beings in Ethiopia and sub-Saharan Africa.

(6) The appearance of a government determined to create ethnic, class, or religious homogeneity among its citizens. Those persons who are incapable of being "homogenized" find themselves in danger of being defined as surplus by a state capable of enforcing its political definitions. This has been the fate of the Jews in World War II, the Armenians in World War I, the non-Communist Russians during the Russian Civil War, the middle-class Kampucheans in 1975, the Vietnamese boat people, and a host of other groups and classes in the twentieth century.[20]

If the Holocaust was a highly successful program for the elimination of a group rendered superfluous, one of the most disturbing aspects of the Holocaust is that none of the economic or political factors leading to the growth of massive surplus populations throughout the world has been alleviated since the end of World War II.[21] On the contrary, the intensified, worldwide competition in international trade compels almost all producers, whether in agriculture or industry, to shift from labor-intensive to automated, computer-assisted methods of production wherever possible. Throughout the world tens of millions of human beings have been uprooted from the land and from simple craft production to face an uncertain future in urban centers that offer little hope of employment to the unskilled and the unlettered. When we read of famine in Africa or of the debt crisis of some Third World country, we do not normally link these phenomena to the problem of surplus people. Yet, that is the context in which the phenomena must be understood. Throughout the world, the modernization of agriculture and industry has rendered millions of human beings hopelessly redundant for the foreseeable future. For the technologically sophisticated, modernization has been the source of unprecedented wealth and opportunity. For the millions displaced by "progress," modernization has meant loss of a meaningful place in the world.

This loss is the sword of Damocles hanging over contemporary civilization. We do not predict yet other state-sponsored extermination programs as a means of "solving" the problem of surplus people. Neither can we be certain that in times of stress, such as war or other social catastrophe, government elites will avoid approaching Auschwitz as a program that worked rather than as a supreme example of human inhumanity.

Epilogue

Some Concluding Reflections
on a Century of Progress

Satellites circle the earth. The moon has been reached, and the planets have been probed. Ours is an age of astonishing technical competence, an amazing electronic era of microchips and computers. It is also the day of heart transplants and other medical wonders that enable people to live longer, if not better, than ever. Polio is a scourge of the past. No longer must children's arms be scarred by smallpox vaccinations, for that once-dreaded disease has been virtually eradicated, too. Quite possibly scientific research will soon have the answer for cancer. Repeatedly the twentieth century has witnessed the surmounting of barriers assumed to be unbreachable. Progress, one might conclude, is its most important product. In all likelihood, no one who reads these words can deny unhypocritically that he or she has benefited immensely from the advances produced by modernity. Indeed, this book itself would not exist without them. Supposing, moreover, that we could turn the clock back to a premodern day, few of us would choose to do so. Unfortunately, the progress that adds so much of worth to human life is a two-edged sword. Nuclear threats make that fact abundantly clear. So does Auschwitz. Progress might well make us more ambivalent than we are.

The twentieth century is both continuous with and yet different from the past. Modernized economic systems, technological capabilities, and political structures produce not only countless blessings but also surplus people, unique forms of human domination, efficient strategies of population elimination, and unprecedented quantities of mass murder. As the Holocaust exemplified, the modern political state may not flinch from putting its apparatus of destruction into action. If a ruling elite still retains control over this overwhelming power, the more ordinary man or woman seems to fall impotently before it. The Holocaust dwarfed most individuals. Typically it showed them to be either defenseless victims, compliant cogs in the machinery of death, or bystanders, largely silent even if not incredulous or stunned, who did too little too late in opposing pressures that drove millions to extinction. Yet, however valid it may be, the impression that individuals and small groups were helpless to intervene effectively against that destructive process—or any other—must be challenged.

Ironically, much twentieth-century progress consists in our imprisoning each other, whether intentionally or unintentionally, in what Max Weber called an iron cage. Soon enough the Holocaust would become the unprecedented paradigm for what he foresaw in 1905. Nonetheless, it also revealed that courageous resistance did from time to time save lives and prevent the Nazis from doing their worst. Countless Jews resisted. Many Gentiles did, too, including a few from deep within the German bureaucracy itself.[1] If Jewish losses did not exceed two-thirds of European Jewry and one-third of the Jewish people worldwide, the credit does not belong entirely to Allied military might. Persons acting as individuals or within small groups made their contributions as well.

As one contemplates the global enormity of the Holocaust, as one ponders how the might of twentieth-century states may progressively squeeze the individual into obedience devoid of dissent, it becomes more important than ever to appraise what individuals can and cannot do. Thus, consider the question put to an imprisoned Franz Stangl, formerly the commandant of Sobibor and Treblinka, on 27 June 1971 by the journalist Gitta Sereny. "Do you think," she asked near the end of a long series of interviews, "that that time in Poland taught you anything?"[2]

The immensity of the Holocaust becomes too impersonal and more inevitable than it really was if one overlooks the fact that individuals did make the decisions and obey the orders that destroyed millions of Europe's civilians, Gentiles as well as Jews. One thing "that time in Poland" has to teach involves exploring how particular persons came to occupy middle-management positions where they saw that the murderous responsibilities handed to them were implemented by others. To be more specific, it is crucial to ask: could Franz Stangl have left the path that took him to Treblinka? And if he could have done so, would it have made any difference if he had?

Simon Wiesenthal, the famed Nazi-hunter, was once quoted as saying that "if I had done nothing else in life but to get this evil man Stangl, then I would not have lived in vain."[3] At the time, Stangl was on trial in Düsseldorf, Germany, having been extradited from Brazil where on 28 February 1967 he was arrested in Brooklin, one of the better residential areas of Sao Paulo. Although Stangl had never flaunted his past, neither was he in hiding. In 1945 American authorities knew about his activity at Treblinka, but Stangl fled to Rome. Assisted by clergy in the Vatican, he obtained a Red Cross passport—it reversed his name to Paul F. Stangl—and then moved on to Damascus, following a route used before and since by his SS peers. Before long he sent for his wife and children who traveled under their own names and told the Austrian police of their destination. In 1954 the Stangls openly entered Brazil, registering at the Austrian consulate in Sao Paulo. Eventually employed by Volkswagen, Stangl had made a new beginning.

Although the surprise was less that Stangl had been found than that he had ever been lost, his court appearance brought the darkness of his past to light. On 22 December 1970 he was sentenced by a West German court to life imprisonment. Early in April of the next year, Gitta Sereny met him for the first time. This meeting occurred because Sereny, who had covered Stangl's trial, became convinced that he was "an individual of some intelligence" and that "things had happened to and inside him which had happened to hardly anyone else, ever."[4] Stangl used the initial interview to rebut accusations made against him, but Sereny was after something more, "some new truth which would contribute to the understanding of things that had never yet been understood." She encouraged Stangl to provide it, promising "to write down exactly what he said, whatever it would be, and that I would try—my own feelings notwithstanding— to understand without prejudice."[5]

After deliberating, Stangl agreed. In fits and starts the layers of his life unfolded in the seventy hours of conversation held in April and June 1971. First published in the *Daily Telegraph Magazine*, these dialogues were later elaborated into book form. In addition to keeping her promise to Stangl, Sereny provides an account more valuable than Rudolf Höss's autobiographical description of his career as the commandant of Auschwitz.[6] For Sereny went on to interview Stangl's family, many of his associates, and other Holocaust authorities in compiling her narrative. Even after all of the cross-checking, elements of the Stangl story remain open to conjecture, but Sereny's work has the advantage of multiple dimensions missing in Höss's confession.

Born in 1908 in the small Austrian town of Altmünster, Stangl claims that he was "scared to death" of his father, a former soldier, who died of malnutrition when his son was eight.[7] Leaving school at fifteen to become an apprentice weaver, he was good at the work and soon supervised others. Music and sailing were his diversions. Looking back, Stangl called these years "my happiest time." In the Austria of the 1930s, however, the young man saw that a lack of higher education would prevent him from further promotions in the textile field. Police work attracted him as an alternative, particularly since it might enable him to assist in checking the turbulence that economic depression had brought to his country. He passed the required entrance examination in 1931 and was notified to report to the Linz barracks for training. Upon announcing his departure, Stangl learned that his textile employer had been planning to send him to Vienna for additional schooling. When Sereny asked whether he still could have seized that opportunity, Stangl responded that his boss "didn't ask me."[8]

Stangl's account frequently reveals his passivity, a sense of being conscripted into circumstances beyond his control. A case in point is his early affiliation with the Nazis. It remains unclear whether Stangl was an illegal Nazi in Austria prior to the *Anschluss* (March 1938), but he offered the following story. As a young police officer, he was decorated for meritorious service, including special recognition for seizing a Nazi arms cache shortly after Engelbert Dollfuss, the Austrian chancellor, was assassinated in July 1934. That achievement would plague Stangl, but the immediate result was his posting to Wels as a political investigator "to ferret out anti-government activities." Stangl, now married, claims to have had no Nazi sympathies at this time, but in 1938 his situation changed. Early on the National Socialists purged the Austrian police. Among the first victims were three of Stangl's colleagues who had received the same decoration that had come to him for his raid against the Nazis some years before. Out of fear, Stangl told Sereny, he arranged for a friend to enter his name on a list that would certify his having been a Nazi party member for the previous two years.

According to Stangl, the die was cast: "It wasn't a matter of choosing to stay or not stay in our profession. What it had already become, so quickly, was a question of survival."[9] Thus, Stangl remained in police work after his branch was absorbed into the Gestapo in January 1939. Over his wife's objections, he also signed the standard statement that identified him as a *Gottgläubiger*, a believer in God, but severed his ties with the Roman Catholic Church. The next decisive step on the path to Treblinka came in November 1940 when Stangl was ordered to Berlin.

These orders, signed by Himmler, transferred Stangl to the General Foundation for Institutional Care (*Gemeinnützige Stiftung für Heil und Anstaltspflege*). This foundation, one unit in the larger network code-named T-4 because its headquarters were at Tiergartenstrasse 4, helped to administer T-4's program of "mercy-killing" for the mentally and physically handicapped in Germany and Austria. Stangl was to be a leading security officer in this secret operation. He reports that the assignment was presented to him as a choice, though prudence ruled out the alternatives. Thus, when Stangl returned to Austria, his new post was a euthanasia center not far from Linz, Schloss Hartheim, which later on would kill Jews from the concentration camp nearby at Mauthausen.

Details of the Nazi euthanasia program have been spelled out previously, but it bears remembering that T-4's activities were under Hitler's personal control. Moreover, the euthanasia project, utilizing carbon monoxide gas, had the blessing of influential German scientists and physicians. It lasted many months and claimed about one hundred thousand lives. Public protest led by prominent German Christians helped stall this death machine in August 1941, but by then the project's goals were virtually achieved. The euthanasia program was probably not consciously devised as a training ground for staff to carry out the Final Solution, but it cannot be sheer coincidence that personnel from Schloss Hartheim and other centers regrouped in Poland to officiate at the death camps. In February 1942, for example, T-4 offered Franz Stangl a new choice: either report back to Linz, where he would be subject to a superior whom he feared, or take a position in the east near Lublin. This "either-or" was no accident either. The Berlin officials were confident that Stangl would choose Poland, and he did. Soon after his arriving there, he learned that his commanding officer, SS General Odilo Globocnik, "intended confiding to me the construction of a camp called Sobibor."[10]

Recall that Nazi objectives called for much of western Poland to be incorporated into the Reich. Jews from that area would be deported to the Polish interior, an area referred to as the *Generalgouvernement*, where they would be ghettoized with countless other Jews from this region and eventually exterminated. In the *Generalgouvernement*, Globocnik, assisted by Christian Wirth and a team of T-4's euthanasia experts under Wirth's direction, had overall command of "Operation Reinhard," named for its mastermind, Reinhard Heydrich, who had been assassinated in the spring of 1942 by Czech patriots.

The pure death camps opened by Globocnik in the *Generalgouvernement* during 1942 —Belzec (March), Sobibor (May), and Treblinka (July)—were in administrative channels that led directly to Hitler's chancellery. In contrast, Auschwitz and Majdanek, the latter also in this zone, remained under authority of the Main Office of Economic Administration (WVHA) because they were labor installations as well. Himmler often sought to intensify the zeal of his underlings through competition, and thus he had given Höss sole charge of Auschwitz. Rivalry ensued, but if Globocnik, Wirth, and their associates finished second to Höss as architects of mass death, they certainly were not failures. Before Belzec, Sobibor, and Treblinka were shut down less than two years later, they destroyed nearly two million Jews and thousands of Gypsies, children making up one-third of the total. Sereny reports that the survivors of these camps—"work-Jews" who had to help run them—numbered less than one hundred.

Stangl claims not to have known at first the purpose of his construction project at Sobibor, but ignorance vanished when he was taken to Belzec to witness the first large-scale extermination with permanent chambers using exhaust gas. He learned that Sobibor would do likewise and that he would be in charge. Back at Sobibor, Stangl discussed the options with a friend: "We agreed that what they were doing was a crime. We considered deserting—we discussed it for a long time. But how? Where could we go? What about our families?"[11] Stangl applied for a transfer. He got no reply, but in June he did receive a letter from his wife. She wrote that his superiors were arranging for her to bring the Stangl children to Poland for a visit.

Sobibor opened in May 1942 and operated for two months. Then the equipment malfunctioned, and exterminations ceased until October. Meanwhile the Stangl family arrived, lodging at an estate about three miles from the camp.

Heretofore Franz had kept Theresa Stangl in the dark about the particulars of his work at Schloss Hartheim and in Poland. Now she learned the truth about Sobibor from one of her husband's subordinates. Apparently the possibility of an open confrontation that might lead to Theresa's rejection of him was more than Stangl could risk. He not only told her that he had no direct responsibility for any killing but also arranged a speedy departure for his family. By the time they were back home in Austria, Franz had been transferred to Treblinka.

Franciszek Zabecki, one of the persons interviewed by Gitta Sereny, was a member of the Polish underground. As traffic supervisor at the Treblinka railway station, he tracked German military movements and also became "the only trained observer to be on the spot throughout the whole existence of Treblinka camp." Zabecki counted the extermination transports, recording the figures marked on each car. "The number of people killed in Treblinka was 1,200,000," he testifies, "and there is no doubt about it whatever."[12]

Dr. Irmfried Eberl, formerly in charge of a euthanasia center at Bernburg near Hanover, was the builder and first commandant of Treblinka. His administration had been wanting in Globocnik's eyes, and thus Stangl replaced him, describing his arrival there as an entry into Dante's Inferno. Stangl rationalized that his major assignment was to care for the riches left behind by those on their way to the gas. "There were enormous—fantastic—sums involved and everybody wanted a piece of it, and everybody wanted control." Indeed, Stangl argued, the main reason for the extermination of the Jews was that the Nazis were after their money. At least one Jewish survivor, Alexander Donat, does not disagree completely. He credits Stangl with being "sober enough to realize that behind the smoke-screen of Nazi propaganda and racist mystique there was no sacred mission but only naked greed."[13] In any case, Stangl tried to convince himself that his involvement was limited to handling Treblinka's windfall. Actually he headed the entire extermination process, which destroyed five to six thousand Jews per day. The system worked, says Stangl, "and because it worked, it was irreversible." With unintended irony, he reiterates that his work was "a matter of survival—always of survival." "One did become used to it," he adds.[14]

Stangl made "improvements" at Treblinka, among them a fake railroad station to deceive the arriving victims. It was unveiled at Christmas 1942. Meanwhile Stangl was in Austria on furlough. He obtained such leaves every three or four months, but his relationship with his wife was strained throughout his time at Treblinka. The gassing and burning continued under Stangl's administration during the first half of 1943. However, on August 2, a Monday, which usually was a light working day because transports were less frequently loaded on Sundays, Treblinka's death machine temporarily jammed when a long-planned revolt broke out among the Jewish workers. Although the camp was set ablaze, the gas chambers remained intact. Transports from Bialystok would still end there, the last one arriving on August 19. Thereafter the camp itself was liquidated, disguised with plantings and a small farm "built from the bricks of the dismantled gas chambers."[15] Stangl was reassigned to Trieste.

That same Christmas of 1942, Stangl had become fully assimilated into the SS, and at the war's end his SS uniform led to his arrest by Americans in an Austrian village on the Attersee. Two years later, as Austrian officials investigated Schloss Hartheim's euthanasia campaign, Stangl came to their attention. They requested jurisdiction, which was granted. Interned in an "open" prison at Linz, Stangl walked away as the Hartheim trial proceeded. Twenty years passed before he was brought to justice.

In conversation with Gitta Sereny, Stangl never stopped implying that he was himself a victim of the Holocaust. He reckoned that he was caught in a web from which he could not escape. Yet his excuses were less than iron-clad, even in his own eyes. Responding to Sereny's question—"Do you think that that time in Poland taught you anything?"—Stangl's final words included these: "Yes, that everything human has its origin in human weakness."[16] Not twenty-four hours later, Franz Stangl died of heart failure.

Could anything have strengthened Stangl's heart enough to divert him from the course he took? That issue climaxes *Into That Darkness* and at this point, surprisingly, not Franz but Theresa Stangl, takes center stage. In October 1971, Gitta Sereny ended her last conversation with Frau Stangl by inquiring:

> Would you tell me, . . . what you think would have happened if at any time you had faced your husband with an absolute choice; if you had said to him: "Here it is; I know it's terribly dangerous, but either you get out of this terrible thing, or else the children and I will leave you." What I would like to know is: if you had confronted him with these alternatives, which do you think he would have chosen?

Theresa Stangl contemplated that painful question for a long time. At last she expressed the belief that her husband given the choice—Treblinka or his wife— "would in the final analysis have chosen me."[17]

The next day Sereny received a note from Frau Stangl qualifying her previous statement. Franz Stangl, wrote his wife, "would never have destroyed himself or the family."[18] Sereny, however, believes that the first appraisal contains the greater truth, no matter how difficult it may have been for Frau Stangl to accept it. If Gitta Sereny is correct, the web of responsibility—and of human frailty, too—spreads out.

Yet one also must ask a second question: would resistance really have made any difference? Franz Stangl, for one, had his doubts. Quizzed about what might have happened if he had refused his orders, Stangl replied: "If I had sacrificed myself, if I had made public what I felt, and had died . . . it would have made no difference. Not an iota. It would all have gone on just the same, as if it and I had never happened." Sereny accepted the answer but pressed on to ask whether such action might at least have given courage to others. "Not even that," insisted Stangl. "It would have caused a tiny ripple, for a fraction of an instant—that's all."[19]

Such testimony cannot be discounted. Fear and insecurity are never easily dislodged, and even if every SS man had shared Stangl's professed ambivalence about the Final Solution, an isolated defection from the ranks would hardly have halted the destruction process. Those truths, however, detract nothing from others that should be stressed as well. First, Sobibor and Treblinka testify that Stangl's despair, however realistic, does not deserve to be the last word. Second, those death camps, as Theresa Stangl helps to show, also signify that such despair moves closer to self-fulfillment whenever people, especially those nearest and dearest to each other, fail to help one another oppose the weakness that enables the powers that be to consign defenseless victims to misery and death. Third, had more individuals done for each other what was very much within their power, to call each other into account for their actions, the Holocaust need not have gone on just the same. We are and must be responsible for each other as well as for ourselves. We must be born again as men and women blessed with the capacity to confront and care for each other here and now. If those points are obvious, they are anything but trivial. Not to underscore them is to create a silence in which personal responsibility can be too easily shirked and in which helpless people can be too easily found redundant and killed.

Gitta Sereny's encounters with Franz Stangl drove home to her "the fatal interdependence of all human actions."[20] If those actions are to forestall progress that culminates tragically in a paralyzing doom, Theresa Stangl must be taken no less seriously than her husband, his superiors, and their obedient underlings. To discern what she and other individuals, ordinary ones like ourselves, could and could not do—including the ways in which her voice dissolves sanguine illusions about the costs of resistance—is a vital lesson to learn from that time in Poland.

On 9 October 1974, some three years after Franz Stangl's heart finally failed in a German prison, advanced hardening of the arteries felled a person who played a Holocaust role quite different from the Treblinka commandant's. Black-marketeer and *bon vivant*, Oskar Schindler had a "life-of-the-party" style that frequently made him an unfaithful husband.[21] By some moral conventions, Stangl was a better man than this tall, blond Czech-German who pursued his fortune in the Polish city of Krakow in 1939. Before the war, Schindler joined the Sudeten German Party. Wearing its swastika lapel pin proved good for business. Hence, this industrial speculator followed the Wehrmacht's invasion into Poland and took over an expropriated enamelware factory. Soon he realized handsome returns by using Jewish labor, which cost him practically nothing—at first. That qualification, however, spells the difference between Schindler's remaining a pleasure-seeking profiteer and his becoming an individual whose personal initiative saved more than a thousand Jews from annihilation.

The tyranny that followed Hitler's seizure of Bohemia and Moravia in March 1939 both surprised and disillusioned Schindler but in the latter case not completely. Indeed, Schindler would go on to lend his services to Admiral Wilhelm Canaris's *Abwehr* (the foreign and counterintelligence department of the German High Command). What decisively changed Schindler's mind was the violence he witnessed as special squads recruited from Heydrich's *Sicherheitsdienst* began to attack Krakow's Jews. Insofar as those tactics targeted productive laborers, Schindler found them utterly counterproductive to the war effort. More than that, this wasting of human life struck him as profoundly morally wrong. Deciding that he could intercede from within the German system itself, Schindler negotiated a daring series of bargains. If his initial purpose was to keep healthy the labor he needed to sustain his factory's productivity, before the war ended, Schindler's obsession was more fundamental. He was determined that the hundreds of workers in his care would survive and have a future.

Schindler kept a list. It contained the names of some thirteen hundred men and women who came to call themselves *Schindlerjuden*. As liberation approached in the spring of 1945, Schindler promised he would "continue doing everything I can for you until five minutes after midnight."[22] His promise was good, just as his word had been for years. During that time in Poland, when his Jewish workers had been forced to live in a slave labor camp under the sadistic Amon Goeth, Schindler spent a fortune in bribes to set up his own subcamp haven at the factory. With the dedicated help of his wife, Emily, that practice continued when Oskar had to relocate his factory in Czechoslovakia as the Red army advanced. Schindler's efforts even plucked from Auschwitz some of those whose names were written in his list of life.

With the war's end, Oskar and Emily Schindler were refugees. They had lost everything—except that they were not forgotten by the *Schindlerjuden*. Under the leadership of Leopold and Mila Pfefferberg, they rallied to help the Schindlers when their own recovery permitted. Among many other kindnesses, they saw that Schindler's last wish—a Jerusalem burial—was granted. Today a tree at Yad Vashem grows in honor of Oskar Schindler. It testifies that he took to heart the Talmudic verse he heard in Krakow in 1939 from Yitzhak Stern, a Jewish accountant: "He who saves the life of one man saves the entire world." Even now, however, the *Schindlerjuden* do not know exactly why Oskar Schindler performed his life-saving missions.

Although the Jewish philosopher Jean Améry was not on Schindler's list, he did survive Auschwitz. Decades after his release from Bergen-Belsen, he observed that "the expectation of help, the certainty of help, is indeed one of the fundamental experiences of human beings."[23] But the gravest loss produced by the Holocaust, he went on to suggest, was that it radically undermined that "element of trust in the world, . . . the certainty that by reason of written or unwritten social contracts the other person will spare me—more precisely stated, that he will respect my physical, and with it also my metaphysical, being.''[24] Hoping to revive at least some of the trust that Améry lost, there are social scientists who are trying to determine why people like Schindler helped the defenseless while so many others did not.[25] Just as it is clear that very few of the rescuers regard themselves as moral heroes, it may be that an "altruistic personality" will emerge from these Holocaust studies. Whatever we can learn on that score is important. As another Jewish survivor, Pierre Sauvage, aptly puts the point:

> If we do not learn how it is possible to act well even under the most trying circumstances, we will increasingly doubt our ability to act well even under less trying ones. If we remember solely the horror of the Holocaust, we will pass on no perspective from which meaningfully to confront and learn from that very horror. If we remember solely the horror of the Holocaust, it is we who will bear the responsibility for having created the most dangerous alibi of all: that it was beyond man's capacity to know and care. If Jews do not learn that the whole world did not stand idly by while we were slaughtered, we will undermine our ability to develop the friendships and alliances that we need and deserve. If Christians do not learn that even then there were practicing Christians, they will be deprived of inspiring and essential examples of the nature and requirements of their faith. If the hard and fast evidence of the possibility of good on earth is allowed to slip through our fingers and turn into dust, then future generations will have only dust to build on. If hope is allowed to seem an unrealistic response to the world, if we do not work towards developing confidence in our spiritual resources, we will be responsible for producing in due time a world devoid of humanity—literally.[26]

Our study of approaches to Auschwitz began with words from Hannah Arendt. Following her lead, we have tried to comprehend the burden that "progress" has placed upon us. If we neither deny our century's wounds nor submit meekly to the Holocaust scars that deface humankind, perhaps we can have more than dust to build on. The mending of the earth and the healing of trust depend on determination to resist the world's horror with undeceived lucidity.

Notes

(The Selected Bibliography contains full publication data for works cited in the Notes.)

PROLOGUE
WHAT IS THE HOLOCAUST?

1. Sigmund Freud, *Civilization and Its Discontents*, p. 92. In addition to the information contained in the Notes and Bibliography for this book, four excellent guides for other sources about the Holocaust are provided by Harry James Cargas, *The Holocaust: An Annotated Bibliography*; Abraham J. Edelheit and Hershel Edelheit, eds., *Bibliography on Holocaust Literature*; Vera Laska, *Nazism, Resistance & Holocaust in World War II: A Bibliography*; and David M. Szonyi, ed., *The Holocaust: An Annotated Bibliography and Resource Guide*.
2. Anne Frank, *Anne Frank: The Diary of a Young Girl*, p. 237.
3. Support for these claims can be found in the recent work of a German geneticist at the University of Cologne. See Benno Müller-Hill, *Tödliche Wissenschaft: Die Aussonderung von Juden, Zigeunern und Geisteskranken 1933–1945*.
4. See Karl A. Schleunes, *The Twisted Road to Auschwitz: Nazi Policy Toward German Jews 1933–1939*.
5. Uriel Tal, "Excursus on the Term: Shoah," *Shoah* 1 (1979): 10–11.
6. Sigmund Freud, *The Future of an Illusion*, pp. 98, 74, 66.
7. Walter Laqueur, *The Terrible Secret: Suppression of the Truth about Hitler's "Final Solution,"* p. 7.
8. See Rosemary Radford Ruether, *Faith and Fratricide: The Theological Roots of Anti-Semitism*.
9. See Franklin H. Littell, *The Crucifixion of the Jews*.
10. See Emil L. Fackenheim, *God's Presence in History: Jewish Affirmations and Philosophical Reflections*.
11. Raul Hilberg, *The Destruction of the European Jews*, rev. ed., 3 vols., 1:8–9.
12. Many of the following themes are set forth in two previous books by Richard L. Rubenstein: *The Cunning of History: Mass Death and the American Future* and *The Age of Triage: Fear and Hope in an Overcrowded World*.
13. See Hannah Arendt, *The Origins of Totalitarianism* and *The Jew as Pariah*, ed. Ron H. Feldman. For an instructive account of how people in the twentieth century have increasingly been pushed into refugee and "unwanted" status, see Michael R. Marrus, *The Unwanted: European Refugees in the Twentieth Century*. Pp. 27–39, 51–68, 141–45, and 208–95 are especially relevant for our concerns.
14. Rubenstein, *The Cunning of History*, p. 72.
15. See Raphael Lemkin, *Axis Rule in Occupied Europe*, p. 79.
16. Helen Fein, *Accounting for Genocide: National Responses and Jewish Victimization during the Holocaust*, p. 3.
17. Yehuda Bauer, *A History of the Holocaust*, p. 332.
18. Cited by Yehuda Bauer, *The Holocaust in Historical Perspective*, pp. 37, 160 n. 16.
19. Fein, *Accounting for Genocide*, p. 4.

CHAPTER 1

THE JEW AS OUTSIDER:
THE GRECO-ROMAN AND EARLY CHRISTIAN WORLDS

1. Albert Camus, *The Rebel: An Essay on Man in Revolt*, p. 297.
2. For a comprehensive treatment, see H. H. Ben-Sasson, ed., *A History of the Jewish People*.
3. Often "antisemitism" and its variants are hyphenated and/or capitalized (for example, anti-Semitism or Antisemitism). We prefer to follow Hannah Arendt's practice of dropping both the hyphen and the capitalization. As Franklin H. Littell observes, the term is "unsatisfactory and finally misleading." "The daily newspapers," Littell continues, "still carry owlish letters informing us that 'the Arabs' cannot be 'anti-Semites' because they are 'Semites' themselves. Since the word is here to stay, it should be used in its plain meaning: hatred of the Jews (*Judenhass*), and it should be spelled without the hyphen." See Littell, *The Crucifixion of the Jews*, p. 6 n. 2.
4. One recent study argues persuasively that Jesus is best regarded not only as a rabbi but as a Pharisee as well. Only apparently at odds with the New Testament, this revisionist view has much to commend it. See Clark M. Williamson, *Has God Rejected His People?: Anti-Judaism in the Christian Church*, pp. 11–29. This book also provides an excellent overview of the development of anti-Jewish teaching within the Christian tradition. For more in this vein about Jesus, see Harvey Falk, *Jesus the Pharisee*, and Leonard C. Yaseen, *The Jesus Connection: To Triumph over Anti-Semitism*.
5. Josephus, *The Jewish War*, 6.3.420.
6. On Rabbi Yochanan, see Jacob Neusner, *First-Century Judaism in Crisis*.
7. On the Pharisees, see Jacob Neusner, *From Politics to Piety: The Emergence of Pharisaic Judaism*.
8. See Neusner, *First-Century Judaism in Crisis*, pp. 145–47.
9. Judah Goldin, ed., *The Fathers According to Rabbi Nathan*, Ch. IV, p. 36, as quoted by ibid., p. 147.
10. Eleazar's speech is found in Josephus, *The Jewish War*, VII, 331–94.
11. Norman Perrin, *The New Testament: An Introduction*, pp. 40–41.
12. These include W. D. Davies, *The Setting of the Sermon on the Mount*, and S. G. F. Brandon, *The Fall of Jerusalem and the Christian Church*.
13. See Norman Perrin, *Rediscovering the Teaching of Jesus*.
14. See Brandon, *The Fall of Jerusalem and the Christian Church*, pp. 185–205.
15. Neusner, *First-Century Judaism in Crisis*, p. 167.
16. See Leon Festinger, Henry W. Riecken, and Stanley Schacter, *When Prophecy Fails*; Leon Festinger, "Cognitive Dissonance," *Scientific American* 207 (October 1962): 93–102; and Elliot Aronson, "The Rationalizing Animal," *Psychology Today*, May 1973, pp. 46–52.
17. See Richard L. Rubenstein, "The Dean and the Chosen People," in *After Auschwitz: Radical Theology and Contemporary Judaism*, pp. 47–58.

CHAPTER 2

THE TRIUMPH OF CHRISTIANITY
AND THE "TEACHING OF CONTEMPT"

1. The term is Jules Isaac's. See his *The Teaching of Contempt*. See also Ruether, *Faith and Fratricide*.

2. The quotations in this paragraph are from Léon Poliakov, *The History of Anti-Semitism*, vol. 1: *From the Time of Christ to the Court Jews*, p. 25. For more on the subject of Jewish-Christian relations during this period, see John Gager, *The Origins of Anti-Semitism: Attitudes toward Judaism in Pagan and Christian Antiquity*, and Robert L. Wilken, *John Chrysostom and the Jews: Rhetoric and Reality in the Late Fourth Century*.

3. Poliakov, *History of Anti-Semitism*, 1:123.

4. Ibid., 1:222.

5. For more detail on Luther and the Jews, see Mark U. Edwards, Jr., *Luther's Last Battles: A Study of the Polemics of the Older Luther, 1531–1546*. See also Heiko A. Oberman, *Wurzeln des Antisemitismus: Christenangst und Judenplage im Zeitalter von Humanismus und Reformation* and *Luther: Mensch zwischen Gott und Teufel*.

6. Ernst Troeltsch, *The Social Teachings of the Christian Churches*, 2:468.

7. Ibid., 2:468–69.

8. Ibid., 2:469.

9. Ibid., 2:470.

10. Martin Luther, "On the Jews and Their Lies," in *Luther's Works*, 47:192.

11. See Walther Bienert, *Martin Luther und die Juden: Ein Quellenbuch mit zeitgenössichen Illustrationen, mit Einführungen und Erlauterungen*, pp. 130–32.

12. Ibid., p. 130.

13. Luther, "On the Jews and Their Lies," 47:137.

14. Ibid., 47:138.

15. Ibid., 47:138–39.

16. "Ein Wort zur Judenfrage, der Reichsbruderrat der Evangelischen Kirche in Deutschland" (8 April 1948), in *Der Ungekündigte Bund: Neue Begegnung von Juden und Christlicher*, ed. Dietrich Goldschmidt and Hans-Joachim Kraus, pp. 251–54.

17. Luther, "On the Jews and Their Lies," 47:139.

18. Ibid., 47:154.

19. Ibid., 47:172.

20. Ibid., 47:156–57. For the reference to the Persians, see Esther 9:5ff.

21. See Norman Cohn, *Warrant for Genocide: The Myth of the Jewish World-Conspiracy and the Protocols of the Elders of Zion*.

22. Bienert, *Martin Luther*, pp. 174–77.

23. Luther, "On the Jews and Their Lies," 47:267–69.

24. Ibid., 47:268 n. 173.

25. H. H. Borchert and Georg Merz, eds. *Martin Luther: Ausgewählte Werke*, 3:61ff. See also Aarne Siirala, "Reflections from a Lutheran Perspective," in *Auschwitz: Beginning of a New Era?*, ed. Eva Fleischner, pp. 135–48.

26. See John S. Conway, *The Nazi Persecution of the Churches, 1933–45*, pp. 1–44, 261–67. On Dibelius, see Conway, p. 411.

27. Additional views about the Enlightenment's impact on Jewish life can be found in Jacob Katz, *From Prejudice to Destruction: Anti-Semitism, 1700–1933*.

28. See, for example, Bauer, *A History of the Holocaust*, pp. 11–25.

CHAPTER 3

THE IRONY OF EMANCIPATION: A FRENCH CONNECTION

1. See Katz, *From Prejudice to Destruction*, pp. 108, 119–20.

2. See Rubenstein, *The Age of Triage*, pp. 128–67.

3. See Arthur Hertzberg, *The French Enlightenment and the Jews*, pp. 280–313. See also Katz, *From Prejudice to Destruction*, pp. 34–47.

4. Hertzberg, *French Enlightenment*, pp. 365–66.

5. We take this term from C. B. Macpherson, *The Political Theory of Possessive Individualism: Hobbes to Locke*.

6. On socialist antisemitism, see Edmund Silberner, *Sozialisten zur Judenfrage*, and George Lichtheim, "Socialism and the Jews," *Dissent* 15 (July-August 1968): 314–42.

7. On Fourier, see Silberner, *Sozialisten zur Judenfrage* pp. 16–27; Lichtheim, "Socialism and the Jews," pp. 316–24; and Katz, *From Prejudice to Destruction*, pp. 120–22.

8. See Karl Marx, "On the Jewish Question," in *Karl Marx: Selected Writings*, ed. David McLellan, pp. 39–62. See also Robert F. Byrnes, *Antisemitism in Modern France: The Prologue to the Dreyfus Affair*.

9. Pierre Haubtmann, ed., *Carnet de P. J. Proudhon: Text inédit et intégral*, 2:337–38. Cited by Lichtheim, "Socialism and the Jews," p. 322.

10. Lichtheim, p. 323.

11. "Paris," *Encyclopedia Judaica*, 13:107–8.

12. See Byrnes, *Antisemitism in Modern France*, pp. 96–97, 41.

13. Ibid., p. 41.

14. A. M. Carr-Saunders, *World Population*, pp. 49, 56.

15. Byrnes, *Antisemitism in Modern France*, p. 126.

16. See *Actes de Lén XIII*, 1:242–77. Cited ibid., p. 127.

17. On the Dreyfus affair, see Guy Chapman, *The Dreyfus Case, a Reassessment*, and Nicholas Halasz, *Captain Dreyfus: The Story of a Mass Hysteria*.

18. Halasz, *Captain Dreyfus*, pp. 20–21.

19. Cited ibid., p. 57.

20. Maurice Paléologue, *An Intimate Journal of the Dreyfus Case*, p. 53.

21. On the identification of the Jews with Judas, see Rubenstein, *After Auschwitz*, pp. 30–31.

22. This conversation is quoted in Carl Schorske, *Fin-de-Siècle Vienna: Politics and Culture*, p. 162.

23. For a biographical note on Esterhazy, see Chapman, *The Dreyfus Case*, pp. 119–21.

24. See Max Weber, "Bureaucracy," in *From Max Weber: Essays in Sociology*, ed. H. H. Gerth and C. Wright Mills.

25. The text of "*J'Accuse!*" is to be found in *Modern Jewish History: A Source Reader*, ed. Robert Chazan and Marc Lee Raphael, pp. 103–13.

26. Cited by Chapman, *The Dreyfus Case*, p. 199.

27. Cited by Halasz, *Captain Dreyfus*, p. 123.

28. Ibid.

29. *Gazette de France*, 6–7 September 1898.

30. See Eugen J. Weber, *Action Française: Royalism and Reaction in Twentieth-Century France*.

31. Ibid., p. 445.

32. See Michael R. Marrus and Robert O. Paxton, *Vichy France and the Jews*.

33. *The Jewish Chronicle*, London, 17 January 1896. The text is to be found in *The Jew in the Modern World: A Documentary History*, ed. Paul R. Mendes-Flohr and Jehuda Reinharz, p. 423.

CHAPTER 4
TOWARD TOTAL DOMINATION

1. Cited by Howard Morley Sachar, *The Course of Modern Jewish History*, p. 246. The discussion in the first two sections of this chapter is indebted to Rubenstein, *The Age of Triage*. For more detail, see especially pp. 135–64.
2. For more on this subject, see Robert F. Byrnes, *Pobedonostsev, His Life and Thought*.
3. See, for example, the following: Karl Dietrich Bracher, *The German Dictatorship*; Alan Bullock, *Hitler: A Study in Tyranny*; Joachim Fest, *Hitler*; Sebastian Haffner, *The Meaning of Hitler*; John Toland, *Adolf Hitler*; and Robert L. Waite, *The Psychopathic God: Adolf Hitler*. Also of great relevance for our purposes are Gerald Fleming, *Hitler and the Final Solution*, and Sarah Gordon, *Hitler, Germans, and the "Jewish Question."* The latter volume especially has influenced our interpretations.
4. Cited by A. J. Ryder, *Twentieth-Century Germany from Bismarck to Brandt*, p. 40.
5. Oscar Handlin, *The Uprooted*, p. 32.
6. Carr-Saunders, *World Population*, pp. 49ff.
7. Hitler was, of course, only one of thousands of wounded German veterans who survived the war. Their disillusionment and discontent proved to be a rich resource on which Hitler and the Nazis could later draw. For a discussion of these matters, see Robert Weldon Whalen, *Bitter Wounds: German Victims of the Great War*.
8. Our discussion of *Mein Kampf* is indebted to Michael D. Ryan, "Hitler's Challenge to the Churches: A Theological Political Analysis of *Mein Kampf*," in *The German Church Struggle and the Holocaust*, ed. Franklin H. Littell and Hubert G. Locke, pp. 148–64.
9. The concept of *Lebensraum* also figures prominently in Hitler's so-called *Zweites Buch*, which he wrote in the late twenties but never published. See Adolf Hitler, *Hitler's Secret Book*.
10. Gordon, *Hitler, Germans, and the "Jewish Question,"* pp. 83–84.
11. Congressional Committee on Immigration, *Temporary Suspension of Immigration*, Sixty-sixth Congress, Third Session, House of Representatives, Report no. 1109, 6 December 1920.
12. Celia S. Heller, *On the Edge of Destruction: Jews of Poland between the Two World Wars*, pp. 101–7. For more on Poland, see Richard C. Lukas, *The Forgotten Holocaust: The Poles under German Occupation 1939–1944*; Yisrael Gutman and Shmuel Krakowski, *Poles and Jews Between the Wars*; and Jan Karski, *The Great Powers and Poland 1919–1945: From Versailles to Yalta*. Karski is one of the heroes of the Polish resistance. His eyewitness accounts of Nazi death camps in Poland were communicated in person to Western leaders, including Franklin D. Roosevelt, in November 1942. A tree grows in his honor at Yad Vashem, Israel's Holocaust Memorial, in Jerusalem.
13. Toland, *Adolf Hitler*, p. 384. Further background on the German situation during this period is available in Harold James, *The German Slump: Politics and Economics 1924–1936*.
14. Toland, p. 439.
15. Adolf Hitler, *Mein Kampf*, p. 398.
16. For more detail on these matters, particularly insofar as they relate to the broader history of economic and political modernization in the West, see Rubenstein, *The Age of Triage*, especially pp. 146–50.

17. Schleunes, *The Twisted Road to Auschwitz*, p. viii. See also Christopher R. Browning, *Fateful Months: Essays on the Emergence of the Final Solution.*
18. See Lucy S. Dawidowicz, *The War Against the Jews 1933–1945*, pp. 16–22. For two views that differ from those of Dawidowicz, see Yehuda Bauer, "Genocide: Was It the Nazis' Original Plan?" in *Reflections on the Holocaust*, ed. Irene G. Shur, Franklin H. Littell, and Marvin E. Wolfgang, pp. 35–45; and John K. Roth, "How to Make Hitler's Ideas Clear?" *The Philosophical Forum* 16 (1984–85): 82–94.
19. Gordon, *Hitler, Germans, and the "Jewish Question,"* pp. 143–44.
20. Heinz Höhne, *The Order of the Death's Head: The Story of Hitler's SS*, p. 17.
21. Adolf Hitler, Letter to Staff-Captain Karl Mayr, 16 September 1919, in *Hitler's Letters and Notes*, ed. Werner Maser, p. 215.
22. Gordon, *Hitler, Germans, and the "Jewish Question,"* p. 163.
23. Raul Hilberg, "The Nature of the Process," in *Survivors, Victims and Perpetrators: Essays on the Nazi Holocaust*, ed. Joel E. Dimsdale, p. 5
24. For a discussion of the Nazis' use of the 1936 Olympic Games see Duff Hart-Davis, *Hitler's Games: The 1936 Olympics.*
25. See Nora Levin, *The Holocaust: The Destruction of European Jewry 1933–1945*, p. 108.
26. Schleunes, *The Twisted Road to Auschwitz*, p. 230.
27. Ibid., p. 237.
28. Ibid., p. 241.
29. Höhne, *Order of the Death's Head*, p. 15.
30. Schleunes, *The Twisted Road to Auschwitz*, p. 175.
31. For more on Eichmann, see Jochen von Lang and Claus Sibyll, eds., *Eichmann Interrogated: Transcripts from the Archives of the Israeli Police.*
32. Cited by Schleunes, *The Twisted Road to Auschwitz*, p. 255.
33. Cited by Dawidowicz, *The War Against the Jews*, p. 106.
34. Schleunes, *The Twisted Road to Auschwitz*, p. 260.
35. More detail on British policy toward the European Jews before and during the Holocaust can be found in Bernard Wasserstein, *Britain and the Jews of Europe, 1939–1945.* American policy is probed by David S. Wyman, *Paper Walls: America and the Refugee Crisis, 1938–1941.*
36. See Louis P. Lochner, ed., *The Goebbels Diaries 1942–43*, p. 241.

CHAPTER 5

WAR AND THE FINAL SOLUTION

1. See Höhne, *Order of the Death's Head*, pp. 405–6. For further detail on the eastern front in World War II, see Omer Bartov, *The Eastern Front, 1941–45, German Troops and the Barbarisation of Warfare.* Additional information on the *Einsatzgruppen* is available in Shmuel Krakowski, ed., *Einsatzgruppen.*
2. For a brief discussion of the organizational structure of the RSHA, see Raul Hilberg, *Destruction*, 1:274–90.
3. Cited by Gerald Reitlinger, *The Final Solution: The Attempt to Exterminate the Jews from 1939–1945*, p. 21.
4. Höhne, *Order of the Death's Head*, p. 406. Italics added.
5. Léon Poliakov, *Harvest of Hate: The Nazi Program for the Destruction of the Jews of Europe*, p. 119.
6. Joachim Remak, ed., *The Nazi Years: A Documentary History*, p. 152.

7. See Hilberg, *Destruction*, 1:287–89, and Höhne, *Order of the Death's Head*, pp. 403–5. The leading character of the NBC miniseries on the Holocaust, Dorf, is said to have been modelled after Ohlendorf.
8. See Poliakov, *Harvest of Hate*, pp. 122-26. Poliakov gives the full text of the testimony of Hermann Graebe, a German engineer who witnessed a massacre in the Ukraine. Graebe, it should be emphasized, was one of only a few German civilian professionals who risked his own life to save Jews from the Nazis. His affidavit about these killings provided crucial evidence in some of the postwar trials. For a biography of Graebe, see Douglas K. Huneke, *The Moses of Rovno*.
9. Verdict against Erich Jahnke, Riga Trial (50) 9/72, 23 February 1973, pp. 69–73, Staatsanwaltschaft Hamburg. For this reference, we are indebted to Gerald Fleming, *Hitler and the Final Solution*, pp. 78–79.
10. See Poliakov, *Harvest of Hate*, p. 119.
11. Hilberg, *Destruction*, 1:275.
12. See Kunrat von Hammerstein, *Spähtrupp*, p. 192. For this reference, we are again indebted to Fleming, *Hitler and the Final Solution*, p. 58.
13. Hilberg, *Destruction*, 1:334–41.
14. RSHA IV-A-1, Operational Report USSR No. 54, 16 August 1941, NO-2849, cited by Hilberg, *Destruction*, 1:308.
15. Höhne, *Order of the Death's Head*, p. 575.
16. Hilberg, *Destruction*, 1:341.
17. Remak, ed., *The Nazi Years*, p. 154.
18. Poliakov, *Harvest of Hate*, pp. 133, 135, 137.
19. Hans Bernd Gisevius, *Wo Ist Nebe?*, p. 244. Caution is to be exercised in accepting Gisevius's portrait of his friend Nebe.
20. Höhne, *Order of the Death's Head*, p. 411.
21. Reitlinger, *The Final Solution*, p. 200.
22. Höhne, *Order of the Death's Head*, p. 411.
23. Helmut Heiber, "Aus den Akten des Gauleiters Kube," *Vierteljahrshefte für Zeitgeschichte* 4 (1956): 57. See also Hilberg, *Destruction*, 1: 386–87; Höhne, *Order of the Death's Head*, pp. 419–22; and Fleming, *Hitler and the Final Solution*, pp. 116–19.
24. See Erich von dem Bach-Zelewski's account in *Aufbau*, a German-Jewish newspaper published in New York, 23 August 1946, pp. 1–2. For this reference, we are indebted to Hilberg, *Destruction*, 1:333. See also Reitlinger, *The Final Solution*, p. 208.
25. See Höhne, *Order of the Death's Head*, pp. 434–38 for the story of Morgen's attempt to root out "corruption" at the camps.
26. Ibid., p. 415.
27. Cited by Remak, ed., *The Nazi Years*, p. 159.
28. "Pogrom," *Encyclopedia Judaica*, 13:694.
29. On Stangl, see Gitta Sereny, *Into That Darkness: An Examination of Conscience*, p. 232. On Eichmann, see von Lang and Sibyll, eds., *Eichmann Interrogated*, p. 57.
30. See Gideon Hausner, *Justice in Jerusalem*, p. 11.
31. See Stephan L. Chorover, *From Genesis to Genocide: The Meaning of Human Nature and the Power of Behavior Control*, pp. 30–55. A definitive discussion of how biologists, geneticists, and physicans contributed to the Holocaust is Robert Jay Lifton, *The Nazi Doctors: Medical Killing and the Pyschology of Genocide*.
32. See Richard Hofstadter, *Social Darwinism in American Thought*, pp. 170–201.
33. Ernst Haeckel, *Die Lebenswunder*, p. 128.

34. See Chorover, *From Genesis to Genocide*, pp. 97–98.

35. Robert J. Waldinger, *The High Priests of Nature: Medicine in Germany, 1883–1933* (B.A. Thesis, Harvard University, 1973), p. 75; cited by Chorover, *From Genesis to Genocide*, p. 98.

36. See ibid., pp. 98–99.

37. Remak, ed., *The Nazi Years*, pp. 133–34.

38. The agency responsible for financing the program was known as the *Gemeinnützige Stiftung für Anstaltspflege* (General Foundation for Institutional Care). The organization of doctors responsible for administering the program was known as the *Reichsarbeitsgemeinschaft Heil und Pflegeanstalten* (Reich Coordinating Agency for Therapeutic and Medical Establishments). The agency responsible for transporting the victims to the death establishments was called the *Allgemeine Kranken-Transport Gesellschaft* (General Ambulance Service).

39. Poliakov, *Harvest of Hate*, p. 185, 321 n. 4.

40. For a typical letter, see Remak, ed., *The Nazi Years*, pp. 138–39.

41. Ibid., p. 134.

42. See Hilberg, *Destruction*, 1:149–54, 356–68; Rubenstein, *The Cunning of History*, p. 25; and Myron Winick, ed., *Hunger Disease: Studies by the Jewish Physicians in the Warsaw Ghetto*.

43. Fleming, *Hitler and the Final Solution*, p. 27.

44. The substance of Bishop von Galen's sermon is reprinted in Remak, ed., *The Nazi Years*, pp. 139–40.

45. Sereny, *Into That Darkness*, p. 74.

46. See ibid., pp. 60–77. The subject of euthanasia in the Third Reich has been dealt with authoritatively by Lothar Gruchmann, *Euthanasie und Justiz im Dritten Reich* and Lifton, *The Nazi Doctors*.

47. See Sereny, *Into That Darkness*, pp. 62–74.

48. Ibid., p. 77; Reitlinger, *The Final Solution*, p. 139.

49. Poliakov, *Harvest of Hate*, p. 187.

50. Two definitive studies of the Nazi concentration and death camps, both having influenced our account, are Konnilyn Feig, *Hitler's Death Camps: The Sanity of Madness*, and Claude Lanzmann, *Shoah: An Oral History of the Holocaust*. The latter is the complete text of Lanzmann's epic documentary film about the Holocaust. The detail of this account is impressive and moving.

51. See Rubenstein, *The Cunning of History*, pp. 48–68.

52. The text of the letter is found in Poliakov, *Harvest of Hate*, p. 188.

53. The phrase is from Höhne, *Order of the Death's Head*, p. 423.

54. "Chelmno," in *Encyclopedia Judaica*, 5:374. See also Poliakov, *Harvest of Hate*, p. 196.

55. The text of Gerstein's report is to be found in Poliakov, *Harvest of Hate*, pp. 192–96; this section is found on p. 194.

56. Affidavit by Blobel, 18 June 1947, NO-3947, cited by Hilberg, *Destruction*, 1:389.

57. While in a Polish prison, Höss wrote his memoirs, which were published in Poland in 1951. Although they must be read with a critical eye, they are an important source of information. See Rudolf Höss, *Commandant of Auschwitz*.

58. See ibid., p. 69 n. 1.

59. When World War II began there were some ten thousand Roman Catholic priests in Poland. One-third of them ended up in concentration camps, and of that number more than twenty-five hundred perished. One of the number was Maximilian Kolbe, a Franciscan, who was canonized by Pope John Paul II on 10 October 1982. For

more detail on this aspect of Nazi persecution and on Kolbe in particular, see Patricia Treece, *A Man for Others.*

60. For the story of I. G. Auschwitz, see Joseph Borkin, *The Crime and Punishment of I. G. Farben*, pp. 111–28.
61. *Trial of War Criminals Before the Nuremberg Military Tribunals, Under Control Council No. 10*, 7:56–58, as quoted by Borkin, *Crime and Punishment*, pp. 138–39.
62. Borkin, *Crime and Punishment*, p. 143.
63. See Hilberg, *Destruction*, 3:1093, 1107–8; see also ibid., p. 162.
64. "Auschwitz," *Encyclopedia Judaica*, 3:856.
65. Miklós Nyiszli, *Auschwitz: A Doctor's Eyewitness Report*, pp. 42–43.
66. Reitlinger, *The Final Solution*, pp. 159–60.
67. See Nyiszli, *Auschwitz*, pp. 44–48.
68. Sereny, *Into That Darkness*, p. 101.
69. Nyiszli, *Auschwitz*, pp. 68–71.
70. See Rubenstein, *The Cunning of History*, pp. 48–54; Lifton, *The Nazi Doctors*; and Alexander Mitscherlich and Fred Mielke, *Doctors of Infamy: The Story of the Nazi Medical Crimes.*
71. Hilberg, *Destruction*, 3:936–47; Rubenstein, *The Cunning of History*, pp. 48–54.
72. Höhne, *Order of the Death's Head*, p. 642.
73. Affidavit by Kurt Becher, 8 March 1946. See Fleming, *Hitler and the Final Solution*, pp. 168–69.
74. Hilberg, *Destruction*, 3:984.
75. See Bauer, *A History of the Holocaust*, p. 335; Dawidowicz, *War Against the Jews*, pp. 402–3; and Hilberg; *Destruction*, 3:1219–20.

CHAPTER 6

VICTIMS AND SURVIVORS

1. Abba Kovner, "A First Attempt to Tell," in *The Holocaust as Historical Experience*, ed. Yehuda Bauer and Nathan Rotenstreich, p. 81. For more on Kovner, see Bauer, *A History of the Holocaust*, pp. 250–51, 269–71, and 340–41.
2. Dawidowicz, *War Against the Jews*, p. 286.
3. Kovner, in *Holocaust*, ed. Bauer and Rotenstreich, pp. 81, 252. See also the biblical roots of the reference: Psalms 44:11 and Isaiah 53:7.
4. A sensitive discussion of these controversial issues is provided by Hilberg, *Destruction*, 3:1030–44.
5. Hannah Arendt, *Eichmann in Jerusalem: A Report on the Banality of Evil*, p. 111. Arendt covered the Eichmann trial in Jerusalem for *The New Yorker*. Her book emerged from that experience. Eichmann had escaped to Argentina at the end of World War II. On 11 May 1960, the Israeli secret service captured him and took him to Israel. Charged with crimes against the Jewish people, crimes against humanity, and war crimes, he stood trial from 11 April to 14 August 1961. Found guilty as charged, he was hanged on 31 May 1962. The Eichmann trial aroused worldwide attention. As this book goes to press, another Israeli trial could do the same. On 28 February 1986, United States authorities extradited to Israel John Demjanjuk, 66, who is accused of operating the gas chambers at Treblinka in 1942 and 1943. Demjanjuk had entered the United States in 1952 and lived in Cleveland. The United States has no applicable war crimes laws that would have enabled it to indict and try Demjanjuk. He is the first accused Nazi war criminal to be extradited to Israel by the United States. The first person since Eichmann to be charged under Israel's Nazis and Nazi Collaborators Law, his trial in that state will be only the second of its kind.

6. Leonard Tushnet, *The Pavement of Hell*, pp. 162, 169, 170, 169.
7. Raul Hilberg, "Discussion: The *Judenrat* and the Jewish Response," in *Holocaust*, ed. Bauer and Rotenstreich, pp. 231–32.
8. Hilberg, *Destruction*, 3:1030.
9. Cited by Isaiah Trunk, *Judenrat: The Jewish Council in Eastern Europe Under Nazi Occupation*, p. 2.
10. Cited by Dawidowicz, *War Against the Jews*, p. 350.
11. Trunk, *Judenrat*, p. 356.
12. Raul Hilberg, "The Ghetto as a Form of Government: An Analysis of Isaiah Trunk's *Judenrat*," in *Holocaust*, ed. Bauer and Rotenstreich, p. 159.
13. Adam Czerniakow, *The Warsaw Diary of Adam Czerniakow*, p. 385.
14. Cited by Hilberg, *Destruction*, 2:841.
15. Yehuda Bauer makes much of this latter point. See *A History of the Holocaust*, pp. 155–67.
16. Yehuda Bauer, "Jewish Leadership Reactions to Nazi Policies," in *Holocaust*, ed. Bauer and Rotenstreich, pp. 173–74.
17. Dawidowicz, *War Against the Jews*, p. 241. For more on Rumkowski and the Lodz ghetto in general, see Lucjan Dobroszycki, ed., *The Chronicle of the Lodz Ghetto, 1941–1944*.
18. Tushnet, *Pavement of Hell*, p. 53.
19. Dawidowicz, *War Against the Jews*, p. 325.
20. George M. Kren and Leon Rappoport, *The Holocaust and the Crisis of Human Behavior*, p. 121.
21. From an affadivit by Hermann Friedrich Graebe (10 November 1945), cited by Hilberg, *Destruction*, 3:1043–44.
22. Isaiah Trunk, *Jewish Responses to Nazi Persecution: Collective and Individual Behavior in Extremis*, p. 55.
23. Kren and Rappoport, *The Holocaust and the Crisis*, p. 100.
24. Ibid., p. 111. For details about armed resistance in Poland, see Shmuel Krakowski, *The War of the Doomed: Jewish Armed Resistance in Poland, 1942–1944*.
25. Zivia Lubetkin, *In the Days of Destruction and Revolt*, p. 153. Zivia Lubetkin survived, arrived in Israel in 1946, and lived there until her death in 1979. Along with her husband, Itzhak Zuckermann, she was one of the leaders in the Jewish resistance movement in Warsaw. (Incidentally, Zuckermann, too, survived the Holocaust. Shortly before his death in 1981, Claude Lanzmann asked him for his impressions of the Holocaust. In one of the most trenchant summaries any survivor has ever offered, Zuckermann replied: "If you could lick my heart, it would poison you." See Lanzmann, *Shoah*, p. 196.) Lubetkin's book is her memoir about life in the Warsaw ghetto and specifically about the ghetto uprising. For further detail on the unique aspects of women's struggle for life in the ghettos, resistance movements, and during the Holocaust generally, see *Women Surviving: The Holocaust*, ed. Esther Katz and Joan Miriam Ringelheim. Another detailed study of the Warsaw ghetto, especially of the underground and resistance movements within it, is to be found in Yisrael Gutman, *The Jews of Warsaw, 1939–1943: Ghetto, Underground, Revolt*.
26. On these matters, see Bauer, *A History of the Holocaust*, especially pp. 309–25 and 329–30.
27. For more detail, see Martin Gilbert, *The Holocaust*, pp. 16–22, and *The Holocaust: A History of the Jews of Europe during the Second World War*, pp. 807, 824–25; Richard C. Lukas, *The Forgotten Holocaust: The Poles under German Occupation, 1939–1944*, and Bohdan Wytwycky, *The Other Holocaust: Many Circles of Hell*.

The latter two volumes especially focus on non-Jews in eastern Europe who were victims of Nazi racism. For discussion of the fate of homosexuals under the Nazis, see Heinz Heger, *The Men with the Pink Triangle*; Richard Plant, *The Pink Triangle: The Nazi War Against Homosexuals*; and Frank Rector, *The Nazi Extermination of Homosexuals*. The fate of the Gypsies is explored by Donald Kenrick and Gratton Puxon, *The Destiny of Europe's Gypsies*.

28. Hilberg, *Destruction*, 3:1220.
29. Filip Müller, *Eyewitness Auschwitz: Three Years in the Gas Chambers*, p. 12.
30. Jack Nusan Porter, "Social-Psychological Aspects of the Holocaust," in *Encountering the Holocaust: An Interdisciplinary Survey*, ed. Bryon L. Sherwin and Susan G. Ament, p. 198.
31. Trunk, *Jewish Responses to Nazi Persecution*, p. 70–71. Most of the child survivors were orphaned. Much research remains to be done on how they endured the Holocaust and continue to cope with its effects on their lives. For more detail, see Doug Smith, "Bond Unites Children of Holocaust," *Los Angeles Times*, 29 May 1986.
32. For more detail on these matters, see Fein, *Accounting for Genocide*.
33. To supplement this account, see Marrus and Paxton, *Vichy France and the Jews*.
34. See Laqueur, *Terrible Secret*, pp. 202, 204; Wasserstein, *Britain and the Jews*; and David S. Wyman, *The Abandonment of the Jews: America and the Holocaust, 1941–1945*. Also significant is Walter Laqueur and Richard Breitman, *Breaking the Silence*, which discusses German industrialist Eduard Schulte, who leaked information about the Final Solution to Jewish leaders in Switzerland in late July 1942.
35. For more detail on these points, see Wyman, *Abandonment*, especially pp. x–xi, 255–87; and Sharon R. Lowenstein, *Token Refuge: The Story of the Jewish Refugee Shelter at Oswego, 1944–1946*.
36. See Martin Gilbert, *Auschwitz and the Allies*, and Hilberg, *Destruction*, 3:1114–32 for further details.
37. Cited by Dawidowicz, *War Against the Jews*, p. 316.
38. Arthur J. Goldberg and Arthur Hertzberg, "Holocaust: Questions of Guilt," *Los Angeles Times*, 25 March 1984. See also Wyman, *Abandonment*, pp. 79–103, 327–30, and Seymour Maxwell Finger, *Their Brothers' Keepers: American Jewry and the Holocaust*. For more detail on the commission's findings, see *American Jewry during the Holocaust: A Report Sponsored by the American Jewish Commission on the Holocaust*, ed. Seymour Maxwell Finger.
39. Cited by Lawrence L. Langer, "The Writer and the Holocaust Experience," in *The Holocaust: Ideology, Bureaucracy, and Genocide*, ed. Henry Friedlander and Sybil Milton, p. 313. Salmen Lewental's testimony can be found in *Amidst a Nightmare of Crime: Manuscripts of Members of Sonderkommandos*, ed. Jadwiga Bezwinska, p. 147.
40. Leo Eitinger, *Concentration Camp Survivors in Norway and Israel*, p. 80. Eitinger was captured by the Nazis in Norway, imprisoned, and eventually deported to Auschwitz. He survived and has done significant psychological research on persons who endured the Holocaust.
41. Terrence Des Pres, *The Survivor: An Anatomy of Life in the Death Camps*, p. 188.
42. For an account of the liberators' experiences, see Robert H. Abzug, *Inside the Vicious Heart: Americans and the Liberation of Nazi Concentration Camps*.
43. See ibid., pp. 141–68; Leonard Dinnerstein, *America and the Survivors of the Holocaust*; and Abram L. Sachar, *The Redemption of the Unwanted: From the Liberation of the Death Camps to the Founding of Israel*.

44. An invaluable guide in this area is provided by Leo Eitinger, Robert Krell, and Miriam Rieck, *The Psychological and Medical Effects of Concentration Camps and Related Persecutions on Survivors of the Holocaust: A Research Bibliography.*

45. See Trunk, *Judenrat*, pp. 548–69.

46. Elie Wiesel, *A Jew Today*, pp. 205, 204, 202, 188.

47. The story of the attempt to secure even token compensation from German corporations for the former slaves is told in Benjamin B. Ferencz, *Less Than Slaves: Jewish Forced Labor and the Quest for Compensation.*

48. Fein, *Accounting for Genocide*, pp. 4, 9.

49. For the idea of the victim as "non-person," see Kren and Rappoport, *The Holocaust and the Crisis*, pp. 73–98.

50. On slavery in the ancient world, see Thomas Weidemann, *Greek and Roman Slavery.*

51. Aristotle, *The Politics*, 1.3.31.

52. See Rubenstein, *The Cunning of History*, pp. 31–35.

53. See Michael Harner, "The Enigma of Aztec Sacrifice," *Natural History* (April 1977): 46–51.

54. Primo Levi, *Survival in Auschwitz: The Nazi Assault on Humanity*, p. 25. Other Holocaust memoirs by the same author include *Moments of Reprieve, The Periodic Table,* and *The Reawakening.* The latter recounts Levi's journey back to Italy after his liberation from Auschwitz.

55. See Max Weber, "Politics as a Vocation," in *From Max Weber,* ed. Gerth and Mills, p. 78.

CHAPTER 7

THEIR BROTHERS' KEEPERS?
CHRISTIANS, CHURCHES, AND JEWS

1. Cited by Franklin H. Littell, "Church Struggle and the Holocaust," in *German Church Struggle,* ed. Littell and Locke, p. 15.

2. Bormann's "Circular on the Relationship of National Socialism and Christianity," from which the quotation is taken, is reproduced in Conway, *The Nazi Persecution of the Churches 1933–1945,* pp. 383–86.

3. Littell, "Church Struggle and the Holocaust," in *German Church Struggle,* ed. Littell and Locke, p. 16.

4. Littell, *The Crucifixion of the Jews,* p. 75.

5. See Guenther Lewy, *The Roman Catholic Church and the Third Reich.*

6. Cited by John S. Conway, "The Churches," in *The Holocaust,* ed. Friedlander and Milton, p. 204.

7. For a study of some important German theologians who took positions quite different from those of Barth and Tillich, see Robert P. Erickson, *Theologians under Hitler: Gerhard Kittel, Paul Althaus, and Emanuel Hirsch.*

8. See Conway, *The Nazi Persecution,* p. 5.

9. In addition to being influenced by Conway, Lewy, and Littell, our interpretations of the religious situation in Germany are indebted to Arthur C. Cochrane, *The Church's Confession under Hitler,* 2d ed.; Richard Gutteridge, *Open Thy Mouth for the Dumb: The German Evangelical Church and the Jews 1879–1950;* Ernst Christian Helmreich, *The German Churches under Hitler: Background, Struggle, and Epilogue;* and Frederic Spotts, *The Churches and Politics in Germany.* Note that the significance of "Evangelical" is not to be confused with connotations lately at-

tached to it within American Protestantism. The German Evangelical churches were much more akin to the mainline Protestant denominations than to the communities of "born-again" Christians who have recently cornered the term.

10. Cited by Conway, *The Nazi Persecution*, p. 15.
11. Ibid., p. 84.
12. Cited by Eberhard Busch, *Karl Barth: His Life from Letters and Autobiographical Texts*, p. 223.
13. Letter to E. Steffens, 10 January 1934, cited by Busch, *Karl Barth*, p. 235.
14. Cited by Eberhard Bethge, "Troubled Self-Interpretation and Uncertain Reception in the Church Struggle," in *German Church Struggle*, ed. Littell and Locke, p. 167. Also relevant is Robin W. Lovin, *Christian Faith and Public Choices: The Social Ethics of Barth, Brunner, and Bonhoeffer.*
15. See Busch, *Karl Barth*, pp. 255, 256.
16. Ibid., p. 290.
17. See Cochrane, *The Church's Confession*, p. 275.
18. Dietrich Bonhoeffer, *No Rusty Swords*, p. 226.
19. Karl Barth, *Church Dogmatics*, II, 2, p. 235. The 1949 assertions are from Karl Barth, "The Jewish Problem and the Christian Answer," in *Against the Stream*, pp. 196, 198. The latter passages are cited by Emil Fackenheim, *To Mend the World: Foundations of Future Jewish Thought*, p. 133. In that work, Fackenheim, one of the twentieth century's most important philosophers, describes Barth as "the last great Christian supersessionist thinker" (p. 284).
20. Cited by Conway, *The Nazi Persecution*, p. 30.
21. For more on Grüber, who was the only German to testify for the prosecution at the trial of Adolf Eichmann in Israel (1961), see Rubenstein, "The Dean and the Chosen People," in *After Auschwitz*, pp. 46–58.
22. Littell, *The Crucifixion of the Jews*, pp. 51–52.
23. Conway, *The Nazi Persecution*, p. 232.
24. Cited by Franklin H. Littell in his foreword to Hubert G. Locke, ed., *Exile in the Fatherland: Martin Niemöller's Letters from Moabit Prison.* Also relevant in this context are Martin Niemöller, *Of Guilt and Hope* and James Bentley, *Martin Niemöller, 1892–1984.*
25. The following discussion draws extensively on John F. Morley, *Vatican Diplomacy and the Jews during the Holocaust 1939–1943.* Other relevant sources are Saul Friedlander, *Pius XII and the Third Reich: A Documentation*; Lewy, *The Catholic Church and Nazi Germany*; and Gordon Zahn, *German Catholics and Hitler's Wars.* See also Gordon Zahn, "Catholic Resistance? A Yes and a No," in *German Church Struggle*, ed. Littell and Locke, pp. 103–37.
26. Morley, *Vatican Diplomacy*, p. 196.
27. Ibid., p. 125.
28. Ibid., p. 206.
29. Fein, *Accounting for Genocide*, p. 33.
30. See ibid., especially pp. 50–120.
31. Noteworthy discussions of the situations in these two countries are provided by Frederick B. Chary, *The Bulgarian Jews and the Final Solution 1940–1944*; Harold Flender, *Rescue in Denmark*; and Leni Yahil, *The Rescue of Danish Jewry.*
32. Cited by Fein, *Accounting for Genocide*, pp. 101–2. The statement was made by Monsignor Domenico Tardini. Along with Monsignor Giovanni Battista Montini (later Pope Paul VI), he was one of the two principal assistants to the Vatican's secretary of state during the Holocaust.

33. The following discussion, including the outline of the five failures by American Protestants, draws upon Robert W. Ross, *So It Was True: The American Protestant Press and the Nazi Persecution of the Jews*. The quotation is from p. 258. For further discussion about the reporting of the Holocaust in the American press, see Deborah E. Lipstadt, *Beyond Belief: The American Press and the Coming of the Holocaust* and Wyman, *Abandonment*.

34. Wyman, *Abandonment*, pp. 318, 413.

35. Ross, *So It Was True*, p. 287.

36. Ibid., p. 290.

37. Cited by Richard Hanser, *A Noble Treason: The Revolt of the Munich Students Against Hitler*, pp. 152–53. See also Annette E. Dumbach and Jud Newborn, *Shattering the German Night: The Story of the White Rose*.

38. Ibid., p. 274.

39. The Bible likens a righteous person to "a tree planted by streams of water that yields its fruit in season, and its leaf does not wither" (Psalms 1:3). At Yad Vashem, which means "place and name" (see Isaiah 56:5), evergreen carob trees honor the "Righteous Gentiles." Durable in Israel's climate, this tree is also a Christian symbol. Tradition holds that John the Baptist came from a spring-fed valley nearby; the bean pods produced by the carob tree are probably the "locusts" that sustained him in the wilderness (see Mark 1:6).

40. A representative sample of works about the "Righteous Gentiles" includes Arieh L. Bauminger, *Roll of Honour*; John Bierman, *Righteous Gentile: The Story of Raoul Wallenberg, the Missing Hero of the Holocaust*; Philip Friedman, *Their Brothers' Keepers*; Peter Hellman, *Avenue of the Righteous*; Douglas K. Huneke, *The Moses of Rovno*; Thomas Keneally, *Schindler's List*; Alexander Ramati, *The Assisi Underground: The Priests Who Rescued Jews*; and Carol Rittner and Sondra Myers, eds., *The Courage to Care*.

41. The following account is indebted to Philip P. Hallie, *Lest Innocent Blood Be Shed: The Story of the Village of Le Chambon and How Goodness Happened There*.

42. At the time of this writing, Philip P. Hallie is completing a book about Major Schmäling, an intriguing Nazi whom Hallie has described as "a good man in an evil cause."

CHAPTER 8

BUSINESS AS USUAL?

PROFESSIONS AND INDUSTRIES DURING THE HOLOCAUST

1. This SS document is cited in Jacob Robinson, *And the Crooked Shall Be Made Straight: The Eichmann Trial, the Jewish Catastrophe, and Hannah Arendt's Narrative*, p. 285. Another telling example of efficiency calculations in the Nazi destruction process is cited by Lanzmann, *Shoah*, pp. 103–4. He quotes from a document dated 5 June 1942 and sent from the killing center at Chelmno to Berlin. The memorandum urges that ten vans ordered from the Saurer Company and slated for delivery at Chelmno must meet the technical requirements "shown by use and experience to be necessary." The vans were slated for use as mobile gas chambers utilizing carbon monoxide.

2. See, for example, Rainer C. Baum, *The Holocaust and the German Elite: Genocide and National Suicide in Germany 1871–1945*, and Henry Ashby Turner, Jr., *German Big Business and the Rise of Hitler*.

3. Further information about German resistance to Hitler, including the degree to which the Jewish question did and did not play a part in it, is available in Peter Hoffmann, *The History of the German Resistance 1933-1945*.

4. For more detail on Mengele see Gerald Astor, *The Last Nazi: The Life and Times of Dr. Joseph Mengele*, and Gerald L. Posner and John Ware, *Mengele: The Complete Story*. Further insights about the role of the German medical profession during the Hitler era can be found in Mitscherlich and Mielke, *Doctors of Infamy: The Story of the Nazi Medical Crimes*; Richard Grunberger, *The 12-Year Reich: A Social History of Nazi Germany 1933-1945*; Hilberg, *Destruction*, 3:936–47; Lifton, *The Nazi Doctors*; Müller-Hill, *Tödliche Wissenschaft*; and Rubenstein, *The Cunning of History*, pp. 48–67. Also relevant are Jack S. Boozer, "Children of Hippocrates: Doctors in Nazi Germany," in *Reflections on the Holocaust*, ed. Shur, Littell, and Wolfgang, pp. 83–97; Gert H. Brieger, "The Medical Profession," in *The Holocaust*, ed. Friedlander and Milton, pp. 141–50; and Robert Jay Lifton, "Medicalized Killing in Auschwitz," in *Psychoanalytic Reflections on the Holocaust: Selected Essays*, ed. Steven A. Luel and Paul Marcus, pp. 11–33.

5. See Grunberger, *12-Year Reich*, pp. 116–36, and also Telford Taylor, "The Legal Profession," in *The Holocaust*, ed. Friedlander and Milton, pp. 133–40.

6. See Grunberger, *12-Year Reich*, pp. 285–323, and also Waite, *The Psychopathic God*, pp. 385–86.

7. Two relevant discussions of these topics are Gilmer W. Blackburn, *Education in the Third Reich: A Study of Race and History in Nazi Textbooks*, and Christa Kamenetsky, *Children's Literature in Hitler's Germany*.

8. See Alan Beyerchen, "The Physical Sciences," in *The Holocaust*, ed. Friedlander and Milton, pp. 151–63. For even more detail, see Alan Beyerchen, *Scientists Under Hitler: Politics and the Physics Community in the Third Reich*.

9. See Thomas P. Hughes, "Technology," in *The Holocaust*, ed. Friedlander and Milton, pp. 165–81.

10. See Christopher R. Browning, "The Government Experts," in *The Holocaust*, ed. Friedlander and Milton, pp. 183–97, for a summary elaboration of some aspects of this dimension of the Holocaust. For more detail, see Christopher R. Browning, *The Final Solution and the German Foreign Office: A Study of Referat D III of Abteilung Deutschland 1940–43*.

11. A significant study of the *Reichbahn's* activity in the Holocaust is available in Raul Hilberg, "German Railroads, Jewish Souls," *Society* 14 (November-December 1976): 60–74. See also Hilberg, *Destruction*, 2:407–16, 486–88.

12. Hilberg, *Destruction*, 2:411.

13. Cited by Joesph Borkin, *The Crime and Punishment of I. G. Farben*, p. 62.

14. Ibid., p. 18.

15. Hilberg, *Destruction*, 3:892.

16. For more detail on these matters, see Irving Greenberg, "Cloud of Smoke, Pillar of Fire: Judaism, Christianity, and Modernity after the Holocaust," in *Auschwitz*, ed. Fleischner, pp. 10–11. See also the comments of Filip Müller, a Czech Jew who worked in the gas chambers and crematoria and survived, in Lanzmann, *Shoah*, pp. 57–60, 68–70, 123–27, 145–46, 149–50, 158–59, and 163–65. Among other things, Müller notes that the struggle in the gas chambers was horrible. The gas rose from the ground upward. In the dark, the strongest would instinctively try to climb higher where the air was. People were crushed. But where the gas crystals had been poured in there would be an empty space. Müller adds that it was useless to tell anyone what awaited them once they had entered the place of death. No one who got that far

could be saved, and no one wanted to know that. In any case a hideous death awaited any prisoner who was caught telling the truth.

17. See Höss, *Commandant of Auschwitz*, p. 122.
18. Joachim C. Fest, *The Face of the Third Reich: Portraits of the Nazi Leadership*, p. 276.
19. Lord Russell of Liverpool, Introd., Höss, *Commandant of Auschwitz*, p. 24.
20. Höss, ibid., pp. 121, 217.
21. Ibid., p. 83.
22. Ibid., p. 233.
23. Ibid., pp. 231, 133.
24. Ibid., pp. 197–98, 198, 199, 202.
25. Ferencz, *Less Than Slaves*, p. 188.
26. Ibid., p. 192.
27. Bradley F. Smith, *Reaching Judgment at Nuremberg*, p. 14. Other helpful accounts of the Nuremberg trials include Eugene Davidson, *The Trial of the Germans: An Account of the Twenty-two Defendants before the International Military Tribunal at Nuremburg*; Bradley F. Smith, *The Road to Nuremberg*; and John and Ann Tusa, *The Nuremberg Trial*. See also M. Cherif Bassiouni, "International Law and the Holocaust," in *Encountering the Holocaust*, ed. Sherwin and Ament, pp. 146–88; Henry Friedlander, "Nuremberg and Other Trials," in *Genocide: Critical Issues of the Holocaust*, ed. Alex Grobman, Daniel Landes, and Sybil Milton, pp. 381–83; and Robert Wolfe, "Putative Threat to National Security as a Nuremberg Defense for Genocide," in *Reflections on the Holocaust*, ed. Shur, Littell, and Wolfgang, pp. 46–67.
28. Smith, *Reaching Judgment*, p. 14.
29. Hilberg, *Destruction*, 3:1077, n. 72.
30. Lee Mays, "Reagan Expert Under Attack For Ties to Nazi War Criminal," *St. Petersburg Times*, 25 April 1982. The story is identified as having originated in the *Los Angeles Times*.
31. Allan A. Ryan, Jr., *Quiet Neighbors: Prosecuting Nazi War Criminals in America*, p. 344. A view less sanguine than Ryan's can be found in Rochelle G. Saidel, *The Outraged Conscience: Seekers of Justice for Nazi War Criminals in America*.
32. Ferencz, *Less Than Slaves*, p. 156.
33. Ibid., p. 155.
34. Rubenstein, *The Cunning of History*, p. 65.
35. Karl Marx, "Theses on Feuerbach," in *Marx and Engels: Basic Writings on Politics and Philosophy*, ed. Lewis S. Feuer, p. 245.
36. For a useful discussion of the various defense mechanisms employed by Nazis to justify the Holocaust, see Hilberg, "The Nature of the Process," in *Survivors*, ed. Dimsdale. See also Wolfe, "Putative Threat to National Security as a Nuremberg Defense for Genocide," in *Reflections on the Holocaust*, ed. Shur, Littell, and Wolfgang.
37. G. W. F. Hegel, *Philosophy of Right*, pp. 13, 12.

CHAPTER 9

WHAT CAN—AND CANNOT—BE SAID?
LITERARY RESPONSES TO THE HOLOCAUST

1. Chaim A. Kaplan, *Scroll of Agony: The Warsaw Diary of Chaim A. Kaplan*, p. 400.
2. Three important books about art during the Holocaust, including reproductions, are Janet Blatter and Sybil Milton, *The Art of the Holocaust*; Miriam Novitch, et al.,

Spiritual Resistance: Art from Concentration Camps 1940–1945; and Nelly Toll, *Without Surrender: Art of the Holocaust*. For a discussion of music during the period, see Susan G. Ament, "Music and Art of the Holocaust," in *Encountering the Holocaust*, ed. Sherwin and Ament, pp. 383–406.

3. Stories that emerged from the Holocaust, orally passed from one person to another and from one community to another, form a significant category in their own right. Yaffa Eliach has collected and traced to their origins almost ninety examples. See her *Hasidic Tales of the Holocaust: The First Original Hasidic Tales in a Century*. See also Azriel Eisenberg, ed., *Witness to the Holocaust*; Jacob Glatstein, Israel Knox, and Samuel Margoshes, eds., *Anthology of Holocaust Literature*; Claude Lanzmann, *Shoah;* and Sylvia Rothchild, ed., *Voices from the Holocaust*.

4. Noteworthy studies of Holocaust literature include Alan L. Berger, *Crisis and Covenant: The Holocaust in American Jewish Fiction*; Sidra Dekoven Ezrahi, *By Words Alone: The Holocaust in Literature*; two works by Alvin H. Rosenfeld, *A Double Dying: Reflections on Holocaust Literature* and *Imagining Hitler*; and three works by Lawrence L. Langer, *The Holocaust and the Literary Imagination*, *The Age of Atrocity: Death in Modern Literature*, and *Versions of Survival: The Holocaust and the Human Spirit*. Film treatments of the Holocaust are discussed in Annette Insdorf, *Indelible Shadows: Film and the Holocaust*.

5. David Rousset, *The Other Kingdom*, p. 168.

6. Yitzhak Katzenelson, *The Song of the Murdered Jewish People*, p. 45.

7. Ibid., pp. 12, 13, 14, 15.

8. Ibid., pp. 17, 18, 19. Katzenelson knew the Bible well. Themes from Lamentations and Ezekiel are governing motifs in *The Song of the Murdered Jewish People*. As the poem's opening suggests, Psalm 137 plays a central role as well.

9. Ibid., pp. 23, 25.

10. Ibid., pp. 27, 29, 30.

11. Ibid., pp. 32, 34, 35.

12. Ibid., pp. 38, 39.

13. Ibid., pp. 40, 42, 44.

14. Ibid., pp. 54, 55.

15. Ibid., pp. 60, 62, 65.

16. Ibid., pp. 67, 68.

17. Ibid., p. 70.

18. Ibid., pp. 75, 82.

19. Ibid., pp. 82, 83, 85.

20. Cited by Lubetkin, *In the Days of Destruction*, p. 151.

21. André Schwarz-Bart, *The Last of the Just*, pp. 4, 6.

22. Ibid., p. 315.

23. Ibid., pp. 375, 404.

24. Ibid., p. 412.

25. Ibid., pp. 422, 417, 421.

26. Ibid., pp. 421, 422, 421.

27. Ibid., pp. 422, 393.

28. Yehiel Dinur (Ka-tzetnik 135633), *Star Eternal*, pp. 50, 51, 52.

29. Ibid., p. 11.

30. Ibid., p. 26.

31. Ibid., pp. 30, 36.

32. Ibid., pp. 47, 58.

33. Ibid., pp. 60, 55, 66, 69.

34. Ibid., pp. 76, 79.

35. Ibid., pp. 80, 88, 89.
36. Ibid., p. 100.
37. Ibid., p. 102.
38. Ibid., pp. 109, 111, 112.
39. Ibid., p. 119.
40. Ibid., pp. 124, 126.
41. Charlotte Delbo, *None of Us Will Return*, vol. 1: *Auschwitz and After*, pp. 7, 128. Our interpretation of Delbo is indebted to Lawrence L. Langer, *The Age of Atrocity*, especially pp. 201–44.
42. Delbo, ibid., pp. 6, 7.
43. Ibid., p. 31.
44. Ibid., p. 14.
45. Ibid., p. 33.
46. Ibid., pp. 38, 73, 76, 127.
47. Charlotte Delbo, *Une Connaissance inutile*, vol. 2: *Auschwitz and After*, pp. 48, 60, 49. The translations are by Lawrence L. Langer.
48. Ibid., p. 145.
49. Ibid., pp. 185, 190, 191.
50. Charlotte Delbo, *Mesure de nos jours*, vol. 3: *Auschwitz and After*, p. 17. The translations are by Lawrence. L. Langer.
51. Ibid., pp. 60, 66.
52. Ibid., pp. 83, 184.
53. Ibid., pp. 200, 187.
54. Ibid., p. 212.
55. Tadeusz Borowski, *This Way for the Gas, Ladies and Gentlemen*, p. 175.
56. Ibid., pp. 176, 122.
57. Ibid., pp. 29, 30, 31.
58. Ibid., pp. 38, 46, 49.
59. Ibid., pp. 58, 83, 84.
60. Ibid., pp. 110, 90, 89.
61. Ibid., pp. 110, 98, 100.
62. Ibid., pp. 112, 113, 115–16.
63. Ibid., pp. 122, 131, 142.
64. Ibid., pp. 163, 168, 166–67.
65. Ibid., pp. 177, 179.
66. Ibid., p. 180.
67. Ibid., pp. 115–16.
68. Rosenfeld, *A Double Dying*, p. 164.
69. William Styron, *Sophie's Choice*, p. 483.
70. Ibid., pp. 513–15.
71. Rosenfeld, *A Double Dying*, p. 159.
72. Styron, *Sophie's Choice*, p. 219.
73. Ibid., p. 466.
74. Elie Wiesel, *Night*, p. 28. In his review of *Shoah*, Claude Lanzmann's nine and one-half hour film documentary on the Holocaust (see *The New York Times*, 3 November 1985), Wiesel notes that it took him a long time to understand the anger of the prisoners who met his transport at Auschwitz. Later he learned that this squad was the one to which Rudolf Vrba belonged. With Alfred Wetzler, he had escaped Auschwitz months before to warn the Hungarian Jews and to tell the world about Auschwitz. Apparently the effort had been in vain—hence the anger.
75. Ibid., pp. 32, 1, 109.

76. For more detail on Elie Wiesel's authorship, see Irving Abrahamson, ed., *Against Silence: The Voice and Vision of Elie Wiesel*, 3 vols; Michael Berenbaum, *The Vision of the Void: Theological Reflections on the Works of Elie Wiesel*; Robert McAfee Brown, *Elie Wiesel: Messenger to All Humanity*; Harry James Cargas, *Harry James Cargas in Conversation with Elie Wiesel*; Ellen S. Fine, *Legacy of Night: The Literary Universe of Elie Wiesel*; and John K. Roth, *A Consuming Fire: Encounters with Elie Wiesel; and the Holocaust.*

77. Elie Wiesel, "Why I Write," trans. Rosette C. Lamont, in *Confronting the Holocaust: The Impact of Elie Wiesel*, ed. Alvin H. Rosenfeld and Irving Greenberg, p. 201.

78. Ibid., pp. 201, 202; Elie Wiesel, *The Oath*, p. 154.

79. Elie Wiesel, *Legends of Our Time*, p. 230.

80. Wiesel, *A Jew Today*, p. 164.

81. Ibid., pp. 140, 141.

82. Ibid., p. 143.

83. Wiesel, *Legends of Our Time*, p. viii.

84. Wiesel, *A Jew Today*, pp. 144, 145.

85. Ibid., pp. 147, 146.

86. Elie Wiesel, *The Trial of God*, p. 129.

87. Ibid., p. 133.

88. Robert McAfee Brown notes this tale in "Wiesel's Case Against God," *The Christian Century*, 30 January 1980, pp. 109–12.

89. Wiesel, *A Jew Today*, p. 136.

90. Ibid., pp. 149, 152.

91. Elie Wiesel, *Messengers of God*, pp. 35–36.

92. Elie Wiesel, *The Testament*, p. 9.

CHAPTER 10

THE SILENCE OF GOD:

PHILOSOPHICAL AND RELIGIOUS REFLECTION ON THE HOLOCAUST

1. Elie Wiesel, *One Generation After*, p. 215.

2. Reeve Robert Brenner, *The Faith and Doubt of Holocaust Survivors*, pp. 21, 103, 95, 94.

3. Ibid., pp. 103, 119.

4. Ibid., p. 112.

5. Ibid., pp. 246, 206.

6. Ibid., p. 215.

7. See Paul M. van Buren, *Discerning the Way*, Part I of *A Theology of the Jewish Christian Reality*, and *A Christian Theology of the People Israel*, Part II of *A Theology of the Jewish Christian Reality*. For a worthwhile study of recent conversations among some German Christians and between these Christians and Jews on the meaning of Judaism for Christianity and Christianity for Judaism, see Robert T. Osborne, "The Christian Blasphemy," *Journal of the American Academy of Religion* 53, no. 3 (September 1985): 339–63.

8. Van Buren, *Discerning the Way*, p. 116.

9. Ibid., p. 117.

10. Van Buren, *A Christian Theology of the People Israel*, pp. 62–63.

11. Van Buren, *Discerning the Way*, p. 119.

12. Ibid., p. 153.

13. Ibid., pp. 151, 181.

14. Ibid., p. 115.
15. Ibid., p. 99.
16. Brenner, *Faith and Doubt*, pp. 230, 231.
17. Van Buren, *A Christian Theology of the People Israel*, pp. 122, 101, 102. See also David G. Roskies, *Against the Apocalypse: Responses to Catastrophe in Modern Jewish Culture*.
18. Joseph Hertz, ed., *The Authorized Daily Prayer Book*, pp. 819, 821, italics added. See also Richard L. Rubenstein, *The Religious Imagination*, pp. 127–30.
19. Ignaz Maybaum, *The Face of God After Auschwitz*, p. 36.
20. Rubenstein, *After Auschwitz*, pp. 93–112.
21. Maybaum, *Face of God*, p. 67.
22. Ibid., p. 63. For this citation, we are indebted to Steven T. Katz, *Post-Holocaust Dialogues: Critical Studies in Modern Jewish Thought*, p. 162.
23. Maybaum. *Face of God*, p. 67.
24. Cited by Rubenstein, *After Auschwitz*, pp. 54, 54–55.
25. "Ein Wort zur Judenfrage, der Reichsbruderrat der Evangelischen Kirche in Deutschland," 8 April 1948, in *Der Ungekündigte Bund*, ed. Goldschmidt and Kraus, pp. 251–54.
26. Rubenstein, *After Auschwitz*, p. 153.
27. Ibid., pp. 151–52.
28. Ibid., pp. 153–54.
29. Hertz, ed., *Prayer Book*, p. 143.
30. Richard L. Rubenstein, *Morality and Eros*, pp. 185–86. For a Buddhist parallel to Rubenstein's mysticism, see Keiji Nishitani, *Religion and Nothingness*.
31. Richard L. Rubenstein, "Naming the Unnameable; Thinking the Unthinkable: A Review Essay of Arthur Cohen's *The Tremendum*," *Journal of Reform Judaism* 31 (Spring 1984): 43–54. See also below, pp. 330–32.
32. Emil L. Fackenheim, *Encounters Between Judaism and Modern Philosophy*, p. 21.
33. Emil L. Fackenheim, "The People Israel Lives," in *The Christian Century*, 6 May 1970, pp. 563–68.
34. Fackenheim, *To Mend the World*, p. 13.
35. Greenberg, "Cloud of Smoke, Pillar of Fire," in *Auschwitz*, ed. Fleischner, p. 11. See also Fackenheim, *To Mend the World*, p. 11.
36. Emil L. Fackenheim, "Can There Be Judaism Without Revelation?" in Fackenheim, *Quest for Past and Future: Essays in Jewish Theology*, pp. 80–81. Reprinted from *Commentary* (December 1951).
37. Fackenheim, *God's Presence in History*, p. 11.
38. In traditional Judaism, the number of commandments given by God to Israel in Scripture is said to be 613. Emil L. Fackenheim, "Transcendence in Contemporary Culture: Philosophical Reflections and a Jewish Theology," in *Transcendence*, ed. Herbert W. Richardson and Donald R. Cutler, p. 150. The passage originally appeared in *Judaism* 16 (Summer 1967): 272–273. See also Fackenheim, *God's Presence in History*, pp. 84–92.
39. Emil L. Fackenheim, *The Jewish Return into History: Reflections in the Age of Auschwitz and a New Jerusalem*, p. 31, italics added.
40. Fackenheim, *To Mend the World*, p. 10.
41. Kren and Rappoport, *The Holocaust and the Crisis*, p. 13.
42. Fackenheim, *To Mend the World*, p.13.
43. Des Pres, *The Survivor*, pp. 51–71.
44. Gisella Perl, *I Was a Doctor in Auschwitz*, pp. 32–33.

45. Levi, *Survival in Auschwitz*, p. 82, as cited by Fackenheim, *To Mend the World*, pp. 99–100.
46. G.W.F. Hegel, *Phenomenology of the Mind*, p. 676.
47. G.W.F. Hegel, "Introduction: Reason in History," in *Lectures on the Philosophy of World History*, p. 43.
48. Fackenheim, *To Mend the World*, p. 248.
49. Pelagia Lewinska, *Twenty Months at Auschwitz*, pp. 41–50, as quoted by Fackenheim, *To Mend the World*, p. 25.
50. Fackenheim, *To Mend the World*, p. 250.
51. Ibid., p. 304.
52. Arthur A. Cohen, *The Natural and the Supernatural Jew*.
53. Arthur A. Cohen, *The Tremendum: A Theological Interpretation of the Holocaust*, pp. 34–35.
54. Rubenstein, *After Auschwitz*, pp. 177–88.
55. Cohen, *The Tremendum*, p. 36.
56. Ibid., pp. 17, 18–19.
57. Ibid., p. 97, italics added.
58. Ibid., pp. 97–98.
59. See Eliezer Berkovits, *Faith after the Holocaust, Crisis and Faith*, and *With God in Hell: Judaism in the Ghettos and Death Camps*.
60. Berkovits, *Faith after the Holocaust*, p. 106. We are indebted to Katz, *Post-Holocaust Dialogues*, p. 271, for this citation.
61. Cohen, *The Tremendum*, p. 11.
62. Ibid., p. 101.
63. Ibid., p. 108.
64. For the New Testament source of these ideas, see Romans 9–11.

CHAPTER 11
THE LEGACY OF THE HOLOCAUST

1. On the question of anticipations of the Holocaust, see Rubenstein, *The Age of Triage*.
2. Kren and Rappoport, *The Holocaust and the Crisis*, p. 13.
3. On what was known in Germany and when, see Laqueur, *The Terrible Secret*, pp. 17–40, and Laqueur and Breitman, *Breaking the Silence*. Also relevant is Gordon, *Hitler, Germans and the "Jewish Question."*
4. For an account of the attitudes of Cardinals Wyszynski and Glemp, see the letter which Abraham Brumberg, an informed authority on Eastern Europe, sent to the editor of *The New York Times Book Review*, 27 January 1985, p. 37.
5. Our intention is not to oversimplify the complexities of the Polish response to the Holocaust. We call attention to Walter Laqueur's cautionary admonition concerning the Poles: "That there has been a great deal of anti-semitism in modern Polish history is not a matter of dispute, but it is also true that help was extended to the Jews after 1939 precisely by some who had been their bitterest enemies. . . . If the Poles showed less sympathy and solidarity with Jews than many Danes and Dutch, they behaved far more humanely than Rumanians or Ukrainians, than Lithuanians and Latvians. A comparison with France would be by no means unfavorable for Poland. In view of the Polish pre-war attitudes toward Jews, it is not surprising that there was so little help, but that there was so much." See Laqueur, *The Terrible Secret*, p. 107. See also Lukas, *The Forgotten Holocaust*.
6. On the German churches and the Jews in the Hitler period, see Conway, *The Nazi Persecution*, pp. 1–44 and 261–67.

7. See Heller, *On the Edge of Destruction*, pp. 77–139.
8. Rubenstein, *The Cunning of History*, p. 89.
9. See Rubenstein, *The Age of Triage*, pp. 165–67.
10. See Leo Kuper, *Genocide: Its Political Use in the Twentieth Century*, p. 173.
11. Kren and Rappoport, *The Holocaust and the Crisis*, p. 133.
12. Ibid., p. 134.
13. See Alan A. Clark, *Barbarossa: The Russian-German Conflict*, 1941–45, pp. 233–35.
14. See Hilberg, *Destruction*, 1:271–390. For further detail about the Bitburg controversy, see Geoffrey H. Hartman, ed., *Bitburg in Moral and Political Perspective*.
15. Poliakov, *Harvest of Hate*, p. 185.
16. Franz Halder, *Kriegstagebuch*, 2:335.
17. Fest, *Hitler*, p. 649.
18. Richard Lowenthal, "The German Question Transformed," *Foreign Affairs* (Winter 1984/85): 314.
19. See Clark, *Barbarossa*, p. 235.
20. The subject of the rise of surplus people and the way governments have dealt with them is discussed extensively in Rubenstein, *The Age of Triage*.
21. As this book goes to press, the United States Census Bureau has reported that the world's population will reach 6.2 billion by the year 2000. The significance of that figure is underscored when one notes that there were about 2.6 billion people in the world in 1950 and 4.9 billion in mid-1985.

EPILOGUE
SOME CONCLUDING REFLECTIONS
ON A CENTURY OF PROGRESS

1. See, for example, Browning, "The Government Experts," in *The Holocaust*, ed. Friedlander and Milton. Browning discusses the case of Bernhard Lösener and Wilhelm Melchers. Concentrating on the latter, who used his position in the Middle Eastern section of the German Foreign Office to argue successfully against the deportation of denaturalized Turkish Jews from Germany and France and of Palestinian Jews held by the Germans, Browning observes that "such incidents demonstrate that even in the civil service of Nazi Germany, individuals with courage and ingenuity could act to save thousands of lives." To keep the record straight, he also adds: "Unfortunately, such obstruction was offered by a mere handful, while the vast majority of their colleagues passively or actively abetted the Final Solution." See p. 194.
2. Sereny, *Into That Darkness*, p. 363.
3. Ibid., p. 351.
4. Ibid., pp. 13, 23.
5. Ibid., pp. 23–24.
6. See Höss, *Commandant of Auschwitz*.
7. Sereny, *Into That Darkness*, p. 25.
8. Ibid., pp. 27, 28.
9. Ibid., pp. 29, 35.
10. Ibid., p. 103.
11. Ibid., p. 113.
12. Ibid., pp. 149, 250.

13. Ibid., pp. 157, 162, 232. See also Alexander Donat, ed., *The Death Camp Treblinka: A Documentary*, p. 14. Donat's book, which features eyewitness accounts by survivors of Treblinka, is a valuable complement to Sereny's work.

14. Sereny, *Into That Darkness*, pp. 202, 164, 200.

15. Ibid., p. 249.

16. Ibid., p. 363.

17. Ibid., pp. 361.

18. Ibid., p. 362.

19. Ibid., pp. 231, 232.

20. Ibid., p. 15.

21. For more detail on Oskar Schindler, see Thomas Keneally, *Schindler's List*. The title of this account is apt, for in addition to referring to Schindler's record about his Jewish workers, the German word *List* means "cunning." Schindler possessed it abundantly and for good ends. Another remarkable story—that of Hermann "Fritz" Graebe—is told by Douglas K. Huneke in *The Moses of Rovno*. Graebe, the only German citizen who volunteered to testify against the Nazis at Nuremberg, was a structural engineer during World War II. Assigned to the Ukraine by the Railroad Administration of the Third Reich, he was horrified by the murder of nearly 1,500 Jewish men by Nazi killing squads. His response was to build a rescue network that protected hundreds of Jews. At the war's end, he used his own train to bring scores of them across Allied lines to freedom.

22. Keneally, *Schindler's List*, p. 371.

23. Jean Améry, *At the Mind's Limits: Contemplations by a Survivor on Auschwitz and Its Realities*, p. 28. Born in Austria as Hans Maier in 1912, Améry fled Nazism by going to Belgium in 1938. There he later joined the resistance. Captured by the Nazis in 1943, he was tortured and sent to a series of concentration camps, including Auschwitz. He took his own life in 1978, but not before writing a series of remarkable essays about his Holocaust experiences. See also his *Radical Humanism: Selected Essays*.

24. Améry, *At the Mind's Limits*, p. 28.

25. Perhaps the most ambitious and promising work of this kind—incomplete at the time of this writing—is the Altruistic Personality Project, which is headed by Samuel P. Oliner. This sociologist is a Holocaust survivor who was hidden by Polish Catholics during World War II. His important autobiography, *Restless Memories*, tells that story. Oliner has interviewed hundreds of rescuers and survivors to clarify the factors and motivations that led people to save Jewish lives during the Nazi era. The findings of his study are scheduled for publication in 1987 under the title *Roots of Heroism: Rescue Behavior in Nazi-Occupied Europe*. Although exceptions to them exist, among Oliner's more important discoveries are the following: (1) rescuers, women and men alike, came from different social classes and diverse occupations; (2) they had learned and deeply internalized values such as helpfulness, responsibility, fairness, justice, compassion, and friendship; (3) they had friends in groups outside of their own family circles or immediate communities; (4) they were tolerant of differences and felt responsible for many kinds of people; (5) they had high levels of self-confidence and self-esteem and were not afraid to take calculated risks; (6) they knew what was happening around them, and, in addition, benefited from a supportive emotional network—their rescue efforts met with approval from family members or others who could be trusted. Oliner believes that, if he were in trouble and could identify persons with these qualities, his chances of receiving assistance would be excellent.

26. Pierre Sauvage was born during the Holocaust in the French village of Le Chambon, which is discussed in Chapter 8. A distinguished filmmaker, he has produced a documentary, *Weapons of the Spirit*, about that place. He also heads "The Friends of Le Chambon," an organization that honors those who saved Jews during the Holocaust. His words are quoted by permission.

Selected Bibliography

I. BOOKS

Abrahamson, Irving, ed. *Against Silence: The Voice and Vision of Elie Wiesel*. 3 vols. New York: Holocaust Library, 1985.

Abzug, Robert H. *Inside the Vicious Heart: Americans and the Liberation of Nazi Concentration Camps*. New York: Oxford University Press, 1985.

Améry, Jean. *At the Mind's Limits: Contemplations by a Survivor on Auschwitz and Its Realities*. Translated by Sidney Rosenfeld and Stella P. Rosenfeld. New York: Schocken Books, 1986.

————. *Radical Humanism: Selected Essays*. Edited and translated by Sidney Rosenfeld and Stella P. Rosenfeld. Bloomington: Indiana University Press, 1984.

Arendt, Hannah. *Eichmann in Jerusalem: A Report on the Banality of Evil*. New York: The Viking Press, 1963.

————. *The Jew as Pariah: Jewish Identity and Politics in the Modern Age*. Edited by Ron H. Feldman. New York: Grove Press, 1978.

————. *The Origins of Totalitarianism*. New York: Harcourt Brace Jovanovich, 1973.

Aristotle. *The Politics*. Translated by T. A. Sinclair. Baltimore: Penguin Books, 1962.

Astor, Gerald. *The Last Nazi: The Life and Times of Dr. Joseph Mengele*. New York: Donald I. Fine, 1985.

Barth, Karl. *Church Dogmatics*, II/2. Translated by G. W. Bromiley et al. Edinburgh: T & T. Clark, 1957.

Bartov, Omer. *The Eastern Front, 1941–45, German Troops and the Barbarisation of Warfare*. New York: St. Martin's Press, 1986.

Bauer, Yehuda. *American Jewry and the Holocaust*. Detroit: Wayne State University Press, 1981.

————. *A History of the Holocaust*. New York: Franklin Watts, 1982.

————. *The Holocaust in Historical Perspective*. Seattle: University of Washington Press, 1978.

————. *They Chose Life: Jewish Resistance in the Holocaust*. New York: American Jewish Committee, 1973.

————, and Rotenstreich, Nathan, eds. *The Holocaust as Historical Experience*. New York: Holmes & Meier, 1981.

Baum, Rainer C. *The Holocaust and the German Elite: Genocide and National Suicide in Germany, 1871–1945*. Totowa, NJ: Rowman and Littlefield, 1981.

Bauminger, Arieh L. *Roll of Honour*. Tel Aviv: "Hamenora" Publishing House, 1971.

Belth, Nathan C. *A Promise to Keep: A Narrative of the American Encounter with Anti-Semitism*. New York: Times Books, 1979.

Ben-Sasson, Haim Hillel, ed. *A History of the Jewish People*. Cambridge, MA: Harvard University Press, 1976.

Bentley, James. *Martin Niemöller, 1892–1984*. New York: The Free Press, 1984.

Berenbaum, Michael. *The Vision of the Void: Theological Reflections of the Works of Elie Wiesel*. Middletown, CT: Wesleyan University Press, 1979.

Berger, Alan L. *Crisis and Covenant: The Holocaust in American Jewish Fiction.* Albany: State University of New York Press, 1985.

Berkovits, Eliezer. *Crisis and Faith.* New York: Sanhedrin Press, 1976.

———. *Faith after the Holocaust.* New York: KTAV, 1973.

———. *With God in Hell.* New York: Sanhedrin Press, 1979.

Beyerchen, Alan D. *Scientists Under Hitler: Politics and the Physics Community in the Third Reich.* New Haven: Yale University Press, 1977.

Bienert, Walther. *Martin Luther und die Juden: Ein Quellenbuch mit zeitgenössichen Illustrationen, mit Einführungen und Erläuterungen.* Frankfurt am Main: Evangelisches Verlagswerk, 1982.

Bierman, John. *Righteous Gentile: The Story of Raoul Wallenberg, the Missing Hero of the Holocaust.* New York: Viking, 1981.

Blackburn, Gilmer W. *Education in the Third Reich: A Study of Race and History in Nazi Textbooks.* Albany: State University of New York Press, 1984.

Blatter, Janet, and Milton, Sybil. *The Art of the Holocaust.* London: Pan Books, 1982.

Blum, Howard. *Wanted!: The Search for Nazis in America.* New York: Fawcett Crest Books, 1977.

Bonhoeffer, Dietrich. *Letters and Papers from Prison.* Edited by Eberhard Bethge. Rev. ed. New York: Macmillan, 1973.

———. *No Rusty Swords.* Translated by H. Robertson and John Bowden. London: Fontana, 1974.

Borchert, H. H., and Merz, Georg, eds. *Martin Luther: Ausgewählte Werke,* Munich: 1936.

Borkin, Joseph. *The Crime and Punishment of I. G. Farben.* New York: The Free Press, 1978.

Borowski, Tadeusz. *This Way for the Gas, Ladies and Gentlemen; and Other Stories.* Translated by Barbara Vedder. New York: Penguin Books, 1967.

Bracher, Karl Dietrich. *The German Dictatorship.* New York: Praeger, 1970.

Braham, Randolph L. *The Politics of Genocide: The Holocaust in Hungary.* New York: Columbia University Press, 1981.

Brandon, S. G. F. *The Fall of Jerusalem and the Christian Church.* London: S.P.C.K., 1968.

Brenner, Reeve Robert. *The Faith and Doubt of Holocaust Survivors.* New York: The Free Press, 1980.

Broszat, Martin. *The Hitler State: The Foundation and Development of the Internal Structure of the Third Reich.* Translated by John W. Hiden. New York: Longman, 1981.

Brown, Robert McAfee. *Elie Wiesel: Messenger to All Humanity.* Notre Dame, IN: University of Notre Dame Press, 1983.

Browning, Christopher. *Fateful Months: Essays on the Emergence of the Final Solution.* New York: Holmes & Meier, 1985.

———. *The Final Solution and the German Foreign Office.* New York: Holmes & Meier, 1978.

Bullock, Alan. *Hitler: A Study in Tyranny.* New York: Bantam Books, 1961.

Busch, Eberhard. *Karl Barth: His Life from Letters and Autobiographical Texts.* Translated by John Bowden. Philadelphia: Fortress Press, 1976.

Byrnes, Robert F. *Antisemitism in Modern France:* Vol. I: *The Prologue to the Dreyfus Affair.* New Brunswick, NJ: Rutgers University Press, 1950.

———. *Pobedonostsev: His Life and Thought.* Bloomington: Indiana University Press, 1968.

Camus, Albert. *The Rebel: An Essay on Man in Revolt*. Translated by Anthony Bower. New York: Vintage Books, 1956.

Cargas, Harry James. *A Christian Response to the Holocaust*. Denver: Stonehenge Books, 1981.

————. *Harry James Cargas in Conversation with Elie Wiesel*. New York: Paulist Press, 1976.

————. *The Holocaust: An Annotated Bibliography*. 2d ed. Chicago: American Library Association, 1985.

————, ed. *When God and Man Failed: Non-Jewish Views of the Holocaust*. New York: Macmillan, 1981.

Carr-Saunders, A. M. *World Population*. Oxford: Clarendon Press, 1936.

Chapman, Guy. *The Dreyfus Case, a Reassessment*. New York: Reynal and Company, 1955.

Charny, Israel W. *How Can We Commit the Unthinkable?: Genocide, the Human Cancer*. New York: Hearst Books, 1982.

Chary, Frederick B. *The Bulgarian Jews and the Final Solution, 1940–1944*. Pittsburgh: University of Pittsburgh Press, 1972.

Chazan, Robert, and Raphael, Marc Lee, eds. *Modern Jewish History: A Source Reader*. New York: Schocken Books, 1974.

Chorover, Stephan L. *From Genesis to Genocide: The Meaning of Human Nature and the Power of Behavior Control*. Cambridge, MA: MIT Press, 1979.

Cipolla, Carlo M. *The Economic History of World Population*. Harmondsworth, Middlesex: Penguin Books, 1970.

————, ed. *The Fontana Economic History of Europe*. London: Collins/Fontana, 1973.

Clare, George. *Last Waltz in Vienna*. New York: Holt, Rinehart and Winston, 1980.

Clark, Alan. *Barbarossa: The Russian-German Conflict, 1941–45*. New York: William Morrow, 1965.

Cochrane, Arthur C. *The Church's Confession under Hitler*, 2d ed. Pittsburgh: The Pickwick Press, 1976.

Cohen, Arthur A. *The Natural and the Supernatural Jew*. New York: Pantheon Books, 1962.

————. *The Tremendum: A Theological Interpretation of the Holocaust*. New York: Crossroad Publishing Company, 1981.

Cohen, Asher. *The Halutz Resistance in Hungary 1942–1944*. Translated by Carl Alpert. New York: Institute for Holocaust Studies, 1986.

Cohen, Elie A. *Human Behavior in the Concentration Camp*. Translated by M. H. Braaksma. New York: W. W. Norton, 1953.

Cohn, Norman. *Warrant for Genocide: The Myth of the Jewish World-Conspiracy and the Protocols of the Elders of Zion*. New York: Harper & Row, 1967.

Conway, John S. *The Nazi Persecution of the Churches, 1933–45*. New York: Basic Books, 1968.

Czerniakow, Adam. *The Warsaw Diary of Adam Czerniakow*. Edited by Raul Hilberg, Stanislaw Staron, and Josef Kermisz. Translated by Stanislaw Staron, et al. New York: Stein and Day, 1979.

Davidson, Eugene. *The Trial of the Germans: An Account of the Twenty-two Defendants before the International Military Tribunal at Nuremburg*. New York: Macmillan, 1966.

Davies, William David. *The Setting of the Sermon on the Mount*. Cambridge: Cambridge University Press, 1964.

Dawidowicz, Lucy S. *The Holocaust and the Historians*. Cambridge, MA: Harvard University Press, 1981.

————. *The War Against the Jews, 1933-1945*. Tenth Anniversary Edition. New York: The Free Press, 1985.

Delbo, Charlotte. *None of Us Will Return*, vol. I of *Auschwitz and After*. Translated by John Githens. Boston: Beacon Press, 1978.

————. *Une Connaissance inutile*, vol II of *Auschwitz and After*. Paris: Les Éditions de Minuit, 1970.

————. *Mesure de nos jours*, vol. III of *Auschwitz and After*. Paris: Les Éditions de Minuit, 1971.

Des Pres, Terrence. *The Survivor: An Anatomy of Life in the Death Camps*. New York: Oxford University Press, 1976.

Dimsdale, Joel E., ed. *Survivors, Victims, and Perpetrators: Essays on the Nazi Holocaust*. New York: Hemisphere Publishing Company, 1980.

Dinnerstein, Leonard. *America and the Survivors of the Holocaust*. New York: Columbia University Press, 1982.

Dinur, Yehiel (Ka-tzetnik 135633). *Star Eternal*. Translated by Nina Dinur. New York: Arbor House, 1971.

Dobroszycki, Lucjan, ed. *The Chronicle of the Łódź Ghetto*. Translated by Richard Lourie. New Haven: Yale University Press, 1984.

Donat, Alexander. *The Holocaust Kingdom*. New York: Holocaust Library, 1978.

————, ed. *The Death Camp Treblinka: A Documentary*. New York: Holocaust Library, 1979.

Dumbach, Annette E., and Newborn, Jud. *Shattering the German Night: The Story of the White Rose*. Boston: Little, Brown and Company, 1986.

Edelheit, Abraham J., and Edelheit, Hershel, eds. *Bibliography on Holocaust Literature*. Boulder, CO: Westview Press, 1986.

Edwards, Mark U., Jr. *Luther's Last Battles: A Study of the Polemics of the Older Luther, 1531–1546*. Ithaca: Cornell University Press, 1983.

Eisenberg, Azriel, ed., *Witness to the Holocaust*. New York: The Pilgrim Press, 1981.

Eitinger, Leo. *Concentration Camp Survivors in Norway and Israel*. London: Allen & Unwin, 1964.

————; Krell, Robert; and Rieck, Miriam. *The Psychological and Medical Effects of Concentration Camps and Related Persecutions on Survivors of the Holocaust: A Research Bibliography*. Vancouver: The University of British Columbia Press, 1985.

Eliach, Yaffa. *Hasidic Tales of the Holocaust: The First Original Hasidic Tales in a Century*. New York: Oxford University Press, 1982.

Elliot, Gil. *Twentieth Century Book of the Dead*. New York: Charles Scribner's Sons, 1972.

Epstein, Helen. *Children of the Holocaust: Conversations with Sons and Daughters of Survivors*. New York: G. P. Putnam's Sons, 1979.

Erickson, Robert P. *Theologians under Hitler: Gerhard Kittel, Paul Althaus, and Emanuel Hirsch*. New Haven: Yale University Press, 1985.

Ezrahi, Sidra Dekoven. *By Words Alone: The Holocaust in Literature*. Chicago: The University of Chicago Press, 1980.

Fackenheim, Emil L. *Encounters between Judaism and Modern Philosophy*. New York: Basic Books, 1973.

————. *God's Presence in History: Jewish Affirmations and Philosophical Reflections*. New York: Harper & Row, 1972.

————. *The Jewish Return into History: Reflections in the Age of Auschwitz and a New Jerusalem*. New York: Schocken Books, 1978.

————— . *Quest for Past and Future: Essays in Jewish Theology*. Bloomington: Indiana University Press, 1968.

————— . *To Mend the World: Foundations of Future Jewish Thought*. New York: Schocken Books, 1982.

Falk, Harvey. *Jesus the Pharisee: A New Look at the Jewishness of Jesus*. Ramsey, NJ: Paulist Press, 1985.

Fanon, Frantz. *The Wretched of the Earth*. Translated by Constance Farrington. New York: Grove Press, 1968.

Feig, Konnilyn G. *Hitler's Death Camps: The Sanity of Madness*. New York: Holmes & Meier, 1981.

Fein, Helen. *Accounting for Genocide: National Responses and Jewish Victimization during the Holocaust*. New York: The Free Press, 1979.

Feingold, Henry L. *The Politics of Rescue: The Roosevelt Administration and the Holocaust, 1938–1945*. New York: Holocaust Library, 1980.

Fenelon, Fania. *Playing for Time*. New York: Atheneum, 1977.

Ferencz, Benjamin. *Less than Slaves: Jewish Forced Labor and the Quest for Compensation*. Cambridge, MA: Harvard University Press, 1979.

Fest, Joachim. *The Face of the Third Reich*. Translated by Michael Bullock. New York: Pantheon Books, 1970.

————— . *Hitler*. New York: Harcourt Brace Jovanovich, 1974.

Festinger, Leon. *A Theory of Cognitive Dissonance*. Evanston: Row, Peterson, 1957.

————— ; Riecken, Henry W.; and Schachter, Stanley. *When Prophecy Fails*. Minneapolis: University of Minnesota Press, 1956.

Feuer, Lewis S., ed. *Marx and Engels: Basic Writings on Politics and Philosophy*. Garden City, NY: Doubleday, 1959.

Fine, Ellen. *Legacy of Night: The Literary Universe of Elie Wiesel*. Albany: State University of New York Press, 1982.

Finger, Seymour Maxwell, ed. *American Jewry During the Holocaust: A Report Sponsored by the American Jewish Commission on the Holocaust*. New York: Holmes & Meier, 1985.

————— . *Their Brothers' Keepers: American Jewry and the Holocaust*. New York: Holmes & Meier, 1986.

Flannery, Edward H. *The Anguish of the Jews: Twenty-three Centuries of Anti-Semitism*. New York: Macmillan, 1976.

Fleischner, Eva, ed. *Auschwitz: Beginning of a New Era?* New York: KTAV, 1977.

Fleming, Gerald. *Hitler and the Final Solution*. Berkeley and Los Angeles: University of California Press, 1984.

Flender, Harold. *Rescue in Denmark*. New York: Simon and Schuster, 1963.

Flinker, Moshe. *Young Moshe's Diary: The Spiritual Torment of a Jewish Boy in Nazi Europe*. Edited by Shaul Esh. Jerusalem: Yad Vashem, 1976.

Frank, Anne. *Anne Frank: The Diary of a Young Girl*. Translated by B. M. Mooyaart-Doubleday. New York: Pocket Books, 1974.

Freud, Sigmund. *Civilization and Its Discontents*. Translated by James Strachey. New York: W. W. Norton, 1961.

————— . *The Future of an Illusion*. Translated by W. D. Robson-Scott. New York: Doubleday, 1957.

Friedlander, Henry, and Milton, Sybil, eds. *The Holocaust: Ideology, Bureaucracy, and Genocide*. Millwood, NY: Kraus International Publications, 1980.

Friedlander, Saul. *Pius XII and the Third Reich: A Documentation*. Translated by Charles Fullman. New York: Alfred A. Knopf, 1966.

Friedman, Philip. *Roads to Extinction: Essays on the Holocaust*. Edited by Ada June Friedman. New York: The Jewish Publication Society of America, 1980.

————. *Their Brothers' Keepers*. New York: Holocaust Library, 1978.

Gager, John C. *The Origins of Anti-Semitism: Attitudes toward Judaism in Pagan and Christian Antiquity*. New York: Oxford University Press, 1983.

Gerth, H. H., and Mills, C. Wright, eds. *From Max Weber: Essays in Sociology*. New York: Oxford University Press, 1946.

Gilbert, Martin. *Auschwitz and the Allies*. New York: Holt, Rinehart and Winston, 1981.

————. *Exile and Return: The Jewish Struggle for a Jewish Homeland*. Philadelphia: J. P. Lippincott, 1978.

————. *The Holocaust*. New York: Hill and Wang, 1978.

————. *The Holocaust: A History of the Jews of Europe during the Second World War*. New York: Holt, Rinehart and Winston, 1985.

Gisevius, Hans Bernd. *Wo Ist Nebe?* Zurich: Droemer, 1966.

Glatstein, Jacob; Knox, Israel; and Margoshes, Samuel, eds. *Anthology of Holocaust Literature*. New York: Atheneum, 1975.

Goldin, Judah, ed. *The Fathers According to Rabbi Nathan*. New Haven: Yale University Press, 1955.

Goldschmidt, Dietrich, and Kraus, Hans-Joachim, eds. *Der Ungekündigte Bund: Neue Begegnung von Juden und Christlicher*. Stuttgart: Gemeinde Kreuz-Verlag, 1962.

Gordon, Sarah. *Hitler, Germans, and the "Jewish Question."* Princeton, NJ: Princeton University Press, 1984.

Greenberg, Louis. *The Jews in Russia*. New York: Schocken Books, 1976.

Grobman, Alex; Landes, Daniel; and Milton, Sybil, eds. *Genocide: Critical Issues of the Holocaust*. Los Angeles: Simon Wiesenthal Center, 1983.

Gruchmann, Lothar. *Euthanasie und Justiz im Dritten Reich*. Stuttgart: Deutsche Verlags-Anstalt, 1972.

Grunberger, Richard. *Red Rising in Bavaria*. New York: St. Martin's Press, 1973.

————. *The 12-Year Reich· A Social History of Nazi Germany 1933–1945*. New York: Holt, Rinehart and Winston, 1971.

Gutman, Yisrael. *The Jews of Warsaw, 1939–1943: Ghetto, Underground, Revolt*. Translated by Ina Friedman. Bloomington: Indiana University Press, 1982.

Gutman, Yisrael, and Krakowski, Shmuel. *Poles and Jews Between the Wars*. New York: Schocken Books, 1986.

Gutteridge, Richard. *Open Thy Mouth for the Dumb: The German Evangelical Church and the Jews 1879–1950*. Oxford: Basil Blackwell, 1976.

Haeckel, Ernest. *Die Lebenswunder*. Stuttgart: A. Kröner, 1904.

Haffner, Sebastian. *The Meaning of Hitler*. Translated by Ewald Osers. Cambridge, MA: Harvard University Press, 1983.

Halasz, Nicholas. *Captain Dreyfus: The Story of a Mass Hysteria*. New York: Simon and Schuster, 1955.

Halder, Franz. *Kriegstagebuch*. 2 vols. Stuttgart: W. Kohlhammer, 1963.

Hallie, Philip P. *Lest Innocent Blood Be Shed: The Story of the Village of Le Chambon and How Goodness Happened There*. New York: Harper & Row, 1979.

Hamerow, Theodore S. *Restoration, Revolution, Reaction: Economics and Politics in Germany, 1815–1871*. Princeton, NJ: Princeton University Press, 1958.

Handlin, Oscar, *The Uprooted*. 2d ed. enl. Boston: Atlantic, Little, Brown, 1973.

Hanser, Richard. *A Noble Treason: The Revolt of the Munich Students Against Hitler*. New York: G. P. Putnam's Sons, 1979.

Hart-Davis, Duff. *Hitler's Games: The 1936 Olympics*. New York: Harper & Row, 1986.

Hartman, Geoffrey H., ed. *Bitburg in Moral and Political Perspective.* Bloomington: Indiana University Press, 1986.

Haubtmann, Pierre, ed. *Carnets de P.-J. Proudhon: Texte inédit et intégral.* 2 vols. Paris: M. Rivière, 1961.

Hausner, Gideon. *Justice in Jerusalem.* New York: Harper & Row, 1966.

Hay, Malcolm. *Europe and the Jews: The Pressure of Christendom on the People of Israel for 1900 Years.* Boston: Beacon Press, 1960.

Hegel, Georg W. F. *Lectures on the Philosophy of World History: Introduction, Reason in History.* Translated by H. B. Nisbet. Cambridge: Cambridge University Press, 1975.

_____. *The Phenomenology of Mind.* Translated by J. B. Baillie. London: Allen & Unwin, 1949.

_____. *Philosophy of Right.* Translated by T. M. Knox. New York: Oxford University Press, 1967.

Heger, Heinz. *The Men with the Pink Triangle.* Translated by David Fernbach. Boston: Alyson Publications, 1980.

Heller, Celia S. *On the Edge of Destruction: Jews of Poland between the Two World Wars.* New York: Columbia University Press, 1977.

Hellman, Peter. *Avenue of the Righteous.* New York: Atheneum, 1978.

Helmreich, Ernst Christian. *The German Churches under Hitler: Background, Struggle, and Epilogue.* Detroit: Wayne State University Press, 1979.

Hertz, Joseph H., ed. *The Authorized Daily Prayer Book.* New York: Bloch, 1948.

Hertzberg, Arthur. *The French Enlightenment and the Jews.* New York: Columbia University Press, 1968.

Herzstein, Robert Edwin. *The Nazis.* Alexandria, VA: Time-Life Books, 1980.

Heyman, Eva. *The Diary of Eva Heyman.* Translated by Moshe M. Kohn. Jerusalem: Yad Vashem, 1974.

Hilberg, Raul. *The Destruction of the European Jews.* 3 vols., rev. ed. New York: Holmes & Meier, 1985.

_____. *Documents of Destruction: Germany and Jewry, 1933–1945.* Chicago: Quadrangle Books, 1971.

Hillesum, Etty. *An Interrupted Life: The Diaries of Etty Hillesum, 1941–1943.* Translated by J.G. Gaarlandt. New York: Washington Square Press, 1985.

Hitler, Adolf. *Mein Kampf.* Translated by Ralph Manheim. Boston: Houghton Mifflin, 1971.

_____. *Hitler's Secret Book.* Translated by Salvator Attanasio. New York: Grove Press, 1983.

Hoffman, Peter. *The History of the German Resistance 1933–1945.* Translated by Richard Barry. Cambridge, MA: The MIT Press, 1977.

Hofstadter, Richard. *Social Darwinism in America.* Boston: Beacon Press, 1955.

Höhne, Heinz. *The Order of the Death's Head: The Story of Hitler's SS.* Translated by Richard Barry. New York: Ballantine Books, 1971.

Holborn, Hajo, ed. *Republic to Reich: The Making of the Nazi Revolution.* Translated by Ralph Manheim. New York: Pantheon Books, 1972.

Höss, Rudolf. *Commandant of Auschwitz.* Translated by Constantine Fitzgibbon. London: Pan Books, 1974.

Hovannisian, Richard G. *Armenia on the Road to Independence, 1918.* Berkeley and Los Angeles: University of California Press, 1967.

_____. *The Armenian Holocaust: A Bibliography Relating to the Deportations, Massacres of the Armenian People, 1915–1923.* Cambridge, MA: Armenian Heritage Press, 1978.

Huneke, Douglas K. *The Moses of Rovno*. New York: Dodd Mead, 1986.

Insdorf, Annette. *Indelible Shadows: Film and the Holocaust*. New York: Random House, 1983.

Isaac, Jules. *The Teaching of Contempt: Christian Roots of Anti-Semitism*. Edited by Claire Huchet-Bishop. Translated by Helen Weaver. New York: Holt, Rinehart and Winston, 1964.

Jaeckel, Eberhard. *Hitler in History*. Hanover, NH: University Press of New England, 1984.

————. *Hitler's Weltanschauung: A Blueprint for Power*. Translated by Herbert Arnold. Middletown, CT: Wesleyan University Press, 1972.

James, Harold. *The German Slump: Politics and Economics 1924–1936*. Oxford: Clarendon Press, 1986.

Josephus. *The Jewish War*. Translated by H. St. J. Thackeray. Cambridge, MA: Harvard University Press, 1968.

Kamenetsky, Christa. *Children's Literature in Hitler's Germany*. Athens: Ohio University Press, 1984.

Kaplan, Chaim A. *Scroll of Agony: The Warsaw Diary of Chaim A. Kaplan*. Edited and translated by Abraham I. Katsh. New York: Collier Books, 1973.

Karski, Jan. *The Great Powers and Poland 1919–1945: From Versailles to Yalta*. Lanham, MD: University Press of America, 1985.

Kater, Michael H. *The Nazi Party: A Social Profile of Members and Leaders, 1919–1945* Cambridge, MA: Harvard University Press, 1983.

Katz, Esther, and Ringelheim, Joan Miriam, eds. *Proceedings of the Conference on Women Surviving—the Holocaust*. New York: The Institute for Research in History, 1982.

Katz, Jacob. *From Prejudice to Destruction: Anti-Semitism, 1700–1933*. Cambridge, MA: Harvard University Press, 1980.

Katz, Steven T. *Post-Holocaust Dialogues: Critical Studies in Modern Jewish Thought*. New York: New York University Press, 1983.

Katzenelson, Yitzak. *The Song of the Murdered Jewish People*. Translated by Noah H. Rosenbloom. [Tel Aviv]: Hakibbutz Hameuchad Publishing House, 1980.

Kazarian, Haigaz K. *Minutes of Secret Meetings Organizing the Turkish Genocide of the Armenians*. Boston: Commemorative Committee on the 50th Anniversary of the Turkish Massacres of the Armenians, 1965.

Keneally, Thomas. *Schindler's List*. New York: Penguin Books, 1983.

Kenrick, Donald, and Puxon, Gratton. *The Destiny of Europe's Gypsies*. New York: Basic Books, 1972.

Kieniewicz, Stefan. *The Emancipation of the Polish Peasantry*. Chicago: University of Chicago Press, 1969.

Klépfisz , Hészel. *Culture of Compassion: The Spirit of Polish Jewry from Hasidism to the Holocaust*. New York: KTAV, 1983.

Korczak, Janusz. *Ghetto Diary*. Translated by Jerzy Bachrach and Barbara Krzywicka (Vedder). New York: Holocaust Library, 1978.

Krakowski, Shmuel. *The War of the Doomed: Jewish Armed Resistance in Poland, 1942–1944*. New York: Holmes & Meier, 1984.

————, ed. *Einsatzgruppen*. New York: Schocken Books, 1984.

Krausnick, Helmut; Bucheim, Hans; Brozat, Martin; and Jacobsen, Hans-Adolf. *Anatomy of the SS State*. Translated by Richard Barry, Marian Jackson, and Dorothy Long. New York: Walker, 1968.

Kren, George, and Rappoport, Leon. *The Holocaust and the Crisis of Human Behavior*. New York: Holmes & Meier, 1980.

Kuper, Leo. *Genocide: Its Political Use in the Twentieth Century*. New Haven: Yale University Press, 1981.

Landes, David S. *The Unbound Prometheus: Technological Change and Industrial Development in Western Europe from 1750 to the Present*. Cambridge: Cambridge University Press, 1969.

Langer, Lawrence L. *The Age of Atrocity: Death in Modern Literature*. Boston: Beacon Press, 1978.

————. *The Holocaust and the Literary Imagination*. New Haven: Yale University Press, 1975.

————. *Versions of Survival: The Holocaust and the Human Spirit*. Albany: State University of New York Press, 1982.

Langer, Walter C. *The Mind of Adolf Hitler: The Secret Wartime Report*. New York: Basic Books, 1972.

Lanzmann, Claude. *Shoah: An Oral History of the Holocaust*. New York: Pantheon Books, 1985.

Laqueur, Walter. *The Terrible Secret: Suppression of the Truth about Hitler's "Final Solution."* Boston: Little, Brown and Company, 1980.

————, and Breitman, Richard. *Breaking the Silence*. New York: Simon and Schuster, 1986.

Laska, Vera. *Nazism, Resistance & Holocaust in World War II: A Bibliography*. Metuchen, NJ: Scarecrow, 1985.

Lederer, Zdenek. *Ghetto Theresienstadt*. New York: Howard Fertig, 1982.

Legters, Lyman H., ed. *Western Society after the Holocaust*. Boulder, CO: Westview Press, 1983.

Lemkin, Raphael. *Axis Rule in Occupied Europe*. Washington: Carnegie Endowment for International Peace, 1944.

Lengyel, Olga. *Five Chimneys: The Story of Auschwitz*. New York: Howard Fertig, 1983.

Levi, Primo. *Moments of Reprieve*. Translated by Ruth Feldman. New York: Summit Books, 1986.

————. *The Periodic Table*. Translated by Raymond Rosenthal. New York: Schocken Books, 1984.

————. *The Reawakening*. Translated by Stuart Woolf. New York: Summit Books, 1985.

————. *Survival in Auschwitz: The Nazi Assault on Humanity*. Translated by Stuart Woolf. New York: Collier Books, 1958.

Levin, Nora. *The Holocaust: The Destruction of European Jewry 1933–1945*. New York: Schocken Books, 1973.

Lewinska, Pelagia. *Twenty Months at Auschwitz*. Translated by Albert Teichner. New York: Lyle Stuart, 1968.

Lewy, Guenther. *The Roman Catholic Church and the Third Reich*. New York: Mc-Graw-Hill, 1964.

Lifton, Robert Jay. *The Nazi Doctors: Medical Killing and the Psychology of Genocide*. New York: Basic Books, 1986.

Lipstadt, Deborah E. *Beyond Belief: The American Press and the Coming of the Holocaust, 1933–1945*. New York: The Free Press, 1986.

Littell, Franklin H. *The Crucifixion of the Jews*. New York: Harper & Row, 1975.

————, and Locke, Hubert G., eds. *The German Church Struggle and the Holocaust*. Detroit: Wayne State University Press, 1974.

Locke, Hubert G., ed. *Exile in the Fatherland: Martin Niemöller's Letters from Moabit Prison.* Translated by Ernst Kaemke, Kathy Elias, and Jacklyn Wilferd. Grand Rapids: William B. Eerdmans, 1986.

Lovin, Robin W. *Christian Faith and Public Choices: The Social Ethics of Barth, Brunner, and Bonhoeffer.* Philadelphia: Fortress Press, 1984.

Lowenstein, Rudolph M. *Christians and Jews: A Psychoanalytic Study.* New York: Delta Books, 1961.

Lowenstein, Sharon R. *Token Refuge: The Story of the Jewish Refugee Shelter at Oswego, 1944–1946.* Bloomington: Indiana University Press, 1986.

Lubetkin, Zivia. *In the Days of the Destruction and Revolt.* Translated by Ishai Tubbin. [Tel Aviv]: Hakibbutz Hameuchad Publishing House, 1981.

Luel, Steven A., and Marcus, Paul. *Psychoanalytic Reflections on the Holocaust: Selected Essays.* New York: KTAV, 1984.

Lukas, Richard C. *The Forgotten Holocaust: The Poles under German Occupation, 1939–1944.* Lexington: University of Kentucky Press, 1986.

Luther, Martin. *On the Jews and Their Lies.* Translated by Martin H. Bertram. In *Luther's Works,* 47:137–306. Edited by Franklin Sherman and Helmut T. Lehman. Philadelphia: Fortress Press, 1971.

Macpherson, C. B. *The Political Theory of Possessive Individualism: Hobbes to Locke.* Oxford: Clarendon Press, 1962.

Marcus, Joseph. *Social and Political History of the Jews in Poland, 1919–1939.* New York: Mouton, 1983.

Marrus, Michael R. *The Unwanted: European Refugees in the Twentieth Century.* New York: Oxford University Press, 1985.

———, and Paxton, Robert O. *Vichy France and the Jews.* New York: Basic Books, 1981.

Maser, Werner, ed. *Hitler's Letters and Notes.* Translated by Arnold Pomerans. New York: Harper & Row, 1973.

Massing, Paul. *Rehearsal for Destruction: A Study of Political Anti-Semitism in Imperial Germany.* New York: Harper & Brothers, 1949.

Maybaum, Ignaz. *The Face of God After Auschwitz.* Amsterdam: Polak & Van Gennep, 1965.

McLellan, David, ed. *Karl Marx: Selected Writings.* Oxford: Oxford University Press, 1977.

Mendes-Flohr, Paul R., and Reinharz, Jehuda, eds. *The Jew in the Modern World: A Documentary History.* New York: Oxford University Press, 1980.

Mitchell, Allan. *Revolution in Bavaria.* Princeton: Princeton University Press, 1965.

Mitscherlich, Alexander, and Mielke, Fred. *Doctors of Infamy: The Story of the Nazi Medical Crimes.* Translated by Heinz Norden. New York: Henry Schuman, 1949.

Morley, John F. *Vatican Diplomacy and the Jews during the Holocaust 1939–1943.* New York: KTAV, 1980.

Morse, Arthur D. *While Six Million Died: A Chronicle of American Apathy.* New York: Hart Publishing Company, 1967.

Mosse, George. *The Crisis of German Ideology: Intellectual Origins of the Third Reich.* New York: Grosset & Dunlap, 1964.

———. *Toward the Final Solution: A History of European Racism.* New York: Harper & Row, 1978.

Müller, Filip. *Eyewitness Auschwitz: Three Years in the Gas Chambers.* Edited and translated by Suzanne Flatauer. New York: Stein and Day, 1979.

Müller-Hill, Benno. *Tödliche Wissenschaft: Die Aussonderung von Juden, Zigeunern und Geisteskranken 1933–1945*. Reinbeck bei Hamburg: Rowohlt Taschenbuch Verlag, 1985.

Neusner, Jacob. *First-Century Judaism in Crisis*. Nashville: Abingdon, 1975.

_____ . *From Politics to Piety: The Emergence of Pharisaic Judaism*. Englewood Cliffs, NJ: Prentice-Hall, 1973.

Niemöller, Martin. *Of Guilt and Hope*. Translated by Renee Spodheim. New York: Philosophical Library, 1947.

Niewyk, Donald. *The Jews in Weimar Germany*. Baton Rouge: Louisiana State University Press, 1980.

Novitch, Miriam, et al. *Sobibor: Martrydom and Revolt*. New York: Holocaust Library, 1980.

_____ . *Spiritual Resistance: Art from Concentration Camps 1940–1945*. Philadelphia: The Jewish Publication Society, 1982.

Nyiszli, Miklós. *Auschwitz: A Doctor's Eyewitness Report*. Translated by Tibere Kremer and Richard Seaver. Greenwich, CT: Fawcett, 1960.

Oberman, Heiko A. *Luther: Mensch zwischen Gott und Teufel*. Berlin: Severin Siedler, 1982.

_____ . *Wurzeln des Antisemitismus: Christenangst und Judenplage im Zeitalter von Humanismus und Reformation*. Berlin: Severin und Siedler, 1981.

Oliner, Samuel P. *Restless Memories*. 2d ed. Berkeley: Judah Magnus Museum, 1986.

Paléologue, Maurice. *An Intimate Journal of the Dreyfus Case*. Translated by Eric Mosbacher. New York: Criterion Books, 1957.

Pawelczynska, Anna. *Values and Violence in Auschwitz: A Sociological Analysis*. Translated and with an Introduction by Catherine S. Leach. Berkeley and Los Angeles: University of California Press, 1979.

Perl, Gisella. *I Was a Doctor in Auschwitz*. New York: International Universities Press, 1948.

Perrin, Norman. *The New Testament: An Introduction*. New York: Harcourt Brace Jovanovich, 1974.

_____ . *Rediscovering the Teaching of Jesus*. New York: Harper & Row, 1967.

Peters, Joan. *From Time Immemorial: The Origins of the Arab-Jewish Conflict Over Palestine*. New York: Harper & Row, 1984.

Plant, Richard. *The Pink Triangle: The Nazi War Against Homosexuals*. New York: New Republic/Henry Holt, 1986.

Polanyi, Karl. *The Great Transformation: The Political and Economic Origins of Our Time*. Boston: Beacon Press, 1957.

Poliakov, Léon. *Harvest of Hate: The Nazi Program for the Destruction of the Jews of Europe*. New York: Holocaust Library, 1979.

_____ . *The History of Anti-Semitism: From the Time of Christ to the Court Jews*. Translated by Richard Howard. New York: Schocken Books, 1974.

_____ , and Sabille, Jaques. *Jews under the Italian Occupation*. New York: Howard Fertig, 1983.

Posner, Gerald L., and Ware, John. *Mengele: The Complete Story*. New York: McGraw-Hill, 1986.

Potok, Chaim. *Wanderings*. New York: Alfred A. Knopf, 1978.

Presser, Jacob. *The Destruction of the Dutch Jews*. Translated by Arnold Pomerans. New York: E. P. Dutton, 1969.

Pridham, Geoffrey. *Hitler's Rise to Power: The Nazi Movement in Bavaria, 1923–1933* New York: Harper & Row, 1974.

Rabinowitz, Dorothy. *New Lives: Survivors of the Holocaust Living in America*. New York: Avon, 1976.

Ramati, Alexander. *The Assisi Underground: The Priests Who Rescued Jews*. New York: Stein and Day, 1978.

Rector, Frank. *The Nazi Extermination of Homosexuals*. New York: Stein and Day, 1981.

Reitlinger, Gerald. *The Final Solution: The Attempt to Exterminate the Jews of Europe 1939–1945*. New York: Beechhurst Press, 1953.

Remak, Joachim, ed. *The Nazi Years: A Documentary History*. Englewood Cliffs, NJ: Prentice-Hall, 1969.

Rezwinska, Jadwiga, ed. *Amidst a Nightmare of Crime: Manuscripts of Members of Sonderkommandos*. Translated by Krystyna Michalik. Oświęcim: 1973.

Richardson, Herbert W., and Cutler, Donald R., eds. *Transcendence*. Boston: Beacon Press, 1969.

Ringelblum, Emmanuel. *Notes from the Warsaw Ghetto*. New York: Schocken Books, 1974.

_____ . *Polish-Jewish Relations during the Second World War*. Jerusalem: Yad Vashem, 1974.

Rittner, Carol, and Myers, Sondra, eds. *The Courage to Care*. New York: New York University Press, 1986.

Robinson, Jacob. *And the Crooked Shall Be Made Straight: The Eichmann Trial, the Jewish Catastrophe, and Hannah Arendt's Narrative*. New York: Macmillan, 1965.

Rogger, Hans, and Weber, Eugen, eds. *The European Right: A Historical Profile*. Berkeley and Los Angeles: University of California Press, 1965.

Rosenbaum, Irving J. *The Holocaust and Halakhah*. New York: KTAV, 1976.

Rosenberg, Alfred. *Race and Race History: and Other Essays*. Edited by Robert Pois. New York: Harper & Row, 1974.

Rosenfeld, Alvin H. *A Double Dying: Reflections on Holocaust Literature*. Bloomington: Indiana University Press, 1980.

_____ . *Imagining Hitler*. Bloomington: Indiana University Press, 1985.

Rosenfeld, Alvin H. and Greenberg, Irving, eds. *Confronting the Holocaust: The Impact of Elie Wiesel*. Bloomington: Indiana University Press, 1978.

Roskies, David G. *Against the Apocalypse: Responses to Catastrophe in Modern Jewish Culture*. Cambridge, MA: Harvard University Press, 1984.

Ross, Robert W. *So It Was True: The American Protestant Press and the Nazi Persecution of the Jews*. Minneapolis: University of Minnesota Press, 1980.

Rotenstreich, Nathan. *Jews and German Philosophy*. New York: Schocken Books, 1984.

Roth, John K. *A Consuming Fire: Encounters with Elie Wiesel and the Holocaust*. Atlanta: John Knox Press, 1979.

Rothchild, Sylvia, ed. *Voices from the Holocaust*. New York: New American Library, 1981.

Rousset, David. *The Other Kingdom*. Translated by Ramon Gutherie. New York: Reynal & Hitchcock, 1947.

Rubenstein, Richard L. *After Auschwitz: Radical Theology and Contemporary Judaism*. Indianapolis: Bobbs-Merrill, 1966.

_____ . *The Age of Triage: Fear and Hope in an Overcrowded World*. Boston: Beacon Press, 1983.

_____ . *The Cunning of History: The Holocaust and the American Future*. New York: Harper & Row, 1975.

_____ . *Morality and Eros*. New York: McGraw-Hill, 1970.

_____ . *The Religious Imagination*. Indianapolis: Bobbs-Merrill, 1968.

Ruether, Rosemary Radford. *Faith and Fratricide: The Theological Roots of Anti-Semitism*. New York: Seabury, 1974.

Ryan, Allan A., Jr. *Quiet Neighbors: Prosecuting Nazi War Criminals in America*. San Diego: Harcourt Brace Jovanovich, 1984.

Ryder, A. J. *Twentieth-Century Germany from Bismarck to Brandt*. New York: Columbia University Press, 1973.

Sachar, Abram L. *The Redemption of the Unwanted: From the Liberation of the Death Camps to the Founding of Israel*. New York: St. Martin's Press, 1983.

Sachar, Howard Morley. *The Course of Modern Jewish History*. New York: Dell Publishing Company, 1977.

Saidel, Rochelle G. *The Outraged Conscience: Seekers of Justice for Nazi War Criminals in America*. Albany: State University of New York Press, 1984.

Sandmel, Samuel. *Anti-Semitism in the New Testament?* Philadelphia: Fortress Press, 1978.

Schleunes, Karl A. *The Twisted Road to Auschwitz: Nazi Policy Toward German Jews, 1933–1939*. Urbana: University of Illinois Press, 1970.

Schorsch, Ismar. *Jewish Reactions to German Anti-Semitism, 1870–1914*. New York: Columbia University Press, 1972.

Schorske, Carl. *Fin-de-Siècle Vienna: Politics and Culture*. New York: Alfred A. Knopf, 1980.

Schwarz-Bart, André. *The Last of the Just*. Translated by Stephen Becker. New York: Bantam Books, 1976.

Sereny, Gitta. *Into That Darkness: An Examination of Conscience*. New York: Vintage Books, 1983.

Sheehan, James J., ed. *Imperial Germany*. New York: Franklin Watts, 1976.

Sherwin, Byron L., and Ament, Susan G., eds. *Encountering the Holocaust: An Interdisciplinary Survey*. Chicago: Impact Press, 1979.

Shirer, William L. *The Rise and Fall of the Third Reich*. New York: Simon and Schuster, 1960.

Shur, Irene G.; Littell, Franklin H.; and Wolfgang, Marvin E,, eds. *Reflections on the Holocaust*. Philadelphia: American Academy of Political and Social Science, 1980.

Silberner, Edmund. *Sozialisten zur Judenfrage*. Berlin: Colloquium Verlag, 1962.

Smith, Bradley. *Reaching Judgment at Nuremberg*. New York: Basic Books, 1977.

————. *The Road to Nuremberg*. New York: Basic Books, 1981.

Snell, John L. *The Nazi Revolution: Hitler's Dictatorship and the German Nation*. Revised by Allan Mitchell. Lexington, MA: D. C. Heath, 1973.

Snoek, Johan M., *The Grey Book: A Collection of Protests Against Anti-Semitism and the Persecution of the Jews Issued by non-Roman Catholic Churches and Church Leaders during Hitler's Rule*. New York: Humanities Press, 1970.

Snyder, Louis Leo. *Encyclopedia of the Third Reich*. New York: McGraw-Hill, 1976.

———— *Hitler and Nazism*. New York: Franklin Watts, 1961.

Sosnowski, Kiryl. *The Tragedy of Children Under Nazi Rule*. New York: Howard Fertig, 1983.

Speer, Albert. *Inside the Third Reich*. Translated by Richard and Clara Winston. New York: Macmillan, 1970.

Spotts, Frederic. *The Churches and Politics in Germany*. Middletown, CT: Wesleyan University Press, 1973.

Steiner, George. *In Bluebeard's Castle: Some Notes Towards the Redefinition of Culture*. New Haven: Yale University Press, 1971.

———— *Language and Silence: Essays on Language, Literature and the Inhuman*. New York: Atheneum, 1972.

_____ *The Portage to San Cristóbal of A. H.* New York: Washington Square Press, 1983.

Steiner, Jean-François. *Treblinka.* Translated by Helen Weaver. New York: New American Library, 1979.

Stern, J. P. *Hitler: The Fuhrer and the People.* Berkeley and Los Angeles: University of California Press, 1975.

Styron, William. *Sophie's Choice.* New York: Random House, 1979.

Suhl, Yuri, ed. *They Fought Back: The Story of the Jewish Resistance in Nazi Europe.* Translated by Yuri Suhl. New York: Schocken Books, 1975.

Szonyi, David M. *The Holocaust: An Annotated Bibliography and Resource Guide.* New York: KTAV Publishing House, Inc., 1985.

Tal, Uriel. *Christians and Jews in Germany: Religion, Politics and Ideology in the Second Reich, 1870–1914.* Ithaca: Cornell University Press, 1975.

Tec, Nechama. *Dry Tears: The Story of a Lost Childhood.* New York: Oxford University Press, 1984.

Thomas, Gordon, and Witts, Max Morgan. *Voyage of the Damned.* New York: Stein and Day, 1974.

Toland, John. *Adolf Hitler.* New York: Ballantine Books, 1977.

Toll, Nelly. *Without Surrender: Art of the Holocaust.* Philadelphia: Running Press, 1978.

Treece, Patricia. *A Man for Others.* New York: Harper & Row, 1982.

Troeltsch, Ernst. *The Social Teaching of the Christian Churches.* 2 vols. Translated by Olive Wyon. New York: Harper & Row, 1960.

Trunk, Isaiah. *Jewish Responses to Nazi Persecution: Collective and Individual Behavior in Extremis.* Translated by Joachim Neugroschel and Gabriel Trunk. New York: Stein and Day, 1979.

_____ . *Judenrat: The Jewish Councils in Eastern Europe under Nazi Occupation.* New York: Stein and Day, 1977.

Turner, Henry Ashby, Jr. *German Big Business and the Rise of Hitler.* New York: Oxford University Press, 1985.

Tusa, Ann, and Tusa, John. *The Nuremberg Trial.* New York: Atheneum Publishers, 1984.

Tushnet, Leonard. *The Pavement of Hell.* New York: St. Martin's Press, 1972.

Uhlman, Fred. *Reunion.* New York: Penguin Books, 1978.

Van Buren, Paul M. *Discerning the Way,* Part I of *A Theology of the Jewish Christian Reality.* New York: The Seabury Press, 1980.

_____ . *A Christian Theology of the People Israel,* Part II of *A Theology of the Jewish Christian Reality.* New York: Seabury Press, 1983.

Vital, David. *The Origins of Zionism.* Oxford: Oxford University Press, 1975.

von Hammerstein-Equord, Kunrat Freiherr. *Spähtrupp.* Stuttgart: H. Goverts, 1963.

von Lang, Jochen, and Sibyll, Claus, eds. *Eichmann Interrogated: Transcripts from the Archives of the Israeli Police.* Translated by Ralph Manheim. New York: Vintage Books, 1984.

von Rad, Gerhard. *Old Testament Theology.* London: S. P. C. K., 1953.

Waite, Robert G. L. *The Psychopathic God: Adolf Hitler.* New York: Basic Books, 1977.

Walker, Mack. *Germany and the Emigration, 1816–1885.* Cambridge, MA: Harvard University Press, 1964.

Wasserstein, Bernard. *Britain and the Jews of Europe, 1939–1945.* Oxford: Oxford University Press, 1979.

Weber, Eugen J. *Action Française: Royalism and Reaction in Twentieth-Century France.* Stanford: Stanford University Press, 1962.

Weidemann, Thomas. *Greek and Roman Slavery.* Baltimore: Penguin Books, 1981.

Weinreich, Max. *Hitler's Professors: The Part of Scholarship in Germany's Crimes against the Jewish People.* New York: YIVO, 1946.

Wells, Leon Weliczker. *The Death Brigade.* New York: Holocaust Library, 1978.

Whalen, Robert Weldon. *Bitter Wounds: German Victims of the Great War, 1914–1939.* Ithaca: Cornell University Press, 1984.

Wiesel, Elie. *A Jew Today.* Translated by Marion Wiesel. New York: Random House, 1978.

————. *Legends of Our Time.* Translated by Stephen Donadio. New York: Avon Books, 1970.

————. *Messengers of God.* Translated by Marion Wiesel. New York: Random House, 1976.

————. *Night.* Translated by Stella Rodway. New York: Bantam Books, 1982.

————. *The Oath.* Translated by Marion Wiesel. New York: Random House, 1973.

————. *One Generation After.* Translated by Lily Edelman and the author. New York: Avon Books, 1972.

————. *The Testament.* Translated by Marion Wiesel. New York: Summit Books, 1981.

————. *The Trial of God.* Translated by Marion Wiesel. New York: Random House, 1979.

Wiesenthal, Simon. *The Sunflower.* New York: Schocken Books, 1976.

Wilken, Robert L. *John Chrysostom and the Jews: Rhetoric and Reality in the Late Fourth Century.* Berkeley and Los Angeles: University of California Press, 1983.

Williamson, Clark M. *Has God Rejected His People?: Anti-Judaism in the Christian Church.* Nashville: Abingdon, 1982.

Winick, Myron, ed. *Hunger Disease: Studies by the Jewish Physicians in the Warsaw Ghetto.* New York: John Wiley and Sons, 1979.

Wischnitzer, Mark. *To Dwell in Safety: The Story of Jewish Migration Since 1800.* Philadelphia: The Jewish Publication Society, 1948.

Wyman, David S. *The Abandonment of the Jews: America and the Holocaust, 1941–1945.* New York: Pantheon Books, 1984.

————. *Paper Walls: America and the Refugee Crisis, 1938–1941.* Amherst: University of Massachusetts Press, 1968.

Wytwycky, Bohdan. *The Other Holocaust: Many Circles of Hell.* Washington, D.C.: The Novak Report on the New Ethnicity, 1980.

Yahil, Leni. *The Rescue of Danish Jewry.* Philadelphia: The Jewish Publication Society, 1969.

Yaseen, Leonard C. *The Jesus Connection: To Triumph Over Anti-Semitism.* New York: The Crossroad Publishing Company, 1985.

Zahn, Gordon. *German Catholics and Hitler's Wars.* New York: Sheed and Ward, 1962.

II. ARTICLES

Ament, Susan G. "Music and Art of the Holocaust." In *Encountering the Holocaust: An Interdisciplinary Survey,* pp. 383–406. Edited by Bryon L. Sherwin and Susan G. Ament. Chicago: Impact Press, 1979.

Armengaud, Andre. "Population in Europe, 1700–1914." Translated by A. J. Pomerans. In *The Fontana Economic History of Europe.* Edited by Carlo M. Cipolla. Vol. 3: *The Industrial Revolution,* pp. 22–76. London: Fontana/Collins, 1973.

Aronson, Elliot. "The Rationalizing Animal." *Psychology Today*, May 1973, pp. 46–52.

Barth, Karl. "The Jewish Problem and the Christian Answer." In *Against the Stream*, pp. 193–201. London: SCM Press, 1954.

Bassiouni, M. Cherif. "International Law and the Holocaust." In *Encountering the Holocaust: An Interdisciplinary Survey*, pp. 146–88. Edited by Byron L. Sherwin and Susan G. Ament. Chicago: Impact Press, 1979.

Bauer, Yehuda. "Genocide: Was It the Nazis' Original Plan?" In *Reflections on the Holocaust*, pp. 35–45. Edited by Irene G. Shur, Franklin H. Littell, and Marvin E. Wolfgang. Philadelphia: The American Academy of Political and Social Science, 1980. "Jewish Leadership Reactions to Nazi Policies." In *The Holocaust as Historical Experience*, pp. 173–92. Edited by Yehuda Bauer and Nathan Rotenstreich. New York: Holmes & Meier, 1981.

Berk, Stephen M. "The Russian Revolutionary Movement and the Pogroms of 1881–1882." *Soviet Jewish Affairs* 7 (1977).

Bethge, Eberhard. "Troubled Self-Interpretation and Uncertain Reception in the Church Struggle." In *The German Church Struggle and the Holocaust*, pp. 167–84. Edited by Franklin H. Littell and Hubert G. Locke. Detroit: Wayne State University Press, 1974.

Beyerchen, Alan. "The Physical Sciences." In *The Holocaust: Ideology, Bureaucracy, and Genocide*, pp. 151–63. Edited by Henry Friedlander and Sybil Milton. Millwood, NY: Kraus International Publications, 1980.

Boozer, Jack S. "Children of Hippocrates: Doctors in Nazi Germany." In *Reflections on the Holocaust*, pp. 83–97. Edited by Irene G. Shur, Franklin H. Littell, and Marvin E. Wolfgang. Philadelphia: The American Academy of Political and Social Science, 1980.

Brieger, Gert H. "The Medical Profession." In *The Holocaust: Ideology, Bureaurcracy, and Genocide*, pp. 141–50. Edited by Henry Friedlander and Sybil Milton. Millwood, NY: Kraus International Publications, 1980.

Brown, Robert McAfee. "Wiesel's Case Against God." *The Christian Century*, 30 January 1980, pp. 109–12.

Browning, Christopher R. "The Government Experts." In *The Holocaust: Ideology, Bureaucracy, and Genocide*, pp. 183–97. Edited by Henry Friedlander and Sybil Milton. Millwood, NY: Kraus International Publications, 1980.

Conway, John. "The Churches." In *The Holocaust: Ideology, Bureaucracy, and Genocide*, pp. 199–206. Edited by Henry Friedlander and Sybil Milton. Millwood, NY: Kraus International Publications, 1980.

"Ein Wort zur Judenfrage der Reichsbruderrat der Evangelichen Kirche in Deutschland." In *Der Ungekundigte Bund: Neue Begegnung von Judischen und Christlicher*, pp. 251–54. Edited by Dietrich Goldschmidt and Hans-Joachim Kraus. Stuttgart: 1962.

Encyclopedia Judaica. Articles: "Auschwitz," 3:856. "Berlin," 4:644. "Chelmno," 5:374. "May Laws," 11:1147–48. "Paris," 13:107–08. "Pobedonostsev," 13:633. "Pogroms," 13:695–98. "Poland," 13:735–49. "Population," 13:889–92. "Vienna," 16:1247.

Ettinger, Shmuel. "Anti-Semitism as Official Policy in Eastern Europe." In *A History of the Jewish People*, pp. 881–90. Edited by H. H. Ben-Sasson. Cambridge, MA: Harvard University Press, 1976.

Fackenheim, Emil L. "Can There Be Judaism Without Revelation?" In *Quest for Past and Future: Essays in Jewish Theology*. Bloomington: Indiana University Press, 1968. Reprinted from *Commentary*, December 1951. "Transcendence in Contemporary Culture: Philosophical Reflections and a Jewish Theology." In *Transcendence*, pp. 143–52. Edited by Herbert W. Richardson and Donald R. Cutler. Boston: Beacon Press, 1969.

Festinger, Leon. "Cognitive Dissonance." *Scientific American* 207 (October 1962): 93–102.

Friedlander, Henry. "Nuernberg and Other Trials." In *Genocide: Critical Issues of the Holocaust*, pp. 381–83. Edited by Alex Grobman, Daniel Landes, and Sybil Milton. Los Angeles: The Simon Wiesenthal Center, 1983.

Goldberg, Arthur J., and Hertzberg, Arthur. "Holocaust: Questions of Guilt." *Los Angeles Times*, 25 March 1984.

Greenberg, Irving. "Cloud of Smoke, Pillar of Fire: Judaism, Christianity, and Modernity after the Holocaust." In *Auschwitz: Beginning of a New Era?*, pp. 7–55. Edited by Eva Fleischner. New York: KTAV, 1977.

Harner, Michael. "The Enigma of Aztec Sacrifice." *Natural History* 86 (April 1977): 46–51.

Heiber, Helmut. "Aus den Akten des Gauleiters Kube." *Vierteljahrshefte fur Zeitgeschichte* 4 (1956): 67–92.

Hilberg, Raul. "Discussion: The *Judenrat* and the Jewish Response." In *The Holocaust as Historical Experience*, pp. 223–71. Edited by Yehuda Bauer and Nathan Rotenstreich. New York: Holmes & Meier, 1981. "German Railroads, Jewish Souls." *Society* 14 (November–December 1976): 60–74. "The Ghetto as a Form of Government: An Analysis of Isaiah Trunk's *Judenrat*." In *The Holocaust as Historical Experience*, pp. 155–71. New York: Holmes & Meier, 1981. "The Nature of the Process." In *Survivors, Victims and Perpetrators*, pp. 5–54. Edited by Joel E. Dimsdale. New York: Hemisphere Publishing Company, 1980.

Hughes, Thomas P. "Technology." In *The Holocaust: Ideology, Bureaucracy, and Genocide*, pp. 165–81. Edited by Henry Friedlander and Sybil Milton. Millwood, NY: Kraus International Publications, 1980.

Kovner, Abba. "A First Attempt to Tell." In *The Holocaust as Historical Experience*, pp. 77–94. Edited by Yehuda Bauer and Nathan Rotenstreich. New York: Holmes & Meier, 1981.

Langer, Lawrence, L. "The Writer and the Holocaust Experience." In *The Holocaust: Ideology, Bureaucracy, and Genocide*, pp. 309–22. Edited by Henry Friedlander and Sybil Milton. Millwood, NY: Kraus International Publications, 1980.

Lichtheim, George. "Socialism and the Jews." *Dissent* 15 (July–August 1968): 314–42.

Lifton, Robert Jay. "Medicalized Killing in Auschwitz." In *Psychoanalytic Reflections on the Holocaust: Selected Essays*, pp. 11–33. Edited by Steven A. Luel and Paul Marcus. New York: KTAV, 1984.

Littell, Franklin H. "Church Struggle and the Holocaust." In *The German Church Struggle and the Holocaust*, pp. 11–30. Edited by Franklin H. Littell and Hubert G. Locke. Detroit: Wayne State University Press, 1974.

Lowenthal, Richard. "The German Question Transformed." *Foreign Affairs* 63 (Winter 1984/85): 303–15.

Marx, Karl. "On the Jewish Question." In *Karl Marx: Selected Writings*, pp. 39–62. Edited by David McLellan. Oxford: Oxford University Press, 1977. "Theses on Feuerbach." In *Marx and Engels: Basic Writings on Politics and Philosophy*, pp. 243–45. Edited by Lewis S. Feuer. Garden City: Doubleday, 1959.

Mays, Lee. "Reagan Expert under Attack for Ties to Nazi War Criminals." *St. Petersburg Times*, 25 April 1982.

Osborn, Robert T. "The Christian Blasphemy." In *Journal of the American Academy of Religion* 53, no. 3 (September 1985): 339–63.

Porter, Jack Nusan. "Social-Psychological Aspects of the Holocaust." In *Encountering the Holocaust: An Interdisciplinary Survey*, pp. 189–222. Edited by Byron L. Sherwin and Susan G. Ament. Chicago: Impact Press, 1979.

Rosenberg, Hans. "Political and Social Consequences of the Great Depression of 1873–1896 in Central Europe." In *Imperial Germany*, pp. 39–60. Edited by James J. Sheehan. New York: Franklin Watts, 1976.

Roth, John K. "How to Make Hitler's Ideas Clear?" *The Philosophical Forum* 16 (1984–85): 82–94.

Rubenstein, Richard L. "The Dean and the Chosen People." In *After Auschwitz*, pp. 47–58. Indianapolis: Bobbs-Merrill, 1966. "Naming the Unnameable; Thinking the Unthinkable: A Review Essay of Arthur Cohen's *The Tremendum*." *Journal of Reform Judaism* 31 (Spring 1984): 43–55.

Ryan, Michael D. "Hitler's Challenge to the Churches: A Theological Political Analysis of *Mein Kampf*. In *The German Church Struggle and the Holocaust*, pp. 148–64. Edited by Franklin H. Littell and Hubert G. Locke. Detroit: Wayne State University Press, 1974.

Siirala, Aarne. "Reflections from a Lutheran Perspective." In *Auschwitz: Beginning of a New Era?*, pp. 135–48. Edited by Eva Fleischner. New York: KTAV, 1977.

Smith, Doug. "Bond Unites Children of Holocaust." *Los Angeles Times*, 29 May 1986.

Tal, Uriel. "Excursus on the Term: *Shoah*." *Shoah* 1 (1979): 10–11.

Taylor, Telford. "The Legal Profession." In *The Holocaust: Ideology, Bureaucracy, and Genocide*, pp. 133–40. Edited by Henry Friedlander and Sybil Milton. Millwood, NY: Kraus International Publications, 1980.

Weber, Max. "Bureaucracy." "Science as a Vocation." "The Social Psychology of the World Religions." "Capitalism and Rural Society in Germany." In *From Max Weber: Essays in Sociology*, pp. 196–244, 129–56, 267–301, 363–85. Edited by H. H. Gerth and C. Wright Mills. New York: Oxford University Press, 1946.

Wiesel, Elie. "Why I Write." Translated by Rosette C. Lamont. In *Confronting the Holocaust: The Impact of Elie Wiesel*, pp. 200–06. Edited by Alvin H. Rosenfeld and Irving Greenberg. Bloomington: Indiana University Press, 1978.

Wolfe, Robert. "Putative Threat to National Security as a Nuremberg Defense for Genocide." In *Reflections on the Holocaust*, pp. 46–67. Edited by Irene G. Shur, Franklin H. Littell, and Marvin E. Wolfgang. Philadelphia: The American Academy of Political and Social Science, 1980.

Yahil, Leni. "Select British Documents on the Illegal Immigration of Palestine (1939–1940)." In *Yad Vashem Studies*, 10:241–76. Jerusalem: Yad Vashem, 1974.

Zahn, Gordon C. "Catholic Resistance? A Yes and a No." In *The German Church Struggle and the Holocaust*, pp. 203–37. Edited by Franklin H. Littell and Hubert G. Locke. Detroit: Wayne State University Press, 1974.

Zmarzlik, Hans-Gunter. "Social Darwinism in Germany, Seen as a Historical Problem." In *Republic into Reich: The Making of the Nazi Revolution*, pp. 435–74. Edited by Hajo Holborn. New York: Pantheon Books, 1972.

Index of Names

Index of Subjects